MW00809205

ROADBLOCKS TO FREEDOM

Slavery and Manumission in the United States South

BY

ANDREW FEDE

Legal History and Biography Series

Quid Pro Books

New Orleans, Louisiana

ROADBLOCKS TO FREEDOM

Published by Quid Pro Books.

QUID PRO, LLC
5860 Citrus Blvd., Suite D-101
New Orleans, Louisiana 70123
www.quidprobooks.com

ISBN 1610271084 (hc)
ISBN-13 9781610271080 (hc)
ISBN-13 9781610271073 (pbk)
ISBN-13 9781610271097 (ePub)

Also available in softcover edition and in all standard eBook formats.

Front cover image copyright © by Robert Fouts, exhibited in his collection at *www. HistoricMontgomery.com*. Depicting the Montgomery, Alabama, Court House in 1854, the image is used by permission of Mr. Fouts and with the gratitude of the author and publisher. Cover design copyright © 2011 by Michele Veade.

Publisher's Cataloging-in-Publication

Fede, Andrew.
    Roadblocks to freedom: slavery and manumission in the United States South / Andrew Fede.
        p. cm. — (Legal history and biography)
        Includes bibliographical references, table of cases, and index.
        ISBN 978-1-61027-108-0 (hc)
1. Slavery—United States—history. 2. Slaves—Legal status, laws, etc.—United States—history. 3. Courts—Southern States—History—19th century. 4. Slavery—Law and legislation—United States—history. 5. African Americans—Legal status, laws, etc.—United States—history. I. Title. II. Series.
KF 4564.F61 2011   342.5'77'0788—dc22
                                                              2011049892

FOR DANIELE

CONTENTS

Preface

A Note on Methods and Acknowledgments

This book furthers the interpretation of the law of slavery in the United States South that I advanced in *People Without Rights: An Interpretation of the Fundamentals of the Law of Slavery in the U.S. South*.[1] That book was first published in 1992 after my initial ten years studying slavery law and my publication of one review essay and two longer articles on slavery law in the United States.[2]

In chapter 7 of *People Without Rights*, I discussed the statutes and cases that regulated and eventually prohibited the masters' power to free their slaves.[3] This book began as an article that I intended to write as an initial chapter in a second edition of *People Without Rights*. Instead, I found the need to write this book to further analyze these legal trends, to develop the fundamental procedural and practical aspects of the law of slavery as applied in real trials and appeals, and to incorporate and consider the books and articles that have more recently been published on the manumission and freedom suits in the United States and elsewhere.

After *People Without Rights* was written, scholars published important monographs and articles on slave law in the United States South, including surveys written by Robert B. Shaw[4] and Thomas D. Morris.[5] Judith Schafer wrote a thorough study of the Louisiana Supreme Court's slavery decisions.[6] Jenny Bourne Wahl contributed an economic history analysis of slave law.[7] William Wiethoff reviewed the judges' rhetoric in their antebellum slave law opinions.[8] A. Leon Higginbotham, Jr. wrote a monograph on the history of race in American law, and co-authored a series of law review articles that included discussions of what he called slave law's "Ten Precepts."[9] Glenn McNair, James M. Campbell, Ariela J. Gross, Walter Johnson, and Sally E. Haddon also published books discussing the law of slave criminal justice, slave sales, slaves' suits for freedom, and slave patrols.[10] Bernie D. Jones, Adrienne D. Davis, and Jason A. Gillmer, among others, have recently written about the law of manumission and miscegenation.[11]

Judith Schafer's 2003 monograph on the Louisiana manumission statutes and freedom suits is a most noteworthy contribution.[12] The present book can be read to complement her study because, as in my earlier work, I will focus on the way that the judges and legislators in the common law states integrated slavery law into the law that the English colonists brought to the New World.

These and other scholars whose works I will cite in this book have made valuable contributions toward an understanding of the cases in which people held as slaves sought to be released from bondage. Still, I believe that the issues that I could further discuss, and contribute a different perspective, include those that were raised in the cases in which people held as slaves won their freedom while slavery was legal in the United States South.

To this end, I draw upon my three decades of experience as a practicing lawyer to consider these cases and statutes, not as abstract expressions of legal doctrines or principles, but as the products of the conscious decisions made by lawmakers and judges. These decisions had real world effects on ordinary lawyers like me and of course even more so on their clients—the enslaved, their owners, and other free people—and the perceived public interest. This practical experience enables me to apply a somewhat different perspective to the legal materials from the years that the United States was a slave nation.

In my earlier works, I examined the fundamental nature of the legal relationship between slaves, masters, and third parties, and addressed the question: Why did the law of slavery in the United States South treat people held as slaves as both people and property? I contended that this slavery law was true to slavery's logic as a social and cultural institution—and to avoid confusion and enhance our understanding of this law, we should not think of slave rights in the law.

As a general rule, the law in the United States defined slaves as human property with no legal rights. Of necessity, however, the lawmakers sometimes treated slaves as people because, after all, they were people. Consequently, the lawmakers included slaves among the people who could commit crimes and who also could be the victims of crime. But, as Randall Kennedy noted, the way that the lawmakers defined crimes that could be committed by and against slaves was one instance in which blacks and other people of color were the victims of both "racially invidious over-enforcement of the criminal law" and "under-enforcement" that "purposefully denies African-American victims of violence" the criminal law's equal protection.[13]

Accordingly, the lawmakers burdened slaves with extra legal duties while they also denied to slaves the most basic human rights. This was so even though the law regulated the masters' right to treat their slaves as cruelly and as leniently as they wished. These regulatory laws included those that at times provided that masters could not free their slaves and that defined who could legally be held as a slave. These regulations did not create slave rights. Instead, they legitimated while regulating the masters' powers, and furthered ends that the lawmakers perceived to be necessary to perpetuate and advance their slave society.[14]

In *People Without Rights*, I explained why it follows that the references in the law to the slaves' humanity constituted cruel ironies. The judges and legislators—often in the name of humanity—denied to slaves the rights that the common law afforded to free people, imposed additional legal duties upon slaves, legitimized the powers of others over slaves, and defined the relative property rights of free people to own and control slave property.[15]

The law allocating the slave's legal rights and duties in this way epitomized in the law slavery's oppressive social relationships. Accordingly, upon further reflection, the phrase "people without rights," although useful in explaining slave law's fundamentals, is an understatement. It captures only one side of slave law's equation of oppression. The statutes and cases that imposed extra legal duties and liabilities on slaves illustrate this equation's other half.[16]

To test and advance this interpretation, I studied those instances in which it appeared that the law recognized slaves as persons. These examples I argued were revealed—one by one—to be rhetorical devices that legitimized slave law's inherent inhumanity. Indeed, slaves were people who according to the law were the property of others. Therefore, the law of people differed from the law of people who were slaves. This was slavery law's fundamental reality.[17]

Southern legislators and judges acknowledged that slavery differed fundamentally from other relationships that exhibited inequality. It does not necessarily follow that all masters treated slaves as property without recognizing the slaves' humanity, but the law permitted masters to think of and treat their slaves as property. Nor does this mean that the judges and legislators anticipated that masters would dehumanize their slaves; but the lawmakers allowed for this possibility, and it was a foreseeable consequence of the law.[18]

Slavery's abolitionist critics and twentieth-century historians including Kenneth Stampp advanced similar interpretations of the slave's legal status.[19] I have attempted to further this interpretation by noting that Southern judges also at times expressed in their judicial opinions similarly frank acknowledgments of slavery's essence. Occasionally, these judges looked into what Henry Wadsworth Longfellow called "the abyss" that was slavery and they saw and expressed the real meaning of slavery's legal suppression of the slave's humanity.[20] For one example, Louisiana Supreme Court Justice Alexander Buchanan wrote, in an 1856 opinion, that the slave

> is the object of contracts, not a legal party to contracts. He may be sold or mortgaged, but he cannot sell or mortgage. He can neither inherit, nor make a will, because he can possess nothing as owner. He is inadmissible as a witness in any civil suit whatever. And if accused of crime, he is tried by a special tribunal, to which the safeguards of the common law are unknown.[21]

Judges like Buchanan "were not 'abolitionist fanatics' bent on the destruction of a perceived moral evil, but were pro-slavery jurists."[22]

At other times, however, judges looked into the same abyss and deluded themselves into thinking that the law that they made and upheld was not so bad.[23] Thus, in an 1821 Mississippi Supreme Court opinion, Justice Joshua G. Clarke asked: "Has the slave no rights, because he is deprived of his freedom?" Clarke answered his own question by asserting that the slave "is still a human being, and possess all of those rights, of which he is not deprived by the positive provisions of law[.]"[24]

Clarke was "only half correct" because slavery law's first principles defined slaves as property. This definition cut slaves off from all claims to legal rights.

But slaves were unique property because they could commit crimes. "Thus, slaves were considered persons by the criminal law. This added insult to injury," because the lawmakers burdened slaves with additional duties and punishments. "Consequently, the slave had a dual legal status that was consistent with and epitomized the oppression of slavery. Slaves were denied the benefits of personhood and were saddled with burdens that exceeded the obligations of 'real' people."[25]

I also emphasized the notion that the law of slavery in the American colonies and states was constantly changing by tracing the origin and constant development of the legal relationships between masters, slaves, and third parties in the common law states of the United States South. This inquiry's goal was to show how slavery was accommodated into the common law that was evolving in the pre-Civil War South.[26]

This approach was to some extent an attempt to address what Paul Finkelman called a "neglected" area of slavery law: "the interaction between slave law and legal doctrine, and the theoretical underpinnings of the law of slavery."[27] This study centered on legal materials—cases, statutes, and constitutions. Nevertheless, I also argued that the social, political, economic, and intellectual background of the law of slavery provides the necessary context within which we can best analyze these legal materials.[28]

This book's analysis is informed by the approaches to legal history that I used in my earlier works, except that I will make a greater use of a comparative approach to evaluate the development in the Southern common law states of substantive legal standards and procedural rules with reference to the law in the civil law state of Louisiana and in other slave societies. Scholars have applied comparative approaches to better understand the possible legal rules that different slave societies adopted or rejected, and "to identify the circumstances in which law changes and hence to uncover the reasons for legal development."[29]

According to Peter Kolchin, historians interested in the United States South "have differed sharply in their definitions of 'comparative history[.]'" He nevertheless suggested "three different comparative approaches: (1) comparisons between the South and the North (the 'un-south'); (2) internal comparisons among various components of the South ('many souths'); and (3) comparisons between the South and other societies sharing some of the same attributes ('other souths')."[30] Although they often reach different conclusions, "a wide variety of scholars have recognized that Southern society is best understood in the context of slavery and other forms of unfree labour elsewhere in the modern world."[31] This book is not a comprehensive comparative study, but it will at times use all three of these comparisons.

Kolchin also stated that most of us think of the third approach when we refer to comparative history, and some historians consider this as "the only real form of comparison."[32] I will use the third approach by referring to the ancient Roman and more modern slave codes, including the Spanish law *Las Siete Partidas de Rey don Alfonso el Sabio*, which was compiled in the Middle Ages under Alfonso X and contained slavery provisions that later influenced slave law in Spain's colonies, and the French *Code Noir*, which was adopted in 1685 under Louis XIV as "the first integrated slave code written specifically for the Americas."[33]

A growing body of literature compares South American slavery and law with that of the French, English, and Dutch colonies, but scholars have hotly debated the proper methods to use and conclusions to draw.[34] Indeed, as Eugene Genovese argued, while critiquing the work of Frank Tannenbaum and others, "the comparative method is a treacherous business, and we have yet to learn to recognize all of its pitfalls or understand its limits."[35] Scholars are still debating the merits of Tannenbaum's thesis concerning the provisions in the South American slave law that apparently were less oppressive than the analogous North American slave law.[36] One does not have to agree with all of the components of Tannenbaum's thesis to use "its rich potential in assessing whether the law enabled slaves to exercise agency or self-sufficiency."[37] Although the comparative approach must be applied with care so as not to "exaggerate or magnify differences[,]" legal historical issues involving race and slavery "are brought into sharper focus when viewed through a comparative lens."[38]

As to Kolchin's first comparison, I refer at times to the law of Great Britain and the free states and to New Jersey law from the years before that state abolished slavery. New Jersey was the last Northern state to adopt a gradual emancipation act, and this process was so gradual that slavery continued in New Jersey in modified form until the Thirteenth Amendment went into effect.[39] In addition, I examine the rules that the American courts applied to analogous proceedings that did not involve slaves. This analysis can at times provide a context for evaluating slave law.[40]

Applying Kolchin's second approach, I again will review the patterns of social and legal change over time within the different Southern colonies, states, and regions to emphasize both continuities and discontinuities. This approach permits us to discern larger patterns and trends within Southern slavery law and society.[41]

I again find it helpful to draw upon ideas and methodological approaches from traditional doctrinal legal history, instrumentalist legal history, and the Critical Legal Studies authors.[42] From the instrumentalists, I argue that the complex and shifting structure of slavery law in the South can best be understood as a process by which the judges and legislators accommodated slavery's essential social elements into the common law, for which slavery was a long-forgotten institution. They achieved this by balancing what they perceived to be the salient interests implicated in the issues presented. These interests included the slave master class's perceived need: (1) to foster slave control, obedience, and submissiveness; (2) to perpetuate the plantation economy and preserve slave property values; (3) to regulate the behavior of overseers and slave hirers; and (4) to control poor white violence and slave abuse, while co-opting poor whites into becoming supporters of the slave economy.[43]

The social, economic, political, and intellectual/religious developments appear to have over time caused the dominant slave owners' perceptions of the balance of these interests to shift. The judges and legislators who created the new legal standards also for the most part shared these new attitudes and concerns. Therefore, the courts and legislatures changed the civil and criminal law to protect slave property, but they also used the law as an instrument of social control asserted against poor whites, overseers, slave hirers, and even against slave owners who did not properly maintain and discipline their slaves.[44]

To evaluate the effect of these social and cultural conditions on slavery law, we should examine relevant non-legal materials in addition to the statutes, constitutions, and case law reports that Robert Gordon called law box data. According to Gordon, the law box contains "whatever appears autonomous about the legal order—courts, equitable maxims, motions for summary judgment; outside lies society, the wide realm of the nonlegal, the political, economic, religious, social...."[45] I have again grounded my interpretation upon an external approach to legal history, which reaches outside of the law box for nonlegal data to help evaluate the law box data. This approach is in contrast to an internal legal history, which confines its inquiry to the law box.[46]

Implicit in each approach, however, is an important answer to the key question concerning the relationship between law and social change: Whether legal change was caused only by autonomous forces at work inside the law box, or whether changes in law, at least to some degree, occurred in response to changes in the society at large.

The way one defines the concept of legal autonomy influences how one views the relationship between law and social change. Gordon suggested two ways to perceive of the contents of the law box. The first is a theory "asserting that law derives its shape almost wholly from sources within the box (i.e., that it is really autonomous as well as seeming so)[.]" According to the second, "the box is really empty, the apparent distinctiveness of its contents illusory, since they are all products of external social forces."[47]

I again assert that slavery law in the United States can best be described as a process by which the judges and legislators legitimized and accommodated slavery's social and cultural elements into the law. The legal and non-legal data support the interpretation that these legislators and judges formulated and reformulated legal standards and doctrine concerning slave law in response to the social, political, economic, and intellectual/religious changes that accompanied slavery's development. This legal evolutionary process was, in essence, more a reaction to non-legal changes and was less an expression of autonomous legal forces.

I thus used different terms to emphasize what Philip Schwarz, Ariela Gross, Laura Edwards, and others have called legal history from the bottom up. This is an approach by which the historians use trial court testimony and other primary sources to reveal the cultural and political interactions that masters and the people they enslaved experienced, as well as the inquiry into how those interactions influenced changes in slavery law.[48] Like Schwarz, however, "I cannot confine myself to 'history from the bottom up,' like a cave explorer who looks down at the stalagmites and ignores the stalactites. I must investigate both 'history from the top down' and 'history from the bottom up.'"[49]

We need to look at how those at the bottom and at the top interacted to form and reform the legal rules both in the books and in action. Robert Olwell explained this interaction well when, in describing colonial South Carolina criminal slave law, he noted that "no system of law can exist apart from the ongoing process of its creation and legitimization." He added that when we speak of the law we "describe the consequence of myriad individual actions, not a single prescient actor." Thus, he concluded that the colonial criminal law of slavery "was constructed each day by the decisions and choices of the living men and women, white and black, who cooperated with or contested against one another in the legislature, at the slave court, or upon the gallows."[50]

Indeed, people held as slaves and their lawyers, from the bottom up, influenced those who wrote the slave laws and court decisions, and this process included cases in which slaves asserted freedom claims. The lawmakers at the top often responded to these claims coming from the bottom, however, by cutting off potential legal routes to freedom. For example, judges and legislators in different jurisdictions and at different times imposed greater or lesser legal constraints upon individual slave masters who wished to free their slaves, and thus confined or expanded the claims to freedom that slaves potentially could assert based upon proof of their masters' intentions to free their slaves. The lawmakers also responded to freedom claims by limiting the potential substantive theories on which slaves could claim their freedom independent of proof that the slaves' masters' intentions to free them. These lawmakers also adopted procedural rules that created burdens and barriers for freedom claimants.

The legislators and judges thus created a legal reality that confronted the freedom claimants, and their lawyers, whose cases are discussed in this book. This law also influenced potential claimants who, by definition, simply could not assert viable legal cases under the legal rules of substance and procedure that were imposed from above.[51]

This interaction between those at the top and at the bottom was not the same in all slave societies, however. In the British colonies that later became states in the United States, the lawmakers and judges at the top were not the kings, queens, or parliaments of the mother country or their colonial administrators. Instead, they were almost from the beginning locally elected or selected legislators and judges who were slave owners themselves, or who were at least not unsympathetic to the interests of the slaveholders.[52] Moreover, except in Louisiana and at the start in South Carolina, these lawmakers and judges did not base their slave law on a code of Roman, medieval, or non-local origin. They instead made up the law as they went along to advance the salient public and private interests in the slave societies that they established and developed.[53]

This interpretation of legal change is akin to the instrumentalist model because it asserts that Southern judges and legislators viewed this law as an instrument of social policy that they used to encourage certain nonlegal changes and to alleviate the harmful effects of others.[54] I do not suggest, however, that the law box was always empty, that statutes and case law reports necessarily reflected dominant interests, or that they did so by means of a simple, unthinking reflex action. In fact, we must account for the important institutional differences between courts and legislatures, along with the different natures of case law and statute law materials. Moreover, we must interpret case law reports with a lawyer's expertise, which accounts for the way lawyers and judges argue from precedents, and which focuses on the specific issues that the litigants have asked the courts to decide.[55]

Therefore, from the traditional legal history approach, we need to carefully distinguish the holdings from the *dicta* in slave law cases, a basic but essential principle of legal research and analysis.[56] Karl Llewellyn said it best when he wrote that the only "law" in a judicial opinion is created when the court "speaks to the question before it[.]" As to any other question the court "says mere words, which no man needs to follow." These words are not "worthless." "We know them as judicial *dicta*; ... words dropped along the road, wayside remarks. Yet even wayside remarks shed light on the remarker. They may be very useful in the future to him, or to us. But he will not feel bound to them, as to his ex cathedra utterance."[57]

Consequently, I again argue that traditional legal doctrinal analysis can help us to reconcile the court opinions in which judges sometimes referred to slave rights with other decisions in which the judges did not feel bound by claims to slave humanity or rights when reaching the holdings in their decisions. These *dicta* and holdings, when read together, tell us that the judges' various references to slave humanity or right do not reconcile the cases. In some cases the courts explicitly discussed the relevant interests that the courts balanced in the slave law judicial opinions. In other opinions, however, the judges' concerns about social changes were implicit in the complex and changing structure of the legal rules and results that flowed from the case and statutory law.

We can reconcile the evolving legal standards only if we reflect on how the judges' and legislators' perceptions of the balance of the relevant interests changed over time. Thus, the judges' and legislators' changing perceptions about the balance of these relevant interests were the motivating force behind legal change. The law does not appear to change for its own strictly autonomous reasons.[58]

From the Critical Legal Studies authors,[59] I will again borrow the notion of reification.[60] Reification is a mode of thought and expression by which we substitute an abstract and positive word or idea in the place of the complex reality of oppressive personal relations.[61] Gordon again provided a helpful analysis: "'Law' is just one among many ... systems of meaning people construct in order to deal with one of the most threatening aspects of social existence: the danger posed by other people, whose cooperation is indispensable to us..., but who may kill us or enslave us."[62]

Slave owners already had enslaved the people held as slaves. They sought to preserve their dominant position over their slaves as well as poor whites, whose cooperation was indispensable. These classes, of course, could combine and rebel. Because of these perceived threats, Gordon stated that the elites in society create legal "belief structures," along with economic and political ones, to rationalize "their dominant power positions[.]" These belief systems "define rights" in ways that reinforce "existing hierarchies of wealth and privilege."[63]

This the master class did with the pro-slavery ideology and the law of slavery. The followers of this ideology in the South, through racism, denied the slave's humanity—or at least placed the slave on a level between humanity and other animals. Similarly, the law defined slaves as chattels to cut them off from all claims to the ordinary rights enjoyed by humanity. These were the "belief structures" that the Southern elites constructed to rationalize their dominant position.[64]

Gordon stated, moreover, that these belief systems make "the social world as it is come to seem natural and inevitable." This occurs when people "externalize" beliefs by attributing "to them existence and control over and above human choice; and, moreover [people] believe that these structures must be the way they are."[65] Gordon thus concluded that reification "is a way people have of manufacturing necessity: they build structures, then act as if (and genuinely come to believe) that the structures they have built are determined by history, human nature, [and] economic law."[66]

Accordingly, slave owners and the legislators and judges in the slave states came to believe that the slavery law that they made was determined by history, human nature, and economic law. With this belief, they rationalized slavery's inhumanity. They thought they were merely acting out the perceived dictates of the reality that they created. The epitome of this process was the rise of the positive good theory of slavery, which did indeed influence the law of slavery, as illustrated by many of the statutes and cases cited in this book.[67] "[O]ne [does not] have to be a Marxist to accept that one of the reasons why people believe in certain shared ideals ('ideology') is to enable them to come to terms with and tolerate practices which would be intolerable when looked at from some alternative point of view."[68]

The definition of slaves as property was the key to the belief system that included slavery law. It rendered all references to slave rights and humanity into rationalizations that masked slavery's total oppression. For example, in *James v. Carper*,[69] the Tennessee Supreme Court in 1857 rejected the contention that the law could deprive a master of her right to recover damages from a hirer of one of her slaves who perpetrated a battery against the slave. Justice Robert J. McKinney's opinion stated that a rule denying the owner her right to sue and recover her damages would "ignore the plainest principles of reason and of right," and "would be justly esteemed a reproach to humanity in any condition of civil society above the level of barbarism."[70]

According to Daniel Flanigan, this decision "demonstrated how slavery could warp the values of the slaveholders. Civil suits to recompense masters for the value of the labor or lives of their slaves did not reduce but instead encouraged 'barbarism.'"[71] Indeed, the court applied the general rule of the common law by which a hirer or bailee of a chattel, such as a horse, can be held liable to the owner for damages caused by the intentional misuse of the chattel.[72] This opinion provides just one example of how slavery's "barbarism" was reified; the court's references to humanity and right helped to obscure the oppression of the fundamentals of the master and slave relation.[73]

Indeed, phrases such as slave "humanity" and slave "rights" expressed—in legal terms—the slave's economic value, and defined the relative property rights and duties of individuals and the state in the slave. Slave law thus expressed the conflicting interests of free people that were embodied in slaves. The notions of slave rights and humanity became reifications.[74]

In this book, I will build on the interpretation that I advanced in *People Without Rights* by again using all of these approaches to legal history, as well as my experience as a practicing lawyer, to further reveal slavery law's essential nature through an analysis of the manumission and freedom suits and the related statutes.[75]

* * * * *

This book is the latest chapter in my 31-year effort to understand and write about slavery law in the United States. I began this inquiry as a second-year law student at Rutgers Law School, in Newark, New Jersey, during a Fall 1980 seminar on law and social change taught by Professor James C. N. Paul. I again wish to note my thanks to Professor Paul and my Rutgers professors John Anthony Scott and Arthur Kinoy, who encouraged me to continue my research and writing in this important field of study while I completed my traditional law school course of study.

In addition to my law practice and continuing research into historical sources and interpretation, since 1986 I have worked as an adjunct professor teaching law classes at Montclair State College, now University, in Upper Montclair, New Jersey. I wish to thank the Sprague Library personnel at Montclair for assisting me in obtaining books that were not available in the Library's collection.

This book, like my earlier works, is the product of my independent efforts. Nevertheless, I thank all of those who have commented on my publications, both in print and in communications that I have received over these many years.

I also wish to acknowledge the many online sources of information, especially Google Books, which have made it easier for independent scholars to obtain access to materials that previously were readily available only to those who were associated with elite institutions. The following data sources also were especially helpful to me in completing this project: Archives of Maryland Online, http://aomol.net/html/, which is the source of most of the Maryland materials I have cited, and Paul Axel-Lute, ed., "The Law of Slavery in New Jersey: An Annotated Bibliography" (January 2005, revised October 9, 2009), http://njlegallib.rutgers.edu/slavery/bibliog.html/, which is the source of many of the New Jersey materials.

Of course, I thank Alan Childress for agreeing to publish the book and for assisting me in my efforts to get the manuscript into publishable form. But my most important thanks go to my wife, Daniele Fede. Also a lawyer, she has had to endure for three years the storage boxes in our dining room filled with copies of the fruits of my research efforts, compounded by my occupation of our dining room table with books, notes, and drafts of the chapters that have finally found their way into this book. For these reasons, and countless others, this book is dedicated to her.

ANDREW T. FEDE

Bogota, New Jersey
October, 2011

Notes to the Preface

[1] Andrew Fede, *People Without Rights: An Interpretation of the Fundamentals of the Law of Slavery in the U.S. South* (1992), and the reprint edition published in 2011 by Routledge [hereinafter Fede, *People Without Rights*].

[2] In *People Without Rights*, I advanced an interpretation of the criminal law, manumission law, and commercial law of Southern slavery, which I had outlined in a 1984 review essay, Andrew Fede, "Toward a Solution of the Slave Law Dilemma: A Critique of Tushnet's 'The American Law of Slavery,'" 2 *Law & Hist. Rev.* 301 (1984) [hereinafter Fede, "Toward a Solution"]. I applied that approach to the criminal law of slavery in Andrew Fede, "Legitimized Violent Slave Abuse in the American South, 1619-1865: A Case Study of Law and Social Change in Six Southern States," 29 *Am. J. Legal Hist.* 93 (1985) [hereinafter Fede, "Legitimized Violence"], reprinted in *Articles on American Slavery: Law, the Constitution, and Slavery* (Paul Finkelman, ed.) (1989); and to the law of slave sales in Andrew Fede, "Legal Protection for Slave Buyers in the U.S. South: A Caveat Concerning *Caveat Emptor*," 31 *Am. J. of Legal Hist.* 322 (1987) [hereinafter Fede, "Slave Buyers"]. *See also* Andrew T. Fede, "Slave Codes," in 2 *Macmillan Encyclopedia of World Slavery* 801 (Paul Finkelman and Joseph C. Miller, eds.) (1998); Andrew T. Fede, "Gender in the Law of Slavery in the Antebellum United States," 18 *Cardozo L. Rev.* 411 (1996) [hereinafter Fede, "Gender"].

[3] Fede, *People Without Rights*, *supra* at 41, 131-58.

[4] Robert B. Shaw, *A Legal History of Slavery in the United States* (1991).

[5] Thomas D. Morris, *Southern Slavery and the Law, 1619-1860* (1996) [hereinafter

Morris, *Slavery*]; *see* Andrew T. Fede, "Book Review," 41 *Am. J. of Legal Hist.* 406 (1997) [hereinafter Fede, "Morris Book Review"] (for a review by this author).

[6] Judith Kelleher Schafer, *Slavery, the Civil Law, and the Supreme Court of Louisiana* (1994) [hereinafter Schafer, *Supreme Court*].

[7] Jenny Bourne Wahl, *The Bondsman's Burden: An Economic Analysis of the Common Law of Southern Slavery* (1998) [hereinafter Wahl, *Burden*]; Jenny Bourne Wahl, "Legal Constraints on Slave Masters: The Problem of Social Cost," 41 *Am. J of Legal Hist.* 1 (1997) [hereinafter Wahl, "Constraints"]; *see* Andrew T. Fede, "Book Review," 42 *Am. J. of Legal Hist.* 433 (1998) (for a review by this author).

[8] William E. Wiethoff, *A Peculiar Humanism: The Judicial Advocacy of Slavery in High Courts of the Old South, 1820-1850* (1996).

[9] A. Leon Higginbotham, Jr., *Shades of Freedom: Racial Politics and Presumptions of the American Legal Process* (1996); A. Leon Higginbotham, Jr., "The Ten Precepts of American Slavery Jurisprudence: Chief Justice Roger Taney's Defense and Justice Thurgood Marshall's Condemnation of the Precept of Black Inferiority," 17 *Cardozo L. Rev.* 1695 (1996); *see* Anita F. Hill, "The Scholarly Legacy of A. Leon Higginbotham, Jr.: Voice, Storytelling, and Narrative," 53 *Rutgers L. Rev.* 641 (2001) (for a bibliography and evaluation of Judge Higginbotham's legal history writings).

[10] Glenn McNair, *Criminal Injustice: Slaves and Free Blacks in Georgia's Criminal Justice System* (2009); James M. Campbell, *Slavery on Trial: Race, Class, and Criminal Justice in Antebellum Richmond Virginia* (2007); Ariela J. Gross, *What Blood Won't Tell: A History of Race on Trial in America* 1-110 (2007) [hereinafter Gross, *Blood*]; Ariela J. Gross, *Double Character: Slavery and Mastery in the Antebellum Southern Courtroom* (2000) [hereinafter Gross, *Double Character*]; Sally E. Hadden, *Slave Patrols: Law and Violence in Virginia and the Carolinas* (2001); Walter Johnson, *Soul by Soul: Life Inside the Antebellum Slave Market* (1999) [hereinafter Johnson, *Soul*].

[11] Bernie D. Jones, *Fathers of Conscience: Mixed-Race Inheritance in the Antebellum South* (2009) [hereinafter Jones, *Fathers*]; Jason A. Gillmer, "Suing for Freedom: Interracial Sex, Slave Law, and Racial Identity in the Post-Revolutionary and Antebellum South," 82 *N.C. L. Rev.* 535 (2004) [hereinafter Gillmer, "Suing for Freedom"]; Adrienne D. Davis, "The Private Law of Race and Sex: An Antebellum Perspective," 51 *Stanford L. Rev.* 221 (1999) [hereinafter Davis, "Race and Sex"]; *see* chapter 1, *infra* at notes 19 and 20 for other sources.

[12] Judith Kelleher Schafer, *Becoming Free, Remaining Free: Manumission and Enslavement in New Orleans, 1846-1862* (2003) [hereinafter Schafer, *Becoming Free*].

[13] *See* Randall Kennedy, "The State, Criminal Law, and Racial Discrimination: A Comment," 107 *Harv. L. Rev.* 1255, 1267 (1994); *see also* Randall Kennedy, *Race, Crime, and the Law* 29-36, 76-80 (1997) [hereinafter Kennedy, *Race*].

[14] *See* Fede, *People Without Rights, supra* at 9-12.

[15] *Id.* at ix.

[16] Many writers have used the phrase "people without rights." For example, some have used it in connection with slavery. *See, e.g.*, Philip D. Morgan, *Slave Counterpoint: Black Culture in the Eighteenth-Century Chesapeake and Lowcountry* 259 (1998) [hereinafter Morgan, *Slave Counterpoint*]; Laura F. Edwards, "Enslaved Women and the Law:

Paradoxes of Subordination in the Post Revolutionary Carolinas," in *Women and Slavery: The Modern Atlantic* 129 (Gwyn Campbell, *et al.*, eds.) (2008); Paul Marshall, "Rights Talk and Welfare Policy," in *Welfare in America: Christian Perspectives on a Policy Crisis* 281 (Stanley W. Carlson-Thies and James W. Skillen, eds.) (1996); *see also* Laura F. Edwards, "Status Without Rights: African Americans and the Tangled History of Law and Governance in the Nineteenth-Century U.S. South," 112 *Am. Hist. Rev.* 365 (2007). Plato used it to describe people who, like slaves, were subject to violence and the confiscation of their property. *See Plato on Rhetoric and Language: Four Key Dialogues* 145 (Jean Nienkamp, ed.) (1999). Hannah Arendt and others used it when writing about the status of European Jews. *See* Peg Birmingham, *Hannah Arendt and Human Rights: The Predicament of Common Responsibility* 98 (2006); Leon I. Yudkin, *Jewish Writing and Identity in the Twentieth Century* 103 (1982) (quoting French poet André Spire). Writers also have used the phrase to describe the disenfranchised people in the Soviet Union before 1936, Golfo Alexopoulos, *Stalin's Outcasts: Aliens, Citizens, and the Soviet State, 1926-1936* 3, 23, 28-31 (2003); the people in the nations captured by the Germans during World War II, Konrad H. Jarausch and Michael Geyer, *Shattered Past: Reconstructing German Histories* 139 (2003); Australia's Aboriginal people, John Chesterman and Brian Galligan, *Citizens Without Rights: Aborigines and Australian Citizenship* 1-10 (1997), and Hannah McGlade, "Aboriginal Women and the Commonwealth Government's Response to Mabo—An International Human Rights Perspective," in *Words and Silences: Aboriginal Women, Politics and Land* 139 (Peggy Brock, ed.) (2001); and those in Kosovo and East Timor, Noam Chomsky, *People Without Rights: Kosovo, Ost-timor und der Westen [Kosovo, East Timor and the West]* (2002).

[17] Fede, *People Without Rights, supra* at x.

[18] *Id.* at ix-x.

[19] Kenneth M. Stampp, *The Peculiar Institution: Slavery in the Ante-Bellum South* 193-236 (1956); *see, e.g.*, Fede, *People Without Rights, supra* at 6-12; and Thomas D. Russell, "A New Image of the Slave Auction: An Empirical Look at the Role of Law in Slave Sales and a Conceptual Reevaluation of Slave Property," 18 *Cardozo L. Rev.* 473, 488-502 (1996) [hereinafter Russell, "New Image"] for reviews of the literature. The anti-slavery treatises include George M. Stroud, *A Sketch of the Laws Relating to Slavery in the Several States of the United States of America* (photo. reprint 1968) (2d ed. 1856); Richard Hildreth, *Despotism in America: An Inquiry Into the Slave-Holding System in the United States* 169-303 (photo. reprint ed. 1970) (1854); William Goodell, *The American Slave Code in Theory and Practice* (photo. reprint 1968) (1853); Harriet Beecher Stowe, *The Key to Uncle Tom's Cabin* (reprint ed. 1968) (1853). Other essential antebellum studies include: Thomas R.R. Cobb, *An Inquiry Into the Law of Negro Slavery in the United States of America* (photo. reprint 1968) (1858); John B. O'Neall, *Negro Law of South Carolina* (1848), in 2 *Statutes on Slavery: The Pamphlet Literature* 117-72 (Paul Finkelman, ed.) (1988) [hereinafter *Statutes on Slavery*]; Jacob D. Wheeler, *A Practical Treatise on the Law of Slavery* (photo. reprint 1968) (1837). For cases, statutes, and commentary, *see, e.g.*, Helen T. Catterall, ed., *Judicial Cases Concerning American Slavery and the Negro* (5 volumes) (reprint ed. 1968) (1926-1937); John C. Hurd, *The Law of Freedom and Bondage in the United States* (2 volumes) (reprint ed. 1968) (1858, 1862); Alexander Karst, "Slaves," in 36 *Cyclopedia of Law and Procedure* 465-95 (William Mack, ed.) (1910).

[20] *See* Jill Lepore, "Paul Revere's Ride Against Slavery," *N.Y. Times*, December 19, 2010 (Week in Review), at 8, discussing Longfellow's anti-slavery views and writings, including the quotation in the text from the poem "The Witness."

[21] *State v. Harrison*, 11 La. Ann. 722, 1856 WL 4823 at *3 (La. 1856).

[22] Fede, *People Without Rights*, *supra* at x; *see* Schafer, *Supreme Court*, *supra* at 51-52, 135, 140, 167, 190-91, 212, 214, 257-60, 285 (discussing Buchanan's opinions).

[23] Fede, *People Without Rights*, *supra* at x.

[24] *State v. Jones*, 1 Miss. (Walker) 83, 1820 WL 1413 at *1 (1821).

[25] Fede, *People Without Rights*, *supra* at 3.

[26] *See id.* at 17-25.

[27] Paul Finkelman, "Exploring Southern Legal History," 64 *N.C. L. Rev.* 77, 89, n. 65 (1985) [hereinafter Finkelman, "Exploring"]. *See* A. E. Keir Nash, "In re Radical Interpretations of American Law: The Relation of Law and History," 82 *Michigan L. Rev.* 274, 274-76 (1983) [hereinafter Nash, "Radical Interpretations"]. Nash called for a "radical" but "non Marxist" theory of slave law, in response to Mark V. Tushnet, *The American Law of Slavery 1810-1860: Considerations of Humanity and Interest* (1981) [hereinafter Tushnet, *Humanity*].

[28] *See* Fede, *People Without Rights*, *supra* at ix.

[29] Alan Watson, *Slave Law in the Americas* xi (1989) [hereinafter Watson, *Americas*]; *see id.* at xi-xv; Alan Watson, "Roman Slave Law: An Anglo-American Perspective," 18 *Cardozo L. Rev.* 591 (1996) [hereinafter Watson, "Anglo-American"].

[30] *See* Peter Kolchin, "The American South in Comparative Perspective" [hereinafter Kolchin, "Comparative Perspective"], in *The American South and the Italian Mezzogiorno: Essays in Comparative History* 26 (Enrico Dal Lago and Rick Halpern, eds.) (2002) [hereinafter *Italian Mezzogiorno*]; *see also* Peter Kolchin, *A Sphinx on the American Land: The Nineteenth Century South in Comparative Perspective* (2003) [hereinafter Kolchin, *Sphinx*] (for Kolchin's further elaboration of these concepts).

[31] *See* Kolchin, "Comparative Perspective," *supra* at 39; *see also* Kolchin, *Sphinx*, *supra* at 74-115.

[32] *See* Kolchin, "Comparative Perspective," *supra* at 37, citing, e.g., George M. Fredrickson, "From Exceptionalism to Variability: Recent Developments in Cross-National Comparative History," 82 *Am. J. of Am. Hist.* 587 (1995).

[33] On *Las Siete Partidas*, see *Las Siete Partidas, Volume 4: Family, Commerce and the Sea: The Worlds of Women and Slaves* xxiii-xxv (Samuel Parsons Scott, tr., Robert I. Burns, ed.) (2001) [hereinafter *Las Siete Partidas, Volume 4*]; Watson, *Americas*, *supra* at 40-42; Herbert S. Klein, *Slavery in the Americas: A Comparative Study of Virginia and Cuba* 57-59 (1967); Michelle McKinley, "Fractional Freedoms: Slavery, Legal Activism, and Ecclesiastical Courts in Colonial Lima, 1593-1689," 28 *Law & Hist. Rev.* 749, 752-53 (2010); Manuel Barcia, "Fighting with the Enemy's Weapons," 3 *Atlantic Studies* 159, 165 (2006); Alejandro de la Fuente, "Slave Law and Claims-Making in Cuba: The Tannenbaum Debate Revisited," 22 *Law & Hist. Rev.* 339, 349, 367-68 (2004) [hereinafter de la Fuente, "Slave Law"]. On *Code Noir*, see "Introduction: Slavery, Freedom, and the Law," in *Slavery, Freedom, and the Law in the Atlantic World: A Brief History with*

Documents 5-10 (Sue Peabody and Keila Grinberg, eds.) (2007) [hereinafter *Brief History*], and "French Crown, The *Code Noir* 1685," in *id*. at 31-36 (the quotation is from page 31). On Roman slave law, which, like American slave law, changed over time, *see generally* Paul du Plessis, *Borkowski's Textbook on Roman Law* 85-109 (4th ed. 2010); Alan Watson, *Roman Slave Law* (1987).

[34] *Compare, e.g.*, Stanley M. Elkins, *Slavery: A Problem in American Institutional Life* 52-80, 223-42 (3d ed. 1976); Klein, *supra* at 37-85; Frank Tannenbaum, *Slave and Citizen: The Negro in the Americas* 48-82 (1946); Mary Wilhelmine Williams, "The Treatment of Negro Slaves in the Brazilian Empire: A Comparison with the United States of America," 15 *J. of Negro Hist*. 315, 331-36 (1930), *with* Carl N. Degler, *Neither Black nor White: Slavery and Race Relations in Brazil and the United States* 3-92 (1971); Eugene D. Genovese, *In Red and Black: Marxian Explorations in Southern and Afro American History* 79-92 (1971); David Brion Davis, *The Problem of Slavery in Western Culture* 100-06, 223-88 (1966) [hereinafter, Davis, *Western Culture*]; Marvin Harris, *Patterns of Race in the Americas* 65-94 (1964); David C. Rankin, "The Tannenbaum Thesis Reconsidered: Slavery and Race Relations in Antebellum Louisiana," 18 *Southern Studies* 5 (1979); Mark Tushnet, "The American Law of Slavery, 1810-1860: A Study in the Persistence of Legal Autonomy," 10 *Law & Soc'y Rev*. 119, 181-84 (1975); Eugene D. Genovese, "Materialism and Idealism in the History of Negro Slavery in the Americas," 1 *J. of Social Hist*. 371 (1968); Sidney W. Mintz, "Book Review," 33 *Am. Sociological Rev*. 471 (1968) (review of Degler); Arnold A. Sio, "Interpretations of Slavery: The Slave Status in the Americas," 7 *Comparative Studies in Society and History* 289 (1965); Sidney W. Mintz, "Book Review," 63 *Am. Anthropologist* 579 (1961) (review of Elkins). *See also* Alejandro de la Fuente and Ariela Gross, "Comparative Studies of Law, Slavery and Race in the Americas," 6 *Ann. Rev. of Law & Soc. Sci*. 469 (2010) (recent survey of literature); Keila Grinberg, "Alforria, direito e direitos no Brasil e nos Estados Unidos [Enfranchisement, Law and Rights in Brazil and the United States]," 27 *Estudios Historicos, Rio de Janeiro* 63 (2001) [Grinberg, "Alforria"] (comparing freedom suits in the United States and Brazil and the English language version, Keila Grinberg, "Freedom Suits and Civil Law in Brazil and the United States," 22 *Slavery & Abolition* 66, 76-77 (2001) [Grinberg, "Freedom"]); Robert J. Cottrol, "The Long Lingering Shadow: Law, Liberalism, and Cultures of Racial Hierarchy and Identity in the Americas," 76 *Tulane L. Rev*. 11 (2001) (comparing Latin American and North American legal history) [hereinafter Cottrol, "Long Lingering Shadow"]; Robert J. Cottrol, "Outlawing Outcasts: Comparative Perspectives on the Differing Functions of the Criminal Law of Slavery in the Americas," 18 *Cardozo L. Rev*. 717 (1996) (comparing articles on the criminal law of slavery in the British colonies and Louisiana) [hereinafter Cottrol, "Outcasts"]; Fredrickson, *supra* at 593-94, 597-98; Judith Kelleher Schafer, "The Long Arm of the Law: Slave Criminals and the Supreme Court in Antebellum Louisiana," 60 *Tulane L. Rev*. 1247 (1986) (comparing law in Louisiana and the common law states).

For other comparisons involving the American South, *see* Enrico Dal Lago, *Agrarian Elites: American Slaveholders and Southern Italian Landowners, 1815-1861* (2005); Don H. Doyle, *Nations Divided: America, Italy, and the Southern Question* (2002); Shearer Davis Bowman, *Masters and Lords: Mid-19th Century U.S. Planters and Prussian Junkers* (1993); Peter Kolchin, *Unfree Labor: American Slavery and Russian Serfdom* (1987); and the essays in *Slave Systems Ancient and Modern* (Enrico Dal Lago and Constantina Katsani, eds.) (2008) [hereinafter *Slave Systems*], and in *Italian Mez-*

zogiorno, supra.

[35] Eugene D. Genovese, "The Comparative Focus in Latin American History," 12 *J. of Interamerican Studies & World Affairs* 317, 318 (1970).

[36] *See* McKinley, *supra* at 752-61 (citing, e.g., the articles in "Forum: What Can Frank Tannenbaum Teach Us about the Law of Slavery," 22 *Law & Hist. Rev.* 339 (2004)); de la Fuente, "Slave Law," *supra* at 339-53.

[37] *See* McKinley, *supra* at 755.

[38] *See* Cottrol, "Long Lingering Shadow," *supra* at 15, 79. This book does not purport to be what Peter Kolchin called a rigorous comparative study of the subject; it is, at best, what Kolchin called a soft comparison. *See* Kolchin, *Sphinx*, *supra* at 3-4; Enrico Dal Lago and Constantina Katsani, "The Study of Ancient and Modern Slave Systems: Setting an Agenda for Comparison," in *Slave Systems*, *supra* at 7. It is an effort to advance an understanding of slave law, manumission, and freedom in the context of what David Brion Davis called "the Big Picture" consisting of "the interrelationship that constituted an Atlantic Slave system as well as the place of such racial slavery in the evolution of the Western and modern worlds." Davis, "Looking at Slavery from Broader Perspectives," 105 *Am. Hist. Rev.* 452, 454 (2000) [footnote omitted]; *see also* Peter Kolchin, "The Big Picture: A Comment on David Brion Davis's 'Looking at Slavery from Broader Perspectives,'" 105 *Am. Hist. Rev.* 452, 454 (2000). For recent wide-ranging comparative studies, *see* Robin Blackburn, *The American Crucible: Slavery, Emancipation and Human Rights* (2011); Seymour Drescher, *Abolition: A History of Slavery and Antislavery* (2009); Stanley L. Engerman, *Slavery, Emancipation, and Freedom: Comparative Perspectives* (2007).

[39] *See* Kolchin, *Sphinx*, *supra* at 7-38; Kolchin, "Comparative Perspective," *supra* at 30-32; *see also* Shaw, *supra* at 266-68; Henry Scofield Cooley, *A Study of Slavery in New Jersey* 20-30 (1896); Gary K. Wolinetz, "New Jersey Slavery and the Law," 50 *Rutgers L. Rev.* 2227, 2228, 2246 (1998).

[40] *See* Fede, "Slave Buyers," *supra* (comparing law of sales of slave and other goods); *see generally* Wahl, *Burden*, *supra* at 9-11.

[41] *See* Kolchin, *Sphinx*, *supra* at 39-73; Kolchin, "Comparative Perspective," *supra* at 32-37. Kolchin's second and third categories may be combined when we consider the development of slavery law in Florida and Louisiana during the respective periods of Spanish, French, British, and United States rule. *See, e.g.*, Larry Eugene Rivers, *Slavery in Florida: Territorial Days to Emancipation* 1-15, 66-67 (2000).

[42] *See* Fede, *People Without Rights*, *supra* at 22-25; Bernie D. Jones, "Southern Free Women of Color in the Antebellum North: Race, Class, and a 'New Women's Legal History,'" 41 *Akron L. Rev.* 763, 771 (2008) [hereinafter Jones, "Southern Free Women"] (also suggesting that the instrumentalist approach and the Critical Legal Studies approaches be combined when reviewing race, class, and gender issues in law).

[43] Fede, *People Without Rights*, *supra* at 22. Thomas D. Morris offered a similar "multi-factored" analysis of the development of slave law in his 1996 monograph. Morris, *Slavery*, *supra* at 9. He stated that the slave law cases and statutes that he studied represented "policy judgments" expressed by judges and legislators, which "involved nonlegal matters." These "included concerns that grew out of class relationships among

whites, a racist commitment to keep people of color subordinate to whites, market demands and theories of political economy, and even evangelical Christianity." *Id.* at 2-3; *see* Fede, "Morris Book Review," *supra* at 406-07.

44 Fede, *People Without Rights*, *supra* at 22-23.

45 Robert W. Gordon, "J. Willard Hurst and the Common Law Tradition in American Historiography," 10 *Law & Soc'y Rev.* 9, 10 (1975).

46 *See id.* at 11.

47 *See id.* at 10; *see also* Fede, *People Without Rights*, *supra* at 23. For an "internal" approach to slave law, *see* Watson, *Americas*, *supra* at 1-21, 113-33.

48 *See* Philip J. Schwarz, *Slave Law in Virginia* xiii, 1-12 (1996) [hereinafter Schwarz, *Slave Law*] (discussing this approach and "the study of the impact of human customs and behavior on the law"); Ariela Gross, "Reflections on Law, Culture, and Slavery," in *Slavery and the American South* 57-82 (Winthrop D. Jordan, ed.) (2003) [hereinafter *Slavery, South*]; Laura F. Edwards, "Commentary," in *id.* at 82-92 (discussing the need to combine legal and cultural history from the bottom up).

49 Schwarz, *Slave Law*, *supra* at 5.

50 *See* Robert Olwell, *Masters, Slaves and Subjects: The Culture of Power in the South Carolina Low Country, 1740-1790* 99 (1998); Jones, "Southern Free Women," *supra* at 771.

51 *See* Walter Johnson, "On Agency," 37 *J. of Social Hist.* 113, 115-16 (2003) (suggesting need for new approaches to issues of slave humanity, agency, and resistance).

52 *See, e.g.,* Jack P. Greene, *Peripheries and Center: Constitutional Development in the Extended Polities of the British Empire and the United States 1607-1788* 10 (1986); Jack P. Greene, "Transatlantic Colonization and Redefinition of Empire in the Early Modern Era: The British-American Inheritance," in *Negotiated Empires: Centers and Peripheries in the Americas 1550-1820* 267-82 (Christine Daniels and Michael V. Kennedy, eds.) (2002); Jonathan A. Bush, "Free to Enslave: The Foundations of Colonial American Slave Law," 5 *Yale J.L. & Humanities* 417, 456-70 (1993) [Bush, "Free to Enslave"], and the sources cited in notes 29-41 *supra*.

53 *See, e.g.,* discussing how colonial slave practices and law developed in the absence of direct legal authority in English law, Lorena S. Walsh, *Motives of Honor, Pleasure, and Profit: Plantation Management in the Colonial Chesapeake, 1607-1763* 113-45 (2010); Fede, *People Without Rights*, *supra* at 17, 29-30, 51-53; Lynn D. Wardle, "From Slavery to Same-Sex Marriage: Comity Versus Public Policy in Inter-Jurisdictional Recognition of Controversial Domestic Relations," 2008 *B.Y.U. L. Rev.* 1855, 1865-78; Steven M. Wise, "The Entitlement of Chimpanzees to the Common Law Writs of Habeas Corpus and De Home Replegiando," 37 *Golden Gate U.L. Rev.* 219, 241-45 (2007) [hereinafter Wise, "Writs"]; Joyce E. McConnell, "Beyond Metaphor: Battered Women, Involuntary Servitude and the Thirteenth Amendment," 4 *Yale J.L. & Feminism* 207, 207-08 (1992); *but see*, discussing English statutes that, it is suggested, may have provided analogies for colonial slave codes, Christopher Tomlins, *Freedom Bound: Law, Labor, and Civic Identity in Colonizing English America, 1580-1865* 418-20 (2010) [hereinafter Tomlins, *Freedom Bound*]; Christopher Tomlins, "Transplants and Timing: Passages in the Creation of an Anglo-American Law of Slavery," 10 *Theoretical Inquiries in Law* 389 (2009)

[hereinafter Tomlins, "Transplants"]; Jonathan A. Bush, "The First Slave (and Why He Matters)," 18 *Cardozo L. Rev.* 599, 600-10, 626-29 (1996) [hereinafter Bush, "First Slave"]; Bradley J. Nicholson, "Legal Borrowing and the Origins of Slave Law in the British Colonies," 38 *Am J. of Legal Hist.* 38 (1994); Bush, "Free to Enslave," *supra* at 420-56; David Konig, "'Dale's Laws' and the Non-Common Law Origins of Criminal Justice in Virginia," 26 *Am. J of Legal Hist.* 354 (1982); *see also* Morris, *Slavery, supra* at 37-57, and Thomas D. Morris, "'Villeinage...as it existed in England, reflects but little light on our subject': The Problem of the 'Sources' of Southern Slave Law," 32 *Am. J. Legal Hist.* 95 (1988) [hereinafter Morris, "Villeinage"] (discussing common law origins of slave law in property law).

On Louisiana, *see* Vernon Valentine Palmer, "The Strange Science of Codifying Slavery—Moreau Lislet and the Louisiana Digest of 1808," 24 *Tulane Eur. & Civ. L.F.* 83, 89 (2009) [hereinafter Palmer, "Codifying"]; Hans W. Baade, "The Bifurcated Romanist Tradition of Slavery in Louisiana," 70 *Tulane L. Rev.* 1481, 1490-93 (1996) [hereinafter Baade, "Bifurcated"]; Vernon Valentine Palmer, "The Origins and Authors of the Code Noir," 56 *La. L. Rev.* 363, 387 (1995) [hereinafter Palmer, "Origins"].

On South Carolina's first slave laws that were based on the slave codes that the British colonists on Barbados previously developed, *see* Tomlins, *Freedom Bound, supra* at 427-52; Fede, *People Without Rights, supra* at 30; A. Leon Higginbotham, Jr., *In the Matter of Color: Race and The American Legal Process: The Colonial Period* 151-215 (1978) [hereinafter Higginbotham, *Color*]; Nicholson, *supra* at 49-53; M. Eugene Sirmans, "The Legal Status of the Slave in South Carolina, 1670-1740," 28 *J. of So. Hist.* 462 (1962).

[54] *See generally, e.g.*, Morton Horwitz, *The Transformation of American Law, 1780-1860* 30 (1977); J. Willard Hurst, *The Growth of American Law: The Law Makers* 1-19 (1950); *see also* Kermit Hall, *The Magic Mirror: Law in American History* 3-8 (1991); and Lawrence M. Friedman, *A History of American Law* xi-xx and *passim* (3d ed. 2005). *Compare* David J. Langum, "The Role of Intellect and Fortuity in Legal Change: An Incident from the Law of Slavery," 28 *Am. J. of Legal Hist.* 1 (1984) (for a critique of this view as applied to slave law).

[55] Fede, *People Without Rights, supra* at 23-24.

[56] *See id.* at 23-24, 61, 75, 111, 146; *but see* Wiethoff, *supra* at 162 (for another inter-pretation).

[57] Karl N. Llewellyn, *The Bramble Bush: The Classic Lectures on the Law and Law School* 39 (OUP reprint edition, 2008). Patrick Brady also noted the need to observe these insights when reading slave law decisions. *See* Patrick S. Brady, "Slavery, Race, and the Criminal Law in Antebellum North Carolina: A Reconsideration of the Thomas Ruffin Court," 10 *N.C. Cent. L.J.* 248, 249 (1979).

[58] Fede, *People Without Rights, supra* at 24.

[59] *See, e.g.*, Pierre Schlag, "Critical Legal Studies," in *The Oxford International Ency-clopedia of Legal History* 295-99 (Stanley N. Katz, et al., eds.) (2009); Mark V. Tushnet, "Critical Legal Studies: A Political History," 100 *Yale L.J.* 1515 (1991); Robert W. Gordon and William Nelson, "An Exchange on Critical Legal Studies between Robert W. Gordon and William Nelson," 6 *Law & Hist. Rev.* 139 (1988), for discussions of and debates on these approaches. *See also* Stephen B. Presser & Jamil S. Zanaldin, *Law and Jurispru-dence in American History: Cases and Materials* 939-92 (2d ed. 1989); Mark Kelman, *A*

Guide to Critical Legal Studies 213, 241 (1987).

[60] Fede, *People Without Rights, supra* at 241-45

[61] *See generally* Louis B. Schwartz, "With Gun and Camera Through Darkest CLS-Land," 36 *Stanford L. Rev.* 413, 442 (1984), for a non-C.L.S. analysis. *See, e.g.*, Peter Gabel, "Reification to Legal Reasoning," in 3 *Research in Law and Sociology* 25-51 (Stephen Spitzer, ed.) (1980), and Kelman, *supra* at 269-75, for C.L.S. discussions.

[62] Robert W. Gordon, "New Developments in Legal Theory," in *The Politics of Law: A Progressive Critique* 288 (David Kairys, ed.) (1982) [hereinafter Gordon, "New Developments"].

[63] *Id.*

[64] Fede, *People Without Rights, supra* at 241-42.

[65] Gordon, "New Developments," *supra* at 288.

[66] *Id.* at 289.

[67] *See* Fede, *People Without Rights, supra* at 54-56.

[68] Thomas E. J. Wiedemann, "The Regularity of Manumission at Rome," 35 *The Classical Quarterly, New Series* 162, 163 (1985) [hereinafter Wiedemann, "Regularity"].

[69] 36 Tenn. (4 Sneed) 397, 1857 WL 2493 (1857).

[70] *James v. Carper*, 1857 WL 2493 at *4, quoted in Daniel Flanigan, *The Criminal Law of Slavery and Freedom 1800-1868* 171 (1987).

[71] *Id.*

[72] *See Wentworth v. McDuffie*, 48 N.H. 402, 1869 WL 2774 (1869) (suit by owner against hirer of a horse that died allegedly because the hirer's immoderate and violent driving); 19 *Williston on Contracts* §53.12 (Richard A. Lord, ed.) (4th ed. 2009).

[73] *See* Wahl, *Burden, supra* at 58-77; Fede, *People Without Rights, supra* at 100-01, 242 (discussing civil liability of slave abusers). For other views of *James, see, e.g.*, Jonathan D. Martin, *Divided Mastery: Slave Hiring in the American South* 122-23 (2004); Note, "What We Talk About When We Talk About Persons: The Language of a Legal Fiction," 114 *Harv. L. Rev.* 1745, 1749, n. 21 (2001).

[74] *See* Fede, *People Without Rights, supra* at 243, citing *Ex parte Boylston*, 33 S.C.L. (2 Strob.) 41, 43, 1847 WL 2155 at *2 (1847), and *id.* at 3-15. I recognized that some might call this a harsh indictment of the slave owners who lobbied for the slave codes and the lawmakers and judges who made and enforced slave law, and that Mark Tushnet employed the Critical Legal Studies analysis to arrive at a different interpretation. *See* Fede, *People Without Rights, supra* at 245, n. 13, citing "Toward a Solution," *supra* at 303-11, for a discussion of Tushnet's views and a critique. Mitchell Crusto also wrote of reification in relation to slavery law in the United States. *See* Mitchell F. Crusto, "Blackness as Property: Sex, Race, Status, and Wealth," 1 *Stan. J. of Civ. Rts. & Civ. Liberties* 51, 58, n. 19 (2005).

[75] For reviews of *People Without Rights, compare* Arthur Howington, "Book Review," 60 *J. of Southern Hist.* 580 (1994), *with* William J. Cooper, "Book Review," 99 *Am. Hist. Rev.* 970 (1994); Ruth Wedgwood, "The South Condemning Itself: Humanity and Property in American Slavery," 68 *Chi.-Kent L. Rev.* 1391, 1391-92 (1993) (book review); for

more general consideration of the analysis and criticism of legal history, *see also* William Nelson, *The Literature of American Legal History* 312-30 (1985) (discussing A.W.B. Simpson's critique of Morton Horwitz's interpretation and the criteria that reviewers should use when reviewing interpretations of legal materials with which they simply do not agree). For other comments, *see* Manfred Berg, "Historical Community and Counterfactual History in the Debate over Reparations for Slavery," in *International Perspective: How Societies Are Trying to Right the Wrongs of the Past* 74, n. 10 (Manfred Berg and Bernd Schaefer, eds.) (2009); Manfred Berg and Martin H. Geyer, "Introduction," in *Two Cultures of Right: The Quest for Inclusion and Participation in Modern America and Germany* 5, n. 13 (Manfred Berg and Martin H. Geyer, eds.) (2002).

ROADBLOCKS
TO
FREEDOM

1

The Manumission and Freedom Suits and the Law as a Compact Among the Slaves' Rulers

Many Americans are familiar with only one slavery law case: the United States Supreme Court's 1857 ruling in *Dred Scott v. Sandford*.[1] That decision ended Dred and Harriet Scott's unsuccessful eleven-year effort to obtain freedom judgments, first in the Missouri state courts and later in the United States courts. The Scotts' claims to liberty arose out of their long-term residence on free soil. Their arguments were contrary to their owners' intentions to continue to own the Scotts and their descendants as slaves. Because of deaths in their owners' family, however, the Scotts were freed two months after Chief Justice Roger B. Taney read the Supreme Court's opinion.[2]

Other slaves were not so lucky. In contrast, there can be little doubt that Alabama slave owner James Doran intended that thirteen of his slaves be freed after he and his wife died. In 1832 and 1833, he convinced the Alabama legislature to adopt two special acts permitting him to free these slaves. His will of 1840 stated that, upon his wife's death, these slaves were to be freed, and he bequeathed 640 acres of his land to the freed slaves, so that they would not become public charges. After Doran and his wife died, however, his executors deprived Doran's slaves of their freedom and removed the slaves to Tennessee. While these people still were held as slaves, they pursued two unsuccessful suits for their freedom—one in Tennessee and the other in Alabama. The highest courts in both of these states affirmed the lower court decisions denying Doran's slaves' claims, in 1852 and in 1861 respectively. Accordingly, despite Doran's clearly expressed intentions, these slaves may have been among those enslaved people who were not freed until after about 620,000 Americans in the military lost their lives in the Civil War.[3]

Enslaved people in the United States South who sought their freedom "had only three options: short- or long-term escape, manumission, and freedom suits."[4] Indeed, some people who were held as slaves in the United States used "extralegal" means, such as an escape to a state that abolished slavery, to Canada, or to Florida when, under Spanish rule, it offered sanctuary to slaves fleeing the British colonies and until 1790 the American states.[5] But others turned to the legal system to obtain their release from unjust enslavement. Some of these litigants won their cases in the courts before slavery was abolished in their state or in the nation. Nevertheless, the Scotts and the Doran slaves, and many others discussed in this book, lost their cases because of the substantive and procedural barriers that the judges and legislators placed in the way of persons held in slavery who sought their freedom in the courts.

The Issues to be Analyzed in the Freedom and Manumission Suits

According to Thomas Cobb's 1858 slave law treatise: "[I]n all the States the negro may institute proceedings to recover his freedom, when unlawfully detained in bondage."[6] These suits were not a unique feature of slavery in the United States. "From ancient times judges and lawmakers had recognized that a man might be unjustly held in bondage, and that slaves should therefore be allowed the right to plead for freedom."[7]

Therefore, two types of slavery existed during slavery times in the United States: just or legal slavery, and unjust or illegal slavery.[8] People held as slaves in the Southern states who sued for a court order releasing them from slavery sought to be included in the category of people unjustly or illegally held as slaves. These claimants "thus risked affirming the legitimacy of the institution that oppressed them. They had first to acquiesce to the idea of *just* subjection under slave law before petitioning courts for emancipation based on *wrongful* enslavement[.]"[9]

The slavery laws that permitted people held as slaves to sue for their freedom were consistent with the logic of slavery.[10] Cases in which slaves won their individual freedom "paradoxically *reinforced* the institution of slavery as a whole because [they] functioned as a kind of safety valve. If slaves could see that a few among them could gain their freedom (especially through compliance with the master's demands), then perhaps they would be more likely to behave well in hopes that they, too, would someday be freed. Indeed, some slave societies reinforced this contradiction by granting freedom to slaves who helped capture runaways or who fought in maroon wars."[11]

Similarly, an individual master's decision to free one or several slaves is not necessarily evidence that the master harbored "an unspoken (or perhaps even unconscious) anti-slavery sentiment." Although some masters freed all of their slaves during their lifetimes, or after their deaths, as an expression of their opposition to slavery, the acts of others who freed "a tiny minority of especially favoured slaves might just as accurately be taken as the ultimate bestowal of patriarchal benevolence. Like the modern lottery's Midas touch, the example of a fortunate few may have served to validate an inherently unequal system."[12]

Consequently, we should distinguish cases in which people held as slaves won their own freedom from a general emancipation, by which "a state or national government abolished slavery throughout its territory."[13] Following Judith Schafer's suggestion, I will use the term manumission to describe the action of the master or the state freeing slaves "during a time in which slavery existed under law," rather than emancipation, which I will use to describe the governmental act freeing slaves immediately, or in the future, when slavery was abolished under law.[14]

"From a just consideration of the rights of *property*, it would seem ... plain that the master might, at his pleasure, relinquish his dominion over the slave."[15] In most slave societies the lawmakers did not perceive manumission as an anti-slavery act, and "'manumission became an intrinsic part of the process of slavery' as masters found it in their best interests 'to exploit their slaves' yearning for freedom as a preferred form of incentive,' and then to rely on cheap and easily obtainable replacements."[16] "Manumission constituted the means of release for almost all ex-slaves. While some running away occurred, in the vast majority of slaveholding societies insignificant numbers of slaves were released by these means."[17]

The master's property right to free his or her slaves was not absolute, however. "Manumission is as universal as slavery; wherever the latter existed, the privilege of being relieved therefrom has concurrently been acknowledged, more or less trammeled by formalities or conditions, according to the policy of the State."[18]

In the United States South the law did indeed trammel the masters' power to free their slaves. This law varied over time and it varied in different places, but, on the whole, it was among the most restrictive in the slave societies. Moreover, its trend of development ended in the late antebellum years with the statutes abolishing all domestic or even foreign manumissions, and encouraging manumission's antithesis, the voluntary enslavement of free blacks. Many antebellum Southern legislators and judges began to perceive manumission as an anti-slavery act that they could not endorse, even if the master directed that the slaves be freed outside of their state.

Nevertheless, some freedom claimants won their court cases even in the late antebellum period. The successful claimants generally asserted two primary theories of relief. Some plaintiffs, like the Doran slaves, tried to convince the courts to enforce their masters' alleged intentions to free them, or one of their ancestors, in cases that I will call the *manumission suits*.[19] Others, like Dred and Harriet Scott, tried to prove that, according to the applicable statute or case law, they were not among the people who could be held as slaves. These plaintiffs sought their freedom in opposition to their purported owners' property ownership claims. I will refer to these cases as the *freedom suits*.

In turn, the freedom suits can be subdivided into two categories. First are the suits in which the claimants asserted their rights to freedom based on the local law of the forum slave state.[20] Second are the cases in which the claimants asserted freedom rights arising out of their travels between slave and free jurisdictions, which depended upon the forum slave state's court's willingness to enforce the free state's or nation's laws.[21]

Of course these categories overlap to some degree, as do any categories for the analysis of legal cases. For example, the judges in the travel cases inferred from the masters' move to free territories, states, or nations an implied intention on the masters' part to free their slaves. In contrast, some courts held that the masters' travels or temporary visits to free jurisdictions did not evince an intention on the masters' part to free their slaves. These travel issues also arose in suits that masters or people held as slaves filed while they were on free soil after the masters took their slaves to a free territory, state, or nation.[22]

This first chapter begins with a summary of the interpretation of slave law that I advanced in my earlier work. I will discuss the significance of the manumission and freedom suits in relation to that interpretation in the later chapters.

Chapter two discusses the nature of the master's manumission right, and chapter three the limits that the legislatures and the courts imposed on that right. Chapter four reviews the procedural rules establishing who could file manumission and freedom suits and the causes of action that could form the basis for these suits. Chapters five to eight analyze how those standards played out in the manumission and freedom suits. Chapter nine reviews the evidence that was admissible to prove or disprove these claims and the damages that successful claimants could recover for wrongful detention in slavery.

Chapter ten analyzes these suits as one example of the South's failure to condemn or to reform itself and its legal institutions. Indeed, the prevailing trend of slave law "reform," under the influence of the pro-slavery ideology in the years before the Civil War, was made up of laws prohibiting manumission and authorizing "voluntary" enslavement, even in Louisiana.

In both the manumission suits and the freedom suits, the legal battle was between the slave's rulers. In the manumission cases, the courts decided whether the master intended to free the slave, and whether that intention should be enforced against the restrictions imposed by the statutes or the property rights or claims of other persons, such as the master's heirs or creditors. In the freedom suits, the courts generally decided whether the claimant's owner could legally hold the claimant in slavery. The courts thus determined who could be held as a slave or they enforced the statutes that defined who could be a slave and who could not be held in bondage, often contrary to the alleged master's wishes. These decisions generally were based on the proofs of what the lawmakers decided was the freedom claimant's relevant status, such as his or her racial appearance and ancestry. They rarely focused on the owner's misconduct or the slave's exemplary conduct, which the legislators decided could lead to a forfeiture of the owner's interest in his or her slaves.

The courts and legislatures created the rules of law governing both the manumission and freedom suits to resolve real disputes that real people brought to the courts in their efforts to obtain the just resolution of the fundamental issues of freedom and bondage. I will, therefore, analyze these issues as the lawyers and litigants might have in the past when they evaluated their relative chances of winning or defending a suit, by considering the effects that the substantive and procedural rules of law would have in action in real cases. This approach to how lawyers and litigants acted in legal history, as Martha S. Jones suggests, can reveal "the connections between everyday legal claims-making and broader contests over power and rights."[23]

One of the key substantive issues in the manumission and freedom suits was: How did the substantive law define just and unjust slavery? People held as slaves and their lawyers and supporters confronted this threshold substantive question and tried to fit their case into the unjust slavery category. On the procedural side, the lawyers and their clients probably asked which side generally had the advantage in these suits: the claimant alleging freedom, or the "owner" who was advocating bondage?

Evaluating the Fairness of the Law Regulating the Manumission and Freedom Suits

The law that the judges and legislators developed in and for these suits fares poorly when we consider it within the context of the law and society in which it was created and applied. Time after time, when the legislators and judges faced a choice between alternative results they sided with slavery over liberty.

The substantive and procedural law that limited the cases that could be heard allows us to better understand the raw trial court and appellate court data that scholars have analyzed. For example, Ariela Gross and Loren Schweninger examined the surviving trial court records in the Southern manumission and freedom cases. They found that claimants whose cases were heard by the courts apparently enjoyed a high success rate. Gross's study of trial court records involving racial identity revealed that twelve of fourteen plaintiffs were successful in their manumission or freedom suits.[24] Schweninger studied 546 freedom and manumission petitions filed by or on behalf of women, either individually or with others, in fifteen Southern states and the District of Columbia. He found an 83% success rate in these cases.[25]

An earlier study by Marion J. Russell, compiled from the mostly appellate cases summarized and collected by Helen Catterall, included 670 "suits for freedom" in which the slaves won 48.9% and lost 37% of the cases, with 14.1% being reported "undecided." These data also reveal an interesting difference, however, based on geography. In the Southern states, 591 cases were reported and the slaves won 47.2%, lost 37.9%, and 14.9% were undecided. But in the other states, these percentages were 60.8% in the slaves' favor, 30.3% against, and 8.9% undecided.[26]

We must evaluate these trial and appellate court data in the context of the substantive and procedural hurdles and burdens that the legislators and the courts created and imposed on persons seeking to win their freedom in the courts. In his book-length 1979 law review article, A. E. Keir Nash asked several salient questions while analyzing the relative fairness of the judicial outcomes and opinions addressing the issues that the courts decided in the manumission cases and in some of the freedom suits.[27] I will include many of these issues in this book. But I also will subdivide the concept of "fairness" into more discrete substantive and procedural components, with which we may analyze and judge the freedom and manumission suits on their own terms.

Judgments about the past must be made with care, but they are worth the effort. They give meaning to the historical data, in what Sanford Levinson called "the linked necessity to judge political actors, both past and present," provided that we "recognize the perils of exercising such judgment."[28] I thus agree with Eric Muller's rejection of the "hindsight defense," by which historians often assert that we in the present cannot "fairly or accurately judge historical figures because we inevitably do so by reference to the morality and customs of our own day rather than the morality and customs" of the past.[29]

I also agree, however, with Nash's assertion that we should not "forget our prime duty of understanding the past on its own terms[,]" and that we must avoid "project[ing] our contemporary moral righteousness back upon a complex past incapable of response." We, in the present, must avoid "setting up a moral double-standard whereby we hold the past, for which we have no culpability, to a stiffer standard than we hold the present in which we live, and for which in varying measure we have some culpability."[30]

We need to have a clear understanding of the manumission and freedom suits. Writers refer to these cases while explaining the history of the legal standards for race relations in the United States, and even the origin and nature of the concept of race itself.[31] Others have cited these cases as evidence of interracial sexual patterns,[32] or to support arguments in favor of animal rights, reparations for slavery, or same-sex marriages.[33] Moreover, an interpretation of slavery and its laws is a necessary component of the jurisprudence of the Civil War amendments to the constitution.[34]

In order to fairly understand and evaluate the role of the manumission and freedom suits in slave society and law, however, we first need to examine the essential elements of slave society and its legal system. Before we can review these suits in their proper context, we need to have a clear understanding of slavery's fundamentals as a social relationship and the role of law in a slavery society.

The Fundamental Nature of Slavery

People held as slaves in the United States South were not legal persons with unequal rights. Instead, they were people who were by law defined as property, and thus they lacked any legal rights.[35] This was no metaphor; slaves and masters experienced this reality each day in what Saidiya Hartman called scenes of subjection, such as those seen on the slave auction block or on the plantation.[36]

According to Ayn Rand, a slave is a person "who produces while others dispose of his product[.]"[37] This definition expresses only one part of the master slave relationship, however. As Moses I. Finley explained, "[t]he slaveowner's rights over his slave-property were total in more senses than one. The slave ... suffered not only total loss of control over his labour but total loss of control over his person and his personality[.]"[38] Slavery was unique because "the labourer himself was a commodity, not merely his labour-power. His loss of control, furthermore, extended to the infinity of time, to his children and his children's children—unless ... the owner by a unilateral act broke the chain through unconditional manumission."[39]

Among others, Harriet Beecher Stowe and Thomas Jefferson captured slavery's essence when they described slavery's underlying logic as "absolute despotism, of the most unmitigated form," and "the most unremitting despotism on the one part [the master], and degrading submission on the other."[40] Orlando Patterson's cross-cultural study of slavery's fundamentals through the ages helps to explain why Stowe and Jefferson did not exaggerate when they asserted that despotism was at the heart of the master and slave relationship. Patterson began with Max Weber's view that "all human relationships are structured and defined by the relative power of the interacting persons." Power forces one person to act, or refrain from acting, contrary to his own will and, instead, to act or refrain from acting as a reflection of another person's will.[41]

Human power relationships differ in degree and kind. According to Patterson, slavery's three constituent elements, in their extremes, distinguish it from other forms of human relationships that evidence inequality. These three elements are: (1) the master's power to use violence against the slave; (2) the slave's "natal alienation," which is defined as the absence of "all 'rights' or claims of birth";[42] and (3) the slave's dishonored condition.[43] Slavery's particular incidents all flowed, directly or indirectly, from the "despotism" that the master exercised over the slave.[44]

Indeed, the masters' power began with their use of force, or the threat that they would use force, to coerce the powerless slave to behave in accordance with the masters' will. Patterson identified this element of slavery with the social level of interaction. On the cultural level, the concept of natal alienation captures the slaves' isolation from the dominant community and their perpetual state of "otherness." The lack of honor relates to psychological coercion. It reinforces the notion that the master is all powerful and honorable and that the slave is powerless and dishonorable.[45]

Finley also identified "three components of slavery—the slave's property status, the totality of the power over him, and his kinlessness," which Finley stated "provided powerful advantages to the slaveowner as against other forms of involuntary labour[.]"[46] The notion of "kinlessness" made the slave a "deracinated outsider" who lacked all family ties. This "[c]omplete and brutal withdrawal of the kinship privilege also took the form of dispersing a slave family through sale."[47]

David Brion Davis offered some helpful modifications to Patterson's analysis. Like Finley, he "would restore the crucial element of chattel property," which "is closely related to Patterson's 'natal alienation' and 'generalized dishonor.'" Davis argued that "[t]he key to this relationship ... lies in the 'animalization' or 'bestialization' of slaves. This is not to say that masters literally saw slaves as 'only animals,' or as an entirely different species, except in extreme cases or in response to the scientific racism that emerged in the mid-nineteenth century."[48]

Davis cited as an extreme example the words of an overseer in the United States South, whom he quoted: "Why, sir, I wouldn't mind killing a nigger more than I would a dog." In contrast, for most people "viewing slaves as 'human animals' meant focusing on and exaggerating the so-called animal traits that all humans share and fear, while denying the redeeming rational and spiritual qualities that give humans a sense of pride, being made in the image of God, of being only a little lower than angels." He also quoted the philosopher Nietzsche for the notion that "Man didn't even want to be an 'animal.'"[49] Therefore, the modes of thought and action of those in power in slave society evidenced the dehumanization or animalization of slaves, and these ideas reinforced the slave's dishonored and alienated condition.[50]

Accommodating Slavery into the Common Law

One of Patterson's and Finley's essential points is that "the master and slave relationship is qualitatively different" from other forms of human relationships that evidence "inequality and domination."[51] Jedediah Purdy called this "the *anomaly* model," which understands "slavery as essentially different from other relationships and as resisting both conceptual and practical assimilation to the law of labor relations." He contrasts this with "the *conciliatory* model," which treats "the master-slave relationship as part of a spectrum, analogous to the other legal bonds arising from agreement or status."[52]

Similarly, I argued in *People Without Rights* that "the law had to recognize that slavery was fundamentally different from other forms of inequality and domination. To legitimize the slave's status," the judges and legislators adapted legal concepts "to fit the mold" of slavery's "social reality."[53] Christopher Tomlins has recently articulated the same conclusion. He stated that "slavery's absolute difference becomes obvious, both in nature and extent. That absolute difference was produced in and reproduced by the Anglo-American law of slavery."[54]

I also argued that slavery law in the United States South is best understood as a process by which legislators and judges were creating a body of law. This law was not a static set of rules and doctrines; it was always changing in relation to variables of time and location, although "it always played a legitimizing role in slave society." This was so because "[s]lavery consisted of oppressive human relations that were unknown to the common law that was brought to the New World by the English colonists." As slavery became a social reality, those who made the law accommodated slavery's "fundamental elements into the body of the English common law."[55]

This process of accommodating the social reality of slavery within the common law began with the definition of slaves as persons who were defined at law as property:

> By defining slaves as property, the law stripped slaves of all legal rights. The concomitant definition of slaves as persons for other purposes was necessary and it accomplished two ends not inconsistent with this paramount aim. First, it protected the public interest and the owner's interest, and second, it burdened slaves with special legal duties and obligations that marked the complete oppression of the system. Consequently, the law created legal duties in slaves while it denied slaves' legal rights. This is the despotism of the slavery relationship expressed in legal terms.[56]

Although the American slave law was constantly evolving, these fundamental constants underlie the seemingly conflicting statutes, cases, and legal categories.

The master's power or control over the slave and the slave's children was the singular characteristic of the master and slave relationship that the judges and legislators in the United States other than Louisiana had to accommodate into the common law, for which slavery was a distant and almost forgotten institution. The legislators and judges in the United States South legitimized this unique master and slave power relationship through the development of slave law.[57]

As explained in chapter four, the legislatures and courts in the Southern common law states confirmed the law's legitimizing function in the manumission and freedom suits with the prevailing pleading convention, with which the alleged master admitted that he was a common law *prima facie* tortfeasor. The law acknowledged that slave masters were by definition presumptively empowered to commit—on a routine and daily basis—acts that otherwise would be intentional torts under the common law.[58] Although this may sound like a harsh judgment from the present projected on the past, it is not when we understand these suits within the context of slavery's internal logic, and the social, political, economic, and intellectual background, which some refer to as the cultural history of slavery.

The Law as a Compact Between the Slave's Rulers

Slave law expressed slavery's unique characteristics in many ways. South Carolina Judge David L. Wardlaw related this understanding of slavery's social reality to the law when he wrote: "In the very nature of things, [the slave] is subject to despotism. Law as to him is only a compact between his rulers, and the questions which concern him are matters agitated between them."[59] Wardlaw's insight, to some extent, foreshadowed Derrick Bell's "interest-convergence" theory. Bell suggested that, at least in some contexts, "[t]he interest of blacks in achieving racial equality will be accommodated only when it converges with the interests of whites."[60] In slavery, the law appeared to at times enforce rights for the benefit of slaves. In reality, however, the law resolved disputes among non-slaves or the state, whose rights were or were not embodied in the slave.

The definition of slaves as property is the essential starting point for the analysis of the internal logic of slave law in the United States. When the lawmakers defined people as property, they expressed in legal terms the unique everyday reality of the master-slave power relationship; "slaves *were* bartered, deeded, devised, pledged, seized, and auctioned. They were awarded as prizes in lotteries and raffles; they were wagered at gaming tables and horse races. They were, in short, property in fact as well as law."[61]

The lawmakers therefore transformed slaves into people who were denied all legal rights. Accordingly, the criminal law legitimized violence directed against slaves, which would have lead to criminal liability if the victim had not been a slave. Slaves who misbehaved could be "convicted" and punished extra-judicially by their masters, overseers, patrollers, and sometimes even by white strangers. The courts and legislators thus deprived slaves the full measure of protection that the common law provided to others against the criminal and other wrongful conduct of others. The cases and statutes granted to a slave's masters, hirers, and overseers, as well as strangers to a slave, differing degrees of legalized power to use violence against the slave, which otherwise would have lead to criminal prosecution or civil tort liability.[62]

This was only one half of the legal equation of oppression, however; the law also burdened slaves with legal duties that exceeded the duties that the law required of free people. The criminal law statutes defined exclusive slave crimes and enhanced punishments for people held as slaves.[63] The cases and statutes did not give to slaves all of the common law's criminal procedural protections and rights, although the levels of protection varied. As Judge Leslie Atchison Thompson explained in an 1853 Florida Supreme Court opinion, the "perpetuation" of slavery,

> indeed the common safety of the citizens during its continuance, would seem to require that the superiority of the white or Caucassian [sic] race over the African negro, should be ever demonstrated and preserved so far as the dictates of humanity will allow—the degraded caste should be continually reminded of their inferior position, to keep them in a proper degree of subjection to the authority of the free white citizens. And thus there is an obvious propriety in visiting their offences with more de-grading punishment than is inflicted on the white citizens, while the humanity of the law is demonstrated by securing to them the same forms of law in making defence [sic]—a trial by jury—compulsory process for their witnesses—the aid of counsel—and indeed, as full, fair, and impar-tial a trial, as can or may be claimed by a white person.[64]

Fair slave trials also served several interests in slave society: they deterred slave crimes, punished wrongdoers, and protected the individual master's property interest that the accused slave embodied. This economic interest was likely to become more pressing in the lawmakers' minds as slave property values in-creased in the nineteenth century.[65]

Slavery was such an extreme form of oppression that it was distinguishable from other forms of legal inequality, including the inequality between a hus-band and wife. This was confirmed in slave law by the "cruel and unusual" pun-ishment statutes and by cases such as *State v. Mann*[66] and its essential com-panion case, *Commonwealth v. Turner*,[67] which legitimized the masters' power to use almost unlimited violence on their slaves to enforce the masters' exclusive right to reap the fruits of slaves' labor and to enforce discipline. The *Mann-Turner* rule held that masters and hirers could not be indicted for the crimes of assault or battery upon their slaves, thus rejecting the common law doctrine of "moderate correction," which limited superiors' power to correct their servants and children. This rule was one component of the criminal law of slavery that subjected slaves to excessive legitimized violence that no free person faced.[68]

Karen A. Getman made a similar argument, stating "slavery adversely affected not only Blacks, but white women as well. While the controls exerted over white women by the southern slaveholding class differed both in degree and kind from those exerted over blacks, they are a vital element of southern legal and social history."[69] I also agree with Getman's view that slavery was more terrible for women who were more likely to suffer sexual abuse.[70] Nevertheless, at law, male and female slaves were equally disadvantaged, although their everyday lives may have differed in the particular forms of oppression they had to endure.[71]

The inequality of others, such as free women, was qualitatively different from the inequality of slaves. Therefore, the Southern judges and legislators created slave law that was fundamentally different from the common law that it supplanted, even though the common law legitimated other unequal relationships.[72]

The lawmakers confirmed the masters' unique power over their slaves when they permitted owners to decide whether to free their slaves, and when they limited the paths to freedom that did not rely on proof of the masters' intention. The lawmakers confirmed this power even while they regulated it, until when, in their changing perceptions of the public interest, the legislators in several Southern states voted to ban all manumissions or all domestic manumissions.

When the legislators and judges defined slaves as property, they confirmed the slaves' lack of honor and the slaves' "natal alienation." This definition permitted, among other things, slave sales on the open market and slave family divisions. Slave families could be disrupted after masters died, if they did not free their slaves, and potentially even if they freed their slaves, if the masters' estates were insolvent or if the courts would not enforce the masters' intention.[73]

The *partus sequitur ventrem* doctrine evidenced the slave's natal alienation. This rule abrogated the contrary common law presumption that applied to free people, according to which the child's social standing followed from that of his or her father. The lawmakers applied to slaves the common law rule that vested the owner of domesticated animals with the right to own his female animals' offspring. George Stroud and others have noted that this is a "genuine and *degrading* principle of slavery," because it "places the slave upon a level with *brute* animals[.]"[74] The lawmakers also thus rejected a rule that would have favored freedom by providing that a child was born free if either parent was free.[75]

Following the lead set by statutes adopted in 1667 in Virginia and in 1671 in Maryland, the Southern slave law also provided that slaves were not freed even if they converted to Christianity or were baptized. These acts indicated the slave's lowly status and eliminated another potential path to freedom.[76]

The following chapters will show how these substantive rules limited the number of people who could claim their freedom by operation of law while confirming that slaves lacked status and honor.

Race, Slavery, and Freedom

The prevailing notions of race also influenced the substantive and procedural rules that had effects on the potential success of manumission and freedom suits in the United States South. Patterson did not identify racism as one of slavery's universal elements, but it was a fundamental element of slavery in the United States.[77] Slavery law in the United States South was based upon coherent considerations of power and race. Beginning with seventeenth century Maryland and Virginia statutes, lifetime slavery was presumed for blacks.[78] Some Native Americans were enslaved by the British settlers, but this form of slavery eventually was abolished.[79] Slavery was almost exclusively reserved for blacks, although not all blacks were slaves and not all slaveholders were white.[80]

The freedom suits help illustrate race's role in slave law, as well as the law's role in defining the concept of race. Thus, the Virginia Supreme Court of Appeals opinions in *Hudgins v. Wrights*[81] established in the Virginia manumission and freedom suits presumptions of slavery or freedom based upon the plaintiff's perceived racial appearance.

That 1806 case was a successful freedom suit for the plaintiffs. Nevertheless, scholars have criticized the judges' opinions in that case for contributing toward the racial basis of slavery in the United States, and even for helping to create the very construct of race itself as a form of oppression.[82] For example, according to Alan Hyde, "race was a necessary concept with which to divide people into enslavable and not enslavable[,]" and the *Hudgins* case "marks the moment when the legal concepts of race changed from genotype to include also phenotype (appearance); when race ceased to be simply a kind of shorthand for genetic background and became rather a kind of embodied spectacle."[83]

The Interests at Issue in the Manumission and Freedom Suits

The law in the United States South permitted people held as slaves to advance claims to freedom as exceptions to the general rule that denied slaves the right to seek relief in the courts.[84] When slaves sued to enforce the master's intention to free them, however, the courts did not enforce any independent right of the slave to be set free. They instead enforced the master's right to free his or her own property. The courts heard and decided a manumission suit "*because* it did not implicate slave rights in any real sense."[85]

The Southern law almost always regulated and at times even prohibited the masters' right to free their slaves. But the law rarely compelled masters to free any slaves, and it did so only to advance policies that the lawmakers perceived to be in the public interest. Manumission thus is best understood as an expression of the masters' power over their property. It confirmed the slaves' status as property and the owners' rights to relinquish their property rights embodied in their slaves. "Therefore, the slave's 'right' to manumission was based solely on the master's will and intent. The master could grant or deny freedom as he elected—the 'right' was his, not that of the slave."[86] The slave's "right" to self-purchase also could be enforced only with the master's consent.[87]

The law permitting people held in bondage to pursue freedom suits that defied the alleged slave owners' intentions vindicated the power of judges and legislators to decide who may be held in slavery, often contrary to their purported masters' intentions. This law also was consistent with the notion that slaves were people without legal rights.

We need to clearly distinguish, however, between two types of slave legal claims. First are claims that legally enslaved people could assert in the courts or could otherwise enforce against their masters or third parties to obtain remedies while the slaves remained in slavery. Included in this category was the "right" of slaves in some slave societies, such as those in Cuba and Latin America, to ask the authorities to order that the slaves be sold to new owners if their current owners subjected them to illegal mistreatment.[88] Second are claims to freedom asserted in the courts by people alleging that they were held as slaves contrary to the law. In a 1993 study of Virginia law, Leon Higginbotham and Michael Higginbotham wrote of this distinction:

> Although slaves had no personal rights, they were nonetheless permitted to sue for their freedom in state courts. How could Virginia legislators justify this contradiction—granting standing to slaves who had no legal rights or remedies? Freedom suits existed not as a means for blacks to alter their legal status from slave to free, but as recourse for those who were in fact free, and who thus possessed a remedy for illegal enslavement. De jure, those enslaved illegally were not slaves at all, but free persons wrongfully deprived of their legal rights. Thus, a claimant's right to petition the court was not predicated on the assumption that a slave had any legal rights, but instead on her rights as a presumptively free person illegally held in slavery.[89]

This analysis suggests several salient questions: Do these assertions apply to the law in the other Southern states? Who did the Southern legislators and judges decide could be held in slavery? How fair was the law that the courts applied in the freedom suits? Can we fairly make judgments about the legal process of the past?

Slave Rights and the Manumission and Freedom Suits

Some will argue that the Southern slave law permitting some potentially successful manumission and freedom suits is an example of the inherent complexity, inconsistency, incoherence, "complete confusion," or even ambivalence in the law that sometimes treated slaves as persons but at other times treated them as property.[90] To the contrary, this law was consistent when it provided that people being held as slaves could not assert in court any claims except when they were permitted to claim their freedom, either directly or through their legal guardian or next friend, on the theory that they were being held illegally in slavery.

As Wilbert Moore wrote, it is not surprising that the law of slavery was not "thoroughly worked out, complete with the formulation of logical implications of accepted principles. Actually, ... there is no necessity of such a complete logical exposition until cases arise which require a clear formulation of principle."[91] The process by which slavery was accommodated into the common law presented difficult problems for the colonial and later the antebellum legislators and judges because slavery strained the common law's tools of analysis. John Codman Hurd argued that the law usually distinguished persons and things in a fundamental way. Persons can act upon other persons and things, and, accordingly, people can have legal rights and duties in reference to their actions. Things, however, can be only the objects of action and embody the relative rights of persons and the state; things cannot have rights.[92]

Slavery challenged this formulation because it is, by definition, the absence of legal right in persons who are held as slaves. The lawmakers solved this dilemma by defining slaves as property, most often chattels. This definition cut slaves off from claims of legal rights and legitimized slavery's social reality, even though the judges could find no common law precedents on the key issues that arose in the law of slavery.

The law regulated the masters' power both to free their slaves and to claim people as their slaves "in view of the interests of society, without vesting the rights of a legal person in the slave."[93] The legislators and judges imposed these standards of conduct according to their perceptions of the public interest.[94] Finley—describing ancient slavery—concluded that this legal control of the slave master's powers was consistent with the slave's status as a "commodity" and "property."

> [S]ome sociologists and historians have persistently tried to deny the significance of that simple fact, on the ground that the slave is also a human being or that the owner's rights over a slave are often restricted by the law. All this seems to me to be futile: the fact that a slave is a human being has no relevance to the question whether or not he is also property; it merely reveals that he is a peculiar property, Aristotle's "property with a soul"....[95]

Similarly, in the United States, slave law was not illogical when it defined slaves as property for most purposes and as people for others, or when it regulated the masters' rights that were embodied in their slaves.

Chief Justice Richmond Pearson explained the slave's legal duality in a North Carolina case:

> A slave, being property, has not the legal capacity to make a contract, and

is not entitled to the rights or subjected to the liabilities incident thereto. He is amenable to the criminal law, and his person (to a certain extent) and his life, are protected. This, however, is not a concession to him of civil rights, but is in vindication of public justice, and for the prevention of public wrongs.[96]

Pearson thus implied that talk of "slave rights" was grounded in delusion. When the law treated slaves as people or regulated the master's conduct, it vindicated "public justice" to prevent "public wrongs;" it did not concede to the slave any civil rights that were inconsistent with the slave's property status.

We can derive some insights from Wesley Newcomb Hohfeld's early twentieth century writings to further explain the fallacy of the notion of slave rights in the law. Hohfeld asserted or is associated with asserting a number of points that are essential for this analysis.[97]

First, Hohfeld explained the distinctions among the legal concepts of rights, privileges, powers, and immunities. He analyzed the interrelationships among these concepts as "jural opposites" and "jural correlatives." The jural opposite of right was no-right, of privilege was duty, of power was disability, and of immunity was liability. The jural correlatives were right and duty, privilege and no-right, power and liability, and immunity and disability.[98]

Second, Hohfeld advanced the notion that property rights are best thought of as "a divisible collection of legal entitlements: a bundle of sticks rather than a giant log."[99] Third, he said that "there is only one unit in the law . . . and that is a human being[.]" And fourth, he concluded that "the only legal fact . . . is a relation between two such human beings. No relation that has legal relevance exists between a human being and a thing[.]"[100]

Consequently, according to Hohfeld's analysis, only people can have legal rights, privileges, powers, and immunities. When humans are defined as property they can be only the holders of duties, no-rights, liabilities, and disabilities. As between the owner and property, however, the property has no legal identity. This notion applies to objects of human property and non-human property.[101]

The owner's property interests are absolute, however, only as to the object of property. The property owner possesses rights, privileges, powers, and immunities that the courts consider in relation to the rights, privileges, powers, and immunities of other persons in reference to and embodied in the property. These incidents of ownership are relative to the rights of other people who may have an interest in one or more of the sticks in the bundle of rights. They also are subject to the interests of the state, which may regulate, in the public interest, the owners' use of their property. The owners' authority over their property thus is not absolute in relation to the state and other people.[102]

Hohfeld's writings, according to his friends and followers, including Walter Cook and Arthur Corbin, highlighted and clarified "the social and political dimensions of legal decisions recognizing (or not recognizing) a right or privilege in a person."[103] When applied to property ownership, this analysis "illuminated the complex and relational character of ownership. It revealed that ownership is not the simple and nonsocial relationship between a person and a thing that Blackstone's description suggested. Rather, ownership is complex and fundamentally social."[104]

Therefore, according to Gregory Alexander, Hohfeld's efforts thinking and writing about property ownership as human relationships and in a nonphysicalist way "had important practical consequences." The "whole thrust" of this analysis

> was to demonstrate that no single constituent element or set of elements was essential to ownership. Ownership was a complex set of legal relations in which individuals were interdependent. Some degree of social interference with one person's ownership interest not only did not negate ownership, it was unavoidable. Precisely because ownership *is* relational, no person can enjoy complete freedom to use, possess, enjoy, or transfer assets regarded as theirs. The real question is which interferences should be legally prohibited and which permitted. There was no analytical, or deductive answer to that question; it depended strictly on what policies society decides to promote.[105]

And so it was with the ownership of people held as slaves.

According to Jane B. Baron, "[i]t does not seem to have occurred to Hohfeld, or his many critics and followers, to consider what would happen if someone were to be in a situation in which they only owed duties to right holders, had no-rights against privilege holders, were subject to liabilities created by the holders of powers, and were under disabilities because of others' immunities."[106] She referred to people in this state as "no property," which is an expression of their "negative collection of lacks."[107]

People with all of these lacks were slaves. The slavery law referred to them as property, and I referred to them as people without rights. The law that defined slaves as property subjected slaves to the physical, psychological, and social power of their masters and others. The law also regulated this power to promote the "public interest," or the relative property claims of the owners and others in the slave.[108]

Consequently, the law had a crucial role in slave society. It lent its approval to the powerlessness of the slave through the concept of chattel slavery. The law thus served a legitimizing function in slave society; it permitted, encouraged, and, when necessary, regulated the master's domination of the slave. Max Weber argued that in modern society the law legitimized state power and domination.[109] Power plus authority became legitimate—or the law. Slave law had a similar effect; it legalized the master's power to dominate the slave. The law lent its "authority" to the master's power over the slave, as well as the power of other non-related whites to control slaves, all as the law allowed. The white man's word, therefore, was the law to the powerless slaves, who had "no rights which the white man was bound to respect[.]"[110]

This is a point upon which there has been much confusion. For example, James Oakes argued that the laws granting procedural fairness in slave criminal trials or regulating the masters' behavior toward their slaves created slave "rights." According to Oakes, "the intrinsic ambiguity of slave law" was "the total subordination of the slave to a master who himself owed allegiance to the state[.]" He called this a "profound dilemma," adding, "it was all but impossible for a liberal political culture to place limits on the masters' power without implicitly granting rights to slaves." Oakes concluded that slavery law in the United States was "intrinsically subversive," because, when the law limited the master's power over the slave, it "necessarily 'diminished' the essence of slavery."[111]

Thomas D. Morris, although emphasizing the importance of the definition of slaves as property, argued that Southern slave law created legal "civil rights" in slaves, although not civil liberties, when it acknowledged slave personhood. He cited examples including laws prohibiting slave abuse and mistreatment and requiring masters to provide criminal defense lawyers for their slaves who were accused of committing crimes.[112] Thomas Cobb advanced similar arguments in his 1858 pro-slavery treatise. He contended that when the law extended to slaves the criminal law's protection of their personal security this was "*quasi* a right belonging to the slave as a person."[113]

Oakes, Morris, and Cobb do not explain why these slave rights or *quasi*-rights should be thought of as rights at all if one accepts slavery law's initial premise, which defined slaves as property. This slave rights theory does not withstand scrutiny when we take into account the law's legitimizing role and the jurisprudential meaning of the term "right."

Indeed, the manumission and freedom suits help illustrate why the notion of slave rights, whether real or *quasi*, is an oxymoron. In the manumission suits, the legislators and judges in the slave states limited the masters' power to free their slaves. And, with limited exceptions, they did not enforce the masters' promises to free their slaves over the masters' objections. The Southern state legislatures also adopted laws that "impeded self-purchase by prohibiting slaves from 'go[ing] at large and trad[ing] as freemen.'"[114] The law permitting people held in bondage to pursue freedom suits confirmed the judges' and legislators' power to decide who may be held in slavery, often contrary to their purported masters' intentions. But this law also confirmed the notion of legal slavery when it defined illegal slavery that violated public policies that had nothing to do with any rights of persons who were legally held as slaves.

Accordingly, these laws regulated the masters' behavior and confirmed the masters' "allegiance to the state," but they did not create any rights in people who were legally held as slaves, nor did they diminish slavery's essence. They were similar to any other legal regime that regulated and legitimated property owners' rights in their property, according to Finley. He called "[l]egal restrictions on the rights of a slaveowner ... a side issue" because "in modern sociological and juridical theories of any school, all property is understood to be a matrix of rights, rarely if ever unlimited. The precise rights that constitute the matrix vary with kinds of property and kinds of society."[115]

Of course, law in the books does not always reflect the conduct of people in the society. Some masters refrained from subjecting their slaves to the restraints and cruelty that the law allowed or even required, provided their slaves with extra-legal privileges, including permitting slaves to exercise the "right" to self-hire their time and keep the excess money they earned, and honored their manumission promises.[116] These facts "[are] interesting, even important, but [they do] not undermine the slave-property link conceptually."[117]

With the limited exceptions noted in this book, people who were legally held as slaves in the United States South had no legal right to demand freedom or to enforce their master's promises of liberty. When a master decided to recognize slave privileges, including manumission, this "was always a unilateral act on his part, never binding, always revocable."[118] Eugene D. Genovese cited other examples of masters' acts or omissions that he called "customary rights." Genovese stated, "if the law said [slaves] had no right to property ... but local custom accorded them private garden plots, then woe to the master or overseer who summarily withdrew the 'privilege.'"[119]

But, contrary to Professor Genovese, these privileges, including property "ownership," self-hiring, and manumission, were not legal rights if his initial premise, that "the law" provided the slave had no right to a privilege that the courts would enforce, is correct. In response to Genovese's views on the law of slavery and paternalism, John Anthony Scott wrote: "To argue that slaves fled from this cruel system of law into the waiting arms of paternalistic 'protectors' is to fly in the face of historical facts. The 'protectors,' after all, were the very ones who had set the law up, who supported it, and who continued to benefit from its operation."[120] The question of whether the slave thought of any privilege as an entitlement and whether the master thought it best to allow the privilege was indeed a different issue—and not a legal issue.

Slaves and masters on occasion found their way around the legal restrictions on self-hiring and manumission, but they did this to effectuate the individual master's intentions to bestow these benefits on all or some of his or her slaves. If the authorities intervened to enforce the law, or if the master died, failed to pay his debts, or just changed his or her mind, the slave's privileges would be unenforceable at law.[121]

This is not to demean the resourcefulness of people held in slavery. They were not "entirely without force in the relationship of slaves and masters; they were not necessarily passive in the face of the legal claim that someone owned them."[122] By filing freedom and manumission suits, slaves influenced and often caused legal change, but the result often was a new law or court decision putting new roadblocks or obstacles in the way of freedom claimants. Slaves could obtain relief in the courts only if they relied on the substantive legal theories and followed the legal procedures that were authorized by "the written texts of state institutions."[123]

According to Jon-Christian Suggs, the authors of the antebellum slave narratives and novels understood full well the import of the written law's definition of slaves as property and its effect on the lives of slaves. He found telling "the number of times 'the law' is mentioned directly" in these documents as well as indirectly by "the references to property and to justice."[124] Accordingly, he concluded that "black essayists, memorialists, autobiographers, [and] novelists of the century were all responding to the single most salient fact of their lives as Americans, enslaved or free: they were creatures of the law and their stories were stories of the law."[125]

Of course, we also must take into account evidence of the customary "law" on the plantations or in the neighborhoods that "governed" the master slave relationship. These norms, it is argued, regulated the "masters' behavior, a modus vivendi enforced by opinion among neighbors, by scorn or exclusion, even by the resistance of slaves whose labor power needed to be mobilized."[126]

This "*modus vivendi*" may have benefited people held as slaves if their masters opted to bestow upon them the blessings of freedom, no matter what was the source of the masters' motivation. But it did not help the claimants who sought their freedom and who were denied relief by laws that negated their masters' intentions, or that limited the paths to freedom that did not rely on proof of the masters' intentions to release their slaves from bondage.

Conclusion

We in the twenty-first century can evaluate the "fairness" of the substantive and procedural law that the legislators and judges applied to the colonial and antebellum Southern manumission and freedom suits if we study these cases within their social, political, economic, intellectual, and legal context. Indeed, these judgments provide an essential part of the context within which we can understand the data demonstrating that some people who were held as slaves in the South won their freedom.

The Southern courts and legislatures adopted and enforced substantive and procedural principles that narrowed the types of suits that lawyers could successfully file, and thus hindered the chances of those seeking their release from slavery when this law is measured, not against today's norms, but against those of the past. This was especially so for the claimants who appeared to be black. The law developed in the freedom suits created a double standard based upon the claimants' perceived racial appearance.

Moreover, the manumission and freedom suits illustrate how not every legal rule that controlled the masters' power over their slave created "rights" in slaves, was "intrinsically subversive" of slavery's fundamentals, or diminished the "essence of slavery," as James Oakes and others have argued.[127] Instead, the law confirmed the master's unique power even when it regulated that power, including laws regulating the master's power to grant his or her slaves privileges, to free his or her slaves, to inflict upon the slave cruel and unusual punishment, or to take the slave's life or limb without what was perceived to be a "good" reason. These regulations furthered what the lawmakers perceived to be the requirements of the public interest in slavery's orderly but necessary oppression, while confirming that slaves were property without legal rights.[128]

With so much at stake in the distinctions between slavery and freedom, the

Southern courts and legislatures decided that they had to allow people held in slavery the right to assert their freedom claims in the manumission and freedom suits. These suits prevented what was perceived to be the unjust and illegal enslavement of people whose masters intended to free them, or people who could not legally be held as slaves because they were members of the dominant or a less disfavored race, or in rare cases because of their own conduct that advanced favored public policies or their owners' misconduct that violated other public policies. Slave law thus legitimized the just and legal bondage of "others" while securing "white economic and liberty interests."[129]

Notes to Chapter 1

[1] 60 U.S. (19 How.) 393, 15 L. Ed. 691 (1857). *See, e.g.,* Tomlins, *Freedom Bound, supra* at 509-69; Stephen Breyer, *Making Our Democracy Work: A Judge's View* 32-48 (2010); Lea S. VanderVelde, *Mrs. Dred Scott: A Life on Slavery's Frontier* (2009) [hereinafter VanderVelde, *Mrs. Dred Scott*]; Earl M. Maltz, *Dred Scott and the Politics of Slavery* (2007); Austin Allen, *Origins of the Dred Scott Case: Jacksonian Jurisprudence and the Supreme Court, 1837-1857* (2006); Mark A. Graber, *Dred Scott and the Problem of Constitutional Evil* (2006); Paul Finkelman, *Dred Scott v. Sandford: A Brief History with Documents* (1997); Walter Ehrlich, *They Have No Rights: Dred Scott's Struggle for Freedom* (1979); Don E. Fehrenbacher, *The Dred Scott Case: Its Significance in American Law and Politics* (1978).

[2] *See* VanderVelde, *Mrs. Dred Scott, supra* at 320-33; Fehrenbacher, *supra* at 420-21, 568; Ehrlich, *supra* at 180-82.

[3] *See Jack, et al. (slaves) v. Doran's Executors,* 37 Ala. 265, 1861 WL 368 (1861); *Doran v. Brazelton,* 32 Tenn. (2 Swan) 149, 1852 WL 1834 (1852); John Keegan, *The American Civil War: A Military History* 77 (2009); James McPherson, *Battle Cry of Freedom: The Civil War Era* 854 (2003).

[4] *See* Edlie L. Wong, *Neither Fugitive nor Free: Atlantic Slavery, Freedom Suits, and the Legal Culture of Travel* 3 (2009).

[5] *See* John Hope Franklin and Loren Schweninger, *Runaway Slaves: Rebels on the Plantation* (1999); John Anthony Scott, *Hard Trials on My Way: Slavery and the Struggle Against It 1800-1860* 87-107 (1974) [hereinafter Scott, *Hard Trials*]: John W. Blassingame, *The Slave Community: Plantation Life in the Antebellum South* 107-08, 112-16 (1972); A. Leon Higginbotham, Jr. & F. Michael Higginbotham, "'Yearning to Breathe Free:' Legal Barriers Against and Options in Favor of Liberty in Antebellum Virginia," 68 *N.Y.U. L. Rev.* 1213, 1271 (1993) [hereinafter Higginbotham & Higginbotham].

Slaves who escaped into Florida between 1683 and 1790 could earn their freedom if they converted to Christianity and satisfied other conditions that varied over time, but only during the years during which the Spanish controlled Florida. *See* Christina Snyder, *Slavery in Indian Country: The Changing Face of Captivity in Early America* 199-200,

216 (2010); Rivers, *supra* at 4-6; Patrick Riordan, "Finding Freedom in Florida: Native Peoples, African Americans, and the Colonists, 1670-1816," 75 *Fla. Hist. Q* 24, 26, 30 (1996), Jane Landers, "Spanish Sanctuary: Fugitives in Florida, 1687-1790," 62 *Fla. Hist. Q.* 296 (1984).

[6] Cobb, *supra* at 248.

[7] Davis, *Western Culture, supra at* 264-65; *see* Grinberg, "Freedom Suits," *supra* at 76-77.

[8] Wong, *supra* at 153-54; *but see* Ariela Gross, "When is the Time of Slavery? The History of Slavery in Contemporary Legal and Political Argument," 96 *Cal. L. Rev.* 282 (2008) (arguing that we are living in slavery time, or at least its aftermath). I refer to slavery times as the years when slavery was permitted by law in the society. Analogies between slavery and other forms of inequality or oppression, both before and after emancipation, made by those on the both the "left" and the "right," although providing powerful political arguments, "should not be accepted if they do not coincide with [the] legal analysis of the fundamentals of the master and slave relationship." Fede, "Gender," *supra* at 432, citing McConnell, *supra* at 207-08; *see* Scott W. Howe, "Slavery as Punishment: Original Public Meaning, Cruel and Unusual Punishment, and the Neglected Clause in the Thirteenth Amendment," 57 *Ariz. L. Rev.* 983 (2009) (discussing the continued legality of slavery as punishment for crime); David Eltis, "Was Abolition of the U.S. and British Slave Trade Significant in the Broader Atlantic Context," 66 *Wm. &. M. Q. 3d Ser.* 715, 735 (2009); Karen E. Bravo, "Exploring the Analogy Between Modern Trafficking in Humans and the Trans-Atlantic Slave Trade," 25 *B.U. Int'l L.J.* 207 (2007) (both urging caution in analogies between historical slave trade and current traffic in human beings).

[9] Wong, *supra* at 153-54.

[10] *See id.* at 154; Fede, *People Without Rights, supra* at 152-53.

[11] "Introduction: Slavery, Freedom, and the Law," in *Brief History, supra* at 26.

[12] *See* Robert Olwell, "Becoming Free: Manumission and the Genesis of a Free Black Community in South Carolina, 1740-90," 17 *Slavery & Abolition* 1, 7 (1996) [hereinafter Olwell, "Becoming Free"].

[13] *See* "Introduction: Slavery, Freedom, and the Law," in *Brief History, supra* at 26; *see also* Arthur Zilversmith, *The First Emancipation: The Abolition of Slavery in the North* (1967) (on the pre-Civil War emancipation).

[14] *See* Schafer, *Becoming Free, supra* at xxiii, n. 13; John H. Russell, *The Free Negro in Virginia, 1619-1865* 42 (1913) [hereinafter Russell, *Free Negro*].

[15] Stroud, *supra* at 96; *see also* Tushnet, *Humanity, supra* at 191-93.

[16] David Brion Davis, *Slavery and Human Progress* 20 (1984) [hereinafter Davis, *Progress*], quoting Orlando Patterson, *Slavery & Social Death: A Comparative Study* (1982) [hereinafter Patterson, *Social Death*].

[17] Patterson, *Social Death, supra* at 431, n 1.

[18] Cobb, *supra* at 278; *see Atwood's Heirs v. Beck, Adm'r*, 21 Ala. 590, 1852 WL 212 at *12 (1852).

[19] *See, e.g.*, Wahl, *Burden, supra* at 160-63; Morris, *Slavery, supra* at 371-423; Shaw, *supra* at 76-109; Loren Schweninger, "Slave Women, County Courts and the Law in the

United States South: A Comparative Perspective," 16 *European Rev. of Hist.* 383, 386-89 (2009) [hereinafter Schweninger, "Slave Women"]; Gillmer, "Suing for Freedom," *supra* at 565-69; Michael L. Nicholls, "'The squint of freedom': African-American Freedom Suits in Post-Revolutionary Virginia," 20 *Slavery & Abolition* 47, 54 (2001) [hereinafter Nicholls, "Squint of Freedom"]; *see also* Fede, "Toward a Solution," *supra* at 301.

On manumission and miscegenation, *see, e.g.,* Jones, "Southern Free Women," *supra*; Davis, "Race and Sex," *supra*; and Mitchell F. Crusto, "Blackness as Property: Sex, Race, Status, and Wealth," 1 *Stan. J. of Civ. Rts. and Civ. Liberties* 51 (2005).

[20] *See, e.g.,* Gross, *Blood, supra* at 1-110; Frank W. Sweet, *Legal History of the Color Line: The Real Triumph of the One-Drop Rule* 159-77 (2005); Shaw, *supra* at 47-63, 152-53; Duncan J. MacLeod, *Slavery, Race, and the American Revolution* 109-26 (1974); Schweninger, "Slave Women," *supra* at 389-90; Gillmer, "Suing for Freedom," *supra* at 569-619; Nicholls, "Squint of Freedom," *supra* at 47-53; Ariela J. Gross, "Litigating Whiteness: Trials of Racial Determination in the Nineteenth-Century South," 108 *Yale L. Rev.* 109 (1998) [hereinafter Gross, "Litigating Whiteness"].

[21] *See* Paul Finkelman, *An Imperfect Union: Slavery, Federalism, and Comity* 2-6, 181-235, 285-98 (1981) [hereinafter Finkelman, *Imperfect Union*]; Fehrenbacher, *supra* at 28-73; Robert M. Cover, *Justice Accused: Antislavery and the Judicial Process* 83-99 (1975) [hereinafter Cover, *Justice Accused*] (discussing comity principles and how they broke down in the nineteenth century); *see also, e.g.,* Wong, *supra* at 127-82; Schafer, *Becoming Free, supra* at 15-33; Peter Kolchin, *American Slavery 1619-1877* 128 (1993) [hereinafter Kolchin, *American Slavery*]; Fede, *People Without Rights, supra* at 150-53; David Brion Davis, *The Problem of Slavery in the Age of Revolution, 1770-1823* 513-22 (1975) [hereinafter Davis, *Revolution*]; Cobb, *supra* at 216-20; Robert C. Schwemm, "*Strader v. Graham*: Kentucky's Contribution to National Slavery Litigation and the Dred Scott Decision," 97 *Ky. L.J.* 353, 364-66 (2009); Wardle, *supra* at 1855-93; David Thomas Konig, "The Long Road to Dred Scott: Personhood and the Rule of Law in the Trial Court Records of St. Louis Freedom Suits," 75 *U.M.K.C. L. Rev.* 53 (2006) [hereinafter Konig, "Dred Scott"]; Michael P. Mills, "Slave Law in Mississippi from 1817-1861: Constitutions, Codes, and Cases," 71 *Miss. L.J.* 153, 178-88, 211-29 (2001); Dennis K. Boman, "The Dred Scott Case Reconsidered: The Legal and Political Context in Missouri," 44 *Am. J. of Legal Hist.* 405, 406-28 (2000) [hereinafter Boman, "Dred Scott"]; Louise Weinberg, "Methodological Interventions and the Slavery Cases; or, Night-Thoughts of a Legal Realist," 56 *Md. L. Rev.* 1316, 1323-45 (1997); Nash, "Radical Interpretations," *supra* at 282-314. For a discussion of these issues under French law, *see* Sue Peabody, *"There Are No Slaves in France": The Political Culture of Race and Slavery in the Ancien Regime* (1996).

[22] *See generally, e.g.,* Wong, *supra* at 1-18; Finkelman, *Imperfect Union, supra* at 1-19; Fehrenbacher, *supra* at 50-73; Cobb, *supra* at 201-16.

[23] *See* Martha S. Jones, "Leave of Court: African-American Claims-Making in the Era of *Dred Scott v. Sandford*," in *Contested Democracy: Freedom, Race and Power in American History* 55 (Manisha Sinha & Penny VonEschen, eds.) (2007); Jones, "Southern Free Women," *supra* at 771.

[24] *See* Gross, "Litigating Whiteness," *supra* at 122, n. 32, and 186-88.

[25] *See* Schweninger, "Slave Women," *supra* at 391, 399.

26 *See* Marion J. Russell, "American Slave Discontent in Records of the High Courts," 31 *J. of Negro Hist.* 411, 418-26 (1946). Russell excluded "34 cases testing wills." *See id.* at 418.

John B. Parks's analysis of the trial court complaints and petitions for freedom in the North American British colonies and in the United States evidences the same pattern. Claimants won 63.7% of the 91 cases that Parks lists during various time periods in nine free states, and claimants won 44.8% of the 901 cases that he lists during various time periods in 15 slave states and the District of Columbia. The case selection process also may be evident in the small numbers of cases listed, fewer than one per year, in the states with the most slaves. For example, Parks lists 19 suits in North Carolina in 135 years, 79 in Louisiana in 133 years, 15 suits in South Carolina in 71 years, 19 in Delaware in 74 years, 9 in Mississippi in 41 years, 10 in Georgia in 39 years, 18 in Alabama in 30 years, 9 in Arkansas in 15 years, 4 in Florida in 30 years, and 8 in Texas in 10 years. In contrast, 341 suits are listed in Missouri in 57 years, 99 in Kentucky in 61 years, and 70 in the District of Columbia in 59 years. *See* Parks, "Freedom v. Slavery: Lawsuits, Petitions and the Legitimacy of Slavery in the British Colonies and the United States," 177-222 (Ph.D. Dissertation, Howard University, 2008).

27 *See* A. E. Keir Nash, "Reason of Slavery: Understanding the Judicial Role in the Peculiar Institution," 32 *Vand. L. Rev.* 7, 98-104 (1979) [hereinafter Nash, "Reason of Slavery"]. I came to very different conclusions about the relative fairness of the manumission cases. Fede, *People Without Rights, supra* at 131-58.

28 Sanford Levinson, "Allocating Honor and Acting Honorably: Some Reflections Provoked by the Cardozo Conference on Slavery," 17 *Cardozo L. Rev.* 1969, 1980 (1996).

29 Eric L Muller, "Judging Thomas Ruffin and the Hindsight Defense," 87 *N.C. L. Rev.* 757, 760 (2009).

30 Nash, "Reason of Slavery," *supra* at 216-17.

31 *See, e.g.*, Gross, *Blood, supra*, at 1-110; Alan Hyde, *Bodies of Law* 213-32 (1997); Daniel J. Sharfstein, "Crossing the Color Line: Racial Migration and the One-Drop Rule, 1600-1860," 91 *Minn. L. Rev.* 592, 620-26 (2007); Adrienne D. Davis, "Identity Notes Part One: Playing in the Light," 45 *Am. U.L. Rev.* 695, 702-11 (1996) [hereinafter Davis, "Identity Notes"]; Ian F. Haney Lopez, "The Social Construction of Race: Some Observations on Illusion, Fabrication, and Choice," 29 *Harv. C.R.-C.L. L. Rev.* 1, 1-7 (1994).

32 *See, e.g.*, Gillmer, "Suing for Freedom," *supra* at 541-43.

33 *See, e.g.*, R. A. Lenhardt, "Beyond Analogy: *Perez v. Sharp*, Antimiscegenation Law, and the Fight for Same-Sex Marriage," 96 *Cal. L. Rev.* 839, 869-80 (2008); Wise, "Writs," supra at 241-80; Donald Aquinas Lancaster, Jr., "The Alchemy and Legacy of the United States of America's Sanction of Slavery and Segregation: A Property Law and Equitable Remedy Analysis of African American Reparations," 43 *How. L.J.* 171, 173-77 (2000); David Favre, "Equitable Self-Ownership for Animals," 50 *Duke L.J.* 473, 491-92 (2000); Steven M. Wise, "Hardly a Revolution—The Eligibility of Nonhuman Animals for Dignity—Rights in a Liberal Democracy," 22 *Vermont L. Rev.* 793, 819-21 (1998).

34 *See, e.g.*, Alexander Tsesis, *The Thirteenth Amendment and American Freedom: A Legal History* (2004); Michael Vorenberg, *Final Freedom: The Civil War, the Abolition of Slavery, and the Thirteenth Amendment* (2001); the articles in *The Promises if Liberty: The History and Contemporary Relevance of the Thirteenth Amendment* (Alex-

ander Tsesis, ed.) (2010) [hereinafter *Promises of Liberty*]; Jennifer Mason McAward, "The Scope of Congress's Thirteenth Amendment Enforcement Power after *City of Boerne v. Flores*," 88 *Wash. U.L. Rev.* 77 (2010); Howe, *supra*; George A. Rutherglen, "State Action, Private Action, and the Thirteenth Amendment," 94 *Va. L. Rev.* 1367 (2008); William M. Carter, Jr., "Race, Rights, and the Thirteenth Amendment: Defining Badges and Incidents of Slavery," 40 *U.C. Davis L. Rev.* 1311 (2007); Lea S. VanderVelde, "The Thirteenth Amendment of Our Aspirations," 38 *U. Toledo L. Rev.* 855 (2006); Tobias Barrington Wolff, "The Thirteenth Amendment and Slavery in the Global Economy," 102 *Colum. L. Rev.* 973 (2002); Marco Masoni, "The Green Badge of Slavery," 6 *Geo. J. on Fighting Poverty* 97 (1994); Guyora Binder, "Did the Slaves Author the Thirteenth Amendment? An Essay in Redemptive History," 5 *Yale J. of Law & Humanities* 471 (1993); Andrew Koppleman, "Forced Labor: A Thirteenth Amendment Defense of Abortion," 84 *Northwestern U.L. Rev.* 480 (1990); Lea S. VanderVelde, "The Labor Vision of the Thirteenth Amendment," 138 *U. Pa. L. Rev.* 437 (1989); G. Sidney Buchanan, "The Quest for Freedom: A Legal History of the Thirteenth Amendment," 12 *Houston L. Rev.* 1, 331, 357, 593, 610, 844, 871, 1070 (1974-1975); Arthur Kinoy, "The Constitutional Right of Negro Freedom," 21 *Rutgers L. Rev.* 387 (1967); Harry H. Shapiro, "Involuntary Servitude: The Need for a More Flexible Approach," 19 *Rutgers L. Rev.* 65 (1964); Jacobus ten Broek, "Thirteenth Amendment to the Constitution of the United States: Consummation to Abolition and Key to the Fourteenth Amendment," 39 *Cal. L. Rev.* 171 (1951).

[35] Fede, *People Without Rights*, *supra* at 17, 29-30.

[36] *See* Saidiya V. Hartman, *Scenes of Subjection: Terror, Slavery, and Self-Making in Nineteenth-Century America* 7 (1997).

[37] *See* D. Benjamin Barros, "Property and Freedom," 4 *N.Y.U. J. L. & Liberty* 36, 55 (2009), quoting Ayn Rand, *Man's Rights*, reprinted in *The Virtue of Selfishness: A New Concept of Egoism* 94 (1964).

[38] Moses I. Finley, *Ancient Slavery and Modern Ideology* 74 (1980) [citation and internal quotation omitted].

[39] *Id.* at 74-75.

[40] Harriet Beecher Stowe, *The Key to Uncle Tom's Cabin* 233 (reprint ed. 1968) (1853); Thomas Jefferson, *Notes on the State of Virginia* 174 (reprint ed. 1853) (1787); *see* Charles S. Sydnor, "The Southerner and the Laws," 6 *J. of So. Hist.* 3, 9 (1940).

[41] *See* Patterson, *Social Death*, *supra* at 1.

[42] *Id.* at 5.

[43] *Id.* at 1-14; *see generally id.* at 17-101. For a critique of Patterson's approach, especially his use of the term "social death," *see* Vincent Brown, "Social Death and Political Life in the Study of Slavery," 114 *Am. Hist. Rev.* 1231 (2010).

[44] *See* David Brion Davis, *Inhuman Bondage: The Rise and Fall of Slavery in the New World* 27-47 (2006) [hereinafter Davis, *Inhuman Bondage*] (discussing Patterson's work and slavery's origins).

[45] Patterson, *Social Death*, *supra* at 1-14.

[46] *See* Finley, *supra* at 77.

47 *Id.* at 75.

48 Davis, *Inhuman Bondage, supra* at 32 [footnote omitted].

49 *Id.* [footnote omitted].

50 *Id.* at 32-47.

51 *See* Fede, *People Without Rights, supra* at 18.

52 *See* Jedediah Purdy, *The Meaning of Property: Freedom, Community, and the Legal Imagination* 89 (2010).

53 *See* Fede, *People Without Rights, supra* at 18; *see id.* at 3-44. The conciliatory model leads to arguments such as those of early twentieth century slavery apologist historian Ulrich B. Phillips. He contended that slave owners who had property rights in slaves were somehow analogous to twentieth century women who had "a property right which the law maintains" in their divorced husbands who were "legally required to pay periodic alimony to their ex-wives, and if one seeks to escape from the levy upon his earnings, he may be clapped into prison until he gives adequate pledges of compliance." *See* Ulrich Bonnell Phillips, *Life and Labor in the Old South* 160 (1929); *see also* Patterson, *Social Death, supra* at 22, 369, n. 22; Fede, "Gender," *supra* at 431.

54 *See* Tomlins, *Freedom Bound, supra* at 411; *see also* Drescher, *supra* at 11; David Eltis, "Europeans and the Rise and Fall of African Slavery in the Americas: An Interpretation," 98 *Am. Hist. Rev.* 1399, 1408-15 (1993).

Christopher Leslie Brown summarized the British laws and practices that to some appeared to have approached slavery's essence, such the general notion that one person can have a type of property right in another, including the relationships between husbands, wives, and children; masters and apprentices, servants, and day laborers; and the navy and impressed sailors; as well as villienage and the Tudor era statutes that sought to enslave vagrants and criminals. Brown, *Moral Capital: Foundations of British Abolitionism* 44-45 (2006) [hereinafter Brown, *Moral Capital*]. He concluded that "enslaved Africans suffered a degree of powerlessness in the colonies wholly without equal elsewhere in the British dominions." *Id.* at 45. He based this conclusion on the slaves' length of service, the treatment of slave parents and children, the slaves' lack of access to legal protections, and the degrees of dishonor and physical abuse that were characteristics of slavery. *Id.* at 45-46. And as to the law, he concluded: "The legal apparatus constructed to define the place of African slaves, however, was an innovation, a deviation from customary English practice." *Id.* at 46; *see also* Teresa Michals, "'That Sole and Despotic Dominion': Slaves, Wives, and Game in Blackstone's *Commentaries*," 27 *Eighteenth-Century Studies* 195, 202 (1993-94) ("The slave differs from such persons [wives, children, and servants] not in being property, but rather in being nothing but property.").

55 Fede, *People Without Rights, supra* at 17; *see* the authorities cited in the present book's preface, *supra* at notes 52-53; *see also* Robin Blackburn, *The Making of New World Slavery: From the Baroque to the Modern, 1492-1800* 31-63 (1997); Robert J. Steinberg, *The Invention of Free Labor: The Employment Relation in English and American Law and Culture, 1350-1870* 1-121 (1991); Parks, *supra* at 39-104, 244-55.

56 Fede, *People Without Rights, supra* at 17; *see* Fede, "Legitimized Violence," *supra* at 94; Fede, "Toward a Solution," *supra* at 312. For similar statements, *see* Tomlins, *Freedom Bound, supra* at 411; Tomlins, "Transplants," *supra* at 390-93; Margaret A.

Burnham, "An Impossible Marriage: Slave Law and Family Law," 5 *Law & Inequality* 187, 188 (1987). For another interpretation, *see* Tushnet, *Humanity, supra* at 37-43, 154-57, and for comment on Tushnet's interpretation, *see* Fede, "Toward a Solution," *supra* at 303-11.

[57] *See* Fede, *People Without Rights, supra* at 17, 29-30. And see Tomlins, *Freedom Bound, supra* at 507-08 for a similar argument, Tomlins emphasizing that the essence of slavery law is "as absolute a degree of control as (humanly) possible" by masters over slaves, including the master's control of the slave's "exit" from slavery by manumission or by the death of the slave.

[58] *See* chapter 4, *infra* at notes 125-37. "Moreover, ... the courts often justified the inevitable inhumanity of slavery by referring to humanity. This cruel irony was a reification of the oppression of slavery...." Fede, *People Without Rights, supra* at 11; *see id.* at 241-45.

[59] *See Ex parte Boylston*, 33 S.C.L. (2 Strob.) 41, 43, 1847 WL 2155 *2 (1847), quoted in Fede, *People Without Rights, supra* at 4-5; *see also* Diane J. Klein, "Naming and Framing the 'Subject' of Antebellum Slave Contracts: Introducing Julia, 'A Certain Negro Slave,' 'A Man,' Joseph, Eliza, and Albert," 9 *Rutgers Race & L. Rev.* 243, 244 (2008) (noting that, in slave law cases, "[s]ometimes the most important person in the case isn't identified in the caption[,]" or "isn't named at all[.]").

[60] *See* Derrick A. Bell, Jr., "*Brown v. Board of Education* and the Interest-Convergence Dilemma," 93 *Harv. L. Rev.* 518, 523 (1980); *see also* Crusto, *supra* at 51, 61-63 (applying Bell's view to slavery).

[61] Stampp, *Slavery, supra* at 201; *see* Fede, *People Without Rights, supra* at 34-37.

[62] *See* Morris, *Slavery, supra* at 161-208; Fede, *People Without Rights, supra* at 19-24, 34-41, 61-130; Shaw, *supra* at 162-64; Philip J. Schwarz, *Twice Condemned: Slaves and the Criminal Laws of Virginia 1705-1865* 6-13 (1988) [hereinafter Schwarz, *Twice Condemned*]; Flanigan, *supra* at 145-88; Edmund S. Morgan, *American Slavery, American Freedom: The Ordeal of Colonial Virginia* 311-15 (1975) [hereinafter Morgan, *American Slavery*]; Stampp, *Slavery, supra* at 210-11; Judith Kelleher Schafer, "'Details are of a most revolting character': Cruelty to Slaves in Appeals of the Supreme Court of Louisiana," 68 *Chi.-Kent L. Rev.* 1283 (1993); Fede, "Legitimized Violence," *supra*.

[63] *See, e.g.*, Glenn McNair, *Criminal Injustice: Slaves and Free Blacks in Georgia's Criminal Justice System* 58-81, 143-65 (2009); Schwarz, *Slave Law, supra* at 63-72; Morris, *supra* at 262-353; Fede, *People Without Rights, supra* at 159-79; Shaw, *supra* at 174-87; Schwarz, *Twice Condemned, supra* at 13-321; Flanigan, *supra* at 1-72; Philip J. Schwarz, "Forging the Shackles: The Development of Virginia's Criminal Code for Slaves," in *Ambivalent Legacy: A Legal History of the South* (David J. Bodenhamer and James W. Ely, Jr., eds.) (1984); *see also* Michael Stephen Hindus, *Prison and Plantation: Crime, Justice, and Authority in Massachusetts and South Carolina, 1767-1878* (1980).

[64] *Luke, a Slave v. State*, 5 Fla. 185, 1853 WL 1268 at *3 (1853) (holding that a slave can be convicted of a crime even if his defense was based upon obedience of his master's order).

[65] *See, e.g.*, on the procedures in slave criminal trials, McNair, *supra* at 82-142; Morris, *Slavery, supra* at 209-61; Fede, *People Without Rights, supra* at 181-99; Flanigan, *supra* at 73-144; Judith Kelleher Schafer, "'Under the present mode of trial, improper verdicts

are very often given': Criminal Procedure in the Trials of Slaves in Antebellum Louisiana," 18 *Cardozo L. Rev.* 635 (1996) Daniel J. Flanigan, "Criminal Procedure in Slave Trials in the Antebellum South," 40 *J. of Southern Hist.* 536 (1974); *see also* Schwarz, *Slave Law, supra* at 73-96 (discussing reasons why in Virginia the number of slaves hanged tended to decrease in the antebellum years).

[66] 13 N.C. (2 Dev.) 263 (1829).

[67] 26 Va. (5 Rand.) 678 (1827).

[68] *See* Fede, *People Without Rights, supra* at 61-130; Fede, "Legitimized Violence," *supra*. Authors analyzing the *Mann* case are numerous. *See, e.g.*, Mark V. Tushnet, *Slave Law in the American South: 'State v. Mann' in History and Literature* (2003); Kennedy, *Race, supra* at 33-34; James A. Wynn, Jr., "*State v. Mann*: Judicial Choice or Judicial Duty?," 87 *N.C. L. Rev.* 991 (2009); Laura F. Edwards, "The Power of Presentism in the History of Slave Law," 87 *N.C. L. Rev.* 855 (2009); Muller, *supra* at 760; Sally Greene, "*State v. Mann* Exhumed," 87 *N.C. L. Rev.* 701 (2009); Sally Hadden, "Judging Slavery: Thomas Ruffin and *State v. Mann*," in *Local Matters: Race, Crime, and Justice in the Nineteenth Century South* (Christopher Waldrep and Donald G. Nieman, eds.) (2001); Brady, *supra* at 248-51; A.E. Keir Nash, "A More Equitable Past? Southern Supreme Courts and the Protection of the Antebellum Negro," 48 *N.C. L. Rev.* 197, 221-23 (1970) [hereinafter Nash, "Equitable Past?"]; Julius Yanuck, "Thomas Ruffin and North Carolina Slave Law," 21 *J. S. Hist.* 456, 461-64 (1955); *see also* Tushnet, *Humanity, supra* at 54-65, and my comment on same in Fede, "Toward a Solution," *supra* at 308-11.

For extended discussions of the *Turner* case, *see* Morris, *Slavery, supra* at 188-90; Watson, *Americas, supra* at 10-15; A. Leon Higginbotham, Jr. & Anne F. Jacobs, "The 'Law Only As An Enemy': The Legitimization of Racial Powerlessness Through the Colonial and Antebellum Criminal Laws of Virginia," 70 *N.C. L. Rev.* 969, 1048-55 (1992). For my views, *see* Fede, *People Without Rights, supra* at 109-11; Fede, "Gender," *supra* at 411, 418-26; and Fede, "Legitimized Violence," *supra* at 134-47.

[69] *See* Fede, "Gender," *supra* at 413, n. 6, quoting Karen A. Getman, "Sexual Control in the Slaveholding South: The Implementation and Maintenance of a Racial Caste System," 7 *Harv. Women's L.J.* 115, 151-52 (1984).

[70] *See* Getman, "Sexual Control in the Slaveholding South," 7 *Harv. Women's L.J.* 115, 142-51 (1984).

[71] *See* Fede, "Gender," *supra* at 413, n. 6, quoting Anita L. Allen, "Surrogacy, Slavery, and the Ownership of Life," 13 *Harv. J.L. & Pub. Pol'y* 139, 142 (1990) (rejecting the argument that surrogate motherhood and slavery should be equated).

[72] *See* Fede, *People Without Rights, supra* at 244; John A. Scott, "Book Review," *Challenge* 65, 66-67 (May-June 1975) [hereinafter Scott, "Book Review"].

[73] *See* Fede, *People Without Rights, supra* at 221-40.

[74] *See* Stroud, *supra* at 2; *see also, e.g.*, Tomlins, *Freedom Bound, supra* at 455-59; Kathleen M. Brown, *Good Wives, Nasty Wenches, and Anxious Patriarchs: Gender, Race, and Power in Colonial Virginia* 132-35 (1996) [hereinafter Brown, *Good Wives*]; Morris, *Slavery, supra* at 43-49, 411-15; Fede, *People Without Rights, supra* at 33, 234; Shaw, *supra* at 47-49; Patterson, *Social Death, supra* at 132-47; Higginbotham, *Color, supra* at 42-44, 159, 194; Cobb, *supra* at 68-81; Taunya Lovell Banks, "Dangerous Woman: Elizabeth Key's Freedom Suit—Subjecthood and Racialized Identity in

Seventeenth Century Colonial Virginia," 41 *Akron L. Rev.* 799, 809-33 (2008); Gillmer, "Suing for Freedom," *supra* at 560, n. 144; Barbara Jeanne Fields, "Slavery, Race and Ideology in the United States of America," *New Left Rev.* 95, 101 (May/June 1990); Morris, "'Villeinage," *supra* at 108-21; William M. Wiecek, "The Statutory Law of Slavery and Race in the Thirteen Mainland Colonies of British America," 34 *Wm. & Mary Q.* 258, 262-63 (1977) [hereinafter Wiecek, "Statutes"].

A limited exception in the majority of Southern states held that, unlike the offspring of farm animals born during a life tenant's term or the term of a tenant for a term of years, the children of slaves born during the relevant term were the property of the holders of the remainder interest. *See* chapter 5, *infra* at notes 141-42. Morris, disagreeing with Stroud, asserted that slavery was not "any less 'degrading'" under the rule providing that the child's status followed the father's status. *See* Morris, *Slavery, supra* at 45-46. Morris did not consider the social and psychological effect, on both free people and slaves, of replacing the rule that applied to people with the rule that applied to animals. *See also* Brown, *Good Wives, supra* at 135; Camille A. Nelson, "American Husbandry: Legal Norms Impacting the Production of (Re)Productivity," 19 *Yale J. L. & Feminism* 1, 17-20 (2007) (discussing *partus sequitur ventrem* and slave breeding).

[75] *See* chapter 7, *infra* at notes 10-15.

[76] *See* Tomlins, *Freedom Bound, supra* at 460-62; Anthony S. Parent, Jr., *Foul Means: The Formation of Slave Society in Virginia, 1660-1740* 112-13, 243-44 (2003); Higginbotham, *Color, supra* at 36-37; 127-28, 198-201; 2 William W. Hening, ed., *Statutes at Large of Virginia* 260 (13 volumes) (1819-1823) (for the Virginia act); 4 Catterall, *supra* at 1-2; Jeffrey R. Brackett, *The Negro in Maryland: A Study of the Institution of Slavery* 29 (reprint ed. 1969) (1889); Jonathan L. Alpert, "The Origin of Slavery in the United States—The Maryland Precedent," 14 *Am. J. Legal Hist.* 189, 196 (1970) (for the Maryland act).

And see, discussing anti-miscegenation laws, which also contributed to the slave's dishonored condition in society, Peggy Pascoe, *What Comes Naturally: Miscegenation Law and the Making of Race in America* 19-44 (2009); Higginbotham, *Color, supra* at 40-47; Kevin Mumford, "After Hugh: Statutory Race Segregation in Colonial America, 1630-1725," 43 *Am. J. of Legal Hist.* 280 (1999); Note, "Sexual Control in the Slaveholding South: The Implementation of a Racial Caste System," 7 *Harv. Women's L.J.* 115 (1984); Alpert, *supra* at 209-12; Walter Wadlington, "The Loving Case: Virginia's Anti-Miscegenation Statute in Historical Perspective," 52 *Va. L. Rev.* 1189 (1966). In contrast, slaves who escaped into Florida between 1683 and 1790 could obtain sanctuary and earn their freedom if they converted to Christianity and satisfied other conditions that varied over time, but only during the years during which the Spanish controlled Florida. *See supra* note 5 in this chapter.

[77] *See Phillips v. Lewis*, 1 Del. Cas. 417, 1796 WL 28 (Del. Com. Pl. 1796) (Asians could not be slaves absent a statute, only "Negroes and mulattoes descended from a female Negro."); Fede, *People Without Rights, supra* at 37. On the rejection of slavery for Europeans, *see* Tomlins, *Freedom Bound, supra* at 270-71; Drescher, *supra* at 46-59; David Eltis, *The Rise of African Slavery in the Americas* 1-28 (2000) [hereinafter Eltis, *Rise of African Slavery*].

[78] *See*, for the Virginia statutes, Higginbotham, *Color, supra* at 37; Cobb, *supra* at 63-67; Higginbotham & Higginbotham, *supra* at 1238; A. Leon Higginbotham, Jr. & Barbara K.

Kopytoff, "Racial Purity and Interracial Sex in the Law of Colonial and Antebellum Virginia," 77 *Geo. L.J.* 1967, 1973-75 (1989) [hereinafter Higginbotham & Kopytoff]; and, for the Maryland statutes, 4 Catterall, *supra* at 1-2; Alpert, *supra* at 195.

[79] *See* 1 Catterall, *supra* at 60-71; Stroud, *supra* at 1-9; Wiecek, "Statutes," *supra* at 263-64. On Native American slavery, *see State v. Van Waggoner*, 6 N.J.L. 374 (Sup. Ct. 1797) (presumption of slavery applied to Indians as well as blacks, denying freedom claims of plaintiff); Deborah A. Rosen, *American Indians and State Law: Sovereignty, Race, and Citizenship, 1790-1880* 9-11, 84-101 (2007); Morris, *Slavery, supra* at 19-21; Shaw, *supra* at 65-75; Gregory Ablavasky, "Comment, Making Indians 'White': The Judicial Abolition of Native Slavery in Revolutionary Virginia and its Racial Legacy," 159 *U. Pa. L. Rev.* 1457, 1461, 1463-72 (2011).

The salience of race is also revealed by the unequal treatment that free blacks faced in the law. *See, e.g.*, Ira Berlin, *Slaves Without Masters: The Free Negro in the Antebellum South* (1974) [hereinafter Berlin, *Slaves Without Masters*]; Ellen D. Katz, "African-American Freedom in Antebellum Cumberland County, Virginia," 70 *Chi.-Kent L. Rev.* 927 (1995); A. Leon Higginbotham, Jr. & Greer C. Bosworth, "'Rather Than the Free': Free Blacks in Colonial and Antebellum Virginia," 26 *Harv. C.R.-C.L. L. Rev.* 17 (1991); David Skillen Bogen, "The Maryland Context of Dred Scott: The Decline in the Legal Status of Maryland Free Blacks 1776-1810," 34 *Am. J. Legal Hist.* 381 (1990).

[80] *See, e.g.*, Morgan, *American Slavery, supra* at 295-337. On black slaveholding, *see, e.g.*, Ira Berlin, *Generations of Captivity: A History of African-American Slaves* 37-38, 138-39, 144-45 (2003) [hereinafter Berlin, *Generations*]; Ira Berlin, *Many Thousands Gone: The First Two Centuries of Slavery in North America* 30-32 (1998) [hereinafter Berlin, *Many Thousands*]; Loren Schweninger, *Black Property Owners in the South 1790-1915* 104-09 (1997) [hereinafter Schweninger, *Black Property*]; Eugene D. Genovese, *Roll, Jordan, Roll: The World the Slaves Made* 406-08 (1974) [hereinafter Genovese, *Roll*]; Stampp, *supra* at 194-95; Katz, *supra* at 963-64; Philip J. Schwarz, "Emancipators, Protectors, and Anomalies: Free Black Slaveowners in Virginia," 95 *Va. Mag. of Hist. & Biography* 317 (1987) [hereinafter Schwarz, "Emancipators"].

Dinesh D'Souza noted that whites were not the only slave owners in the United States South; black slaves were owned by both Native Americans and free blacks. *See* D'Souza, *The End of Racism: Principles for a Multiracial Society* 74-79 (1995). "[A]lthough slavery and racism are not intrinsically related ... what distinguished the American experience from the rest of the world was the evolution over time of racial slavery, specifically black slavery. The American institution of slavery became driven and maintained by the assumptions of racial superiority." *Id.* at 86; *see* Crusto, *supra* at 135-36. Some Southern court decisions and statutes eventually found that blacks could not own slaves because of racist public policy notions. *Ewell v. Tidwell*, 20 Ark. 136 (1859); *Davis v. Evans*, 18 Mo. 249 (1853); *Tindal v. Hudson*, 2 Del. (2 Harr.) 441 (1838); Morris, *Slavery, supra* at 30-31. A Virginia statute permitted free "people of color" to buy only a spouse or child after July 1, 1832. *See* Schwarz, "Emancipators," *supra* at 332.

[81] 11 Va. (1 Hen. & M.) 134 (1806).

[82] *See, e.g.*, Eva Sheppard Wolf, *Race and Liberty in the New Nation: Emancipation in Virginia from the Revolution to Nat Turner's Rebellion* 149-52 (2007) [hereinafter Wolf, *Race*]; George Warnke, *After Identity: Rethinking Race, Sex, and Gender* 50-51 (2007); Rosen, *supra* at 84-101; H. Jefferson Powell, *A Community Built on Words: The Consti-*

tution in History and Politics 100-10 (2005); Peter Wallenstein, *Tell the Court I Love My Wife: Race, Marriage, and Law—An American History* 32-37 (2002); Cover, *Justice Accused, supra* at 51-55; Angela Onwuachi-Willig, "Multiracialism and the Social Construction of Race: The Story of *Hudgins v. Wrights*," in *Race Law Studies* 145-73 (Rachel F. Moran, *et al.*, eds.) (2008); Wythe Holt, "George Wythe: Early Modern Judge," 58 *Ala. L. Rev.* 1009, 1031-38 (2007); Paul Finkelman, "The Crime of Color," 67 *Tulane L. Rev.* 2063, 2107-10 (1993) [hereinafter Finkelman, "Crime of Color"]; Higginbotham & Higginbotham, *supra* at 1237-42; Higginbotham & Kopytoff, *supra* at 1985-87 (all discussing this case).

[83] Hyde, *supra*, at 231. In fact, Judge John Louis Taylor had previously charged a North Carolina jury with a similar presumption. *See Gobu v. Gobu*, 1 N.C. (Tay.) 100 (1802).

[84] *See, e.g.*, Fede, *People Without Rights, supra* at 140; Cobb, *supra* at 247; Wheeler, *supra* at 197; *Susan, A Free Woman of Color v. Wells*, 5 S.C.L. (3 Brev.) 11 (1811) (dismissing plaintiff's assault and battery action, plaintiff's witnesses testified plaintiff had been a slave). Freed slaves and free blacks, such as Sojourner Truth and Polly Berry, used the courts to enforce their legal rights during the slavery times. *See* Wong, *supra* at 137-43; Lucy A. Delaney, "Struggles for Freedom," in *Six Women's Slave Narratives* 9-51 (William L. Andrews, introduction, 1988) (narrative of Lucy A. Delaney, whose mother Polly, then a free black girl, was kidnapped into slavery, and who through the courts obtained her freedom and Lucy's freedom); Fede, "Gender," *supra* at 418-26 (discussing Sojourner Truth's efforts to obtain the return of her son from slavery); Allen, *supra* at 142-43 (discussing Lucy A. Delaney's narrative).

[85] Fede, *People Without Rights, supra* at 138.

[86] *Id.*

[87] *See* Berlin, *Generations, supra* at 42-43, 66, 94-95, 135, 142, 145, 156; Berlin, *Many Thousands, supra* at 29-31, 36-38, 213-14, 235-36, 280-81, 319, 331-34.

[88] *See, e.g.*, Patterson, *Social Death, supra* at 202-05; Alejandro de la Fuente, "Slaves and the Creation of Legal Rights in Cuba: *Coartación* and *Papel*," 87 *Hispanic Am. Hist. Rev.* 652, 669-72 (2007) [hereinafter de la Fuente, "Legal Rights"]; Barcia, *supra* at 169-77. According to Orlando Patterson, this change of masters procedure "was more a mild punishment of the master than a 'right' of the slave." Patterson, *Social Death, supra* at 202.

[89] Higginbotham & Higginbotham, *supra* at 1234-35.

[90] *See, e.g.*, Gross, *Double Character, supra* at 3-5; Daniel W. Hamilton, "Emancipation and Contract Law," in *The Dred Scott Case: Historical and Contemporary Perspectives on Race and Law* 100-01 (David Thomas Konig, Paul Finkelman, and Christopher Alan Bracey, eds.) (2010) [hereinafter *Dred Scott Perspectives*]; Walter Johnson, "The Slave Trader, the White Slave, and the Politics of Racial Determination in the 1850s," 87 *J. of Am. Hist.* 13, 37-38 (2000); Walter Johnson, "Inconstancy, Contradiction, and Complete Confusion: The Everyday Life of the Law of Slavery," 22 *Law & Soc. Inquiry* 405, 429-30 (1997) (book review); William W. Fisher, III, "Ideology and Imagery in the Law of Slavery" (a revised and expanded version of an article published in 68 *Chi.-Kent L. Rev.* 1051 (1993)), in *Slavery and the Law* 43-59 (Paul Finkelman, ed.) (1997) [hereinafter *Slavery and the Law*].

[91] *See* Wilbert E. Moore, "Slave Law and the Social Structure," 26 *J. Negro Hist.* 171, 188,

n. 36 (1941) [hereinafter Moore, "Slave Law"].

[92] 1 Hurd, *supra* at 18-20, 36-43.

[93] *Id.* at 42 [footnote omitted].

[94] *See* Fede, *People Without Rights*, *supra* at 22-23; *see also* Wahl, *Burden*, *supra* at 142-73.

[95] Finley, *supra* at 73 [citation omitted].

[96] *Howard v. Howard*, 51 N.C. (6 Jones) 235, 236 (1858).

[97] Hohfeld stated his theories in two articles, Wesley N. Hohfeld, "Fundamental Legal Conceptions as Applied in Judicial Reasoning," 26 *Yale L.J.* 710 (1917) [hereinafter Hohfeld, "Fundamental"], and Wesley N. Hohfeld, "Some Fundamental Legal Conceptions as Applied in Judicial Reasoning," 23 *Yale L.J.* 16 (1913) [hereinafter Hohfeld, "Some Fundamental"], and in Wesley N. Hohfeld, *Fundamental Legal Conceptions as Applied in Judicial Reasoning and Other Legal Essays* (Walter W. Cook, ed., 1923); *see, e.g.*, Gregory S. Alexander, *Commodity and Property: Competing Visions of Property in American Legal Thought 1776-1970* 319-23 (1997); L.W. Sumner, *The Moral Foundation of Rights* 18-53 (1987); Gary L. Francione, *Animals, Property, and the Law* 43, 96 (1995); Joseph Singer, "The Legal Rights Debate in Analytical Jurisprudence from Bentham to Hohfeld," 1982 *Wisconsin L. Rev.* 975, 986-95 (1982); Max Radin, "A Restatement of Hohfeld," 51 *Harv. L. Rev.* 1141 (1938); Arthur L. Corbin, "Legal Analysis and Terminology," 33 *Yale L.J.* 501 (1924); Arthur L. Corbin, "Rights and Duties," 29 *Yale L.J.* 163 (1919).

For discussions of Hohfeld's analysis and slavery law, *see* Fede, *People Without Rights*, *supra* at 19-21, 34; Russell, "New Image," *supra* at 502-04; *see also* Jeanne L Schroeder, "Hegel's Slaves, Blackstone's Objects, and Hohfeld's Ghosts: A Comment on Thomas Russell's Imagery of Slave Auctions," 18 *Cardozo L. Rev.* 525 (1996) (critiquing Russell's article and Hohfeld's theory).

[98] *See* Hohfeld, "Fundamental," *supra* at 710; Hohfeld, "Some Fundamental," *supra* at 30-58.

[99] *See* Alexander, *supra* at 319-23; Fede, *People Without Rights*, *supra* at 34; Russell, "New Image," *supra* at 503. Russell correctly quotes my reference to the slave owner possessing the "bundle of rights" embodied in the slave, *id.* at 520, but in the same paragraph to which Russell refers I also stated that "the characterization of slaves as property presented a means of ordering the relationships between the slave, the master, and third parties." Fede, *People Without Rights*, *supra* at 34. Thus, I did not mean to imply that the master possessed all of the rights in the slave, and my unclear expression makes it appear that my views differ from those that Russell more clearly and thoroughly explained.

[100] *See* Radin, *supra* at 1147; *see also* 1 Hurd, *supra* at 19 ("all legal relations are relations of persons to persons—directly or through things").

[101] Fede, *People Without Rights*, *supra* at 19.

[102] *See* Alexander, *supra* at 323.

[103] *See id.* at 320.

[104] *See id.* at 321 [footnote omitted].

[105] *See id.* at 323.

[106] *See* Jane B. Baron, "Property and 'No-Property,'" 42 *Houston L. Rev.* 1425, 1429 (2006). For critiques of Hohfeld's theory, *see, e.g.,* Schroeder, *supra*; Jeanne L Schroeder, "Chix Nix Bundle-O-Stix: A Feminist Critique of the Disaggregation of Property," 93 *Mich. L. Rev.* 239 (1994); Singer, *supra*; Kenneth J. Vandevelde, "The New Property of the Nineteenth Century: The Development of The Modern Concept of Property," 29 *Buffalo L. Rev.* 325 (1980).

[107] *See* Baron, *supra* at 1429.

[108] Fede, *People Without Rights, supra* at 19-20.

[109] For a general discussion of Max Weber's views of the legitimizing function of law, *see* David Trubeck, "Max Weber on Law and the Rise of Capitalism," 1972 *Wisconsin L. Rev.* 720, 720-26 (1972).

[110] *See* Fede, *People Without Rights, supra* at 19-20, quoting Chief Justice Roger B. Taney in *Scott v. Sandford*, 60 U.S. (19 How.) at 407.

[111] *See* James Oakes, *Slavery and Freedom: An Interpretation of the Old South* 159 (1990), *quoting* 1 Hurd, *supra* at 42.

[112] *See* Morris, *Slavery, supra* at 193-96.

[113] *See* Cobb, *supra* at 93. Cobb also stated that he disagreed with Wardlaw's analysis in *Boylston. See id.* at 93-94, n. 5.

[114] *See* Guyora Binder, "The Slavery of Emancipation," 17 *Cardozo L. Rev.* 2063, 2089 (1996), quoting Tushnet, *Humanity, supra* at 199; *see, e.g., Jarman v. Patterson*, 23 Ky. (7 T.B. Mon.) 644, 1828 WL 1332 (1828) (rejecting challenge to statute permitting arrest of self-contracting slaves); Schweninger, *Black Property, supra* at 52-54; Paul Finkelman, *The Law of Freedom and Bondage: A Casebook* 127-28 (1986) [hereinafter Finkelman, *Casebook*].

[115] *See* Finley, *supra* at 73.

[116] On the practice of self-hiring by slaves, *see* Martin, *supra* at 159-87; Berlin, *Generations, supra* at 222-26; Berlin, *Many Thousands, supra* at 69, 136-37, 156-57, 317; Schweninger, *Black Property, supra* at 54-56; Stampp, *supra* at 72-73, 96, 228.

[117] Finley, *supra* at 74.

[118] *Id.*

[119] Genovese, *Roll, supra* at 30.

[120] Scott, "Book Review," *supra* at 67. For Scott's interpretation, *see* Scott, *Hard Trials.*

[121] Morris, *Slavery, supra* at 388-92.

[122] *See* Wedgwood, *supra* at 1394; *see also, e.g.,* Anthony E. Kayne, *Joining Places: Slave Neighborhoods in the Old South* (2007) (discussing slave neighborhoods); Steven Hahn, *A Nation Under Feet: Black Political Struggles in the Rural South from Slavery to the Great Migration* (2003) (discussing what he calls slave political relationships); Gross, *Double Character, supra* (discussing how slaves influenced civil court proceedings); Johnson, *Soul, supra* (discussing how slaves influenced civil court proceedings and slave sales transactions); Blassingame, *supra* (discussing slave communities and families). And see this book's preface, *supra* at notes 50-51, discussing slave agency.

123 *Compare* Wedgwood, *supra* at 1394.

124 *See* Jon-Christian Suggs, *Whispered Consolidations: Law and Narrative in African American Life* 27 (2000).

125 *See id.* at 30; *see also* Jon-Christian Suggs, "African American Literature and Legal History," 22 *Law & Literature* 325 (2010); Jon-Christian Suggs, "African American Literature and the Law," in *Studies in Law (Volume 43) Special Issue: Law and Literature Reconsidered* 153-72 (Austin Sarat, ed.) (2008). Ariela Gross added to her agreement with Suggs's views the assertion that "[s]laves were also acutely aware of themselves as objects of property relations and commercial transactions." *See* Gross, *Double Character, supra* at 42.

126 *See* Wedgwood, *supra* at 1394; *see also* Ulrich B. Phillips, *American Negro Slavery: A Survey of the Supply, Employment and Control of Negro Labor as Determined by the Plantation Régime* 514 (1918) (contending that slavery law described "a hypothetical régime, not an actual one.") [hereinafter Phillips, *American Negro Slavery*].

127 *See* Fede, *People Without Rights, supra* at 19-22, discussing the views of James Oakes in Oakes, *supra* at 159, *see also* 1 Hurd, *supra* at 42.

128 *See* Fede, *People Without Rights, supra* at 61-121; *see also* Hartman, *supra* at 88-101; Peter W. Bardaglio, *Reconstructing the Household: Families, Sex and the Law in the Nineteenth-Century South* 6, 21-30 (1995).

Laura F. Edwards refers to a similar concept of the public peace while discussing Southern law and culture. Edwards, *The People and Their Peace: Legal Culture and the Transformation of Inequality in the Post-Revolutionary South* 105-07 (2009) [hereinafter Edwards, *People*]; *see* Fede, *People Without Rights, supra* at 83-84, 210-15 (discussing the disruption of slavery's orderly oppression by acts including slave theft), and *id.* at 190-97; Flanigan, *supra* at 140-44 (discussing the disruption of slavery's orderly oppression by lynch mobs). On the related issue of the kidnapping of free blacks, *see* Carol Wilson, *Freedom at Risk: The Kidnapping of Free Blacks in America, 1780-1865* (1994).

129 *See* Davis, "Identity Notes," *supra* at 708.

2

The Fundamental Nature of Manumission and Manumission Contracts

Manumission in the United States South is best thought of as the master's gift of liberty to the person he or she holds as a slave. The English word manumission is derived from the Latin *manumittere*, which means "to let go from the hand or set at liberty."[1] According to Thomas Cobb's treatise on slave law in the United States, manumission "derives its name from the Roman law. The English writers adopted with the name, the definition and explanation."[2] Thus, Cobb cited Littleton stating that manumission placed "one beyond or without the hand (*manum*) or power of another."[3] Cobb also quoted Glanville's treatise, which called manumission "the gift of liberty; for one in slavery is supposed to be in the hand or power of his master, and when he is manumitted, he is liberated from the hand and power of his master."[4]

This chapter will address several questions about manumission's essential nature that are suggested by these definitions, including: Who could free a person held as a slave? In his multi-cultural study of slavery, Orlando Patterson defined manumission as "the legal release of an individual from slavery either *by the master or by a superior authority, such as the state.*"[5] North Carolina Chief Justice Thomas Ruffin, in an 1838 opinion, however, referred to manumission as "*the act of the master*, by which he renounces his right to the services of his slave, and sets her free from him."[6] The difference between these two definitions is telling; in the United States South the state rarely manumitted slaves contrary to the master's intent.

This chapter also will demonstrate how the concept of manumission as a gratuity was the foundation of the general rule in the South by which the courts did not enforce manumission contracts in suits by slaves who performed their end of the bargain.

The Nature of the Slave Owner's Manumission Rights/Powers

When the statutes did not prohibit manumission, masters could during their lifetimes free their slaves. Masters also could express in their wills their intention to free their slaves after the masters died. Manumissions took effect immediately, immediately upon the masters' death, at a fixed time in the future, or upon the satisfaction of a condition by the slaves or by others.[7]

As noted in chapter one, Hohfeld did not consider slavery in his analysis. Under Hohfeld's theory, when masters freed their slaves, their acts can be understood as the exercise of their legal power to relinquish their property rights in the slaves. "'Powers' are state-enforced abilities to change legal entitlements held by oneself or others[.]"[8] Hohfeld cited a property owner's decision to abandon personal property as an example of the exercise of a power. The owner extinguishes "his own legal interest (rights, powers, immunities, etc.) through ... abandonment; and—simultaneously and correlatively—to create in other persons privileges and powers relating to the abandoned object, *e.g.*, the power to acquire title to" the property object.[9] An owner who abandons property leaves "himself with precisely the same sort of privileges and powers as any other person."[10]

The courts generally enforced the master's intentions to abandon his or her property rights in a slave when they permitted a manumitted slave to continue to live in freedom after the master released his or her rights in the slave according to law.[11] Even this right was subject, however, to the superior property rights of the master's creditors and others. The Southern judges and legislators recognized that an insolvent master's decision to free his or her slaves had to be balanced against the rights of the master's legitimate creditors.[12]

But masters who freed their slaves did more than just release their own individual property rights and interests in slave property. They also had an impact on the public interest because the freed slaves no longer were items of human personal property who were people without rights. Manumission transformed slaves from property to people with all of the rights that the law vested in them upon their release from bondage.[13]

Accordingly, a slave owner's decision to free a slave differed conceptually from an owner's decision to abandon personal property.[14] Under the common law rule, the finder of abandoned personal property acquires good title against all others including the rightful owner and the owner of the real estate on which the chattel may have been found, unless the finder was trespassing when the find occurred.[15]

In contrast, freed slaves generally no longer were property. Manumission was "an utter destruction of the right of property."[16] It severed the entire bundle of property rights of the owner and all others in the slave, and it created for the freed slave new legal rights and obligations. Exceptions to this rule included the statutes in some Southern states that permitted the re-enslavement of freed slaves who did not leave the state after manumission, contrary to the statute. These freed slaves were subject to be returned to slavery "as if they were abandoned property."[17]

Manumission's better analogy, therefore, may be with the owner's right to use and destroy his or her property. Both Roman law and the Anglo-American common law included this right—called *jus abutendi et abutendi*—among the property owners' powers and rights.[18] This right's legal nature and its justifications are not "well developed." The owner destroys not only his or her own right to obtain the benefits of property ownership; he or she also destroys that right for "future generations."[19] Thus, "[t]he law of property destruction ... governs whether and under what circumstances the owner may deprive a resource of its immortality."[20]

The destruction of property may also have a wider effect on what is perceived to be the public interest. Courts in the United States have recently placed greater limits on this power in view of the effects that property destruction may have on the owner's heirs and its effect on society at large, depending on the perceived value of the property, such as that of an historic building. This is especially so when the owner's will calls for the destruction of the owner's property after his or her death, because of the effect that the destruction would have on the present and future rights of others in the property.[21]

Moreover, scholars have recently advocated greater legal limits on the owner's right to destroy or waste objects of personal property. For example, Joseph L. Sax suggested that an owner's decision to destroy "a major work of art or science is felt as a loss to the community because it undermines pursuit of a common agenda."[22] He contrasted this with the destruction of physical objects that are "devoid of any public element except a broad obligation to avoid doing conventional harm such as trespassing on the rights of others."[23] Thus, Sax called for legal rules or procedures to regulate the owner's right to destroy those objects that implicate the public interest as to which "a larger community has a legitimate stake because they embody ideas or scientific and historical information."[24]

And so it was with slaves in the South. The lawmakers believed that the master's power to abandon or destroy property rights embodied in a slave had to be regulated in the public interest. "Free blacks were considered dangerous to the slave South, and thus their increase was strictly regulated."[25] Many legislators and judges concluded that manumission was an anti-slavery act. They eventually prohibited, in the public interest, the owners' power to destroy, by manumission, the relational property interests that other people or the state had—or in the future might have—in slave property.

Who Was a Master Who Possessed the Manumission Rights/Powers?

It follows, then, that most of the manumission cases decided in the South centered on proof of the master's intention to exercise his or her power to free a slave. When the courts consider a person's alleged exercise of a power, they determine whether the person had a purpose to exercise the power, "and whether the person was in fact clothed with a power to create a demand—or privilege—right against another; or whether the particular person in the particular case, whatever his purpose, was without such power, *i.e.*, was under a disability."[26]

Accordingly, even if manumission was not then prohibited by a statute, the heirs of masters who were intent on challenging wills freeing slaves could hire lawyers to claim that the masters suffered from "some disability, such as nonage, or coverture, or lunacy, or duress."[27] Heirs also could assert that undue influence or the violation of some requirement of form voided the masters' wills freeing slaves.[28]

Moreover, a person could acquire title to a slave by adverse possession. Therefore, a master's manumission could not be effective against another person who by adverse possession acquired ownership of the slave to be freed.[29]

Just like other forms of property, slaves often were the subjects of multiple present and future claims of right and ownership. Some slaves were jointly owned by more than one person. Slaves also could be held by a life tenant or widow with a dower interest for her lifetime in the slave. The slave would become the property of the persons entitled to the remainder interest upon the death of the life tenant or widow.[30]

Consequently, the courts also needed to ascertain if the person claiming to be entitled to free the slave had a sufficient ownership interest to do so. According to Cobb, one joint owner could not free the slave without the consent of the other owner or owners.[31] He referred to but questioned the 1848 opinion of Kentucky Court of Appeals Judge James Simpson in *Tom Davis, (of color) v. Tingle*.[32] Citing an 1817 New York opinion, Judge Simpson suggested that owners of a majority interest in a slave could free their slave, but they would be liable for conversion as to the other co-owners.[33] Judge Simpson stated, however, that a partial manumission by the owner or owners of less than a half interest in the slave must yield to the rights of the majority owners, because the states of freedom and slavery cannot exist "united together in the same person." The partial manumission authorized by a minority interest holder or holders is "postponed ..., until such time if ever, as it may become efficacious by the concurrence of the other owners[.]"[34]

The Southern courts also held that life tenants and widows with lifetime dower rights in slaves could not free "their" slaves because their right of sale extended only to their limited interest in the slave. Therefore, they could not by manumission destroy the future property rights of the holders of the remainder, although the holders of the remainder could free the slave effective upon the life tenant's or dowager's death.[35]

This rule giving one owner a veto over a proposed manumission was not the only possible option available to the Southern judges. According to the Spanish law *Las Siete Partidas*, "if a slave were owned by more than one master and if only one of the masters wanted to free the slave, the slave could be freed."[36] The law required the other co-owners to sell their shares to the owner who wanted to free the slave "at a just and suitable price."[37] Because some slaves who became the heirs of their masters were automatically freed, if the inheriting slaves were co-owned by another, that master was required to "accept a price in reason for that part of the slave which belonged to him."[38]

The Louisiana Code of 1825 in effect repealed this Spanish law provision and stated that masters could not be compelled to free their slaves. It also stated that "no master shall be compelled to sell his slave," with two exceptions. According to the first, a master who was "only co-proprietor of the slave" could be ordered to sell his interest if "his co-proprietor demands the sale in order to make partition of the property[.]" And the second occurred "when the master shall be convicted of cruel treatment of his slave, and the judge shall deem proper to pronounce, besides the penalty established for such cases, that the slave shall be sold at public auction, in order to place him out of the reach of the power which the master has abused."[39]

The law in the United States therefore could have provided for different rules if it truly did favor liberty, but it did not. Any co-owner, life tenant, or widow with a dower interest in a slave could have been allowed to free the slave, provided that the other co-owners or the holders of the remainder interest received a judgment for their share of the slave's value.[40]

State Manumission, the Slaves' Good Conduct, and the Masters' Misconduct

The state could reserve to itself the legal power to free a person who legally was held as a slave, without regard to that person's owner's intentions, to advance what the lawmakers perceived to be important public interests. Patterson called this process political manumission.[41] The law often provided that by their good conduct slaves could earn their freedom, and the master may or may not have been compensated for the property loss. Masters also could forfeit their property rights through their own misconduct that the lawmakers perceived to be contrary to the public interest.

For example, the Spanish law *Las Siete Partidas*, following Roman law, included provisions that authorized manumissions contrary to the master's intentions. These manumissions generally were based on a slave's good conduct or a master's bad conduct. Slaves could earn their freedom by their "good actions," which included informing on one who "violated or carried off a virgin," identifying counterfeiters, informing on guards and soldiers who had deserted their posts, accusing or avenging the killer of the slaves' masters, or revealing treason against the crown. The government would reimburse the masters for their slaves' value in all of these cases except the last, which can be viewed as a governmental taking of the slaves for public purposes.[42]

Moreover, a master who mistreated a slave ran the risk that the slave could be sold to another owner. But a master who ordered a female to commit prostitution could be ordered to forfeit his slave, "on account of such depravity as this[.]" The local authorities also were charged with the duty to prevent the master from again enslaving the woman declared to be free.[43]

A slave also was freed if he became a cleric with his master's consent, and without the master's consent, if the master did not reclaim him as a slave within one year of learning of the ordination, or if the slave became "a priest qualified to say mass" and the slave provided the master with another slave in his place.[44] "A Christian slave living among the Moors might return to live among the Christians as a free man."[45]

People held as slaves in Portuguese Brazil also could be freed for good cause without their masters' consent. For example, the King had a monopoly over lucrative enterprises in the colonies, such as diamond mines. A slave who found and presented to the authorities a diamond larger than twenty carats was to be freed by the state, which compensated the slave's owner for the slave's value. A slave who reported on another person who did not properly surrender a diamond of more than twenty carats also was to be freed, and the slave's owner was to be paid the slave's value, unless the slave reported on his or her owner, in which case the slave would be freed and would be paid one-half of his or her value.[46] And slaves would be freed upon being baptized only if their masters so intended.[47]

Moreover, people held as slaves in nineteenth century Brazil could assert several grounds for freedom suits, which included those based on the master's consent and those that were not. These were: (1) the enforcement of the master's letters of manumission; (2) the declaration of slaves as free after the master allowed them to live as free people for a period of time; (3) the enforcement of the rights of people who were the descendants of free women who could not be held as slaves because of their race; (4) the illegality of slavery for people who arrived in Brazil after the slave trade was outlawed; (5) the right to freedom if a master inflicted excessive violence or abuse on the slave, including holding the slave in prostitution; and (6) the enforcement of a master's promise or contract to free the slave.[48]

The legislators on the island of Jamaica in 1733 adopted a statute that permitted mixed race people to be treated as if white, and, therefore, no longer eligible for the bonds of slavery. The act stated that "no Person who is not above three Degrees removed from the Negro Ancestor exclusive, shall be allowed to vote or poll in Elections; and no one shall be deemed a Mulatto after the Third Generation, as aforesaid, but that they shall have all the Privileges and Immunities of His Majesty's white Subjects of this Island, providing they are brought up in the Christian Religion."[49] Carl Degler called this a "mulatto escape hatch" out of slavery. "In short," mixed race people "after the third generation" according to this law "would be legally white."[50] This law applied apparently if the mixed race person had a female African ancestor who was legally held as a slave and was not freed.

In contrast, the law in the United States South rarely mandated manumission without the master's consent and did not provide for an escape hatch out of slavery for some mixed race people who had a female African ancestor. For example, Louisiana's legislators limited the involuntary manumission principles of *Las Siete Partidas* after Spain's rule ended.[51] The 1825 Civil Code, in Article 191, following Louisiana's 1808 Digest, stated that masters could not "be compelled, either directly or indirectly," to free their slaves. The statute included an exception "only in cases where the [manumission] shall be made for services rendered to the State, by virtue of an act of the Legislature of the same, and on the State satisfying to the master the appraised value of the manumitted slave."[52]

As noted in chapter seven, Southern slave owners' misconduct also rarely could lead to freedom for their slaves. In three Southern states—Delaware, Virginia, and Maryland—statutes provided that masters who illegally imported slaves into the state as merchandise, and not for their own use as *bona fide* settlers, risked forfeiting those slaves. Delaware was the only Southern state that extended involuntary slave forfeiture to someone who, without a license, either exported slaves from Delaware or sold slaves with the intention of exporting them from the state.[53]

The good conduct of enslaved people in the United States South was on occasion asserted in freedom suits, which also are discussed in chapter seven. In most of the Southern freedom suits in which the claimants did not base their claim on direct or indirect expressions of their masters' intentions, the proofs centered on the freedom claimants' race. Some freedom claimants sought to prove that their non-African race or ancestry prevented them from being held in bondage. These claimants sought to defeat their alleged masters' right to hold the claimants in bondage by offering to prove their whiteness—either by showing that they had "acted white" or that they were accepted as white by the white community, or both.[54]

In addition, Southern state legislatures adopted acts freeing an individual slave or slaves. These statutes often indirectly reflected the masters' intentions, however, because masters petitioned the legislature to free favored slaves who may have been relatives or long time favored servants. For example, in 1833, Samuel H. Osborne filed a petition with the Mississippi legislature on behalf of a child whom he purchased. He alleged that the child, who was of white parentage, "by fraud or some disgraceful device" was brought into the state and was sold as a slave. Osborne asked the legislature "to restore to her what he honestly believes to be her natural rights." After Osborne exhibited the child to the Mississippi legislature, it adopted an act freeing her.[55] And on March 6, 1856, Georgia's General Assembly adopted an act freeing a slave named Boston. The legislators found that "during a long life" Boston "served his owners with uniform fidelity[.]" In addition, the act cited as a basis for the manumission Boston's service "during the War of 1812 ... with his master in the company from Liberty county, which marched to Darien, and remained there under arms in momentary expectation of an engagement with the British who threatened a landing, and other important services to the public." Boston thus was freed with the consent of his six owners, to "enjoy all the rights and privileges to which free negroes in the State of Georgia are entitled."[56]

State/Political Manumission, War, and Public Safety

War and public safety concerns also constituted public interests that at times persuaded the lawmakers in slave societies to provide people held as slaves with opportunities to win their freedom in return for good conduct in military service, without regard to the slaves' owners' intentions. According to Orlando Patterson, the most common causes for political manumissions were "exceptional acts of valor on the part of the slave, usually in warfare."[57] He stated that "[a]lmost all" slave societies "used manumission at some time" to motivate slaves to help defend their home territory or to invade other territory. "Civil wars were also important in the history of mass manumissions," because "slaves tended to benefit from both sides." Patterson argued that "there has been a tendency to underestimate" the significance of these manumissions, which "often contributed substantially to the size of the freed population."[58]

Patterson suggested that military manumissions most often occurred in times of crisis, even in societies that, as a general rule, otherwise prohibited slave soldiers. He cited examples from ancient Greece and Rome, medieval Europe, the Islamic islands, Korea, and the European colonies in South America and the Caribbean.[59] Other scholars have noted that slave soldiers were used elsewhere, including in eighteenth century Cuba and Suriname and in nineteenth century Buenos Aires, and that some of these slaves were freed after their military service.[60]

According to Patterson, the North American British settlers in the "early colonial times ... regularly recruited [slaves] in the defense of the colonies against Indians and foreign Europeans. Usually the reward was freedom."[61] Moreover, in 1710, Virginia's General Assembly adopted a special act freeing a slave named Will for similarly exemplary conduct in support of the slaveholding government. The legislators found that Will was "signally serviceable" in discovering a conspiracy of "negroes ... for levying war in this colony[.]" The manumission was "a reward of his fidelity and for encouragement of such services[.]" The act does not state if Will's owner was compensated for his property loss.[62]

Carl Degler compared the white colonists' use of slaves in the military in Portuguese Brazil and in Britain's North American colonies. He found that Brazilian slaves were more often employed in the militia and then freed.[63] Degler did not attribute this difference to any perceived religious or moral imperative to protect or advance "the humanity of the Negro." He argued, instead, that these differences arose from factors including the larger slave population percentages in Brazil's early years than in the North American colonies and the Brazilians' greater perceived security threats. "Use of Negroes as soldiers in the colonial period in Brazil, in short, was not the result of the prior acceptance of the colored man as an equal, but of the need of him as a fighter."[64]

Social and military circumstances similar to those in Brazil also explain South Carolina's and Georgia's early eighteenth century laws permitting slaves in the militia and freeing some of the slaves who served in the colonies' defense. South Carolina had to defend against attacks from the Spanish and also from Native Americans. The colony also had a larger percentage of slave population than the other North American British colonies. "Despite constant complaints from whites about the independence of black slaves, for the first half-century of South Carolina's history black soldiers proved to be indispensable in repelling attacks from the west by Indians and from the south by the Spanish."[65]

In the early eighteenth century, Carolina's legislature adopted a series of acts in apparent response to these conditions. A 1704 act compelled masters to furnish slaves for the militia. The owners were to be paid out of the public funds for these services of their slaves.[66]

Moreover, in 1703 and 1708, the legislature adopted statutes stating the perceived need to enlist "our trusty slaves" in the militia in response to an invasion. The acts freed slaves who "in actual invasion" killed or captured an enemy combatant. Slaves who were disabled while fighting also were to be freed, and were to be supported "at the charge of the public[.]" Proof "by any white person" was required.[67] Higginbotham called this a "curious feature" of the statute; "while freedom was theoretically obtainable, it was possible that deserving slaves would not be able to provide satisfactory proof."[68] The legislature reversed its position after the Stono rebellion of 1739, however, thus putting "[a] permanent damper ... on Negro enlistment in the militia."[69]

The Georgia legislators adopted a similar provision in the colony's 1755 militia act. Like the South Carolinians, early Georgia settlers perceived the need to enlist at least some slaves in the colony's defense against the threats posed by France and Spain.[70] The statute therefore stated that slaves and white servants who "shall actually engage the Enemy, in times of Invasion of the Province, and Shall Couragiously [sic] behave themselves in Battle so as to kill any one of the Enemy, or take a prisoner alive or Shall take any of their Colours," were to be freed, if white officers witnessed those actions. The masters of the slaves freed under this provision were to be compensated out of the public treasury.[71]

"By the late seventeenth century the colonial legislatures had become increasingly alarmed at the sight of armed slaves, and throughout most of the eighteenth century there were laws prohibiting their employment as soldiers."[72] This policy precluding slave soldiers prevailed even when the colonies began to fight for their independence.

The American Revolution obviously was a crisis in which slaves could have been recruited for military service in return for political or state-mandated manumission. General George Washington initially was among those who opposed the use of enslaved or free black soldiers in the Continental Army, and the colonies at first prohibited black soldiers in their militias. Nevertheless, Massachusetts, New Hampshire, Rhode Island, North Carolina, Virginia, Delaware, and Maryland later recruited free blacks or at least permitted them to serve as substitutes in their forces. Maryland and North Carolina also permitted slaves to serve if their masters agreed. Thus, a Maryland act of October 1780 permitted "able bodied" slaves between the ages of sixteen and forty to volunteer for military service with their masters' consent. This act did not, however, provide for the manumission of these slaves.[73]

Only two of the new states adopted statutes that clearly required that slaves who served in the military during the war be freed after their service. A Rhode Island act of February 1778 permitted "every able-bodied negro, mulatto, or Indian man slave, in this state," to enlist in the military. The act provided each enlisting slave's owner with compensation, and stated that every enlisting slave "shall, upon passing muster ..., be immediately discharged from the service of his master or mistress, and be absolutely free[.]" New York followed with a March 1781 law that authorized slave owners to deliver one or more "able-bodied male slaves" to serve in two regiments that the act created. The masters were entitled to grants of 500 acres of unoccupied land and they were discharged from any liability for the future support of the slaves they enlisted. The slaves were to be freed, not immediately upon their enlistment, but after serving for three years or until they were "regularly discharged[.]"[74]

Georgia and South Carolina continued to resist the use of slaves in their defense, however, even after the British invaded Georgia in November 1778. In May 1779, the Continental Congress adopted an act asking South Carolina and Georgia to enlist 3,000 black recruits. Congress offered to pay to slave owners $1,000 for each able bodied "man of standard size, not exceeding thirty-five years of age[,]" and offered to pay for these soldiers' food and clothing. The slave soldiers would not be paid any wages for their service, but if they served "well and faithfully" until the war ended they were to be freed and paid $50. Both Georgia and South Carolina rejected this proposal even though Alexander Hamilton and General Washington supported it, and despite the efforts of South Carolinians Henry Laurens, a member of Congress, and his son John, a Continental Army officer and a South Carolina legislator.[75]

The majority of Georgia's and South Carolina's leaders thus continued to resist the enlistment of their slaves in the defense of their slave societies. This resistance did not cost the rebels this war. But the repetition of this obstinacy on a grander scale may have contributed to the Confederate States' defeat in the Civil War.

There is evidence that some enslaved men were freed after the war in recognition of their military service, including a 1782 Rhode Island act freeing a slave named Quaco, a 1784 North Carolina act freeing Ned Griffin, and three acts of Virginia's general assembly, adopted between 1786 and 1792, freeing five slaves.[76] And at least one slave soldier won his liberty in a post-war freedom suit. The Superior Court of Connecticut, in 1784, discharged the claimant Jack. With the consent of his master, Ivers, Jack enlisted in the Continental Army, apparently pursuant to New York's 1781 law. Ivers later claimed Jack "as his servant." Jack fled "eastward" from Ivers, who lived in New York, apparently to Connecticut. Ivers pursued and recovered Jack. On his way back home, Ivers stayed in New Haven, "and for safe-keeping..., he got the gaoler [sic] to commit Jack to prison[.]" The court then issued a writ of *habeas corpus* in response to Jack's application "complaining of being unlawfully and unjustly holden in prison[.]" Ivers was summoned, "and upon a summary hearing, Jack was discharged from his imprisonment, upon the ground that he was a freeman, absolutely manumitted from his master by enlisting and serving in the army...."[77]

Both the Northern and Southern states also were slow to offer the promise of freedom to recruit slaves as soldiers in the Civil War. The North acted first, with the adoption of the July 17, 1862 Militia Act. Among other things, this Act authorized the president to accept in the military service "persons of African descent." It freed "any man or boy of African descent" who served as a Union soldier and whose owner, "during the present rebellion, has levied war or has borne arms against the United States, or adhered to their enemies by giving them aid and comfort[.]" The Act also freed these "African" soldiers' "mother, wife and children" if their owners also fought for or supported the rebel cause.[78]

Nevertheless, it was not until February 24, 1864 that the Northern side amended the Enrollment Act to free enslaved men living in Union territory who fought for the United States. This act required that "all able-bodied male colored persons, between the ages of twenty and forty-five" be enrolled in the draft. When a "loyal" master's slave was "drafted and mustered into the service of the United States," the master was to receive "a certificate thereof" and the slave was freed. The government was to pay to the freed slave's owner the $100 bounty that otherwise would be payable to the draftee. The act also required the Secretary of War to appoint commissioners in all of the Union's slave states "to award to each loyal person to whom a colored volunteer may owe service a just compensation not exceeding three hundred dollars, for each such colored volunteer[.]" The Act declared to be free all slave volunteers, "on being mustered into service[.]" It applied retroactively to all slaves who were enlisted in or who volunteered for military service for the United States.[79]

The Confederate Congress, after much military, political, and public debate, refused to offer freedom to slaves to encourage them to serve as soldiers who would fight to preserve the society that enslaved them and their families. The Congress initially rejected even General Robert E. Lee's recommendations, made in a January 1865 letter, suggesting that slaves who enlisted in the Confederate forces be offered "immediate freedom," and that freedom after the war be extended "to the families of those who discharge their duties faithfully (whether they survive or not), together with the privilege of residing in the South. To this might be added a bounty for faithful service."[80]

It was not until March 13, 1865, however, when the war was all but lost, that the Confederate Congress adopted a statute titled: "An act to increase the military force of the Confederate States."[81] This act permitted the president to "ask for and accept from the owners of slaves, the services of such number of able-bodied Negro men as he may deem expedient for and during the war to perform military service in whatever capacity he may direct." The act also stated that slave soldiers, while serving, were to "receive the same rations, clothing and compensation as are allocated to other troops in the same branch of service."

If the president determined that this voluntary recruitment method was not sufficient, the act authorized him to call on each state to provide its quota of 300,000 soldiers in addition to those already enlisted or eligible to serve. These soldiers were "to be raised from such classes of the population, irrespective of color, in each State, as the proper authorities thereof may determine[.]" The act also provided, however, that not more than twenty-five per cent "of the male slaves between the ages of eighteen and forty- five, in any State, shall be called for under the provisions of this Act."

Accordingly, contrary to Lee's recommendations, the statute required the slave's master and his home state's laws to consent before any slave soldier would be freed. This intention of the legislators was confirmed by section five of the act stating: "That nothing in this Act shall be construed to authorize a change in the relation which the said slaves shall bear toward their owners, except by consent of the owners and of the States in which they may reside, and in pursuance of the laws thereof."[82]

Adjutant and Inspector General Samuel Cooper repeated and rephrased these provisions in his March 23, 1865 General Order Number 14. According to that order: "No slave will be accepted as a recruit unless with his owner's consent and with the approbation of his master by a written instrument conferring, as far as he may, the rights of a freedman[.]"[83] This order thus appears to accept as binding any state laws that might or might not permit masters to free slaves. The order also called for the kind and humane treatment of the former slave troops, to protect them from "injustice and oppression."[84]

Even when they were facing apparent defeat, the Southern lawmakers therefore accommodated the pre-Civil War laws of the Confederate States, as noted in chapter three, which prohibited either all manumissions or all domestic manumissions. The Southern leaders' antebellum aversion to manumission may have contributed to their own rebellion's defeat and to their government's downfall. This policy delayed what some military and political leaders came to believe was the South's last hope for a military victory—the mobilization of the slave population to defend the slaveholding regime.

The Law of Peculium, Coartación, Self-Purchase, and Manumission

Because political manumission was so rare, the master's right and power usually were at issue in the manumission cases in the United States South. According to Patterson, manumission was based upon the master's "freely given decision ... to part with something—his power—for nothing." Sometimes the slave gave or paid something as a "redemption fee," but the slave did not really pay for the master's loss of power because "whatever the slave has already belongs to the master." Even if the parties structured a manumission as an exchange by which the master released his or her power for some benefit given by the slave, Patterson stated that the slave was not "really paying for his [or her] freedom." The slave's part of the exchange "is usually conceived of as making a gift offering in gratitude for the master's freely given decision to release" the slave from bondage.[85]

In the United States South, people who were legally held as slaves generally did not have a legal right to buy, earn, or contract for their manumission. Masters could grant or deny freedom to one or more of their slaves as they elected. The slave's potential "right" to freedom in the manumission cases was based solely on the master's will and intent, except when, as noted in chapter three, the statute and case law regulated or prohibited that right in the public interest. Among the legal rights generally denied to slaves in the United States South, other than those in Louisiana and Delaware, was the right to contract for their freedom and the related right of self-purchase.

Most slave societies permitted slaves to acquire some legal rights in property called the slaves' *peculium*. This was property distinct from the master's other property, with which the slaves could buy their freedom.[86] According to Orlando Patterson, "[r]ecognition of the slave's peculium was very nearly universal. Societies varied only in the degree to which the peculium was legally or socially sanctioned."[87] "In theory, ... slaves should not have been able to redeem themselves with earnings from their peculium," because the slave paid the master for his property, the slave, with another part of the master's own property, the slave's peculium. "In practice, most slaveholding societies found ways of getting around this nice legal problem."[88]

Alan Watson explained the advantages of the peculium as a matter of "fact," and not "law":

It would be common practice, I believe, for an owner to make a bargain with his slave to free him once the slave could pay him his value from his peculium. The bargain struck would be unenforceable, but it would be in the owner's interest to keep it: the slave (and his fellows) would work harder for the reward of freedom and would be more docile. The owner could use the price paid by the slave for his freedom to replace the slave with another of the same value.[89]

Patterson reached a similar conclusion, stating that "[t]he universality of the peculium is not difficult to explain."

It solved the most important problem of slave labor: the fact that it was given involuntarily. It was the best means of motivating the slave to perform efficiently on his master's behalf. It not only allowed the slave the vicarious enjoyment of the capacity he most lacked—that of ownership of property—but also held out the long-term hope of self-redemption for the most diligent slaves. The master lost nothing, since he maintained an ultimate claim on the peculium, and he had everything to gain.[90]

Patterson also found that: "Neither race, ethnicity, nor size of the servile population relate in any significant way to attitude toward the peculium."[91]

In the Spanish American colonies, the law permitted slaves the right to buy their way out of slavery under the more expansive doctrine of *coartación*.[92] "By what is called *coartación* a slave who by himself or through another presented his just price to his master became free."[93] Slaves could have their values appraised and fixed so that they might purchase their freedom, even over the master's objection. "An owner who refused to negotiate could be carried before a tribunal which would fix the price and order forced execution, though this was usually not necessary."[94] Cuban law evolved to permit slaves to buy their freedom under what Hans Baade called "an installment plan," which provided slaves "with the double advantage of their purchase price being established at an early stage, and more 'free time' was available to obtain funds through outside employment to pay the balance owed on their freedom."[95] *Coartación* gave "slaves working for their freedom an interest in the system, making them unlikely to participate in insurrectionary plots and motivating them to be industrious laborers."[96]

Slavery law in Brazil permitted slaves also to purchase their liberty in installments by a procedure called *coartação*, which was similar to *coartación*. It was most evident in *Minas Gerais*, where slaves participated in mining and an urban cash economy.[97]

After almost nine years of debate and only three years before slavery was abolished in France's Atlantic colonies, French slave law in 1845 authorized a process that was similar to *coartación*. This law permitted slaves to negotiate with their owners for the purchase in installments of their own freedom, or that of their parents, grandparents, spouses, and children, in a process that was called *rachat amiable*. If the parties could not agree on a price, the law authorized a commission to fix the price in what was called *rachat forcé*. The owner was allowed six months to oppose a proposed price, and the slave to be freed also was required to work for a free person as a form of indentured servant.[98]

In contrast, slavery law in the United States was more disadvantageous to people held as slaves. Other than in Louisiana, the law did not recognize the slaves' "right" to earn and accumulate any interest in property such as *peculium* that they potentially could use to fund a self-purchase. Slaves in the United States also did not have any legal right to enforce self-purchase through a procedure similar to *coartación*.[99] Moreover, the Southern state legislatures adopted laws that "impeded self-purchase by prohibiting slaves from 'go[ing] at large and trad[ing] as freemen.'"[100]

The 1846 Alabama case *Shanklin v. Johnson*[101] illustrates these principles. The plaintiff, Johnson, owned a slave named Moses. The defendant, Shanklin, was a free black man. A prior owner of Moses, Mrs. Owen, permitted Moses to work in Mobile in return for agreed wages that Moses paid to Mrs. Owen, who also apparently permitted Moses to save any excess money that he earned. From these funds, Moses gave $200 to Shanklin to buy a parcel of real estate for Moses. Shanklin bought the lot in his own name, and later sold it for $700. He then counted out the money for Moses. Shanklin proposed to use some of the money to buy his daughter and promised to return the funds to Moses.[102]

Johnson sued Shanklin for money paid, laid out, and expended, and for money had and received. The jury found for Johnson. On appeal, the Alabama Supreme Court affirmed the judgment for $818.21.[103] Chief Justice Henry W. Collier wrote the Supreme Court's opinion. He did not explicitly refer to the Roman law doctrine of *peculium*. But, as Robinson and Hardy noted, the court's reasoning, at least by implication, rejected this doctrine when it held that Johnson was entitled to the funds.[104]

Collier began his opinion with a citation to Roman law and the law "in this country ... that slaves can do nothing in their own right, can hold no property, can neither buy, sell, barter or dispose of any thing, without express permission from their master[.]" Therefore, any property purchased by or on behalf of a slave belonged to the master.[105] It followed, then, that at Johnson's option he could legally claim the funds at issue. The court reasoned that if Johnson could not obtain a judgment, then Shanklin may retain the money "against all the rest of the world. This would be exceedingly unjust to the slave, as we must suppose, that whatever is recovered [by Johnson] will be appropriated to his [Moses'] benefit, although the law might not coerce the performance of such a duty."[106]

Robinson and Hardy stated that "the Court's presumption was probably wrong," and Moses' transaction with Shanklin was "more likely to redound to the slave's benefit." Shanklin already had exhibited his good faith by accounting for the profits of the sale and asking Moses' permission for the loan to buy Shanklin's daughter. "It is more likely that Johnson simply sought to recover the money for his own use and benefit."[107]

Although both Roman and Alabama law provided that slaves could not own property, under Roman law, slaves had "administrative control" over their *peculium*.[108]

If slaves were allowed to hold *peculium*, then perpetual slavery was highly unlikely since *peculium* afforded slaves the means to purchase their freedom as well as the tacit recognition of their basic "humanity." But in Alabama, persons of color were generally assumed to be unassimilable into the prevailing social structures in any capacity other than slave. Free persons of color were regarded as a potential threat to civil peace, and the Legislature sharply restricted emancipation during the ante-bellum period. Since freedom for, and property ownership by, black people was considered an undesirable public policy, it is hardly surprising that judge-made law was unprepared to recognize the legitimacy of peculium, which did imply, after all, that the slave was both human and partly free.[109]

Thus, the issue the court resolved was "which free person got Moses' property since Moses couldn't[.]"[110]

Under Judge Wardlaw's formula, the case can be understood as a contest between the slave's rulers. Johnson won the right to the profits earned by Shanklin's efforts buying and selling the real property at issue for Moses. In Hofeldian terms, the proceeds of the real estate sale were part of the bundle of sticks that Moses embodied. That stick did not belong to Moses. As between Johnson and Shanklin, the court awarded that stick to Johnson.

Indeed, "the opinion stopped short of even recognizing [that Moses had a] 'moral' claim to the 'gift' from his former owner. Sanctions for an owner's failure to recognize this moral claim by the slave would have to come in the form of obloquy and shame rather than from the courts."[111]

Louisiana's law confirms that another alternative was available to the lawmakers in the United States South. The 1825 Louisiana Code recognized the slave's *peculium* in Article 175, which stated: "All that a slave possesses, belongs to his master; he possesses nothing of his own, except his *peculium*, that is to say, the sum of money, or moveable estate, which his master chooses he should possess."[112] According to Vernon Valentine Palmer, the Code's drafters stated that they based the *peculium* "on previously existing local custom: 'We here are in the habit of permitting our slaves to enjoy what they acquire by their industry.'"[113]

Even this more "liberal" Code left to the master's own discretion the creation, continued existence, and enforceability of these slave property "rights;" these permissive "rights" did not have the force of law. Nor did the Code adopt *coartación* or a similar right of self-purchase.[114]

Manumission Contracts between Master and Slave: The Majority Rule

The courts in the majority of the Southern states applied the principle of manumission-as-a-gratuity to the cases in which slaves sought to enforce their master's promise to free them. These courts generally refused to enforce manumission agreements made by masters and slaves in suits filed by slaves, even after the slaves performed their agreed part of the bargain.[115] The judges reasoned that people held as slaves did not have any legal rights, and, therefore slaves could not enter into or enforce legally binding agreements.[116] This rule also applied to marriage contracts, thus barring the legal recognition and enforcement of slave marriages.[117]

The majority of the Southern courts held that "[t]he promises of a master to a slave, are binding only in conscience and honor; at law, notwithstanding any such promise, that the slave shall have acquisitions, all the acquisitions of the slave in possession, are the property of the master."[118] A promise or executory contract for freedom between an owner and a slave "is not obligatory, and cannot be enforced in law or in equity. A slave is not competent to make a valid contract. He has no ability to enter into an agreement, nor will any promise made to him by his owner, authorize him to maintain suit against him for his freedom."[119] A slave only could be "the recipient of his master's bounty, and receive from him manumission."[120]

The 1821 Virginia case *Lewis v. Fullerton*[121] illustrates how the courts applied this general rule, even if the master and slave exchanged mutual promises or if the slave acted in reliance on the master's promises. Lewis, who was an infant, sought his freedom in a suit that was filed by his mother, Milly. The defendants were William Fullerton and Jane Rodgers. A jury trial ended in a verdict for the defendants. Lewis then filed an appeal with the Supreme Court of Appeals of Virginia, which affirmed the judgment, in an opinion by Judge Spencer Roane.

The statement of facts in the officially reported case lacks detail, but this is an important case on several of the points of law that Lewis's lawyer raised. Some time during or before March 1808, John Rodgers brought Milly and her husband Naise to Ohio, apparently from John's home in Virginia. Milly and Naise then obtained a writ of *habeas corpus*, seeking an order releasing them from John's custody, who claimed them as his slaves. A Gallia County Ohio judge held "a hearing of the parties and witnesses at a subsequent day[.]" The judge rendered a judgment that Milly and Naise "go hence, be discharged, and set at liberty."

The next day, John went to Edward Tupper and asked "him to prevail on Milly to live with him as an indentured servant for two years[.]" John promised that if Milly agreed to do this "he would execute to her a complete deed of manumission, which should put the question of her liberty at rest[.]" John also promised not to file an appeal from the Ohio court's order. Milly and Naise agreed to these terms, provided that John would sign a manumission deed.

On April 2, 1808, John signed a manumission deed, and this execution was attested to by two witnesses. John also acknowledged the deed's execution before an associate judge in Gallia County, and this was certified by the county recorder, the county clerk, and the President of the Court of Common Pleas.[122]

Milly and Naise returned to Virginia with John, and Lewis was born after they returned to Virginia. Milly also apparently performed her end of the bargain, but John later apparently reneged on his promise, and would not free Lewis. It appears from the report of the case that Milley was not freed, nor is it clear who the defendants were, other than John's successors in interest to Lewis.

Lewis's lawyer asserted three claims to Milly's freedom, which the defendants conceded would also free Lewis "as a necessary consequence."[123] First, he claimed that Milly was freed by "having sojourned" in Ohio, where slavery was prohibited and where at least for one day she worked for her master. Second, he claimed that the Ohio court judgment freed Milly. Third, he relied on John's own manumission deed, which confirmed his intention to free Milly, and the exchange of promises, which included John's promise to free Milly if she served him for two years.[124]

Judge Roane's opinion acknowledged John's undisputed promise to free Milly in two years if she returned with him to Virginia and if she served him for two years. It also appeared that Milly performed her end of the bargain, and John and his successors did not perform as agreed, at least as to their refusal to free Milly's son, Lewis. Nevertheless, Judge Roane gave the deed and oral contract no effect. He applied Virginia law, not the law of Ohio, where the deed and contract were made.[125]

Therefore, in April 1808, John had no right to detain Milly as a slave in Ohio or to force her to return to Virginia without committing common law torts of assault, battery, or false imprisonment. His promise induced a legal detriment to Milly, who gave up the right to remain free in Ohio when she agreed to return to Virginia in reliance on the promise that in two years John would free her. Judge Roane nevertheless did not enforce John's promise. Lewis remained a slave because the manumission deed and the exchange of promises between the master and "slave" were unenforceable under Virginia law. Kentucky's highest court came to the same conclusion in a very similar case.[126]

The courts in the majority of the Southern states would not even enforce written manumission contracts between masters and slaves. Thus, in *Redmond v. Murray*,[127] an 1860 Missouri case, Redmond sued to enforce the written promise of his master Edward B. Osborn. On January 10, 1855, Osborn signed a document stating: "Received of Elijah Dehart and Redmond the sum of five hundred and one dollars, it being part of a sum of five hundred and fifty dollars, bearing ten per cent interest from the date of this bill of sale held by Osborn, which being paid he is to have his freedom." In August 1855, Redmond alleged that he tendered the balance due to Osborn, plus interest, but Osborn "disregarded his agreement," and sold Redmond to Wigginton, who sold Redmond to Murray.[128]

The Missouri Supreme Court affirmed the dismissal of Redmond's suit on the defendants' demurrer. Justice Ephraim B. Ewing's opinion explained that this result flowed from the nature of the master and slave relationship and manumission, which was "a mere gratuity, under our laws[.]"[129] Even an equity court cannot enforce a master's promise "that he will emancipate his slave after a certain condition is performed, which condition has been complied with by the slave," because equity jurisdiction "only extends to cases where the pauper has a *legal* right to freedom, but there is some impediment to the assertion of that right in a court of law."[130] Redmond's gross hardship was not an equitable interest "of which the law can take cognizance ..., however strongly it might appeal ... to conscience or the moral sense."[131]

The courts applied this rule even if the master's written promise was made not to his slave, but to another white person. In *Jackson v. Bob*,[132] an 1857

Arkansas case, the plaintiff Bob won a jury verdict after a trial on his petition for freedom. Bob based his claim primarily on the written agreement between George A. Brown and Robert Hamilton. That agreement was dated February 15, 1835, and apparently was made when Brown sold Bob to Hamilton. It stated that Hamilton would have Bob "appraised six years after [this] date by disinterested persons, and when said negro shall have worked out the sum he may be appraised to," he shall be set free. Hamilton promised to pay $600 if he breached this contract, which was binding on Hamilton and his "heirs, executors or administrators."[133]

Hamilton refused to comply with the agreement before his death. The Arkansas Supreme Court would not enforce the contract against Hamilton's estate, and thus reversed Bob's judgment. The opinion of Chief Justice Elbert Hartwell English held that the same result follows if a master entered into a contract to free a slave with that slave or with a third party. If a master promised his slave "that the slave shall be emancipated upon his paying to his master a sum of money, or rendering him some stipulated amount of labor," even if the slave fully performed his end of the bargain, the slave "cannot compel his master to execute the contract, because both the money and the labor of the slave belong to the master and could constitute no legal consideration for the contract."[134]

The courts did, however, enforce manumission provisions in contracts between slave owners and other persons, such as a slave buyer, when the free litigant was one of the parties to the contract.[135] For example, in an 1809 case, *Thompson v. Wilmot*,[136] the Kentucky Court of Appeals enforced a manumission provision in a contract between a buyer and seller of the slave, Will. The plaintiff, Ruth Wilmot, was one of the parties to the contract. Wilmot alleged that, in October 1790 in the State of Maryland, she agreed to exchange Will for a slave named Harry, who was owned by the defendant, Thomas A. Thompson. Thompson was about to move to Kentucky, and "one of the moving considerations" in the exchange was Thompson's promise "that he would manumit ... Will in seven years[.]" Wilmot also alleged that this agreement was confirmed in writing, and that Will "was persuaded by Thompson, to leave her and go with him to Kentucky, by the prospect of freedom thus held out to him; that in said instrument it was inserted that if the said Will did not choose to live with said defendant in Kentucky, he should be at liberty to return to Maryland after one year of the term had expired[.]"[137]

According to Wilmot, Thompson refused to free Will after the seven years passed. Will "had instituted a suit at law ... to recover his freedom, but had failed because the said instrument was held not to amount to an actual and formal emancipation, and the *slave* therefore not entitled to sue." She therefore filed her own suit for specific execution of the agreement, "and for an account and payment for the value of the service of the slave beyond the said term of seven years, during the illegal detention of the said slave[.]"[138]

Thompson admitted that he signed the agreement, but he raised several defenses. He alleged that "the agreement was made with the *slave* only, but under the inspection of the complainant." He also asserted "that Will was refractory and discontented for the first four or five years," that the agreement permitted him to at any time return Will for Harry, although this term was omitted from the written agreement, and that Wilmot would not agree to the re-exchange because "she has been informed that by an act of Maryland, slaves which have been kept out of the State more than a year were prohibited from being carried back; that therefore he must keep Will, as she can't think of giving up Harry, and running the risk of losing Will by that act." He also alleged "that he is yet willing to return Will to the complainant and receive Harry."[139]

The Circuit Court ruled in Wilmot's favor. It freed Will and empanelled a jury "to assess the damages by the said detention of Will, beyond the said period of seven years in the bill complained of; which being assessed at 691 dollars 25 cents, were decreed to be paid by the defendant to the complainant in trust for said negro Will[.]"[140]

The Court of Appeals affirmed this judgment in an opinion by Chief Justice George M. Bibb. He found that Wilmot proved her allegations, and that "Thompson does not afford a colorable pretext for withholding a performance of his engagement, solemnly made, under circumstances interesting to humanity and most obligatory upon a man of good conscience and unpolluted faith. The contract in itself was not forbidden by any political institution, but is in unison with the dictates of natural right, and was a most becoming subject for the Court of Chancery to act upon specifically."[141]

Bernie D. Jones cited this decision to support her contention that the Kentucky legislators and judges were less hostile to manumission than those in the other Southern states.[142] She stated: "Thomson's behavior shocked the conscience of the court, indicating the extent to which early in the court's history interests of humanity were to be negotiated within the law of slavery[.]" She thus includes this case as evidence that "early on in the state's history the solicitude at the foundation of Kentucky's liberal manumission jurisprudence had been laid[.]"[143]

The Kentucky judges and legislators may on other issues have been more liberal than their counterparts elsewhere in most of the South. But the *Thompson v. Wilmot* decision is consistent with the notion that the real issue was what Wilmot and Thompson intended. Will's humanity was indeed irrelevant, as confirmed by his own unsuccessful freedom suit. He was freed only because Wilmot was willing to honor her promise and be his white champion who funded and filed a suit in Kentucky for Will's benefit when Thompson did not honor his promise to Wilmot and to Will.

The other Kentucky cases confirm that a person held in slavery could not sue his or her master, or the master's executors, if the master, or his or her executors, heirs, or assigns simply decided not to honor the master's written promise to free the slave. The "dishonorable" behavior that Thompson evidenced did not shock the conscience of the judges in Kentucky or the other Southern courts, if the plaintiff was a slave.[144]

Thus, as Cobb concluded, the slave was not at law a party to the contract and could not "apply for its execution in his favor."[145] These cases are consistent with the underlying principles providing that slaves were property and that enslaved people had no legal rights that the courts would enforce.

Tennessee is the one common law Southern state with decisions on this issue that are not clear. One source of this lack of clarity is Justice Nathan Green's assertion in the 1846 case of *Ford v. Ford*:[146] "A slave is not in the condition of a horse or an ox. ... [W]hile he is a slave, he can make a contract for freedom, which our laws recognize[.]"[147] The issues that the court decided in that case, however, did not include whether a court would enforce a manumission contract over the master's objection.[148]

Notwithstanding the dictum in *Ford*, I have not found a case in which the Tennessee courts held that a manumission contract was enforceable in law over the master's objection. The decision that came the closest was the Tennessee Supreme Court's 1859 decision in *Isaac (a man of color) v. Farnsworth*,[149] a freedom suit that a slave referred to only as Isaac filed by his next friend.

The facts are indeed unique. In 1829, Isaac's owner Frederick Dewitt died. In his will, he left his two slaves to his wife for her life with the remainder to his children. But the will also stated: "no Court nor power of law, either of county or State, shall have anything to do with my estate, but that at *any* time my wife shall have full power to rent out or sell my tract of land, *hire or sell* my two negro boys, or remove any part or all that is movable, to any other county or State as may seem good unto her."

"[A]fter some years," Mrs. Dewitt "broke up house-keeping[.]" She then lived with her son-in-law, William Gilbert. She later sold one of the slaves, and "she proposed to Isaac that if he would procure any one to advance $300, in gold or silver, to her, she would give him his freedom, and gave him, or caused the same to be done by her said son-in-law, Mr. Gilbert, who acted as her agent, a written authority to make the best arrangement he could for the money."

In August 1846, Gilbert "succeeded in making a contract with Michael George[.]" George agreed to pay in advance "for eight years' [of Isaac's] services." Mrs. Dewitt "executed an absolute bill of sale to George, with an understanding or verbal agreement on his part, that he would, at the end of the term, emancipate Isaac." Isaac then served "George, under this contract, ... faithfully, with the settled and avowed purpose on the part of George, all the time, to give [Isaac] his freedom at the end of the term."

Things went according to plan for Isaac until "[a]bout fifteen months before the termination of the eight years[.]"

> [U]nder some influence or other, the old lady, then being near eighty, at the instance of one Henry A. Farnsworth, one of the defendants, sold Isaac to McCampbell, another defendant, and made him an absolute bill of sale, to take effect in possession at the termination of the eight years. Upon application to George to acknowledge this title, he refused, and insisted upon his title by said bill of sale, coupled with the trust for the benefit of the slave. A bill was then filed in the name of the old lady, to reform the bill of sale of George, so as to make it a contract for eight years' service only, which suit was compromised by the surrender, by George, both of his title

and the slave, upon the payment to him, by McCampbell, of $100 for the balance of the term—he not choosing to enter into litigation about the matter, as to which he had no pecuniary interest.

Isaac then persuaded a next friend to file a suit for freedom on Isaac's behalf, and the Chancery Court found in Isaac's favor.

The Tennessee Supreme Court affirmed the judgment in an opinion by Justice Robert L. Caruthers. He found that the defendants' conduct was worthy of condemnation:

> There is a great amount of swearing and false swearing, crediting and discrediting of parties and witnesses in the case; but we conclude, upon a full consideration of the evidence, that the facts are substantially as above stated. Perhaps in no case was the proof ever more irreconcilably conflicting. But it would be as useless as disagreeable to comment upon the picture of depravity and the perversion of truth among near relations and speculators which the record in this case exhibits. It is revolting to see to what an extent some men will go against the rights of the weak, in eager pursuit of gain.

He added: "We prefer not to develop the deformity of this case by an analysis of the proof, but simply to state our conclusions as to the facts, which we regard as established by the weight of the evidence in the record, and upon which our judgment as to the law must be based."[150]

Justice Caruthers first held that the defendants could not dispute Mrs. Dewitt's power to sell Isaac, in view of the terms of Mr. Dewitt's will and their own conduct in the transactions. He stated that, instead of freeing Isaac herself, Mrs. Dewitt consented to Isaac's manumission

> for a satisfactory consideration, and passed the title out of herself to another with this parol trust attached. It is true that no consideration passed from the slave, as she was entitled to his time and labor, not only for the eight ensuing years, but as long as he might live; and perhaps such a promise or contract could not have been enforced by the slave against her. But then she executed the purpose so far as could be done by her, it being prospective, by parting with the title, and, in effect, conferring the right of freedom, incumbered [sic] with the eight years' service. She had no other act to perform in the case, and could not revoke what she had done. Neither could George, by any compromise to which the complainant was not a party, surrender the trust he had taken upon himself to the prejudice of Isaac's rights. He was allowed by his mistress to become a party to this contract and arrangement for his benefit, and is entitled to the advantages of it, subject alone to the legal condition, that the judicial authorities acting for the State shall sanction it.

Justice Caruthers also found that "Isaac has established an excellent character for a slave, and proved that he is worthy of freedom[.]" He also noted that "the provision of our recent statutes, that emancipation can only be allowed upon condition that the subject shall be sent out of the State to Liberia, in Africa, abrogates this provision of the law as it formerly existed in these cases, as it does away the reason for it."[151]

This case is best understood as a limited holding on its unique facts.[152] Justice Caruthers presumed, consistently with the majority rule, that Isaac could not have enforced his freedom contract with Mrs. Dewitt had she not divested herself of all ownership interests in Isaac. Indeed, this opinion is more telling for what it does not say than for what it says. Caruthers did not rely on or even cite a line of cases in which the Tennessee courts "consistently held" that manumission contracts between masters and slaves were "valid and enforceable."[153] This suggests that this line of authority did not exist; certainly if it did the decision would have been much shorter.

The reported Tennessee cases do, however, include evidence confirming that other masters, unlike Mrs. Dewitt, voluntarily entered into and later performed the manumission contracts that they made with their slaves.[154] But in an 1860 opinion, Justice John McKinney stated in *dictum* a view that is consistent with the majority rule: "A pecuniary consideration moving from the slave to the owner is not essential [for manumission]. The right is not imparted by force of formal contract in the legal sense, for the slave, as such, is incapable of making a contract for his freedom or of paying a valuable consideration, as he can have nothing to give."[155]

An 1833 Tennessee statute also referred to manumission contracts, but it did not grant to slaves "the right to contract for their freedom," as Robert Shaw stated.[156] An 1831 act mandated that all manumissions, which by acts of 1777 and 1801 had to be approved by the county courts, be conditioned on the immediate removal of the freed slaves from the state.[157] The 1833 act exempted from this removal requirement slaves "who had *bona fide* contracted" for their freedom before the 1831 act was adopted and those who were freed by the wills of masters who died before the 1831 act was adopted.[158] This act thus did not require the courts to enforce pre-1831 freedom contracts over a master's objection, and an 1849 act repealed this exemption.[159]

A 1783 Virginia statute provided a limited exception to the general rule barring the enforcement of freedom contracts or promises. During the Revolutionary War, Virginia law permitted free blacks to enlist in Virginia's military, but slaves could not serve in the military. Some masters nevertheless enlisted their slaves as substitutes for themselves or for other free people who were otherwise required to serve in the military. These owners in effect lied about their slaves' servile status to avoid military service when they represented to the "recruiting officers that the slaves so enlisting by their direction and concurrence were freemen[.]" After the War, some of these masters reclaimed their slaves, and attempted to return them to servitude.

The Virginia legislators declared that slaves who honorably served in the military as substitutes were entitled to be freed. The owners' efforts to again enslave these soldiers were found to be "contrary to the principles of justice, and their own solemn promise." The statute required the attorney general to file actions *in forma pauperis* to obtain the release of any slaves so detained in servitude, and to seek an award of damages from a jury.[160]

This Virginia statute was unique, but the problem it addressed apparently was not confined to Virginia, as illustrated by a 1784 North Carolina act freeing Ned Griffin, a former slave soldier. Griffin filed a petition dated April 4, 1784 with the legislature, seeking his liberty "by Contract and merit." He alleged that he was "a Man of Mixed Blood" who, during the Revolutionary War, was sold to William Kitchen—"a Soldier Deserted from his line"—to serve as Kitchen's substitute in the "Continental Service," on the promise that Griffin would be freed after his service. Griffin alleged that, after he completed his term of service, Kitchen re-enslaved him and sold him as a slave.

A legislative committee reviewed Griffin's petition, and on May 4, 1784, it recommended that the legislature free Griffin in view of his "meritorious services." The legislature then adopted an act freeing Griffin, noting that he had been promised his freedom if he served in the "continental line" for twelve months, and that he "did faithfully on his part perform" his end of the bargain.[161]

These statutes freeing slave soldiers prove the general rule making a master's manumission promises unenforceable, however, because the promises of freedom made to the Virginia slave soldiers and to Griffin were not enforceable absent legislative action. The legislators created a form of estoppel with these statutes. They in effect stated that slave owners could not benefit from frauds committed on the military authorities by representing that their substitutes were free blacks, and later claiming these same former soldiers as slaves.

As the next section illustrates, Louisiana and Delaware law permitted slaves to sue in court and enforce a master's written manumission contract, and Maryland presented a mixed result. These distinctions suggest important questions: Why did the lawmakers and judges in the other Southern states not enforce the masters' promises as legal obligations owed to their slaves? And because they did not, were these obligations truly perceived to be moral obligations that were among the masters' requirements in action, and not just in words?

Louisiana, Delaware, and Maryland Law on Manumission Contracts

Louisiana and Delaware statutes permitted slaves to enforce their written manumission contracts, providing an exception to the general rule that prevailed elsewhere in the South. The Louisiana law could at least in part have been caused by the influence of Spanish law. While it was under Spain's rule, some of Louisiana's slaves purchased their freedom under provisions similar to the doctrine of *coartación*.[162] The Louisiana Civil Code later abolished *coartación*, and provided, in Article 177, that a slave was incapable of making contracts, "except those which relate to his own emancipation."[163] Judith Schafer called this contract right "a watered-down version of the Spanish *coartación*, as it did not force the master to sell the slave if the slave got up the purchase price and slaves could accumulate property and money only with the consent of their owner."[164]

Schafer discusses the Louisiana Supreme Court and the District Court in

New Orleans cases in which people held as slaves sued to enforce their rights to freedom under the contracts that they alleged they made with their masters.[165] Her analysis of these suits confirms that not all masters were honorable people who abided by their promises made to their slaves. This was so even in Louisiana, where the law mandated that the master's alleged moral obligations be enforced. "Unscrupulous owners sometimes used ignorance or inattention to proper legal forms to continue to hold bondservants in slavery even though they had fulfilled the contract and remitted the agreed price."[166]

For example, the Louisiana Supreme Court in 1816 held that a slave could not establish by parol testimony her owner's promise to free her upon reimbursement for her purchase price. The court held that freedom contracts had to be in writing because the Civil Code defined slaves as real property.[167]

Indeed, not all of the people held as slaves who filed suits in Louisiana were successful. But at least the Louisiana plaintiffs who based their claims on written evidence, unlike slaves such as Redmond and Bob, had a chance to win their freedom in Louisiana's courts if they also could prove that they performed their promises, or that they were ready and willing to do so, and provided that they otherwise were qualified to be freed under the state's then prevailing statutes regulating who was entitled to benefit from manumission.[168]

"[A] number of slaves found ingenious ways to prove that they had purchased themselves, using the courts and the law to win their freedom."[169] For example, Schafer cited a successful suit in an unreported 1854 Louisiana Supreme Court decision, *Henriette, statu liber, v. Arroyo.*[170] Henriette and her two children were sold at auction to settle their late owner's estate. Before the sale, the auctioneer announced that Henriette and her children wanted to be freed and that their owner's heirs did not object. Therefore, the buyer "would have to agree to give [Henriette] her liberty when reimbursed for her value and that of her children." The defendant, Oscar Arroyo, purchased Henriette and her children, but he did not free them. Henriette then filed a suit. She proved that she paid Arroyo $700 toward the agreed $1,000 purchase price, and that Arroyo refused to accept the $300 balance. The lower court ruled against Henriette. She appealed her case to the Supreme Court, which "remanded the case for a new trial, stating that [Henriette] had a 'clear cause of action.'"[171]

The Louisiana Supreme Court also ruled in favor of freed slaves in two cases that illustrate how even an honorable master's intentions could be foiled if his or her creditors, executors, or heirs did not share the master's intention to honor his or her contract. In an 1855 decision, *Hardesty v. Wormley,*[172] the freed slave, Sukey Wormley, proved that she paid for her own freedom and that of her child pursuant to a contract that was confirmed in writing. M.C. Hardesty had purchased Wormley from her prior master, Wright, on the condition that Hardesty would free her when she paid Hardesty for the balance of her purchase price that he advanced. In an opinion by Chief Justice Thomas Slidell, the court affirmed the lower court ruling and the jury verdict rejecting the claim of Hardesty's heirs that this freedom contract was void because of concubinage. Slidell wrote that even if Hardesty "had degraded himself by debauching the slave under his dominion," this would not discharge the freedom contract.[173] "This suit is a cruel experiment upon the liberty and hard earnings of an [sic] humble and deserving woman, and has been righteously discountenanced by the verdict of a jury of the vicinage with whom her character for industry, honesty and thrift stood her in good stead."[174]

The Louisiana Supreme Court ruled against the claims of a master's creditors and in favor of a freed slave in an 1824 case, *Doubrere v. Grillier's Syndic*.[175] The court's opinion by Justice Alexander Porter reversed the lower court's ruling that was contrary to the plaintiff, who was claimed by the creditors of his last owner, Pierre Grillier, who allegedly was insolvent. The plaintiff was owned by Louis Doubrere before 1819. The plaintiff was able to earn or borrow $1,800 to buy his freedom. Grillier agreed to buy the plaintiff from Doubrere for $1,800, for the purpose of freeing the plaintiff. Grillier then freed the plaintiff and signed a receipt dated May 1819 acknowledging that he received a payment of $1,700 from the plaintiff. Grillier also signed as surety for the plaintiff in 1821, so that the plaintiff could obtain a license, thus again confirming that the plaintiff was free.[176] Grillier's creditors nevertheless claimed that the freedom contract was fraudulent or otherwise unenforceable. The Supreme Court disagreed and ordered that the plaintiff be freed upon the payment of $100.[177]

Some authors suggest that few Louisiana slaves could afford to enforce the rights created by contracts to buy their freedom, or to enforce self-purchase rights under the doctrine of *coartación*.[178] Even if these doctrines did not provide practical remedies for all of the people who were held as slaves, they were denied to all people held as slaves in the other Southern states.[179]

Nevertheless, people held as slaves in Louisiana lost this right to enforce contracts for freedom after March 6, 1857. On that date, the legislature adopted a statute stating: "That from and after the passage of this Act no slave shall be emancipated in this State."[180] The Louisiana Supreme Court, in *Julienne f.w.c. v. Touriac*,[181] afforded this statute retroactive effect to bar the enforcement of manumission contracts that predated March 6, 1857, if the slaves had not actually been freed before that date.[182]

Written deeds promising freedom were enforceable under Delaware law after 1797. In that year, the legislature adopted a statute stating that it was "necessary for the security of negro and mulatto slaves, whose masters or mistresses may intend to manumit them, and also for the safety of persons holding such property," that freedom contracts "be rendered certain, and not depend upon verbal [oral] contracts or manumissions, which are often misunderstood and forgotten[.]" The act thus declared all oral freedom contracts made by masters to be "null and void" and not binding on the master. All manumissions had to be by a written will or by a deed that was witnessed and attested by a competent white citizen and filed with the state. If these formalities were satisfied, a master's promises could be enforceable, and the freed slave could seek redress in the courts.[183] This statute "ensured that slaves who were promised freedom by their masters were protected from petulant heirs and aggressive creditors."[184] It also protected slaves from owners who may have been inclined to dishonor their promises of freedom made to their slaves.

In 1810, the Delaware legislators adopted a statute regulating masters' manumission promises that were to take place in the future. This practice was known as delayed manumission, and slaves benefiting from these delayed manumissions were called term slaves or *statu liberi*. According to the 1810 act, term slaves remained slaves in law until the end of their agreed term of servitude, and the children born of women who were term slaves also were to be slaves until they reached the age of 21 if they were female, and 25 if they were male, when they were to be freed. The statute stated that an owner could not sell a term slave out of the state without court permission, and that owners who violated this provision were subject to a $500 fine.[185]

Nevertheless, a term slave's legal rights were created only if the master decided to bestow the benefit of freedom on the slave. A slave for life had no right to become a term slave contrary to the master's wishes.

Maryland's courts followed the majority rule providing that manumission contracts between masters and slaves were unenforceable, with one exception for some term slaves. Historians including T. Stephen Whitman, Christopher Phillips, and Seth Rockman have written extensively about deeds for delayed manumissions in Maryland. They asserted that these manumission deeds created contract rights in people held as term slaves, because the slaves could win their freedom in court if they faithfully performed their required terms of service or the deed's other conditions.[186]

Beginning with the 1752 Maryland statute that prohibited manumission by will and oral manumission promises, manumission deeds that were to take effect immediately or in the future were binding and enforceable only if the deeds were prepared, signed, and witnessed in accordance with the statute's formal requirements. Manumission deeds that were to take effect in the future also had to be recorded within six months of execution.[187]

The Maryland legislature nevertheless provided some protections for term slaves. An 1810 act stated that "no person shall hereafter sell or dispose of any servant or slave, who is or may be entitled to freedom after a term of years, after any particular time, or upon a contingency, to any person who is not a bona fide resident of this state, and who has not resided therein for the space of at least one year next preceding such sale[.]" The statute also stated that no one may "sell such servant or slave for a term of years longer than he or she is bound to serve[.]" The act imposed a fine of "five hundred dollars for any such servant or slave so sold, to be recovered by action of debt in the county court of the county where such seller may reside, one half whereof to the use of the county in which the recovery may be had, and the other to the person who may prosecute for the same."[188] And a statute adopted on February 3, 1818, moreover, required masters to register all term slaves, and provided that owners could not sell term slaves beyond their required term of service or out of the state.[189]

Although an 1832 law required all newly freed slaves to leave Maryland, it contained a clause exempting persons who were freed by deeds recorded or wills probated before the act's effective date.[190] In 1833, the legislators adopted a supplemental act, which in part was similar to Tennessee's freed slave exclusion statute, exempting persons who were the subjects of existing future freedom contracts. The exemption applied, however, only if all or some "of the stipulated price or consideration for such freedom" had been paid, and if the full consideration later was paid and the slave was freed.[191]

Nevertheless, term slaves seeking freedom under a future manumission deed faced several obstacles, and the courts denied many valid claims to liberty. As noted further in chapter six, the Maryland courts strictly applied the statutory execution and recording requirements. If the masters did not follow the statutory execution procedure or did not properly record the deeds calling for future manumission, the people held as slaves could not enforce the masters' promises.[192] Thus, in 1837, the Court of Appeals held that the property rights of a good faith purchaser of a term slave were entitled to greater weight than the term slave's right to liberty under an unrecorded future manumission deed. The court also invalidated a special act of the legislature that was intended to validate the unrecorded manumission deed.[193]

The slave's rights under these delayed manumission deeds also were subject to the superior rights of the master's creditors as of the manumission's actual effective date.[194] In addition, the slave had to be of an age at which manumission could take effect when the term of servitude ended, at least until 1831, when the statutes were amended to permit a slave of any age to be freed.[195]

As will be noted in chapter six, these statutory requirements created roadblocks for some slaves who were promised their freedom, even if the master truly intended to free the slaves as promised and this promise was confirmed in writing. Thus, in 1837, Maryland's Court of Appeals, in *Bland and Woolfolk v. Negro Beverly Dowling*,[196] confirmed the majority rule denying the enforceability of manumission contracts, although it affirmed a freedom verdict for the claimant, Beverly Dowling. Judge Stevenson Archer based the court's decision on his finding that Dowling's return to slavery in Maryland, after he lived as a free person out of state, would violate the intention of Maryland's anti-importation act.[197]

Archer expressly rejected Dowling's breach of manumission contract claim, however, while cogently restating the majority rule. Archer wrote that in view of "the state of slavery [in Maryland], and the relations between the slave and his master growing out of such condition, we cannot maintain the principle that a slave can enter into any binding contract with his master, or that he could appear as a suiter in any of our courts of justice, legal or equitable, to enforce any alleged contract."[198]

The notion that these deeds should be thought of as contracts also is diminished by the 1849 Maryland Court of Appeals decision holding that masters who did not honor their promises and held people as slaves beyond the promised freedom date would not be liable to the slaves for the net value of the services that the slaves provided without compensation after the promised freedom date.[199] This ruling was consistent with Maryland's line of cases, noted in chapter nine, holding that defendants were not liable to people wrongfully held as slaves for damages caused by their wrongful detention in slavery.[200]

These delayed manumission deeds apparently were at least in part intended to encourage slaves to exhibit good behavior when they were held as term slaves. The Maryland statutes provided that owners could apply to the courts to extend the terms of slaves who ran away or whose conduct was "notoriously vicious and turbulent[.]" In the alternative, the masters could apply for permission to sell out of the state slaves exhibiting these undesirable behaviors.[201]

As in Louisiana, however, the Maryland legislature eventually found that manumission should be prohibited. In 1860, the legislature adopted an act "prohibiting manumission of negro slaves, and authorizing free negroes to renounce freedom and become slaves."[202] The act prohibited manumissions by deed or by will. It also stated that a presumption of freedom should not arise for blacks who were "going at large and acting as free," or who were unclaimed by an owner. Unlike the Louisiana law, the Maryland statute excepted term slaves who were previously freed by a will or deed, but whose date with freedom had not arrived.[203]

Alternative Ways to Enforce Promises of Freedom

The majority rule of law adopted in the United States South paralleled Roman slave law, which prohibited suits by slaves against masters, with few exceptions. But an indirect route developed in Roman law by which some slaves could buy their freedom and enforce their freedom contracts.[204] Slaves entered into contracts to purchase their freedom with third parties who would buy the slaves from their masters with the intention of freeing the slaves. Slaves also were allowed to institute legal proceedings against these third party buyers, not the masters, asserting the slaves' alleged right to freedom if the slaves paid the agreed price for their liberty using money "not proceeding" from the slaves' owners. The law did not compel owners to sell their slaves. It meant only that if the new owners accepted money based on the promise to free the slaves and later refused to do so, the slaves were permitted "to institute such proceedings."[205]

The law in Spain and its colonies and in Brazil allowed people held as slaves the right to enforce in court their masters' promises to free their slaves.[206] For example, Keila Grinberg discussed the case of a Brazilian slave, Joaquim, who in 1823 sued to enforce his deceased owner's promise of freedom after the owner's son refused to honor his mother's promise to allow Joaquim to buy his freedom. After three years, the High Court of Rio de Janeiro enforced the deceased owner's promise to free Joaquim. The court ordered that he be freed upon the payment of his value or that he be sold to an owner who would agree to free him upon receipt of the payment.[207]

The courts in the United States South could have taken the lead by enforcing the master's promises under the doctrines of promissory estoppel or moral consideration, but they did not.[208] This possibility is best illustrated by the 1792 South Carolina decision in *Guardian of Sally v. Beaty*.[209] The plaintiff filed the suit "in nature of *ravishment of ward*," pursuant to a 1740 South Carolina statute, to establish the freedom of the plaintiff's ward, who was described only as "a negro girl Sally."[210]

The master's promise at issue was not made to Sally; it was instead made to a slave of the master Beaty. The report refers to that slave only as "a negro wench slave[.]" Beaty allowed the "wench slave" to work "in town" on her own. "[B]y her industry, [she] acquired a considerable sum of money, over and above what she stipulated to pay for her monthly wages, to her master[.]"[211]

Beaty's unnamed slave used her own money to purchase Sally, whom she later set free. "For a considerable time after the purchase was made, the defendant never claimed any property in [Sally]—never paid taxes for her; but," on the contrary, acknowledged he had no property in her." Nevertheless, Beaty later refused to "deliver up the girl as free," and the suit followed. Beaty's counsel argued that his client owned Sally because all the money that Beaty's slave earned was Beaty's property. Therefore, all of the property that his slave purchased with "her" money also was Beaty's property, which he could claim at any time at his own whim.[212]

Chief Judge John Rutledge instructed the jury to the contrary. He stated that, "although the case was a new one," he found "no difficulty whatever, in forming an opinion on it[.]"

> [I]f the master got the labour of his wench or what he agreed to receive for her monthly wages, (which was the same thing) he could not be injured; on the contrary, he was fully satisfied; and all that she earned over, ought to be at her own disposal; her extra labour, to the purchase of this girl, or in order afterwards to set her free-would a jury of the country say no? He trusted not. They were too humane and upright, he hoped, to do such manifest violence to so singular and extraordinary an act of benevolence.

After hearing this charge, "*[t]he jury*, without retiring from their box, returned a verdict for the plaintiff's ward."[213]

Rutledge's charge to the jury was a legal ruling that more or less directed the jury to find for the plaintiff. The charge can be read as a judicial decision applying the equitable doctrines of promissory estoppel, equitable estoppel, or moral consideration to enforce Beaty's promise as a moral obligation. The courts could have used these doctrines to require that masters honor their promises made to and relied upon by their slaves, as substitutes for the flow of legal consideration, especially when the slave fully performed his or her end of the bargain, but they did not.[214]

This decision is an exception that illustrates the rule. According to Thomas Cobb, in *Guardian of Sally*, "[b]oth Judge and jury seemed carried away with enthusiasm, at the 'extraordinary benevolence of the wench.'"[215] George Stroud called *Sally* "an *isolated* case" that was "in opposition to other *later* decisions."[216] Peter Hoffer wrote that Rutledge's "appeals to humane feelings ... grew increasingly rare in the 1850s."[217] Jenny Bourne Wahl called this case "[t]he celebrated exception" to the rule that rendered manumission contracts between masters and slaves unenforceable.[218] The Southern courts did not follow it to, in Justice John B. O'Neall's words, "get back alongside of such men as C.J. Rutledge[.]"[219] The

South Carolina Court of Equity and Appeals confirmed this when it stated, after the Civil War, that "no change of law was wrought by this verdict[.]"[220] Even Justice O'Neall questioned Rutledge's charge in an 1842 opinion, stating: "That case goes further than I desire to go; but it is ample authority to prove, that by the law of this State a slave might acquire personal property[.]"[221]

Moreover, in 1846 the South Carolina Court of Appeals effectively overruled this decision in *Gist v. Toohey*.[222] A hired slave, William, had paid $100 on account to the defendant so that the defendant could purchase William's two children. William saved this money from wages that he earned in addition to the agreed wages that he paid to his master. After William advanced the initial $100 payment, the defendant purchased William's children. William's master then sued the defendant for the money had and received. The court held that William could not acquire property rights in the money that he earned and saved. William, in effect, bought his children for his master, because he had no property right in his surplus earnings. Therefore, the court held that the master was entitled to a judgment for $100 against the defendant.[223]

The law that might have been also is illustrated by an 1851 decision, *Guess v. Lubbock, Adm'r*.[224] Texas Supreme Court Justice Abner Lipscomb suggested in *dictum* that on remand the trial court might indeed find that an estoppel *in pais* applied to enforce an alleged slave's rights to her freedom and to own real property.[225] He stated that the doctrine of estoppel, "though questioned at first, is now too firmly established by the decisions in England and the courts of the several states of the Union to be shaken."[226]

The issue arose in a suit that Margaret Guess filed against the defendant, Francis Lubbock, who was the administrator of the estate of Adam Smith. Guess claimed that Lubbock improperly listed her, her child, and her real estate as assets of Smith's estate. Although Lubbock's answers to the complaint omitted this contention, at trial he apparently asserted that Guess and her daughter were Smith's slaves when he died, and that Smith did not purchase the real estate at issue in trust for Guess. After a jury trial, Lubbock obtained a judgment in his favor, and Guess appealed. The Supreme Court reversed the judgment for a number of reasons, and remanded the case for a new trial.[227]

One of these reasons leading to the reversal and remand concerned Lubbock's claim that Guess was Smith's slave. Justice Lipscomb wrote that even if the trial court were to grant Lubbock leave to amend his answer to properly assert this defense, according to the evidence it was not clear whether Guess paid for herself or that Smith paid for her when Smith "acquired" her in February 1836. It was clear, however, that "from the time of purchase or nearly so down to 1846 Smith lived with [Guess] as his wife; that he at all times disclaimed being her owner, but said on all occasions that she was free; that she claimed and exercised ownership of property in her own right; that Smith always called it her property, and there is but slight evidence that he ever exerted any control over her property or her own actions[.]" Thus, it appeared that Smith "never in his life claimed the plaintiff as his slave, and by his continued acts treated her as a free woman[.]" Smith also signed a document when he and Guess ended their cohabitation. The document was dated March 19, 1840, and it stated that "Margaret, a negro woman, about thirty years of age, is free and at liberty to go and do the best she can to make an honest livelihood in the world."[228]

Justice Lipscomb opined that these facts suggested an estoppel that could bar Lubbock's claim to Guess, her daughter, and her property. He stated that the facts also suggested a presumption that Smith freed Guess before Texas law would have prevented it.[229]

On May 20, 1852, the case again was tried before Judge C.W. Buckley, who was the judge in the first trial. Buckley, a slave owner himself, heard the case without a jury. He ruled "that Guess was a free person and awarded her the property claimed by Lubbock. Given the hostility shown to Lubbock's position by the Supreme Court, it does not come as a surprise that there was not a second appeal to that court."[230]

The case thus took almost five years and included two trials and one appeal to the state's highest court. But, in the end, Guess and her daughter won their freedom, and Guess kept her property. According to Mark Davidson, Guess sold her real estate soon after winning her judgment, "possibly to pay attorney's fees, and then [she] dropped out of the public records."[231]

If Southern judges really were inclined to favor freedom, they could have been guided by the "justice of the heart" rather than the "justice of the head" that it is argued the Northern judges promulgated in the nineteenth century law of contracts. The Southern jurists could have been the innovators who employed "honorable" and equitable doctrines such as estoppel or moral consideration to prevent masters from reneging on their promises made to and relied upon by their slaves, even without any flow or exchange of legal consideration between the master and the slave.[232] To the contrary, however, the manumission contract decisions confirmed that the "justice of the head" prevailed. The courts did not enforce the master's promises made to and relied upon by his or her slaves.

Are we asking too much of the Southern judges? I say not necessarily. An Alabama case from 1845, *Kirksey v. Kirksey*,[233] is one of the cases cited most often for the strict nineteenth century consideration doctrine. Nevertheless, in other contexts, Southern antebellum judges applied the moral consideration doctrine to enforce promises.[234] Moreover, in a related context, not all of the Southern courts followed the Northern antebellum cases employing the doctrine of *caveat emptor* in slave sale cases.[235]

The law in the common law Southern states also could have enforced slave master promises of freedom, without undermining slavery's fundamentals. The Louisiana and Delaware examples confirm this. It thus does not appear that it would be overly harsh on the Southern lawmakers and judges to suggest that the majority rule making freedom contracts unenforceable was contrary not only to the common law that otherwise would have applied to promises made and actions performed in reliance thereon, but also to notions of common sense, fairness, and honor. This was especially ironic in a society such as the antebellum South, where the concept of "honor" allegedly was of great import to the slave holding class.[236]

If honorable conduct by slave owners was a value that was important to the slave holding class in action rather than rhetoric, then why did its members not prevail upon their duly elected representatives to follow Louisiana's and Delaware's lead and change the prevailing law to comport with the prevailing values of society? The legislatures of the other Southern states could have created an exception to the general rule barring contracts by slaves by permitting the courts to enforce manumission contracts between masters and slaves, but they did not.[237]

The Southern courts enforced this concept of honor in the law when they awarded specific performance of contracts for the sale of slaves because "[t]here is at least as much reason for enforcing the specific execution of a contract for the sale of slaves, as of a contract for the sale of real estate."[238] The Southern law thus, at other times, acted in compliance with the principle that

> it is simply right that one get what he was promised. This is not the place to figure out why we enforce promises, but surely there is a reason beyond efficient allocation of resources. The origins of enforcement may be religious, or religion may have been used to achieve utility, but I think that today most people believe that one should stand by one's word. This is as it should be, for when a person bargains for a promise he puts his trust in the promisor. This is especially true in noncommercial transactions and in transactions involving idiosyncratic values[.] ... Predictability is an important value in law, as should be the promotion of economic efficiency. But most important are fairness and justice.[239]

In these manumission contract suits, however, the substantive law negated these concepts of "fairness and justice" when the alleged slave was the plaintiff. The law limited the claims on which an alleged slave could obtain a finding that he or she was not legally being held in bondage.

It thus was conceivable that the Southern courts could have applied the doctrines of moral consideration or estoppel to enforce the masters' express and implied promises of freedom. This rule would have confirmed in action this alleged ideal of the honorable conduct of slave masters in Southern slave society.

This law also suggests the need to question the ideal of the honorable master. Marion B. Lucas noted that slave owners promised their slaves manumission "both idly and seriously, for a wide variety of reasons." She cited examples of Kentucky slave owners who "never intended to [free] a slave when they pledged eventual freedom. They usually made the promise to ensure the slave's continued good service and good behavior. Such pledges had no immediate costs, though falsely raising a slave's hopes could prove troublesome in the long run."[240] The law did not, however, contribute to the troubles of the dishonorable master.

Robert Olwell summed the issues up well when he wrote that slave owners who dangled "the carrot of freedom as well as the whip" provided "a powerful incentive with which to extract slaves' labour." But because the masters' promises were not enforceable contracts at law, "[a] slave promised freedom in eight years upon good behaviour could be sold after seven." He also noted that slaves who were the victims of "such betrayals" and these agreements that "were not carried through ... would have left little trace in the records."[241]

Conclusion

Maryland's Chief Justice Thomas B. Dorsey, in an 1849 opinion, wrote that when his state's legislature repealed a 1752 statute prohibiting manumission by will it did so not out of hostility to slavery or to benefit people held as slaves. Indeed, he believed that "slaves, for the most part, were far better fed and clothed; more contented and happy; and in point of sobriety, virtue and moral character, far above the free coloured population of this State." According to Dorsey, the legislators who permitted manumission intended "to gratify the masters of slaves, to enlarge their privileges, and to give them an authority to dispose of their slaves in a way which otherwise they did not possess."[242]

Therefore, manumission in the United States South generally was one of the masters' privileges of property ownership. Masters, with only limited exceptions, were not legally obligated to free any slaves, including those who offered to pay their market value or who performed their freedom contract obligations. [243] Moreover, the state rarely manumitted slaves for public policy reasons contrary to the master's wishes not to free his or her slaves.

Some will no doubt dismiss this analysis of the substantive law as simplistic "statist positivism" because it focuses on statutes and case law and "gives short shrift to customary law and customary rights."[244] Notwithstanding this positive law, however, some masters in the United States South allowed slaves to self-hire out their services, keep their excess earnings, and purchase their freedom when their masters made and honored promises of freedom if the slaves paid an agreed price or satisfied other conditions of manumission.[245] It is not true, however, that these promises were contractual, or that "manumission was available to any slave who could afford the price[.]"[246]

Notes to Chapter 2

[1] Orlando Patterson, "Three Notes of Freedom," in *Paths to Freedom: Manumission in the Atlantic World* 15 (Rosemary Brana-Shute and Randy J. Sparks, eds.) (2009) [hereinafter *Paths to Freedom*].

[2] Cobb, *supra* at 278.

[3] *Id.* at 279.

[4] *Id.* at 278-79.

[5] *See* Patterson, *Social Death*, *supra* at 431, n. 1 [emphasis added].

[6] *See Sampson v. Burgwin*, 20 N.C. (3 & 4 Dev. & Bat.) 21, 1838 WL 470 at *3 (1838) [emphasis added].

[7] Cobb, *supra* at 283, 296.

[8] Singer, *supra* at 986.

[9] *See* Hohfeld, "Some Fundamental," *supra* at 45.

[10] *See id.* at 45, n. 66.

[11] *See, e.g., Shue v. Turk*, 56 Va. (15 Gratt.) 256, 263-65 (1859) (enforcing contract to prevent execution on judgment debtor/master's former slave because the master had freed the slave); *Fulton v. Shaw*, 25 Va. (4 Rand.) 597, 1827 WL 1188 (1827) (declaring void a provision in a manumission deed freeing a female slave, Mary Shaw, but attempting to retain for the master the right to own as slaves Mary's children born even after Mary was freed).

[12] *See* Morris, *Slavery, supra* at 388-92; Suzanna Sherry, "The Early Virginia Tradition of Extratextual Interpretation," in *Toward a Usable Past: Liberty under State Constitutions* 171-72 (Paul Finkelman & Stephen E. Gottlieb, eds.) (1991).

[13] *See Fulton v. Shaw*, 25 Va. (4 Rand.) 597, 1827 WL 1188 at *2; Favre, *supra* at 491-92 (discussing manumission as a model for changing the legal status of non-human animals). Freed slaves generally did not benefit from equal legal rights or opportunities after manumission. *See* Morris, *Slavery, supra* at 372; Ira Berlin, *Slaves Without Masters: The Free Negro in the Antebellum South* (1974) [hereinafter Berlin, *Slaves Without Masters*].

[14] *See* Morris, *Slavery, supra* at 371-72; 1 Hurd, *supra* at 214, n. 2.

[15] *See* John V. Orth, "What's Wrong with the Law of Finders and How to Fix It," 4 *Green Bag 2d* 391, 391-94 (2001); Eric W. Neilsen, "Is the Law of Acquisition of Property by Find Going to the Dogs?" 15 *T. M. Cooley L. Rev.* 479, 485-86 (1998). The courts applied this general rule also to a person coming into possession of an estray animal. *See id.* at 493-98.

[16] *See Maria v. Surbaugh*, 23 Va. (2 Rand.) 228, 1824 WL 1192 at *2 (1824).

[17] *See* Linda O. Smiddy, "Judicial Nullification of State Statutes Restricting the Emancipation of Slaves: A Southern Court's Call for Reform," 42 *S.C. L. Rev.* 589, 604 (1991); *see also Linam v. Johnson*, 18 S.C.L. (2 Bail. 137) (1831); Morris, *Slavery, supra* at 372-73.

[18] *See, e.g.,* Lior Jacob Strahilevitz, "The Right to Destroy," 114 *Yale L.J.* 781, 783-96 (2005); Edward J. McCaffery, "Must We Have The Right to Waste?," in *New Essays in the Legal and Political Theory of Property* 76-84 (Stephen R. Munzer, ed.) (2001); *but see* Joseph L. Sax, *Playing Darts with a Rembrandt: Public and Private Rights in Cultural Treasures* 203, n. 2 (1999) (questioning the historical basis of this concept).

[19] *See* Strahilevitz, *supra* at 793.

[20] *See id.* at 795; McCaffery, *supra* at 84-91.

[21] *See* Strahilevitz, *supra* at 796-854.

[22] *See* Sax, *supra* at 2.

[23] *See id.* at 3.

[24] *See id.* at 6-9; *see also id.* at 199-201 for Sax's proposal for law reform, and McCaffery, *supra* at 91-105, for McCaffery's proposal to use the tax code to discourage "nonurgent" or "dissipatory" waste that he states has similar effects on society as property destruction.

[25] Paul Finkelman, "Fugitive Baseballs and Abandoned Property: Who Owns the Home

Run Ball?" 23 *Cardozo L. Rev.* 1609, 1618 (2002) (analyzing home run baseballs as abandoned property, and the law prohibiting abandonment of some forms of property).

[26] *See* Radin, *supra* at 1158.

[27] Cobb, *supra* at 279.

[28] *See* chapter 6, *infra* at notes 2-71; Jones, *Fathers, supra*; Davis, "Race and Sex," *supra*.

[29] *Givens and Reynolds v. Manns*, 20 Va. (6 Munf.) 191, 1818 WL 1120 at *7 (1818); Cobb, *supra* at 280; *see Simons v. Fox*, 46 S.C.L. (12 Rich.) 392, 1859 WL 4920 (1859); *Bryan v. Weems*, 29 Ala. 423, 1856 WL 404 (1856); *Winburn's Ex'rs v. Cochran*, 9 Tex. 123, 1852 WL 4036 *2-*3 (1852); *Little's Adm'r v. Chauvin*, 1 Mo. 626, 1826 WL 1702 at *4 (1826); Schafer, *Supreme Court, supra* at 115-17 (on adverse possession of slaves).

[30] The law in the Southern colonies and then states generally provided widows with at least a life estate interest in one-third of her husband's real and personal property, except South Carolina, which excluded personal property including slaves. *See* Morris, *Slavery, supra* at 93-96; Marylynn Salmon, *Women and the Law of Property in Early America* 141-84 (1986); 1 Catterall, *supra* at 270. The widow's dower interest could void some or all of the manumissions called for by her husband's will, if the estate was not sufficient. *Negro William v. Kelly*, 5 H. & J. 59, 1820 WL 913 (Md. 1820) (freedom claim under will denied because slave was allotted to widow in satisfaction of one-third elective share). In Kentucky, however, the courts held that husbands had the right to free their slaves by will, and their widows did not have any dower rights in the freed slaves. *See Graham's Executor v. Sam*, 46 Ky. (7 B. Mon.) 403, 1847 WL 2843 (1847); *Lee v. Lee's Executors*, 31 Ky. (1 Dana) 48, 1833 WL 2414 (1833).

[31] Cobb, *supra* at 280-81.

[32] 47 Ky. (8 B. Mon.) 539, 1848 WL 3338 (1848).

[33] *Tom Davis, (of color) v. Tingle*, 1848 WL 3338 at *5, citing *Oatfield v. Waring*, 14 Johnson Rep. 188 (N.Y. Sup. Ct. 1817); *see* 1 Catterall, *supra* at 270-71.

[34] *Tom Davis, (of color) v. Tingle*, 1848 WL 3338 at *6; *see Berry v. Hamilton*, 64 Ky. (1 Bush) 361, 1867 WL 6923 at *4 (1866) (owner of one-quarter interest in slaves could not free any of them); *Nunnally v. White's Ex'rs*, 60 Ky. (3 Met.) 584, 1861 WL 3525 at *8 (1861) (will of three-fifths owner freeing slaves destroyed tenancy in common, and heirs of one-fifth owner entitled to monetary damages).

[35] *See Williams' Adm'r v. McClanahan*, 60 Ky. (3 Met.) 420, 1861 WL 3485 (1861); *Lark v. Linstead*, 2 Md. 420, 1852 WL 3059 (1852); *King v. Sharp*, 25 Tenn. (6 Hum.) 255, 1845 WL 1853 (1845); *Tom Davis, (of color) v. Tingle*, 1848 WL 3338 at *2, *7; Cobb, *supra* at 280-81, 306-07; *but see Mimms v. Lawrence*, 91 S.W. 715 (Ky. 1906) (estate of holder of slaves for life not liable to remainder holders when slaves were freed by general emancipation during life term); *Isaac (a man of color) v. Farnsworth*, 40 Tenn. (3 Head) 275, 1859 WL 3454 (1859) (husband's will gave widow the right to sell slaves).

[36] William D. Phillips, Jr., "Manumission in Metropolitan Spain and the Canaries in the Fifteenth and Sixteenth Centuries, in *Paths to Freedom, supra* at 43 [hereinafter Phillips, "Manumission"].

[37] *See Las Siete Partidas, Volume 4, supra*, Part 4, Title 22, Law 2 at 981; Watson, *Americas, supra* at 45; Tannenbaum, *supra* at 50.

[38] *See Las Siete Partidas, Volume 5: Underworlds: The Dead, the Criminal, and the Marginalized* Part, 6, Title 3, Law 23 at 1201 (Samuel Parsons Scott, tr., Robert I. Burns, ed., 2001) [hereinafter *Las Siete Partidas, Volume 5*]; Tannenbaum, *supra* at 52.

[39] *See* Willie Lee Rose, *A Documentary History of Slavery in North America* 177-78 (1976), quoting *Civil Code of the State of Louisiana*, Art. 191, 192 (1825) [hereinafter *Civil Code*].

[40] *See Burgess v. Heape*, 10 S.C. Eq. (1 Hill Eq.) 397, 1833 WL 1699 (S.C. App. 1833) (co-owner who removed slave from the state could be ordered to account to the other owner for the appropriate portion of the slave's value); Cobb, *supra* at 307.

[41] *See* Patterson, *Social Death, supra* at 234-36.

[42] *See Las Siete Partidas, Volume 4, supra*, Part 4, Title 22, Law 3 at 982; Klein, *supra* at 63; Tannenbaum, *supra* at 50; Phillips, "Manumission," *supra* at 33, 36-37.

[43] *See Las Siete Partidas, Volume 4, supra*, Part 4, Title 21, Law 6 at 979; Title 22, Law 4 at 982; Klein, *supra* at 63.

[44] *See Las Siete Partidas, Volume 4, supra*, Part 4, Title 22, Law 6 at 983; Watson, *Americas, supra* at 45; Klein, *supra* at 64. Slaves who became bishops had to supply two slaves. *See id.*; Phillips, "Manumission," *supra* at 39.

[45] Tannenbaum, *supra* at 50; *see Las Siete Partidas, Volume 4, supra*, Part 4, Title 22, Law 7 at 983; Phillips, "Manumission," *supra* at 37-39. This sanctuary doctrine was applied in Spanish Florida from 1683 until 1790. *See* chapter 1, *supra* at note 5.

[46] *See* Portuguese Crown, Law of December 24, 1734, in *Brief History, supra* at 136-37; Watson, *Americas, supra* at 99-100.

[47] *See id.*

[48] *See* Keila Grinberg, "Manumission, Gender, and the Law in Nineteenth-Century Brazil: Liberata's Legal Suit for Freedom," in *Paths to Freedom, supra* at 221-28.

[49] *See* Winthrop D. Jordan, "American Chiaroscuro: The Status and Definition of Mulattoes in the British Colonies," 19 *Wm. & Mary Q.* 183, 198 (1962); *see also* Samuel J. Hurwitz & Edith F. Hurwitz, "A Token of Freedom: Private Bill Legislation for Free Negroes in Eighteenth-Century Jamaica," 24 *Wm. & Mary Q.* 423 (1967).

[50] *See* Degler, *supra* at 240. Degler defined this escape hatch, which he stated was in existence in Brazil and not the United States, as "the recognition of a special place for mixed bloods." *See id.* at 245; *see also, e.g.*, discussing this concept, Robert J. Cottrol, "Brown and the Contemporary Brazilian Struggle Against Racial Inequality: Some Preliminary Comparative Thoughts," 66 *U. Pitt. L. Rev.* 113, 121 (2004); Julissa Reynoso, "Race, Censuses, and Attempts at Racial Democracy," 39 *Colum. J. of Transnat'l L.* 533, 545 (2001); Tanya Hernandez, "'Multiracial' Discourse: Racial Classifications in an Era of Color-Blind Jurisprudence," 57 *Md. L. Rev.* 97, 122 (1998).

[51] *See* Jennifer M. Spear, *Race, Sex, and Social Order in Early New Orleans* 193-94 (2009); Schafer, *Becoming Free, supra* at 3-4; Vernon Valentine Palmer, "The Strange Science of Codifying Slavery – Moreau Lislet and the Louisiana Digest of 1808," 24 *Tulane Eur. & Civ. L. F.* 83, 109 (2009) [hereinafter Palmer, "Digest"]; *see generally* Shaw, *supra* at 99-102 discussing the development of Louisiana slave law, which Shaw suggests, because of its French and Spanish heritage, was "somewhat in contrast with, and generally

milder than, that prevailing in most of the English colonies." *Id.* at 99; *see also* Vernon Valentine Palmer, "The Customs of Slavery: The War Without Arms," 48 *Am. J. of Legal Hist.* 177, 182-193 (2006) (discussing the development of Louisiana slave law) [hereinafter Palmer, "Customs"].

[52] *See* Schafer, *Becoming Free, supra* at 3-4; Rose, *supra* at 177, quoting *Civil Code,* Art.191. The first Mississippi, Alabama, and Arkansas constitutions contained similar provisions. *See* A. Hutchinson, ed., *Code of Mississippi from 1798 to 1848* 34 (1848) [hereinafter *Code of Mississippi*]; Harry Toulmin, ed., *A Digest of the Laws of the State of Alabama* 638-39 (1823); Orville W. Taylor, *Negro Slavery in Arkansas* 43 (1958) [hereinafter Taylor, *Negro Slavery in Arkansas*].

[53] *See* chapter 7, *infra* at notes 24-38, 185-95.

[54] *See* chapter 7, *infra* at notes 19-21, 57-165.

[55] Loren Schweninger, *et al.*, eds., *The Southern Debate Over Slavery: Petitions to Southern Legislatures, 1775-1864* 143 (2001) [hereinafter *Petitions to Legislatures*]; *but see id.* at 18-20 (petitions of slave owner and 39 others seeking manumission of a woman and child held as slaves in North Carolina, alleging woman's mother was white, no legislation passed).

[56] "An Act to manumit a negro man slave, named Boston, the property of E. B. Way, Catherine P. Wheeler, Thomas B. Wheeler, H.R. Wheeler and Eugene Bacon of Georgia, and County of Liberty, and John Savage of the County of Chatham, and State aforesaid," in *Acts of the General Assembly of the State of Georgia, 1855-56* 539 (John W. Duncan, ed.) (1856); *see generally* Stampp, *supra*, at 233; *see also Jack et al. (slaves) v. Doran's Executors*, 37 Ala. 265 (1861) (discussing legislation permitting manumission on conditions); Jones, *Fathers, supra*, at 102-11 (petitions to Mississippi legislature); Schafer, *Becoming Free, supra*, at 4-6 (petitions to Louisiana legislature); John Hope Franklin, *The Free Negro in North Carolina, 1790-1860* 28-34 (1995) [hereinafter Franklin, *Free Negro*] (39 North Carolina acts freed 89 slaves between 1791 to 1855); Charles S. Sydnor, "The Free Negro in Mississippi before the Civil War," 32 *Am. Hist. Rev.* 769, 773-74 (1927) [hereinafter Sydnor, "Free Negro"] (petitions filed with Mississippi legislature).

[57] *See* Patterson, *Social Death, supra* at 234.

[58] *See id.* at 287.

[59] *See id.* at 288-93.

[60] *See* Peter M. Voelz, *Slave and Soldier: The Military Impact of Blacks in the Colonial Americas* 1-32, 431-50 (1993); Brana-Shute, *supra* at 189; Evelyn P. Jennings, "Paths to Freedom: Imperial Defense and Manumission in Havana, 1762-1800," in *Paths to Freedom, supra* at 121-41 [hereinafter Jennings, "Imperial Defense"]; Lyman L. Johnson, "Manumission in Colonial Buenos Aires, 1776-1810," 59 *Hispanic Am. Hist. Rev.* 258, 274 (1979); *see also* the essays in *Arming Slaves: From Classical Times to the Modern Age* (Christopher Leslie Brown and Philip D. Morgan, eds.) (2006) [hereinafter *Arming Slaves*].

[61] *See* Patterson, *Social Death, supra* at 292; Benjamin Quarles, "The Colonial Militia and Negro Manpower," 45 *Miss. Valley Hist. Rev.* 643 (1959) [hereinafter Quarles, "Militia"].

[62] 3 Hening, *supra* at 537; *see* Russell, *Free Negro, supra* at 42.

[63] *See* Degler, *supra* at 75-82.

[64] *See id.* at 79, 80.

[65] See Davis, *Inhuman Bondage, supra* at 137; Berlin, *Many Thousands, supra* at 66-67; Peter H. Wood, *Black Majority: Negroes in Colonial South Carolina from 1670 through the Stono Rebellion* 124-30 (1974) [hereinafter Wood, *Black Majority*].

[66] *See* 7 *Statutes at Large of South Carolina* 347-49 (David J. McCord, ed.) (1840) [hereinafter *Statutes at Large of South Carolina*]; *see also* Degler, *supra* at 82; Quarles, "Militia," *supra* at 648-49.

[67] *See* 7 *Statutes at Large of South Carolina, supra* at 33, 349-51. The 1703 act is listed among the acts relating to Charleston. The 1708 act's duration was for two years. *Id.; see also* Higginbotham, *Color, supra* at 175; Wood, *Black Majority, supra* at 125-26; Quarles, "Militia," *supra* at 649.

[68] Higginbotham, *Color, supra* at 175. *But see* Wood, *Black Majority, supra* at 126, stating that several slaves were freed after hostilities that occurred in 1706.

[69] Quarles, "Militia," *supra* at 650; *see* Peter Charles Hoffer, *Cry Liberty: the Great Stono River Slave Rebellion of 1739* 126-31 (2010); Davis, *Inhuman Bondage, supra* at 139-40; Berlin, *Many Thousands, supra* at 64-76; Wood, *Black Majority, supra* at 308-30; *see also* Jack Shuler, *Calling Out Liberty: The Stono Slave Rebellion and the Universal Struggle for Human Rights* (2009); and the materials and comments in *Stono: Documenting and Interpreting A Southern Slave Revolt* (Mark M. Smith, ed.) (2005).

[70] *See* Betty Wood, *Slavery in Colonial Georgia, 1730-1775* 117-19 (2007) [hereinafter Wood, *Georgia*]; Gloria J. Browne-Marshall, *Race, Law, and American Society: 1607 to Present* 139 (2007); Higginbotham, *Color, supra* at 259-61.

[71] *See* Wood, *Georgia, supra* at 119; Higginbotham, *Color, supra* at 261.

[72] Patterson, *Social Death, supra* at 292; *see* Browne-Marshall, *supra* at 139; Philip D. Morgan and Andrew Jackson O'Shaughenessy, "Arming Slaves in the American Revolution," in *Arming Slaves, supra* at 183-87.

[73] *See* Drescher, *supra* at 125; Davis, *Inhuman Bondage, supra* at 147; William James Cooper, Jr., *Liberty and Slavery: Southern Politics to 1860* 35-36 (2000); Michael Lee Lanning, *African Americans in the Revolutionary War* 65-66 (2000); James Oliver Horton & Lois E. Horton, *In Hope of Liberty: Culture, Community, and Protest Among Northern Free Blacks, 1700-1860* 63-76 (1998); Benjamin Quarles & Vincent P. Franklin, *The Negro in the Making of America* 56-69 (3d. ed. 1996); William H. Williams, *Slavery and Freedom in Delaware, 1639-1865* 146 (1996) [hereinafter Williams, *Slavery and Freedom in Delaware*]; Patterson, *Social Death, supra* at 292; Berlin, *Slaves Without Masters, supra* at 18-20; Jack D. Foner, *Blacks in the Military in American History: A New Perspective* 11 (1974); Benjamin Quarles, *The Negro in the American Revolution* 9-18, 51-60 (1961) [hereinafter Quarles, *Revolution*]. For the Maryland act, *see* "An act to procure recruits," in *Archives of Maryland Muster Rolls and other Records of Service of the Maryland Troops in the American Revolution 1775-1783* 367 (1900); *see also* Quarles, *Revolution, supra* at 56; Brackett, *supra* at 196-97. The Virginia militia acts of July 1775 and May 1777 applied to all free males older than 16 and younger than 50 years of age, but, according to the latter act, "free mulattoes" were to be employed as "drummers, fifers, or

pioneers." 9 Hening, *supra* at 27, 267-68. Another May 1777 act required the enlisting officer to obtain a freedom certificate issued by a justice of the peace before enlisting a free "negro or mulatto." *Id.* at 280. According to Benjamin Quarles, "Virginia drew the line against slave enlistments in any form." The legislature in 1780 rejected a plan, supported by James Madison, to free and enlist some slave soldiers. *See* Quarles, *Revolution, supra* at 57-58. For North Carolina, *see University v. Cambreling*, 14 Tenn. (6 Yerg.) 79, 1834 WL 993 (Err. & App. 1834).

[74] For Rhode Island, *see* 8 John Russell Bartlett, ed., *Records of the State of Rhode Island and Providence Plantations in New England, 1776-1779* 358-60 (1863); *Corbin v. Marsh*, 63 Ky. (2 Duv.) 193, 1865 WL 2310 at *18 (1865) (Williams, J., dissenting) (discussing this and other statutes); Davis, *Inhuman Bondage, supra* at 147; Gary B. Nash, *The Unknown American Revolution: The Unruly Birth of Democracy and the Struggle to Create America* 229 (2005) [hereinafter Nash, *Unknown Revolution*]; Paul F. Dearden, *The Rhode Island Campaign of 1778: Inauspicious Dawn of Alliance* 23 (1980); Sidney Kaplan, *The Black Presence in the Era of the American Revolution 1770-1800* 55-57 (1973); Donald L. Robinson, *Slavery in the Structure of American Politics, 1765-1820* 116 (1971); Quarles, *Revolution, supra* at 55; Morgan & O'Shaughenessy, *supra* at 192-93; Gregory D. Massey, "The Limits of Antislavery Thought in the Revolutionary Lower South: John Laurens and Henry Laurens," 63 *J. of S. Hist.* 495, 495 (1997); Lorenzo Greene, "Some Observations on the Black Regiment of Rhode Island in the American Revolution," 37 *J. of Negro Hist.* 143, 143-44 (1952). In May 1778, the legislature repealed the act effective on June 10, 1778, but black enlistments nevertheless continued until the war ended. *See* Bartlett, *supra* at 399; Greene, *supra* at 162-63. For New York, *see* "An act for raising two Regiments for the Defense of this State on Bounties of Unappropriated Lands," in 1 Thomas Greenleaf, ed., *Laws of the State of New York* ch. 32, §6 at 42 (1792); David N. Gellman, *Emancipating New York: The Politics of Slavery and Freedom, 1777-1827* 37 (2006); Edgar J. McManus, *Negro Slavery in New York* 161 (1966); Quarles, *Revolution, supra* at 56; A. Judd Northrup, "Slavery in New York, A Historical Sketch," 4 *State Library Bulletin, History* 287 (May 1900). The Connecticut legislators in May 1777 considered but rejected a plan to enlist freed slaves and compensate their owners. Nevertheless, according to Benjamin Quarles, the legislature adopted two acts in May and October 1777 that encouraged masters to use freed slaves as substitutes and that relieved the masters of what otherwise would have been their obligations to support their former slaves. *See* Quarles, *Revolution, supra* at 54; "An Act for raising and compleating [sic] the Quota of the Continental Army to be raised in this State," in Charles J. Hoadly, ed., *The Public Records of the State of Connecticut, from Oct., 1776, to Feb., 1778, inclusive* 240 (1894); "An act in Addition to and in Alteration of An Act concerning Indian, Molatto [sic] and Negro Servants and Slaves," in *Id.* at 415. The North Carolina legislature, in a 1779 act, extended a provision calling for the seizure and sale of slaves to those who were improperly freed before a 1777 act was adopted, but it excepted any slave who was freed and not sold under a court order who had "enlisted into the service of this or the United States previous to the passing of this Act." *See* Walter Clark, ed., *The State Records of North Carolina, Vol. XXIV, Laws, 1777-1788* 221 (1905) [hereinafter Clark, *1777-1788*]; Franklin, *Free Negro, supra* 102; *see also* chapter 3, *infra* at note 95 (discussing these statutes).

[75] *See* Jack Rakove, *Revolutionaries: A New History of the Invention of America* 198-241 (2010); Drescher, *supra* at 125; Douglas R. Egerton, *Death or Liberty: African Americans*

and Revolutionary America 82-85 (2009); Davis, *Inhuman Bondage, supra* at 147-48; Nash, *Unknown Revolution, supra* at 328-31; Lanning, *supra* at 67-72; Edward Ball, *Slaves in the Family* 222-24 (1998); Charles Patrick Neimeyer, *America Goes to War: A Social History of the Continental Army* 77-80 (1996); Quarles & Franklin, *supra* at 60-61; Sylvia R. Frey, *Water from the Rock: Black Resistance in a Revolutionary Age* 81-142 (1991); Degler, *supra* at 77; Robinson, *supra* at 117-28; Quarles, *Revolution, supra* at 60-67; Morgan & O'Shaughenessy, *supra* at 193-94; Massey, *supra* at 495-96, 509-27.

[76] *See* Quarles, *Revolution, supra* at 182-85. For the Rhode Island act, *see* 9 John Russell Bartlett, ed., *Records of the Colony of Rhode Island and Providence Plantations in New England, 1780-1783* 493-94, 509-10 (1864). For the North Carolina act, *see* Clark, *1777-1788, supra* at 639; Franklin, *Free Negro, supra* 102; Quarles, *Revolution, supra* at 59-60, 183-84 (a 1784 North Carolina act freeing Ned Griffin, who was a slave of William Kitchen, based upon the legislature's finding that Griffin was promised liberty if he served in the military for twelve months as a substitute for Kitchen, and that Griffin "did faithfully perform" his end of the bargain, but was re-enslaved); *see also* note 161 *infra*. For the Virginia acts, *see* 13 Hening, *supra* at 619 (1792 act freeing Saul); *Id.* at 103 (1789 act freeing Jack Knight and William Boush); *Id.* at 102 (1789 act freeing Caesar); 12 *Id.* at 380 (1786 act freeing James). For a 1783 Virginia statute that was adopted in response to masters who enlisted slaves as free blacks but who later attempted to re-enslave them, *see* note 160 *infra*.

[77] *See Arabas v. Ivers*, 1 Root 92, 1784 WL 10 at *1 (Conn. Super. 1784); *see also* Quarles, *Revolution, supra* at 184.

[78] 12 *Statutes at Large, Treaties and Proclamations of the United States of America from December 5, 1859 to December 3, 1863* ch. 201, §§12 & 13 at 599 (George P. Sanger, ed.) (1863) [hereinafter 12 *Statutes at Large*]. *See* Eric Foner, *The Fiery Trial: Abraham Lincoln and American Slavery* 215-16 (2010) [hereinafter Foner, *Lincoln*]; Amy Dru Stanley, "Instead of Waiting for the Thirteenth Amendment: The War Power, Slave Marriage, and Inviolate Human Rights," 115 *Am. Hist. Rev.* 732, 745-46, n. 23 (2010) [hereinafter Stanley, "Instead of Waiting"]. With this Act, the 1861 Confiscation Act, and the 1862 Second Confiscation Act, the North duplicated Virginia Royal Governor Lord Dunmore's war strategy. On November 7, 1775, he offered to free rebel-owned slaves who joined the British forces. *See, e.g.*, Maya Jasanoff, *Liberty's Exiles: American Loyalists in the Revolutionary World* 48-49 (2011); Egerton, *supra* at 129-30; Davis, *Inhuman Bondage, supra* at 148-49; Nash, *Unknown Revolution, supra* at 150-66; Berlin, *Many Thousands, supra* at 257-59; Quarles, *Revolution, supra* at 19-32; Morgan & O'Shaughenessy, *supra* at 189-92. On this Union law's evolution, *see* Foner, *Lincoln, supra* at 166-289; Hahn, *supra* at 65-102; Ira Berlin, Joseph Patrick Reidy, and Leslie Rowland, eds., *Freedom's Soldiers: The Black Military Experience in the Civil War* 2-6, 19, 21 (1998); Ira Berlin, Barbara J. Fields, and Steven F. Miller, *Slaves No More: Three Essays on Emancipation and the Civil War* 21-26, 40-44, 103, 107-24, 194, 205, 207 (1992); Eric Foner, *Reconstruction: America's Unfinished Revolution, 1863-1877* 1-76 (1988).

[79] 13 *Statutes at Large, Treaties and Proclamations of the United States of America from December 1863 to December 1865* ch. 13, §24 at 11 (George P. Sanger, ed.) (1866) [hereinafter 13 *Statutes at Large*]; *see Corbin v. Marsh*, 1865 WL 2310 at *8-*27 (1865) (Williams, J., dissenting). On the breakdown of slavery in Kentucky during the Civil War, *see* Victor B. Howard, "The Civil War in Kentucky: The Slave Claims His Freedom," 67 *J. of*

Negro Hist. 245, 250-51 (1982). The statute's compensation provisions for loyal slave owners were similar to those in the District of Columbia Emancipation Act of 1862. *See* 12 *Statutes at Large, supra* at ch. 54, 376-78; *see also* Kate Masur, *An Example for All the Land: Emancipation and the Struggle over Equality in Washington, D.C.* 25 (2010); Paul Finkelman, "The Civil War, Emancipation, and the Thirteenth Amendment: Understanding Who Freed the Slaves," in *Promises of Liberty, supra* at 43-45. A March 3, 1865 Congressional resolution "To encourage Enlistments and to promote the Efficiency" of the Union military freed any Union soldier's wife and children who were held as slaves in Confederate territory controlled by the Union forces or in the slave states of Kentucky and Delaware that were loyal to the Union. *See* 13 *Statutes at Large, supra* at 571; Foner, *Lincoln, supra* at 253; Stanley, "Instead of Waiting," *supra* at 732-33, 762. The Kentucky Supreme Court declared this resolution to be unconstitutional in *Corbin v. Marsh*, 1865 WL 2310 at *1-*7.

[80] *See, e.g.,* Charles H. Wesley, "The Employment of Negroes as Soldiers in the Confederate Army," 4 *J. of Negro. Hist.* 239, 242-50 (1919) (reprinted in J. H. Segars and Charles Kelly Barrow, eds., *Black Soldiers in Confederate Armies: A Collection of Historical Accounts* 1-26 (2001)). In December 1863, General Patrick Cleburne authored a memorandum calling on the Confederacy to enlist and free slave soldiers, but this proposal met with resistance in the military, and President Jefferson Davis banned its publication. Nevertheless, President Davis's November 7, 1864 address to the Confederate Congress called upon the legislators to authorize the use of up to 40,000 slaves, if necessary, to support the war effort as laborers, pioneers, engineers, and in other similar roles, with the promise of freedom after their discharge. Thus, he called for an expansion of a February 17, 1864 act that authorized the impressment of up to 20,000 slaves in support of the war effort, if a sufficient number of free blacks could not be pressed into service for these defensive support roles. According to that act, the slaves were not to be freed as a result of their service; instead, their owners were to be compensated for lost wages and they were to be paid the slaves' values if, during the slaves' service, the slaves should die, be captured, or escape. *See generally, e.g.,* Stephanie McCurry, *Confederate Reckoning: Power and Politics in the Civil War South* 311-50 (2010); Scott Reynolds Nelson & Carol Sheriff, *A People at War: Civilians and Soldiers in America's Civil War, 1854-1877* 283-84 (2008); Bruce Levine, *Confederate Emancipation: Southern Plans to Free Slaves During the Civil War* 1-3, 27-29, 135 (2006); Ervin J. Jordan, Jr., *Black Confederates and Afro-Yankees in Civil War Virginia* 232-51 (1995) [hereinafter Jordan, *Black Confederates*]; Robert Franklin Durden, *The Gray and the Black: The Confederate Debate on Emancipation* 101-06 (1972); Degler, *supra* at 77-78; Benjamin Quarles, *The Negro in the Civil War* 276-81 (1953) (reprint ed. 1988); N. W. Stephenson, "The Question of Arming the Slaves," 18 *Am. Hist. Rev.* 295 (1913); *see also* Gerardo Gurza-Lavalle, "Slavery Reform in Virginia, 1816-1850" 242-50 (Ph.D. Dissertation, University of North Carolina at Chapel Hill, 2008). For the February 17, 1864 act, *see* "An act to increase the efficiency of the Army by the employment of free negroes and slaves in certain capacities," in Fred C. Ainsworth & Joseph W. Kirkley, *The War of the Rebellion: A Compilation of the Official Records of the Union and Confederate Armies, Series IV, Vol. III* 208 (1900) [hereinafter *Rebellion Records*]. For Davis's message, *see id.* at 797-99. For Lee's letter, *see id.* at 1012-13; Wesley, *supra* at 249-50.

[81] "An act to increase the military force of the Confederate States," in *Rebellion Records*,

supra at 1161; *see* McCurry, *supra* at 350-51; Levine, *supra* at 110-30; Jordan, *Black Confederates, supra* at 237-42; Durden, *supra* at 202-03; Degler, *supra* at 77; Gerardo Gurza-Lavalle, *supra* at 250-51; Wesley, *supra* at 251.

[82] *See Rebellion Records, supra* at 1161.

[83] *See id.; see also* Durden, *supra* at 268-70.

[84] *See Rebellion Records, supra* at 1162; McCurry, *supra*, at 350-51; Gerardo Gurza-Lavalle, *supra* at 251.

[85] Patterson, *Social Death, supra* at 211.

[86] Fede, *People Without Rights, supra* at 138; Oakes, *supra* at 32-33; Watson, *Americas, supra* at 24-25, 54-55, 89, 99, 121-22; Alan Watson, *Roman Slave Law* 90-101 (1987); Patterson, *Social Death, supra* at 182-86; Palmer, "Digest," *supra* at 112-13.

[87] Patterson, *Social Death, supra* at 185.

[88] *Id.* at 184.

[89] Alan Watson, "Roman Slave Law: An Anglo-American Perspective," 18 *Cardozo L. Rev.* 591, 595 (1996) [hereinafter Watson, "Anglo-American"].

[90] Patterson, *Social Death, supra* at 185-86; Thomas E. J. Wiedemann, *Greek and Roman Slavery* 47 (1981) [hereinafter Wiedemann, *Greek and Roman*].

[91] Patterson, *Social Death, supra* at 186.

[92] *See* Laird W. Bergad, *The Comparative Histories of Slavery in Brazil, Cuba, and the United States* 196 (2007); Rebecca Jarvis Scott, *Slave Emancipation in Cuba: The Transition to Free Labor, 1860-1899* 13-14 (2000); Berlin, *Many Thousands, supra* at 331-33; Morris, *Slavery, supra* at 380; Laird W. Bergad, Fe Iglesias Garcia, and Maria Del Carmen Barcia, *The Cuban Slave Market, 1790-1880* 123-44 (1995) [hereinafter Bergad, *Slave Market*]; Oakes, *supra* at 33; Watson, *Americas, supra* at 50-62, 121; Klein, *supra* at 196-200; Tannenbaum, *supra* at 54-56; Jennings, "Imperial Defense," *supra* at 124; Kimberly Welch, "Coartación," in 1 *Encyclopedia of Antislavery and Abolition* 173-74 (2007); de la Fuente, "Legal Rights," *supra* at 676-92; de la Fuente, "Slave Law," *supra* at 358-60; Barcia, *supra* at 168-69; Thomas N. Ingersoll, "Slave Codes and Judicial Practice in New Orleans, 1718-1807," 12 *Law & Hist. Rev.* 23, 43-46 (1995) [hereinafter Ingersoll, "Slave Codes"]; Hubert H. S. Aimes, "Coartación: A Spanish Institution for the Advancement of Slaves into Freedmen," 17 *Yale Rev.* 412 (1909); *see also* Johnson, *supra* at 261, 274.

[93] Watson, *Americas, supra* at 50.

[94] Palmer, "Digest," *supra* at 93, 107; *see* de la Fuente, "Legal Rights," *supra* at 659-61 (discussing a case in which a slave's price was decided).

[95] Hans W. Baade, "The *Gens de Couleur* of Louisiana: Comparative Slave Law in Microcosm," 18 *Cardozo L. Rev.* 535, 545-46 (1996) [footnote omitted] [hereinafter Baade, "Comparative"]; *see* de la Fuente, "Legal Rights," *supra* at 679-92 (after 1842 *curtados* had the legal right to demand a forced sale to another owner); Welch, *supra* at 174 (noting that Cuba's governor mandated to the contrary in 1871). On *coartación* in Spanish Florida, *see* Jane Landers, *Black Society in Spanish Florida* 2, 139-44 (1999).

[96] *See* Schafer, *Supreme Court, supra* at 3.

[97] *See Brief History, supra* at 22, 137-39; Herbert S. Klein and Francisco Vidal Luna, *Slavery in Brazil* 259-65 (2010); Watson, *Americas, supra* at 100 (noting that in 1830 it was held that a female slave who offered to pay a price for her freedom would be manumitted, and in 1831 a female slave was to be freed because the owner demanded an exorbitant price); *see also* Bergad, *Slave Market, supra* at 134-35 (discussing differences between laws and practices in Brazil and Cuba). Brazilian law also permitted freed slaves to purchase their spouses and children. *See* Watson, *Americas, supra* at 98.

[98] *See* Rebecca Hartkopf Schloss, *Sweet Liberty: The Final Days of Slavery in Martinique* 208 (2009); Bernard Moitt, *Women and Slavery in the French Antilles, 1635-1848* 151-72 (2001) [hereinafter Moitt, *Women and Slavery*]; Lawrence C. Jennings, *French Anti-Slavery: The Movement for the Abolition of Slavery in France 1802-1848* 83, 218 (2000); Bernard Moitt, "Pricing Freedom in the French Caribbean: Women, Men, Children, and Redemption from Slavery in the 1840s," in *Women and Slavery, Vol. 2, The Modern Atlantic* 159-69 (Gwyn Campbell, Suzanne Miers, and Joseph Calder Miller, eds.) (2008) [hereinafter Moitt, "Pricing Freedom"]. Slavery was abolished in the French colonies in 1848. *See* Drescher, *supra* at 281-82; *Brief History, supra* at 10.

[99] *See Brandon v. Planters' and Merchants' Bank of Huntsville*, 1 Stew. 320, 1828 WL 478 at *13 (Ala. 1828); T. Stephen Whitman, *The Price of Freedom: Slavery and Manumission in Baltimore and Early National Maryland* 113-14 (1997) [hereinafter Whitman]; Morris, *Slavery, supra* at 380-85; Oakes, *supra* at 33; Cobb, *supra* at 235, 240; Palmer, "Digest," *supra* at 93; de la Fuente, "Slave Law," *supra* at 368-69; Watson, *Americas, supra* at 121; Robert B. Robinson and James D. Hardy, Jr., "An Actio de Peculio in Ante-Bellum Alabama," 11 *J. of Legal Hist.* 364 (1990).

[100] Guyora Binder, "The Slavery of Emancipation," 17 *Cardozo L. Rev.* 2063, 2089 (1996), quoting Tushnet, *Humanity, supra* at 99; *see, e.g., Jarman v. Patterson*, 23 Ky. (7 T.B. Mon.) 644, 1828 WL 1332 (1828) (rejecting challenge to statute permitting arrest of self-contracting slaves); Schweninger, *Black Property Owners, supra* at 52-54; Finkelman, *Casebook, supra* at 127-28; Sumner Eliot Matison, "Manumission by Purchase," 33 *J. of Negro Hist.* 146, 155-56 (1948). On self-hiring, *see* Martin, *supra at* 159-87; Berlin, *Generations, supra* at 222-26; Berlin, *Many Thousands, supra* at 69, 136-37, 156-57, 317; Schweninger, *supra* at 54-56; Stampp, *supra* at 72-73, 96, 228.

[101] 9 Ala. 271 (1846).

[102] *Shanklin v. Johnson*, 9 Ala. at 271-72, 274-75.

[103] *Id.* at 271, 276.

[104] *See* Robinson and Hardy, *supra* at 368-69. The Court had previously noted, in *Brandon v. Planters' and Merchants' Bank of Huntsville*, 1 Stew. 320, 1828 WL 478 at *13, that the *peculium* was not adopted in the United States, and Johnson's counsel cited that case in *Shanklin*. *See Shanklin v. Johnson*, 9 Ala. at 274.

[105] *Id.*

[106] *Id.* at 275-76.

[107] *Id.* at 370, n. 14.

[108] *See* Robinson and Hardy, *supra* at 367.

[109] *Id.* at. 368 [footnote omitted].

[110] *Id.* at 369.

[111] *See id.* at 366-67.

[112] *See* Rose, *supra* at 176, quoting *Civil Code,* Art. 175; Palmer, "Digest," *supra* at 113.

[113] *See* Palmer, "Customs," *supra* at 217, n. 176, quoting I *Project of the Civil Code of 1825* 14 (1937).

[114] *See* Spear, *supra* at 194; Palmer, "Customs," *supra* at 217-18.

[115] *See, e.g., Redmond v. Murray,* 30 Mo. 570 (1860); *Jackson v. Bob,* 18 Ark. 399 (1857); *Norris, (of color) v. Patton's Adm'r,* 54 Ky. (15 B. Mon.) 575 (1855); *Major, (of color) v. Winn's Adm'r,* 52 Ky. (13 B. Mon.) 250 (1852); *Henry v. Nunn's Heirs,* 50 Ky. (11 B. Mon.) 239 (1850); *Wills, (of color) v. Bruce and Warfield,* 47 Ky. (8 B. Mon.) 548 (1848); *Stevenson v. Singleton,* 28 Va. (1 Leigh) 72 (1829) (and cases cited in note thereto); *Sawney v. Carter,* 27 Va. (6 Rand.) 173 (1828); *Richard v. Van Meter,* 20 F. Cas. 682 (D.C. Cir. 1827) (No. 11,763); *Letty v. Lowe,* 15 F. Cas. 411 (D.C. Cir. 1825) (No. 8,285); *Cooke v. Cooke,* 13 Ky. (3 Litt.) 238 (1823); *Fanny v. Kell,* 8 F. Cas. 995 (D.C. Cir. 1823) (No. 4,639); *Contee v. Garner,* 6 F. Cas. 361 (D.C. Cir. 1818) (No. 3,139); *Brown v. Wingard,* 4 F. Cas. 438 (D.C. Cir. 1822) (No. 2,034); *Beall v. Joseph,* 3 Ky. (Hard.) 51 (1806). *See also Anderson v. Poindexter,* 6 Ohio St. 622, 1856 WL 85 (1856) (under Kentucky law denying enforcement of promissory note given by slave and sureties to purchase freedom); *Blackman v. Gordon,* 19 S.C. Eq. (2 Rich. Eq.) 43 (1845) (anti-emancipation act could be retroactively applied to slave not freed); *Bland and Woolfolk v. Dowling,* 9 G. & J. 19, 1837 WL 1911 (Md. 1837) (master and slave cannot enter into contracts under Maryland law, but affirming freedom claimant's verdict on anti-importation statute).

[116] *See, e.g., Hall v. United States,* 92 U.S. 27, 30-31, 23 L. Ed. 597 (1875); *Woodland v. Newhall's Adm'r,* 31 F. 434, 438 (C.C. W.D. Va. 1887); *Bedford Trustee v. Williams, Adm'r,* 45 Tenn. (5 Cold.) 202, 1867 WL 2269 at *3 (1867); *Sanders v. Devereaux,* 25 Tex. Supp. 1, 1860 WL 5729 at *7 (1860); Wahl, *Burden, supra* at 163; Morris, *Slavery, supra* at 380-85; Fede, *People Without Rights, supra* at 138-39; Finkelman, *Casebook,* at 127-29; Stampp, *supra* at 197; Cobb, *supra* at 242, 303-04; Anthony R. Chase, "Race, Culture, and Contract Law: From the Cottonfield to the Courtroom," 28 *Conn. L. Rev.* 1, 31 (2005); Wahl, "Constraints," *supra* at 12-13 and n. 41; A. Leon Higginbotham, Jr. & Barbara K. Kopytoff, "Property First, Humanity Second: The Recognition of the Slave's Human Nature in Virginia Civil Law," 50 *Ohio State L.J.* 511, 525-28 (1989).

[117] *See* Shaw, *supra* at 166; Michael Grossberg, *Governing the Hearth: Law and the Family in Nineteenth-Century America* 129-33 (1985); Kolchin, *American Slavery, supra* at 122-27; Elkins, *supra* at 53-55; Genovese, *Roll, supra* at 32, 458-81; Stampp, *supra* at 198; Cobb, *supra* at 242-46; Goodell, *supra* at 106; Stroud, *supra* at 41; Burnham, *supra* at 206-14; Darlene C. Goring, "The History of Slave Marriage in the United States," 39 *J. Marshall L. Rev.* 299, 306-10, 316 (2006). Laws that did not permit interracial sex or slave marriage limited a path to freedom by which male slaves could employ "reproductive strategies ... to secure free birth for their children." *See* Paul Lokker, "Marriage as Slave Emancipation in the Seventeenth Century Rural Guatemala," 58 *The American* 175, 179 (2001).

[118] *Gist v. Toohey,* 31 S.C.L. (2 Rich.) 424, 1846 WL 2221 at *1 (1846).

[119] *Wills, (of color) v. Bruce and Warfield,* 47 Ky. (8 B. Mon.) 548, 1848 WL 3339 at *2

(1848) (affirming dismissal of plaintiff's freedom claim).

[120] *Id.*

[121] 22 Va. (1 Rand.) 15, 1821 WL 967 (1821).

[122] *Lewis v. Fullerton,* 1821 WL 967 at *1.

[123] *See id.* at *4.

[124] *See id.* at *3-*4.

[125] *See id.* at *5-*6.

[126] *See* Shaw, *supra* at 132; Finkelman, *Imperfect Union, supra* at 89, 189, n. 17; Cover, *Justice Accused, supra* at 97-98; Nash, "Reason of Slavery," *supra* at 133-34 (discussing the *Lewis* case); *see also* Timothy S. Huebner, *The Southern Judicial Tradition: State Judges and Sectional Distinctiveness, 1790-1890* 10-39 (1999) [hereinafter Huebner, *Tradition*] (biography including references to many of Roane's opinions during his 27 years on the Court of Appeals, but not *Lewis*). For the other issues in *Lewis, see* chapter 5 and chapter 8, *infra.* For the Kentucky decision affirming the dismissal of a similar freedom suit, *see Norris, (of color) v. Patton's Adm'r,* 54 Ky. (15 B. Mon.) 575 (1855).

[127] 30 Mo. 570, 1860 WL 6177 (1860).

[128] *Redmond v. Murray,* 1860 WL 6177 at *1.

[129] *Id.* at *3.

[130] *Id.,* citing *Sawney v. Carter,* 27 Va. (6 Rand.) 173 (1828) (affirming dismissal of claim filed based on freedom contract, even if slave had performed as agreed).

[131] *Id.* at *3.

[132] 18 Ark. 399, 1857 WL 607 (1857).

[133] *Jackson v. Bob,* 1857 WL 607 at *2-*3.

[134] *Id.* at *9 [citations omitted], *see* Stampp, *supra* at 199; L. Scott Stafford, "Slavery and the Arkansas Supreme Court," 19 *U. Ark. Little Rock L.J.* 413, 451-53 (1997).

[135] *See* Cobb, *supra* at 304.

[136] 4 Ky. (1 Bibb.) 422, 1809 WL 759 (1809), *see also Thompson v. Thompson,* 43 Ky. (4 B. Mon.) 502, 1844 WL 3503 (1844) (enforcing promissory note, consideration was co-owner's promise to free slave and obtain consent from the other co-owners); *Negro Cato v. Howard,* 2 H. & J. 323, 1808 WL 659 (Md. 1808) (reversing judgment against freedom claimant who was sold as a slave for life by the same seller who previously sold the slave for a term, and the first buyer executed and filed a manumission deed).

[137] *Thompson v. Wilmot,* 1809 WL 759 at *1.

[138] *Id.*

[139] *Id.* at *2.

[140] *Id.*

[141] *Id.* The appellate court also affirmed the money judgment. *Id.* at *3, *see* chapter 9, *infra* at notes 126-29.

[142] *See* Jones, *Fathers, supra* at 68-97.

143 *Id.* at 75.

144 *See, e.g., Norris (of color) v. Patton's Adm'r*, 54 Ky. (15 B. Mon.) 575, 1855 WL 4178 (1855); *Hawkins v. Hawkins*, 52 Ky. (13 B. Mon.) 245, 1852 WL 3401 (1852); *Wills, (of color) v. Bruce and Warfield*, 47 Ky. (8 B. Mon.) 548, 1848 WL 3339 (1848); *Peter Cooke (a person of color) v. Cooke*, 13 Ky. (3 Litt.) 238, 1823 WL 1154 (1823) (all affirming dismissal of plaintiffs' freedom claims); *see also Winn v. Sam Martin (of color)*, 61 Ky. (4 Met.) 231, 1863 WL 2544 at *3-*4 (1863) (reversing freedom judgment and dismissing petition, noting that alleged manumission agreement between freedom claimant and his owner "could not be enforced."); *Gatlif's Adm'r v. Rose*, 47 Ky. (8 B. Mon.) 629, 1848 WL 3356 at *4 (1848) (reversing freedom judgment, ordering new trial, and noting that freedom claimant cannot sue to enforce executory contract between free persons for her manumission); *Dunlap and Collins v. Archer*, 37 Ky. (7 Dana.) 30, 1838 WL 2266 at *2 (1838) (reversing judgment denying manumission and ordering new trial, and noting that freedom claimant could claim rights based upon a manumission deed and not an executory manumission contract).

145 *See* Cobb, *supra* at 304.

146 26 Tenn. (7 Hum.) 92, 1848 WL 1497 (1846).

147 *Ford v. Ford,* 1848 WL 1497 at *2.

148 On the Ford case, *see* Jones, *Fathers, supra* at 35-36; Fede, *People Without Rights, supra* at 146-47; Arthur F. Howington, *What Sayeth the Law: The Treatment of Slaves and Free Blacks in the State and Local Courts of Tennessee* 1-27 (1986) [hereinafter Howington, *What Sayeth*]; Arthur F. Howington, "Not in the Condition of a Horse or an Ox: Ford v. Ford, the Law of Testamentary Manumission and the Tennessee Courts' Recognition of Slave Humanity," 34 *Tenn. Historical Q.* 269 (1975).

149 40 Tenn. (3 Head.) 275, 1859 WL 3454 (1859).

150 *See Isaac (a man of color) v. Farnsworth*, 1859 WL 3454 at *1.

151 *See id.* at *3. The Supreme Court modified the judgment only to allow McCampbell "a credit for the unexpired term of about fifteen months, for which he satisfied George on obtaining possession." *Id.* at *3.

152 This decision is cited and discussed by Morris, *Slavery, supra* at 382-83 and Howington, *What Sayeth, supra* at 66.

153 *See* Shaw, *supra* at 92.

154 *See* Morris, *Slavery, supra* at 381-83, citing *McCloud and Karnes v. Chiles*, 41 Tenn. (1 Cold.) 248 (1860); *Isaac v. Sigler*, 40 Tenn. (3 Head.) 214 (1859); *Lewis v. Simonton*, 27 Tenn. (8 Hum.) 185 (1847); Howington, *What Sayeth, supra* at 56 (citing petitions to free slaves by owners who entered into contracts freeing slaves).

155 *McCloud and Karnes v. Chiles*, 41 Tenn. (1 Cold.), 1860 WL 3046 at *2 (finding for slaves freed by will that testator did not revoke).

156 *See* Shaw, *supra* at 92.

157 "An act concerning free persons of colour, and for other purposes," in *Public Acts of the State of Tennessee 1831*, ch. 102, §2 at 121-22 (1832) [hereinafter *Tennessee Acts, 1831*]; Howington, *What Sayeth, supra* at 34.

158 "An act to explain an act entitled, 'an act concerning free persons of color, and for other purposes, passed December 16, 1831,'" in *Public Acts of the State of Tennessee 1833*, ch. 81 at 99-100 (1833) [hereinafter *Tennessee Acts, 1833*]; *see* Howington, *What Sayeth*, *supra* at 35; *Jameson Adm'rs v. McCoy*, 52 Tenn. (5 Heisk.) 108, 1871 WL 3741 at *4 (1871); *Greenlow v. Rawlings*, 22 Tenn. (3 Hum.) 90, 1852 WL 1885 at *2-*3 (1842) (discussing 1777, 1801, 1831, and 1833 statutes); Wahl, *Burden*, *supra* at 253, n. 116; 2 Catterall, *supra* at 479-80.

159 "An act to Amend the Act of 1842, ch. 191," in *Acts of the State of Tennessee 1849-50*, ch. 107 at 300 (1850) [hereinafter *Tennessee Acts, 1849-50*]; *see* Howington, *What Sayeth*, *supra* at 39; *see also* chapter 3, *infra* at notes 108-14.

160 11 Hening, *supra* at 308; *see* Shaw, *supra* at 103; Finkelman, *Casebook*, *supra* at 111; Quarles, *Revolution*, *supra* at 184.

161 *See* note 76, *supra*; Herbert Aptheker, ed., *A Documentary History of the Negro People in the United States* 13-14 (1951); Walter Clark, ed., *The State Records of North Carolina, Vol. XIX, 1782-1784* 552 (1901) (legislative committee's May 4, 1784 report recommending a statute freeing Griffin for "meritorious services"); *see also* Neimeyer, *supra* at 88. Herbert Aptheker noted Griffin was honorably discharged after serving from June 1781 to July 1782, and that Griffin's petition was supported by his honorable discharge dated July 1, 1782 and a March 27, 1784 affidavit of Joseph Fort. *See* Aptheker, "Edward Griffin, Revolutionary Soldier," 13 *Negro Hist. Bulletin* 38 (November 1949). Douglas Egerton suggested that the legislature's action may have been influenced by Griffin's allegation that Kitchen was a deserter, and its "disdain for Kitchen's cowardice rather than any general support for black liberation." Egerton, *supra* at 159. *See also Payne v. Richardson*, 67 Ky. (4 Bush) 207, 1868 WL 4076 (1868) (in an action to collect on a loan allegedly made by one former slave soldier to another, holding that slave owners who during the Civil War offered slaves as suitable substitutes for themselves or others in the United States military thereby manumitted slaves and were not entitled to compensation).

162 *See* Berlin, *Generations*, *supra* at 94-95; Berlin, *Many Thousands*, *supra* at 331-33; Tannenbaum, *supra* at 54-55; Palmer, "Customs," *supra* at 210; Baade, "Comparative," *supra* at 545-46.

163 *See* Schafer, *Becoming Free*, *supra* at 3-4; Morris, *Slavery*, *supra* at 384; Schafer, *Supreme Court*, *supra* at 224; Rose, *supra* at 176, quoting *Civil Code*, Art. 177; Palmer, "Digest," *supra* at 93, 107; Baade, "Comparative," *supra* at 574, 581; *see also* Cobb, *supra* at 242 (noting that Louisiana enforced manumission contracts between masters and slaves).

164 Schafer, *Supreme Court*, *supra* at 224; *see also* Palmer, "Customs," *supra* at 210; Shawn Cole, "Capitalism and Freedom: Manumissions and the Slave Market in Louisiana, 1725-1820," 65 *J. of Economic Hist.* 1008, 1012-14 (2005).

165 *See* Schafer, *Becoming Free*, *supra* at 3-4, 45-58; Schafer, *Supreme Court*, *supra* at 220-34.

166 *Id.* at 225.

167 *Victoire v. Dussuau*, 4 Mart. (o.s.) 212, 1816 WL 970 (La. 1816) (affirming dismissal of freedom suit in which plaintiff offered parol testimony to prove contract).

[168] After 1807, slaves could be manumitted if they were thirty years old and had exhibited "honest conduct" during the four years before manumission. *See* Schafer, *Becoming Free*, *supra* at 4.

[169] *Id.* at 58.

[170] Louisiana Supreme Court Case No. 3706 (1854), cited in Schafer, *Supreme Court*, *supra* at 231.

[171] *See id.*

[172] 10 La. Ann. 239, 1855 WL 4414 (La. 1855).

[173] *Hardesty v. Wormley*, 1855 WL 4414 at * 1.

[174] *Id.* at *2.

[175] 2 Mart. (n.s.) 171, 1824 WL 1613 (La. 1824).

[176] *Doubrere v. Grillier's Syndic*, 1824 WL 1613 at *1.

[177] *Id.* at *3. Schafer suggests that the result may have been different if any of the creditors were secured rather than unsecured creditors. *See* Schafer, *Supreme Court, supra* at 227.

[178] *See* Berlin, *Generations, supra* at 95; Morris, *Slavery, supra* at 380, 384-85; Watson, *Americas, supra* at 50-62, 121-22. On the debate on the number of slaves in Cuba who were *coratados*, *see* Jarvis Scott, *supra* at 13-14.

[179] *See* Schafer, *Supreme Court, supra* at 224; Stampp, *supra* at 96-97; Schweninger, "Slave Women," *supra* at 391-92; *but see* Ingersoll, "Slave Codes," *supra* at 36-37, 61-62 (suggesting the need to compare customs and practices as well as the legal provisions when analyzing these issues).

[180] "An Act to prohibit the emancipation of slaves," in *Acts Passed by the Legislature of Louisiana, 1857* No. 69 at 55 (1857); *see* chapter 3, *infra* at note 107.

[181] 13 La. Ann. 599, 1858 WL 5217 (La. 1858).

[182] *See id.* (judgment for non-suit entered instead of dismissal); *see also, e.g.*, enforcing the 1857 Act and entering non-suit against slaves in other contexts, *Price. v. Ray*, 14 La. Ann. 697, 1859 WL 5929 (La. 1858); *Pauline, f.w.c. v. Hubert*, 14 La. Ann. 161, 1859 WL 5785 (La. 1859); *George v. Demouy*, 14 La. Ann. 145, 1859 WL 6041 (La. 1859); *Pelagie Brown, f.w.c. v. Raby*, 14 La. Ann. 41, 1859 WL 5770 (La. 1859); *Jamison v. Bridge*, 14 La. Ann. 31, 1859 WL 5762 (La. 1859); *Delphine v. Guillet*, 13 La. Ann. 248, 1858 WL 5097 (La. 1858); Schafer, *Becoming Free, supra* at 54-58, 89-90; Schafer, *Supreme Court, supra* at 248-49.

[183] 2 *Laws of the State of Delaware, 1700 to 1797* 1321 (1797) [hereinafter *Laws of Delaware*]. *See Wilson v. George*, 2 Del. Cas. 413, 1818 WL 1171 at *6 (Err. & App. 1818); Patience Essah, *A House Divided: Slavery and Emancipation in Delaware, 1638-1865* 41 (1996); Williams, *Slavery and Freedom in Delaware, supra* at 156-57; 2 Hurd, *supra* at 76-77.

[184] Lacy K. Ford, *Deliver Us from Evil: The Slavery Question in the Old South* 32 (2009); *see Wilson v. George*, 2 Del. Cas. 413, 1818 WL 1171 at *6-*7 (oral manumission contracts invalid).

[185] *Revised Statutes of the State of Delaware to 1852* 253 (1852) [hereinafter *Revised*

Delaware Statutes]; Ford, *supra* at 32; Essah, *supra* at 104-07; Williams, *Slavery and Freedom in Delaware, supra* at 157-58; 2 Hurd, *supra* at 78.

[186] *See* Seth Rockman, *Scraping By: Wage Labor, Slavery, and Survival in Early Baltimore* 60, 112-14 (2009); Whitman, *supra* at 96-118; Christopher Phillips, *Freedom's Port: The African American Community of Baltimore, 1790-1860* 36-56 (1997) [hereinafter Phillips, *Freedom's Port*]; *see also* Ford, *supra* at 33; Stephen Whitman, "Diverse Good Causes: Manumission and the Transformation of Urban Slavery," 19 *Social Science Hist.* 333, 350-51 (1995).

[187] *See Laws of Maryland*, 1796, ch. 67, §29; Proceedings and Acts of the General Assembly, 1752-1754, ch. 1; Brackett, *supra* at 149-53.

[188] *Laws of Maryland*, 1810, ch. 15, §3.

[189] *Laws of Maryland, 1817*, ch. 112; Whitman, *supra* at 101, 111.

[190] *Laws of Maryland, 1831*, ch. 281, §12; Brackett, *supra* at 164-67.

[191] *Laws of Maryland, 1832*, ch. 296, §4; Whitman, *supra* at 98.

[192] *See Bland and Woolfolk v. Dowling*, 1837 WL 1911 at *6-*8; Whitman, *supra* at 102.

[193] *See Negro Anna Maria Wright v. Rogers*, 9 G. & J. 181, 1837 WL 1204 (Md. 1837).

[194] *See, e.g., Wilson v. Negro Ann Barnett*, 9 G. & J. 158, 1837 WL 1917 (Md. 1837); Morris, *Slavery, supra* at 390-92; Barbara Jeanne Fields, *Slavery and Freedom on the Middle Ground: Maryland during the Nineteenth Century* 36 (1985) [hereinafter Fields, *Slavery and Freedom*].

[195] *See Anderson v. Negro Julia Ann Baily*, 8 G. & J. 32, 1836 WL 1867 (Md. 1836) (reversing freedom judgment because of claimant's age when "right" to freedom arose); *but see Negro Henry Rozier v. Holliday*, 8 Md. 381, 1855 WL 3827 (1855); *Tongue v. Negroes Crissy, Rhody and others*, 7 Md. 453, 1855 WL 3801 (1855) (reversing judgments against freedom claimant based upon 1831 statute that permits slaves of any age to receive freedom by will).

[196] 9 G. & J. 19, 1837 WL 1911 (Md. 1837).

[197] *See Bland and Woolfolk v. Negro Beverly Dowling*, 1837 WL 1911 at *8; *see also* Rockman, *supra* at 183-84 (discussing the facts in the *Dowling* case).

[198] *See Bland and Woolfolk v. Negro Beverly Dowling*, 1837 WL 1911 at *6; *see also Wicks v. Chew*, 4 H. & J. 543, 1819 WL 947 (Md. 1819) (reversing freedom judgment because manumission deed was not recorded and was not a contract that slaves could enforce); *Brown v. Wingard*, 4 F. Cas. 438 (D.C. Cir. 1822) (No. 2,034) (denying claim based on manumission contract confirmed in writing and partly performed by slave).

[199] *See Negro Andrew Franklin v. Waters Exc'r*, 8 Gill 322, 1849 WL 3212 (Md. 1849).

[200] *See* chapter 9, *infra* at notes 104-21.

[201] *See* 1 *The Maryland Code*, Art. 66, §§38-41 at 457 (1860) [hereinafter *Maryland Code*]; Rockman, *supra* at 60; Whitman, *supra* at 112-13; *Patterson v. Crookshanks*, 7 Gill 211, 1848 WL 2976 (Md. 1848) (discussing statutes).

[202] *See* 1 *Maryland Code, supra*, Art. 66, §§42-43 at 458; Brackett, *supra* at 171, 173; 2 Hurd, *supra* at 24.

[203] *See* 1 *Maryland Code, supra,* Art. 66, §42, at 458.

[204] Baade, "Bifurcated," *supra* at 1490-93; Watson, "Anglo-American," *supra* at 594.

[205] Watson, *Americas, supra* at 36.

[206] *See, e.g.,* Phillips, "Manumission," *supra* at 43; Debra G. Blumenthal, "The Promise of Freedom in Late Medieval Valencia," in *Paths to Freedom, supra* at 51-68; Jennings, "Imperial Defense," *supra* in *id.* at 124; Grinberg, "Manumission," in *id.* at 219-34; Baade, "Bifurcated," *supra* at 1493-97; *see also* Robert J. Cottrol, "Normative Nominalism: The Paradox of Egalitarian Law in Inegalitarian Cultures—Some Lessons from Recent Latin-American Historiography," 81 *Tulane L. Rev.* 889, 905 (2007) [hereinafter Cottrol, "Normative Nominalism"].

[207] Grinberg, "Alforria," *supra* at 64-65.

[208] For discussions of cases invoking promissory estoppel, *see* Kevin M. Teeven, "A Legal History of Binding Gratuitous Promises at Common Law: Justified Reliance and Moral Obligation," 43 *Duq. L. Rev.* 11, 14-60 (2004); Eric Mills Holmes, "Restatement of Promissory Estoppel," 32 *Willamette L. Rev.* 263, 277-88 (1996).

[209] 1 S.C.L. (1 Bay) 260 (1792).

[210] *Guardian of Sally v. Beaty,* 1 S.C.L. (1 Bay) at 260. *See* Chapter 4, *infra* at notes 140-46, discussing the 1740 statute.

[211] *Guardian of Sally v. Beaty,* 1 S.C.L. (1 Bay) at 260. Although the Southern states outlawed his practice of self-hiring, it apparently persisted in practice, especially in South Carolina, into the nineteenth century. *See, e.g.,* Martin, *supra* at 165.

[212] *Guardian of Sally v. Beaty,* 1 S.C.L. (1 Bay) at 260.

[213] *Id.*

[214] *See* Teeven, *supra* at 60-90; Holmes, *supra* at 277-88. It appears that the Connecticut Superior Court enforced a master's promise to free a slave when the slave reached the age of 25 years. *See* David Menschel, "Abolition Without Deliverance: The Law of Connecticut Slavery 1784-1848," 111 *Yale L.J.* 183, 200-01 (2001), citing *Geer v. Huntington,* 2 Root 364 (Conn. Super. Ct. 1796). The Pennsylvania Supreme Court also suggested that a master's promise to free two captured runaway slaves if they served him for four years was enforceable after the slaves performed their end of the bargain. The court awarded damages to a plaintiff who bought one of the slaves as a slave for life, because the manumission contract was not disclosed. *See Stiles v. Richardson,* 4 Yeats 82, 1804 WL 943 (Pa. 1804); *see also State v. Adm'ns of Prall,* 1 N.J.L. 4 (Sup. Ct. 1790) (suggesting that master's oral declarations that he intended to free a slave upon his death were either evidence of a present conditional manumission or that "the obligation of this promise is binding" on the decedents' representatives).

[215] Cobb, *supra* at 242, n.7, 304, n. 3.

[216] Stroud, *supra* at 32.

[217] Peter Charles Hoffer, *The Law's Conscience: Equitable Constitutionalism in America* 112 (1990).

[218] Wahl, *Burden, supra* at 253, n. 116; Wahl, "Constraints," *supra* at 13, n. 41. Morris discussed the decision twice in his book. Morris, *Slavery, supra* at 49-50, 381; *see* Wendy

Brown-Scott, "Anita Hill Meets Godzilla: Confessions of a Horror Movie Fan," 70 *Tulane L. Rev.* 1921, 1941 (1996) (discussing the decision); Nash, "Reason of Slavery," *supra* at 73; A. E. Keir Nash, "Negro Rights, Unionism, and Greatness on the South Carolina Court of Appeals: The Extraordinary Chief Justice John Belton O'Neall," 21 *S.C. L. Rev.* 141, 176, n. 138 (1969) [hereinafter Nash, "Negro Rights"].

[219] The quotation is from Justice O'Neall's dissenting opinion in *Vinyard v. Passalaigue*, 33 S.C.L. (2 Strob.) 536, 1848 WL 2463 at *8 (1848) (dissenting from majority holding that presumption of manumission no longer applied if evidence produced that slaves were permitted to be free for 20 years).

[220] *See Blakely v. Tisdale*, 35 S.C. Eq. (14 Rich. Eq.) 90, 1868 WL 2633 at *6 (1868) (holding that slaves freed in 1865 could recover nothing under the will of their former master).

[221] *Carmille v. Carmille's Administrator*, 27 S.C.L. (2 McMul.) 190, 198 (1842).

[222] 31 S.C.L. (2 Rich.) 424 (1846).

[223] *Id.; see also, e.g., Sanders v. Devereaux*, 25 Tex. Supp. 1, 1860 WL 5729 at *7-*8 (1860) (contract with slaves for sale of cotton not enforceable).

[224] 5 Tex. 535, 1851 WL 3918 (1851).

[225] *Guess v. Lubbock, Adm'r*, 1851 WL 3918 at *6, *8.

[226] *Id.* at *6, citing *Swenson v. Walker's Administrator*, 3 Tex. 93, 1848 WL 3871 (1848) (in which Lipscomb stated the court examined estoppel "with a great deal of care and attention").

[227] *See Guess v. Lubbock, Adm'r.*, 1851 WL 3918 at *2; *see also* Mark Davidson, "One Woman's Fight for Freedom: *Guess v. Lubbock*," 45 *Houston Lawyer* 10 (Jan./Feb. 2008) (discussing the case in detail).

[228] *Guess v. Lubbock, Adm'r.*, 1851 WL 3918 at *6.

[229] *Id.* at *6-*9.

[230] Davidson, *supra* at 14.

[231] *Id.*

[232] Peter Karstens, *Heart Versus Head: Judge Made Law in Nineteenth Century America* 15-20 (1997); *see* Kevin M. Teeven, "The Advent of Recovery on Market Transactions in the Absence of a Bargain," 46 *Am. Bus. L.J.* 289 (2002); Kevin M. Teeven, "Origins and Scope of the American Moral Obligation Principle," 46 *Cleveland St. L. Rev.* 585 (1998); Alfred L. Brophy, "Reason and Sentiment: The Moral Worlds of Reasoning of Antebellum Jurists," 79 *Boston U.L. Rev.* 1161, 1181 (1997) (book review). *See also* James W. Fox, Jr., "The Law of Many Faces: Antebellum Contract Law Background of Reconstruction-Era Freedom of Contract," 49 *Am. J. of Legal Hist.* 61, 66-112 (2007) (discussing the literature on antebellum contract law).

[233] 8 Ala. 131 (1845) (plaintiff denied damages after relocating in reliance on brother-in-law's promise of residence on his land). *See* William R. Casto and Val D. Ricks, "'Dear Sister Antillico...': The Story of *Kirksey v. Kirksey*," 94 *Geo. L.J.* 321 (2006); Holmes, *supra* at 301, n. 94.

[234] *See, e.g., Vance v. Wells & Co.,* 8 Ala. 399 (1845); *Scott v. Carruth,* 17 Tenn. (9 Yer.) 418 (1836); *McMorris v. Herndon,* 18 S.C.L. (2 Bail.) 56 (1831); *Cardwell's Adm'rs v. Strother,* 16 Ky. (Litt. Sel. Cas.) 429, 1821 WL 1239 (1821).

[235] *See* Fede, "Slave Buyers," *supra;* Judith K. Schafer, "'Guaranteed Against the Vices and Maladies Prescribed by Law': Consumer Protection, the Law of Slave Sales, and the Louisiana Supreme Court, 1809-1862," 31 *Am. J. of Legal Hist.* 306 (1987); *see also* Karstens, *supra* at 53-56; Robert E. Mensel, "'A Diddle at Brobdingag': Confidence and Caveat Emptor During the Market Revolution," 38 *U. Memphis L. Rev.* 97, 100, 134 (2007).

[236] *See, e.g.,* Gross, *Double Character, supra* at 47-71; Edward L. Ayers, *Vengeance and Justice: Crime and Punishment in the 19-th-Century American South* 9-33 (1984); Jason A. Gillmer, "Poor Whites, Benevolent Masters and Ideologies of Slavery: The Local Trial of a Slave Accused of Rape," 85 *N.C. L. Rev.* 489, 527-40 (2007); William W. Fisher, III, "Ideology and Imagery in the Law of Slavery" (a revised and expanded version of an article published in 68 *Chi.-Kent L. Rev.* 1051 (1993)) (discussing concept of honor and pro-slavery thought), in Paul Finkelman, ed., *Slavery and the Law* 59-68 (1997) [hereinafter *Slavery and the Law*].

[237] In fact, Jenny Bourne Wahl noted an Alabama statute of 1834 "forbade manumission by contract[.]" Wahl, *Burden, supra* at 253, n. 116; Wahl, "Constraints," *supra* at 13, n. 41.

[238] *Summers v. Bean,* 56 Va. (13 Gratt.) 404, 413 (1856); *see* Fede, *People Without Rights, supra* at 202-06.

[239] Peter Linzer, "On the Amorality of Contract Remedies—Efficiency, Equity and the Second *Restatement,*" 81 *Colum. L. Rev.* 111, 138-39 (1981) [footnotes omitted].

[240] *See* Marion Brunson Lucas, *A History of Blacks in Kentucky: From Slavery to Segregation, 1760-1891* 52 (2d ed. 2003); *see also id.* at 52-57 (discussing examples).

[241] *See* Olwell, "Becoming Free," *supra* at 8 (discussing the records of the manumission of Tartar, who was promised that he would be freed in 1748 and instead was freed in 1768).

[242] *See Spencer v. Negro Dennis,* 8 Gill 314, 1849 WL 3211 at *4 (Md. 1849).

[243] *See* Michael Les Benedict, "Comment on Guyora Binder, 'The Slavery of Emancipation,'" 17 *Cardozo L. Rev.* 2103, 2109 (1996).

[244] Wedgwood, *supra* at 1394.

[245] Guyora Binder, "The Slavery of Emancipation," 17 *Cardozo L. Rev.* 2063, 2086-97 (1996).

[246] *See id.* at 2087.

3

The Statutes Regulating and Prohibiting Manumission and Permitting Voluntary Enslavement

The masters' right to free their slaves did not require "permission or sanction of the law to give it validity and effect" because slave masters, like any other property owners, had the power "to renounce" their property rights.[1] Writing for the United States Supreme Court, Justice Smith Thompson noted that "it would seem a little extraordinary to contend, that the owner of property is not at liberty to renounce his right to it, either absolutely, or in any modified manner he may think proper. As between the owner and his slave, it would require the most explicit prohibition by law, to restrain this right." Nevertheless, Thompson also stated that "[c]onsiderations of policy, with respect to this species of property, may justify legislative regulation, as to the guards and checks under which such manumission shall take place; especially so as to provide against the public's becoming chargeable for the maintenance of slaves so manumitted."[2]

We therefore should not be surprised to read that lawmakers in the United States South, as in most slave societies, enacted laws regulating the owners' rights to exercise this power. What is surprising, however, is the trend in the late antebellum law by which some legislatures eliminated the masters' right to renounce their property in slaves through manumission.

The common law required property owners to maintain their property so that it did not become a threat to the public health, safety, and welfare. Those who breached this duty and failed to properly maintain their property, such as owners who abandoned sick animals on the public square, committed a public nuisance. These property owners were potentially liable in civil tort actions for damages that the nuisance caused to others.[3] They also could be prosecuted under the common law of crimes for creating a public nuisance.[4]

When people began to hold slaves in a state or colony, they presumed that they, like other chattel owners, had the right to hold, use, or dispose of their slaves as they wished, as long as they did not create a public nuisance or thereby injure any other person's rights or the perceived public interest. The Southern legislators and courts, at various times and in different ways, therefore expressly limited the individual master's manumission rights, based upon the way the lawmakers evaluated public policy considerations. The law thus regulated the owner's power to abandon slaves who could not support themselves, or whose liberty was to be at the expense of the master's creditors.[5]

The general trend in the law in the Southern states shifted from a pro-manumission or neutral approach that merely mitigated manumission's potentially harmful effects in individual cases, to one that increasingly regulated and eventually prohibited manumission in the years leading up to the Civil War. "The master's right to free his slaves shrank as slavery expanded."[6]

This chapter first reviews Virginia's manumission laws to illustrate these trends. This pattern of change in law provides an example of how the Southern elected leaders' changing attitudes toward manumission law paralleled the social, political, economic, and intellectual/religious developments in the South. These legal changes illustrate how the pattern by which slave law evolved in Virginia and the other Southern states can best be described in relation to these non-law box developments, and not as a more or less autonomous process.

This chapter also refers to the law regulating manumission in other slave societies, to shed light on the Southern manumission law. This approach also helps us to fully understand the significance of the truly unique ultimate legal trend prohibiting all manumissions and encouraging the "voluntary" enslavement of free blacks.

The Changing Pattern of the Virginia Manumission Statutes

In the early years of settlement in Virginia, the law legitimized slavery as it became an accepted practice in custom.[7] Consistent with common law property ownership principles, the early colonists apparently presumed that the law permitted them to enslave, buy, hold, and free both Africans and Native Americans, and masters began exercising the right to free their slaves as early as the 1640s.[8] Some of the former slaves, such as Anthony Johnson, even owned land and slaves.[9]

This is not surprising. The first settlement phase consisted of years of "rough equality" in Virginia, as well as most of the other slave colonies and later the slave states. Settlement began with this frontier period, which was a time of great opportunity and hardship. The settlers of a new territory initially were preoccupied with subsistence agriculture and establishing a permanent settlement. Plantation agriculture eventually began to replace subsistence agriculture, but slaves were still relatively few in number, and slave holdings remained relatively small.[10]

A more defined law of slavery began to emerge in what I have called the slave boom. This period of development started when the settlers discovered a profitable combination of crop, soil, and climate, and when farmers began to grow this crop for sale. Farms tended to increase in size, and the sizes of slave holdings also grew. The relative size of slave populations also increased during this period.[11]

In Virginia, tobacco was the "magic" cash crop. It did not require large slave holdings; thus, plantation agriculture began before the slave boom. Nevertheless, slave labor became widely employed by the end of the seventeenth century when the tobacco boom took off.[12]

After first attempting to enslave some Indians and Africans, Virginia's colonists relied on black slaves in greater numbers after 1680. Virginia's population statistics illustrate this general development pattern. Between 1620 and 1680, Virginia's black population grew steadily but slowly from .09% to 6.9%. In the next decade, however, the black population tripled, to 17.6%, and by 1700 it grew to 28%.[13] In that period, the predominant social and legal concerns apparently shifted from survival to slave control. Accordingly, the Virginia colonists adopted a series of laws addressing their concerns about slavery, and in 1705, they adopted the colony's first comprehensive slave code.[14]

Of course, not all of Virginia's slaves were black and not all blacks were slaves, but by 1690 the free black population became "an object of suspicion and fear."[15] The increasing number of free blacks apparently was one of the main concerns that motivated the legislators to impose restraints on the masters' right to free their slaves.

This fear of free blacks is confirmed by Virginia's 1691 act, which was the first of the free black exclusion statutes in what would become the United States. In the act's preamble, the lawmakers found that "great inconveniences may happen to this country by the setting of negroes and mullatoes free, by either entertaining negro slaves from their masters['] service, or receiving stolen goods, or being grown old bringing a charge upon" the public.

The act therefore declared that "no negro or mulatto be ... set free by any person," unless that person, or his "heirs, executors, or administrators pay for the transportation" of the freed slave "out of the country [sic]" within six months, "upon penalty of paying of tenn [sic] pounds sterling to the Church wardens of the parish where such person shall dwell with, which money, or so much thereof as shall be necessary, the said Church wardens are to cause the said negro or mulatto to be transported out of the countrey[.]" Any remainder of the fine was to be for "the use of the poor of the parish."[16]

According to Anthony Parent, we should read this and other acts regulating manumission in the context of Virginia's legislators' efforts "to undermine free black society." He stated that the act's preamble confirms the legislators' intent to end a "mean-spirited and cruel practice" of some slave owners, who apparently were manumitting older and infirm slaves and sending them off the plantations "to fend for themselves." Parent added that this 1691 act should not be understood as "a humanitarian gesture, however, but [as] an effort to halt superannuated blacks from being wards of the parish. Limiting the local burden was only a part of the government's larger project to restrict the manumission of the enslaved and thus impede the accretion of free blacks."[17]

Some Virginians nevertheless read the 1691 statute in favor of freedom. They understood the act's preamble to express the legislators' intention to permit masters to free slaves if the masters provided a means to prevent the freed slaves from becoming charges to the community. Others responded with the belief that the act thus did not sufficiently limit the colony's free black population's growth. "In 1713, the Council of State, responding to a directive from the governor, reviewed a report from the justices of Norfolk County in which it was related that the late John Fulcher, a planter in Norfolk, had used this qualification to free, through his will, sixteen blacks and had given them a 'considerable Tract of Land in fee simple.'" The council asked the assembly to pass a law prohibiting these manumissions, "fearing the potential damage over time of the freed slaves' 'increase and correspondence with other Slaves.'"[18] The assembly did not immediately adopt the recommended manumission reform legislation.

In the years that followed the 1691 act, Virginia's black population growth continued to increase to 28% in 1700, 29.5% in 1710, and 30.2% in 1720. It hovered between 40% and 45% from 1750 to 1860.[19] These statistics illustrate how Virginia progressed through its slave population boom to the mature plantation period. During this period, the size of the larger slaveholdings generally increased and an elite planter class emerged. Parent noted that "Virginia's white society" evidenced "dangerous fissures" as tensions developed among members of the classes of planters, small slave owners, and non-slave owning whites. Therefore, white social and economic issues began to compete with slave control as the dominant concerns of the elite planter class, causing the elite to believe that the greater public interest required the law to at times regulate the freedom of non-slave owning whites and even individual masters.[20]

The legislature finally responded to the call for manumission reform legislation in 1723 with a statute that prohibited manumissions of "negro, mulatto, or Indian slaves, ... except for some meritorious service, to be adjudged and allowed by the governor and council," which were to issue a license before the slave was freed. If a master freed a slave without obtaining this approval, the statute "authorized and required" the "churchwardens of the parish" where the freed slave lived for one month "to take up and sell" the slave. The church was permitted to apply the sale proceeds to the use of the parish.[21]

The governor and council apparently did not readily approve manumissions under this meritorious service standard.[22] For one example, in 1729, they freed "a very old" man slave known as James Pawpaw or Papan, who discovered "a concoction of roots and barks" with which "wonderful cures could be effected," and, accordingly, it was then "known how to cure slaves without mercury."[23]

Between 1777 and 1783, Virginia's general assembly adopted acts freeing nine slaves.[24] Only two of these acts mentioned the meritorious service standard; an October 1779 act freed a slave named Kitt because he exposed a counterfeiting ring and the act approved a payment to his owner, and an October 1783 act freed a slave named Aberdeen for his years of "public service in the lead mines."[25]

In the years before the Revolution, some of Virginia's slave owners, most notably the Quakers, sought legislation restoring their right to manumit some or all of their slaves.[26] It was not until 1782, however, and on the fourth try, that Virginia's legislators adopted legislation that permitted masters to free their slaves. Other bills that were not adopted were introduced in 1769, 1778, and 1780, and Thomas Jefferson was a legislative supporter of the first of these proposals.[27]

The 1782 act was a general manumission statute. It permitted masters, in their wills or in their lifetimes, to free some or all of their slaves, as long as the masters satisfied certain conditions. "As one would expect from an act written largely by slaveholders elected by fellow slaveholders," this act "protected the safety and interests of white society, especially property rights, as the previous bills had done."[28]

In an apparent attempt to limit fraudulent manumission claims, the act required that the master express his or her intention "in writing, under his or her hand and seal, attested and proved to the county court by two witnesses," or that the master's intention be acknowledged by the court in the county in which the master resided. Masters had to pay for and provide the freed slaves with a certified copy of their freedom papers. Justices of the peace were authorized to jail any freed slaves "traveling out of his or her county of residence" without a copy of these papers.

To protect the public fiscal interest, the statute required masters to support their freed slaves who were "not being in the judgment of the court, of sound mind and body, or being above the age of forty-five years, or being males under the age of twenty-one, or females under the age of eighteen years[.]" If the master or his successors failed to support these freed slaves, the county court and sheriff were authorized to "distrain and sell so much of the person's estate as shall be sufficient for such purpose." The statute also authorized the county court or sheriff to hire out any freed slave who did not pay his or her taxes for the time necessary to raise the funds necessary to pay the taxes, "if sufficient distress cannot be made upon his or her estate...."[29]

The legislators later concluded that the general manumission statute did not adequately protect the interests of an insolvent master's creditors. Therefore, a 1792 statute provided that any manumitted slave may be liable to be taken in execution to satisfy the master's pre-manumission debts.[30]

After 1782, Virginia's free black population grew as masters freed some or all of their slaves, and as the courts began to enforce expressions of the master's intentions, if they complied with the statute.[31] Some masters with large slave-holdings, including George Washington, Robert Carter, and John and Jonathan Pleasants, freed all of their slaves during their lifetimes or in their wills because of their philosophical or religious beliefs. The emerging trend, however, consisted of masters who freed some of their favorite slaves. These slaves were chosen generally because of their good behavior, because they were the master's sexual partners, or because they were the master's children.[32] St. George Tucker estimated that Virginia's free black population in 1782 was about 1,800 or 2,800. It rose to 12,766 in 1790, to 20,124 in 1800, and to 30,570 in 1810.[33]

Many Virginians nevertheless began to favor a revival of restrictions on manumission soon after the 1782 act was adopted. "Slaveholders saw no contradiction in doling out liberty with one hand and tightening the chains of bondage with the other."[34] For example, in the 1790s "an angry neighbor" wrote to Robert Carter to complain about the nuisance that Carter's manumission caused, stating "that a man has almost as much right to set fire to his own

building though his neighbor[']s is to be destroyed by it, as to free his slaves...."
As Ira Berlin noted:

> If the opponents of manumission dared to challenge Robert Carter, one
> of the most powerful planters in Virginia, little wonder that they intim-
> idated lesser men. After 1800, the number of manumissions declined
> sharply. The glare of hostile public opinion not only dissuaded many
> would-be manumitters but also encouraged avaricious heirs and creditors
> to challenge the slave's right to freedom. Once promised liberty, slaves
> often faced new hurdles which delayed freedom or quashed it alto-
> gether.[35]

Indeed, Carter's heirs "stubbornly sought to nullify the deeds of manumission he had executed in his lifetime and to neutralize his testamentary
intentions."[36] And in a case discussed at several points in this book, some of the
heirs of the Pleasants resorted to litigation in their efforts to defeat the manumissions provided for in the wills of their father and brother.[37]

"Public opposition [to manumission] was soon transformed into legislative
prohibitions."[38] A bill requiring that freed slaves be excluded from Virginia
twelve months after their manumission was introduced but defeated in 1787.[39]
This defeat did not end the debate about the state's manumission laws, however. In 1804-1805 and 1805-1806, the legislature considered bills that would
have banned all manumissions. Instead, the legislators in January 1806
adopted a statute that revived the 1691 removal act, except that the new act
required the freed slaves, and not their masters, to pay for their removal from
the state. The act stated that slaves freed after May 1, 1806 forfeited their liberty
if they remained in Virginia for one year after their "right to freedom shall have
accrued." The statute authorized the overseers of the poor to apprehend these
freed slaves and sell them "for the benefit of the poor" of the county.[40]

The legislature in the same January 1806 act also amended the state's 1778
anti-importation law, which authorized the manumission of persons held as
slaves who were illegally imported into Virginia. The 1806 statute deleted this
forfeiture provision. It provided instead that the local overseers of the poor were
to sell illegally imported slaves for "cash."[41]

These statutes slowed but did not stop Virginia's free black population
growth.[42] "For a number of years there was almost no effort made to punish
violators of this law; consequently there accumulated a considerable number of
free colored persons who were not by law entitled to reside in the State. By and
by spasmodic efforts began to be made to give the act life."[43]

White Virginians had ambivalent feelings about the freed slave exclusion
law. "Part of the problem was the difficulty of legislating complicated human
relationships. As in their view of slaves, a disjunction existed between white
Virginians' views of free blacks generally, a view that held them as threatening
and violent, and the ideas about the individual free black people whom they
knew as members of their communities and whom they counted as friends."[44]

Virginia legislators apparently reflected these ambivalent public attitudes, and they modified the free black exclusion law in 1815 and 1819. These amend-ments permitted the county courts to grant freed slaves permission to stay in their county, if the slaves were manumitted because of "an act or acts of extra-ordinary merit." The 1819 statute declared, however, that "proof of good general character and conduct alone" was not sufficient. The legislature provided procedures for public notice of the freed slave's application to remain and for the recording of the court's determination. An applicant's spouse or children also could obtain permission to remain in the county on proof of their "general good character and conduct," again after public notice and a hearing. This per-mission could be revoked, however, if any freed slave committed a crime, or if "any descendant, however remote," of a female slave granted permission to remain committed a crime. The convicted free person was required to leave Virginia within twelve months, or be sold into slavery, under provisions similar to the 1806 removal act.[45]

This statute appears to have had the effect of totally blocking the path to freedom for some slaves. For example, a Virginia slave owner named Rucker stated in his will: "[I]t is my will and desire that my mulatto man James Gilbert should be free; but finding there would be some difficulty for it to be so, and for him to remain here," Rucker directed his executors to set Gilbert up on a three acre corner of Rucker's land to live in a state of *quasi*-freedom under the execu-tors' control during Gilbert's "natural life on good behaviour[.]" Gilbert won a freedom judgment in the trial court, but the Virginia Supreme Court of Appeals in its 1831 decision reversed the judgment.[46] The appellate court's opinion of Judge Francis T. Brooke stated: "However much [Rucker] desired that Gilbert should be free, it was very clear, that he was deterred by the difficulties which the law presented with respect to residence here; and, under the circumstances, determined to do what he considered the next best for him; to settle him for life on a piece of land, there to enjoy the fruits of his own labor." Therefore, Gilbert remained a *quasi*-slave because the statutes prohibited his master's "will and desire."[47]

In response to this statute, many freed slaves presented petitions to the Virginia General Assembly seeking special legislation permitting them to remain in Virginia.[48] Therefore, in 1837, the legislature adopted an act that permitted the county courts to allow a freed slave to remain in Virginia upon proof "that the applicant is a person of good character, peaceable, orderly and industrious, and not addicted to drunkenness, gaming, or any other vice[.]" The applicant's right to remain in the state was conditioned, however, on his or her continued good behavior. The court was empowered to revoke the permission, and the freed slave would be sold into slavery if he or she continued to remain in Virginia.[49]

The courts granted to some freed slaves permission to remain in Virginia in the years that followed, and free blacks continued to petition the legislature for permission to remain in Virginia.[50] But Virginia's 1852 Constitution, which was drafted in 1850-1851, confirmed that a stronger anti-manumission trend was gaining force in the South, and that it had supporters in Virginia. That state's new constitution provided that all slaves who were freed after it was adopted would forfeit their freedom if they remained in the commonwealth for more than twelve months. The constitution empowered the general assembly to impose restrictions on the masters' power to free slaves, and to pass "laws for the relief of the commonwealth from the free negro population, by removal or otherwise." It also denied the general assembly the authority to "emancipate any slave, or the descendant of any slave, either before or after the birth of such descendant."[51]

Virginia did not, however, follow the antebellum trend of thought in the South that found all domestic and foreign manumission to be incompatible with slavery. The Virginia legislature, on October 3, 1862, adopted a statute holding any judges or other officials of the United States liable for double damages and a fine for emancipating under the laws of the United States a slave owned by a Virginia citizen.[52] The legislature also debated a total ban on manumissions, but never approved this legislation.[53]

Accordingly, Virginia's masters had the greatest freedom to decide whether to liberate some or all of their slaves during the years before 1691 and in the 24 years from 1782 to 1806. At other times, the legislators weighed public and private interests against the master's individual property interests, and these lawmakers passed laws restricting the masters' property rights.

Moreover, Eva Sheppard Wolf argued that we should keep in check our enthusiasm about the 1782 act as an expression of anti-slavery thought or as an extension of the principles of the American Revolution to slavery. She stated that this act "was in many ways a conservative piece of legislation, careful to restrict manumission in accord with white interests[.]" Nevertheless, the act "marked a meaningful break from the past, especially because it did not require freed slaves to leave Virginia."[54] She also noted, however, that soon after the legislature adopted this manumission act, it approved a statute that limited the practice by which masters permitted slaves to hire out their own time. Thus, the legislators both recognized and regulated the masters' rights to treat their slaves as they wished, in the public interest.[55]

She also cited a 1782 act "for the recovery of slaves, horses, and other property, lost during the war." The act empowered the local justices of the peace to jail any slaves found wandering and directed that the slaves be returned to their masters. "But by treating slaves and horses together in one law the legislators revealed that revolutionary ideology had not changed their view that slaves and horses were merely two different species of the same legal category."[56]

Of course, only twenty-four years later, the legislators revived the free black exclusion act. This act illustrates how the legislators "mediated between important rights and the practical imperative to provide for public safety. But the intent of the law was to curtail manumission, and that was its effect; the number of manumissions in Virginia dropped drastically, and the growth of the free black population slowed markedly after 1806."[57]

The Manumission Statutes in the Other Southern States

Virginia's shifting manumission law provides a pattern with which we can evaluate the other Southern states' laws. These laws generally permitted manumission in the early years of settlement in a colony or state. For example, the South Carolina and Georgia slave codes initially did not prohibit or regulate manumission.[58] This permissive regime in the slave states other than Delaware and Missouri ultimately gave way to laws that increasingly regulated the masters' right to free their slaves, and to some laws that prohibited manumission.[59] "Manumission became, at first, vexatious, then difficult, and finally almost impossible. While absolute prohibitions against manumission were not commonplace, or were enacted only late in the slavery period, conditions attached to the process often rendered it a practical impossibility."[60]

In the years following the American Revolution, Maryland (1790 and 1796), Kentucky (1794, 1798, and 1800), Missouri (1804), Louisiana (1807), and later Arkansas (1838) adopted general manumission statutes similar to Virginia's 1782 act.[61] Even these relatively permissive statutes regulated the masters' right to free their slaves to protect the interests of other legal persons and the state. These limits fell into three categories that furthered several policy goals.

The first of these limits was intended to control masters who might free young, old, or infirm slaves who could not support themselves. For example, the Maryland legislators found that some masters advanced their own interests by freeing "disabled and supernated slaves" who "have either perished through Want, or otherwise become a Burthen [sic] to others[.]"[62] Consequently, the legislatures in Delaware (1740 and 1767), North Carolina (1801 and 1831), Tennessee (1801 and 1831), Kentucky (1794, 1798, and 1842), Louisiana (1830 and 1855), and Florida (1829) adopted statutes requiring masters to post bonds before freeing some or all of their slaves. The bonds were to be used to indemnify the state or county for any costs incurred by the public if, because of their age or health, the freed slaves required support.[63]

Other statutes imposed a continuing support obligation on masters freeing some or all slaves. For example, a 1787 Delaware act, among other things, permitted slave owners to free healthy slaves who were 18 to 35 years of age without posting a bond, and it legalized all prior manumissions of healthy slaves 21 to 35 years of age. But the law also stated that this manumission without a bond did not discharge the masters' obligation, or that of their estates, to support the slaves who were or became incapable of earning a livelihood.[64] An 1819 statute permitted masters to free slaves without posting a bond, but if the slave was younger than ten years and older than thirty five, or unhealthy or incapable of earning a livelihood, the master or his or her estate remained liable for maintaining the slave.[65] The Louisiana Code stated that manumission "imports an obligation" on the masters' part "to provide for the subsistence" of their freed slaves who "should be unable to support [themselves]."[66] The Missouri and Arkansas statutes also required that the masters or the estates of masters freeing slaves support freed slaves who were not of sound mind, who were older than forty-five years, or if male, who were younger than twenty-one, and, if female, who were younger than eighteen.[67]

Other statutes specified the ages and condition of slaves who could be manumitted. Maryland's acts of 1752, 1790, and 1796, for example, permitted masters to free slaves only if the slaves were younger than fifty years of age, forty-five after 1796, and if the slaves were able to work and "gain a sufficient livelihood" when they were to be freed.[68] The 1752 act also required masters to support slaves who when freed were "disabled to work, or gain a sufficient Livelihood and Maintenance[.]"[69] Louisiana's Civil Code permitted masters to free slaves who were at least thirty years of age and who "behaved well" during the four years before the manumission.[70] The statute allowed exceptions for slaves who saved the lives of their master, their master's spouse, or one of their master's children.[71]

The legislatures in states including Maryland, Arkansas, Kentucky, Missouri, and Louisiana adopted statutes similar to Virginia's 1792 act that protected the rights of creditors. A master's creditors could, at times, override a master's decision to free his or her slaves if the master's estate was insolvent. And if a widow of a deceased male master was entitled to a share of her deceased husband's estate, statutes adopted in Virginia and Mississippi disallowed slave manumissions to the extent that it was necessary to satisfy this requirement.[72]

The Louisiana Code extended this protection to "the portion [of an estate] reserved by law to forced heirs[.]" It defined a "fraud against creditors" as occurring "when it shall appear that at the moment of executing the [manumission], the person granting it had not sufficient property to pay his debts or to leave his heirs the portion to them reserved by law[.]" The Code also protected the rights of those who held mortgages in slaves who were proposed to be freed by their owner. The manumission could take effect if "the slave or any one in his behalf shall pay the debt for which the mortgage was given."[73]

The legislators also were concerned about slaves who might assert fraudulent manumission claims. Under the common law, the courts held that a master's intention to manumit his or her slaves could be proven without any formal requirements. Some courts found that evidence of a master's oral statements was sufficient proof of his or her intent to free his or her slaves.[74] The legislatures of the eighteenth and nineteenth centuries, including those in the more "liberal" states of Delaware, Maryland, Kentucky, Louisiana, Arkansas, and Missouri, enacted statutes requiring masters to state their intention to free slaves in a written deed or will. Some of these statutes also required that manumission documents be witnessed and recorded to memorialize the master's intention to free the slaves. If the master did not satisfy the statutory mandates, the slaves could not enjoy their freedom.[75]

For example, the Louisiana Code permitted masters to free their slaves either by will or if they appeared before their parish judge and declared their intentions. The judge was required to post a notice of the proposed manumission on the court house door for forty days. The judge was to grant permission for the manumission if no opposition to the proposed manumission was received. The owner could then sign a manumission deed before a notary noting the judge's authorization. Masters and notaries faced a $100 fine if they did not follow the act's pre-manumission procedures.[76]

A Maryland act of 1752 prohibited oral manumission, manumission by will, and manumission arising out of the master's "last sickness." It permitted manumission only by a written instrument that a master had to sign before two witnesses and the instrument had to be recorded within six months of its execution.[77]

These were the least restrictive limits that the legislators placed on the master's right to free his or her slave. Nevertheless, as the antebellum years wore on, the Southern legislators enacted a progressively more stringent anti-manumission regime.

These anti-manumission acts fell into three categories.

First were statutes that were similar to Virginia's 1723 act prohibiting manumissions unless the master's decision to free the slaves was based upon proof of good cause for freedom and was approved by a special act of the legislature or by a court ruling.[78]

The North Carolina legislature adopted a statute in 1741 stating that no black or mulatto slaves may be freed "upon any Pretence whatsoever, except for meritorious services," as determined by the local county court and after a license was issued permitting the manumission. The legislature in 1777 and 1796 reenacted this meritorious services requirement. The 1777 act was based on the finding that "the evil and pernicious Practice of freeing Slaves in this State, ought at this alarming and critical Time to be guarded against by every friend and Wellwisher to his Country[.]"[79] Because the Quaker minority was influential in certain counties, some county courts were perceived to be too lenient in favor of freedom. Therefore, an 1818 statute required the state's Superior Court to hear all applications for the approval of manumissions.[80]

Tennessee masters, during their lifetimes, could free their slaves under the 1777 North Carolina law, which after 1790 continued to be applied in Tennessee, only if the meritorious services standard was satisfied. The Tennessee legislature in 1801 adopted a more liberal standard, however, which required a finding that the freed slave would not become a public charge.[81] Although manumissions contrary to these statutes were valid in Tennessee as between the masters and the slaves, they were not binding on the state, which could prosecute the masters for illegally permitting the slaves to act as free persons. "The master cannot, by parting with his right to the slave, elude these responsibilities [imposed by these statutes], and turn the slave loose upon society without those guarantees the law demands in such cases."[82]

The South Carolina legislators first limited the masters' right to free their slaves in an 1800 act. The legislature found that there had been "a practice for many years past in this State, for persons to ... set free their slaves, in cases where such slaves have been of bad or depraved character, or, from age or infirmity, incapable of gaining their livelihood by honest means[.]" To prevent these evils, the act required masters wishing to free their slaves to show good cause before a judge and five freeholders demonstrating that their slaves were "not of bad character" and were "capable of gaining a livelihood in an honest way[.]" If the master proved his or her case, a manumission deed was required to be recorded within six months from the date of execution, otherwise the manumission was to be "void and of noneffect[.]" Any person could capture and keep as their slaves and property people who were freed contrary to the act.[83] These freed slaves were treated "as if they were abandoned property."[84] An 1820 act found that the 1800 act did not prevent a "great and rapid increase" in the state's free black population, and declared: "No slave shall hereafter be emancipated but by act of the Legislature."[85]

Georgia's permissive approach to manumission ended with the act of 1801, which stated that it was not "lawful" for any person to free a slave "in any manner or form, [other] than by application to the legislature for that purpose." The act also established fines for owners who violated the act and for public officials who recorded manumission deeds contrary to the act.[86]

The Legislative Council of the Mississippi Territory in 1805 adopted the first statute regulating manumissions in Alabama and Mississippi; its title was "An act to prevent the liberation of slaves, only in cases hereinafter named, and for other purposes." It required that masters obtain legislative approval for all manumissions. Masters had to "first prove to the satisfaction of the general assembly" that the slaves to be freed performed "some meritorious act" either for the owners' benefit "or for the benefit of this territory[.]" The owners also were required to enter into bonds for security against the slaves' becoming charges upon the territory. The freed slaves remained liable for the satisfaction of their owners' existing debts.[87]

The first Mississippi and Alabama constitutions, which were ratified in 1817 and 1819, vested the legislatures with the "power to permit the owner of slaves to emancipate them, saving the rights of creditors, and preventing them from becoming a public charge."[88] The Alabama legislature continued to approve all manumissions by private acts until 1834, when the legislature adopted an act authorizing judicial approval of manumissions for good cause. It stated that

> whenever the owner or owners of any slave or slaves shall be desirous of emancipating such slave or slaves, such owner or owners shall make publication in some newspaper, printed in the county where such slave or slaves reside, (or if there be no paper printed in said county, then in the nearest paper thereto,) for at least sixty days previously to the making [of the] application, in which shall be set forth the time and place that such application will be made, together with the names and description of the slave or slaves sought to be emancipated; and at the time appointed, the judge of the said county court may, upon petition filed, proceed to hear and determine upon the application so made; and if, in his opinion, said slaves should be emancipated, in consideration of long, faithful and meritorious services performed, or for other good and sufficient cause shown,

said judge may proceed to emancipate and set free such slave or slaves; and the clerk of the said court shall make record of the same in a book to be kept for that purpose[.][89]

The act also required that the freed slave leave the state within twelve months "never more to return, and that such emancipation shall not take effect until after such removal"; if the freed slaves returned to the state, they were to be arrested and sold into slavery. The act also stated that it was not to be "construed as to prejudice" the master's creditors' rights.[90]

The Mississippi legislature also at first approved individual manumissions and, in 1822, adopted an act permitting a master to free his or her slaves by his or her "last will and testament, or by any other instrument in writing," under his or her "hand and seal, attested and proved, in the manner required by law by two credible witnesses, or the instrument of writing acknowledged by the party or parties in the court of the county or corporation where he, she, or they reside[.]" Masters also were required to prove to the General Assembly's "satisfaction ... that such slave or slaves have done and performed some meritorious act for the benefit of the owner or owners, or some distinguished service for the benefit of this state[.]" The will or other document was declared not to be effective until the legislature adopted an act approving it, and until the owner "complied with the conditions" of the legislative act.[91]

The *second class of acts* followed the lead of Virginia's acts of 1691 and 1806. These statutes, like Alabama's act of 1834, required freed slaves to remove themselves from the state within a specified time period, or, in some cases, they ran the risk of being sold back into slavery.[92] A 1722 South Carolina act required masters freeing slaves to "make provision for [the slave's] departure out of this Province[.]" A slave who did not depart twelve months after his or her manumission was to "lose the benefit of such manumission, and continue to be a slave," unless both houses of the legislature approved the manumission.[93]

North Carolina's legislators adopted a statute in 1715 permitting masters to free slaves as a "reward" for "honest and Faithful service." But the act required freed slaves to leave the state in six months or they would be sold back into slavery for five years to a buyer who would provide security to pay for the export of the slave out of the state. According to a 1723 act, many freed slaves evaded this removal requirement by leaving North Carolina for a short time and then returning. That act provided that freed slaves who returned to North Carolina were required to serve as slaves for seven more years. The 1741 act that required court approval for manumissions on proof of meritorious services also stated that slaves who were otherwise freed and who did not leave the state after six months were to be sold as slaves by the local churchwardens. If a freed slave left the state and later returned, he or she could be sold back into slavery after only one month.[94]

In the years following independence, the North Carolina legislature adopted several measures to better enforce this limitation on manumission. A 1777 law abolished the six-month grace period, and provided that any slave who was freed contrary to these statutes could be seized immediately by any freeholder, taken to a sheriff, and then sold back into slavery. The freeholder seizing the slave would receive a finder's fee of one fifth of the sale's net proceeds. The legislature in 1779 extended this seizure and sale provision to slaves who were improperly freed before the 1777 act was adopted, except for any slave who was freed and not sold under a court order who had "enlisted into the service of this or the United States previous to the passing of this Act." In 1788, the legislators authorized a procedure for the apprehension and seizure by local sheriffs of illegally freed slaves.[95]

An 1830 North Carolina statute permitted masters to petition the Superior Court for permission to free slaves without establishing good cause, and authorized manumissions by will. Nevertheless, the freed slaves were required to leave the state in 90 days, and the masters were required to post $1,000 bonds for each freed slave. Slaves who were older than fifty could be freed for meritorious services, which meant "more than general performance of duty," and could remain in the state if the owner posted a $500 bond.[96]

In November 1829, the Florida territorial legislature adopted a freed slave removal statute that was unique because it applied only to slaves who were brought into Florida after the act was adopted. If the freed slaves in that category did not leave the state within thirty days after their manumission, they could be seized under a court order by a county marshal or sheriff and sold back into slavery at a public sale. The sale proceeds were to be paid to the state treasury.[97]

The Louisiana legislature adopted several statutes between 1830 and 1857 that were intended to limit the growth of the state's free black population by requiring freed slaves to leave the state. An 1830 act required that freed slaves leave the state within one month of their manumission, and it required owners who freed slaves to post a $1,000 bond as security for this new removal requirement.[98] In 1831, the legislature adopted an exception to this rule, which permitted the police jury of the parish, by a three-fourths vote, to permit freed slaves to remain, and it exempted slaves who were freed in reward for "long, faithful, or important services[.]"[99] According to a study of the New Orleans Police Parish Jury records between 1831 and 1846, each request that was made under this law was granted.[100] In 1846, the legislature created a new court to hear these cases, and it too granted every request.[101]

In 1852, Louisiana's legislature responded with an act that required all persons freeing slaves to send them to Liberia within one year of the manumission. The owner freeing a slave was required to pay $150 for the slave's passage to Africa. Freed slaves who stayed in the state, or who returned after being freed, were to "forfeit their freedom and become slaves and revert to their former owners."[102] Slave owners who wished to free slaves "besieged the legislature with requests for individual exceptions, and the number of legislative manumissions with permission to remain in the state increased."[103]

In 1855, the Louisiana legislature again responded with a statute that included provisions requiring the district courts to decide whether to permit freed slaves to remain in the state. The master was required to file a suit in the district court and pay all of the court costs. The district attorney was "to represent the State, and to urge all legal objections, and to produce such proofs as may be in his power to defeat plaintiff's demand." The master had the burden to prove his or her ownership of the slave and to establish that the slave to be freed was "'of good character and sober habits' by producing character witnesses as well as proof that the slaves in question had no criminal convictions." The act provided for a trial by jury. It also required the owner to advertise a notice of the proposed manumission in the local newspapers at least five times during the 30 days before filing the suit, and to post a $1,000 bond to serve as a pledge that the slave would not become a public charge if the court granted permission to remain.[104]

The change in the court apparently did not sufficiently stem the tide of local manumissions. Judith Schafer has stated that the New Orleans district court records reveal that, between 1855 and 1856, slave owners filed 159 suits seeking permission to free 289 slaves who would remain in the state.[105] In December 1856, the Louisiana Supreme Court invalidated the 1855 law, finding that it was adopted in violation of the state constitution's single subject provision.[106]

On March 6, 1857, the Louisiana legislature prohibited manumission. It adopted a statute stating: "from and after the passage of this Act no slave shall be emancipated in this State."[107]

The Tennessee legislature, on December 16, 1831, adopted legislation requiring that the courts approve manumissions pursuant to the 1777 and 1801 acts only if the freed slaves were to be "immediately removed" from Tennessee. A master seeking to free a slave was required to post a bond in an amount equal to the slave's value. The bond would serve to guarantee that the slave would leave the state.[108] A November 23, 1833 act exempted from the statute's removal requirement slaves "who had, *bona fide* contracted" for their freedom before the 1831 removal act's adoption and those who were freed by the wills of masters who died before the 1831 act was adopted [109] A February 4, 1842 act "widened the loophole of 1833 by giving county courts power to permit [a freed] slave to remain in the state if that slave had been born in Tennessee or had become a Tennessee resident prior to 1836."[110] The statute required that the county court be satisfied that the slave would not become indigent, and would "keep the peace and be of good behavior towards all free white citizens of this state[.]" The act also mandated that a $500 bond guarantee the slave's good behavior, and if the slave was found to violate these behavioral requirements, he or she would be subject to deportation within twenty days under the 1831 act. The bond was to be renewed every three years, when the county court was permitted to "again institute an enquiry into the character and conduct of the applicant[.]" Slaves exhibiting bad behavior could be deported within twenty days under the 1831 act.[111]

Tennessee's legislators closed these loopholes with a December 31, 1849 act that required all slaves be manumitted pursuant to the 1831 act's terms.[112] The final Tennessee freed slave removal act, adopted on February 24, 1854, required that all freed slaves be "transported to the western coast of Africa." It provided an exception for slaves "who from age or disease were unable to go with safety" to Africa.[113] According to Arthur Howington, in many but not all cases the local courts granted petitions nevertheless permitting freed slaves to remain in Tennessee.[114]

The Maryland legislature in 1832 adopted a statute titled: "An act relating to the People of Color in this state." Among other things, it required freed slaves to leave the state, and it provided procedures to colonize freed slaves in Liberia or elsewhere. The act stated that slaves who "cannot be removed without separating families," and who thus were "unwilling" to leave the state, could in open court "renounce the freedom so intended by" the master's will and remain in Maryland as slaves. The statute also authorized the orphan's court and the Baltimore city court "to grant annually a permit" to freed slaves wishing to stay in Maryland as free persons, if the court was "satisfied by respectable testimony" that the slaves "deserve such permission on account of their extraordinary good conduct and character[.]" This permission did not, however, exempt the master or his or her estate from liability to maintain a freed slave who, when freed, "may be unable to gain a livelihood, or be over forty-five years of age at said time, and afterwards become unable to maintain himself or herself."[115]

An 1831 Mississippi statute required that all free blacks between the ages of 16 and 50 leave the state within ninety days, and they were not to return "under any pretense whatsoever." The act included an exception, however, stating that "any free negro or mulatto" could apply to a local county or probate court for a license granting him or her permission to remain in the state if he or she could "prove ... that he or she is of good character and honest deportment."[116] An 1842 act extended this provision to slaves who were freed elsewhere and who returned to Mississippi. They could be treated as if they were free blacks or "mulattos" who were illegally in the state. They thus could be brought before a justice of the peace and made to post security for their good behavior. If they misbehaved, these freed slaves could be jailed and sold back into slavery.[117]

An 1834 Alabama statute permitted manumission on court approval, but it also required that the freed slave leave the state within twelve months "never more to return[.]" The manumission was not to "take effect until after such removal."[118] Alabama's 1852 Code was even more restrictive. It required all freed slaves to leave the state within six months or "be seized and sold as slaves for life."[119]

In the 1840s, the Missouri legislators adopted statutes requiring qualified free "negroes and mulattos," including slaves who were manumitted in the state, to obtain a license permitting them to remain in the state. The statute required free blacks and "mulattos" to apply to the county courts for a license and demonstrate that they were "of good character and behavior[.]" The license applicants also were required to post a bond of no more than $1,000 as a guarantee of their good behavior. Blacks or "mulattos" who were in Missouri without a license could be fined and sent out of the state.[120]

The 1850 Kentucky state constitution empowered the legislature with the authority to "pass laws to permit owners of slaves to emancipate them, saving the rights of creditors, and to prevent them from remaining in this State after they are emancipated."[121] The legislature, on March 24, 1851, adopted a statute providing that slaves could be manumitted only upon the condition that they be removed from the state.[122]

The version of this statute that the legislators adopted in the 1852 *Revised Statutes of Kentucky* also stated that the manumission did not take effect until the freed slave was removed from the state. If the master did not make provisions for the slave's removal, the county courts were authorized to hire the slave out from year to year until enough money was raised, except for slaves who were older than 65 years of age or who "by disease or infirmity" were "incapable of labor for a support[.]" The master was required to provide a means for the removal of slaves "and one year's support." When the court was satisfied that sufficient funds were available, the court was to "ascertain, by personal examination of the slave in open court, his willingness to be removed out of the state, and to accept his freedom upon the conditions prescribed by law[.]" Slave families who were freed were to have the proceeds of this hiring "united in one common fund," which was to be "applied for the removal of all at the same time, and to the same place." Slaves who were freed but who refused to consent to the removal were to be "hired out, ... for the benefit of the county, in such mode as the county court may direct, until such time as they shall give their assent, and actually remove out of the state."[123]

In Texas, the Supreme Court, in the 1854 case of *Purvis v. Sherrod*,[124] interpreted the Texas 1845 Constitution to require that manumitted slaves be removed from the state. The provision on which Justice Abner Lipscomb relied stated that the legislature "shall have the right to pass laws to permit the owners of slaves to emancipate them, saving the rights of creditors, and preventing them from becoming a public charge."[125] This text said nothing about the removal of freed slaves from Texas. Justice Lipscomb nevertheless found that this removal requirement was implied in the text. He construed the constitution against liberty, by reference to the Constitution of the Republic of Texas, which did require the removal of freed slaves, and an 1840 act of the Congress of the Republic, which prohibited free blacks from moving into Texas and remaining there.[126] The Texas Supreme Court followed this interpretation in later cases. The Texas legislature never acted to overturn this interpretation, although it did on more than one occasion adopt special acts to permit individual freed slaves to remain in Texas.[127]

These freed slave deportation requirements may have been unevenly enforced, but the threat of their enforcement posed many obvious practical difficulties to the newly freed slaves. Many would have been "reluctant to leave family and familiar surroundings[.]" And, moreover, "almost every other southern state, and many of those in the North as well, prohibited the entry of free negroes."[128]

Nevertheless, the legislators in several states found that even these freed slave removal laws were too lenient or too difficult to enforce; they therefore adopted the *third type of anti-manumission statute*, which prohibited some or all manumissions.[129] These anti-manumission laws are in two categories. Some statutes prohibited all manumissions by will. Maryland's legislators in 1752 found that manumission by will "may be attended with many Evils[.]" They therefore prohibited manumission by will or at the time of the master's "last sickness," and required that the slaves to be freed be not older than fifty years of age and be able to support themselves. But this act was in effect repealed by the 1790 and 1796 statutes that allowed masters to free slaves of the specified ages by a written deed or a will.[130] The South Carolina acts requiring the master to come before a court, or later the legislature, to obtain approval for manumission also in effect appear to have been intended to prohibit manumissions by will.[131] The North Carolina legislators, after permitting manumission by will for thirty years, in 1861 adopted a statute again barring manumissions by will, deed, or any other writing, which is not to take effect in the life of the owner.[132]

Between 1857 and 1860, legislators in Maryland, Georgia, Alabama, Mississippi, and Arkansas went a step further and attempted to outlaw all manumissions within the state and all *post-mortem* manumissions anywhere. The Georgia legislators foreshadowed what became this trend when they adopted an act in 1818 stating that masters could not directly or indirectly free their slaves by wills, by deeds, or by parol evidence. The same statute prohibited the settlement in Georgia of free blacks from other states.[133] On December 14, 1859, the legislature closed a loophole through which the Georgia courts permitted out-of-state manumissions by will. The statute stated that "after the passage of this act, any and every clause in any deed, will, or other instrument made for the purpose of conferring freedom on slaves, directly or indirectly, within or without the State, to take effect after the death of the owner, shall be absolutely null and void."[134]

South Carolina's legislature in 1841 passed an act that prohibited all in-state and out-of-state manumissions.[135] That statute consisted of four sections. It voided all manumissions intended to be effectuated by removal of the slave from South Carolina. Second, it voided trusts created to fund slave removal and liberation. Third, it voided attempts to create trusts to support in-state "nominal servitude." Fourth, the statute declared illegal all gifts to slaves through trusts to be held for the benefit of slaves.[136]

An 1842 Mississippi statute barred all manumissions by will, including a will that directed that the master's slaves be removed from Mississippi and freed elsewhere. The act provided for an exception for wills freeing slaves who performed meritorious services to the masters, but only upon legislative approval.[137] In 1857, the Mississippi legislators adopted a comprehensive statute that apparently was intended to close off all possible loopholes in the 1842 law. The new act provided that it was not "lawful" for "any person either by will, deed, or other conveyance, directly or in trust, either express or secret, or otherwise," to dispose of slaves "for the purpose, or with the intent to emancipate" the slaves in the state, "or to provide that such slaves be removed to be emancipated elsewhere, or by any evasion or indirection so to provide that the colonization society, or any donee or grantee, can accomplish the act, intent or purpose designed, to be prohibited by this article." The act also stated that all wills, deeds, trusts, or other conveyances "intended to accomplish the emancipation of any slave after the death of the owner, no matter when made" were declared "void."[138]

A February 2, 1859 Arkansas statute banned further manumissions. Another statute enacted ten days later required, among other things, that all free blacks twenty-one years of age or older leave the state by January 1, 1860.[139]

Alabama's January 25, 1860 statute voided all wills, trusts, or other documents freeing slaves, even if the slaves were to be taken elsewhere and freed. It also repealed all laws that permitted the courts to free slaves, but stated that it did not apply to wills or other documents, "which may have become effective before its passage."[140]

In 1860, the Maryland legislature adopted an act "prohibiting manumission of negro slaves, and authorizing free negroes to renounce freedom and become slaves."[141] The act went beyond the prohibitions of the 1752 act and stated that: "No slaves shall henceforth be manumitted by deed or by last will and testament[.]" It also stated that freedom will not be presumed for blacks who were "going at large and acting as free," or who were unclaimed by an owner. The Maryland statute excluded term slaves who were previously freed by a will or deed, but whose date with freedom had not arrived.[142]

In two states the anti-manumission policy was made a part of the state constitution. The Florida constitution of 1838 and the Texas constitution of 1861 prohibited manumissions to take effect both in and out of those states.[143]

These statutory and constitutional provisions confirm that the trend in the antebellum South lead to increased regulation and the statutes prohibiting manumission. In these Southern states, the legislators and the drafters of two constitutions apparently determined that the anti-manumission rule furthered several salient policy goals. The lawmakers in other slave societies did not always arrive at this calculation of the relevant interests.

Manumission Regulations in Other Slave Societies

The anti-manumission trend generally was not duplicated in the laws of other slave societies. The lawmakers elsewhere did not prohibit this prerogative of slave ownership because it usually was not found to be contrary to slavery's essence.

Roman law permitted manumission "*inter vivos* or by will."[144] Although, like that of the United States South, Roman manumission law evolved over time, it "imposed very few restrictions on manumission."[145] Adult slave owners, during their lifetimes, had the right to free their slaves without any showing of good cause or without obtaining governmental approval, although a master could not free his slaves to defraud his creditors or his patron.[146] Masters younger than twenty years of age were required to establish good cause before freeing their slaves, and masters seeking to free slaves who were younger than thirty years of age also were required to establish good cause. But good cause was broadly defined to include the freeing of an owner's parent, child, sibling, teacher, nurse, general agent, or a woman to be married by the owner within six months of the manumission.[147] "The persons who could thus be freed would be those that an owner was likely to want to free, so the practical restrictions on even young owners were minimal."[148]

"Augustus in 2 B.C. introduced restrictions on the numbers [of slaves] who could be freed by [a master's] will[.]"[149] Masters could free from one-half to one-fifth of their slaves, up to a maximum of 100 slaves, depending on the size of the masters' slaveholding.[150] Justinian later abolished this restriction.[151]

These Roman laws indicate that the lawmakers were not hostile to manumission, nor did they think that it was inconsistent with slavery or a threat to slavery. According to Alan Watson, slavery's "primary purpose ... is to maximize the benefits for the owners while minimizing the risks to them, which requires a mixture of carrots and sticks." He called manumission "the juiciest carrot."[152] Roman law sought only to regulate the manner in which a master was permitted to offer that carrot to his or her slaves, so as to avoid any unnecessary detrimental effects on a master's creditors and heirs.

The law in Spain's colonies "made manumission easy," according to Watson. This law was consistent with the Roman legal tradition and the pro-manumission provisions of *Las Siete Partidas*. Watson cites this as an example of the transplanting of Roman and Castilian law in the New World.[153]

Masters who were at least twenty years of age had the right to free their slaves as long as their intention was stated before a judge, in their will, or in writing or in an oral statement, both of which required five witnesses. A showing of good cause before a judge was required only if the master was between the ages of twenty and seventeen. Good cause was defined as the freeing of a slave who was a child, a parent, a sibling, a teacher, a person who brought the master up, a foster child, a person who suckled at the same breast, a person who saved the master from death or bad reputation, a person who was to act as general agent to receive goods for the master and was at least seventeen years old, or a woman who the master intended to marry within six months. Masters freeing slaves in their wills could be as young as fourteen years of age.[154]

The law also recognized the rights of the masters' creditors. Masters could not free all of their slaves if they did not have sufficient goods to pay their debts.[155]

The law of manumission in Portuguese Brazil was similar to that of Rome and Spain. The law also did not require formalities for a valid manumission. "There were few restrictions, and they were the familiar ones such as to prevent fraud against creditors, or to avoid prejudice to the *herdeiros necessarios*."[156]

The French Caribbean colonies and later Louisiana, after the end of Spanish rule, eventually enacted a more restrictive approach that was similar to the early manumission law in the English common law colonies. This legal change was all the more remarkable because the French *Code Noir* of 1685 initially contained, in Article 55, a manumission provision that was even less restrictive than Roman law. It provided that masters as young as twenty years of age were free to manumit their slaves by will or during their lifetimes without obtaining official approval or that of their parents, and without providing reasons for the manumission.[157]

Nevertheless, apparently it was perceived that too many masters were offering to free slaves for a price, which it was alleged caused slaves to "undertake the most illicit acts" to obtain funds to buy their freedom. Accordingly, amendments followed in 1713, 1724, and 1736 that required masters to obtain written approval from the local Governor-General and the Intendant or the Governor and Superintendent-General before manumitting slaves, increased to twenty-five the minimum age of masters who could free their slaves, and authorized the re-enslavement of people who were freed contrary to these legal requirements.[158] The law changed again, however, with a Royal Ordinance of July 12, 1832, which permitted the manumission of enslaved people after applications were made on public notice, and if no objections were filed.[159]

The slave law of the Dutch colony of Suriname exhibits a similar evolution in the approach to manumission as the eighteenth century French law. According to Watson, the Dutch colonies generally accepted Roman slave law.[160] Nevertheless, in 1733, Suriname's planters' elected representatives decided from their own experience that they needed to regulate "the customary practice of freeing slaves."[161] They required masters to obtain court permission before freeing their slaves, and the masters had to guarantee the freed slaves' self-sufficiency by making a financial pledge or posting a bond. Masters also were required to educate their freed slaves in Christianity. If the owner did not follow these provisions, "the manumission would remain illegal, and the would-be manumitted [slave was] subject to confiscation by the government."[162]

Rosemary Brana-Shute stated that the lawmakers did not declare their reasons for adopting this law. But she concluded that "this legislation was intended to control both the manumitters and the emerging manumitted— though a very small group." The law protected the colonial treasury from the need to support ex-slaves. The lawmakers later heavily taxed manumission because they "knew that they could collect these heavy taxes, as many slaves and free residents valued manumission...."[163]

The New Jersey statutes also provide another contrasting approach to manumission. These laws sought to regulate manumission, but they never prohibited manumission, nor did they ever require masters to obtain legislative or judicial approval before manumitting slaves.[164] The first New Jersey statute regulating manumission was contained in a 1713-14 law titled: "An Act for Regulating Slaves." It stated the legislators' finding that "Free Negroes are an Idle Slothful People, and prove very often a charge" to the place where they live. The statute therefore required masters manumitting their "Negro or Mulatto" slaves to give security to the king or queen of 200 pounds for each slave with two sureties, and to pay 20 pounds yearly to each slave to be manumitted. The executors of masters freeing slaves by their wills also were required to comply with these provisions "immediately upon proving the said Will and Testament." If the masters or executors refused to comply with these requirements, "the said Manumission [was to] be void, and of none Effect."[165]

The legislature later adopted a 1769 act that contained a provision requiring that a master manumitting a "Negro, Indian or Mulatto Slave," in his or her lifetime or by will, give a bond to the king of 200 pounds, with one or more sufficient sureties, to indemnify the master's local government against all charges of maintenance if the slave to be manumitted were to become incapable of supporting himself or herself. The master's heirs, executors, and administrators also were required to comply with these requirements for manumissions by will. The statute added that "on Failure whereof, such Manumission shall be utterly void, and of none Effect[.]"[166]

The act also stated, however, that if masters freed slaves without posting the required bond, they or their heirs, executors, or administrators, remained "obligated and compelled at all times to support and maintain" the freed slaves. If the master "became insolvent, and so incapable of providing for and maintaining his or her" slaves, and if the slaves could not maintain themselves, the colony's overseers of the poor were to provide to the freed slaves "the same Relief as white Servants" were entitled to receive under the colony's laws.[167]

"The financial requirement to post a bond precluded many masters from ... freeing their slaves."[168] In 1773, in response to several petitions, a bill proposing to eliminate the bond requirement was introduced in the New Jersey Assembly. The bill stated that the colony's manumission law "had on experience been found too indiscriminate, the requirement of equal security in all cases working, in some instances, to 'prevent the exercise of humanity and tenderness in the emancipation of those who may deserve it.'" The bill met with both support and opposition; therefore, "the House ordered that the bill be printed and referred to the next session." At the next session in 1775, however, petitions again were filed in support of and against the proposal, and it again was postponed to the next session, "by which time the greater interests of the Revolution crowded out the consideration of the matter."[169]

In 1786, the legislature finally got around to amending the manumission laws. The statute permitted masters to avoid the future support obligations for freed slaves not younger than twenty-one years old and not older than thirty-five years old, provided that the master certified in writing the slave's age and fitness. The certificate also had to be signed by two overseers of the poor, after their examination of the slave to be freed, and the certificate then was to be recorded in the county clerk's office.[170]

In 1798, the New Jersey legislature adopted a comprehensive slave code titled "An Act respecting Slaves." The code's provisions included a section reenacting the 1786 act's provisions regarding certificates from the overseers of the poor discussed above, although the age of the oldest slaves that could be freed without future liability was increased to forty.[171] The statute also extended these provisions to slaves who were freed by will.[172] The legislature increased the required bond to $500 for freed slaves, but masters who freed able bodied slaves within the permitted age group of twenty-one to forty were exempted from the bonding requirement.[173]

The statute also provided, however, that masters freeing slaves for whom certificates were not obtained had to confirm their intent to manumit slaves in a will or by a deed that was signed before two witnesses.[174] "There had been many instances in which deeds of manumission had been executed conformably to law in every respect, excepting that there had been but one witness. These manumissions were made valid by a special act of the legislature in 1844."[175]

In sum, then, the laws of a slave society regulating manumission did not necessarily have to progress to the total prohibition that took hold over the antebellum South on the eve of the Civil War. Other slave societies adopted other approaches. As in the Southern United States, these legal provisions changed over time, apparently as the lawmakers' dominant attitudes toward slavery and freedom changed.

Nevertheless, the total ban on manumissions was not typical. What does this tell us about the law, the lawmakers, and the lawmaking process in the United States South?

The Statutes Prohibiting Manumission and the Pro-Slavery Argument

One of slavery's characteristics in the United States South was a relatively low manumission rate. Orlando Patterson illustrated this by comparing the available manumission data with other slave holding societies, such as those in South Africa, Brazil, and Jamaica.[176]

Eva Sheppard Wolf examined Virginia's manumission data during the 1782 to 1806 period, when that state's laws gave masters the greatest freedom to free their slaves. She found that Virginia's annual manumission rate was only about one-tenth of one percent of all slaves, which was "among the lowest of all slave societies."[177] During this 24-year peak, Virginia's annual manumission rate was only two freed slaves per thousand slaves, or .02 percent. "These rates were not high from an individual slave's viewpoint. Assuming that the average slave life expectancy was about thirty-five years, an annual manumission rate of one per thousand would mean 3.5 percent of all slaves would be manumitted at some point in their lives, [and] 7 percent at the rate of two per thousand[.]"[178] In contrast, the average annual manumission rate on Curacao was 1.2 percent in the mid-nineteenth century and in Buenos Aires it was .04 percent in 1778 and it rose to 1.3 percent in 1810.[179]

This low manumission rate had two obviously negative effects on people held as slaves in the United States South. First, fewer slaves achieved their freedom before slavery was abolished by a general emancipation. Second, as Patterson concluded, in the United States South the promise of freedom generally was not as meaningful as an inducement to slave discipline.[180] Masters instead "used physical punishment 'as an integral part of their system for maintaining social discipline and regulating work activity[.]'"[181] The "few masters (mainly in the cities and border states) who allowed their slaves to buy their freedom 'understood that freedom was the greatest gift they could give their slaves, and they consciously used it as a mechanism of control and a means of encouraging divisions among blacks.'"[182]

The Southern law of slavery that restricted manumission may have contributed to this limited frequency of manumission, or those who made that law may have been influenced by the social views and values that called for limits on the master's right to free his or her slaves. Shawn Cole studied Louisiana's manumission records from the years 1725 to 1820. He found that "[t]he consensus view that manumission was less common in the American period than the Spanish period is correct[.]" The rate of manumission in Louisiana fell from 6.5 per 100 slave sales during the period 1725 to 1803, when Spanish law governed, to 2.3 manumissions per 100 slave sales during the period 1804-1820, when the United States laws governed Louisiana.[183]

Nevertheless, the Southern slave law in the later antebellum years moved toward an even more extreme position—an absolute prohibition of manumission to take effect anywhere. As George Stroud found: "Having degraded a rational and immortal being into a *chattel*,—a thing of bargain and sale,—it has been discovered that certain incidents result from this degradation which it concerns the welfare of the community vigorously to exact and preserve."[184]

In the United States South, "[t]he terms of manumission were set by slaveholders, for the benefit of slaveholders."[185] The democratically elected legislators and the elected or appointed judges, many of whom owned slaves or on whom slave owners did not lack influence, adopted and enforced the manumission laws.[186] Historians who studied Southern politics have concluded that the slave owners and their ideas dominated Southern pre-Civil War politics.[187] Officials did not last long if they opposed the slave masters' interests. For example, the opinions of Kentucky Court of Appeals Justice Benjamin Mills "contained some passages reflecting a clear hostility toward the institution of slavery." Thus, in 1828 Mills lost his seat on the court when the state's senate rejected the governor's nomination of Mills.[188]

The Southern states, beginning with the Virginia act of 1691, adopted various statutes that either regulated or prohibited the master's right to free his or her slaves. Jacob Wheeler's slave law treatise explained the justification for the statutes. He stated that because "slaves are a peculiar species of property, it will not excite surprise that laws are necessary for their regulation, and to protect society from even the benevolence of slave owners, in throwing among the community a great number of stupid, ignorant, and vicious persons, to disturb its peace, and to endanger its permanency."[189]

Wheeler stated that society's right "to regulate and control" slave property "may be justified on the same grounds as some other species of property."

> No one can doubt the right of individuals to acquire, possess, and sell gun powder. But if the possessor chooses to take it to his house or store, in a

city or populous town, the public become interested, and will restrain him within reasonable and proper limits. In New York, Philadelphia, Baltimore, and other populous places, this property, as an article of commerce, is regulated (as to the quantity to be kept in the city,) by the public laws. And the constitutionality of those laws cannot be doubted. So of slaves. The owner may keep as many as he pleases, but if he emancipates them, and turns them loose upon society, they have a right to protect themselves against his improvidence, or even his benevolence and generosity. They have a right to declare the act illegal or to restrain it within such bounds as shall secure their safety.[190]

In short, the lawmakers perceived the need to limit the master's "benevolence," when the perceived needs of society came into conflict with "generosity."

The legislators who adopted the manumission statutes sought primarily to limit the number of free blacks, as confirmed by Virginia's 1691 act. According to Arthur Howington, the lower court records in Tennessee indicate that the various antebellum changes in that state's manumission statutes had the effect of reducing the number of legally manumitted slaves. He also argued that the fears caused among slave owners by the Nat Turner rebellion contributed to the legislative hostility toward manumission in the latter antebellum years.[191] Ira Berlin wrote of a similar effect on manumissions in Virginia and Missouri counties.[192]

The economics of manumission posed a second policy concern. Slave values increased in the nineteenth century after the legal African slave trade was stopped.[193] According to Orlando Patterson, the high replacement costs of slaves, coupled with a limited external supply of new slaves, correlated with the United States South's low manumission rate.[194]

This low manumission rate, in turn, correlated with legislative hostility to a further reduction in the supply of slaves that would be caused by widespread manumission. "At the root of the legislative and judicial opposition to manumission stood the growing Southern commitment to slavery."[195]

The lawmakers' hostility to manumission was in harmony with the pro-slavery and overtly racist ideology that evolved in the nineteenth century South. This doctrine was based on the notions that blacks were inferior to whites and that blacks therefore never could hope to achieve equality with whites. It followed that slavery was better than freedom for blacks; because of their alleged racial defects freedom for them was a cruel joke.[196]

The Virginia judge and law writer St. George Tucker warned, in 1796, that a society based upon the inalienable rights of all people could not accommodate slavery into its law "unless we first degrade [the enslaved] below the rank of human beings, not only politically, but also physically and morally."[197] As Tucker predicted, a racist pro-slavery doctrine emerged in the antebellum years. It was a significant cultural fact in Southern law and society. This was not an ideology of a fringe group. Some of the South's most influential lawyers, judges, politicians, opinion leaders, and writers were among its adherents. Among others, John C. Calhoun, George Fitzhugh, Thomas R. Dew, George Frederick Holmes, James Henry Hammond, Henry Hughes, Chancellor William Harper, and Thomas R. R. Cobb argued that slavery was morally just and necessary.[198] "Virtually all of the major antebellum Southern defenders of slavery were educated in the law."[199]

Fitzhugh, for one example, contended that free laborers must earn sufficient wages to house and support their families. "Slavery relieves our slaves of these cares altogether," according to Fitzhugh, who praised slavery as "the very best form [] of Socialism."[200] He also stated that people of the same race could be slaves and masters, although he thought it generally was better if those who were dominant in a society imposed slavery upon persons of another nationality. He disapproved of black freedom because "the negro has neither energy nor enterprise," and because a freed black slave "finds with his improvident habits, that his liberty is a curse to himself, and a greater curse to the society around him."[201]

The positive good mentality had possibly its most explicit legal influence on the antebellum Southern manumission statutes and case law. The law allowing masters to free their black slaves could not coexist with this ideology. Therefore, in the nineteenth century, both the Southern courts and the legislatures determined that the public interest required them to restrict the masters' power and freedom to release their slaves from bondage.

The pro-slavery ideology found a clear voice in the law in Justice Joseph Lumpkin's opinions. Lumpkin was a long-time Justice of Georgia's Supreme Court. He called slavery a moral necessity "since blacks were divinely condemned to eternal service and since only under the tutelage of the superior white race could the black ever achieve the highest degree of civilization."[202]

Lumpkin wrote of black slavery as a biblical imperative: "To inculcate care and industry upon the descendants of Ham, is to preach to the idle winds. To be the 'servants of servants' is the judicial curse pronounced upon their race." Lumpkin called this principle a "Divine decree" that was "unreversible." He declared that "[i]t will run on parallel with time itself. And heaven and earth shall sooner pass away, than one jot or tittle of it shall abate." According to Lumpkin, only "[u]nder the superior race and no where else, do [blacks] attain to the highest degree of civilization[.]" He thus concluded that God's "ways are higher than ours; and humble submission is our best wisdom, as well as our first duty!"[203]

Lumpkin also called upon more recent history to justify slavery:

Our ancestors settled this State when a province, as a community of white men, professing the christian religion, and possessing an equality of rights and privileges. The blacks were introduced into it, as a race of Pagan slaves. The prejudice, if it can be called so, of caste, is unconquerable. It was so at the beginning. It has come down to our day. The suspicion of taint even, sinks the subject of it below the common level.

Lumpkin thus rejected the notion "that parity or rank would be allowed such a race[.]"[204] This racism fueled Lumpkin's hostility to manumission:

> To [the free black] there is but little prospect, but a life of poverty, of depression, of ignorance, and of decay. He lives amongst us without motive and without hope. His fancied freedom is all a delusion. All practical men must admit, that the slave who receives the care and protection of a tolerable master, is superior in comfort to the free negro. Generally, society suffers, and the negro suffers by manumission.[205]

Thus, Lumpkin was among the Southerners who came to oppose even foreign manumission of Georgia's slaves.[206]

Lumpkin also at times recognized slaves as moral agents capable of human thought, but his ideology was not internally inconsistent.[207] The rationale of slavery's oppression becomes clear when one looks critically at the types of cases in which Lumpkin and his brethren believed that they should recognize slave humanity.[208]

As will be noted in chapter six, Lumpkin and the other judges who explicitly advanced the positive good theory in their opinions often differed with some of their colleagues on points of manumission law. But this did not mean that the more "liberal" judges were anti-slavery. The South's judicial philosophy was pro-slavery. Although judges disagreed at times on the best way to advance slavery through law, they did not differ on the need to uphold that institution.[209]

Moreover, Lumpkin freely invoked the notion of humanity to the slave in his pro-slavery opinions. To Lumpkin, slavery's oppression was more humane than freedom to the black people held as slaves because of their racial inferiority. The harsh results Lumpkin reached were converted, through his ideological filter, to appear as the embodiment of benevolence. Accordingly, these references to slave humanity by Lumpkin and the other pro-slavery advocates became reifications—structures of thought and expression that masked slavery's oppression. Lumpkin's opinions are prime examples of how the concepts of humanity and right came to justify slavery's total despotism by making the state of affairs seem natural, good, and necessary.[210]

The statutes banning manumission and calling for free black exclusion from the slave states also manifested this pro-slavery theory in the law. The preamble to Georgia's 1818 act prohibiting manumission and free black settlement is instructive.[211] It stated that

> the principles of sound policy, considered in reference to the free citizens of this State, and the exercise of humanity towards the slave population within the same, imperiously require that the number of free persons of color within this State should not be increased by manumission, or by the admission of such persons from other States to reside [in Georgia].[212]

With the increasing influence of the positive good, pro-slavery ideology, the law eventually came to reflect a cultural consensus of an increasing hostility to the very idea of manumission, even if individual slave owners still clearly expressed their intention to free their slaves, and the freed slaves were to be sent and freed in a free state.

Southern legislators and judges came to perceive freed slaves to pose so great a sociological, psychological, and ideological threat to the white antebellum South, and all that it represented, that they responded by encroaching on the owner's right to free his chattel from the shackles of bondage. Some judges and legislators also found that any freed slaves anywhere were a real and an ideological threat, and they eventually prohibited manumission out of the state as well as in the state.[213]

Voluntary Enslavement

The positive good theory also was manifested in law by the statutes that the Southern legislatures adopted, beginning in 1856, generally permitting free blacks to enter into "voluntary" slavery. Before these statutes were adopted, the state legislatures entertained and sometimes granted individual enslavement petitions filed by free blacks, as they did for individual manumission requests. While they were either prohibiting manumission, barring the introduction of free blacks, or both, nine Southern states enacted statutes establishing procedures making it easier for free blacks to seek approval for their enslavement.[214]

Statutes adopted in Alabama, Florida, Louisiana, Maryland, Tennessee, Texas, Kentucky, Arkansas, and Virginia authorized the courts to approve the proposed enslavement. In South Carolina and Georgia, special acts of the legislature were required to approve the voluntary enslavement.[215] In Mississippi, the legislature continued to adopt special legislative acts permitting the enslavement of individual free blacks.[216] The North Carolina legislators considered various voluntary enslavement bills between 1858 and 1863, but they never adopted any of these proposals.[217] Nevertheless, during that period North Carolina's legislators considered individual enslavement petitions of free blacks, and some were granted.[218]

"These acts represented a culmination of the 'positive good' theory of slavery—that people of African descent lived happily as slaves and found freedom inconvenient or miserable."[219] These statutes were, in effect, the corollary of the laws that denied to masters the power to bestow freedom on their slaves and the free black exclusion laws. The legislators during the same time period gave to free blacks the power to convert their status, and that of their children, from free people with unequal rights to unfree people who became property without rights.[220]

For example, the Texas legislators adopted their state's voluntary enslavement act on January 27, 1858.[221] The statute was titled: "An Act to permit free persons of African descent to select their own master and become slaves." It permitted a "free person of African descent" over the age of 14 years, either in the state or later coming into the state, "to choose his or her master, and become a slave[.]"[222] If the claimant was a female with children younger than the age of 14, she could choose to enslave her children as well.[223]

Slavery claimants were required to file a petition with the district court in their county of residence. The petition was to state the name of the proposed master that the petitioner requested. It was to be signed by the petitioner and by at least two subscribing witnesses.[224] After the petition was filed, the court clerk was to post the petition on the court house door for four weeks. The clerk also was to issue a summons to the petitioner and the requested master, and to issue subpoenas to the witnesses to appear at a hearing.[225]

At the hearing, the district attorney was required to separately examine the petitioner, the master, and the subscribing witnesses.[226] The court could grant the petition if it was satisfied that there was no evidence of "fraud nor collusion between the parties, that the proposed master was of good repute, and there is no reason to the contrary[.]" The decree would provide that "the property in [the petitioner], as a slave, shall vest in the person so chosen as master, and his rights and liabilities, and the condition of the petitioner shall in all respects be the same as though the petitioner had been born a slave to the master so chosen."[227] The one exception stated that the new slave "shall not be subject to forced sales for any debt incurred by, or judgment rendered against the chosen master prior to the period of enslavement."[228] The act also provided that after the petition was filed, "no proceedings shall be had against the petitioner under any law prohibiting free persons of color from remaining in or coming to this State."[229]

The general voluntary enslavement acts adopted elsewhere contained similar provisions, although some of the details varied, such as the age limits for the enslavement petitioners. Virginia's 1856 act also required the court to determine the petitioner's value, and the new master was to deposit one-half of that value in the public treasury.[230] In March of 1861, the Virginia legislators adopted a new act that streamlined the pre-enslavement procedures and eliminated the cash contribution requirement. Instead, the new master was required to post a bond as security that the new slave would not become a public charge, and the master was required to pay the slave's debts.[231] Kentucky's version of the act provided a $500 fine for those convicted of accepting a free black as a slave, but "not with the *bona fide* intention of making him or her a slave...."[232]

According to Randolph Campbell, "Some free Negroes actually enslaved themselves" under the Texas act, but the district court records "give absolutely no hint as to the motivation" of the petitioners. The local newspapers in Texas nevertheless found these petitions for enslavement to be newsworthy, and they "gleefully reported such cases as evidence that slavery was better than freedom for Negroes."[233]

Enslavement petitions and newspaper reports about them also existed in other Southern states. The petitions speak eloquently of the dilemma that free blacks faced in the late antebellum South. The Southern legislators adopted statutes that so limited free black legal rights and social standing that petitioners of both sexes and of all ages found slavery to be a better alternative.[234]

The Southern newspapers dutifully cited these enslavement requests as triumphs of slavery over freedom instead of being a result of the unjust laws that provided free blacks with inferior legal rights.[235] For example, a Georgia newspaper reported and commented favorably on the 1857 voluntary enslavement of Elizabeth Bickley, a 22-year-old free black woman, as follows: "The woman is very intelligent, and was full aware that a kind master was better able to provide and care for her than she was herself. This is a nut for the Yankee philosophers to crack."[236]

The only officially reported decision interpreting one of these statutes is in the Texas Supreme Court case of *Westbrook v. Mitchell*.[237] The plaintiff, John B. Westbrook, sued the defendant, William L. Mitchell, Jr., "for the recovery of a negro, alleged to have been formerly a free negro, but who had, for a consideration stated in the petition, sold himself to the plaintiff, and who had been enticed out of his possession, by the defendant."[238] Westbrook's petition claimed ownership of the "negro man," alleging that "sometime in the year 1855, [the free black man], did, in the state of Texas, for a consideration in money, sell his freedom to the plaintiff, and agree to be, during the rest of his life, the slave of the plaintiff, in the same manner as if he had been born a slave, the property of the plaintiff." Westbrook sought a declaration that "the relation of master and slave exists between the plaintiff and the negro man named in the petition[,]" and "that the plaintiff may recover the negro man as his slave."[239]

The Texas Supreme Court, in a decision by Justice James H. Bell, affirmed the lower court order that dismissed Westbrook's claim. Justice Bell noted that "slavery could originate, under the Roman law, in three ways, viz., by birth, when the mother was a slave; by captivity in war; and by the voluntary sale of himself, as a slave, by a freeman, above the age of twenty, for the sake of sharing the price."[240] He stated that "[t]he individual who is claimed as a slave in the petition before us, is described as 'a free negro of African descent.' So far as we have been able to inform ourselves, the slavery of negroes of African descent, has its origin in this country, in one way only..., by birth of a slave mother; except where other modes of originating the condition of slavery, as to such persons, have been prescribed by statutes, from considerations of public policy."[241]

Justice Bell stated that, before the legislature adopted the 1858 act, Texas law "did not recognize any persons as slaves, except such as were the offspring of slave mothers. It has never been judicially declared, in this country, so far as we know, that a negro of African descent, or any other person, could sell himself into slavery; and we do not therefore feel at liberty to recognize this as one of the modes in which slavery may originate." He stated that in the voluntary enslavement statute, the legislature

> evinced the greatest caution in prescribing the manner in which free negroes might enter into the condition of slavery. The act requires all the proceedings to be of the most public and formal character. The district

courts must have supervision of the matter. The court must be satisfied that there is no fraud; that the proposed master is a person of good repute, and that no good reason exists, why the relation of master and slave should not be formed in the particular case. This caution of the legislature will suggest to the intelligent mind, that there are reasons of public policy, why the courts of the state should not recognize the right of free negroes to sell themselves into slavery. The recognition of such a right might lead to its exercise for bad purposes. It would be impossible to prevent frauds. Sometimes the negro might be the only sufferer, but at other times, the public might feel the bad effects of permitting negroes to reside amongst us, under the nominal protection of designing men.[242]

Therefore, the court held: "We are not inclined to initiate any new rule not heretofore recognized in the jurisprudence of the country, but to leave the subject to be regulated by the general and well known law of the land, that the slavery of the negro in this country depends upon birth, and subject to such further regulations as the legislature, in its wisdom, has thought proper to prescribe."[243]

These voluntary enslavement petitions and the laws permitting them were the antithesis of the laws permitting the manumission and freedom suits, but the racial basis for slavery was a constant in both. This probably explains why the South Carolina legislature rejected three enslavement petitions that Lucy Adams, a free person of color, filed between 1858 and 1863. The legislators apparently concluded that she could not be a "voluntary" slave because her mother was white.[244]

Orlando Patterson concluded that voluntary or self-enslavement was one of the means by which people have been enslaved in human history. "Poverty was, of course, one of the main reasons for self-sale[.]"[245] He does not cite the United States South as one of the societies in which self-sale was a major source of slaves. The self-enslavement laws of the late antebellum years were not in effect long enough to have had a major effect.

The Re-enslavement of Freed Slaves

According to Patterson, "[t]he act of manumission creates not just a new person and a new life, but a new status[.]"[246] In almost all slave societies, the freed slaves had "a strong patron-client bond" with their former masters, and the law in most societies recognized and enforced this bond. In some of these societies, freed slaves could be re-enslaved if they violated the post-manumission duties of respect that they owed to their former masters.[247]

The Roman law of slavery regulated the freed slaves' conduct, and imposed on them a continuing duty to show respect or *obsequium* toward their former masters. This "involved, among other things, restrictions on a freedman's right to sue his patron and the obligation to support a needy patron."[248]

During the reign of Commodus, between the years 180 and 192, Alan Watson states that a law was enacted providing for the re-enslavement of slaves who committed extreme violations of this duty of respect or who struck or assaulted a former master. These ungrateful former slaves were to be returned to the power of the former master, and if they resisted this command, they could be sold by the governor and the former owner would receive the benefit of the price paid for the slave. This re-enslavement did not apply to slaves who were freed by a master who was obligated to do so under a will or trust or to slaves who purchased their freedom with their own money.[249] A provision in *Las Siete Partidas* imposed similar obligations on freed slaves. It also excluded from re-enslavement slaves who purchased their freedom.[250]

The slave law in the Americas, including the United States, generally did not impose the threat of legal re-enslavement upon freed slaves because the law did not require freed slaves to obey these post-manumission duties of respect. The Portuguese and Dutch colonial laws were exceptions that followed Roman law.[251] In Brazil, however, re-enslavement "fell into disuse over the nineteenth century, and was practically nonexistent from the 1860s onward."[252]

Accordingly, slave law in the United States could be viewed as being more favorable to the freed slave than the Roman, Castilian, and colonial Dutch and Portuguese laws, because it did not hold the threat of re-enslavement over the head of freed slaves for breaches of the client and patron bond between freed slaves and their former masters. To the contrary, in the antebellum years the Southern law was evolving toward a rule that anticipated no relationship between freed slaves and their former owners; the freed slaves were to vacate the state and never return.

Nevertheless, the legislators from time to time adopted statutes that permitted some freed slaves to remain in the state if they were perceived to be of good character and if they had white supporters. Thus, there may have been a similarity in the practice of the client and patron bond. Freed slaves who had good relationships with their former masters and other whites had a greater chance of winning the "right" to remain in their home state with their families and friends.[253]

But this legal permission to remain in the state was tenuous. The Southern colonies and states also at times adopted laws permitting the re-enslavement of freed slaves who did not behave properly. Moreover, the Southern law generally denied freed slaves and other free blacks equal legal rights and opportunities, and these legal restrictions tended to increase in time. Ira Berlin and others have shown that over time the life of freed slaves in the South became so difficult that some free black people decided that they did have to resort to voluntary enslavement.[254]

Conclusion

The antebellum Southern legislators and judges thus increasingly limited the individual master's power to free his or her slaves. These restraints extended to the master's power to permit his or her slaves to self-hire their time.

Nevertheless, even the most liberal laws, like those in Delaware that allowed manumission but required masters to post bonds before freeing slaves, may have prevented some manumissions. How many we may never know. But for one example, a Delaware Quaker who wanted to free his slaves "just prior to the revolution ... did not because of the 'oppressive law in force relative to the freeing of negroes.'"[255]

In chapters five and six, we will see how this legal trend restricting manumission is further illustrated by the judicial decisions interpreting the manumission statutes. Before we can fairly review and evaluate the decisions interpreting and applying these statutes, however, we need to review the procedures that the courts applied in the manumission and freedom suits.

Notes to Chapter 3

[1] *See* Cobb, *supra* at 279.

[2] *M'Cutchen v. Marshall*, 33 U.S. (8 Pet.) 220, 8 L. Ed. 923, 1834 WL 3795 at *13 (1834); *see Jones v. Laney*, 2 Tex. 342, 1847 WL 3563 at *5 (1847).

[3] *See* 3 William Blackstone, *Commentaries on the Laws of England* *216-*221 (1768), on nuisance; and at *211 on an owner's liability in trespass for damage caused by loose cattle. *See also* William L. Prosser, *et al.*, *Prosser and Keeton on the Law of Torts* 616-43 (5th ed. 1984).

[4] *See* Prosser, *et al.*, *Prosser and Keeton on the Law of Torts* 643-50.

[5] *See* Morris, *Slavery*, *supra* at 372; Cobb, *supra* at 279.

[6] Berlin, *Slaves Without Masters*, *supra* at 138.

[7] *See* Allan Kulikoff, *Tobacco and Slaves: The Development of Southern Cultures in the Chesapeake, 1680-1800* 40-42 (1986); Fede, *People Without Rights*, *supra* at 29-38; *see also* this book's preface, *supra* at notes 52-53.

I will not address here two issues that scholars have long debated: (1) when and how the practice or custom of holding people and their children as slaves for life began in each British colony, and (2) when and how the lawmakers first explicitly legitimized this practice or custom. I also will not address the two related issues: (1) whether slavery's beginnings were the result of the colonists' unthinking or intentional decision making, and (2) whether racism or slavery came first in practice and in law. *See generally, e.g.*, Tomlins, *Freedom Bound*, *supra* at 463-75; Parent, *supra* at 105-34; Alden T. Vaughn, *Roots of American Racism: Essays on the Colonial Experience* 128-74 (1995); T. H. Breen & Stephen Innes, *"Myne Owne Ground": Race and Freedom on Virginia's Eastern Shore* 19-25 (1980).

[8] *See* Russell, *Free Negro*, *supra* at 42-50.

[9] *See* Berlin, *Many Thousands*, *supra* at 29-46; Breen & Innes, *supra* at 7-18; and the authorities at chapter 1, *supra* at note 80.

[10] *See* Fede, *People Without Rights*, *supra* at 46; *see also* William E. Nelson, *The Common Law in Colonial America: The Chesapeake and New England 1607-1660* 13-

22 (2008) [hereinafter Nelson, *Common Law*]; Morgan, *Slave Counterpoint, supra* at 11-13; Kulikoff, *supra* at 1-6.

In my 1985 article, I first outlined a general development pattern for plantation slavery in the slave colonies and the later-settled slave states in the United States South. This included four stages: the frontier period, the plantation boom, the mature plantation period, and the decline of plantation slavery. I based this pattern on the relevant social, political, economic, and intellectual developments. Fede, "Legitimized Violence," *supra* at 101-10. I applied this pattern to place the changes in slavery's criminal law into their ever-changing non-legal context. *Id.* at 110-50. I also applied this approach to the law of slave sales, Fede, "Slave Buyers," *supra* at 322-29, 356-58, and later, in *People Without Rights*, to the development of criminal law, manumission law, and commercial law in the South. *See* Fede, *People Without Rights, supra* at 45-60. I cited the early twentieth century economic histories written by Ulrich B. Phillips and Lewis C. Gray. *See id.*, citing 1 Lewis C. Gray, *History of Agriculture in the Southern United States to 1860* 14-22, 42-59, 213-34, 312-41, 437-62 (reprint ed. 1958) (1932); Phillips, *American Negro Slavery, supra* at 73-186; Ulrich B. Phillips, "Introduction," in 1 *A Documentary History of American Industrial Society, Plantation and Frontier Documents: 1649-1863 Illustrative of Industrial History in the Colonial and Ante-Bellum South* 69-104 (Ulrich B. Phillips, ed.) (1909) [hereinafter *Plantation and Frontier Documents*]; Ulrich B. Phillips, "The Origin and Growth of the Southern Black Belts," 11 *Am. Hist. Rev.* 798 (1906) (the latter two articles are reprinted in Ulrich B. Phillips, *The Slave Economy of the Old South: Selected Essays in Economic and Social History* 3-22, 95-116 (Eugene Genovese, ed.) (1968)).

In his 1998 book comparing the early development of the slave societies in the Chesapeake and the South Carolina low country, Phillip D. Morgan used a similar pattern consisting of "a frontier phase, a period of institution building (characterized, above all, by a heavy black migration), and a mature phase (marked among other things, by the natural growth of the slave population and a routinization of slave life)." *See* Morgan, *Slave Counterpoint, supra* at xviii, citing Willie Lee Rose, "The Domestication of Domestic Slavery," in *Slavery and Freedom* 18-36 (William W. Freehling, ed.) (1982); Ira Berlin, "Time, Space, and the Evolution of Afro-American Society in British Mainland America," 85 *Am. Hist. Rev.* 44 (1980).

Robert Olwell also approved of this approach as Morgan applied it, but he expanded it to include seven phases of South Carolina low country slave society evolution, concluding with the Civil War. *See* Robert Olwell, "The Long History of a Low Place: Slavery on the South Carolina Coast, 1670-1870," in *Slavery South, supra* at 123-26. Ira Berlin elaborated on this approach in Berlin, *Generations in Captivity, supra* at 2-144; *see generally, e.g.*, discussing the development of plantations and slavery, Walsh, *supra* and Eltis, *Rise of African Slavery, supra* at 29-84; Kulikoff, *supra*; David W. Galenson, *White Servitude in Colonial America* 117-82 (1981); David W. Galenson, "White Servitude and the Growth of Black Slavery in Colonial America," 41 *J. Econ. Hist.* 39 (1981); Russell W. Menard, "The Africanization of the Lowcountry Labor Force, 1670-1730," in *Race and Family in the Colonial South* (Winthrop D. Jordan and Sheila L. Skemp, eds.) (1987); Russell W. Menard, "From Servants to Slaves: The Transformation of the Chesapeake Labor System," 16 *Southern Studies* 355 (1977) [hereinafter Menard, "Chesapeake"]. Both of Menard's essays are reprinted in Russell W. Menard, *Migrants, Servants and Slaves: Unfree Labor in Colonial British America* (2001).

[11] Fede, *People Without Rights, supra* at 46-47.

12 Nelson, *Common Law*, *supra* at 23-48; Kulikoff, *supra* at 23-44; Fede, *People Without Rights*, *supra* at 57, n. 4; Menard, "Chesapeake," *supra* at 383-85.

13 Fede, *People Without Rights*, *supra* at 31, 35, 46.

14 3 Hening, *supra* at 447-62; *see* Tomlins, *Freedom Bound*, *supra* at 469-70; Walsh, *supra* at 203-05; Kulikoff, *supra* at 320-21; Fede, *People Without Rights*, *supra* at 34-35.

15 *See* Russell, *Free Negro*, *supra* at 51; *see also* Mechal Sobel, *The World They Made Together: Black and White Values in Eighteenth-Century Virginia* 45 (1987); Breen & Innes, *supra* at 107-14.

16 3 Hening, *supra* at 87-88; *see* Tomlins, *Freedom Bound*, *supra* at 468; Morris, *Slavery*, *supra* at 393; Finkelman, *Casebook*, *supra* at 108-09; Higginbotham, *Color*, *supra* at 48.

17 *See* Parent, *supra* at 120. Bradley J. Nicholson cited this 1691 act as one of the examples supporting his view that the early colonial lawmakers in Virginia and on Barbados borrowed non-slave law concepts, such as the transportation of criminals and other undesirables out of the territory, from "English precedents for controlling servants and vagabonds." He argued that "while a body of slave law had to be created in these colonies, it is a mistake to assume that it was created out of nothing." *See* Nicholson, *supra* at 48, 53-54; *compare* Fede, *People Without Rights*, *supra* at 29-30.

18 *See* Parent, *supra* at 120; Adele Hast, "The Legal Status of the Negro in Virginia 1705-1765," 54 *J. of Negro Hist.* 217, 220 (1969).

19 Fede, *People Without Rights*, *supra* at 35, 36.

20 Parent, *supra* at 132; Fede, *People Without Rights*, *supra* at 47.

21 4 Hening, *supra* at 132; *see* Brown, *Good Wives*, *supra* at 216-20; Morris, *Slavery*, *supra* at 393; Finkelman, *Casebook*, *supra* at 109; Hast, *supra* at 220-21. The legislators reenacted this statute in 1753. 6 Hening, *supra* at 111; *see* Russell, *Free Negro*, *supra* at 52-53. For a 1728 case in which this provision was enforced to seize and re-enslave Tom, "an Indian boy slave[,]" *see* Ablavsky, *supra* at 1477.

22 *See* Morris, *Slavery*, *supra* at 393-94; 1 Catterall, *supra* at 72, n. 144; Russell, *Free Negro*, *supra* at 52-53; Hast, *supra* at 221.

23 Russell, *Free Negro*, *supra* at 53, quoting William Gooch's letter to the Board of Trade; *see* Morgan, *Slave Counterpoint*, *supra* at 625; Sobel, *supra* at 99.

24 11 Hening, *supra* at 308 (1783 act freeing Aberdeen); 10 *Id.* at 372 (1780 act freeing Ned and Kate); 10 *Id.* at 211 (1779 act freeing John Hope, William Beck, and Pegg); 10 *Id.* at 115 (1779 act feeing Kitt); 9 *Id.* at 320-21 (1777 act freeing Rachel and her daughter Rachel); *see* Eva Sheppard Wolf, *Race and Liberty in the New Nation: Emancipation in Virginia from the Revolution to Nat Turner's Rebellion* 30-31 (2006) [hereinafter Wolf, *Race*]; 1 Catterall, *supra* at 72.

25 11 Hening, *supra* at 308; 10 *Id.* at 115; *see* Wolf, *Race*, *supra* at 30, n. 40.

26 Morris, *Slavery*, *supra* at 394.

27 Wolf, *Race*, *supra* at 28-34; Paul Finkelman, *Slavery and the Founders: Race and Liberty in the Age of Jefferson* 137-38 (2d ed. 2001) [hereinafter Finkelman, *Founders*]; Russell, *Free Negro*, *supra* at 55.

[28] Wolf, *Race, supra* at 34; *see also* Allison Goodyear Freehling, *Drift Toward Dissolution: The Virginia Slavery Debate of 1831-1832* 88-89 (1982).

[29] 11 Hening, *supra* at 39-40; *see* Morris, *Slavery, supra* at 394; Finkelman, *Casebook, supra* at 109-10; Higginbotham, *Color, supra* at 49.

[30] 1 Benjamin Watkins Leigh, William Waller Hening, and William Mumford, *The Revised Code of the Laws of Virginia* 434 (1819) [hereinafter *Virginia Code 1819*]; *see* Morris, *Slavery, supra* at 389; Russell, *Free Negro, supra* at 82.

[31] Wolf, *Race, supra* at 34; Morris, *Slavery, supra* at 394-98; Russell, *Free Negro, supra* at 61. On December 13, 1787, the legislature adopted two acts that gave retroactive effect to the 1782 statute by enforcing the pre-1782 manumissions intended by Charles Moorman and Joseph Mayo. *See* 12 Henning, *supra* at 611-13; *Mayo v. Carrington*, 8 Va. (4 Call) 472, 1791 WL 338 (1791) (deciding issues relating to the distribution of the remainder of Mayo's estate). In contrast, the legislature later refused to adopt similar legislation that Robert Pleasants sought authorizing the manumissions intended by his father and brother, thus leading to the case of *Pleasants v. Pleasants*, 6 Va. (2 Call) 319, 1800 WL 404 (1800). *See* chapter 6, *supra* at 22-35.

[32] Berlin, *Slaves Without Masters, supra* at 59-61, 159-51; Eva Sheppard Wolf, "Manumission and the Two-Race System in Early National Virginia," in *Paths to Freedom, supra* [hereinafter, Wolf, "Manumission"]; Ellen Eslinger, "Liberation in a Rural Context: the Valley of Virginia, 1800-1860," in *Paths to Freedom, supra*; James H. Kettner, "Persons or Property? The Pleasants Slaves in the Virginia Courts 1792-1799," in *Launching the "Extended Republic": The Federalist Era* (Ronald Hoffman and Peter J. Albert, eds.) (1996).

[33] Berlin, *Slaves Without Masters, supra* at 46-48; *see also* Freehling, *supra* at 88-89.

[34] Kulikoff, *supra* at 433-34; Berlin, *Slaves Without Masters, supra* at 150.

[35] *See* Berlin, *Slaves Without Masters, supra* at 101.

[36] *See* MacLeod, *supra* at 138, citing *Dawson v. Thurston*, 12 Va. (2 Hen. & M.) 132, 1808 WL 572 (1808).

[37] *See Pleasants v. Pleasants*, 6 Va. (2 Call) 319, 1800 WL 404 (1800).

[38] Berlin, *Slaves Without Masters, supra* at 101.

[39] Wolf, *Race, supra* at 113.

[40] 3 Samuel Shepherd, *The Statutes at Large of Virginia from October 1792 to December 1806* 252-53 (1836); 1 *Virginia Code 1819, supra* at 436; *see* Wolf, *Race, supra* at 85-86, 121-26; Morris, *Slavery, supra* at 394; Finkelman, *Casebook, supra* at 111-12; Freehling, *supra* at 116-17; Winthrop D. Jordan, *White Over Black: American Attitudes Toward the Negro, 1550-1812* 574-77 (1968) [hereinafter Jordan, *White Over Black*]; Higginbotham & Higginbotham, *supra* at 1266. The act was later amended to permit slaves who were freed while they were minors to remain in the state until one year after they reached the age of 21. *See Virginia Code 1819, supra* at 436.

[41] 3 Shepherd, *supra* at 251; *see* Wolf, *Race, supra* at 25-27, 126.

[42] *See id.* at 125, 131-38; Katz, *supra* at 948-49.

[43] Russell, *Free Negro, supra* at 156; *see* Eslinger, *supra* at 366 (finding no records of

enforcement in Rockbridge or Augusta Counties "until after mid century"); Katz, *supra* at 949 (noting "lax enforcement" of the act); Luther P. Jackson, "Manumission in Certain Virginia Cities," 15 *J. of Negro Hist.* 278, 298 (1930) (calling the statute a "dead letter"); *see also* Wolf, *Race, supra* at 130-38 (discussing enforcement efforts in Loudoun County in the 1830s and in Accomack County in the 1820s); Melvin Patrick Ely, *Israel on the Appomattox: A Southern Experiment in Black Freedom from the 1790s through the Civil War* 371-72 (2004) (discussing 1850 prosecutions in Prince Edward County of Jesse Woodson and Isaac Coles) [hereinafter Ely, *Israel*]; Morris, *Slavery, supra* at 372 (discussing 1834 Charles County order selling Patty Green and Betty back into slavery); Gurza-Lavalle, *supra* at 56-60 (discussing prosecutions in several counties, and concluding: "There is significant evidence that Virginia communities often looked the other way, and not infrequently even helped free blacks dodge the law.").

44 Wolf, *Race, supra* at 138.

45 1 *Virginia Code 1819, supra* at 436-37; *see* Wolf, *Race, supra* at 138; Finkelman, *Casebook, supra* at 112-13.

46 *Rucker's Adm'r v. Gilbert*, 30 Va. (3 Leigh) 8, 1831 WL 1927 at *1 (1831).

47 *Rucker's Adm'r v. Gilbert*, 1831 WL 1927 at *2; *see Walthall's Ex'or v. Robertson*, 29 Va. (2 Leigh) 189, 1830 WL 1558 (1830) (affirming judgment denying freedom claim, master's will stated desire to free slaves in Virginia, if the law allowed it at his death); *see also* Ely, *Israel, supra* at 379 (stating that the 1806 law "did have a chilling effect on would be emancipators who did not want to put their former slaves at risk of being expelled").

48 *See* Wolf, *Race, supra* at 138-47; Higginbotham & Higginbotham, *supra* at 1267.

49 1 *The Code of Virginia*, title 30, ch. 107, §§2-4, at 466 (1849) [hereinafter *Virginia Code 1849*]; Finkelman, *Casebook, supra* at 114-15; Eslinger, *supra* at 367; Jackson, *supra* at 298.

50 *See* Eslinger, *supra* at 366-67; Katz, *supra* at 948-51; Higginbotham & Higginbotham, *supra* at 1268; Marainne Burhoff Sheldon, "Black-White Relations in Richmond, Virginia, 1782-1820," 45 *J. of Southern Hist.* 27, 41 (1979); Jackson, *supra* at 298-300; *and see* Gurza-Lavalle, *supra* (discussing petitions to the legislature). Eslinger noted evidence that some masters sought to "bypass" this and other legal restrictions on manumission. Eslinger, *supra* at 367-75.

51 *Acts of the General Assembly of Virginia Passed in 1852* 330 (1852) (quoting 1852 constitution, art. IV, §§19-21); *see* Morris, *Slavery, supra* at 394; Finkelman, *Casebook, supra* at 115; Higginbotham, *Color, supra* at 49-50; *see also* John Dinan, *The Virginia State Constitution: A Reference Guide* 7-16 (2006); Freehling, *supra* at 235-50.

52 *See* "An Act to protect and indemnify Citizens of Virginia," in *Acts of the General Assembly of the State of Virginia, Passed at Called Session, 1862* Chapter 6, 112-15 (Richmond 1862); *but see* Higginbotham & Higginbotham, *supra* at 1267 (stating this statute prohibited all manumissions and fined judges). This statute appears to be in response to: (1) the adoption in 1861 and 1862 of the constitution for the counties that, in December 1862, became West Virginia; (2) the July 17, 1862 second confiscation act, authorizing the United States courts to free the slaves of persons "engaged in any rebellion," and permitting the president "to employ as many persons of African descent as he may deem necessary and proper for the suppression of this rebellion"; and (3) the

July 17, 1862 militia act, freeing union soldiers of African descent "who by the laws of any State shall owe service or labor to any person who, during the recent rebellion has levied war or has born arms against the United States, or adhered to their enemies by giving them aid and comfort[.]" The militia act extended freedom to the slave soldiers' mothers, wives, and children. *See* 12 *Statutes at Large, supra* at 589-92, 597-600, 633-34; Silvana R. Siddali, *From Property to Person: Slavery and the Confiscation Acts 1861-1862* 55-94, 120-250 (2005); John Syrett, *The Civil War Confiscation Acts: Failing to Reconstruct the South* 1-54 (2005); Herman Belz, *Abraham Lincoln, Constitutionalism, and Equal Rights in the Civil War Era* 105-13 (1998); Frank J. Williams, "'Doing Less' and 'Doing More': The President and the Proclamation—Legally, Militarily, and Politically," in Harold Holzer, ed., *The Emancipation Proclamation: Three Views, Harold Holzer, Edna Greene Medford, Frank Williams* 48-66 (2006); Robert M. Bastress, *The West Virginia State Constitution: A Reference Guide* 9-15 (1995).

[53] *See Journal of the House of Delegates of the State of Virginia for the Called Session of 1863* 91-92 (Richmond 1863) (referring to special committee a motion to "enquire into the expediency of altogether prohibiting the manumission of slaves in the Commonwealth by will or otherwise"); *Journal of the Senate of the Commonwealth of Virginia* 136 (1849) (rejecting on March 5, 1850 a bill banning manumission by will or by a deed to take effect in the future, by a vote of 11 to 11).

[54] Wolf, *Race, supra* at 35.

[55] *Id.*

[56] *Id.* at 36-37; 11 Hening, *supra* at 23.

[57] Wolf, *Race, supra* at 125; *see* Robert McColley, *Slavery and Jeffersonian Virginia* 161-62 (2d ed. 1973).

[58] *See* Higginbotham, *Color, supra* at 259; Olwell, "Becoming Free," *supra* (discussing South Carolina manumission deeds filed between 1740 and 1790).

[59] *See* Berlin, *Slaves Without Masters, supra* at 138-39; *see also* Shaw, *supra* at 79-103 (state-by-state chronological summary of the manumission laws); Stroud, *supra* at 96-104; James Benson Sellers, *Slavery in Alabama* 236-41 (2d ed. 1964); Charles Sackett Sydnor, *Slavery in Mississippi* 203-38 (reprint ed. 1965) (1933) [hereinafter, Sydnor, *Slavery in Mississippi*]; Howell Meadoes Henry, *The Police Control of the Slave in South Carolina* 168-76 (reprint ed. 1968) (1914); Wheeler, *supra* at 386-88; Benjamin Joseph Klebaner, "American Manumission Laws and the Responsibility for Supporting Slaves," 63 *Va. Mag. of Hist. & Bio.* 443, 443 (1955). On Delaware, *see* Essah, *supra* at 36-41; Williams, *Slavery and Freedom in Delaware, supra* at 71-72, 141-58.

Robert Shaw's chronological summary was very helpful in the preparation of this chapter, as reflected by the many citations to his book, which also was of assistance where I have instead cited the works of others. Nevertheless, in the more analytical summary that follows, and in the preceding discussion of Virginia law, I have added citations to some of the statutes to which Shaw referred without citations. I also have included references to additional statutes and references to secondary sources, which provide the contexts for the adoption of the statutes cited. I believe that the analytical approach that follows can provide further insights into the patterns of legal change.

[60] Shaw, *supra* at 79.

[61] *See* Berlin, *Slaves Without Masters, supra* at 29; Stroud, *supra* at 98-99; *see also* for

Maryland, *Laws of Maryland, 1796*, ch. 67, §§13, 29, & 30; *Laws of Maryland, 1790*, ch. 9, §§2 & 3; Shaw, *supra* at 80; Brackett, *supra* at 151-53; for Kentucky, *see* 2 William Littell, *The Statute Law of Kentucky: With Notes, Praelections, and Observations on the Public Acts* 119-20, 387 (1810) (1798 and 1800 acts); 1 William Littell, *The Statute Law of Kentucky: With Notes, Praelections, and Observations on the Public Acts* 246-47 (1809) (1794 act); *Lee v. Lee's Executors*, 48 Ky. (1 Dana) 48, 1833 WL 2414 (1833); Jones, *Fathers, supra* at 73; Shaw, *supra* at 94-95; 1 Catterall, *supra* at 276; for Louisiana, *see* Rose, *supra* at 177, quoting *Civil Code*, Art. 184-96; and for the Arkansas statute adopted on February 19, 1838, *see Revised Statutes of the State of Arkansas*, ch. 56, §§1-8 at 359-60 (1838) [hereinafter *Revised Statutes of Arkansas*]; *Campbell v. Campbell*, 13 Ark. 513, 1853 WL 540 at *4 (1853); Shaw, *supra* at 96; Taylor, *Negro Slavery in Arkansas, supra* at 237-38; L. Scott Stafford, "Slavery and the Arkansas Supreme Court," 19 *U. Ark. L.R. L.J.* 413, 448 (1997). The Missouri law originated with an 1804 act that was adopted when the area was known as the District of Louisiana. *See* 2 Hurd, *supra* at 166-67; *see also* 2 Charles H. Hardin, *Revised Statutes of Missouri*, ch. 150, art. II, §§1-2 at 1478 (1856) [hereinafter *Revised Statutes of Missouri*].

62 *See, e.g., Proceedings and Acts of the General Assembly, 1752-1754*, ch. 1; Shaw, *supra* at 78-79; Cobb, *supra* at 281-82; Klebaner, *supra* at 443, 451-53.

63 *See* Wahl, *Burden, supra* at 161; Klebaner, *supra* at 443-49; *see also* for Delaware, 1 *Laws of Delaware, supra* at 214, 435-36; Essah, *supra* at 38-40; Williams, *Slavery and Freedom in Delaware, supra* at 143 (Delaware act of 1740 requiring a 30 pound bond for unhealthy slaves and those older than 35, and the act of 1767, requiring a 60 pound bond for all freed slaves); for Kentucky, 2 Littell, *supra* at 119-20; 1 Littell, *supra* at 247; Jones, *Fathers, supra* at 73; for Tennessee, 1 John Haywood & Robert L. Cobbs, eds., *The Statute Laws of the State of Tennessee of Public and General Nature* 327 (1831) (for *Laws of Tennessee 1801*, ch. 27) [hereinafter Haywood & Cobbs, *Laws of Tennessee*]; "An act concerning free persons of colour, and for other purposes," in *Tennessee Acts, 1831, supra* ch. 102, §2 at 121-22; Howington, *What Sayeth, supra* at 33, n. 7, 34, n. 9; for North Carolina, 2 Henry Potter, J. L. Taylor, & Bart Yancey, *Laws of the State of North Carolina* 947-48 (1821); Franklin, *Free Negro, supra* at 27; for Florida, this chapter *infra* at note 97. Missouri's 1820 constitution, at article III, §26, granted to the General Assembly the power: "To permit the owners of slaves to emancipate them, saving the rights of creditors, where the person emancipating will give security that the slave so emancipated shall not become a public charge." The legislature did not adopt an act requiring pre-manumission bonds, and the Missouri Supreme Court declined an invitation to declare the manumission statute unconstitutional. *See Milton (of color) v. McKarney*, 31 Mo. 175, 1860 WL 6210 at *3 (1860).

64 2 *Laws of Delaware, supra* at 886; *Trustees of the Poor of Sussex County v. Hall*, 3 Del. (3 Harr.) 322, 1841 WL 389 at *3 (Del. Super. 1841). *See* Essah, *supra* at 40; Williams, *Slavery and Freedom in Delaware, supra* at 143-44.

65 *See* Williams, *Slavery and Freedom in Delaware, supra* at 144; Klebaner, *supra* at 446-47.

66 *See* Rose, *supra* at 177, quoting *Louisiana Civil Code*, Art. 188.

67 *See* 2 *Revised Statutes of Missouri, supra* at ch. 150, art. II, §4 at 1479; *Revised Statutes of Arkansas, supra* §4 at 360; *Campbell v. Campbell*, 13 Ark. 513, 1853 WL 540 at *4; Stafford, *supra* at 448.

[68] *See Laws of Maryland, 1796,* ch. 67, §§13, 29, & 30; *Laws of Maryland, 1790,* ch. IX, §III; *Proceedings and Acts of the General Assembly, 1752-1754,* ch. 1; Brackett, *supra* at 151-53; Worthington G. Snethen, *The Black Code of the District of Columbia in Force September 1st, 1848* 25-26 (1848); *see also Wilson v. Barnett,* 9 G. & J. 158 (Md. 1837); *Anderson v. Bailey,* 8 G. & J. 32 (Md. 1836); *Hamilton v. Cragg,* 6 H. & J. 16 (Md. 1823).

[69] *Proceedings and Acts of the General Assembly, 1752-1754,* ch. 1.

[70] *See* Schafer, *Becoming Free, supra* at 4; Rose, *supra* at 177, quoting *Louisiana Civil Code,* Art. 185.

[71] *See* Spear, *supra* at 194; Rose, *supra* at 177, quoting *Louisiana Civil Code,* Art. 186. The legislature also adopted special manumission acts that in effect granted exceptions from the minimum age requirement. *See* Spear, *supra* at 195.

[72] *See* Wahl, *Burden, supra* at 163; Morris, *Slavery, supra* at 388-92; Cobb, *supra* at 281-82, 294, 298-301; Stroud, *supra* at 96; *see also* for Maryland, *Laws of Maryland, 1796,* ch. 67, §13; *Laws of Maryland, 1790,* ch. 9, §3; Brackett, *supra* at 158-61; Snethen, *supra,* at 25; for Kentucky, 2 Littell, *supra* at 120; 1 Littell, *supra* at 247; Jones, *Fathers, supra* at 73; for Arkansas, *Revised Statutes of Arkansas, supra* §3 at 360; Stafford, *supra* at 448; for Missouri, 2 *Revised Statutes of Missouri, supra* ch. 150, art. II, §3 at 1478-79; for Louisiana, Rose, *supra* at 177, quoting *Civil Code,* Art. 190.

In Kentucky, however, the courts held that husbands had the right to free their slaves by will, and their widows did not have any dower rights in the freed slaves. *See Graham's Executor v. Sam,* 46 Ky. (7 B. Mon.) 403, 1847 WL 2843 (1847); *Lee v. Lee's Executors,* 31 Ky. (1 Dana) 48, 1833 WL 2414 (1833). Kentucky slaves were real property and were to be sold after an insolvent estate's personal property. *See* Jones, *Fathers, supra* at 73. An 1840 act subjected slaves to sale like an insolvent estate's other assets. *See id.* at 90; Morris, *Slavery, supra* at 61-80, 392.

[73] *See* Rose, *supra* at 177, quoting *Civil Code,* Art. 190.

[74] *See* Shaw, *supra* at 79; *see also Sampson v. Burgwin,* 20 N.C. (3 & 4 Dev. & Bat.) 21, 1838 WL 470 *4 (1838); *State v. M'Donald,* 1 N.J.L. 332 (Sup. Ct. 1795); *State v. Frees,* 1 N.J.L. 259 (Sup. Ct. 1794); *State v. Prall,* 1 N.J.L. 4 (Sup. Ct. 1790); *but see,* denying manumission under a 1798 statute, *State v. Emmons,* 2 N.J.L. 6 (Sup. Ct. 1806).

[75] *See* Cobb, *supra* at 279, 286-90; Stroud, *supra* at 96-100; *see also* for Arkansas, *Revised Statutes of Arkansas, supra* §1 at 359-60; Stafford, *supra* at 448; for Delaware, *Wilson v. George,* 2 Del. Cas. 413, 1818 WL 1171 at *6 (Err. & App. 1818); Essah, *supra* at 41; 2 Hurd, *supra* at 76-77; for Missouri, 2 *Revised Statutes of Missouri, supra* ch. 150, art. II, §1 at 1478; *Schropshire v. Loudon,* 23 Mo. 93, 1856 WL 5271 (1856); *Robert (a man of color) v. Melugen,* 9 Mo. 170, 1845 WL 3835 (1845) (trial court did not err by excluding evidence of testator's oral statements of his intention to free a slave upon his death). Kentucky's 1794 and 1798 acts required that the deed be sealed and acknowledged, but an 1800 act did not. *See* 2 Littell, *supra* at 119, 387; 1 Littell, *supra* at 246-47; *Reuben v. Parrish,* 25 Tenn. (6 Hum.) 122, 1845 WL 1873 (1845); *Winney v. Cartwright,* 10 Ky. (3 A. K. Marsh.) 493, 1821 WL 1145 (1821); Jones, *Fathers, supra* at 73-74. Pursuant to the 1850 Kentucky constitution, which was similar to the 1792 constitution, the legislature again required that manumission deeds be acknowledged or proved in the county court by two subscribing witnesses. *See id.* at 92-93; *see also Smith v. Adam (of color),* 57 Ky. (18 B. Mon.) 685, 1857 WL 4848 (1857) (slave freed by non-conforming

deed remained an asset available to the master's creditors); Ivan E. McDougle, "Slavery in Kentucky," 3 *J. of Negro Hist.* 211, 240-42, 274-75 (1918).

76 *See* Spear, *supra* at 194; Rose, *supra* at 177, quoting *Civil Code*, Art. 187.

77 *See Proceedings and Acts of the General Assembly, 1752-1754,* ch. 1; *see, e.g., Miller v. Herbert*, 46 U.S. (5 How.) 72, 12 L. Ed. 55 (1842); *Bloodgood v. Grasey*, 31 Ala. 575, 1858 WL 430 (1858); *Thrift v. Hannah*, 29 Va. (2 Leigh) 300, 1830 WL 1565 (1830); *Negro James v. Gaither*, 2 H. & J. 176, 1807 WL 480 (Md. 1807) (denying freedom claims when master did not follow this and the successor act's formal execution and recording requirements); Brackett, *supra* at 149.

78 Wahl, *Burden, supra* at 161; Stroud, *supra* at 96-98; Binder, *supra* at 2089.

79 For the 1741 act, *see* Walter Clark, ed., *The State Records of North Carolina, Vol. XXIII, Laws, 1715-1776* 203-04 (1904) [hereinafter Clark, *1715-1776*]; for the 1777 act, *see* Clark, *1777-1788, supra* at 14-15; 2 Hurd, *supra* at 82; and for the 1796 act, *see Laws of North Carolina 1796* ch. V at 2 (1796); Franklin, *Free Negro, supra* at 20-21; 2 Hurd, *supra* at 85; *see also* Shaw, *supra* at 82-83; 2 Catterall, *supra* at 4.

80 *See* Cover, *Justice Accused, supra* at 75; Franklin, *Free Negro, supra* at 21-23; *Sampson v. Burgwin*, 1838 WL 470 at *4 (noting that the county courts often abused their prerogatives, and the legislature transferred jurisdiction to the superior courts).

81 *See* 1 Haywood & Cobbs, *Laws of Tennessee, supra* at 327-28 (citing *Laws of Tennessee*, 1801, ch. 27); Howington, *What Sayeth, supra* at 32-33 (citing *Laws of Tennessee*, 1777, ch. 7 and 1801, ch. 27); *see also* James W. Ely, Theodore Brown, *et al.*, eds., *A History of the Tennessee Supreme Court* 28-29 (2002); 2 Hurd, *supra* at 82; Stroud, *supra* at 98; James W. Patton, "The Progress of Emancipation in Tennessee, 1796-1860," 17 *J. of Negro Hist.* 67, 75 (1932); Charles C. Trabue, "The Voluntary Emancipation of Slaves in Tennessee as Reflected in the State's Legislation and Judicial Decisions," 4 *Tenn. Historical Mag.* 50, 50-51 (1918). Tennessee's Supreme Court of Errors and Appeals in 1826 interpreted these statutes to permit masters to free their slaves by will. *See M'Cutchen v. Marshall*, 33 U.S. (8 Pet.) 220, 237-41, 8 L. Ed. 923 (1823); *Hope v. Johnson*, 10 Tenn. (2 Yer.) 123, 1826 WL 442 at *2 (1826). An 1829 statute required executors and administrators to petition the county court for permission to free slaves manumitted by will, and stated that if these fiduciaries failed to do so, the slaves could file bills in equity, by their next friends, for their freedom. *See* 1 Haywood & Cobbs, *Laws of Tennessee, supra* at 327-28 (quoting *Laws of Tennessee*, 1829, ch. 29); *see also* Howington, *What Sayeth, supra* at 13-14. In 1831, the legislature amended the 1829 act to apply only to post-1829 wills. "An act to explain and amend an act passed December 7th 1829, Chapt. 29, 'more effectually to provide for emancipating slaves,'" in *Tennessee Acts, 1831, supra* ch. 101, at 120-21; *John v. Tate*, 26 Tenn. (7 Hum.) 388, 1846 WL 1572 at *4 (1846); *Hinklin v. Hamilton*, 22 Tenn. (3 Hum.) 569, 1842 WL 1996 at *2-*3 (1842).

82 *See James v. The State*, 28 Tenn. (9 Hum.) 308, 1848 WL 1860 at *2 (1848) (criminal charges against slave freed contrary to statute dismissed, defendant was "punishable" only as a slave).

83 *See* 7 *Statutes at Large of South Carolina, supra* at 442-43, §§VII, VIII, & IX; Shaw, *supra* at 85; 2 Catterall, *supra* at 267-68; Smiddy, *supra* at 603-04, n. 69.

84 *See id.* at 604; *see also Linam v. Johnson*, 18 S.C.L. (2 Bail. 137) (1831); Morris, *Slavery, supra* at 372-73.

[85] *See 7 Statutes at Large of South Carolina, supra* at 459, §I; Shaw, *supra* at 85-86; 2 Catterall, *supra* at 268; Smiddy, *supra* at 612.

[86] Oliver H. Prince, *A Digest of the Laws of Georgia* 787 (2d ed. 1837); *see* Shaw, *supra* at 88; David J. Grindle, "Manumission: The Weak Link in Georgia's Law of Slavery," 41 *Mercer L. Rev.* 701, 704-05 (1991).

[87] Tomlin, *supra* at 632; *see Atwood's Heirs v. Beck, Admr.*, 21 Ala. 590, 1852 WL 212 at *13 (1852); Sellers, *supra* at 236.

[88] John G. Aiken, *A Digest of the Laws of the State of Alabama* xliv (2d ed. 1836); *see Atwood's Heirs v. Beck, Admr.*, 21 Ala. 590, 1852 WL 212 at *14; *Code of Mississippi, supra* at 34.

[89] "An act to authorize the Judges of the County Courts to emancipate Slaves," in Aikin, *supra*, §1 at 647.

[90] *Id.*, §§2-4 at 647-48; *see* Sellers, *supra* at 236. Unlike the Tennessee courts, the Alabama Supreme Court held that this statute by implication precluded manumission by will. *See Trotter v. Blocker*, 6 Port. 269, 1838 WL 1294 (Ala. 1838); Shaw, *supra* at 90-91.

[91] *Code of Mississippi, supra* at 523; *see Mitchell v. Wells,* 37 Miss. 235, 1859 WL 3634 at *3 (1859) and at * 22 (Handy, J., dissenting); *Purvis v. Sherrod*, 12 Tex. 140, 1854 WL 4380 at *17 (1854); *see also* Meredith Lang, *Defender of the Faith: The High Court of Mississippi, 1817-1875* 75-76 (1977); Sydnor, "Free Negro," *supra* at 773-74. For the laws freeing slaves between 1814 and 1821, *see* George Poindexter, ed., *The Revised Code of the Laws of Mississippi* 577-81 (1824).

[92] *See, e.g.*, Wahl, *Burden, supra* at 162-63; Morris, *Slavery, supra* at 372; Binder, *supra* at 2089; Klebaner, *supra* at 447-49.

[93] *See 7 Statutes at Large of South Carolina, supra* at 384, §XXXIX; *see also* Higginbotham, *Color, supra* at 175.

[94] Clark, *1715-1776, supra* at 65, 106-07, 203-04; *see* Morris, *Slavery, supra* at 379; Shaw, *supra* at 83; 2 Catterall, *supra* at 4.

[95] Clark, *1777-1788, supra* at 14-15, 221, 964; *see* Shaw, *supra* at 83; 2 Catterall, *supra* at 4; Rosser Howard Taylor, *The Free Negro in North Carolina* 7-8 (1920) [hereinafter Taylor, *Free Negro North Carolina*].

[96] *See* Morris, *Slavery, supra* at 379; Shaw, *supra* at 83-84; Franklin, *Free Negro, supra* at 23-29; Taylor, *Free Negro North Carolina, supra* at 11; Reuel E. Schiller, "Conflicting Obligations: Slave Law and the Late Antebellum North Carolina Supreme Court," 78 *Va. L. Rev.* 1207, 1229 (1992); *see also Feinster, Ex'r v. Tucker*, 58 N.C. (5 Jones Eq.) 69, 1859 WL 2258 at *4 (1859) (suggesting that slaves older than fifty could be freed by will if the executor can prove meritorious services and otherwise comply with the statute).

[97] John P. Duval, *Compilation of the Public Acts of the Legislative Council of the Territory of the State of Florida Passed Prior to 1840* 228-29 (1839); *see Bryan v. Dennis*, 4 Fla. 445, 1852 WL 1109 at *2-*3 (1852); Shaw, *supra* at 97; 2 Hurd, *supra* at 192; Thelma Bates, "The Legal Status of the Negro in Florida," 7 *Fla. Hist. Q.* 159, 164-65 (1928).

[98] *See* Spear, *supra* at 194; Schafer, *Becoming Free, supra* at 6; 2 Hurd, *supra* at 161-62.

[99] *See* Spear, *supra* at 194-95; Schafer, *Becoming Free, supra* at 7; 2 Hurd, *supra* at 162.

[100] *See* Schafer, *Becoming Free, supra* at 2, n. 2 and 7, citing Lawrence J. Kotlikoff and Anton J. Rupert, "The Manumission of Slaves in New Orleans, 1827-1846," 19 *Southern Studies* 172 (1980).

[101] *See* Schafer, *Becoming Free, supra* at 2, n. 2.

[102] *See* Spear, *supra* at 194; Schafer, *Becoming Free, supra* at 12.

[103] *See* Schafer, *Becoming Free, supra* at 12.

[104] *See* Spear, *supra* at 195; Schafer, *Becoming Free, supra* at 71-72.

[105] *See* Schafer, *Becoming Free, supra* at 73. Schafer stated that many of these trials "seem to have been largely *pro forma.*" *Id.* at 81.

[106] *State v. Harrison,* 11 La. Ann. 722, 1856 WL 4823 (1856); *see Maranthe v. Hunter,* 11 La. Ann. 734, 1856 WL 4829 (1856); Spear, *supra* at 183; Michael D. Gilbert, "Single Subject Rules and the Legislative Process," 67 *U. Pitt. L. Rev.* 803 (2006).

[107] "An Act to prohibit the emancipation of slaves," in *Acts Passed by the Legislature of Louisiana, 1857* No. 69 at 55 (1857); *see Price v. Ray,* 14 La. Ann. 697, 1858 WL 5929 (La. 1858); Schafer, *Becoming Free, supra* at 87-90; Schafer, *Supreme Court, supra* at 248-49; Baade, "Bifurcated," *supra* at 1490, 1499; Baade, "Comparative," *supra* at 581-82.

[108] "An act concerning free persons of colour, and for other purposes," in *Tennessee Acts, 1831, supra* ch. 102, § 2 at 121-22; *see Fisher's Negroes v. Dabbs,* 14 Tenn. (6 Yer.) 119, 126, 129-30 (1834); Howington, *What Sayeth, supra* at 34.

[109] "An act to explain an act entitled, 'an act concerning free persons of color, and for other purposes, passed December 16, 1831,'" in *Tennessee Acts, 1833, supra* ch. 81 at 99-100; *see* Howington, *What Sayeth, supra* at 35. Requests for special acts exempting individual slaves from the 1831 law may have prompted the legislature to adopt this loophole. *See id.* at 35, n. 11.

[110] *See id.* at 37.

[111] "An act to amend the laws now in force in relation to free persons of color," in *Acts of the State of Tennessee 1841-42,* ch. 191 at 229-30 (1842); *see* Howington, *What Sayeth, supra* at 37-38.

[112] "An act to Amend the Act of 1842, ch. 191," in *Tennessee Acts, 1849-50, supra* ch. 107 at 300; *see* Howington, *What Sayeth, supra* at 39.

[113] "An act to regulate the emancipation of slaves, and to provide for the transportation of free persons of color to the western coast of Africa," in *Acts of the State of Tennessee 1853-54,* ch. 50 at 121-22 (1854). The act applied to all slaves who had acquired a right to be freed but who had not been freed by the county court, and to free "persons of color" who, two months after receipt of notice, failed to post the "good behavior" bond that Tennessee law required. *Id.* at 122; *see* Howington, *What Sayeth, supra* at 51-52.

[114] *See* Howington, *What Sayeth, supra* at 35-70; *see also* 2 Catterall, *supra* at 480.

[115] *See Laws of Maryland 1831,* ch. 281 §§1-11 (1832). The statute did not apply to deeds executed and recorded before it was passed, or to wills admitted to probate before it was passed, unless the slave consented. *Id.* at §12; *see also* Ford, *supra* at 387-88; Shaw, *supra* at 81-82; Berlin, *Slaves Without Masters, supra* at 202-12; Brackett, *supra* at 164-

67. According to Shaw, this statute "became almost a dead letter," and in only one case was it enforced to require a slave's removal. *See* Shaw, *supra* at 82, citing Brackett, *supra* at 166.

[116] *Code of Mississippi, supra* at 533; *see* Jones, *Fathers, supra* at 102, citing Act of December 20, 1831, ch. 5, §1; Shaw, *supra* at 91; Sydnor, *Slavery in Mississippi, supra* at 203-04; Sydnor, "Free Negro," *supra* at 780.

[117] *Code of Mississippi, supra* at 537-38; *see* Jones, *Fathers, supra* at 102, citing Act of February 26, 1842, ch. 4, §§1-2; 2 Hurd, *supra* at 148.

[118] *See Trotter v. Blocker*, 6 Port. 269, 1838 WL 1294 at *14; Sellers, *supra* at 236.

[119] John J. Ormand, Arthur P. Bagby, and George Goldthwaite, eds., *The Code of Alabama* §2047 at 391 (1852) [hereinafter *Code of Alabama*]; *see* Shaw, *supra* at 91; Rose, *supra* at 188.

[120] *See* 2 Hurd, *supra* at 170; 2 *Revised Statutes of the State of Missouri*, ch. 114, §§7-20, 26-31 at 1093-99. The statute defined a "mulatto" as a person, "other than a negro," who had at least one grandparent who was "a negro," or a person with "one-fourth or more negro blood[.]" *Id.*, §1 at 1093. It also permitted visitors to Missouri to bring free black servants into the state for more than six months at a time. *Id.*, §32 at 1099. In an unreported 1846 decision, *State v. Charles Lyons*, St. Louis Circuit Court Judge John Krum rejected the free black defendant's constitutional challenge to this statute. *See* Kenneth C. Kaufman, *Dred Scott's Advocate: A Biography of Roswell M. Field* 145-47 (1996).

[121] *See* Lowell H. Harrison and James C. Klotter, *A New History of Kentucky* 117-18 (1997).

[122] *See Smith v. Adam*, 57 Ky. (18 B. Mon.) 685, 1857 WL 4848 at *3 (1857); Jones, *Fathers, supra* at 92-96; Shaw, *supra* at 94-95; 2 Hurd, *supra* at 18-19; McDougle, *supra* at 326.

[123] *See Revised Statutes of Kentucky*, Chapter 93, Article IX, §§1(4)-(5), 2-13 (1852); *Elisha (of color), ex parte*, 57 Ky. (18 B. Mon.) 675, 1858 WL 4846 (1858). The removal requirement did not apply if the slave's right to freedom vested before the statute's effective date. *See Kitty v. Commonwealth*, 57 Ky. (18 B. Mon.) 522, 1857 WL 4427 (1857); *Jackson v. Collins*, 55 Ky. (16 B. Mon.) 220, 1855 WL 4202 (1855); Jones, *Fathers, supra* at 94-95. A March 3, 1860 act stated that, as of January 1861, slaves were not "deemed to be emancipated" until their master posted a bond to secure the slave's removal from Kentucky within 90 days and until the freed slave agreed to leave the state. Slaves who returned would be deemed guilty of a felony. *See* "An act concerning free negroes, mulattoes, and Emancipation," in 1 *Acts of the General Assembly of the Commonwealth of Kentucky, 1860*, ch. 1304, §§1-6 at 129 (1860) [hereinafter *Kentucky Acts, 1860*].

[124] 12 Tex. 140, 1854 WL 4380 (1854).

[125] *Purvis v. Sherrod*, 1854 WL 4380 at *16.

[126] *Id.* at *17. For another interpretation of this case, *see* A. E. K. Nash, "The Texas Supreme Court and Trial Rights of Blacks, 1845-1860," 58 *J. of Am. Hist.* 622, 631-32 (1971) [hereinafter Nash, "Trial Rights"].

[127] *See Hunt, Adm'r v. White*, 24 Tex. 643, 1860 WL 5723 (1860); *Armstrong v. Jowell*,

24 Tex. 58, 1859 WL 6366 (1859); *Philleo v. Holliday*, 24 Tex. 38, 1859 WL 6364 (1859); Shaw, *supra* at 102-03; Randolph B. Campbell, *The Peculiar Institution in Texas, 1821-1865* 112 (1989); 5 Catterall, *supra* at 269-70; John E. Fisher, "The Legal Status of Free Blacks in Texas, 1836-1861," 4 *Texas So. U.L. Rev.* 342, 345-56 (1977) [hereinafter Fisher, "Free Blacks"].

128 Shaw, *supra* at 79.

129 Wahl, *Burden*, *supra* at 163, and 253-54, n. 119; Morris, *Slavery*, *supra* at 398; Stroud, *supra* at 96-97; Binder, *supra* at 2089; Klebaner, *supra* at 443.

130 *See Laws of Maryland, 1796*, ch. 67, §§13, 29, & 30; *Laws of Maryland, 1790*, ch. IX, §III; *Proceedings and Acts of the General Assembly, 1752-1754*, ch. 1; Shaw, *supra* at 80; Brackett, *supra* at 149-53; *see also Spencer v. Negro Dennis*, 8 Gill 314, 1849 WL 3211 at *4-*5 (Md. 1849); *Hughes v. Negro Milly*, 5 H. & J. 310, 1821 WL 1014 (Md. 1821); *Wood v. Negro Stephen*, 1 Serg. & Rawle 175, 1814 WL 1357 (Pa. 1814).

131 *See* Morris, *Slavery*, *supra* at 379; Shaw, *supra* at 85; Smiddy, *supra* at 604.

132 *Public Laws of the State of North Carolina 1860-1861* ch. 37 at 69 (1861); *see* Morris, *Slavery*, *supra* at 379; Shaw, *supra* at 83-84; Franklin, *Free Negro*, *supra* at 28-29; 2 Catterall, *supra* at 6; Taylor, *Free Negro North Carolina*, *supra* at 11; Schiller, *supra* at 1229.

133 Prince, *supra* at 794-96; *see* Shaw, *supra* at 88; Grindle, *supra* at 704-05.

134 "An Act to prohibit the post-mortem manumission of slaves," in *Acts of the General Assembly of the State of Georgia, 1859* 68 (1860) [hereinafter *Georgia Acts 1859*]; *see* Shaw, *supra* at 89-90; 2 Hurd, *supra* at 109; Grindle, *supra* at 714; Nash, "Reason of Slavery," *supra* at 118.
On December 17, 1859, the legislators adopted two apparently related acts. The first prohibited free black immigration into Georgia. It provided that offenders, upon a conviction, would be sold into slavery. *See* "An Act to prevent free persons of color, commonly known as free negroes, from being brought or coming to the State of Georgia," in *Georgia Acts 1859*, *supra* at 68-69. The second declared a vagrant to be "any free person of color wandering or strolling about, or leading an idle, immoral or profligate course of life[.]" On a first conviction a violator was to be sold into slavery for a term not to exceed two years. A second offender "shall be sold into perpetual slavery." *See* "An Act to define and punish Vagrancy in free persons of color," in *id.* at 69.

135 11 *The Statutes at Large of South Carolina, Consisting of Acts from 1838* 168-69 (1873); *see* Shaw, *supra* at 86-87; 2 Catterall, *supra* at 268; Nash, "Negro Rights," *supra* at 166.

136 *See* Nash, "Negro Rights," *supra* at 164; *Jolliffe v. Fanning*, 44 S.C.L. (10 Rich. L) 186, 190 (1856); *Morlon v. Thompson*, 27 S.C. Eq. 146 (6 Rich. Eq.) 370, 375-76 (1854).

137 *Code of Mississippi*, *supra* at 539-40, quoting Act of February 26, 1842, ch. 4, §11; *see Mitchell v. Wells*, 37 Miss. 235, 1859 WL 3634 at *24 (Handy, J., dissenting); Shaw, *supra* at 92; Lang, *supra* at 76, Sydnor, *Slavery in Mississippi*, *supra* at 216-17; 2 Hurd, *supra* at 149.

138 William Lewis Sharkey, *et al.*, eds., *Revised Code of the Statute Laws of the State of Mississippi* ch. 33, art. 9 at 236 (1857) [hereinafter *Revised Mississippi Code*]; *see Mitchell v. Wells*, 37 Miss. 235, 1859 WL 3634 at * 28 (Handy, J., dissenting); Lang, *supra* at

76.

[139] *See* "An Act to prohibit the emancipation of slaves," in *Acts of the General Assembly of the State of Arkansas* no. 68 at 69 (1859), and "An act to remove Free Negroes and Mulattoes from this State," in *id.* no. 151 at 175-78; *see also* Shaw, *supra* at 95-96; Berlin, *Slaves Without Masters*, *supra* at 372-73; Taylor, *Negro Slavery in Arkansas*, *supra* at 255-58; 2 Hurd, *supra* at 174; Georgena Duncan, "Manumission in the Arkansas River Valley: Three Case Histories," 66 *Ark. Hist. Q.* 422, 423, 442 (2005); Stafford, *supra* at 450.

The expulsion act, among other things, required that free blacks be hired out for a year to raise funds to pay for their removal out of the state, and slaves between and seven and twenty-one years of age be hired out until they were required to leave the state, or these free blacks could be sold into slavery. Free blacks wishing to stay in Arkansas could agree to be enslaved and they could select a master. Many free blacks left Arkansas in anticipation of the expulsion act's enforcement. *See id.*; *see also* Billy D. Harris, *A Stranger and a Sojourner: Peter Caulder, Free Black Frontiersman in Antebellum Arkansas* 196-210 (2004); Berlin, *Slaves Without Masters*, *supra* at 373-74; 2 Hurd, *supra* at 174; Billy D. Higgins, "Act 151 of 1859, aka: Act to Remove the Free Negroes and Mulattos from the State, aka: Arkansas's Free Negro Expulsion Act of 1859," in *The Encyclopedia of Arkansas History & Culture* http://encyclopediaofarkansas.net/encyclopedia/entry-detail.aspx?entryID=4430 (last updated November 12, 2008). A January 10, 1861 act extended the expulsion date to January 1, 1863 for "all negroes and mulattoes, now within the limits of this state, who are held in duress or by operation of law[.]" *See* "An Act to permit certain free negroes and mulattoes, still in the state, to remain until the first day of January, 1863," in *Acts of the General Assembly of the State of Arkansas* no. 99 at 206 (1861); Berlin, *Slaves Without Masters*, *supra* at 380; Taylor, *Negro Slavery in Arkansas, supra* at 258; Stafford, *supra* at 450, n. 227; *see also Phebe v. Quillin*, 21 Ark. 490, 1860 WL 770 at *2-*3 (1860) (finding that the statute banning manumission does not apply retroactively to a pre-act manumissions to take place after the act's effective date). On the debates about free black exclusion laws in other slave states, *see* Berlin, *Slaves Without Masters*, *supra* at 374-80; Jonathan M. Atkins, "Party Politics and the Debate over the Tennessee Free Negro Bill, 1859-1860," 70 *J. of So. Hist.* 245 (2005).

[140] "An act to amend the law in relation to the Emancipation of Slaves," in *Acts of the Seventh Biennial Session of the General Assembly of Alabama* No. 36 at 28 (1860) [hereinafter *Acts of Alabama 1860*]; *see* Shaw, *supra* at 91; Sellers, *supra* at 237.

[141] *See Laws of Maryland, 1860*, ch. 322, §1; 1 *Maryland Code*, *supra*, Art. 66, §§42-43 at 458; Shaw, supra at 82; Fields, *Slavery and Freedom*, *supra* at 78-84; Brackett, *supra* at 171,173; 2 Hurd, *supra* at 24.

[142] *See* 1 *Maryland Code*, Art. 66, §42 at 458. On February 11, 1864, Maryland's legislature adopted an act that once again permitted manumission by a written will or deed. It also "ratified and made valid" manumissions attempted after the 1857 act was adopted, and provided that executors or fiduciaries could execute manumission deeds for slaves enlisted in the United States military, so that the estate could receive compensation for the slaves. But it also provided that all freed slaves were not "entitled to vote at any election, or be capable of holding any office of profit or trust, or of giving evidence against any white person." *See Laws of Maryland 1864*, ch. 105 at 130-31; Brackett, *supra* at 171.

[143] *See* Campbell, *supra* at 207, and Fisher, "Free Blacks," *supra* at 355-56, for the 1861

Texas constitution's provision: "No citizen, or other person residing in this State, shall have the power by deed or will, to take effect in this State, or out of it, in any manner whatsoever, directly or indirectly, to emancipate his slave." Also see *Bryan v. Dennis*, 4 Fla. 445, 1852 WL 1109 at *4 (1852), and 3 Catterall, *supra* at 107 n. 5, for the 1838 Florida constitution's provision: "The General Assembly shall have no power to pass laws for the emancipation of slaves."

144 *See* Watson, *Americas*, *supra* at 23; William D. Phillips, Jr., *Slavery from Roman Times to the Early Transatlantic Trade* 30 (1985) [hereinafter Phillips, *Slavery*]; Phillips, "Manumission," *supra* at 32; David Daube, "Two Early Patterns of Manumission," 36 *J. of Roman Studies* 57 (1946).

145 Watson, "Anglo-American," *supra* at 591; *see* Watson, *Americas*, *supra* at 23.

146 Watson, "Anglo-American," *supra* at 591-93.

147 *See* Watson, *Americas*, *supra* at 26-27; Watson, "Anglo-American," *supra* at 591-92.

148 Watson, "Anglo-American," *supra* at at 593.

149 Watson, *Americas*, *supra* at 23-24.

150 Phillips, *Slavery*, *supra* at 31; Wiedemann, *Greek and Roman*, *supra* at 27, 46, 67-68; Watson, "Anglo-American," *supra* at 591-92.

151 Watson, *Americas*, *supra* at 24.

152 *See id.*; Wiedemann, "Regularity," *supra* at 164, 175.

153 *See* Watson, *Americas*, *supra* at 62. Watson made this point as part of his larger argument that Roman slave law allowed slave owners wider "freedom of action" regarding their slaves than did the slave laws adopted in and for the Americas, and that these differences in the law were based upon autonomous legal cause—the reception of Roman law in Europe, but not England. *See* Watson, "Anglo-American," *supra* at 591; Watson, *Americas*, *supra* at 1-21.

154 *See Las Siete Partidas, Volume 4, supra*, Part 4, Title 22, Law 1 at 981; Watson, *Americas*, *supra* at 44; Phillips, "Manumission," *supra* at 34.

155 *Las Siete Partidas, Volume 5, supra*, Part 6, Title 3, Laws 21 & 24 at 1200, 1201-02; Watson, *Americas*, *supra* at 45.

156 *See* Watson, *Americas*, *supra* at 99; *see also* Phillips, *Slavery*, *supra* at 159-60; Degler, *supra* at 40-41; *Brief History*, *supra* at 22.

157 *See* "Edict of the King concerning the Enforcement of Order in the Islands of Americas, Versailles, March 1685," in *Brief History*, *supra* at 35; *see also* Spear, *supra* at 65; Watson, *Americas*, *supra* at 86; Moitt, "Pricing Freedom," *supra* at 157; Palmer, "Origins," *supra* at 387 (noting that the Code permitted manumission "without special formalities, [and] for whatever reasons the owner may have, whether mercenary or kindly."). Spear notes that the provision not requiring parental consent was significant because "persons under the age of twenty-five were ordinarily considered minors." *See* Spear, *supra* at 251, n. 60.

158 *See* "French Royal Decree on Manumitting Slaves, October 24, 1713," in *Brief History*, *supra* at 42-44 (quotation, *id.* at 43); *see also* Spear, *supra* at 65; Watson, *Americas*, *supra* at 86-87; Moitt, "Pricing Freedom," *supra* at 157-58; Palmer, "Origins,"

supra at 389-90. According to Palmer, the French law's pro-manumission policy was changed, "in the light of later *experience*, and in time the Caribbean experience would serve as a proxy for Louisiana." *See id.* at 389.

[159] *See* Moitt, "Pricing Freedom," *supra* at 159; Frank D. Lewis, "Manumission: A Life-Cycle Approach Applied to the United States and Guadeloupe," in *Slavery in the Development of the Americas* 166-67 (David Eltis, Frank D. Lewis, and Kenneth L. Sokoloff, eds.) (2004).

[160] *See* Watson, *Americas, supra* at 102-14.

[161] *See* Rosemary Brana-Shute, "Sex and Gender in Surinamese Manumissions," in *Many Paths, supra* at 176.

[162] *Id.* at 177.

[163] *See id.* The Dutch were the last of the northern Europeans to abolish slavery in their colonies, in 1860 in the East Indies and in 1863 in the West Indies. *See* Drescher, *supra* at 282-83.

[164] For the manumission statutes, *see* Cooley, *supra* at 45-50; Wolinetz, *supra* at 2233-34, 2244; *see also State v. Emmons*, 2 N.J.L. 6, 1806 WL 636 (Sup. Ct. 1806).

[165] *An Act Regulating Slaves*, March 11, 1713-14, §14; *see* Tomlins, *Freedom Bound, supra* at 492-93.

[166] *An Act for laying a Duty on the Purchasers of Slaves imported into this Colony*, November 16, 1769, §4.

[167] *See id.* at §5.

[168] Wolinetz, *supra* at 2234, n. 46, citing Giles R. Wright, *Afro-Americans in New Jersey* 168 (1988).

[169] Cooley, *supra* at 46.

[170] *An Act to prevent the Importation of Slaves into the State of New Jersey, and to authorize the Manumission of them under certain Restrictions, and to prevent the Abuse of Slaves*, March 2, 1786, §5; Cooley, *supra* at 47.

[171] *An Act respecting Slaves*, March 14, 1798, §21.

[172] *Id.* at §22.

[173] *Id.* at §23.

[174] *See id.*; Cooley, *supra* at 47; Wolinetz, *supra* at 2244-45.

[175] Cooley, *supra* at 50, n. 1; *see* "An act to confirm the manumission of certain slaves," February 28, 1844.

[176] Patterson, *Social Death, supra*, at 272-73.

[177] Wolf, "Manumission," *supra* at 311.

[178] Robin Blackburn, "Introduction," in *Paths to Freedom, supra* at 3.

[179] Willem Wurbo Klooster, "Manumission in an Entrepot: The Case of Curacao," in *Paths to Freedom, supra* at 164; Johnson, *supra* at 277.

[180] Patterson, *Social Death, supra* at 284-85.

[181] *Id.* at 285.

[182] *Id.*

[183] *See* Cole, *supra* at 1014.

[184] *See* Stroud, *supra* at 96; *see also* Wheeler, *supra* at 386-88.

[185] Berlin, *Many Thousands, supra* at 331-32.

[186] *See* Fede, *People Without Rights, supra* at 51-52.

[187] *See* Elkins, *supra* at 37-52; Ralph A. Wooster, *Politicians, Planters, and Plain Folk: Courthouse and Statehouse in the Upper South, 1850-1860* 3-21, 33-42, 119-28, 163-72 (1975); Clement Eaton, *A History of the Old South: The Emergence of a Reluctant Nation* 52-54, 65-66 (3d ed. 1975); Eugene Genovese, *The Political Economy of Slavery: Studies in the Economy and Society of the Slave South* 28, 46-47 (1961); Charles Sydnor, *The Development of Southern Sectionalism 1819-1848* 47-49, 52, 275-93 (1948); *see* Campbell, *supra at* 210 (discussing Texas politics).

[188] Robert C. Schwemm, "*Strader v. Graham*: Kentucky's Contribution to National Slavery Litigation and the Dred Scott Decision," 97 *Ky. L.J.* 353, 365 (2009).

[189] Wheeler, *supra* at 387; *see* Cobb, *supra* at 279.

[190] Wheeler, *supra* at 387-88.

[191] *See* Howington, *What Sayeth, supra* at 34-70; *see also* Sellers, *supra* at 236-37, 364-68; Sydnor, *Slavery in Mississippi, supra* at 203; Henry, *supra* at 170-71.

[192] Berlin, *Slaves Without Masters, supra* at 141.

[193] Fede, *People Without Rights, supra* at 50-51.

[194] *See* Patterson, *Social Death, supra* at 284.

[195] Berlin, *Slaves Without Masters, supra* at 141.

[196] *See generally, e.g.,* Alexander, *supra* at 222-28; Fisher, "Ideology," *supra,* at 46-68.

[197] St. George Tucker, *A Dissertation on Slavery: With a Proposal for the Gradual Abolition of It in the State of Virginia* 50-51 (1796) [hereinafter Tucker, *Dissertation*]; Michael Kent Curtis, "St. George Tucker and the Legacy of Slavery," 47 *Wm. & Mary L. Rev.* 1157, 1160 (2006).

[198] *See* Larry E. Tise, *Proslavery: A History of the Defense of Slavery in America, 1701-1840* (1987); *see generally, e.g.,* Ford, *supra* at 9; Davis, *Inhuman Bondage, supra* at 186-92; Alexander, *supra* at 211-40; Fede, *People Without Rights, supra* at 54-55; Elkins, *supra,* at 206-22; Eugene Genovese, *The World the Slaveholders Made: Two Essays in Interpretation* 112-224 (1969) [hereinafter Genovese, *Slaveholders*]; Robert A Garson, "Proslavery as Political Theory: The Examples of John C. Calhoun and George Fitzhugh," 84 *So. Atlantic Q.* 84 (1985). Some Southern religious leaders also argued in favor of slavery. *See, e.g.,* John Patrick Daly, *When Slavery Was Called Freedom: Evangelicalism, Proslavery and the Causes of the Civil War* (2002). On Cobb's views, *see* William B. Cash, *Thomas R. R. Cobb: The Making of a Southern Nationalist* 131-74 (2004).

[199] Alexander, *supra* at 212.

[200] *See* George Fitzhugh, *Sociology for the South, Or the Failure of Free Society* 27-28 (1854).

[201] *See* George Fitzhugh, *Cannibals All! Or, Slaves Without Masters* 294-95 (1857) (re-

print ed. 1960). Fitzhugh also stated: "[O]ur Southern slavery has become a benign and protective institution, and our negroes are confessedly better off than any free laboring population in the world." He therefore asked: "How can we contend that white slavery is wrong, whilst all the great body of free laborers are starving; and the slaves, white or black, throughout the world, are enjoying comfort?" *Id.* at 297; *see also* Purdy, *supra* at 98-100; Davis, *Inhuman Bondage, supra* at 191-92; Alexander, *supra* at 222; Fede, *People Without Rights, supra*, at 54; Genovese, *Slaveholders, supra*, at 118.

[202] *See* Mason W. Stephenson and D. Grier Stephenson, Jr., "'To Protect and Defend': Joseph Henry Lumpkin, The Supreme Court of Georgia, and Slavery," 25 *Emory L.J.* 579, 583 (1976).

[203] *American Colonization Society v. Gartrell*, 23 Ga. 448, 464-65 (1857).

[204] *Bryan v. Walton,* 14 Ga. 185, 202 (1853).

[205] *Id.* at 205-06.

[206] *See* Stephenson, *supra* at 597-607.

[207] *Compare* Stephenson, *supra* at 584-86.

[208] *See* Fede, *People Without Rights, supra* at 55.

[209] *See id.*

[210] *See, e.g.,* Cobb, *supra* at ccxii to ccxxi (discussing his views about slavery's overall benefits while noting evils of the system).

[211] *See* Prince, *supra* at 794-96.

[212] *Id.* at 794.

[213] Shaw, *supra* at 78-79 (listing objections).

[214] *See, e.g.,* Stephanie Li, *Something Akin to Freedom: The Choice of Bondage in Narratives by African American Women* 68-72 (2010); Schafer, *Becoming Free, supra* at 150-62; Morris, *Slavery, supra* at 32-36; Ruthie Winegarten, *Black Texas Women: 150 Years of Trial and Triumph* 1-11 (1995); Campbell, *supra* at 113; Wilbert E. Moore, *American Negro Slavery and Abolition: A Sociological Study* 100 (1980); Marina Wikramanayake, *A World in Shadow: The Free Black in Antebellum South Carolina* 183 (1973); Berlin, *Slaves Without Masters, supra* at 367; Russell, *Free Negro, supra* at 108-09; Emily West, "'She is dissatisfied with her present condition': Requests for Voluntary Enslavement in the Antebellum American South," 28 *Slavery & Abolition* 329, 332-36 (2007); Larry E. Rivers, "Slavery in Microcosm: Leon County Florida, 1824 to 1869," 66 *J. of Negro Hist.* 235, 245 (1981).

[215] *See* Morris, *Slavery, supra* at 32. For Maryland, *see Laws of Maryland, 1860,* ch. 322, §2; for Louisiana, *see* "An Act to permit free persons of African descent to select a master and become slaves for life," in *Acts Passed by the Legislature of Louisiana, 1859* ch. 275 at 214-15 (1859); Shirley Elizabeth Thompson, *Exiles at Home: The Struggle to Become American in Creole New Orleans* 81-82 (2009); Schafer, *Becoming Free, supra* at 150, 153; Winegarten, *supra* at 11-12; Schafer, *Supreme Court, supra* at 179; 2 Hurd, *supra* at 166; for Tennessee, *see* "An act providing for the voluntary enslavement of persons of color in this State," in *Public Acts of the State of Tennessee, 1857-8* ch. 45 at 55-56 (1858); 2 Hurd, *supra* at 94; for Florida, *see* "An act to permit free persons of African descent to select their own masters and become slaves," in *Acts and Resolutions*

of the General Assembly of the State of Florida 1858 ch. 860, 13-14 (1859); Bates, *supra* at 170-71; for Alabama, *see* "An Act Permitting free Negroes to select a Master and become Slaves," in *Acts of Alabama 1860, supra* no. 71 at 63-64; for Arkansas, *see* "An Act to Amend the 8th Section of an Act Approved 12th February, 1859, entitled 'An act to remove free negroes and mulattoes from this state,'" in *Acts of the General Assembly of the State of Arkansas* no. 62 at 135-36 (1861), and the 1859 free black removal act, *supra* at note 139; and for Kentucky, *see* "An Act for the Voluntary Enslavement of Free Negroes, without compensation to the Commonwealth," in 1 *Kentucky Acts, 1860, supra* at ch. 1304, §§9-10 at 130. The Virginia and Texas statutes are noted below.

[216] *See* Mills, *supra* at 172 (citing acts adopted in January and February 1860); Sydnor, "Free Negro," *supra* at 781.

[217] *See* John Hope Franklin, "The Enslavement of Free Negroes in North Carolina," 29 *J. of Negro Hist.* 401, 410-14, 425-28 (1944).

[218] *See id.* at 414-24.

[219] Schafer, *Becoming Free, supra* at 150.

[220] Russell, *Free Negro, supra* at 108.

[221] 4 H.P.N. Gammel, *The Laws of Texas 1822-1897* 947 (Austin 1898); *see* Campbell, *supra* at 113; Fisher, "Free Negro," *supra* at 356-58.

[222] Gammel, *supra* at 947.

[223] *Id.* at 948.

[224] *Id.* at 947.

[225] *Id.* at 948.

[226] The district attorney was to be paid a fee of $10 per examination, and these fees were to be included in the taxed costs to be paid by the new slave owner. *Id.* at 948-49.

[227] *Id.* at 948.

[228] *Id.* at 947.

[229] *Id.* at 949.

[230] "An act providing for the voluntary enslavement of the free negroes of the commonwealth," in *Acts of the General Assembly of Virginia Passed in 1855-6* Chapter 46 at 37-38 (Richmond 1856); *see* William A. Link, *Roots of Secession: Slavery and Politics in Antebellum Virginia* 157-58 (2005); Russell, *Free Negro, supra* at 108-09; 2 Hurd, *supra* at 12.

[231] "An Act for the Voluntary Enslavement of Free Negroes, without compensation to the Commonwealth," in *Acts of the General Assembly of Virginia Passed in 1861* Chapter 26 at 52-53 (Richmond 1861); *see* Aaron Sheehan-Dean, "Politics in Civil War Virginia: Democracy on Trial," in *Virginia at War, 1864* 25 (William C. Davis and James I. Robertson, Jr., eds.) (2009).

[232] "An act concerning free negroes, mulattoes, and emancipation," in 1 *Kentucky Acts, 1860, supra,* ch. 1304, §11 at 130; *see* Schafer, *Becoming Free, supra* at 153.

[233] *See* Campbell, *supra* at 113.

[234] *See* West, *supra* at 339-43 (summarizing petitions from many states); *see also* Link,

supra at 158, 303, nn. 24 and 25 (Virginia petitions); Schafer, *Becoming Free, supra* at 150-62 (Louisiana petitions); *Petitions to Legislatures, supra* at 247-48 (quoting petitions from Mississippi and Virginia); Morris, *Slavery, supra* at 35 (discussing petitions in Florida, Virginia, Georgia, and South Carolina).

[235] *See, e.g.,* Schafer, *Becoming Free, supra* at 151-62 (discussing Louisiana newspaper reports of enslavement petitions).

[236] 2 *Plantation and Frontier Documents, supra* at 162, quoting a news item in the *Federal Union*, Milledgeville, Georgia (October 6, 1857).

[237] 24 Tex. 560, 1859 WL 6468 (1859).

[238] *Westbrook v. Mitchell*, 1859 WL 6468 at *1.

[239] *Id.* at *2.

[240] *Id.* (citing 2 Kent, *Com.* 274).

[241] *Id.*

[242] *Id.* at *3.

[243] *Id.; see also Casey v. Robards*, 60 N.C. 434, 2 Win. 38, 1864 WL 1065 at *2 (1864); *Phillips v. Murphy*, 49 N.C. (4 Jones) 45, 1856 WL 1643 (1856) (free blacks' agreements to serve for 99 and five years respectively did not create slavery relationship).

[244] *Petitions to Legislatures, supra* at 233-34; Morris, *Slavery, supra* at 35-36.

[245] *See* Patterson, *Social Death, supra* at 130. Brazilian law permitted a free man voluntarily to become a slave to serve along with his slave wife and children, and they all would be freed upon their master's death. *See* Watson, *Americas, supra* at 98.

[246] Patterson, *Social Death, supra* at 240.

[247] *See id.* at 240-47.

[248] *See* Watson, *Americas, supra* at 34; Wiedemann, *Greek and Roman, supra* at 48-53.

[249] *See* Watson, *Americas, supra* at 35.

[250] *See Las Siete Partidas, Volume 4, supra*, Part 4, Title 22, Laws 8 & 9 at 983-84; Watson, *Americas, supra* at 45.

[251] *See Brief History, supra* at 22, 135; Watson, *Americas, supra* at 113; Patterson, *Social Death, supra* at 245-47; Brana-Shute, *supra* at 176-77.

[252] *See Brief History, supra* at 22.

[253] *See* Fields, *Slavery and Freedom, supra* at 36-39.

[254] *See* Patterson, *Social Death, supra* at 246; Berlin, *Slaves Without Masters, supra* at 217-49.

[255] *See* Williams, *Slavery and Freedom in Delaware, supra* at 143.

4

The Procedural Roadblocks to the Manumission and Freedom Suits

Procedural rules are necessary so that disputes can be fairly decided. These rules establish norms for the orderly presentation of claims and evidence to the finders of the facts and the law. These decision makers create or apply substantive rules of law to determine which disputants are the winners and which are the losers. Nevertheless, procedural rules can—to some extent—be outcome determinative, and the courts can fashion and enforce substantive legal rules only through some type of procedure.[1]

Consequently, legal scholars have long debated how best to draw the line between substantive and procedural rules. Some contend that the distinction between these two concepts is illusory, or that they are best thought of as being on two ends of a continuum.[2]

The distinction between substantive and procedural rules is easier to explain at the ends of the continuum, and it becomes less clear toward the middle. In an article that discussed four slave law cases and the contemporary Federal Rules of Civil Procedure, Robert M. Cover showed how courts and rule makers can blur this substantive/procedural distinction by manipulating apparently neutral procedural rules to achieve substantive aims and outcomes.[3] For example, procedural rules can have substantive effects by making it easier or more difficult for one side of a dispute to pursue and win a particular class of cases.[4] Cover also stated that procedural rules can influence the development of substantive law, citing as examples rules permitting class actions and intervention.[5]

It follows, then, that we may conclude that the lawmakers and judges who erect barriers to or benefits for some substantive claims, under the guise of neutral procedural rules, know what they are doing—or they should be presumed to know what they are doing. Cover cautioned, however, that procedural rule makers often obscure their substantive objectives when they manipulate procedures to advance substantive ends.[6]

Cover suggested that we look for the substantive effects that followed when lawmakers selected one procedural rule in place of other possible options. With this analysis we can evaluate the "fairness" of the procedural law in the manumission and freedom suits and are not necessarily applying today's norms to the law of the past.

Who Could Be the Plaintiffs in Manumission or Freedom Suits?

The first issue that arises in evaluating the fairness of the manumission and freedom suits process is the question: Who could be the plaintiff? In some Southern states, the persons alleging that they were illegally held in slavery could not be the plaintiffs in their own cases. Only a legal guardian or next friend could file a freedom or manumission lawsuit, by analogy to the procedure that applied to children or others without legal standing. This rule was consistent with the general principle that all slaves were property without legal rights who could not file or pursue actions in the courts.

For example, the 1740 South Carolina slave code provided that "if any negro, Indian, mulatto, or mustizo [sic]" asserted a claim to freedom, a guardian had to be appointed on the alleged slave's behalf. The guardian was entitled "in law, to bring an action of trespass in the nature of ravishment of ward, against any person who shall claim property in, or shall be in possession of" the ward.[7] The legislators thus adopted by analogy a common law writ that the guardian of an infant could assert on the marriage of the infant ward without the guardian's consent.[8] Georgia's 1755 slave code contained an almost identical provision.[9]

These slave codes required persons contesting their enslaved status to first establish a *prima facie* case of freedom to the satisfaction of some white persons who would agree to be the claimants' legal guardians. The alleged slaves thus needed to enlist support from "white sympathizers who were willing to take the slaves' side in lengthy and expensive legal battles."[10] The pre-suit review process could be one reason why Ariela Gross and Loren Schweninger found high success rates in the cases that went to trials in the Southern freedom and manumission cases.[11]

South Carolina's 1690 and 1712 slave codes did not impose this requirement on freedom claimants.[12] According to A. Leon Higginbotham, the 1740 South Carolina slave code, which was adopted at least in part in response to the 1739 Stono slave rebellion, placed "[f]ormidable barriers ... before those who chose to challenge their alleged slave status."[13]

The Tennessee Supreme Court applied this general rule apparently as a matter of common law in an 1852 decision, *Doran v. Brazelton*.[14] The facts in *Doran* were quite compelling. The plaintiffs were "eleven persons of color" who sought to establish their freedom from the defendants, who held them as slaves. The plaintiffs claimed that they were slaves of the late James Doran. They alleged that Doran was an Alabama slave holder whose 1840 will expressed his intention to free the plaintiffs after Doran's wife's death. Instead, Doran's executors moved the slaves to Tennessee and denied them their right to freedom.[15]

The plaintiffs' counsel argued that, under Alabama law, the plaintiffs could not be "emancipated by will unless the Legislature grant the privilege, which was done in this case[.]"[16] He also cited eight Tennessee cases in which the courts decided the claimants' freedom suits without reference to the next friend requirement.[17] He argued that if freedom claimants "cannot be heard without the active agency and responsibility for cost of some free person they will often be deprived, as in this case, of most valued of all boons, the sacred right of freedom[.]" This, he asserted, "would be a reproach upon our laws to deny resort to our courts of justice to the down-trodden and oppressed, because no one could be found to befriend them." The defense argued that if slaves could "harass their owners with suits and costs at pleasure, without some responsible free person to stand forward as their friend, and vouch for their cause, there would be no quiet and subordination in the community, and this species of property would be worthless."[18]

The Supreme Court affirmed the order that dismissed the suit in a decision by Justice Robert L. Caruthers, who held: "A slave can have no *status* in court except by next friend." He added that if a slave filed a suit "a motion to dismiss may be made at any stage of the proceedings. No demurrer or plea is necessary. They are property, and have no rights except such as are extended to them by some law."[19]

Caruthers stated that although "several cases are referred to, in our reports, where there is no notice of a next friend," no case was cited or found "where the question was presented for adjudication."[20] This decision thus illustrates the need for readers of slave law cases to carefully distinguish the holdings from the *dicta* in the cases, a basic but essential principle of legal research and analysis.[21]

Moreover, Caruthers summarized the case's policy implications, which he resolved against the alleged slaves. The courts' "province," he wrote, was not "to weigh and balance these considerations, but to pronounce the law." Therefore, he opined that the legislature should address these policy concerns, not the judiciary. Caruthers nevertheless expressed his own views about the applicable public policy: "Our laws afford ample means to any, who are unlawfully held in slavery, to assert and prosecute their right. The courts are open to them, and an inclination always manifested to favor their claim, where it is at all sustained." He added: "The experience of our country also demonstrates that no difficulty is ever found, where the claim is calculated to inspire the least confidence in its justice, in procuring the agency of responsible citizens to stand forth as next friend, in any suit which may be necessary to establish their claim of freedom. But still, if this were otherwise, our decision would have to be the same, under the present state of our laws upon the subject."[22]

Therefore, the court based its ruling on the alleged slave's status as property without any rights at law other than those provided by statute.[23] Moreover, the plaintiffs in the *Doran* case apparently experienced the very difficulty that Justice Caruthers stated did not exist in Tennessee; they could not persuade a next friend to advance their suit. This failure had profound effects on the *Doran* case plaintiffs, but they did not give up.

These plaintiffs later filed an unsuccessful suit in Alabama.[24] The Alabama state legislature, in 1832 and 1833, had, as alleged in the Tennessee suit, adopted two special acts permitting James Doran to free 13 named slaves. These acts required Doran to convey his 640 acres of farm land, or the equivalent, to the judge of the Jackson County court, to be held in trust for the use of the slaves, as security so the slaves would not become public charges. Doran never complied with this condition to the letter, however, although he clearly stated in his will his intention to free his slaves after his wife's death, and to leave his 640 acres to his former slaves, so they would not be public charges.[25]

The Alabama Supreme Court in 1861 nevertheless rejected the petition for freedom of Doran's slaves, who apparently still were in Tennessee in 1858 when the Alabama suit was filed. The Court held that the will was not properly executed in the form necessary to convey to the slaves title to the real estate, and that a devise of property directly to slaves was void under Alabama law.[26]

Thus, the procedural rule barring the suit in the plaintiffs' names was only one of the roadblocks that Doran's slaves faced in their unsuccessful efforts to effectuate their master's intentions. This rule posed a conceptual dilemma because it anticipated—even before the "official" outset of the case—the unfavorable outcome for the plaintiffs. The primary issue in a manumission or a freedom case, after all, was whether the plaintiff was or was not legally held as a slave.

No common law precedent compelled the court to adopt the rule advanced in *Doran*. The Kentucky Court of Appeals in 1836 arrived at a ruling to the contrary in *Catherine Bodine's Will*.[27] The plaintiffs were slaves of the late Catherine Bodine. Her will, among other things, "declared that her slave Jenny should be 'set free' whenever she should cease child-bearing, and that other slaves should be 'set free' after designated periods not yet expired[.]" The executors, who also were devisees under the will, objected to the probate of the will. The County Court refused to probate the will, and the plaintiffs filed a writ of error with the Court of Appeals.[28]

The Court of Appeals decision by Chief Justice George Robertson addressed the "preliminary question," which was whether the plaintiffs could pursue the writ in their own names. They all were still held in slavery because none had yet satisfied their freedom contingency under the will's terms.[29]

The Chief Justice thus noted that it was asserted "that a slave can not sue. But this objection, though imposing, is not as we must think, insuperable."[30] Indeed, the court created a common law exception to the general rule that barred suits filed by slaves when the object of the proceedings was to secure the slaves' freedom under a will as their master intended. He wrote:

> The reason why a human being doomed to legal slavery can not sue, is, not because he has not, in judgment of law, personal existence or capacity, but is altogether arbitrary, and springs from the felt necessity of withholding from slaves all legal rights. And therefore, the general rule is, and upon reasons of state, must be, that a slave can neither sue nor be sued. But, although the law of this State considers slaves as property, yet it recognizes their personal existence, and, to a qualified extent, their natural rights. They may be emancipated by their owners; and must, of course, have a right to seek and enjoy the protection of the law in the establishment of all deeds, or wills, or other legal documents of emancipation; and, so far, they must be considered as natural persons, entitled to some legal rights, whenever their owners shall have declared, in a proper manner, that they shall, either *in presenti* or *in futuro,* be free; and, to this extent, the general reason of policy which disables slaves as persons, and subjects them to the condition of mere brute property, does not apply; and the reason ceasing, the law ought also to cease.[31]

Therefore, Catherine Bodine's slaves' "right" to sue was at best a derivative of her right to free them. It was created when, and if, the master exercised her legal power to free her slaves. It provided a way for the court to enforce the master's will, even over the objection of her heirs and executors.[32]

Nevertheless, this decision provided a narrow exception to the rule barring slave suits. The Kentucky Court of Appeals in 1850 affirmed the dismissal of a suit in which the claimants sought to enforce their master's manumission contract. The contract required that the slaves be freed after the master's death. Judge James Simpson wrote for the court:

> Persons wrongfully held in slavery, may bring a suit to establish their claim to freedom, and to be delivered from illegal bondage but to be able to sue they must be free when the suit is instituted. Slaves can not maintain a suit in their own names, to have a contract for their emancipation specifically executed, because not being free when the suit is brought, as is apparent from the contract itself and the object of the suit, they can not assert any right, and also because they can not from their condition be regarded as parties to the contract, although it was for their benefit. The contract therefore can be enforced alone by the parties to it, or by some person having a right to do so, growing out of the relation to one of the parties.

The court permitted the master's administrators to sue to enforce the contract if they wished, but found that the law "does not enable the slaves to bring a suit for its enforcement in their own names[.]"[33] Enslaved people thus could not sue in court to enforce manumission contracts even indirectly as intended third party beneficiaries.

The legislators in other Southern states adopted statutes that permitted enslaved people to sue for their freedom, but even these statutes included procedural safeguards in favor of the alleged owners. For example, in Virginia, white servants and enslaved people who were Indians, Africans, or mixed race people began filing freedom suits in the mid-seventeenth century.[34] The courts entertained these suits and apparently established procedures on a case-by-case basis until December 25, 1795, when the Virginia legislature adopted a statute that is known as the Freedom Suit Act.

The legislators stated that their purpose in adopting the Freedom Suit Act was to better protect slave owner property rights in freedom and manumission suits:

> Whereas great and alarming mischiefs have arisen in other states of this Union, and are likely to arise in this by voluntary associations of individuals, who under cover of effecting that justice towards persons unwarrantably held in slavery, which sovereignty and duty of society alone ought to afford; have in many instances been the means of depriving masters of their property in slaves, and in others occasioned them heavy expenses in tedious and unfounded law suits: To the end that a plain and easy mode may be pointed out by law for the recovery of freedom where it is unjustly and illegally denied, and that all such practices may in the future be made

useless and punished.[35]

Further, "The preamble distinctly evinces, that it was suggested, less by an anxiety to facilitate the remedies of the slave, than by 'the great and alarming mischiefs'" that were caused by those who would assist freedom claimants with these "tedious and unfounded law suits[.]"[36]

The Act permitted "any person" who "shall conceive himself or herself illegally detained as a slave in the possession of another" to "make complaint thereof" to a magistrate or to the Superior Court in the county where the complainant resided. A complainant filing a claim with the Superior Court was required, "by affidavit or otherwise," to state "the material facts of the case," seeking the court's permission to sue *in forma pauperis*. If the claimant proved his or her allegations "to the satisfaction of the court," the court was to assign counsel for the petitioner, "who, without fee or reward, shall prosecute the suit[.]" Before process could issue against the defendant, however, the lawyer was required to "make an exact statement to the court of the circumstances of the case, with his opinion thereupon[.]" If the court found this report of counsel to be satisfactory, then process would issue summoning the owner to appear and answer the allegations.[37]

The provision requiring the court to appoint counsel for freedom claimants was a mixed blessing for the claimants. It prevented lawyers associated with Virginia's anti-slavery societies from pursuing cases for alleged slaves.[38] The Southern states also generally provided court-appointed counsel for slaves accused of crimes. Slaves had no right to represent themselves in the courts, and they had no means to afford to hire a lawyer. "Accordingly, the state had to intervene to provide counsel; otherwise slave trials would not serve the truth-finding aim of the criminal law."[39] Similar concerns may explain why the Virginia Freedom Suit Act required the appointment of counsel. The notion of slaves representing themselves in court "was impossible to imagine.... This would have led to a slave cross-examining a white person, and in many other ways acting like a white person and a free person."[40]

The statute also permitted the owner to regain possession of the freedom claimant while the case was pending by depositing a guarantee equal to the claimant's value. If the owner did not do so, the claimant was to be held by the court, and the alleged owner was charged with the expenses.[41]

The Act apparently codified a procedural barrier that the courts created for freedom suits before 1795. In a 1793 case, the Virginia Supreme Court of Appeals stated: "Although suits for freedom may be instituted without leave of the Court, yet it is usual to petition for such leave. The Court generally require the opinion of counsel upon the plaintiff's right; and it if appearing that the plaintiff has probable cause for suing," the court would permit the suits to proceed with "special orders" to protect the claimant "from the master's resentment, or ill treatment" caused by the suit.[42]

A 1798 statute added another procedural safeguard for the slave owner defendants. It required the courts to exclude from the juries in these cases "a member of any society instituted for the purpose of emancipating negroes from the possession of their masters[.]"[43] "[T]here was no corresponding statute requiring the removal of slaveowners from such juries."[44]

This rule excluding anti-slavery jurors found support elsewhere. The Mississippi code contained a similar provision.[45] And the United States Supreme Court held that the trial judge in a freedom suit did not err when he excluded from the jury a potential juror who "appeared to have formed no opinion on the particular case; but ... avowed his detestation of slavery to be such that in a doubtful case he would find a verdict for the plaintiffs[.]"[46] The Missouri Supreme Court arrived at a similar holding in an 1845 decision.[47]

In Missouri, an 1807 act of the Legislature of the Territory of Louisiana and a Missouri act of 1824 required persons claiming that they were illegally held as slaves to first petition the court for permission to sue for freedom. The case could proceed only if the judge found that it had merit, with a lawyer being provided to the alleged slave, who was to sue as a "poor person." The judge was to order process free of costs, and order that the claimant not be taken from the court's jurisdiction "or [be] subjected to any severity because of his or her application for freedom[.]" If it appeared to the court that these orders were going to be violated, the court was authorized to issue a writ of *habeas corpus* and to require the defendant to post a bond.[48]

The Missouri Supreme Court also permitted the plaintiff to sue under the common law, without making the *prima facie* showing to a judge. The court held that if the claimant elected to do so, he or she would not proceed with the procedural safeguards of the statute.[49]

Dennis Boman stated that despite these statutes' favorable provisions, "one must not forget that such a right was inoperative unless slaves were aware [of it] ... and were willing to assert it. Even with the protections provided, slaves understood that suing their master could end very badly for them. The greatest deterrent of all was the threat that slaves and loved ones could be sold 'down South' after the trial."[50] Another deterrent to freedom suits was "the difficult situation that most free blacks found in Missouri and the rest of the South."[51]

By 1845, however, Missouri's legislature had adopted statutory amendments that "sharply modified" the freedom suits procedures. "Petitioners now had to post bond for any costs incurred in cases they lost, the wages they earned during the trial went to the sheriff, and they recovered no damages if successful. The rules of evidence were tightened, and, most significantly, the right to personhood guaranteed by the right to habeas corpus during the trial was repealed."[52]

In other states, the statutes provided that slaves could directly petition the courts to assert their freedom claims in place of the common law. The Maryland Provincial Court began hearing petitions for freedom filed by servants and slaves in the 1650s because both slaves and servants could not file suits at law.[53] In 1699, the Maryland General Assembly confirmed this practice with an act that authorized the provincial and county courts "to hear and Determine any Complaints between Masters and Servants by way of Petition to give Judgement and award Execution upon the Same[.]" The act stated that judgments were not to be reversed on appeal "for want of Judiciall [sic] proofs or that the Same was not tryed [sic] by Jury or any Matter of forme [sic] either in the Entry or giveing [sic] of Judgment provided ... that the Parties Defendant was [sic] Legally Summoned and not Condemned unheard[.]" The statute extended this procedure to "Ser[vants] Imported into this Province," apparently referring to slaves, and to servants bound for a term of years. It also stated that disputes about contracts of indenture or wages "or any other matter of Differences between the Said masters and Servants ... shall be Tryed [sic][,] heard[,] and determined by Petition as aforesaid any law[,] Statute[,] or usage to the Contrary Notwithstanding."54

Maryland's 1796 statute continued to permit slaves to file freedom petitions in their home county, but it did not provide for the appointment of counsel or pre-trial procedures to protect slaves while the case was pending. The statute afforded the claimant and the owner a right to a jury trial, and stated that appeals were to be limited to issues of law after a jury trial. Although the statute did not require a judge to review the complaint for probable cause, in its operation the statute imposed that obligation on the claimant's lawyer. It authorized the court to order a lawyer filing an unsuccessful freedom petition to pay "all legal costs arising therein," unless the court was "of the opinion, under all the circumstances, that there was probable cause to suppose the [claimants] had a right to freedom[.]"55

Delaware's 1760 freedom suit act began with the finding that "the children of white women by negro or mulatto fathers," and their descendants, were entitled to their freedom, but they nevertheless were "frequently held and detained as servants or slaves by persons pretending to be their masters and mistresses[.]" Moreover, some of these mixed-race people were being sold out of Delaware "with a fraudulent design to prevent their procuring proof of their being entitled to their freedom[.]" Thus, the legislators concluded that Delaware's laws were "defective in not prescribing any mode for settling and determining in a short and summary manner the claim or right of any persons pretending to be entitled to their liberty[.]"

Nevertheless, the act was not limited to that class of claimants who could not be enslaved. It permitted all freedom claimants to petition the courts for relief on their own, or by their "parent or friend," alleging that they were "kept, held or detained" as servants or slaves by their "pretended" masters. The courts were directed to issue summonses commanding the alleged masters to appear in court to answer the petitions, but the act did not provide for the appointment of lawyers for the freedom claimants. The courts were to hear the proofs presented "in a summary way[.]" If the proofs were sufficient to satisfy the judges, they were authorized to free the petitioners, who were to "enjoy all the benefits and advantages" accorded to free blacks or mulattos. If the masters did not appear, the courts were authorized to hear "the proofs and allegations on the part of the ... petitioner only." Court costs were to be imposed on the losing defendant masters.

The act also permitted successful freedom claimants to file actions of "trespass and false imprisonment or any other action in the law" against their "pretended" owners to recover money damages caused both before and after the freedom judgments. The act later was amended to require freedom claimants to post a $200 bond as surety for costs if their masters prevailed, and to limit the damages recoverable to those caused by post-freedom suit detentions by masters unless they filed appeals from the freedom judgments.[56]

Louisiana's 1825 Slave Code, in article 177, stated that a slave "cannot be a party in any civil action, either as plaintiff or defendant, except when he has to claim or prove his freedom."[57] The Louisiana Digest of 1808 also permitted Louisiana slaves to sue for their freedom.[58]

Alabama's 1852 slave code included a more detailed procedure. It permitted people held as slaves claiming their freedom to directly file a petition in the circuit court of the county in which the alleged owner resided, or where the petitioner was held as a slave. The clerk was to issue a summons requiring the alleged owner to answer the petition. But if the owner defaulted, the trial was to proceed "as if appearance had been entered, and the truth of the allegations of the petition denied." The alleged owner could retain possession of the slave while the case was pending if he or she posted a bond with the court. The court also was authorized to permit the slave to post a bond, and if the slave did this, "the possession of such slave must be given to his sureties, until the cause is determined." If the slave was not in the alleged owner's possession, he or she was required to execute a bond to secure his or her obligation to pay the costs and damages caused to the owner if the suit failed. The code required the slave or his sureties to pay for the master's costs and damages in an unsuccessful suit. If the petitioner was successful, the code did not state that he could recover his costs and damages from the master; it stated only that "he is thenceforth entitled to his freedom."[59]

Some statutes evidenced efforts by the Southern legislators to discourage people held as slaves and lawyers who might file freedom and manumission suits. For example, the South Carolina and Georgia statutes stated that in a successful suit the jury could award the alleged slave's ward damages and costs of suit. But if the master won, the court was "fully empowered to inflict such corporal punishment, not extending to life or limb, on the ward of the plaintiff, as they, in their discretion shall think fit[.]"[60] The Virginia Freedom Suit Act required any person aiding or abetting any person who asserted an unsuccessful claim for freedom to pay $100 to the slave owner, and "be liable to an action on the case for any damages arising therefrom to the party aggrieved thereby."[61] And, as noted above, Maryland's 1796 freedom statute authorized the court to order an unsuccessful freedom claimant's lawyer to pay "all legal costs" unless the court found that the suit was based upon "probable cause[.]"[62] This provision prompted at least one Maryland lawyer to state that he avoided freedom suits because "I am not yet Abolition-mad enough to run the hazard of the expense."[63]

Who Represented the Slaves in the Freedom and Manumission Suits?

Even under the more "liberal" statutes, the alleged slave would have to find a lawyer, and possibly sureties, who would agree to pursue and fund the matter on the belief that the suit will be successful, and that the freed slave would be able to pay the lawyer and sureties. "Slaves needed competent lawyers to stand up to their masters in court, but public hostility discouraged most attorneys from taking such cases."[64]

Some people held as slaves were lucky enough to find a legal champion who opposed slavery. For example, according to Lucy A. Delaney's narrative, Edward Bates, whom President Abraham Lincoln later appointed to serve as Attorney General, agreed to file a suit in freed slave Polly Berry's effort to free her daughter, Lucy. Bates charged only for his expenses. He was a slave owner of Quaker heritage who opposed slavery.[65]

Francis Scott Key, a Maryland and District of Columbia lawyer, also represented freedom claimants. This work was consistent with his publicly stated anti-slavery and pro-colonization views.[66] Key's brother-in-law, future Chief Justice Roger B. Taney, while he was a Maryland lawyer, also "occasionally worked to secure for African Americans the limited benefits that Maryland law afforded them."[67] In 1821, however, Taney also unsuccessfully argued to the Maryland Court of Appeals a slave owner's appeal that sought to overturn a judgment in favor of several freedom claimants, and unlike Key, Taney did not take a public stand against slavery.[68]

What type of lawyer would agree to pursue an alleged slave's manumission or freedom suit, other than a lawyer who opposed slavery or was allied with abolitionists?[69] Judith K. Schafer's study of the New Orleans cases of the later antebellum years includes the portraits of two rather dubious but colorful lawyers who pursued freedom suits for alleged slaves. One, John Charles David, "emerges as the quintessential sleazy and often pathetically inept attorney."[70] The other, Thomas Jefferson Earhart, was admitted to the Louisiana bar three years after being convicted of a felony. He also filed cases under the 1859 act permitting free blacks to seek voluntary enslavement.[71]

There is evidence, at least in the early antebellum years, that some competent lawyers represented freedom claimants. A "well respected" Louisiana attorney, Christian Roselius, represented an alleged slave in a freedom suit in 1845 before that state's Supreme Court. But sixteen years later, he argued a freedom suit before that court on behalf of a slave owner. Roselius won both cases.[72] In late eighteenth century Virginia, Thomas Jefferson pursued one of the earliest reported freedom suits, and John K. Taylor, a Federalist legislator and respected advocate, was the plaintiffs' lawyer in manumission and freedom cases.[73]

At least two Supreme Court Justices also represented parties in freedom and manumission suits in their pre-judicial law practices. As a Virginia lawyer in the 1780s and 1790s, future Chief Justice John Marshall represented the interests of people held as slaves in freedom suits, including the leading case of *Pleasants v. Pleasants*.[74] Nevertheless, like Taney, Marshall did not take a public stand on slavery, and he also represented slaveholder interests. "In slavery cases, Marshall took the law where his clients wanted it to go."[75] Gabriel Duvall, who later served as a Maryland judge and a United States Supreme Court Justice, also represented late eighteenth century Maryland freedom claimants, including Charles Mahoney in the case *Mahoney v. Ashton*.[76]

Kent Newmyer has warned that "lawyer's arguments, like judge's opinions, however, are not always reliable statements of personal belief."[77] Luther Martin, a Maryland Constitutional Convention delegate and Attorney General, opposed the Constitution because it in effect permitted the slave trade until 1808. He also supported gradual emancipation and was one of the original members of the Maryland Abolition Society. Nevertheless, as Maryland's Attorney General, he argued successfully before the Maryland Court of Appeals for the reversal of the freedom judgment that Charles Mahoney obtained in *Mahoney v. Ashton*, one of the cases in which Duvall for a time represented the slave freedom claimant.[78]

Chief Justice Taney and Abraham Lincoln provide better known examples. In *Scott v. Sandford*,[79] the Supreme Court's 1857 opinion by Taney held that blacks were not citizens who could be parties in federal diversity actions. This portion of Taney's opinion refuted the position that Taney advocated almost thirty years earlier when he was a lawyer for a white plaintiff who sued a black defendant as a citizen in the federal court diversity action *Le Grand v. Darnell*.[80] Abraham Lincoln was one of the lawyers who represented slave owner Robert Matson in an 1847 Illinois freedom case that was heard in Coles County Circuit Court.[81] Brian Dirck stated that because Lincoln's case selection was influenced by "too many variables," it is "futile to read moral choices about slavery into Lincoln's choice of litigation."[82] This probably was true of many lawyers who represented parties for and against liberty in the manumission and freedom suits.

Keila Grinberg found a similar pattern in her study of the lawyers who participated in the nineteenth century Brazilian manumission and freedom suits. She analyzed the lawyers who appeared in appeals filed with the Rio de Janeiro Court of Appeals before 1865, when abolitionist societies and lawyers became involved in these suits. Twenty-six lawyers represented litigants in more than five of these appeals, but none of them represented only slaves or only slave owners in their cases.[83] "[A]ttorneys generally treated the freedom suits as they would ... any other case, sometimes defending masters, sometimes slaves, sometimes winning, sometimes losing and utilizing arguments which might quickly and easily win them their particular case, while rarely advocating a general emancipation."[84]

Unless their lawyers would work with no guarantee of compensation, people held as slaves in most states would have to find a way to pay the fees of lawyers who were willing and able to take on the payment risks that were associated with freedom and manumission suits. As explained in chapter nine, some states permitted slaves who won their suits to also obtain money judgments for the damages caused by their wrongful detention in slavery. A lawyer might agree to take on a strong case for liberty if a monetary recovery could be anticipated. But in some states the courts and legislators did not permit those winning freedom judgments to recover damages, thus removing a potential incentive for lawyers to represent freedom claimants.[85]

Nevertheless, some slaves, such as Dred and Harriet Scott, were lucky to have white supporters who helped finance and guide their cases through the courts, and some whites even helped slaves hire competent legal counsel. The Scotts benefited from the assistance of the adult children of Dred's one-time owner Peter Blow. It is impossible to know how many other slaves who were not so lucky simply did not have a way to bring their case to the courts for a fair hearing.[86]

Other Procedural Approaches to Slaves' Claims to Liberty

The law in other slave regimes permitted slaves to sue for their freedom. According to Alan Watson, Ancient Roman law did not permit slaves to file suits; "a slave had no legal personality and hence at private law he could not sue or be sued. But what if his status was in doubt?" Watson cited a law adopted under Justinian in 528 stating that people who were enslaved but who claimed to be free, "or who seemed to be free but [were] claimed as slave[s], could appear in court on [their] own behalf. In the latter situation, moreover, [they] could appear through the procurator." Watson also noted that before this enactment, "in some cases when a slave was to be given his freedom directly or by a trust ..., he might be given access to an official for relief."[87]

Roman slaves also could sue their owner if they bought themselves with their own money and the owner accepted the money but refused to free the slave. "The proceedings were not in the regular courts but [were] before the prefect of the city or, if in a province, before the governor."[88]

The Spanish law *Las Siete Partidas* established a general rule providing that masters and slaves were not to file suits in the courts against each other. A slave could not sue because he was "under the control of another, and not his own[.]"[89]

Nevertheless, the statute stated exceptions for "special cases." These included, "as, for instance, when someone makes a will in which he orders that a certain slave of his be emancipated, and he who is directed to do this fraudulently conceals the will, in which the grant of emancipation was made; since in the instance of this kind, the slave has a right to bring suit in court against whoever keeps him under restraint." A second exception occurred if "any slave has money which does not belong to his master but which he has received from some other party, and gives it to someone to be kept for him, trusting in him, with the understanding that he will purchase him from his master, and afterwards set him at liberty, and said party, after having received the money, refuses to buy him, or having bought him, is unwilling to set him free[.]" The third example occurred if "a slave makes a contract with anyone to purchase him of his master, and set him free after he has repaid the money which he gave for him, and after this contract was entered into, he, having purchased the said slave, refuses to receive the money for his emancipation, or, having received it, refuses to set him free, as he had agreed to do." People held as slaves could plead their own case, or a representative or family member could do so.[90]

People held as slaves in Spain's colonies also had procedural advantages.

They could obtain "the protection of any person who could represent them as a *padrino*, a term used to denote a person—usually white—who would act on behalf of the slaves before their masters and local authorities."[91] Moreover, beginning in the 1760s, "Spanish lawmakers also created the post of *sindico procurador* in each jurisdiction to look after the proper treatment of the slaves and to serve them as a sort of attorney. The *sindicos procuradores* were 'public servants who acted as protectors of the slaves and who were supposed to know and decide in the first instance about the validity of their demands.'"[92]

The local town councils elected the *sindicos*. The position was considered "an honorable public duty[.]" Thus, Alejandro de la Fuente suggested that many *sindicos* "were themselves slave owners and not particularly concerned with the well-being of the slaves." Nevertheless, at least in Cuba, some *sindicos* were effective advocates for slaves claiming their legal rights under the doctrines of *coartación*, which permitted slave self-purchase against the master's will, and *papel*, which afforded some slaves the right to demand that they be sold to another master.[93]

Slaves in colonial Lima also could seek relief in the ecclesiastical courts as well as the courts of law. Michelle McKinley cited cases filed by two slaves—Catalina Conde and Dominiga de Llanos—who used the process known as *censura* to obtain evidence in support of their freedom and manumission claims.[94] Although the *censuras* "did not end with judgments," McKinley found evidence that Catilina Conde was freed.[95] The Catholic Church's legal process provided a forum in which slaves could air grievances against their masters and seek their freedom.[96]

Slaves in colonial Brazil, in addition to using the courts, could file appeals to the Portuguese monarch or the colonial royal representatives when their claims were not enforced because of "the discrimination inherent to the judiciary, bureaucratic mechanisms and law enforcement."[97] These appeals were few in number and the outcome was never certain. Nevertheless, "the mere existence of this mechanism may have curbed excesses by the ordinary judges and magistrates."[98]

Consequently, Robert Cottrol called it a paradox of legal history that slave law appeared to be more egalitarian in the more inegalitarian legal and social cultures of Latin America than in the republican United States. Although scholars debate how effective these more egalitarian remedies were in practice, these religious and royal venues and remedies were not available to provide even a potential basis for freedom for any people held as slaves in the United States South.[99]

Before the manumission and freedom suits went before the courts in the United States South, they faced roadblocks unlike other suits. These suits first were screened and tried in the informal white court of public opinion. The courts would entertain these claims only if the slave claimants could convince at least one white person of the merit of the slave's case for liberty. The alleged slave had to convince a lawyer to take or pursue the case, and often had to convince a white person to intervene—at his or her own expense—as the slave's next friend. The law did not provide for *sindicos* or formal procedures to facilitate the airing of the slaves' claims or grievance. And there were no ecclesiastical courts to inquire into and police the morality of the slave holders.

Were any or many potentially meritorious claims to freedom screened out by this pre-suit filter? This is a difficult question to answer with certainty because the evidence of claims or potential cases "rejected" at this initial stage would be limited. This preliminary hurdle could not have had a beneficial effect on freedom suits, however, which thus became a class of disfavored cases even before they were filed.

What Cause of Action Could Form the Basis for a Freedom or Manumission Suit?

When analyzing a freedom or a manumission suit, the lawyers on both sides needed to determine the cause of action that might successfully be asserted by or on behalf of the claimant held in bondage. The Southern courts and legislatures generally denied to most people held as slaves the benefits of the common law writs of *habeas corpus* and *de homine replegiando*. These writs were, as a general rule, deemed not to be the "appropriate" remedies for those who were black and who claimed that they were illegally held in slavery. In the place of these writs, the Southern judges and legislators applied other forms of action that they deemed to be less of a threat to their society.[100]

Justice John Paul Stevens called the writ of *habeas corpus* "'an integral part of our common law heritage' by the time the colonies achieved their independence[.]"[101] Almost 50 years earlier, Zecharia Chaffee hailed the writ as "[t]he most important human rights provision in the [United States] Constitution."[102] These comments do not reflect principles of only the twentieth and twenty first centuries. William Blackstone called the writ of *habeas corpus* "[t]he most celebrated writ in English law," and it also is referred to as "[t]he most fundamental legal right" in Anglo-American law.[103] Moreover, Paul Halliday and Edward White have demonstrated the salience of the writ's common law origins, criticizing Blackstone's emphasis on the effect of the Habeas Corpus Act of 1679.[104]

The writ of *habeas corpus* provided a common law remedy, which was supplemented by statutes, to free persons alleging that they were being deprived of their liberty and that they were being held by an illegal restraint.[105] The court could release a successful claimant, but did not punish the defendant, award to the plaintiff a judgment for the damages that the illegal confinement caused, or permit a jury trial on the return of the writ.[106]

The writ of *de homine replegiando* in effect permitted the plaintiff to regain possession of his or her own liberty.[107] It is also called personal replevin because it is a form of the writ of replevin, which is the common law writ that permits a property owner to recover wrongfully detained property.[108] The courts allowed jury trials for claims asserted under the writ of *de homine replegiando*.[109] The writ required the immediate release of the claimant who was seeking his or her freedom, but exceptions developed that caused the writ of *habeas corpus* to be thought of as providing a more efficient procedure.[110]

Lord Mansfield used the writ of *habeas corpus* to free James Somerset from slavery in the landmark case of *Somerset v. Stewart*.[111] According to Paul Halliday, Mansfield's decision is just one example of the English judges' expansive use of the writ "by reasoning not from precedents, but from the writ's central premise; that it exists to empower the justices to examine detention in all forms."[112]

The *Somerset* decision was widely reported in the press in England and the American colonies.[113] It apparently was perceived by some as a precedent for the use of the writ of *habeas corpus* by persons held as slaves in Britain's colonies and later in the new United States.[114] The Northern courts followed the English common law and applied the common law writs of *de homine replegiando* and *habeas corpus* for even non-white persons who claimed that they were illegally held as slaves. All people, including those held in slavery, could file these writs to challenge their alleged illegal confinement or slave status.[115] These writs therefore were available to slave owners seeking to recover runaway slaves and to abolitionists seeking to prevent the removal of slaves from free soil to the South.[116]

There is evidence that the New Jersey Supreme Court permitted blacks held as slaves to obtain their freedom via writs of *habeas corpus* in the 1770s, even before the state legislature adopted the 1804 gradual emancipation act.[117] The Supreme Court then exercised original and appellate jurisdiction.[118] The alleged slave did not directly present his or her claim in court against the purported owner. Instead, the state's Attorney General asserted the freedom claim on the claimant's behalf.[119] The court did not require the claimant or the state to post security for costs, and it permitted oral testimony, but not jury trials, at the hearing on the writ.[120]

In the New Jersey Supreme Court's May 1775 term the Court heard evidence and argument, and, in its November 1775 term, ruled in favor of the freedom claimant in *King v. Esther Barber and others*; this was a manumission suit "on Habeas Corpus for to [sic] bring the Body of Beulah, a Negro Girl."[121] Between 1775 and 1795, the New Jersey Supreme Court judges granted the freedom or manumission claims in 16 of 17 unreported cases and in seven of ten officially reported cases.[122] This trend apparently motivated the legislature to adopt a provision in a 1798 act establishing a new more detailed slave code.[123] The statute "significantly altered the habeas corpus process by which many slaves had previously obtained their freedom." It required, in part, jury trials when *habeas corpus* petitions were filed on behalf of persons held as slaves.[124]

In contrast, the statutes and case law in the Southern states other than Louisiana and Texas required that freedom and manumission suits be filed on behalf of black plaintiffs in the form of common law tort actions against the purported master. The suits usually alleged claims for assault and battery or false imprisonment.[125] These common law torts were derived from the action of trespass, "which first emerged in the thirteenth century," and "was directed at serious and forcible breaches of the King's peace[.]"[126]

Battery and assault are two separate torts. Battery is "[a] harmful or offensive contact with a person, resulting from an act intended to cause the plaintiff or a third person to suffer such contact, or apprehension that such a contact is imminent[.]"[127] Assault protects a person's "interest in freedom from apprehension of a harmful or offensive contact with the person, as distinguished from the contact itself[.]"[128] False imprisonment is a related tort that "protects the personal interest in freedom from restraint of movement."[129]

Freedom and manumission claimants did not have to prove that the defendant committed any of the usual elements of these common law torts.[130] This prompted the judges in several Virginia decisions to call the pleading convention a legal fiction because the suit "is founded upon the concession that the status of the claimant is that of slavery, otherwise the remedy would be inappropriate."[131] This may have been thought to be so in Virginia because its judges, contrary to the majority of Southern courts, denied more than nominal damages for the wrongful retention in slavery to persons winning their freedom.[132]

This form of tort action was not a legal fiction, however, even in the states that did not permit those wrongfully detained in slavery to recover damages along with their liberty. A legal fiction is "either (1) a statement propounded with a complete or partial consciousness of its falsity, or (2) a false statement recognized as having utility."[133] The Southern courts' pleading convention was, instead, the opposite—fundamental legal truth telling, what Nancy Knauer called juristic truth.[134] It was an implied concession that the master and slave relationship was inherently tortious under at least three of the common law torts. Masters who were sued for assault and battery essentially admitted that they were *prima facie* tortfeasors. False imprisonment defendants also in essence admitted that "a person held as a slave is controlled and compelled to act by the will of another, and is in fact and law imprisoned, although not within the four walls of a jail."[135] The alleged owners asserted, as an affirmative defense, that their ownership rights legitimized violence that otherwise would be tortious under the common law. They did not assert any other justification for committing the alleged tort, such as consent or self-defense.[136]

The Southern legislators and judges thus abolished the common law writs of *habeas corpus* and *de homine replegiando* in the freedom and manumission cases because they found that the common law was too favorable to the alleged slave. Under either common law writ, the alleged slave might be set free pending the outcome of the case. The writ of *habeas corpus* also was disfavored because it deprived the alleged property owner of his property rights without a jury trial.[137]

The Virginia courts, for example, allowed writs of *habeas corpus* and *de homine replegiando* in slave freedom cases before the legislators adopted the 1795 Freedom Suit Act. That Act replaced the common law writs, which, according to the legislature, "proved vexatious and unsafe," with a "new proceeding" that better accommodated the relevant interests in a slave society.[138] The courts nevertheless permitted other plaintiffs, including free blacks who were in possession of "free papers," to assert claims of unlawful detention under the common law writs.[139]

The South Carolina and Georgia statutes of 1740 and 1755 stated that the claimant's guardian was entitled "in law, to bring an action of trespass in the nature of ravishment of ward, against any person who shall claim property in, or shall be in possession of," the slave.[140] The legislators' choice of the common law action of trespass in the nature of ravishment of ward instead of the common law writs of *habeas corpus* or *de homine replegiando* caused significant disadvantage to the claimants seeking their freedom.[141]

The South Carolina Court of Appeals illustrated this disadvantage with its decision in *Huger v. Barnwell*.[142] The plaintiff, as next friend of Venus Hunger and her child Sarah, sued the defendant, William Barnwell, by filing a writ *de homine replegiando*. The plaintiff alleged that Barnwell, a free person of color, improperly held his wards as slaves.[143]

The Court of Appeals opinion of Justice Thomas J. Withers affirmed the dismissal of the suit, because the court found that the form of the action was contrary to the 1740 statute. The court noted that the writ *de homine replegiando* was "one of the four forms of process known to the common law, whereby the personal liberty of the individual might be vindicated," but this writ "has grown quite into disuse in England having been superseded by that of *habeas corpus*[.]"[144]

The court held that the writ *de homine replegiando* was an inappropriate procedural form for freedom suits in South Carolina because the person alleged to be illegally held as a slave was "to enjoy his freedom *pendente lite*; whereas according to the statutory mode, the claimant remains *statu quo*, in the mean time." The claimant suing under the writ *de homine replegiando* was to be delivered to be kept in the custody of the prison keeper if she did not give sufficient security to permit her to be set free pending the final judgment in the case. In either case, this writ would work to the disadvantage of the "master," whom the court found, *pendente lite*, was to be presumed the claimant's rightful owner.[145] On the other hand, under the statute the claimant would be subject to his or her master's control while the suit against that master is pending, no doubt a most uncomfortable position for the "slave," even if the "master" was a free black, such as the defendant, Barnwell.

This result appears on first reading to be compelled by the statutory language specifying the form of the pleading that the plaintiff must file for his ward. On further reflection, however, the decision dismissing the case because of an error of pleading form is contrary to the statute's provision stating that in a freedom suit filed under the act "judgment shall be given according to the very right of the cause, without having any regard to any defect in the proceedings, either in form or substance[.]"[146]

Maryland's statutes establishing the right of slaves to file petitions for freedom also apparently precluded common law claims by people held as slaves for writs of *habeas corpus*.[147] The first reported Maryland state court case in which a successful writ of *habeas corpus* was filed on behalf of a slave was not decided until 1866. The court issued this writ after the 1864 Maryland constitution that abolished slavery went into effect.[148] Maryland's statutes did, however, recognize the right of people held as slaves to challenge the legality of their enslavement by filing writs *de homine replegiando*.[149] No reported cases have been found, however, in which this writ was used in place of the petition for freedom.

Louisiana and Texas adopted another approach. People held as slaves in Louisiana filed many *habeas corpus* petitions pursuant to Article 177 of that state's Code, which permitted slaves to sue for their freedom.[150] The Texas legislature did not adopt a statute governing freedom suits, and the *habeas corpus* statute did not exclude slaves.[151]

Thus, it appears that, unlike the other Southern common law slave states, a freedom claimant in Texas had the benefit of the writ of *habeas corpus*, but only after the court appointed a guardian *ad litem*. For example, a case that was heard between 1849 and 1852 began as a suit filed by George S. Gaines against Thomas and Colton to recover the possession of a slave girl named Ann.[152] The defendants did not answer, but suggested that Ann "was a free white girl, without negro blood, and moved the court for the appointment of a guardian *ad litem*, to sustain her rights to her freedom and for a writ of *habeas corpus* to bring" Ann before the court. The trial court appointed the attorneys Neblett and Gould to serve as Ann's guardians and issued the writ. On the return of the writ, the court ordered that a trial be held on Ann's right to freedom, and on the appeal by Gaines, the Texas Supreme Court affirmed this procedure.[153]

Court access did not always ensure success, however. Ann's guardians twice obtained freedom judgments, which the Texas Supreme Court twice reversed for being against the weight of the evidence.[154]

Conclusion

The courts and legislatures established and applied procedural rules in the Southern freedom and manumission suits that directly or indirectly exhibited the legislators' and judges' intentions to make it difficult for people held as slaves to pursue and win their suits. A freedom claimant in the United States South had to convince someone in the white community to be the claimant's lawyer or guardian before the case could be heard in court, and some statutes required a judge to determine on a preliminary basis if the claim had any merit before it could be heard in court and tried on the merits. The law also denied the most fundamental right to pursue the writs of *habeas corpus* and *de homine replegiando* to millions of persons held as slaves, and permitted the purported owners to obtain a trial by a jury of their peers and to retain control over their alleged slaves while the case was pending in court.

These procedural burdens had evident unfavorable substantive effects on the freedom claimants in many of the reported cases discussed in this book. It also is likely that these procedures may have influenced lawyers or guardians to decide not to support, finance, or pursue a freedom claimant's case when they evaluated the claimant's chances of success in view of the legal obstacles they faced.[155]

In one of the many apparent incongruities of slave law, however, slave owners successfully asserted their right to use the great writ of *habeas corpus* to recover their slaves that they alleged were wrongfully "detained" as free people in free states.[156] Moreover, the Mississippi statutes also permitted slave owners to use the writ of *habeas corpus* to recover possession of their slave property. The statute applied to a slave who was "taken or seduced out of the possession of the master, owner, or overseer of such slave, by force, stratagem, or fraud, and [was] unlawfully detained in the possession of any other person."[157]

Dallin Oaks commented on this statute:

> The doctrinal inconsistency between this remedy, where a judge tried the issues and exercised the power to remove the slaves from their existing custodian and restore them to their rightful owner, and the right-to-jury rationale for refusing a similar habeas corpus remedy to slaves for testing their right to freedom, does not seem to have influenced the lawmakers.[158]

Indeed, this statute is not incoherent if it is viewed as an expression of the concerns that the slave owning class, the courts, and the legislatures had about slave theft.[159] It also illustrates how the lawmakers reified slave humanity. The legislators and the courts denied the great writ of *habeas corpus* to people claiming that they were being unjustly held as slaves in Mississippi, but the judges and legislators made the writ available so that slave owners could recover their slaves as property.[160]

Notes to Chapter 4

[1] *See generally* Lawrence B. Solum, "Procedural Justice," 78 *S. Cal. L. Rev.* 181, 215-26 (2004).

[2] *See, e.g.,* Jenny S. Martinez, "Process and Substance in the 'War on Terror,'" 108 *Colum. L. Rev.* 1013, 1019-27 (2008); Walter Wheeler Cook, "'Substance' and 'Procedure' in the Conflict of Laws," 42 *Yale L.J.* 333, 341 (1933).

[3] *See* Robert M. Cover, "For James Wm. Moore: Some Reflections in a Reading of the Rules," 84 *Yale L.J.* 718, 722-732 (1975) [hereinafter Cover, "Reflections"].

[4] *Id.* at 731-32.

[5] *Id.* at 732-40.

[6] *Id.; see* Martinez, *supra* at 1077-92.

[7] *See* 7 *Statutes at Large of South Carolina, supra* at 397-98; *see also* Higginbotham, *Color, supra* at 194-95; 1 Hurd, *supra* at 302-08; Stroud, *supra* at 52-53; O'Neall, *supra* at 8.

[8] *Black's Law Dictionary* 1136 (5th ed. 1979). Ravishment de gard was a common law writ "which lay for a guardian by knight's service or in socage, against a person who took from him the body of his ward." *Id.*

[9] *See* Prince, *supra* at 777; *see also Knight v. Hardeman,* 17 Ga. 253, 1855 WL 1818 *4-*6 (1855) (for 1770, 1835, and 1837 acts); Higginbotham, *supra* at 252-53; 1 Hurd, *supra* at 311; Stroud, *supra* at 53; Wiecek, "Statutes," *supra* at 265.

10 Berlin, *Many Thousands, supra* at 281; *see* William E. Nelson, "The Height of Sophistication: Law and Professionalism in the City-State of Charleston, South Carolina, 1670-1775," 61 *S.C. L. Rev.* 1, 48, n. 446 (2009) [hereinafter Nelson, "South Carolina"], citing cases from 1759 and 1765; *see also* Shaw, *supra* at 168; Goodell, *supra*, at 297-98; Gillmer, "Suing for Freedom," *supra* at 567.

11 *See* chapter 1, *supra* at notes 24-26.

12 *See* 7 *Statutes at Large of South Carolina, supra* at 343-47, 352-65; *see also* Higginbotham, *Color, supra* at 169, 194.

13 *Id.* at 194.

14 32 Tenn. (2 Swan) 149, 1852 WL 1834 (1852). Jason Gillmer quoted an 1817 Tennessee statute that required the defendant in a freedom suit to post a bond to secure a freedom claimant's presence in the state while the suit was pending if the claimant demonstrated to the court "by the affidavit of some respectable person, or otherwise" that there was "probable reason to believe" that the slave was entitled to freedom. If the claimant satisfied this requirement, the sheriff was to take the claimant into custody while the case was pending until the owner provided "good and sufficient security" that the claimant would be in the state until the case could be heard. Gillmer, "Suing for Freedom," *supra* at 568-69, quoting 1 John Haywood & Robert L. Cobbs, eds., *The Statute Laws of the State of Tennessee of Public and General Nature* 328-29 (1831).

15 *Doran v. Brazelton*, 1852 WL 1834 at *2.

16 *Id.* at *1.

17 *Id.* at *2.

18 *Id.*

19 *Id.*

20 *Id.*

21 *See* Fede, *People Without Rights, supra* at 23-24, 61, 75, 111, 146.

22 *Doran v. Brazelton*, 1852 WL 1834 at *3.

23 *Id.* at *3-*4 (the same rule applies, "with few exceptions, to all persons under the age of twenty-one, and *femes covert.*"). For a biographical sketch of Justice Caruthers, *see* Nash, "Reason of Slavery," *supra* at 123-24. Nash omits *Doran v. Brazelton* from his discussion of Caruthers and from his analysis of the Tennessee manumission cases decided between 1835 to 1860. *Id.* at 172-84. For another view of the Tennessee next friend cases, *see* Howington, *What Sayeth, supra* at 12-20.

24 *Jack, et al. (slaves) v. Doran's Executors*, 37 Ala. 265, 1861 WL 368 (1861).

25 *Id.* at *1-*2.

26 *Id.* at *2.

27 34 Ky. (4 Dana) 476, 1836 WL 2089 (1836).

28 *Catherine Bodine's Will*, 1836 WL 2089 at *1-*2.

29 *Id.* at *1.

30 *Id.*

31 *Id.*

32 *See also Aleck v. Tevis*, 34 Ky. (4 Dana) 242, 1836 WL 2053 at *2 (1836) (opinion by Robertson, C.J. holding that a slave can pursue in Chancery a claim to freedom under a will).

33 *Henry v. Nunn's Heirs*, 50 Ky. (11 B. Mon.) 239, 1850 WL 3346, at *4 (1850).
Bernie Jones does not refer to this decision in her discussion of the Kentucky manumission cases. *See* Jones, *Fathers, supra* at 68-97.

34 *See, e.g.*, John Ruston Pagan, *Anne Orthwood's Bastard: Sex and Law in Early Virginia* 7-9, 131-44 (2003); Wallenstein, *supra* at 27-38; Woody Holton, *Forced Founders: Indians, Debtors, Slaves and the Making of the American Revolution in Virginia* 140 (1999); Brown, *Good Wives, supra* at 132, 223-25, 241; Ablavsky, *supra* at 1477-90; Owen Stanwood, "Captives and Slaves: Indian Labor, Cultural Conversion, and the Plantation Revolution in Virginia," 114 *Va. Mag. of Hist. & Bio.* 435, 453-56 (2006); Michael L. Nicholls, "Passing Through this Troublesome World: Free Blacks in the Early Southside," 92 *Va. Mag. of Hist. & Bio.* 50, 56-61 (1984) [hereinafter Nicholls, "Passing Through"].

35 "An Act to amend an act intituled [sic], an act to reduce into one, the several acts concerning slaves, free negroes, and mulattoes, and for other purposes," in *Collection of all such Acts of the General Assembly of Virginia* 346 (1803) [hereinafter *Collection of Virginia Acts*]; *see* Robert McColley, *Slavery and Jeffersonian Virginia* 160 (2d ed. 1973); Higginbotham & Higginbotham, *supra* at 1236.

36 *Nicholas v. Burruss*, 31 Va. (4 Leigh) 289, 1833 WL 2087 at *5 (1833); *see* Wolf, *Race, supra* at 118; MacLeod, *supra* at 124; McColley, *supra* at 160; Nicholls, "Squint of Freedom," *supra* at 55-56; Christopher Doyle, "Judge St. George Tucker and the Case of *Tom v. Roberts*: Blunting the Revolution's Radicalism from Virginia's District Courts," 106 *Va. Mag. of Hist. & Bio.* 419, 431 (1998); Higginbotham & Higginbotham, *supra* at 1236; *but see* Ablavsky, *supra* at 1477, n. 100.

37 *See Collection of Virginia Acts, supra* at 346; *see also* Joseph Tate, *Digest of the Laws of Virginia, Which Are of a Permanent Character and General Operation; Illustrated by Judicial Decisions* 869-71 (1841); Gillmer, "Suing for Freedom," *supra* at 568; Higginbotham & Higginbotham, *supra* at 1235; *see generally* Loren Schweninger, "The Vass Slaves: County Courts, State Laws, and Slavery in Virginia," 114 *Va. Mag. of Hist. & Bio.* 465, 471-72 (2006) (discussing the Virginia statutes as applied in a manumission case).

38 *See* MacLeod, *supra* at 124; Nicholls, "Squint of Freedom," *supra* at 56-57.

39 *See* Fede, *People Without Rights, supra* at 194.

40 Paul Finkelman, "The Dragon St. George Could Not Slay: Tucker's Plan to End Slavery," 47 *Wm. & Mary L. Rev.* 1213, 1224, n. 75 (2006) [hereinafter Finkelman, "Tucker"].

41 *See Collection of Virginia Acts, supra* at 346; *see also* Tate, *supra* at 870-71; Higginbotham & Higginbotham, *supra* at 1235; *Sarah v. Henry*, 12 Va. (2 Hen. & M.) 19 (1808) (slaveholder who did not post bond was required to reimburse state for expenses incurred in holding claimant before trial).

42 *Coleman v. Dick and Pat*, 1 Va. (1 Wash.) 233, 1793 WL 378 at *5 (1793); *see* Gillmer, "Suing for Freedom," *supra* at 568; Doyle, *supra* at 428-31.

43 *See Collection of Virginia Acts, supra* at 347; *see also* Wolf, *Race, supra* at 118; McColley, *supra* at 161; Tate, *supra* at 871; Nicholls, "Squint of Freedom," *supra* at 56; Higginbotham & Higginbotham, *supra* at 1246-47.

[44] *See* Higginbotham & Higginbotham, *supra* at 1246-47, n. 190.

[45] *See* William Lewis Sharkey, *et al.*, eds., *Revised Code of the Statute Laws of the State of Mississippi* ch. 33, art. 13 at 237 (1857) [hereinafter *Revised Mississippi Code*].

[46] *Mima Queen v. Hepburn*, 11 U.S. (7 Cranch) 290, 297 (1813).

[47] *See Chouteau v. Pierre of color*, 9 Mo. 3, 1845 WL 3817 at *2 (1845) (reversing freedom judgment).

[48] *See* "An act to enable persons held in slavery to sue for their freedom," in 1 *Laws of Missouri Revised and Digested to February 21, 1825* 404-06 (St. Louis, 1825) [hereinafter *Laws of Missouri 1825*]; "An act to enable persons held in slavery to sue for their freedom," in *Laws of the Territory of Louisiana* ch 35 at 96-97 (St. Louis, 1808-09) [hereinafter *Laws of the Territory of Louisiana*]; *Tramell v. Adam, a Blackman*, 2 Mo. 155, 1829 WL 1766 at *2 (1829); Kaufman, *supra* at 106; Konig, "Dred Scott," *supra* at 67-68; Boman, "Dred Scott," *supra* at 406-07; Eric T. Dean, Jr., "Reassessing Dred Scott: The Possibilities of Federal Power in the Antebellum Context," 60 *U. Cin. L. Rev.* 713, 724-27 (1992).

On the pre-suit process, *see Joshua, (man of color) v. Purse*, 34 Mo. 209, 1863 WL 2985 (1863); *Jeffrie v. Robdeaux*, 3 Mo. 33, 1831 WL 2580 (1831); *Catiche v. Circuit Court*, 1 Mo. 608, 1826 WL 1721 (1826). According to Loren Schweninger, the Missouri courts granted petitions for leave to sue for freedom among the 115 successful petitions in the 116 Missouri cases that he studied. *See* Schweninger, "Slave Women," *supra* at 391, 399.

[49] *See Tramell v. Adam, A Blackman*, 1829 WL 1766 at *2.

[50] Boman, "Dred Scott," *supra* at 407.

[51] *Id.*; *see generally* Schafer, *Supreme Court, supra* at 220.

[52] Konig, "Dred Scott," *supra* at 77; *see* Evans Casselberry, *The Revised Statutes of the State of Missouri*, "Freedom," 283-84 (1845) [hereinafter *Statutes of Missouri 1845*]; *The Revised Statutes of the State of Missouri*, "Freedom," 284-86 (1835) [hereinafter *Statutes of Missouri 1835*]; Fehrenbacher, *supra* at 251, 657, n. 5; VanderVelde, *Mrs. Dred Scott, supra* at 233-36; Ehrlich, *supra* at 34; Duane Benton, "Lessons for Judges from *Scott v. Emerson*," in Dred Scott *Perspectives, supra* at 201.

[53] *See* 65 *Archives of Maryland: Proceedings of the Provincial Court, 1670/1-1675*, "Introduction" at xxxiii, and 279 (Elizabeth Merritt, ed.) (1952); Brackett, *supra* at 148; Alpert, *supra* at 192, 202-03.

[54] *See Proceedings and Acts of the General Assembly, March 1697 to July 1699* 328. The legislature re-enacted this statute in 1715. *See Laws of Maryland, 1715*, ch. 44, §31.

[55] *See Laws of Maryland, 1796*, ch. 67, §§21-25; Brackett, *supra* at 153; Snethen, *supra* at 30-31.

[56] *See*, for the 1760 act, *Laws of Delaware, supra* at 499-500, and, for the amendments, *see Revised Delaware Statutes, supra* at 255-56. *See also* Williams, *Slavery and Freedom in Delaware, supra* at 113.

[57] *See* Schafer, *Becoming Free, supra* at 3; Rose, *supra* at 188-89, quoting *Civil Code* §177.

[58] *See* Schafer, *Becoming Free, supra* at 4.

[59] *Code of Alabama, supra* §§2049-2055 at 391-92; *see* Rose, *supra* at 188-89; *Farrelly v.*

Maria Louisa, 34 Ala. 284, 1859 WL 731 at *2 (1859) (Alabama Code §2049 applied to all persons held as slaves, not only people "of African blood."); *see also Revised Mississippi Code*, *supra* at ch. 33, art. 10-11 at 236-37; Lang, *supra* at 75 (for the similar Mississippi provisions of 1822).

[60] For South Carolina, *see* 7 *Statutes at Large of South Carolina*, *supra* at 398; *see also* Stroud, *supra* at 52; O'Neall, *supra* at 9; and for Georgia, Prince, *supra* at 777; *Knight v. Hardeman*, 17 Ga. 253, 1855 WL 1818 at *4 (1855) (quoting the 1770 Georgia act).

[61] Tate, *supra* at 871; *see* Wolf, *Race*, *supra* at 118; Higginbotham & Higginbotham, *supra* at 1236; *see also*, for the Mississippi provision, *Revised Mississippi Code*, *supra* at ch. 33, art. 12 at 237.

[62] *Laws of Maryland, 1796*, ch. 67, §25; Whitman, *supra* at 65-66; Stroud, *supra* at 53; Goodell, *supra* at 298; Snethen, *supra* at 31.

[63] *See* Berlin, *Slaves Without Masters*, *supra* at 102; Grinberg, "Freedom," *supra* at 73.

[64] Berlin, *Slaves Without Masters*, *supra* at 102.

[65] *See* Delaney, *supra* at 36-38; Konig, "Dred Scott," *supra* at 72.

[66] *See, e.g., Scott v. Negro Ben*, 10 U.S. (6 Cranch) 3, 3 L. Ed. 135, 1810 WL 1606 (1810); *Queen v. Neale*, 3 H. & J. 158, 1810 WL 592 (Md. 1810); *Negro James v. Gaither*, 2 H. & J. 176, 1807 WL 480 (Md. 1807); *Maria v. White*, 16 F. Cas. 732 (C.C.D.C. 1829) (No. 9,076); *Amelia v. Caldwell*, 1 F. Cas. 596 (C.C.D.C. 1823) (No. 278); *Brown v. Wingard*, 4 F. Cas. 438 (C.C.D.C. 1822) (No. 2,034); *Nan v. Moxley*, 17 F. Cas. 1147 (C.C.D.C. 1808) (No. 10,007). *See generally* Victor Weybright, *Spangled Banner: The Story of Francis Scott Key* 180-203 (1935); Hoffer, *supra* at 117-18; Timothy S. Huebner, "Roger B. Taney and the Slavery Issue: Looking Beyond—and Before—*Dred Scott*," 97 *J. of Am. Hist.* 17, 19 (2010) [hereinafter Huebner, "Taney"].

Key represented the alleged slaves in *The Antelope*, 23 U.S. (10 Wheat.) 66, 6 L. Ed. 268 (1825); *see* Shaw, *supra* at 218-19; *see generally* John T. Noonan, Jr., *The Ordeal of the Recaptured Africans in the Administrations of James Monroe and John Quincy Adams* (1977). But he also represented slave owners in freedom suits. *See Davis v. Wood*, 11 U.S. (1 Wheat.) 6, 4 L. Ed. 22 (1816); *Wood v. Davis*, 11 U.S. (7 Cranch) 271, 3 L. Ed. 339 (1812); *Joice v. Alexander*, 13 F. Cas. 907 (C.C.D.C. 1808) (No. 7,345). Philip Barton Key, Francis Scott Key's uncle and legal mentor, represented slave holders in several Maryland freedom suits. *See, e.g., Higgins v. Allen*, 3 H. & McH. 504, 1796 WL 638 (Md. Gen. Ct. 1796), *aff'd* (Md. Ct. App. 1798); *Rawlings v. Boston*, 3 H. & McH. 139, 1793 WL 394 (Md. Gen. Ct. 1793); David S. Bogen, "The Annapolis Poll Books of 1800 to 1804: African American Voting in the Early Republic," 86 *Md. Historical Mag.* 57, 64, n. 12 (1991).

[67] *See* Huebner, "Taney," *supra* at 19.

[68] *See id.* at 19-35; *Hughes v. Negro Milly*, 5 H. & J. 310, 1821 WL 1014 (Md. 1821); *Dunbar v. Ball*, 7 F. Cas. 1185 (C.C.D.C. 1821) (No. 4,128); *see also Matilda v. Mason & Moore*, 16 F. Cas. 1106 (C.C.D.C. 1822) (No. 9,280), *rev'd sub nom. Mason v. Matilda*, 25 U.S. (12 Wheat.) 590, 6 L. Ed. 738 (1827), a case in which Taney represented the freedom claimants in the lower court, and Key later argued on their behalf before the United States Supreme Court.

[69] *See* Schweninger, "Slave Women," *supra* at 384-85.

[70] Schafer, *Becoming Free*, *supra* at 34, *see id* at 34-44; Loren Schweninger, *et al.*, eds.,

The Southern Debate Over Slavery: Petitions to Southern County Courts, 1775-1867 22 (2008); Judith Kelleher Schafer, "'Voleur de Negres': The Strange Career of John Charles David, Attorney at Law," 44 *Louisiana Hist.* 261 (2003).

[71] *See* Schafer, *Becoming Free, supra* at 160-62.

[72] *See id.* at 35; *Morrison v. White*, 16 La. Ann. 100 (1861); and *Miller v. Belmonti*, 11 Rob. 339 (La. 1845).

[73] *See* Schweninger, "Slave Women," *supra* at 385 (citing lawyers who represented black clients in manumission and freedom suits in the Southern county courts). On Jefferson, *see Howell v. Netherland*, 1 Va. (Jeff.) 90 (Va. Gen. Ct. 1770); Hoffer, *supra* at 68-69; Gillmer, "Suing for Freedom," *supra* at 562-64; Annette Gordon-Reed, "Logic and Experience: Thomas Jefferson's Life in the Law," in *Slavery, South, supra* at 5-11. Howell was of mixed-race ancestry, and was not a slave. Jefferson unsuccessfully sued to release Howell from the remainder of his thirty-one-year term as a servant. A Virginia 1705 statute required white women who had mixed-race children to serve a thirty-one-year term as servants. A 1723 statute extended this obligation to any "bastard child by a negro or mulatto" who the white woman may have while serving the statutory term. Finkelman, *Founders, supra at* 138-39. On Taylor, *see, e.g., Pallas v. Hill*, 12 Va. (2 Hen. & M.) 249, 1808 WL 573 (1808); *Whiting v. Daniel*, 11 Va. (1 Hen. & M.) 390, 1807 WL 433 (1807); *Pegram v. Isabel*, 11 Va. (1 Hen. & M.) 387, 1807 WL 432 (1807); *Hudgins v. Wrights*, 11 Va. (1 Hen. & M.) 134 (1806); *Woodley v. Abby*, 9 Va. (5 Call) 336, 1805 WL 445 (1805); *Charles v. Hunnicutt*, 9 Va. (5 Call) 311, 1804 WL 547 (1804); Powell, *supra* at 101; Wallenstein*, supra* at 32; MacLeod, *supra* at 124, 219 n. 49. *See also* Dennis K. Boman, *Abiel Leonard: Yankee Slaveholder, Eminent Jurist, and Passionate Unionist* 30-33, 133-35 (2002) (discussing freedom suits that Leonard handled as a Missouri lawyer), and *id.* at 194-95 (discussing Leonard's two slave law opinions authored as a Missouri Supreme Court Justice).

[74] 6 Va. (2 Call) 319, 1800 WL 404 (1800).

[75] R. Kent Newmyer, *John Marshall and the Heroic Age of the Supreme Court* 96 (2001); *see, e.g., Shelton v. Barber*, 2 Va (2 Wash.) 64, 1795 WL 504 (1795); *Coleman v. Dick*, 1 Va (1 Wash.) 233, 1793 WL 378 (1793); Newmyer, *supra at* 94-96; 1 Catterall, *supra* at 65; *see also* Newmyer, *supra* at 441 and 1 Catterall, *supra* at 94-95 (discussing *Hannah v. Davis*, a 1787 freedom suit in which Marshall represented Native Americans held in slavery).

[76] *Mahoney v. Ashton*, 4 H. & Mc H. 295, 1799 WL 397 (Md. Gen. Ct. 1799), *rev'd* (Md. Ct. App. 1802), 4 H. & Mc H. 210, 1798 WL 411 (Md. Gen. Ct. 1798), 4 H. & Mc H. 63, 1797 WL 583 (Md. Gen. Ct. 1797). Before he became a Maryland General Court judge in 1796, Duvall was counsel for the freedom claimant Charles Mahoney; he did not sit when the General Court heard the case. *See also Wood v. Davis*, 11 U.S. (7 Cranch) 271, 272, 3 L. Ed. 339 (1812) (Justice Duvall refers to Maryland freedom petitions that he filed including *Rawlings v. Boston*, 3 H. & McH. 139, 1793 WL 394 (Md. Gen. 1793)); Eric Robert Papenfuse, "From Redcompense to Revolution: Mahoney v. Ashton and the Transfiguration of Maryland Culture, 1791-1802," 15 *Slavery & Abolition* 38, 39 (1994).

[77] *See* Newmyer, *supra* at 95.

[78] *See* Gary B. Nash, *Race and Revolution* 26-27, 142-43 (1990) [hereinafter, Nash, *Race and Revolution*]; Davis, *Revolution, supra* at 322-27; Gregory A. Stiverson, "Luther Martin," in 14 *American National Biography* 605-08 (1999); Papenfuse, *supra* at 46-47 and

59, n. 55.

[79] 60 U.S. (19 How.) 393, 15 L. Ed. 691 (1857).

[80] 27 U.S. (2 Pet.) 664, 1849 WL 3173 (1829). *See* chapter 5, *infra* at notes 61-66; Stanton D. Krauss, "New Evidence that Dred Scott was Wrong about whether Free Blacks Could Count for the Purposes of Federal Diversity Jurisdiction," 37 *Conn. L. Rev.* 25, 26, n. 5 (2007).

[81] *See, e.g.*, Foner, *Lincoln, supra* at 48-50; Brian Dirck, *Lincoln the Lawyer* 148-49 (2008); Mark E. Steiner, *An Honest Calling: The Law Practice of Abraham Lincoln* 105-13 (2006); Allen D. Spiegel, *A. Lincoln Esquire: A Shrewd, Sophisticated Lawyer in His Time* 42-43 (2002); David Herbert Donald, *Lincoln* 103-04 (1996); Finkelman, *Imperfect Union, supra* at 149, n 8, 152; Mark E. Steiner, "'The Sober Judgment of Courts': Lincoln, Lawyers, and the Rule of Law," 36 *N. Ky. L. Rev.* 279, 289-92 (2009); Anton-Hermann Chroust, "Abraham Lincoln Argues a Pro-Slavery Case," 5 *Am. J. of Legal Hist.* 299 (1961).

[82] *See* Dirck, *supra* at 149; *see also* Donald, *supra* at 157 (stating that Lincoln's law practice did not suggest that he had a "consistent legal philosophy").

[83] *See* Grinberg, "Manumission," *supra* at 227-28.

[84] *Id.* at 228; *see also* Cottrol, "Normative Nominalism," *supra* at 904-08 (discussing Grinberg's biography of Brazilian politician and lawyer Antonio Pereira Reboucas, and his legal representation of slaves in manumission and freedom suits).

[85] *See* chapter 9, *infra* at notes 84-142.

[86] *See* chapter 8, *infra* at notes 134-35, 143, 146.

[87] *See* Watson, *Americas, supra* at 35-36; Phillips, *Slavery, supra* at 30; Phillips, "Manumission," *supra* at 32.

[88] *See* Watson, *Americas, supra* at 36.

[89] *Las Siete Partidas, Volume 3: Medieval Law: Lawyers and their Work* Part 3, Title 2, Law 8 at 539-40 (Samuel Parsons Scott, tr., Robert I. Burns, ed., 2001) [hereinafter *Las Siete Partidas, Volume 3*]. The statute also stated that a master with complaints against his slave "should exercise his rights over [the slave] by punishing him by reproof, or by blows, in such a way as not to kill or cripple him." A person with a complaint against another person's slave could sue that slave's master, who was "bound to answer." *Id.*

[90] *See id.; see also* Klein, *supra* at 65; Tannenbaum, *supra* at 50-51; Phillips, "Manumission," *supra* at 43.

[91] Barcia, *supra* at 169.

[92] *Id.* at 169-70, quoting Gloria Garcia, *La Esclavitud desde la Esclavitud. La vision de los Siervos* 5 (2003); *see* Klein, *supra* at 78; de la Fuente, "Legal Rights," *supra* at 665.

[93] *See* de la Fuente, "Legal Rights," *supra* at 665; *see also* de la Fuente, "Slave Law," *supra* at 367. On the British parliament's efforts to create similar position of protector of slaves as part of the nineteenth century efforts to ameliorate the conditions of slaves in the British colonies; *see* Parks, *supra* at 115-22; Olwyn M. Blouet, "Earning and Learning in the British West Indies: An Image of Freedom in the Pre-Emancipation Decade, 1823-1833," 34 *Historical J.* 391, 399 (1991); Claude Levy, "Slavery and the Emancipation Movement in Barbados 1650-1833," 55 *J. Negro Hist.* 1, 8, 10 (1970); *see also* Melanie J. Newton, *The Children of Africa in the Colonies: Free People of Color in Barbados in the Age of Eman-*

cipation 97-98 (2008) (discussing the creation of the position on Barbados and its effect in freedom suits).

[94] *See* McKinley, *supra* at 762-63, 773-75.

[95] *See id.* at 775, and e-mail dated August 2, 2010, on file with author.

[96] *See id.* at 765-74.

[97] *See* A.J.R. Russell-Wood, "'Act of Grace': Portuguese Monarchs and their Subjects of African Descent in Eighteenth-Century Brazil," 32 *J. of Latin Am. Studies* 307, 325 (2000).

[98] *See id.* at 326.

[99] *See* Cottrol, "Normative Nominalism," *supra* at 889-92.

[100] *See, e.g., Clark v. Gautier*, 8 Fla. 360 (1859) (reversing plaintiff's judgment, citing cases holding *habeas corpus* inappropriate remedy); *Daniel v. Guy*, 19 Ark. 121, 1857 WL 545 at *7 (1857) (citing statutes permitting all persons except a "negro or mulatto held as a slave" to file writs of *habeas corpus*); *Weddington v. Sloan*, 54 Ky. (15 B. Mon.) 147 (1854) (*habeas corpus* is inappropriate writ to try right to freedom, when on return of the writ the judge finds "reasonable grounds for the claim, the judge, instead of undertaking to investigate the question himself, should only make such an order as would enable petitioner to bring an action and have an opportunity afforded him of establishing the right which he claims."); *Field v. Walker*, 17 Ala. 80 (1849) (reversing plaintiffs' judgment, *habeas corpus* is inappropriate writ under statute when blacks held as slaves); *Thornton v. DeMoss*, 13 Miss. 609 (1846) (*habeas corpus* is inappropriate writ under statute when blacks held as slaves); *Ex parte, Renney v. Mayfield*, 5 Tenn. (4 Hay.) 165 (1817) (*habeas corpus* is inappropriate writ for blacks held as slaves, should be tort action); Thomas D. Morris, *Free Men All: The Personal Liberty Laws of the North 1780-1861* 8-13 (1974); Wise, "Writs," *supra* at 219, 250-53, 273-75; Dallin H. Oaks, "Habeas Corpus in the States—1776-1865," 32 *U. Chi. L. Rev.* 243, 268-70, 276-79, 286-87 (1965).

[101] *Rasul v. Bush*, 542 U.S. 466, 473 (2004), quoting *Preiser v. Rodriguez*, 411 U.S. 475, 485 (1973); *see* Wise, "Writs," *supra* at 272.

[102] Zechariah Chaffee, Jr., "The Most Important Human Right in the Constitution," 32 *B.U. L. Rev.* 143, 143 (1952), citing U.S. Const., art. I, §9 ("The Privilege of the Writ of Habeas Corpus shall not be suspended, unless when in Cases of Rebellion or Invasion the Public safety may require it.").

[103] Wise, "Writs," *supra* at 256, quoting William Blackstone, 3 *Commentaries* *129; David Clark and Gerrard McCoy, *The Most Fundamental Legal Right: Habeas Corpus in the Commonwealth* (2000); Chaffee, *supra* at 143.

[104] *See* Paul D. Halliday and G. Edward White, "The Suspension Clause: English Text, Imperial Contexts, and American Implications," 94 *Va. L. Rev.* 575, 598-613 (2008), *see also* Paul D. Halliday, *Habeas Corpus: From England to Empire* (2010).

[105] *See* Wise, "Writs," *supra* at 255-63; Oaks, *supra* at 243-45.

[106] *See* Wise, "Writs," *supra* at 276, n. 238; *Pirate v. Dalby*, 1 U.S. 167, 1 L. Ed. 84 (1786) (directing action filed by writ of *habeas corpus* be tried as an action *de homine replegiando* before a jury); *State v. Beaver*, 1 N.J.L. 80 (Sup. Ct. 1791); *State v. Farlee*, 1 N.J.L. 41 (Sup. Ct. 1790) (denying alleged owner's demand for jury trials); Wise, "Writs," *supra* at 248-49.

[107] Wise, "Writs," *supra* at 245-49; Oaks, *supra* at 281-82.

[108] *See* Wise, "Writs," *supra* at 246-48. Replevin is "[a]n action whereby the owner or person entitled to repossession of goods or chattels may recover those goods or chattels from the one who has wrongfully distrained or taken or who wrongfully detains such goods or chattels." *Black's Law Dictionary* 1168 (5th ed. 1979). Personal replevin is "a species of action to replevy a man out of prison or out of the custody of any private person. It took the place of the old writ of *de homine replegiando*; but ... it is now superseded by the writ of habeas corpus." *Id.* Replevin is similar to detinue, which is "[a] form of action which lies for the recovery, *in specie*, of personal chattels from one who acquired possession of them lawfully, but retains it [sic] without right, together with damages for the detention." *Id.* at 405. The owner may pursue this action if the defendant acquired possession of the chattel lawfully, as a bailment, but retained the chattel unjustly. *Id.* These actions apply when the plaintiff prefers to recover the specific property and not money damages for conversion. The Southern courts applied these forms actions to permit owners to recover possession of slave property. *See, e.g., Gullett v. Lamberton*, 6 Ark. 109 (1845) (replevin); *Jarman v. Patterson*, 23 Ky. (7 T. B. Mon.) 644 (1828) (replevin); *Willis v. Willis' Admr's*, 36 Ky. (6 Dana) 48 (1837) (detinue). These courts' facile application of these property law causes of action illustrates how the slave's humanity was not deemed relevant in the masters' business dealings. *See* Fede, *People Without Rights*, *supra* at 201-15; Fede, "Gender," *supra* at 415.

[109] *See* Wise, "Writs," *supra* at 248-49.

[110] *See id.* at 248.

[111] Lofft 1, 98 Eng. Rep. 499, 20 How. St. T. 1 (K.B. 1772); *see* Steven M. Wise, *Though the Heavens May Fall: The Landmark Trial that Led to the End of Human Slavery* (2006) [hereinafter Wise, *Heavens*]; *see also, e.g.*, Halliday, *supra* at 174-77; Wong, *supra* at 26-31; Alfred W. Blumrosen and Ruth G. Blumrosen, *Slave Nation: How Slavery United the Colonies and Sparked the American Revolution* 1-11 (2005); James Oldham, *English Common Law in the Age of Mansfield* 305-23 (2004) [hereinafter Oldham, *Common Law*]; Finkelman, *Imperfect Union*, *supra* at 16, 34-40; Higginbotham, *Color*, *supra* at 313-68; Cover, *Justice Accused*, *supra* at 16-18; William M. Wiecek, *The Sources of Antislavery Constitutionalism in America, 1760-1848* 20-39 (1977) [hereinafter Wiecek, *Sources*]; Davis, *Revolution*, *supra* at 469-522; George VanCleve, "Somerset's Case and its Antecedents in Imperial Perspective," 24 *Law & Hist. Rev.* 601 (2006); William M. Wiecek, "Somerset: Lord Mansfield and the Legitimacy of Slavery in the Anglo-American World," 42 *U. Chi. L. Rev.* 86 (1974) [hereinafter Wiecek, *Somerset*].

[112] *See* Halliday, *supra* at 176.

[113] *See* George William VanCleve, *A Slaveholders' Union: Slavery, Politics, and the Constitution in the Early American Republic* 30-39 (2010); Simon Schama, *Rough Crossings: Britain, the Slaves and the American Revolution* 48-58 (2006); Blumrosen and Blumrosen, *supra* at 15-32; Halliday & White, *supra* at 676; Wardle, *supra* at 1876; VanCleve, *supra* at 602, 625.

[114] *See* Wiecek, *Sources*, *supra* at 157, n. 24; Halliday & White, *supra* at 671-76; Wise, "Writs," *supra* at 263-72.

[115] *See, e.g., Jackson v. Bulloch*, 12 Conn. 38, 1837 WL 60 (1837) (granting plaintiff freedom on *habeas corpus*); *Commonwealth ex rel. Negro Lewis v. Holloway*, 6 Binn. 213,

1814 WL 1384 (Pa. 1814) (denying plaintiff freedom on *habeas corpus*); *In re Tom*, 5 Johns. 365 (N.Y. Sup. 1810) (granting plaintiff freedom on *habeas corpus*); Halliday & White, *supra* at 675-76 and n. 312; Wise, "Writs," *supra* at 273, citing *Lemmon v. People*, 20 N.Y. 562 (1860); *Commonwealth v. Aves*, 35 Mass. (18 Pick.) 193 (1836); *State v. Lasselle*, 1 Blackf. 60, 1824 WL 868 (Ind. 1820); *Respublica v. Smith*, 4 Yeates 204 (Pa. 1805); *Respublica v. Blackmore*, 2 Yeates 234 (Pa. 1797); *Arabas v. Ivers*, 1 Root 92 (Conn. Super. Ct. 1784); Oaks, *supra* at 267-68, 278-79, 284-86; *see also* 5 Catterall, *supra* at 359-60, citing *Habeas Corpora*, Grant (Jam.) 344 (1787) (Jamaican decision permitting slaves to file writs *de homine replegiando*).

[116] *See* Oaks, *supra* at 278.

[117] Wolinetz, *supra* at 2243-46.

[118] *Id.* at 2244, n. 124.

[119] *Id.* at 2243-46. This may have created the initial case review that the Southern law required.

[120] *State v. Lyon*, 1 N.J.L. 462, 464-66 (Sup. Ct. 1789); *State v. Oliver* (N.J. Sup. Ct. 1787), in *Cases Adjudged in the Supreme Court of New Jersey Relative to the Manumission of Negroes and Others Holden in Bondage* 18-19 (1794) [hereinafter *Cases Adjudged*] (published by the New Jersey Society for Promoting the Abolition of Slavery); *State v. McKnight*, (N.J. Sup. Ct. 1782), in *Cases Adjudged* at 11-12.

[121] *See Cases Adjudged*, *supra* at 7-8. The case also was reported in *The Pennsylvania Gazette*, January 17, 1776, in 1 *Documents Relating to the Revolutionary History of the State of New Jersey: Extracts from American Newspapers, Volume 1, 1776-1777* 19-22 (William S. Stryker, ed.) (1901) [hereinafter *Revolutionary Documents*].

[122] The reported cases for the claimants are *State v. M'Donald and Armstrong*, 1 N.J.L. 382 (Sup. Ct. 1795); *State v. Heddon*, 1 N.J.L. 377 (Sup. Ct. 1795); *State v. Shreve*, 1 N.J.L. 268 (Sup. Ct. 1794); *State v. Pitney*, 1 N.J.L. 192 (Sup. Ct. 1793); *State v. Anderson*, 1 N.J.L. 40 (Sup. Ct. 1790); *State v. Administrators of Prall*, 1 N.J.L. 4 (Sup. Ct. 1790); and *State v. Lyon*, 1 N.J.L. 462 (Sup. Ct. 1789). The reported cases for the owners are *State v. Mount*, 1 N.J.L. 337 (Sup. Ct. 1795); *State v. Frees*, 1 N.J.L. 293 (Sup. Ct. 1794); and *State v. Beaver*, 1 N.J.L. 80 (Sup. Ct. 1791). The unreported cases and some of the reported cases are noted in *Cases Adjudged*, *supra* at 7-32. *See also* Wolinetz, *supra* at 2243-46.

[123] *See* Wolinetz, *supra* at 2241.

[124] *See id.* at 2243. The later Supreme Court judges also may have had different attitudes. *See State v. Emmons*, 2 N.J.L. 106 (Sup. Ct. 1806) (denying freedom claims of plaintiffs, manumission deeds were signed before one and not two witnesses, as required by 1798 statute); *State v. Van Waggoner*, 6 N.J.L. 374 (Sup. Ct. 1797) (presumption of slavery applied to Indians as well as blacks, denying freedom claims of plaintiff).

[125] *See* Gillmer, "Suing for Freedom," *supra* at 567-68; Andrew Kull, "Restitution in Favor of Former Slaves," 84 *B.U. L. Rev.* 1277, 1279 (2004). Andrew Kull notes that plaintiffs also could assert restitution claims for the value of the services improperly obtained by the "master," either by "waiv[ing] the tort and su[ing] in assumpsit" or by asserting a bill in chancery. In either example, the suit would test the plaintiff's claim to freedom. *Id.*, citing *Jarrot v. Jarrot*, 7 Ill. (2 Gilm.) 1, 13, 24 (1845); *Kinney v. Cook*, 4 Ill. (3 Scar.) 231, 232 (1841); *see also* Wise, "Writs," *supra* at 276, n. 237 (citing the 1845 Missouri Freedom Suit Act authorizing suits for trespass for false imprisonment); Stafford, *supra* at 448-49 (citing

the 1838 Arkansas statute authorizing suits for false imprisonment).

126 *Prosser and Keeton on the Law of Torts* 29 (W Page Keeton, ed.) (5th ed. 1984) [hereinafter *Prosser*].

127 *Id.* at 39.

128 *Id.* at 43.

129 *Id.* at 47.

130 *See, e.g., Tramell v. Adam, a Black Man,* 2 Mo. 155, 1829 WL 1766 at *2 (1829); MacLeod, *supra* at 112.

131 *Peter v. Hargrave,* 46 Va. (5 Gratt.) 12, 14, 8148 WL 2754 at *1-*2 (1848); *Paup's Adm'rs v. Mingo,* 31 Va. (4 Leigh) 163, 1833 WL 2076 at *12 (1833); MacLeod, *supra* at 112.

132 *See* chapter 9, *infra* at notes 84-103.

133 Lon Fuller, *Legal Fictions* 9 (1967), quoted in Aviam Soifer, "Reviewing Legal Fictions," 20 *Ga. L. Rev.* 871, 875 (1986).

134 *See* Nancy J. Knauer, "Legal Fictions and Juristic Truth," 23 *St. Thomas L. Rev.* 23 (2010).

135 *Matilda v. Crenshaw,* 12 Tenn. (4 Yer.) 299, 1833 WL 1102 at *3 (1833).

136 *See* Fehrenbacher, *supra* at 251; *see also* Prosser, *supra* at 108-59 (discussing defenses including discipline, which was limited by the doctrine of moderate correction). These implied concessions are mirrored in the criminal law by the often cited case of *State v. Mann,* 13 N.C. (2 Dev.) 263 (1829), and the less frequently discussed case of *Commonwealth v. Turner,* 26 Va. (5 Rand.) 678 (1827). The *Mann-Turner* rule held that masters and hirers could not be indicted for the crimes of assault or battery upon their slaves, thus rejecting the common law doctrine of "moderate correction," which limited a "superior's" power to correct his servants and children. *See* chapter 1, *supra* at notes 66-68.

137 *See, e.g.,* Wise, "Writs," *supra* at 274; Oaks, *supra* at 268-70, 277-79, 286.

138 *See DeLacy v. Antoine,* 34 Va. (7 Leigh) 438, 1836 WL 1763 at *3-*4 (1836); *Nicholas v. Burruss,* 31 Va. (4 Leigh) 289, 1833 WL 2087 at *5-*6 (1833); Wise, "Writs," *supra* at 275-76; Higginbotham & Higginbotham, *supra* at 1235 and n. 125.

139 *DeLacy v. Antoine,* 1836 WL 1763 at *3. Judge Henry St. George Tucker, the son of St. George Tucker, wrote further: "To suppose that a free negro, in possession of regular 'free papers,' may be falsely imprisoned at the pleasure of any individual, without redress, is indeed to attribute a gross and lamentable omission to the law. To confine that redress to a suit *in forma pauperis* to establish his freedom, when he already has the conclusive evidence of it in his hands, would be a mockery." *Id.* The legislature adopted statutes permitting writs of habeas corpus, but "annulled" the writ *de homine replegiando.* Tate, *supra* at 484-86. The Mississippi Code also permitted free blacks who were arrested as runaway slaves to pursue writs of *habeas corpus. Revised Mississippi Code, supra* at ch. 33, art. 16 at 238; David J. Libby, *Slavery and Frontier Mississippi, 1720-1835* 95 (2004) (discussing 1831 case of John Gibbs, a free black man who was arrested as a runaway slave and was released on a writ of *habeas corpus*).

140 *See supra* at notes 7 and 9, in this chapter.

141 *See, e.g., Cone v. Force*, 31 Ga. 328 (1860) (reversing judgment for claimants seeking freedom because the statutory procedures not followed); *State v. Fraser*, Dud. 43, 1 Ga. Rep. 373 (Super. Ct. 1831) (dismissing *habeas corpus* writ, freedom claimant left to statutory remedy); *but see State v. Philpot*, Dud. 46, 1 Ga. Rep. 375 (Super. Ct. 1831) (defendant held in contempt for failure to produce alleged slave); Wise, "Writs," *supra* at 241-80 (discussing the common law writs, including their use in freedom suits).

142 39 S.C.L. (5 Rich.) 273, 1852 WL 2468 (1852).

143 *Huger v. Barnwell*, 1852 WL 2468 at *1.

144 *Id.* at * 2.

145 *Id.*

146 *See 7 Statutes at Large of South Carolina, supra* at 398; Stroud, *supra* at 52; Wiecek, "Statutes," *supra* at 265. The South Carolina Negro Seamen Act of 1844 stated that free black seamen could not enter the state and they were not entitled to the writ of habeas corpus. *See, e.g.,* Wong, *supra* at 191, and *id.* at 183-230 (discussing these laws).

147 *See supra* notes 53-56, in this chapter.

148 *See Coston v. Coston*, 25 Md. 500, 1866 WL 2033 (1866) (dismissing writ of error from judgment freeing plaintiff's children who the defendant was holding as "apprentices"); *see also In re Turner*, 24 F. Cas. 337 (No. 14,427) (C.C.D. Md. 1867) (granting relief on writ in case arising in Maryland after the effective date of the Maryland constitution of 1864 and the thirteenth amendment).

149 *Laws of Maryland, 1810*, ch. 60, §2; *Johnson v. Medtart*, 4 H. & J. 24, 1815 WL 274 (Md. 1815) (affirming dismissal of writ flied on behalf of soldier; arguments of counsel refer to court jurisdiction to free slaves pursuant to writ).

150 *See* Schafer, *Becoming Free, supra* at 102, 112-14, 123, 139, 142, 145-46.

151 *See* Oliver C. Hartley, ed., *A Digest of the Laws of Texas* 489-91 (1850), quoting Act of January 14, 1840, vol. 4, p. 32.

152 *Gaines' Admr. v. Ann, by Guardian ad Litem*, 26 Tex. 340, 1862 WL 2867 (1862), and *Gaines v. Ann*, 17 Tex. 211, 1856 WL 4994 (1856).

153 *Gaines v. Ann*, 1856 WL 4994 at *2.

154 *See Gaines' Admr. v. Ann, by Guardian ad Litem*, 26 Tex. 340, 1862 WL 2867 at *2-*3; *Gaines v. Ann*, 1856 WL 4994 at *3.

155 *See, e.g.,* Essah, *supra* at 106-07 (discussing the 1802 freedom suit of Molly Moore, which the Delaware Abolition Society decided could not be successful on its lawyer's advice).

156 *See Ex Parte Archy*, 9 Cal. 147, 1858 WL 739 (1858) (owner filed writ of *habeas corpus* to recover alleged slave, affirming use of *habeas corpus* to try issue whether freedom claimant was legally a slave, issue arose in suit in which plaintiff sought recovery of slave he claimed to own); Paul Finkelman, "The Law of Slavery and Freedom in California, 1848-1860," 17 *Cal. W. L. Rev.* 437, 457-62 (1981); *United States ex rel. Wheeler v. Williamson*, 28 F. Cas. 682 (No. 16,725) (D.C. Pa. 1855) (owner filed writ of *habeas corpus* to recover alleged slave); Wong, *supra* 104-12; Finkelman, *Imperfect Union, supra* at 255-65.

157 *Revised Mississippi Code, supra* at ch. 48, art. 18 at 368; *Buckingham v. Levi*, 23 Miss.

590, 1852 WL 1983 at *1 (1852), quoting *Code of Mississippi, supra,* Ch. 65, §19 at 1002-03; *see Covington v. Arrington,* 3 George 144, 1856 WL 2653 (Miss. Er. & Ap. 1856); *Steele v. Shirley,* 21 Miss. (13 Smedes & M.) 196, 1849 WL 2320 (1849); *Steele v. Shirley,* 17 Miss. (9 Smedes & M.) 382, 1848 WL 1946 (1848); *Nations v. Alvis,* 13 Miss. (5 Smedes & M.) 338, 1845 WL 2019 (1845); *Hardy v. Smith,* 3 Smedes & M. 316, 1844 WL 2084 (Miss. Er. & Ap. 1844); *Scudder v. Seals,* 1 Miss. (1 Walk.) 154, 1824 WL 630 (1824).

[158] Oaks, *supra* at 278 [footnote omitted].

[159] *See* Fede, *People Without Rights, supra* at 210-15.

[160] *See id.* at 241-45 (discussing the concept of reification and other examples from slave law in the United States).

5

Interpreting the Master's Will
in the Manumission Cases

According to North Carolina Chief Justice Thomas Ruffin, any act of the master that "purports to have been done" with an intention to free his or her slaves "would upon common law principles suffice; and in favor of liberty, the intention might be inferred from slight acts. The legislature has however upon a ground of public policy, interposed in restraint of the power of the master."[1]

The manumission cases are not easy to summarize because these statutory restraints on manumission are a moving target, and because the statutes are part of the necessary context within which these cases must be considered. Indeed, the extent of the owners' right to manumit their slaves was "considerably obscured by the wide diversity of statutes in the several states and the varying attitudes of the laws of the particular states at various stages of their history[.]"[2]

Nevertheless, the antebellum Southern manumission cases exhibit two trends. First, some courts were more willing than others to effectuate the masters' apparent attempts to free their slaves when the courts considered ambiguous deeds, wills, or the masters' acts allegedly evidencing the masters' intent to free their slaves, weighed against the claims of heirs and creditors or the then-applicable limits imposed by manumission statutes. Second, judicial hostility toward manumission increased during the nineteenth century. This legal change occurred as the pro-slavery ideology became more popular. The proponents of this ideology depicted manumission as a threat to the South's slave society. As this pro-slavery ideology took hold, the legislators adopted statutes that increasingly regulated and then barred manumission. These pro-slavery views also were expressed in some judicial opinions.

The statutes regulating the masters' legal right to free their slaves caused the courts to confront two primary issues in manumission cases: (1) what did the masters intend, and (2) did that intent contravene a statute or a public policy? The judges and legislators resolved these issues in various ways over time and in different states. Accordingly, the freedom claimants' chances of success also were not consistent, even if these claims were based upon unambiguous statements of their owners' intentions.

This chapter will illustrate how the Southern courts increasingly constrained the masters' power to free their slaves by construing the evidence of the masters' intention against liberty when the masters' intentions were in doubt. The next chapter will review cases in which the courts came to "overrule" even unambiguous expressions of the masters' intentions to free or otherwise benefit their slaves.

Construing Intent in Favor of Liberty—Or Not

Unless masters clearly documented their intentions in their manumission deeds or wills, the courts were confronted with issues of interpretation when the interested parties could not agree on what the masters intended. Thomas Cobb, the pro-slavery treatise writer, stated that the courts should apply to manumission deeds of "doubtful construction, the usual rules of interpretation...." These included the rule of construction requiring that the court construe deeds "most strongly against the grantor."[3] Thus, the courts would construe the deed against the grantor-master and in favor of the grantee-slave. At least to some extent, this approach paralleled the notion that manumission deeds should be construed in favor of liberty.

Cobb cited for support Judge John Green's opinion in an 1828 Virginia case *Isaac v. West's Executor.*[4] In that case, Green did indeed state that when construing a "doubtful" manumission deed, the courts should consider the "maxim" stating that deeds will "be taken most strongly against the grantor," and "the spirit of the Laws of all civilized nations which favors liberty."[5]

But the same Judge Green four years earlier advocated a neutral judicial approach to questions of slavery and freedom in the majority opinion in *Maria v. Surbaugh,*[6] a decision that advanced one of the most telling anti-manumission rules of law in the antebellum South. Green started that opinion by stating that when the courts decide "questions of liberty and slavery, such as that presented in this case," it is the court's "duty ... uninfluenced by considerations of humanity on the one hand, or of policy (except so far as the policy of the law appears to extend) on the other, to ascertain and pronounce what the law is[.]" According to Green, the courts should leave these policy decisions "to the Legislature, as the only competent and fit authority, to deal as they may think expedient, with a subject involving so many and such important moral and political considerations."[7]

Cobb also asserted that the courts should not favor liberty or slavery in will construction cases. He noted that "some of the courts have announced that the law favors liberty," and "will incline in favor of manumission," but that others, to prevent the growth of the free black population, "will incline against manumission."[8] Still other judges, such as North Carolina Justice Richmond Pearson, suggested that, when interpreting a will that allegedly expressed the owner's intention to free his or her slaves, the courts have "a single eye to the intention of the testator, without reference to the notion that Courts should favor charities, and lean *in favorem libertatis*; for, however humane we may suppose the feeling that prompts, it is not established that public policy favors the emancipation of our slaves[.]" He acknowledged that "the principles of the common law look with favor upon the transition of a bondsman, or villain [sic], to the state and condition of a *free white man,* yet very different considerations may be involved, when the question is between the condition of a slave and that of a *free negro.*"[9]

Cobb agreed, and he suggested that in the cases in which the parties disputed the proof of a will the courts "should inquire, first, what is the intention of the testator? and, second, has he used sufficient words to carry out his intention? If, in either of these particulars, the bequest is insufficient, it must fail, unless in the latter case the facts make out such a case as, under the general rules of law, will authorize the court to supply words[.]"[10] Cobb did not suggest that the courts apply any special or liberal treatment of wills that expressed the testators' alleged intentions to free some or all of their slaves.

Cobb's and Pearson's will construction approach was consistent with the trend in the antebellum United States wills and estates law. "Post-Revolutionary America saw a marked growth in testamentary freedom in tandem with the abolition of primogeniture, entail, and other common law devices that restricted the ability to make individual dispositions of property."[11] The law as a general rule increasingly granted to individuals the freedom to write wills that determined who would own their property when they died. This right was not unlimited, however; the law balanced the testators' rights with the interests of their spouses and children, as well as with social policy concerns.[12]

In the antebellum South, "these redefinitions of inheritance practices incorporated specific rules to deal with the political economy of slavery."[13] For example, the Southern appellate courts generally enforced male slave owner wills that bequeathed freedom and/or property to the master's female slave with whom the master had a "meretricious" relationship, as well as to the children born of the master's sexual relationship with his slave. The courts resisted "the idea that bondswomen could easily rob masters of their free agency. While mid-century judges were often given to moralizing about these sorts of relationships, they nonetheless strenuously upheld the right of the testator to make what was— in their eyes—an unnatural disposition of his worldly goods."[14]

When the evidence of the masters' intent to manumit was unclear, the courts considered the evidence of the masters' intentions in light of the judges' perceptions of the public policy concerns that the manumission implicated and the interests of third parties, including the master's creditors or potential heirs, whose legal rights might be compromised by the manumission. The courts also applied the statutes limiting the masters' right to free their slaves.

In making their calculations of public versus private interests, the courts gave no weight to the slave's interest in freedom, independent of proof of the master's intention. This was so because throughout the South the slave had no right to sue or to be a party to a non-criminal legal proceeding. Jacob Wheeler's slave law treatise explained this rule as follows: "It would be an idle form and ceremony to make a slave a party to a suit, by the instrumentality of which he could recover nothing; or if a recovery could be had, the instant it was recovered it would belong to the master."[15] Manumission suits were exceptions to this rule because the real dispute in a manumission case was between the slaves' "rulers"—the purported liberator and the state or the individuals who challenged the enforcement of the master's expressed or implied intentions. The courts heard these disputes *because* they did not implicate slave rights in any real sense.

The manumission decisions freeing slaves therefore were not in any real sense libertarian. No court in the South exercised the legal discretion to liberate a person legally held as a slave without some expressed or implied indicia of the master's intent to free the slave. The judges enforced the master's will in the manumission cases. These cases were thus anti-libertarian because they tacitly legitimized the justly held slave's lack of any right to liberty independent of the master's will. The legally enforceable basis for a slave's claim to freedom depended upon the owner's whim. This was another example of the slave owner's all-powerful and despotic position in relation to the rightless and powerless slave.

With this analytical framework in mind, it is not surprising that many judges expressed an interest in affording slaves a "fair hearing" in manumission cases, while slaves were afforded no right to any hearing in other types of potential civil cases. The manumission hearing was "fair" because at issue was the clash between the master's private interests, other private property interests, and public policy. But just how "fair" were the courts in these cases?

The following sections will examine issues that arose when the master's intentions were not clear, and will show how the manumission decisions varied. These issues include whether the courts would apply the doctrines of tacit manumission and implied manumission by prescription, and how the courts would treat the freedom claims of people who were born when their mothers were serving as term slaves.

Implied Manumission by a Gift of Property

The ways that judges and legislators treated ambiguous expressions of the masters' intention to free their slaves illustrate the diverse opinions that these people had regarding manumission. The implied manumission doctrine permitted lawmakers and judges to express in their deeds any inclinations they had in favor of liberty, when they dealt with ambiguous evidence of the masters' intentions to their slaves.

If a master's will devised property to or for the benefit of a slave, should not this be interpreted as an imperfect expression of the master's intention to free the slave, because slaves could not own property? Roman law by the time of Justinian in 531 A.D. applied the doctrine of implied or tacit manumission to free the slave in this situation. "Thus if an owner in his will appointed his slave as his heir or made him a tutor (guardian) to his children, and did not mention freedom, the slave became free." And if a male slave owner had no wife and "made his slave woman his concubine and intended to keep her as such until his death, the slave woman became free, and any children she conceived with her master were treated as freeborn and [were] given the benefit of their *peculia*."[16]

The Spanish law *Las Siete Partidas* also readily recognized the masters' implied intention to free their slaves, when that intention could be inferred from the masters' acts or omissions that were inconsistent with the masters' intention to continue to hold their slaves in slavery. Accordingly, a slave would be freed if, with the master's knowledge, he or she married a free person or became a cleric, or if the master named a slave who was older than twenty-five to be the guardian of the master's children.[17] When a master without heirs named a slave as an heir in the master's will the law presumed that the master intended to free the slave, even if the will did not clearly state the master's intentions to manumit the slave.

This presumption did not apply, however, to a female master who was accused of committing adultery with the slave whom she named as the heir, if the master died before the adultery case was decided.[18] And if a master's will named a slave as an heir, but before his or her death the master sold the slave, it was presumed that the master "changed his [or her] mind," the slave would not be freed, and the slave's new owner would receive the slave's inheritance under the will.[19]

The French *Code Noir* also permitted the tacit or implied manumission of slaves who were to receive a legacy under their master's will.[20] But the 1724 *Code Noir* that was adopted for Louisiana "completely repudiated the liberal policy of the first Code Noir with respect to donations to slaves. The new ban on donations even extended to ex-slaves and freeborn blacks. Acts of manumission could no longer contain valid donations to the erstwhile slave."[21]

Accordingly, the Louisiana Code stated that manumission by will "must be express and formal, and shall not be implied by any other circumstances of the testament, such as a legacy, an institution of heir, testamentary executorship or other dispositions of this nature, which in such case, shall be considered as if they had not been made."[22] The Code also provided, however, that a slave who "acquired the right of being free at a future time, is from that time, capable of receiving by testament or donation." The property in question would be delivered to the slave when he or she was freed.[23] If the slave died before the time of freedom, "the gifts or legacies made him revert to the donor or to the heirs of the donor."[24]

No statute in the other Southern United States provided for tacit or implied manumission by donations to slaves made in wills. The Southern decisions also did not apply this concept of implied or tacit manumission to doubtful cases to favor freedom over slavery. This law confirmed the slave's natal alienation because it was based on the notion that "[a] slave cannot take by descent, there being no inheritable blood."[25]

Cobb made a confusing observation in his treatise when he suggested that the United States courts generally applied the implied manumission doctrine when a master provided in his or her will a devise to a slave.[26] He cited only two cases in support of this assertion: *Hall v. Mullin*[27] and *Guillemette v. Harper*.[28] Helen Catterall and Robert Shaw also cited *Hall v. Mullin* as a decision that adopted this implied manumission rationale.[29] But upon a close reading, these cases provide no support for this rule. Even Catterall called the *Hall* decision a "decided novelty."[30]

Indeed, we can understand the *Hall* decision, in part, by the case's unusual facts. Henry L. Hall's 1817 will left to Dolly Mullin a life tenancy to one hundred and forty-one acres of land, with the remainder after Dolly's life to her son Henry Mullin and his heirs, along with "two young negroes, one called Joan and the other Aaron." The will mentioned by name Hall's other slaves, who were devised to other named beneficiaries. The will also contained a residuary clause stating that Hall wanted to leave "all the remainder part of my negroes free."

Accordingly, it appears that Hall believed that Dolly was already free when he wrote his will. He had sold Dolly in 1810 to her father, Basil, who a month later executed a deed of manumission. Henry Hall apparently believed that Basil was free and therefore was capable of buying Dolly because Benjamin Hall (Henry's father) in his will executed in 1803 declared: "I hereby manumit and set free from the time of my decease, my carpenter, called old Basil."[31]

But Basil was older than forty-five years of age when Benjamin Hall died. Maryland's statutes by then prohibited the manumission of people of that age. If Basil had not been legally manumitted he still was a slave, he could not buy his daughter Dolly, and he could not free her.[32]

The Maryland Court of Appeals majority opinion by Judge John Johnson nevertheless held that Henry Hall's will set Dolly free. According to Johnson, Hall expressed his intention "that none of his slaves should remain slaves after his death, other than those he named and bequeathed as slaves[.]"[33] Johnson stated, in what clearly was *dictum,* that "without the aid of the residuary clause [Dolly] would have a right to freedom, under those parts of the will by which property was given to her; her freedom by implication is indispensably necessary to give efficacy to those clauses of the will."[34] In a concurring opinion, Chief Judge Jeremiah Chase stated: "The testator imagined Dolly was free; she was not free, but a slave, at the time the will was made, and being a slave, the will operated to give her freedom, and the lands devised to her."[35]

The *Hall* holding, therefore, can be attributed at least in part to the master's mistaken belief that Basil was legally freed, or to the effect of the will's residuary manumission clause. It also may reflect a judicial attitude that was more favorable to freedom than was accepted elsewhere in the South.

As Cobb noted in his treatise, South Carolina Justice John B. O'Neall also expressed his support for this implied manumission doctrine in *dicta* in his opinion in an 1850 case *Guillemette v. Harper.*[36] That case involved the will of Edward Quinn, whose slaves included Patrick E. Quinn. Patrick was born as a slave in Georgia while Edward lived there. In 1832 or 1833, Edward returned to Ireland, his place of birth, and brought with him Patrick and Patrick's mother Cherry, who also was a slave of Edward, where they lived for more than two years. While they were in Ireland, Edward died. His will and a codicil were probated in the Irish courts. Edward had a plantation and other slaves in Georgia. His widow remarried and returned to the United States with Patrick, who eventually was sold into slavery to the plaintiffs Charles and Eugenia Guillemette. They filed a suit for trover against the defendant Harper, alleging that he enticed Patrick to run away.[37]

Edward's will directed that all of his slaves in Georgia, as well as Patrick and his mother, who then were in Ireland, "be set free if an Act of the Legislature of the State of Georgia for that purpose could be obtained; and, if not, then that they should be allowed to go wherever they could be free." According to Justice O'Neall, "[i]f the right of freedom depended on this clause, then it might be very well contended that Patrick, in a slave country, such as South Carolina or Georgia, would remain a slave, no matter in what point of view he might have been regarded in Ireland."

O'Neall then quoted the fifth clause of the codicil to Edward's will, which he wrote "gives a very different aspect to the case. For in it the testator says, 'I will and bequeath the sum of £50 sterling to *the black child* whom I brought to this place, called Patrick Edward Quinn, and I allow my wife to take care of him, to give him a good education, and, when he arrives at the proper age, to send him to a decent trade.'"[38] O'Neall continued:

> This clause, where it is permissible by law to manumit a slave by will, would, on being assented to by the executor, confer freedom. In a country where negro *slavery* is not recognized, as in Ireland, and in other parts of the kingdom of Great Britain, it would certainly be regarded as a virtual acknowledgment, on the part of the master, that the negro was free, by his consent. For it is to be remarked that *here* he does not speak of Patrick, as he did the March preceding, in his will. Then he spoke of him as his property. But now, in the codicil of September, he calls him "the black child I brought to this place." This shews [sic] that he had ceased to regard him as property. The bequest to him of a pecuniary legacy, the placing him in the care of his wife to be educated, and then to be put to a trade, are conclusive of his assent to freedom. This therefore establishes that the negro was free in Ireland, both by the general law, and also by the assent of his master, as evidenced by his will.[39]

O'Neall thus suggested that a will that devised property to a slave coupled with an expression of the master's intent to free the slave will be persuasive to show the master's intent to manumit, and his opinion affirmed the dismissal of the Guillemettes' suit.[40]

As in *Hall,* however, Edward's devise of property to Patrick did not stand alone in support of the conclusion that he intended to free Patrick. Justice O'Neall's opinion does not cite any cases for this apparent endorsement of the implied manumission doctrine. Moreover, South Carolina cases decided before and after *Guillemette* held that bequests to slaves were void.[41] As Judge O'Neall himself wrote in an 1830 opinion, "a legacy cannot be given to a slave; for he can have no right, whatever, which does not, the instant it is transferred to him, pass to his master. Every thing which belongs to him, belongs to his owner. In other words, he is in law himself chattels personal; and it would be absurd to say, that property can own property." Therefore, a will directing that a slave be freed is not "to be regarded as bequeathing a legacy to persons, who can take it; but as merely directory to his executors to do an act, on a particular event, which is then to confer freedom on the slaves, and make them capable of acquiring the rights of property."[42]

The other Southern cases that discussed the implied manumission doctrine rejected it or failed to apply it, as illustrated by the following decisions from North Carolina, Kentucky, Arkansas, Florida, and Texas. In the 1801 North Carolina case of *Cunningham's Heirs v. Cunningham's Executors,*[43] Thomas Cunningham's 1792 will stated that portions of his lands should be rented out, and that three of his slaves should work that land for the benefit of his slave Rachel, for "the maintenance and education of her three mulatto children," and for a child with which she then was pregnant. Cunningham left another tract of land to Rachel, her children, and their heirs. Moreover, the will stated Cunningham's "will and desire that Rachel and her children should be set free immediately after my decease."[44]

The North Carolina Court of Conference consisting of Judges John Hall, John Louis Taylor, Samuel Johnston, and Spruce Macay found that the devise of property was void.[45] According to Judge Taylor, the will clearly stated that Cunningham intended to devise property to his slave Rachel and her heirs, whom he also wished to set free upon his death. The court held that the will nevertheless was invalid because "it is indispensable to the validity of every devise, that there be a devisee appointed who is competent to take. Slaves have not that competence; for a civil incapacity results from the nature and condition of slavery." Taylor added that "it would be a solecism that the law should sanction or permit the acquisition of property by those from whom it afterwards withholds that protection without which property is useless."

Judge Taylor distinguished the condition of the villein, who, according to the common law, could inherit property. People held as slaves could not inherit or own property. Judge Hall wrote a concurring opinion in which he stated that he agreed with the result.[46]

This decision was particularly harsh because the testator clearly stated his intention to free Rachel and her children. Nevertheless, the court's decision was in part compelled by the North Carolina statutes that did not permit manumission by will.[47]

The Kentucky Court of Appeals rejected the implied manumission doctrine in the 1853 case of *Jones v. Lipscomb*.[48] The freedom claimants, Dodson and Spicy, were slaves of Humphrey Jones. They relied on a clause in Jones's will that stated: "In consideration of faithful services, I will and require that my executors give my slaves, Dodson and Spicy, $200 each, to be paid out of my estate." The will did not express in so many words Jones's intention to free Dodson and Spicy. Another will provision stated that four other named slaves were to be freed. The will also contained a residuary clause stating that Jones's "other slaves" were to "have liberty to choose their masters at their value."[49]

The Court of Appeals affirmed a judgment against the claimants, in an opinion by Chief Justice Elijah Hise. Hise rejected the implied or constructive manumission doctrine that the claimants' lawyer advanced. In doing so, Hise discussed at length the decision in *Hall v. Mullin*, which he concluded should not be read to support the rule that a bequest to a slave should be construed in favor of liberty as an imperfect expression of the master's intention to free the benefited slave, even though a slave could not inherit any property.[50] Like Taylor in *Cunningham*, Hise distinguished the villein, who, according to the common law, could inherit property. "[A]ccording to the laws of this state contracts with a slave, and grants and conveyances to slaves, are void, and they can only be manumitted by deed, will, or other solemn written instrument."[51]

Therefore, the Kentucky Court of Appeals construed Jones's will against liberty and in favor of bondage. This interpretation rendered void both Jones's bequest to these slaves and any implication that they were to have their freedom to enjoy the bequest.

The Arkansas Supreme Court came to the same conclusion about the implied manumission doctrine in another 1853 decision, *Campbell v. Campbell.*[52] The opinion of Chief Justice George C. Watkins upheld the lower court's decision enforcing the manumission by the will of Duncan G. Campbell of a slave girl named Viney, and the bequest of $5,000 to her that the will stated was to take effect when she was fifteen years old. The relevant provisions in Duncan's January 6, 1845 will stated that he left equal shares of his property to his siblings Samuel Campbell, Jane Bickerstaff, Mary Campbell, and Flora Anne Campbell, "after deducting therefrom five thousand dollars, which I bequeath to Viney, a yellow girl, and one hundred dollars to my uncle, John Nicholson[.]" The will also stated Duncan's "wish" that Mary "take charge of the above named Viney, and take care of her until she arrives to the age of fifteen years, when she is to be free and receive her legacy[.]" Duncan's will also stated that if Viney were to "die before she arrives to the age of fifteen years, it is my wish that the legacy go to my sister Mary." Duncan appointed his brother Samuel as the executor of his estate. According to Watkins, Duncan "died without lawful issue. The girl Viney was his daughter by one of his slaves, and at the time of his death was about three years old."

Samuel Campbell qualified as the estate's executor, but he later was removed by the probate court and letters of administration then were issued to Cornelius Campbell. Samuel Campbell, Jane Bickerstaff, Mary and Flora Anne Campbell, and their spouses then sued to void the manumission and bequest to Viney. While he was executor, Samuel sold Viney as a slave out of the state. The court appointed a guardian, who found Viney in Missouri and recovered her on a writ of *habeas corpus.*[53]

At the time of the hearing before the lower court, Samuel Campbell had absconded and the estate's assets did not amount to the $5,000 bequest to Viney. The chancery court therefore dismissed the complaint.

The Arkansas Supreme Court affirmed this decision. Chief Justice Watkins's opinion upheld the bequest and the manumission, while mentioning his disapproval of the implied manumission doctrine. He began his analysis by citing the "leading rule in the construction of wills," which "is to give effect to what appears to be the intention of the testator, in view of all the provisions of the will; and if this intention can be ascertained, it should be carried out, unless contrary to law or against public policy." The will's text lead the court to conclude that Duncan intended that Viney "should be liberated immediately" after he died,

> not merely by reason of the bequest to her of $5,000 by present words of gift, for we should be loath to sanction the principle at this day, and with reference to the condition of slave property in the southern States of this Union, that a mere bequest to a slave would operate as an emancipation; not merely by reason of the intention of the testator as manifested, that in case of the death of Viney before she arrived at the age of fifteen years, her legacy would go to his sister Mary, but because the will no where contem-

plates, that Viney should serve anyone, or remain in a state of slavery until she attained the age of fifteen years.

Watkins arrived at this interpretation although the will contained the clause stating that Viney was "to be free at the age of fifteen years, and receive her legacy," coupled with Duncan's wish that "Mary should take charge of Viney, and take care of her until she arrived at that age[.]" He read these provisions as if Duncan "had said, in so many words, that he liberated Viney, and committed the testamentary guardianship of her to his sister Mary, until she arrived to the age of fifteen years[.]"

The court also considered it relevant that Viney was Duncan's child, "that she was of tender years, that it was necessary, under our statute, for him to make some adequate provision for her support, to prevent her from becoming a charge on the public," and that he "confid[ed] the care and custody of the child to one of his nearest relations, for whom he signified his preference over all others[.]" Watkins concluded that "the will appears to be as sensible and judicious a one, albeit not technically framed, as any man in the unhappy condition of the testator, could well have made."[54]

Florida's Supreme Court also considered this doctrine in the 1849 case *Sibley v. Maria, a woman of color*,[55] but the court based its decision on other grounds. The plaintiff Maria claimed her freedom under the 1827 will of William Oliphant. Oliphant left his estate to his nephew William C. Hollingsworth on the condition that William allow Oliphant's slave Maria and her four children to live as if they were free persons and receive $250 each, otherwise, he was "to take them to the State of Ohio, and the balance of the money over and above what will be expended in their passage to be paid to them there[.]" If William should not comply with this condition or should die without a legal heir, the will directed that James H. Hollingsworth would inherit Oliphant's property, also provided that he complies with this condition.[56]

Maria filed her trespass action in Florida almost 18 years after Oliphant died. The Florida Supreme Court, in an opinion by Justice George Sidney Hawkins, affirmed a freedom judgment for Maria. Hawkins noted that "[t]here is some diversity in the decisions how far a devise of property to a slave will entitle such slave to his freedom by necessary implication." Hawkins cited *Hall v. Mullin*, among other cases, but stated that "[a] decision of this question is not necessary[.]" Justice Hawkins in effect read into the will Oliphant's intention that the slaves be freed from his direction that the slaves be sent to Ohio. The court took judicial notice of Ohio's free state status. It also assumed "that the taking [of Maria] to Ohio was regarded by the testator as a *dernier* means of giving her freedom."[57]

The Texas Supreme Court also rejected the implied manumission doctrine in its 1860 decision in *Hunt, Ad'mr v. White*.[58] William Bracken had three slave children, Charles, whom he did not own, and Amanda and Harriet, who were his slaves when he dictated his January 1852 will. The will included a provision requiring his executor to purchase Charles and left equal shares of the estate's residuary to Charles, Amanda, and Harriet, among others. But the will did not express Bracken's intention to free these slaves. This intention was set forth in a written explanation that the four witnesses to the will signed in March 1852, when the will was submitted for probate. In May 1853, Bracken's disappointed heirs filed a petition with the county court challenging the will, and the county court ruled in favor of the heirs. The slaves appealed to the probate court, which reversed the judgment and ordered that Bracken's executor purchase Charles and take all three slaves to a state in which they could be freed.[59]

The Texas Supreme Court reversed this judgment in an opinion authored by Chief Justice Royall T. Wheeler. Wheeler held that slaves could not be freed in Texas under the implied manumission doctrine "in any of the modes known to the civil law, or the laws of those states where manumission may be effected without the observance of any legal formalities[.]" Accordingly, "[t]he bequest of property to a slave cannot operate [as a manumission] within this state," because in state manumission violated Texas's "laws and public policy," which prohibited the "introduction" of free blacks into the state. Wheeler noted that the will did not contain any "clause expressly manumitting these slaves." Therefore, Bracken's intention to free his slave children "can be derived only by implication, from the bequest to them of property, and some expressions in the will, which seem to contemplate their continued residence in the state, in the enjoyment of freedom and property." Wheeler held that "these provisions cannot be held to effectuate their freedom, being in contravention of the laws and declared public policy of the state."[60]

The United States Supreme Court approved of *Hall v. Mullin* and the implied manumission doctrine in *dicta* in its 1829 decision in *Le Grand v. Darnall*.[61] Justice Gabriel Duvall wrote the Court's opinion. He had been a Maryland lawyer and state court judge (among other governmental positions) before he was appointed to the United States Supreme Court in 1811. Future Chief Justice Roger B. Taney was the lawyer for the appellant, Claudius F. Le Grand. One commentator called this litigation "[p]robably the friendliest case decided by the Court...."[62]

The Supreme Court affirmed the trial court's decision that confirmed the legality of Nicholas Darnall's manumission by his father and owner, Bennett Darnall. Bennett died in 1814. His will referred to manumission deeds that he executed in 1805 and 1810. Nicholas apparently was to be freed according to one of those deeds, although they were not produced by either party in the litigation. Bennett's will devised lands to Nicholas, who was between the ages of ten and eleven years when his father died.

Nicholas took possession of the properties devised to him upon coming of age. In 1826, he entered into a contract with Le Grand to sell one of the properties, known as Portland Manor, for $13,112, payable in six annual installments. Le Grand entered into possession under this land sale contract, but doubts later were suggested to Nicholas regarding the legality of his title. Maryland law required that a slave to be freed must be "able to work and gain a sufficient maintenance and livelihood at the time the freedom given shall commence."[63]

A suit was filed with the apparent purpose to confirm Le Grand's title. At the trial "[f]our respectable witnesses" from the neighborhood testified "that Nicholas was well grown, healthy and intelligent, and of good bodily and mental capacity: that he and his brother Henry could readily have found employment, either as house servant boys, or on a farm, or as apprentices; and that they were able to work and gain a livelihood."[64]

Accordingly, based upon this undisputed evidence, the trial court found that the manumission was valid, and the Supreme Court affirmed this judgment. Justice Duvall concluded that Nicholas was able to work when his father died and thus he later could convey good title to the property that he inherited and sold to Le Grand. Duvall's reasoning consists of his statement that the Maryland Court of Appeals, in *Hall v. Mullin,* "decided, that a devise of property real or personal by a master to his slave, entitles the slave to his freedom by necessary implication. This Court entertains the same opinion." He did not, however, state why he cited that decision, in view of Bennett's manumission deeds.[65]

Therefore, Justice Duvall did not correctly state the holding of the court in *Hall v. Mullin.* Nevertheless, the Southern courts did not follow the United States Supreme Court's lead, and, with his title confirmed, Le Grand later sold Portland Manor.[66]

Under the implied manumission *dicta* in *Le Grand, Hall,* and *Guillemette,* a master who devised property to a slave could be held to have intended to free the slave as well, to permit his executors to bestow the property on the freed slave. If the Southern courts truly favored liberty, they could have reasoned that the master must have intended to free his slave; otherwise, the devise of property to the slave who could not legally own property would be a futile act with no meaning. But no reported case in the United States Southern reports so held.

The *Hall* and *Guillemette dicta* therefore were novelties. The implied manumission theory collided with the fundamental slave law principle that denied to slaves the right to own or inherit property. The courts and legislatures, either expressly or by their inaction, rejected this doctrine that favored liberty when the master's intentions were ambiguous, even if there was evidence suggesting that the master intended to free the benefited slave.

Implied Manumission by Prescription

Another ambiguity arose if a master permitted a slave to act as if free for a long time period. Would the master's inaction be interpreted as an intention to free the slave? A provision in *Las Siete Partidas* in favor of liberty stated that slaves were to be free if "in good faith and thinking that [they were] free," they lived free for ten years at home, and for twenty years abroad. If the slaves were fugitives who did not act in good faith, they still would earn their freedom, but after thirty years of liberty.[67]

The Louisiana Supreme Court endorsed this doctrine in two decisions from 1818 and 1819. Justice Pierre Derbigny's opinions cited as authority the provisions in *Las Siete Partidas,* even before the Louisiana statutes addressed this concept.[68] The legislators later included the prescription doctrine in the Civil Code of 1825 in Article 3510. That section stated: "If a master suffer a slave to enjoy his liberty for ten years, during his residence in the state, or for twenty years while out of it, he shall lose all right of action to recover possession of the slave, unless the slave be a runaway or fugitive."[69] Thus, the Louisiana legislators did not adopt the Spanish law's manumission by prescription rule for fugitive slaves.

Moreover, the Louisiana Supreme Court, in *Meilleur v. Coupry*,[70] held, pursuant to the 1807 manumission law, Civil Code Article 185, that slaves had to be at least thirty years of age to win their freedom by prescription.[71] The plaintiff, Coupry, appealed from a judgment revoking his appointment as executor of an estate. The heirs successfully argued in the lower court that Coupry was a slave, and thus he could not serve as executor. The Supreme Court affirmed this judgment in an opinion by Justice François-Xavier Martin.[72]

The court found that Coupry "was born of a slave mother, that his mother's owner has ever resided, and still resides, in New-Orleans, that he is twenty-seven or twenty-eight years of age, that he has enjoyed his freedom for fourteen years and been married as a free man." On these facts, Justice Martin held that Coupry continued to be a slave "unless he was emancipated; as he is under the age of thirty years[.]" Because "the lawful emancipation of a slave cannot take place before that age, the presumption of a legal emancipation, which might result from his long possession of his freedom, is repelled, from the evident impossibility of his legal emancipation having taken place, and the legal impossibility of a slave becoming free, without a legal emancipation." The court concluded: "Prescription can no more avail him, than it would the possessor of property evidently out of commerce."[73]

The prescription doctrine met its demise in Louisiana in 1859. The Louisiana Supreme Court held that the 1857 statute banning manumissions precluded any further successful suits based upon the prescription doctrine and Article 3510 of the Code.[74]

Cobb wrote that, elsewhere in the United States, "[s]ometimes the courts presume a deed of manumission when the owner permits the slave, for a number of years, to do acts inconsistent with a state of slavery. It is a question generally submitted to the jury, but upon which the courts, in different States, vary their rulings."[75] The courts in Maryland, South Carolina, Missouri, North Carolina, New York, and New Jersey applied this rule to cases in which masters treated their slaves as if they were free for more than twenty years.[76] These decisions also are analogous to the law of adverse possession that applied when an owner failed to file an action to assert his or her rights to possession of other forms of property.[77]

Nevertheless, the implied manumission doctrine fell into disfavor in the antimanumission climate of the late antebellum period.[78] The courts began to hold that this doctrine conflicted with statutory provisions stating that masters could not allow their slaves to act as if free, and with the statutes establishing formal written requirements for a valid manumission.

The policy behind the former statutes is illustrated by Judge Fredric Nash's opinion for the North Carolina Supreme Court in *State v. Nat.*[79] The defendant, Nat, was a slave of John Carmatt. Nat was indicted and convicted in the Beauford

County Superior Court of hiring his own time in 1850, contrary to the North Carolina statutes. The Supreme Court reversed the conviction on the grounds that the slave could not be indicted for this offense and tried in the Superior Court.[80]

Nash referred to two statutes, a 1794 act, "constituting the 31st sec. of the 111th ch. of the Revised Statutes," and an 1831 act, "constituting the 32d sec. of the same Revised Statute." He explained that these statutes

> operate upon separate and distinct offences. The 31st section forbids persons to suffer their slaves to hire their own time, and punishes them when they do so, by the loss of the services of their slave for a limited time, and the forfeiture of forty dollars, "to be recovered before any Justice of the Peace, to the sole benefit of the party prosecuting." The clause then points out how the slave is to be dealt with. The Grand Juries, both of the County and Superior Courts, are directed to present all slaves, within their respective counties, who do so hire their own time, and are permitted to go at large. If the presentment is made in the Superior Court, a warrant is directed to be issued to the Sheriff, returnable before the next County Court. It is the duty of the Sheriff to have the slave there, and of the Court to empanel a Jury to "inquire into, and try the truth of the presentment;" and, upon conviction, the slave is to be hired out for one year. By this section, the offence of the master is clearly pointed out. The Act of [18]31 made no alteration in the Act of [17]94, but introduced a new offence, to wit: suffering a slave to go at large as a free man. A custom had sprung up in the State, particularly among that class of citizens who were opposed to slavery, of permitting persons of color, who, by law, are their slaves, to go at large as free,—thereby introducing a species of *quasi* emancipation, contrary to the law, and against the policy of the State. It was to repress this evil, that the Act was passed, and, for a violation of its provisions, the master is liable to indictment under the Act of [17]94; for suffering his slave to hire his time, and go at large, the master is not indictable. The law has made a distinction between the two acts of the master.—Both are evils, but not of the same grade. In the one, the master still considers himself the owner of the slave, and the latter is made to feel and act as his slave; in the other, all the restraints of servitude are thrown aside,—a new class of members of society introduced, or attempted to be introduced, contrary to law, and injurious to the community.

Thus, the court held that the Beauford County Superior Court did not have jurisdiction, and reversed the judgment. Nevertheless, the opinion indicates how the implied manumission doctrine, even after twenty years of freedom, came into conflict with these statutory mandates.[81]

South Carolina Judge John S. Richardson, in his 1848 opinion in *Vinyard v. Passalaigue*,[82] questioned this implied manumission rule's continued viability. He also criticized trial Judge John B. O'Neall's use of this rule. The suit was a trover action. The litigants, John Vinyard and John E. Passsalaigue, asserted competing claims to own, or at least to possess, "a mulatto woman, Mary Anne, and her four children[.]" Vineyard filed the action to recover damages. He alleged that Passalaigue converted Mary Anne and her children.

Vinyard based his claim on the August 22, 1822 will of Mrs. E. Peake. Peake appointed Vineyard as her executor, and she bequeathed Dido and her children to Vineyard, but she qualified the gift by adding, "*they by no means to be considered in slavery.*" Dido was Mary Anne's mother.

Mrs. Peake died in August 1822. Thereafter, "Mary Anne was allowed to go at large, and do as she pleased. In the language of one of the witnesses, Metivier, who had known Mary Anne for fifteen or twenty years, she seemed to be 'mistress of her own time.'" Mary Anne "was married to Passalaigue's baker. From the time she married him, perhaps ten years ago, she lived at defendant's father's, to whose possession the defendant succeeded on his failure, until within the last few years, when she and her husband lived in a house in Henrietta-street, rented by them."[83]

In December 1842, Vinyard and several others "entered the house where Mary Anne and her children and her husband lived, and carried her and her children to Vinyard's plantation, where they remained a few days and then escaped." Passalaigue then apparently regained possession of the alleged slaves. Vinyard demanded that Passalaigue return Mary Anne and her children. Passalaigue replied with a December 7, 1842 letter "claiming them as his own by possession." Passalaigue and Vineyard both "declared in Court that their whole object was that the woman and her children should be free."

Judge O'Neall's jury instructions included reference to the 1820 act, which provided that manumission "could only regularly take place by Act of the Legislature[.]" Nevertheless, he also told that jury "that time (twenty years) stood in the place of all written muniments [sic] of title. If, therefore, the negroes had been permitted to go at large, and be free, for 20 years, the jury might presume that they were legally manumitted and set free." The jury returned a verdict for the defendant, stating that they believed "the negroes to be free."[84]

The Court of Appeals reversed the judgment and ordered a new trial, with only Judge O'Neall dissenting. Judge Richardson, writing for the court, relied on the 1740 act's provision stating that "it shall be always presumed that every negro, Indian, mulatto and mustizoe [sic], is a slave, unless the contrary can be made to appear, (the Indian in amity with this government excepted,) in which case the burthen of the proof shall lie on the defendant." He also cited the 1800 and 1820 acts limiting manumissions. He admitted that the common law allowed for presumptions after the passage of twenty years regarding the payment of bonds and the possession of real estate. He distinguished those cases, however, because "[t]he law discourages and forbids" manumission. He also stated that: "The express presumption of the law is, that Africans are slaves. Shall we raise up an antagonistic presumption, to counteract that special one of the Act of 1740? Surely not."[85] He cited the recent case of *McCarthy v. McCarthy*, in which the court held that a couple's divorce would not be presumed even after 44 years of separation because South Carolina law prohibited divorce.[86]

Richardson also stated his own views indicating hostility to manumission because it results in the increase in the number of free blacks:

> Every one is conscious of this instinct of human nature. It consists in no more than justness of conduct to a man's self. In the case now before the Court, this strict State policy, prohibiting all emancipation of slaves within the State, by the owner, has further a necessary and moral justification, arising from the long experience of very many of these United States—all of which, at least all that were once British Colonies, held, by British laws, African slaves.

> And the experience of all these States is, that the white Caucasian and the black African races cannot live together upon terms of equality. Wherever tried, whether in the English settlements on the coasts of Africa, or as coolies in Jamaica, or as apprentices in Illinois, or as emancipated in New York or Philadelphia, Africans become, and do, as fully as in Charleston, constitute the contented menials, or other subordinate servants of white men. There is no where any practical equality. In this brief notice of the State policy, and its reasons, upon which is predicated the prohibitory Act of 1820, a policy plainly developed by the slave Act of 1740, we may perceive the whole argument that forbids, as in the case of marriage, the presumption that an Act of emancipation had been passed by the Legislature. Such a presumption, from only twenty years' of evidently permissive exemption from practical slavery, would be not merely incredible, but would run directly counter to the express presumption of the Act of 1740—that all Africans shall be presumed slaves, until their emancipation be proved.

Thus he concluded: "In a word, the presumption, enacted by the Act, and which expressly requires evidence to rebut it, estops all counter presumption."[87]

Richardson went a step further, however, by acknowledging the questionable efforts of Mrs. Peake to free her slaves without complying with the 1820 act:

> But laying aside all legal rules, who does not know of many instances of negroes, still slaves to their masters, yet commanding their own time, and practically, at least, in the language of Mrs. P. "by no means in slavery." Under such injunction from Mrs. P., the ready acquiescence of Mr. V., and this practical enlargement of faithful or favorite negroes, which is so frequent, what reason is there to strain presumptions, as counter to the policy of the law? As to our knowledge of the subject, and our credence of the probable truth of the case, there can be none.

> The master that would make his slave absolutely free, must send him out of the State. But, if he would indulge further philanthropy, by keeping him here, the negro must run the risk of his being seized by any stranger; and the master, that of being liable for his necessary support. For this see the case of *City Council v. Cohen*, where the negro being abandoned, and unable to support himself, the master was held liable to the city for his reasonable support.

Thus, Richardson concluded that "by our laws, the master cannot free himself from his legal liability, by his own emancipation. Our slave code is consistent and essentially suited to the natural endowments of the white and black man; and in no way is it regardless of just humanity to slaves." He also held that "we cannot presume a Legislative Act of emancipation. It must be proved, before the master and the negro can be divorced from their respective legal ties."[88]

Judge O'Neall's dissent stated that precedent supported his jury instruction. It was

> based upon the doctrine, acknowledged universally in our Courts, that twenty years stands in place of that ancient unremembered period, beyond the reign of the 1st Richard, which, in England, was regarded as that "*beyond which the memory of man runneth not to the contrary.*" In *McClure v. Hill*, 2d Law Rep. by Mill, 424, the Court, by one of its greatest and most distinguished members, (Judge Cheves,) laid down the rule that, after 20 years' possession or enjoyment of lands, a grant was to be presumed. This was, I think, well settled even before that case; and not only in reference to grants, but also as to prescriptive rights, and all other matters to be presumed from lapse of time, it has been ever since uniformly followed. After a lapse of twenty years' possession of lands, or enjoyment of an easement or right, the legal presumption of "*omnia presumuntur esse vite acta*" necessarily arose.[89]

O'Neall admitted that this rule may not apply if the presumption is disfavored in law, such as would be a presumption of divorce in South Carolina. But he contended that although the law regulated manumission it was not yet prohibited.[90]

O'Neall also stated his own opposition to the 1820 act, which he asserted should be repealed: "A law evaded, as it is, and against which public sentiment, within and without the State, is so much arrayed, ought not to stand. It is better by far, that a wise and prudent system of emancipation, like that of 1800, should exist, rather than that unlicensed emancipation, according to private arrangement, should take place."

O'Neall went further, however, and confirmed his policy views in opposition to those of Richardson:

> What is there in the policy of the law of South Carolina to forbid emancipation, by an owner, of a faithful, honest, good slave? Have we anything to fear from such a liberal and humane course? I should be sorry to believe that our domestic institution of slavery required any such restriction upon the rights of owners. Indeed, when any thing is pushed to extremes, injury is done by it; and that is now the case of the Act of 1820, and other kindred provisions in other Acts. They are continually thrust in our faces by those who undertake to meddle with matters which do not concern them, as evidence of our injustice, and our sense of error in our slave system. For one I have no hesitation in declaring, that we ought to do right by repealing all such enactments, and that then we should have nothing to fear from anything which our meddling friends, in other States, may think proper to

say or do against slavery. We are secure, when we can say, as one man, *negro slavery, as it existed at the adoption of the Constitution, as it exists now, is an institution to be regulated by the States in which it exists; and is not to be touched by Congress or the other States, or their people.* The motto of the Thistle, "*noli me tangere,*" ought to be ours on this subject.

Still, as I have already said, our duty is, to think and act right towards the beings who are our slaves. The first thing which ought to be done, is to get back alongside of such men as C. J. Rutledge, who, in the case of the *Guardian of Sally v. Beatley,* 1 Bay, 262 [sic], in speaking of the purchase of a girl by another slave to set her free, asked the emphatic question, "would a jury of the country say no? He trusted not—they were too humane and too upright, he hoped, to do such manifest violence to so singular and extraordinary an act of benevolence." This was the expression of the benevolent feelings which had been tried in the crucible of the revolution; there was perhaps no very correct notion of law in the ruling of the case, yet it spoke what, I think, always belongs to Carolina—a love of mercy, of right, and a hatred of that which is mean or oppressive.

Until fanaticism and folly drove us from that position, the law of our State had uniformly favored emancipation by owners, of their slave property, with such limitations and guards as rendered the free negro, not a dangerous, but an useful member of the community, however humble he might be. It is time we should return to it, and say to all at home or abroad, we have nothing to fear from occasional emancipation. Every one knows, that the free negroes in South Carolina are far, very far, from being a class of people envied by our slaves. Generally, they are worse off in every respect. They throw themselves under the sheltering wing of some benevolent white man, and, instead of being formenters [sic] of insubordination and rebellion among slaves, they pursue a directly contrary course.[91]

O'Neall's eloquent words fell on deaf ears, however, in this case and in the halls of the legislature, which did not heed his calls for his notions of slave law reform.[92]

The Kentucky Court of Appeals, in an 1854 opinion in *Anderson v. Crawford*,[93] also rejected the presumption of freedom in response to the freedom claims of three children of a slave Milly. The claimants based their case on the fact that Milly's owner permitted her to live as if free "for a period of nearly or quite twenty years[.]"[94] Chief Justice Thomas A. Marshall wrote that "it can not be admitted that the illegal act of allowing a slave to act as a freeman gives of itself a title to freedom, since this would be an utter subversion of the laws and policy of the state which impose restraints upon emancipation, and of the objects and policy of that law which prohibits the permission of slaves to act as freemen." He also wrote that the court did not need to decide if "the continued permission so to act for any length of time should authorize the presumption of a written act of emancipation" because "the circumstances disprove any such presumption of fact."[95]

These cases indicated that it was becoming apparent that the implied manumission doctrine also could not exist in states that prohibited all in-state manumissions or those that required legislative or judicial approval of manumissions. These statutes and court decisions can be attributed to attitudes that were less favorable toward manumission, when there was ambiguous evidence that the master intended to free his or her slaves. They foreshadowed the statutes later prohibiting manumission even when the evidence clearly established the master's intention to free his or her slaves.

Maryland's legislature made this clear with its 1860 act prohibiting manumission, and authorizing free blacks to renounce freedom and become slaves.[96] The act not only prohibited manumission by deed or by last will, it also stated that freedom will not be presumed for blacks who were "going at large and acting as free," or who were unclaimed by an owner.[97]

The Treatment of People Who Were Born Before Their Mothers Were to be Freed

"One of the most troubling questions" of slave law, "was whether children born of a female slave who had been promised freedom were entitled to the same benefit."[98] This situation most often arose if the mother had been a slave for life, but gave birth to a child while serving out a term of years under a will or deed of manumission in which the owner stated that the slave would be released from bondage at the end of a term that the owner specified. People in this category were called *statu liberi*.

Often, the master's manumission deed or will did not clearly state how he or she wished to treat the children born to *statu liberi*. Should they be slaves for life and thus remain slaves even after their own mother was freed? Or, under the rule of *partus sequitur ventrem,* would these children be liberated with their mother at the end of their mother's term of bondage?

The majority of the Southern courts came down in favor of slavery over liberty and held that children presumptively would be denied their freedom if, when they were born, their mother was serving out a term of years in slavery. Unless the master clearly stated his or her intention to the contrary in a will or a manumission deed, the majority default rule favored bondage over liberty. It held that a mother's *present or former* state of absolute slavery was inherited by her children and their children.[99]

No common law precedent mandated this rule of law. This is illustrated by the first reported United States case to address the issue, *State v. Anderson.*[100] The New Jersey Supreme Court, in that 1790 decision, adopted a rule favoring freedom for the children of *statu liberi*.

The suit involved a claim to freedom by the "negro Silas." It arose out of a 1761 will of John Horsfield. The will directed Horsfield's executors to sell his two female slaves, Betty and Nelly, "for the term of fifteen years, *and at the end of that term to be free*[.]" The will also stated that the sale proceeds were to be divided equally among Horsfield's daughters, and if the "girls [Betty and Nelly] became chargeable or misbehaved, it should be at the risk of the buyer." Silas was

Betty's son, who was born during the fifteen year period before Betty was to be freed.[101]

The New Jersey Supreme Court freed Silas, holding that children born during that fifteen year period "could not be slaves; they follow the condition of the mother who was not [a slave]. The issue of servants are free."[102] The court rejected the claim of "hardship pretended by the defendant," who was Betty's ultimate purchaser, stating that "the loss he may have sustained by the temporary incapacity of the mother ought not to be recompensed by the slavery of the child. Besides, the will directs that the risk shall be upon the purchaser; this is a general expression, and must be applied generally."[103]

The court also refused to follow cases that distinguished between the lapse of legacies that were vested or that were payable at the age of 21, stating that these rules "are inapplicable to this case of personal liberty. The arbitrary rules of property are applicable only to a certain extent to cases of this description."[104] The court concluded that "the purchaser had no interest in Betty beyond her service for fifteen years; he cannot, therefore, pretend to [have] any rights which result from the mere condition of slavery."[105]

Maryland's legislature codified what would become the contrary majority rule favoring slavery in a statute that it adopted on January 7, 1810. In the statement of the act's purpose, the legislators noted that the "state and condition" of the children of *statu liberi* is often not specified in the manumission deed or will declaring their mother's future rights to freedom, and "the state and condition of such issue seems not to be settled with sufficient legal precision[.]"

Therefore, the act permitted a slave owner's manumission deed or will that was executed after February 1, 1810 to free a "negro or mulatto slave" in the future or subject to a condition. It also confirmed that the deed or will could "fix and determine ... the condition of the issue that may be born of such negro or mulatto slave during their period of service." If, however, the master's deed or will failed to state his or her intention to free or enslave "the issue that may be born of such negro or mulatto female slave..., then the state and condition of such issue shall be of a slave[.]"[106] The legislators considered but rejected a proposed amendment to the statute that would permit the children of *statu liberi* to be freed at the ages of 25 for males and 20 for females. This proposal "was defeated by a large majority."[107]

The Kentucky Court of Appeals in 1811 decided the first reported case adopting this rule disfavoring liberty in the absence of a statute in *Ned v. Beal.*[108] The case involved the will of Isaac Cox, which devised his slaves to his wife "to serve in the following manner, and to be free at the following periods, to-wit: Easter, on the 1st day of May, in the year of our Lord, 1793; Jude, to be free in the year 1804; and Dinah, to be free in the year 1806; and in the meantime, the above named Jude and Dinah shall be schooled in such manner as to be able to read a chapter in the Bible." After Cox died, and before 1804, Jude had several children. After Jude was freed, she filed a suit seeking freedom for her children, who the defendant claimed as slaves. The circuit court found for the defendant. On Jude's appeal, Kentucky's highest court affirmed that judgment.[109]

Chief Justice John Boyle began the court's brief opinion by noting that the court had previously endorsed the maxim *partus sequitur ventrem*.[110]

> Hence it naturally follows, if Jude, the mother of the appellants, were at the time of their birth a slave, that they are also slaves. Whether Jude was a slave or not, when the appellants were born, depends upon the intention of the testator, deducible from the language he has used in the expression of that intention. The language used by the testator is plain and unequivocal; and having, in express words involving no ambiguity, fixed the period when the mother of the appellants should become free, it by necessary implication follows, that the testator intended she should continue to be a slave until that period arrived. To say that she was free at the death of the testator, and that she should *become free* at a future period, is a contradiction in terms wholly irreconcilable by any rule of construction, or upon any principle of common sense.

Justice Boyle also found that no inference favoring liberty for Jude's children would "be deduced from the expression in the will, with respect to the manner in which [Jude] should serve. The only modification of her servitude which is designated by the testator, relates to her education[,]" which the court found was "by no means incompatible with slavery."[111]

The Louisiana Supreme Court, in 1820, also endorsed this rule in favor of slavery and against liberty. The court's short opinion relied on the Roman law rule requiring that the children of *statu liberi* be enslaved.[112]

The authority most often recognized with advancing this rule, however, is in the 1824 Virginia case *Maria v. Surbaugh*.[113] William Holliday's June 17, 1790 will left his slave Mary to his son, William, and stated that Mary was to be freed when she reached the age of 31. After the testator died, his son William, in 1804, sold Mary. The defendant Surbaugh eventually bought Mary, who by then had one child. Mary had four children altogether who were born after the testator's death, but before she reached the age of 31. When Mary turned 31, in 1818, she filed her suit for her freedom and to free her children. The trial judge ruled in Mary's favor, but found that Mary's children were not free.[114]

Virginia's Supreme Court of Appeals affirmed this ruling. Judge John Green's opinion held that Mary's four children were born as slaves for life, and that they remained slaves even after Mary was freed. Green's opinion discussed in detail Virginia law and his understanding of the civil law, unlike the opinions in *Anderson* and *Ned*, which do not cite any authorities for their conflicting conclusions.[115] Judge William H. Cabell concurred without an opinion in *Maria*, and Judge Francis T. Brooke authored a shorter opinion, coming to the same holding as Judge Green.[116]

Both Judges Green and Brooke distinguished the earlier Virginia case of *Pleasants v. Pleasants*.[117] The court in *Pleasants* construed the wills of John Pleasants, a leading Quaker, and his son Jonathan. The wills freed their slaves when they reached the age of 30 if they elected freedom, and extended this right to elect to slaves "now born or hereafter to be born, whilst their mothers are in the service of me or my heirs[.]"[118]

In contrast, both Judges Green and Brooke believed that Holliday's will did not adequately express his intention to free Mary's children as of the day the testator died. Green wrote that Mary's children could be free only if the testator's intention to do so "may be fairly gathered from the will."

> I have no doubt, but that, if the idea had occurred to him, that she would probably have children before she attained her age of 31, he would have expressly provided that they also should be free, which could have been effected by the addition of these words, "and her increase." His not having done so, satisfies me entirely, that he never thought of, or intended to make any provision for the children. And if so, it was a subject in relation to which he had no thought, or will, or intention, and is consequently to be disposed of according to the law of the land.[119]

Green thus declared the rule of law favoring slavery over liberty that would apply in the absence of proof of the testator's intention.[120]

Judge Brooke agreed that Mary's children's claim to liberty had to be based upon the will. He stated that when Holliday wrote his will it was "highly probable" that Mary would have children before she reach the age of 31,

> yet, they are not noticed nor alluded to by the testator. He might have strong reasons for liberating her, when she should arrive at the age of thirty-one, which did not apply to her children, born before that period. It may have been unjust to his family to extend his bounty to them also. However that may be, it is enough, that by no reasonable construction of the will, they can be included in it, or derive any benefit under it. They must claim their freedom on the rule, that the children shall be bond or free, according to the condition of the mother;—a rule, probably adopted from the civil law, by the act of 1662, and repeated in several subsequent acts, down to 1753. As to her condition at the birth of the appellants, according to the will, she was a slave until she attained the age of 31. It only declares her to be free when she shall arrive at that age. If she had never attained that age, it would have been wholly inoperative as to her, and her children would have had no pretensions to freedom.

He also stated that "[t]he idea, that she was free from the death of the testator, and only held to service until she attained the age of 31, is wholly inconsistent with the obvious intention of the testator." He added that this notion also was "inconsistent ... with the provisions of the act of 1782, for the reasons stated by the Judge who has preceded me."[121]

The court in *Maria* thus derived a "default" rule of interpretation that applied when the master's will was not as clear as the will in *Pleasants*. Judge Green also apparently understood the harshness of this rule. He wrote that he was "not ... inattentive to the favor shewn [sic] by the common law to liberty. *Co. Lit.* 124, *b*. But, it is my duty to execute the law as I find it, according to its spirit and policy. And I must say, with the civilians, in relation to this case, *Quod quidem perquam durum est, sed ita lex scripta est.*"[122] Thus, he invoked the maxim, which Blackstone also quoted: "This indeed is exceedingly hard, but so the law is written; such is the written or positive law."[123] This assertion would have been accurate under the Maryland statute that established the rule favoring slavery in this context, but the Virginia statutes contained no such provision. Accordingly, Green's effort to distance himself from the rule that he and his court created is unconvincing.

The majority of Southern courts, and even the United States Supreme Court, eventually adopted the *Maria* rule.[124] Missouri Justice James H. Birch's 1851 opinion in *Lee v. Sprague*[125] applied this presumption against liberty to the claim of the plaintiff who was born while her mother, according to a deed of conveyance, was serving out a ten year term after which she was to be freed. Birch did not express any reservations about this result; he apparently approved of this rule, "which so early and so naturally glided into our jurisprudence from that of Justinian and which but properly ordains and establishes, at least in respect to the polity and policy of the institutions which recognize the relation amongst us, that a person born of a slave is a slave."[126]

The courts endorsed this default rule of will and deed interpretation against liberty unless the master's manumission deed or will clearly stated his or her intention to free all of the master's slaves at a time in the future after his or her death or unless the master expressed or strongly implied his or her intention to free the increase or issue of his or her specifically named favored female slaves.[127] For example, the Kentucky decisions held that proof of a master's strong anti-slavery views expressed in a will could override this presumption.[128] But an 1855 decision held that if the will was unambiguous, parol evidence of the master's Quaker beliefs was not admissible to free the children born to a slave who was to be freed later under the will's terms.[129]

And in *Isaac v. West's Executor*,[130] the Supreme Court of Appeals of Virginia, in an 1828 opinion by Judge Green, read an ambiguous manumission deed and the master's actions thereafter in favor of liberty to free the child of a female slave, who the court found, along with the master's other slaves, were freed as of the date of the deed, with the obligation to serve the testator until his death. Judge Green did not attempt to distinguish or even cite his opinion in *Maria*.[131]

The Tennessee Supreme Court confirmed that the *Maria* rule was not the inevitable product of positive law when it adopted the contrary rule in its 1834 decision, *Harris v. Clarissa*.[132] The facts in *Harris* are similar to *Maria*. Thomas Bond's 1800 will made in Maryland left several named slaves to Bond's children for various periods of time, after which the slaves were to be freed. The will also states that "all the negroes which I have hereinbefore given to my children, which are under the age of twenty-five years, and also all the young negroes which I may have in my possession at the time of my decease, shall have their freedom when they respectively arrive at the age of twenty-five."[133]

Bond died in Maryland in 1800, and his will was probated there in accordance with a 1796 statute that permitted owners to free slaves in their wills.[134] One of Bond's slaves was Clarissa, who was about ten years old when Bond died.

Before she reached the age of twenty-five, Clarissa had three children—Hannah, Delia, and Edward. After she was twenty-five, Clarissa had two more children—Edy and Martha. Clarissa and all of her children were the plaintiffs. The trial judge instructed the jury, and in effect found, that Clarissa and her two youngest children were free, but that Hannah, Delia, and Edward would be freed when they reached the age of twenty-five. The defendant appealed.[135]

Chief Justice John Catron, later a United States Supreme Court Justice, wrote the initial majority opinion for the Court's March 1833 term. He cited with approval the *Anderson* decision, and stated his disagreement with the decisions that by then had established the majority rule.[136] But because the court was uncertain about Maryland's law on the issue of the children of *statu liberi*, the case was reargued.[137]

After the reargument, Chief Justice Catron wrote a second opinion at the Court's March 1834 term discussing the Maryland cases following *Maria*. He nevertheless again sided with the plaintiffs. The Court held that Hannah, Delia, and Edward should not have to wait until they reached the age of twenty-five to be freed.[138] Justice Nathan Green dissented in *Harris*, but without any published opinion.[139]

No doubt, the minority rule was more beneficial to the alleged slaves seeking their release from bondage, and it was less beneficial to heirs who would be deprived of assets that could be eliminated from their presumed inheritance. The *Harris* rule also may have been perceived to be less beneficial to the public interest because it would increase the number of free blacks. The Tennessee court's majority in the *Harris* case may have been less concerned about this effect, however, because the Tennessee legislature had by then adopted an 1831 statute requiring that all freed slaves be "immediately removed from Tennessee."[140]

Moreover, as Chief Justice Catron noted in his second opinion in *Harris*, the *Maria* rule was contrary to the rule establishing a presumption that most Southern courts applied to a similar property law issue, but one in which the liberty of alleged slaves was not at stake.[141] That issue arose when a master willed his slaves for a term of years, or for the life of a life tenant, but with the slaves being the remainder to be inherited by others at the end of the relevant term of years or lifetime. If a slave gave birth during the interim period, the majority of Southern courts held that the person entitled to the remainder—and not the tenant for the term—was entitled to the slave's offspring. This rule was contrary to the general rule that applied to the increase of animals, but it was consistent with the decisions holding that a gratuitous bailee had no right to the issue of bailed chattels. Thus, the beneficiary who was a tenant for a term or for life was equated with a gratuitous bailee.[142]

Similarly, under the *Anderson* and *Harris* rule, title to the issue of the soon-to-be-freed slave would not be in the estate of the life tenant or tenant for a term. This presumption had even greater logical force when a person's freedom was at stake because, by expressing an intention to free the slave at the end of the term, the master—by a logical implication—disclaimed all interest in the remainder, as well as any interest in any of the slave's issue.[143]

Accordingly, although the *Harris* rule had logical support in this analogous situation when a person's liberty was not at issue, if it were applied to the children of *statu liberi* it would have resulted in more successful freedom suits when the master's intentions were somewhat ambiguous. The majority of the Southern courts opted for an asymmetrical result, which, whether intentionally or not, resulted in fewer potential successful freedom suits.

Some Southern legislators apparently came to favor the minority rule, if only for a time. The legislators in Delaware (1810), Louisiana (1838), Virginia (1849), Kentucky (1852), and North Carolina (1854) adopted statutes enacting this rule, or a presumption in favor of the rule.[144] The Delaware statute was adopted as part of an effort to better define the status of term slaves. It provided that the male children of female slaves who were to be freed in the future were slaves until they were 25 years old, and female children were slaves until they were 21 years old.[145]

The Louisiana legislature in 1838 effectively overruled its Supreme Court and adopted a statute stating that "[t]he child born of a woman after she has acquired the right of being free at a future time, follows the condition of its [sic] mother, and becomes free at the time fixed for [the mother's] enfranchisement, even if the mother should die before that time."[146]

The Kentucky statute stated: "The issue of a slave willed to be free, born after the death of the testator, shall have the same right to freedom as the mother, and [will] be treated accordingly, unless it shall manifestly appear by the provisions of the will that such issue is not intended to be emancipated."[147] Virginia's 1849 code provision was similar; it stated: "The increase of any female slave" who was freed according to the code "by deed or will hereafter made, born between the death of the testator, or the record of the deed, and the time when her right to the enjoyment of her freedom arrives, shall also be free at that time, unless the deed or will otherwise provides."[148]

The North Carolina statute created a presumption that was less in favor of freedom. It stated:

> Whenever a female slave shall by will be directed to be emancipated, all her issue, born after the date of the will, shall be deemed to have been likewise intended by the testator to be emancipated; and the court shall so declare, unless a contrary intent appear by the will, or by some disposition of the slave so born, inconsistent with such presumed intent.[149]

This statute thus permitted the courts to consider evidence other that the master's will, such as the master's acts selling or otherwise disposing of the child of a slave who was to be freed in the future.

Thomas Morris wrote of these statutes:

> Obviously, the "authoritative" decision in *Maria* was too much for many Southerners. Whenever they considered the problem as a law-making problem they adopted statutes more favorable to the children than ordinary rules of property law allowed. At the same time, they did accom-

modate the intention of slaveowners, but only in the sense that if an owner wished the children of a woman he freed to be slaves for life, he would have to say so.[150]

There are several problems with this analysis.

First, the majority and minority presumptions were default rules that the judges used to fill the gaps that occurred only when the owners did not clearly express their wishes in a will or manumission deed. These rules thus were irrelevant when a document clearly expressed the owner's "say so" regarding his or her intentions in favor or against liberty. But when a document was unclear, these default rules caused results in individual cases that the decision makers apparently preferred, but were not willing to mandate. These default rules thus were status-confirming; the majority rule perpetuated slavery when the master's intentions were in doubt, and the minority rule perpetuated freedom. These rules also were transformatory; they educated the parties in "what good actions or states of affairs are[,]" and the preferred "structure of social authority" of slave society.[151]

Second, not all statutes adopted the more favorable rule for the children of *statu liberi*. The Maryland legislature codified the rule later announced in *Maria*.

Third, the beneficial pro-liberty regulations were short lived. The Louisiana Supreme Court in 1859 held that its 1838 statute was impliedly repealed by an 1857 statute that barred all manumissions.[152] The North Carolina legislators joined those in the other Southern states that, before the Civil War, prohibited all manumissions, or at least all in state manumissions.[153] What proved in the end to be "too much" for many Southerners was the idea of manumissions leading to any more free blacks in their own states, and, for some, anywhere on the face of the earth.[154]

Fourth, the majority rule was not mandated by the "ordinary rules of property" established by the common law, as illustrated by the *Anderson* and *Harris* opinions. The judges in all of the Southern states except Tennessee nevertheless adopted this rule for people held as slaves. This rule, which was not mandated by any statute or any common law precedent, limited the number of potential successful manumission suits.

Conclusion

These cases in which the courts grappled with ambiguous expressions of the master's alleged intentions indicate a growing anti-manumission trend in the antebellum South. This trend is further confirmed by the cases in which the courts were confronted with objections to the enforcement of relatively unambiguous written expressions of the master's belief that he or she should free or otherwise benefit slaves. The next chapter illustrates that sometimes the judges' thoughts conflicted with the master's clearly-expressed wishes, and the courts "overruled" even the master's clear expressions of his or her intentions to bestow a gratuity on a slave.

Notes to Chapter 5

[1] *See Sampson v. Burgwin*, 20 N.C. (3 & 4 Dev. & Bat.) 21, 1838 WL 470 at *3 (1838); *see also, e.g., Wells v. Lane*, 9 Johns. 144 (N.Y. 1812) (declarations made more than 20 years before by slave's owner that he purchased her to make her free, and that he meant her to be freed, were held to be a manumission in suit for harboring a slave); *State v. M'Donald*, 1 N.J.L. 332, 1795 WL 586 (Sup. Ct. 1795) (freedom judgment where plaintiff was orally promised freedom and was permitted to live free for ten years); *State v. Admn's of Prall*, 1 N.J.L. 4 (Sup. Ct. 1790) (finding that intestate decedent's oral declarations of his intention to free a slave after his death were sufficient proof of intention to manumit).

[2] *See* Karst, *supra* at 489.

[3] *See* Cobb, *supra* at 294.

[4] 27 Va. (6 Rand) 652, 1828 WL 1034 (1828).

[5] *Isaac v. West's Executor*, 1828 WL 1034 at *4.

[6] 23 Va. (2 Rand.) 228, 1824 WL 1192 (1824).

[7] *Maria v. Surbaugh*, 1824 WL 1192 at *1.

[8] *See* Cobb, *supra* at 297-98.

[9] *Cromartie v. Robinson*, 55 N.C. (2 Jones Eq.) 218, 1855 WL 1593 at *3 (1855); *see also Phebe v. Quillin*, 21 Ark. 490, 1860 WL 720 at *5 (1860); *Myers v. Williams*, 58 N.C. (5 Jones Eq.) 362, 1860 WL 1976 at *4 (1860).

[10] *See* Cobb, *supra* at 298 [footnotes omitted], citing, *e.g., Cleland v. Waters*, 16 Ga. 496, 1854 WL 1651 at *4-*10 (1854). Cobb was one of the attorneys in *Cleland*, and his father in law, Justice Joseph Lumpkin, wrote the court's opinion favoring Cobb's side's position. *See* Paul Finkelman, "Introduction: Thomas R. R. Cobb and the Law of Negro Slavery," in *An Inquiry into the Law of Negro Slavery in the United States of America* 3 (Paul Finkelman, ed.) (1999).

[11] *See* Davis, "Race and Sex," *supra* at 232.

[12] *See, e.g.,* Joseph William Singer, *Property Law: Rules, Policies, and Practices* 63-69 (4th ed. 2006); Kevin Noble Maillard, "The Color of Testamentary Freedom," 62 *S.M.U. L. Rev.* 1783 (2009); Susanna L. Blumenthal, "The Deviance of the Will: Policing the Bounds of Testamentary Freedom in Nineteenth-Century America,"119 *Harv. L. Rev.* 959, 969-76, 999-1000 (2006); Melanie B. Leslie, "The Myth of Testamentary Freedom," 38 *Ariz. L. Rev.* 235 (1996).

[13] *See* Davis, "Race and Sex," *supra* at 232.

[14] *See* Blumenthal, *supra* at 999; *see also* Pascoe, *supra* at 24-28.

[15] Wheeler, *supra* at 197; *see* Cobb, *supra* at 247.

[16] Watson, *Americas, supra* at 27; *see* Cobb, *supra* at 311.

[17] *Las Siete Partidas, Volume 4, supra*, Part 4, Title 22, Laws 5 and 6 at 982-83; *Las Siete Partidas, Volume 5, supra*, Part 6, Title 16, Law 7 at 1286; Watson, *supra* at 45; Tannenbaum, *supra* at 52.

[18] *Las Siete Partidas, Volume 5, supra*, Part 6, Title 3, Law 3 at 1193; Watson, *supra* at 45; Tannenbaum, *supra* at 52.

[19] *Las Siete Partidas, Volume 5, supra*, Part 6, Title 3, Law 25 at 1202.

[20] *See Brief History, supra* at 35; Watson, *Americas, supra* at 90; Palmer, "Origins," *supra* at 388.

[21] *See id.* at 389-90.

[22] Rose, *supra* at 177, quoting Civil Code, Art. 184; Cobb, *supra* at 311.

[23] Rose, *supra* at 178, quoting Civil Code, Art. 193.

[24] Rose, *supra* at 178, quoting Civil Code, Art. 195.

[25] Cobb, *supra* at 238; *see, e.g., Graves v, Allen*, 52 Ky. (13 B. Mon.) 190, 1852 WL 3389 (1852); *Bell v. McCormick*, 3 F. Cas. 107 (C.C.D.C. 1838) (No. 1,255); *Bynum v. Bostock & Walker*, 4 S.C. Eq. (4 Des.) 266, 1812 WL 394 (S.C. 1812).

[26] *See* Cobb, *supra* at 311.

[27] 5 H. & J. 190, 1821 WL 476 (Md. 1821).

[28] 38 S.C.L. (4 Rich. 186), 1850 WL 2766 (1850).

[29] *See Shaw, supra* at 81; 4 Catterall, *supra* at 6.

[30] *See* 4 Catterall, *supra* at 6.

[31] *Hall v. Mullin*, 1821 WL 476 at *2.

[32] *Id.* at *3.

[33] *Id.* at *4.

[34] *Id.* at *5.

[35] *Id.*; 4 Catterall, *supra* at 6-7 [footnotes omitted].

[36] 38 S.C.L. (4 Rich.) 186, 1850 WL 2766 (1850).

[37] *See Guillemette v. Harper*, 1850 WL 2766 at *1-*3.

[38] *See id.* at *3.

[39] *See id.* at *4.

[40] *See id.* at *4-*5.

[41] *See, e.g., Mallett v. Smith*, 27 S.C. Eq. (6 Rich. Eq.) 12 (1853); *Thorne v. Fordham*, 24 S.C. Eq. (4 Rich. Eq.) 222 (1852); *Swinton v. Egleston*, 24 S.C. Eq. (3 Rich. Eq.) 201 (1851); *Fable v. Brown*, 11 S.C. Eq. (2 Hill Eq.) 378, 1835 WL 1408 (S.C. App. 1835).

[42] *Lenoir v. Sylvester*, 17 S.C. L. (1 Bail.) 632, 1830 WL 3099 at *6 (1830). For other cases stating that slaves could not take property by descent or by purchase, *see* Stroud, *supra* at 32-33.

[43] 1 N.C. (Cam. & Nor.) 353, 1801 WL 193, 1 N.C. (Tay.) 209, 1801 WL 692 (1801); Wheeler, *supra* at 191-93.

[44] *Cunningham's Heirs v. Cunningham's Executors*, 1801 WL 193 at *1.

[45] The Court of Conference was not an appellate court; it was an advisory court that made recommendations to the trial judges in cases pending in the trial court. *See* Edwards, *supra* at 50.

[46] *Cunningham's Heirs v. Cunningham's Executors*, 1801 WL 193 at *2.

[47] *See* Shaw, *supra* at 82-84; Cover, *Justice Accused*, *supra* at 75; Reuel E. Schiller, "Conflicting Obligations: Slave Law and the Late Antebellum North Carolina Supreme Court," 78 *Va. L. Rev.* 1207, 1229 (1992).

[48] 53 Ky. (14 B. Mon.) 296, 1853 WL 3753 (1853).

[49] *Jones v. Lipscomb*, 1853 WL 3753 at *1-*2.

[50] *See id.* at *1-*2 (citing *Graves v. Allen*, 52 Ky. (13 B. Mon.) 190, 1852 WL 3389 (1852) (slaves cannot take by inheritance)).

[51] *See id.* at *3.

[52] 13 Ark. 513, 1853 WL 540 (1853).

[53] *See Campbell v. Campbell*, 1853 WL 540 at *2.

[54] *See id.* at *3. Watkins concluded that the lower court's decree was "without prejudice to the right of the appellants, to institute proceedings anew against the administrator, whenever it can be made to appear that the assets of the estate exceed the debts and specific legacies." *See id.* at *5.

[55] 2 Fla. 553, 1849 WL 1274 (1849).

[56] *See Sibley v. Maria, a woman of color*, 1849 WL 1274 at *1-*3.

[57] *See id.* at *4; *Leiper v. Hoffman*, 26 Miss. (4 Cushm.) 615, 1853 WL 3718 (1853) (slave who moved to Ohio with master's consent deemed to be a free person).

[58] 24 Tex 643, 1860 WL 5723 (1860).

[59] *See Hunt, Ad'mr v. White*, 1860 WL 5723 at *1-*4.

[60] *See id.* at *5, citing Cobb, *supra* at 310. Wheeler also held that the written explanation could not be used to modify the will and supply the missing provisions. *See id.* at *6-*9.

[61] 27 U.S. (2 Pet.) 664, 1849 WL 3173 (1829).

[62] 13 Charles Alan Wright, *et al.*, *Federal Practice & Procedure, Federal Rules of Evidence* §3530 at n. 69 (2000 & supp. 2008). *See*, on Justice Gabriel Duvall, Christopher L. Tomlins, *The United States Supreme Court: The Pursuit of Justice* 476 (2005); John Paul Jones, "Gabriel Duvall," in *The Supreme Court Justices: A Biographical Dictionary* 153-54 (Melvin I. Urofsky, ed., 1994).

[63] *See Le Grand v. Darnell*, 27 U.S. (2 Pet.) at 667-68. These doubts apparently arose because of the Maryland Court of Appeals' 1823 decision holding that the Maryland statutes did not permit a master to free a young child. *See Hamilton v. Cragg*, 6 H. & J. 16 (Md. 1823).

[64] *See Le Grand v. Darnell*, 27 U.S. (2 Pet.) at 669-70.

[65] *See id.* at 670. He also stated that the court expressed no opinion "as to the correctness of the decision of the court of appeals in the case of Hamilton vs. Cragg. It is unnecessary in reference to the case under consideration." *Id.*

[66] On the debate regarding the merit of Justice Duvall's Supreme Court career, and on the correct spelling of his name, *see* Frank H. Easterbrook, "The Most Insignificant Justice: Further Evidence," 50 *U. Chi. L. Rev.* 481 (1983); David P. Currie, "The Most Insignificant Justice: A Preliminary Inquiry," 50 *U. Chi. L. Rev.* 466 (1983); Nash, "Reason of Slavery," *supra* at 138, n. 428. For other discussions of the case, *see* Jones, *Fathers*, *supra* at 23-24;

Wallenstein, *supra* at 46-47. Le Grand sold Portland Manor and in 1836 moved to Louisiana, where he became a wealthy planter and slave owner. *See* Saul S. Freidman, *Jews and the American Slave Trade* 177 (1998); Lyle Saxon, *Old Louisiana* 133-39 (1989); Clement Eaton, *The Growth of Southern Civilization* 138 (1961).

[67] *Las Siete Partidas, Volume 4, supra*, Part 4, Title 22, Law 7 at 983.

[68] *Metayer v. Metayer*, 6 Mart. (o.s.) 16, 1819 WL 1296 (La. 1819) (affirming freedom judgment after prior decision affirming dismissal); *Metayer v. Noret*, 5 Mart. (o.s.) 566, 1818 WL 1597 (La. 1818) (reversing freedom judgment); Palmer, "Codifying," *supra* at 112, nn. 101-104.

[69] Palmer, "Codifying," *supra* at 112, nn. 101-104; *see Eulalie v. Long & Mabry*, 11 La. Ann. 463, 1856 WL 1856 at *1 (La. 1856); *Eulalie v. Long & Mabry*, 9 La. Ann. 9, 1854 WL 3988 at *1 (La. 1854); Schafer, *Becoming Free, supra* at 30, 66-67 n. 10, 113, 123-24; Schafer, *Supreme Court, supra* at 234-37.

[70] 8 Mart. (o.s.) 128, 1829 WL 1709 (La. 1829).

[71] *Meilleur v. Coupry*, 1829 WL 1709 at *1; *see* Rose, *supra* at 177, quoting Civil Code, Art. 185.

[72] *Meilleur v. Coupry*, 1829 WL 1709 at *1.

[73] *Id.*; *see Carmouche v. Carmouche*, 12 La. Ann. 721, 1857 WL 4752 (La. 1857) (slave's suit dismissed because slave required to be 30 years old, and did not prove ten years' of freedom); Schafer, *Supreme Court, supra* at 234.

[74] *See George v. Demouy*, 14 La. Ann. 145, 1859 WL 6041 (La. 1859); Schafer, *Supreme Court, supra* at 246-48.

[75] Cobb, *supra* at 295; *see* Shaw, *supra* at 150-52; O'Neall, *supra* at 9-10.

[76] *See Lewis v. Hart*, 33 Mo. 535, 1836 WL 535 (1863) (plaintiff and child freed after establishing their purchase by plaintiff's mother, who was a free black who let the plaintiff live as if free for 17 years); *Henderson v. Jason*, 9 Gill 483, 1851 WL 3107 (Md. 1851) (freedom judgment affirmed, plaintiffs' mother was permitted to be free from 1831 to 1851); *Stringer v. Burcham*, 34 N.C., (12 Ired.) 41, 1851 WL 1125 (1851) (freedom judgment affirmed, plaintiff's grandmother had been freed allegedly according to law in 1807); *Anderson v. Garrett*, 9 Gill 120, 1850 WL 3293 (Md. 1850) (reversing freedom judgment for plaintiffs where 20 years' proof of freedom absent); *State v. Hill*, 29 S.C.L. (2 Speers) 150, 1843 WL 2511 (1843) (criminal prosecution 30-year rule recognized); *Miller v. Reigne*, 20 S.C.L. (2 Hill) 592, 1835 WL 1347 (1835) (trover action, 20-year rule cited); *Monk v. Jenkins*, 11 S.C. Eq. (2 Hill Eq.) 9, 1834 WL 1463 (1834) (equity bill filed after death of slave allegedly freed, refers to master's failure to recover slave); *Wilson v. Barnet*, 8 G. & J. 159, 1836 WL 1877 (Md. 1836) (prescription can run only if owner of his or her representatives have knowledge that slave is living as if free); *Burke v. Negro, Joe*, 6 G. & J. 136, 1834 WL 1985 (Md. 1834) (freedom judgment for claimant, whose grandmother, mother, and children were permitted to live as free beginning in 1797 and until 1832, when plaintiff was seized); *Hutchinson v. Noland*, 19 S.C.L. (1 Hill) 222, 1833 WL 1347 (1833) (trover action, 20-year rule cited); *Wells v. Lane*, 9 Johns. 144 (N.Y. 1812) (declarations made more than 20 years before by slave's owner that he purchased her to make her free, and that he meant her to be freed, were held to be a manumission in suit for harboring a slave); *State v. M'Donald*, 1 N.J.L. 332, 1795 WL 586 (Sup. Ct. 1795) (freedom judgment where plaintiff was orally promised freedom and was permitted to live free for ten years).

[77] *See* Fede, *People Without Rights, supra* at 149-50.

[78] *See, e.g., id.* at 150; Cobb, *supra* at 109, 287-90, 295; O'Neall, *supra* at 9-11.

[79] 35 N.C. (13 Ired.) 154, 1851 WL 1243 (1851).

[80] *State v. Nat*, 1851 WL 1243 at *1.

[81] *Id.*, overruling *State v. Clarissa*, 27 N.C. (5 Ired.) 221, 1844 WL 1501 (1844); *see* Morris, *Slavery, supra* at 339.

[82] 33 S.C.L. (2 Strob.) 536, 1848 WL 2463 (1848).

[83] *Vinyard v. Passalaigue*, 1848 WL 2463 at *1, *3.

[84] *Id.* at *1.

[85] *Id.* at *4.

[86] *Id.* at *5.

[87] *Id.* at *5-*6.

[88] *Id.* at *6. Judges Evans, Wardlaw, and Frost concurred in the court's opinion. Chancellors Johnston, Caldwell, and Dunkin concurred in the order for a new trial. *Id.*

[89] *Id.* at *7.

[90] *Id.* at *7-*8.

[91] *Id.* at *8.

[92] *See* O'Neall, *supra* at 9-11; and chapter 10, *infra* at notes 33-40.

[93] 54 Ky. (15 B. Mon.) 328, 1854 WL 3841 (1854).

[94] *Anderson v. Crawford*, 1854 WL 3841 at *5.

[95] *Id.* at *7.

[96] *See Laws of Maryland, 1860*, ch. 322, §1; 1 *Maryland Code, supra*, Art. 66, §§42-43 at 458; Brackett, *supra* at 171, 173; 2 Hurd, *supra* at 24.

[97] *See Laws of Maryland, 1860*, ch. 322, §1; 1 *Maryland Code, supra*, Art. 66, §§42-43 at 458; Brackett, *supra* at 171, 173; 2 Hurd, *supra* at 24.

[98] Davis, *Western Culture, supra* at 270.

[99] *See generally* Morris, *Slavery, supra* at 406-16; Fede, *People Without Rights, supra* at 146-47; Shaw, *supra* at 188-93; Cobb, *supra* at 72-77, 283; Nash, "Reason of Slavery," *supra* at 156, nn. 515-19; *see also* Mariana L. R. Dantas, "Child Abandonment and Foster Care in Colonial Brazil," in *Paths to Freedom, supra* at 206-07 (noting that this rule applied in colonial Brazil and suggesting that mothers may have abandoned their children who were born while the women were terms slaves to enable their children to avoid slavery).

[100] 1 N.J.L. 41 (Sup. Ct. 1790). The case also is unofficially reported in *Cases Adjudged, supra at* 25-27.

[101] *State v. Anderson*, 1 N.J.L. at 42 [emphasis added].

[102] *Id.*

[103] *Id.* at 42-43.

[104] *Id.* at 43.

[105] *Id.* A United States Circuit Court judge for the District of Columbia also apparently applied this rule in *Sarah v. Taylor,* 21 F. Cas. 31, 2 Cranch C.C. 155 (No. 12,339) (C.C. D.C. 1818) (freedom judgment for plaintiff who was born during a nine-year term after which her mother was to be freed according to the terms of sale).

[106] *Laws of Maryland, 1809,* ch. 171; Morris, *Slavery, supra* at 414; *see* Fede *People Without Rights, supra* at 146, n. 65; Brackett, *supra* at 154-55. According to Christopher Phillips and Steven Whitman, in the vast majority of deeds masters did not grant immediate freedom to the children of their female term slaves. *See* Whitman, *supra* at 122; Phillips, *Freedom's Port, supra* at 44-45; *see also* Rockman, *supra* at 113-14.

[107] Brackett, *supra* at 155.

[108] 5 Ky. (2 Bibb.) 298, 1811 WL 298 (1811).

[109] *See Ned v. Beal,* 1811 WL 298 at *1-*2.

[110] *See id.* at *1; *see also Frank v. Milam's Ex'r,* 4 Ky. (1 Bibb.) 615, 1809 WL 837 (1809) (reversing freedom judgment in favor of claimants born in Kentucky whose mother was born in Pennsylvania).

[111] *See Ned v. Beal,* 1811 WL 298 at *1.

[112] *Catin v. D'Orgenoy's Heirs,* 8 Mart. (o.s.) 219 (La. 1820); Morris, *Slavery, supra* at 414-15; Palmer, "Codifying," *supra* at 112, n. 103.

[113] 23 Va. (2 Rand.) 228, 1824 WL 1192 (1824); *see, e.g.,* discussing *Maria,* Morris, *Slavery, supra* at 406-09; Shaw, *supra* at 189-90; Cover, *Justice Accused, supra* at 74-75; Higginbotham & Higginbotham, *supra* at 1256, 1263-65.

[114] *See Maria v. Surbaugh,* 1824 WL 1192 at *1.

[115] *See id.* at *1-*9.

[116] *Id.* at *9.

[117] 6 Va. (2 Call.) 319, 1800 WL 404 (1800); *Maria v. Surbaugh,* 23 Va. (2 Rand.) 228, 1824 WL 1192 at *3-*8, *9.

[118] *Pleasants v. Pleasants,* 1800 WL 404 at *1. The *Pleasants* case involved several important issues, and various authors have emphasized one or more of these issues in books and articles. The other issues in the case and some of these sources are discussed in chapter 6, *infra* at notes 22-35, and chapter 9, *infra* at notes 87-100.

[119] *Maria v. Surbaugh,* 1824 WL 1192 at *8.

[120] *Id.* at *9.

[121] *Id.*

[122] *Id.*

[123] *See* 2 *A New Law Dictionary and Glossary* 573 (Alexander M. Burrill, ed.) (1851).

[124] *See, e.g., McCutchen v. Marshall,* 33 U.S. (8 Peters) 220, 240-41, 8 L. Ed. 923 (1834); *Leary v. Nash,* 56 N.C. (3 Jones Eq.) 356, 1857 WL 1732 (1857); *Lee v. Sprague,* 14 Mo. 476, 1851 WL 4178 (1851); *Sidney v. White,* 12 Ala. 728, 1848 WL 356 (1848); *Mayho v. Sears,* 25 N.C. (3 Ired.) 224, 1842 WL 1055 (1842); *Chew v. Gary,* 6 H. & J. 526, 1825 WL 1051 (Md. 1825); *Hamilton v. Cragg,* 6 H. & J. 16, 1823 WL 1067 (Md. 1823); *Ned v. Beal,*

5 Ky. (2 Bibb.) 298, 1811 WL 298 (1811); Morris, *Slavery, supra* at 411-12, 414-18. The United States Supreme Court cited the majority rule in *dictum* while affirming the dismissal of the plaintiffs' claims for the alleged slaves because the identity of the alleged slaves to be inherited was too vague. *See* Leslie Freidman Goldstein, "Slavery and the Marshall Court: Preventing 'Oppressions of the Minor Party'?," 67 *Md. L. Rev.* 166, 179-80 (2007). The United States Supreme Court incorrectly predicted that the Tennessee Supreme Court would follow the majority rule.

[125] 14 Mo. 476, 1851 WL 4178 (1851).

[126] *Lee v. Sprague,* 1851 WL 4178 at *1. Justice Birch's tenure on the Missouri Supreme Court was short. For his interesting biography as a pro-slavery, anti-secessionist, *see* Jerry E. Wilson, "Birch, James H.," in *Dictionary of Missouri Biography* 74 (Lawrence O. Christensen, ed., 1999).

[127] *See, e.g., Davis (of color) v. Wood,* 56 Ky. (17 B. Mon.) 86, 1856 WL 4274 (1856); *Linstead v. Green,* 2 Md. 82, 1852 WL 3041 (1852); *O'Bryan v. Goslee,* 49 Ky. (10 B. Mon.) 100, 1849 WL 3546 (1849); *Lucy v. Cheminant's Adm'rs,* 43 Va. (2 Gratt.) 36, 1845 WL 2847 (1845); *Anderson's Ex'rs v. Anderson,* 38 Va. (11 Leigh) 616, 1841 WL 2458 (1841); *Campbell v. Street,* 23 N.C. (1 Ired.) 109, 1840 WL 719 (1840) (applying Virginia law); *Crawford v. Moses,* 37 Va. (10 Leigh) 277, 1839 WL 2070 (1839); *Erskine v. Henry & Wife,* 36 Va. (9 Leigh) 188, 1838 WL 1837 (1838); *Hudgens v. Spencer,* 34 Ky. (4 Dana) 589, 1836 WL 2119 (1836); *Charles (a man of color) v. French,* 29 Ky. (6 J.J. Marsh.) 331, 1831 WL 2314 (1831); *Fanny v. Bryant,* 27 Ky. (4 J.J. Marsh.) 368, 1830 WL 1906 (1830); *Hart v. Fanny Ann,* 22 Ky. (6 T.B. Mon.) 49, 1827 WL 1628 (1827); *Hughes v. Negro Milly,* 5 H. & J. 310, 1821 WL 1014 (Md. 1821); *Cobb, supra* at 78; *but see Hamilton v. Cragg,* 6 H. & J. 16, 1823 WL 1067 (Md. 1823) (although will mentioned slaves to be freed "and their increase," freedom claims denied because plaintiffs were not of sufficient age under statute regulating manumission).

For discussions of the post-*Maria* cases in Virginia, *see* Morris, *Slavery, supra* at 409-11; Nash, "Reason of Slavery," *supra* at 127-56; and, discussing the post-*Mayho* cases in North Carolina, *see* Tushnet, *Humanity, supra* at 201; Schiller, *supra* at 1231. I disagree with Schiller's reading of *Leary v. Nash, supra, Caffey v. Davis,* 54 N.C. (1 Jones Eq.) 1, 1853 WL 1489 (1853), and *Wooten v. Becton,* 43 N.C. (8 Ired.) 66, 1851 WL 1305 (1851), because he does not discuss or even cite *Mayho. See id.*

[128] *Hudgens v. Spencer,* 34 Ky. (4 Dana) 589 (1836); *Charles v. French,* 29 Ky. (6 J. J. Marsh.) 331 (1831).

[129] *Spurrier's Heirs v. Parker,* 55 Ky. (16 B. Mon.) 274, 1855 WL 4205 (1855).

[130] 27 Va. (6 Rand) 652, 1828 WL 1034 (1828).

[131] *See Isaac v. West's Executor,* 1828 WL 1034 at *2-*4.

[132] 14 Tenn. (6 Yer.) 153, 1834 WL 1003 (1834). For discussions of this case, *see, e.g.,* Morris, *Slavery, supra* at 413-14; Nash, "Reason of Slavery," *supra* at 156-57; Howington, *What Sayeth, supra* at 13-14.

[133] *Harris v. Clarissa,* 1834 WL 1003 at *1.

[134] *Id.* at *7-*8.

[135] *Id.* at *8.

[136] *Id.* at *8-*10.

[137] *Id.* at *11.

[138] *Id.*

[139] *Id.* Catron concurred with United States Supreme Court majority in *Scott v. Sandford*, 60 U.S. (19 How.) 393, 15 L. Ed. 691 (1857). Justice Nathan Green eventually endorsed the *Harris* holding. *See* Fede, *People Without Rights, supra* at 146-47. On Catron's career, *see* Huebner, *Tradition, supra* at 40-69.

[140] Howington, *What Sayeth, supra* at 34; *see* Huebner, *Tradition, supra* at 61, noting Catron's views that freed blacks were "a very dangerous and most objectionable population where slaves are numerous," and that freed slaves thus should be removed from the United States, citing Catron's opinion in *Fisher's Negroes v. Dabbs*, 14 Tenn. (6 Yer.) 119, 126, 129-30 (1834). Between 1831 and 1854, the Tennessee legislature adopted legislation liberalizing and then tightening this restriction on freed slaves, but in many but not all of the cases the local courts granted petitions nevertheless permitting freed slaves to remain in Tennessee. Howington, *What Sayeth, supra* at 35-70.

[141] *Harris v. Clarissa*, 1834 WL 1003 at *11 (1834).

[142] For the majority rule that the courts applied to life tenancies and tenancies for a term, *see Williamson v. Daniel*, 25 U.S. (12 Wheat.) 568, 6 L. Ed. 713 (1827); *Wilks v. Green*, 14 Ala. 437 (1848); *Miller v. McClelland*, 23 Ky. (7 T.B. Mon.) 231 (1828); *Ellison v. Woody*, 20 Va. (6 Munf.) 368, 1819 WL 877 (1819); *Wheeler, supra* at 23-28; *see also Maria v. Surbaugh*, 1824 WL 1192 at *2. For the Delaware and Maryland rule, *see, e.g., Smith v. Milman*, 2 Del. (2 Harr.) 497, 1839 WL 167 (Del. Super. 1838); *Somerville v. Johnson*, 1 H. & McH. 348, 1770 WL 3 (Md. Ch. 1770); 4 Catterall, *supra* at 214; Brackett, *supra* at 144-46, n. 1; Burnham, *supra* at 217-18, and on the general rules as to bailees of animals and gratuitous bailees, *see* 3B *C.J.S.* "Animals" §6 at 214 (2003 & supp. 2010). *See generally* Morris, *Slavery, supra* at 412-14; Fede, *People Without Rights, supra* at 147; Shaw, *supra* at 194-97.

[143] *Harris v. Clarissa*, 1834 WL 1003 at *11.

[144] Morris, *Slavery, supra* at 411, 415-16.

[145] *See Revised Delaware Statutes, supra* at 253; Essah, *supra* at 104-05; Williams, *Slavery and Freedom in Delaware, supra* at 157-58; 2 Hurd, *supra* at 78. The Delaware Supreme Court in 1832 held that children born to *statu liberi* before the 1810 statute was in effect were slaves for life. *Jones v. Wooten*, 1 Del. (1 Harr.) 77 (Del. Super. 1833). Sixteen years later, the Court of Errors and Appeals overruled that decision. *Elliot v. Twilley*, 5 Del. (5 Harr.) 192 (Del. Err. & App. 1849).

[146] Rose, *supra* at 178, quoting Civil Code, Art. 196; *see* Schafer, *Becoming Free, supra* at 47; Morris, *Slavery, supra* at 414-15; Shaw, *supra* at 192.

[147] *Revised Statutes of Kentucky*, ch. 93, art. IX, §10 at 645 (1852). The Kentucky statutes also stated: "The issue of a slave emancipated by deed, born after the date of the deed, shall have the same right to his freedom that the mother has under said deed, and shall be treated accordingly." *Id.*, §9 at 645.

[148] 1 *Virginia Code 1849, supra*, title 30, ch. 103, §10, at 458-59; *see* Finkelman, *Casebook, supra* at 127.

[149] Morris, *Slavery, supra* at 416, quoting William B. Rodman, Bartholomew F. Moore, & Asa Biggs, *Revised Code of North Carolina Enacted by the General Assembly at the Ses-*

sion of 1854 ch. 107, §48 at 574 (1855) [hereinafter *Revised North Carolina Code*]; *see also* Schiller, *supra* at 1229.

[150] *See* Morris, *Slavery, supra* at 416.

[151] *See* Purdy, *supra* at 49; Alan Schwartz, "The Default Rule Paradigm and the Limits of Contract Law," 3 *S. Cal. Interdisc. L.J.* 389, 413-15 (1993).

[152] *See Pauline, f.w.c. v. Hubert*, 14 La. Ann. 161, 1859 WL 5785 (La. 1859); Schafer, *Supreme Court, supra* at 232-34; *see also Heirs of Henderson v. Rost & Montgomery*, 11 La. Ann. 542 (1856); *Angelina v. Whitehead*, 3 La. Ann. 556 (1848); Morris, *Slavery, supra* at 415; Schafer, *Supreme Court, supra* at 213-14 (discussing the effect of the 1857 statute barring manumissions).

[153] Wahl, *Burden, supra* at 164, n. 119; Fede, *People Without Rights, supra* at 137; Stroud, *supra* at 96-97; Binder, *supra* at 2089; Higginbotham & Higginbotham, *supra* at 1268-69.

[154] On the general trends in the statutes regulating and eventually prohibiting manumission intra state and eventually anywhere, *see* chapter 3, *supra*; Fede, *People Without Rights, supra* at 135-38; Shaw, *supra* at 76-109. *See also* chapter 3, *supra* at notes 197-245, discussing the "positive good" theory that motivated these prohibitions as well as the "voluntary enslavement" statutes.

6

Social Policy Versus the Master's Will
in the Manumission Cases

In some manumission cases, the deceased masters' disappointed would-be heirs or family members argued that the courts should not enforce the deceased masters' relatively unambiguous expressions of their intent to free their slaves. These litigants asked the judges to invalidate what they alleged were impermissible attempts by owners to circumvent their states' anti-manumission statutes or public policies. This chapter reviews five key issues that arose in these cases: (1) whether the courts would liberally or strictly enforce statutory requirements as to the form of documents expressing the masters' intention to free their slaves; (2) whether the courts would enforce wills permitting slaves to make choices or elections as permitted by their masters' will; (3) whether the courts would enforce send/free and free/send wills; (4) whether the courts should use the *cy pres* doctrine to effectuate the masters' apparent intention to free slaves; and (5) whether the courts would enforce wills creating *quasi*-manumissions, either permanently or before slaves were to be set free.

These cases further illustrate the emerging antebellum Southern trend in law and society restricting manumission. The nineteenth century Southern judges, and especially those in Georgia, also became more hostile to all manumissions.[1]

The Cases Enforcing Formal Requirements for Valid Manumission Deeds and Wills

As noted in chapter three, in the eighteenth and early nineteenth centuries, the Southern legislatures adopted statutes that barred oral manumissions and required masters to confirm in writing their intentions to free their slaves. These statutes also established formal requirements for these manumission documents. The legislators apparently intended to prevent people held as slaves from asserting fraudulent oral manumission claims. These laws are not as restrictive as those that prohibited manumissions, but they nevertheless regulated the manner in which the documents were to be executed and in some cases recorded.[2]

According to Thomas Cobb, the Southern courts required freedom claimants who advanced written proof of their masters' intention "to show a compliance with these formalities or restrictions" before the manumission as confirmed in the document could take effect.[3] The Southern courts did not adopt an approach to statutory construction in favor of liberty. Instead, they favored form over substance, and strictly enforced the formal requirements of these "liberal" manumission laws. Accordingly, many slaves were denied their "right" to freedom in cases evidencing little or no doubt about their masters' true intentions to free them. Even under the more "liberal" statutory regimes, some freedom claimants remained as slaves although they produced strong written evidence of their masters' contrary intention. The legislators apparently did not disagree with this illiberal interpretation; they did not amend the liberal statutes to delete these strict requirements of form after the courts construed them against liberty.

One of the early leading cases strictly interpreting Maryland's manumission laws that permitted immediate and delayed manumission deeds was *Negro James v. Gaither*.[4] The Maryland Court of Appeals in 1807 affirmed the reversal of a freedom judgment in favor of the claimant, James. Although the official report of the case does not include a Court of Appeals opinion, the court denied James's claim to liberty while apparently adopting a strict interpretation of Maryland's 1752 manumission law and the 1796 more "liberal" law that readopted the earlier statute's relevant provisions.[5]

James's freedom claim was based on a manumission deed and a will that his former owner B. Gaither signed, and the apparently undisputed testimony of two witnesses. The manumission deed was dated September 13, 1784. It gave freedom after Gaither's death "to sundry of his negro slaves," including James. Gaither signed and sealed the document and acknowledged it before T. Boyd, who was a justice of the peace. The deed was recorded in the county records on November 27, 1784. In his will dated June 20, 1791, Gaither devised to Benjamin Ijams all of his estate "except my negroes[.]" The will also stated Gaither's intention "that all my young negroes, born since my negroes were recorded, shall be absolutely free at my death." Accordingly, Gaither's estate's inventory did not include any of his slaves.

Ignatius Allen testified "that he lived with Gaither" when Gaither sent for Boyd "to take the acknowledgment of a deed to set his negroes free[.]" According to Allen, Boyd went to Gaither's home, prepared the deed, and Gaither then "did sign, seal, and acknowledge the same as his act and deed, and did deliver" the deed to Boyd for recording. Allen also testified that when Gaither signed the deed "he was confined to his bed; that he called upon the witness to assist him in getting up in his bed to sign the deed[.]" Allen stated that he assisted Gaither, he saw Gaither "sign the deed, and acknowledge it as his act and deed[,]" and he also saw Boyd sign the deed as a witness. Allen also recalled that, in response to Gaither's question, Boyd said that it was not "necessary that any one else should sign" the deed. According to Allen, several other persons also saw Gaither sign the deed. Gaither asked that they "all to take notice that he had signed an instrument of writing to set all his negroes free."

Allen also testified that he lived with Gaither for eight or nine years after this deed execution. During those years, Allen "frequently heard [Gaither] declare that all his negroes would be free at his death, as he had them recorded in court." Allen admitted, however, that he "cannot write his name, and did not sign the deed as a witness."

Robert Waters also testified that he prepared Gaither's will. Gaither told Waters that "he had deeded his negroes to be free at his death, and that the deed had been recorded several years." Waters first prepared the clause in the will in favor of Ijams. Gaither then told Waters "to draw a clause in favour of some young negroes," but Gaither then told Waters "to stop, and said it was hardly worth while, the old ones he had deeded free at his death, and the deed had been recorded for several years, and the young ones will be free, if not named in the will. But after some pause he said, however, you may do it, and do it in this way, all my young negroes, born since my negroes were recorded, to be free at my death."

Waters also testified that Gaither "died about the year 1793, and the negroes mentioned in the deed have been at large ever since." No one "ever set up any claim to the negroes, until about two years ago."

The County Court Chief Judge, Henry Ridgely, at the April 1802 term, found for James. The defendant appealed to the General Court, which at its May 1804 term, reversed the judgment and found that James was a slave. On James's further appeal, the Maryland Court of Appeals affirmed that judgment.[6]

The court's reasoning can be surmised from a review of the unsuccessful arguments of James's lawyers, one of whom was Francis Scott Key.[7] James's lawyers cited the 1752 act's provision that permitted a Maryland master to free his or her slaves "who are or shall be of healthy constitutions, and sound in mind and body, capable by labour to procure to him or them sufficient food and raiment, with other requisite necessaries of life, and not exceeding fifty years of age," by a "writing under his, her or their hand and seal, evidenced by two good and sufficient witnesses at least[.]" If the master intended to free slaves in the future, the statute also required, among other things, that the deed be acknowledged by a justice of the peace of the county and be recorded in the county court's records within six months of the execution.[8]

James's lawyers argued that the County Court judgment should be restored, "unless this court think they are bound by a rigid construction of the act of assembly of 1752[.]" After quoting the 1752 statute, "[t]hey insisted that the act does not indispensibly [sic] require that two witnesses should *subscribe* their names to the deed. That an enlarged construction ought to be given to the word *evidenced*[.]"[9] Thus, they in essence argued that Allen's testimony, when combined with Boyd's signature on the deed, which apparently was duly recorded, should be enough to sustain James's freedom, if the statute's purpose truly was to prevent unmeritorious manumission claims.

The Court of Appeals disagreed with James's lawyers and it adopted the rigid rule of construction. It apparently concluded that Allen's testimony confirming that he witnessed the execution of the deed, combined with Water's testimony about Gaither's will referring to that deed, could not overcome Boyd's bad legal advice to Gaither. James lost his freedom for want of another witness's signature on the manumission deed. This result followed even though no one raised any serious doubts about the reliability of the deed as an expression of Gaither's intention to free his slaves, which had been a matter of public record for almost twenty years.

The *Gaither* decision has to be one of the more influential precedents for which there was no opinion of the court. Relying on *Gaither*, the United States Supreme Court and the highest courts in Alabama and Virginia used this "rigid" rule of construction to deny manumission claims based on Maryland's manumission laws.[10]

Maryland's legislature in effect gave its prospective approval to the *Gaither* doctrine on December 23, 1810, when it adopted "An Act relating to Servants and Slaves." That act stated that "any deed heretofore executed for the manumission of any slave or slaves, who by law might have been set free or manumitted by deed, and which has been acknowledged and recorded" as required by the 1796 act "shall be valid and effectual in law to give freedom to any such slave or slaves, and their issue, although such deed of manumission, or writing as aforesaid, may not have been evidenced by two or more good and sufficient witnesses."[11] The legislators added, however, that this act shall not "be so construed as to affect or destroy the right of any person, who, before the passage of this act, was a bona fide purchaser of any slave or slaves claiming his, her or their freedom under such deeds of manumission[.]" The statute also provided "that notwithstanding such deed of manumission, no slave shall be entitled to his or her freedom under the provisions of this act, who has been heretofore adjudged to be a slave by any court of law in this state."[12] The act therefore applied only to some past manumission deeds that were not properly executed, and not to the claimant in *Gaither*.

Maryland's Court of Appeals continued to apply this rule of strict construction to its own state's statute's requirements. Slaves continued to lose their cases if the manumission deeds were not recorded as required. Moreover, in 1837, the Court of Appeals held that the property rights of a good faith purchaser of a term slave were entitled to greater weight than the term slave's right to liberty under an unrecorded future manumission deed. The court also invalidated a special act of the legislature that was intended to validate the unrecorded manumission deed.[13]

Slaves also were unsuccessful if, when the right to manumission accrued, the master's estate was not solvent,[14] or, before the law was amended in 1831 to require freed slaves to vacate Maryland, the slaves were too young[15] or were too old.[16] And in 1820, the Court of Appeals applied this strict approach to the 1797 Delaware manumission statute's formal document execution requirements, when it rejected a freedom claim based upon an imperfectly executed Delaware manumission deed.[17]

The Maryland Court of Appeals even applied this interpretation not favoring liberty to general remedial statutes that were adopted in 1785 and 1792. These acts permitted the courts to order that a deed be filed out of time if it was not timely recorded, "without any fraudulent design or intention of the party claiming under such deed[.]"[18] In the 1819 decision in *Wicks v. Chew*,[19] the plaintiffs sought a chancery court order under these statutes permitting the filing of a May 10, 1805 manumission deed that their owner, Richard Darnall, signed but failed to record. Darnall died on December 25, 1807. The plaintiffs filed suit in 1814. On February 18, 1817, Chancellor William Kilty issued a decree that allowed the plaintiffs six months to file the deed. The order would, in effect, give the plaintiffs their freedom as if Darnall had filed the deed on a timely basis.[20]

In an opinion by Justice John Buchanan, the Court of Appeals reversed this judgment. Buchanan wrote that these remedial acts

> are not intended to give relief in cases which were before without remedy, but to give an additional remedy, by enabling a party acquiring equitable rights, under a deed not operative in law for want of recording, to perfect those rights, by applying to the chancellor to order the original instrument to be recorded, and thus to give it the effect which by law it would have had, if recorded in due time, instead of going into chancery to enforce a specific performance, or compel a conveyance. They are intended to give an accumulative remedy to persons able to contract, and who by deed acquire rights which equity will protect, with the power to prosecute those rights. But by the laws of this state, a negro, so long as he is a slave, can have no rights adverse to those of his master; he can neither sue, nor be sued, nor can he make any contract, or acquire any rights under a deed, which either a court of law or of equity can enforce. And as it is the record-ing of a deed of manumission within the time prescribed by law, which entitles him to his freedom, he continues a slave, and can acquire no rights under such an instrument, until it is so recorded, and consequently cannot go either into a court of law or equity for relief of any kind. And as the acts of assembly only authorise [sic] the recording of a deed, on the application of the party claiming under it, and on the chancellor being satisfied that such party has a fair and equitable claim *to the premises therein men-tioned,* they must be understood to relate alone to deeds creating claims, and to persons capable of acquiring and of prosecuting such claims, and cannot be construed to embrace the case of a deed of manumission, by which no right or claim can be created until it is recorded, and the object of which, while he continues in a state of slavery, is incapable of suing either in a court of law or equity. A master may execute and acknowledge a deed of manumission, and afterwards destroy it, or keep it, and refuse to have it recorded, and the slave remains a slave without redress. Besides, the origi-nal act of 1785 speaks of the *thing or premises* mentioned in the deed, and the language of the supplement of 1792, is "the *land* or *thing* conveyed or intended to be conveyed," by which it is obvious that they only contemplate deeds having relation to *property.*

Therefore, Buchanan concluded that, until a master records a manumission deed, "the slave remains a slave without redress."[21]

The courts in other states found the Maryland court's approach to be per-suasive. One would have guessed that the Virginia Supreme Court of Appeals decision in *Pleasants v. Pleasants*[22] suggests that the Virginia courts should instead adopt a liberal interpretation of the mere technical requirements of Virginia's most liberal manumission law of 1782. That case involved the 1771 will of John Pleasants, and the similar 1776 will of one of his sons, Jonathan Pleas-ants. John's will stated that he intended to free his slaves "if they chuse [sic] it when they arrive to the age of thirty years, and the laws of the land will admit them to be set free without their being transported out of the country." He also extended freedom to "all my slaves now born or hereafter to be born, whilst their mothers are in service of me or my heirs, to be free at the age of thirty years...." Jonathan's will included similar language.[23]

Both of the Pleasants died and their slaves were distributed to various legatees before the Virginia legislature adopted the 1782 law that permitted manumission by will. The estates' executor was Robert Pleasants, one of John's sons who also opposed slavery. Robert and his brother Samuel signed and filed manumission deeds in 1782 and 1783 freeing 139 of the Pleasants' slaves. But the other heirs refused to surrender "their" slaves. Robert tried to free these slaves first by petitioning the legislature in 1790 and 1791. These efforts failed. Robert then sued in the High Court of Chancery to enforce the Pleasants' wills. One of slaves also sued for his own freedom.[24]

Chancellor George Wythe decided the case in September 1798. He overruled the heirs' lawyers' demurrers, which challenged the equity court's jurisdiction. Wythe also held that the Pleasants' slaves were to be freed at the age of thirty, that the children of slaves born before 1782 were to be freed at the age of thirty, that children born after 1782 were freed immediately, and that the slaves were entitled to an accounting and damages from the heirs for their unfree labor after 1782.[25]

The heirs appealed and raised several issues, which centered on the contention that the Virginia statutes did not authorize manumission by will until 1782, although legislation in Virginia proposing this reform had been debated in the years before and after these wills were executed. These issues included: (1) whether the court should apply the 1782 manumission law to these wills that predated the act's adoption, (2) whether the wills violated the rule against perpetuities, (3) whether the children of slaves born after the masters' deaths would be freed when their mothers reached thirty years of age or when they became thirty years old, and (4) whether the slaves were entitled to damages for their work while they were held as slaves after 1782. The court heard argument in November 1798. John Marshall joined John Warden as the appellate counsel for Robert Pleasants. The heirs' lawyers were John Wickham and Edmund Randolph.[26] This was a major case; the "stakes were enormous, involving the freedom of as many as 400 slaves and economic losses that could total hundreds of thousands of dollars."[27]

Each of the judges, President Edmund Pendleton, Spencer Roane, and Paul Carrington, issued opinions on May 6, 1799. They all agreed to apply the 1782 act to the pre-act wills and found ways around the rule against perpetuities, in part based on the notion that manumission claims should be treated more favorably than property claims because the potential liberty of a person held in slavery was at stake, along with the competing property claims of the disappointed heirs or beneficiaries. Pendleton and Carrington disagreed with Wythe's ruling on the immediate manumission of the children of slaves born after 1782, however, with Roane dissenting on this point. All three judges agreed to reverse Wythe's ruling permitting the slaves to obtain an accounting for their services and damages.[28]

Many writers have commented favorably on the *Pleasants* opinions. According to Paul Finkelman, the court in *Pleasants* "strained to enforce two Quaker testators' wishes to emancipate their slaves." He attributed the result to the judges' "humanitarian instincts, even though existing law had to be ignored or rejected."[29] Timothy Huebner credited Judge Roane's appellate court opinion to "the revolutionary generation's preoccupation with liberty," and to Roane's own early "enthusiasm for emancipation[.]"[30] Robert Cover advanced a similar interpretation: "The *Pleasants* case was the product of judicial sympathy with the Pleasants family and with their aspirations; of a vision of the Act of 1782 as reflective of a state policy favoring manumission; and of a sense of residual law favoring freedom. Liberty is to be pursued where law is unformed."[31] He noted further that the court four years later extended this interpretation to the pre-1782 will of another Quaker testator.[32]

Nevertheless, except on the damages issue, the Virginia courts did not follow the *Pleasants* opinions; they did not favor liberty over property rights when applying the technical requirements of the manumission statute. To the contrary, the Virginia courts applied the strict rule of construction to that state's "liberal" 1782 manumission law's formal execution and authentication requirements. Eva Sheppard Wolf wrote, "[a]fter about 1820 the intent of the manumitter was clearly less important to Virginia's high judges than whether the would-be manumitter had complied with the letter of the law. The judges began consistently to treat suits for freedom like other questions of property."[33]

This change in the judge's reasoning and results cannot entirely be explained by changes in the court's personnel. As Huebner noted, Roane remained on the court until his death in 1822. He did not dissent as the court began to elevate form over substance and favor bondage over liberty in the manumission cases, and as his "sentiments favoring liberty clashed with the realities of slave society."[34] To the contrary, it appears the Court of Appeals judges' attitudes to a significant degree reflected the Virginians' ever changing attitudes toward manumission. As noted in chapter three, these attitudes also are evidenced in Virginia's statutes, which by 1806 had once again required freed slaves to leave the state.[35]

In opinions that mirrored the Maryland approach, the nineteenth century Virginia courts denied manumission claims based on the 1782 law's technical requirements, even when the written proof of the masters' intentions was clear. This was foreshadowed by the Supreme Court of Appeals' 1818 decision in *Givens v. Manns*.[36] Among other things, the court's opinion reversing a freedom judgment in favor of the plaintiffs stated that a manumission deed cannot be effective if it was not authenticated and acknowledged as the 1782 law required.[37] The court later followed this line of reasoning to reject other freedom claims.[38]

Moreover, in its 1828 decision in *Moses v. Denigree*,[39] the Supreme Court of Appeals read the *Pleasants* holding narrowly while it applied the rule of technical construction to affirm the denial of the manumission claim of Moses. Moses was a slave of Samuel Pretlow. On November 13, 1781, Pretlow signed a deed stating his intention to free Moses, who then was "about six years," on December 31,

1796, when Moses would be about twenty-one years old. Pretlow executed a will on November 14, 1781. The will, among other things, devised Moses and three other slaves to Pretlows's daughter, Mary, but only until these slaves "become free."[40]

When Pretlow signed the manumission deed and his will, the 1723 manumission act was in effect, which prohibited manumission by will or deed. But in May 1782 the law changed to permit manumission by a properly executed will or deed. Nevertheless, in a decision by Dabney Carr, the Court of Appeals held that the manumission deed was invalid under the 1782 act because "it has never been recorded according to the directions of that Act and this Court ... have declared, that unless the Law is pursued in that respect, the Deed is void." Carr distinguished *Pleasants* because Pretlow's deed did not call for manumission when the law allowed it. Instead, Pretlow directed that Moses be freed in 1796. The law then allowed manumission by a deed only if it was duly prepared and recorded. Judge Carr thus retroactively applied the 1782 act's formal requirements to the pre-act deed. He stated that this result follows "even under the decision of *Pleasants v. Pleasants*, ... a case which has surely carried this doctrine as far as it ought to go."[41]

The Virginia Supreme Court of Appeals, in contrast, applied a liberal approach to an imperfectly prepared deed conveying property in slaves in its 1807 decision in *Whiting v. Daniel*.[42] The Court reversed a manumission judgment in favor of Daniel and twenty-three other claimants, who were slaves of Mary Robinson. The Court enforced a deed by which Robinson allegedly conveyed her slaves to her nephew, Mathew Whiting. The deed was witnessed by only one person, James Kerney, Jr., and it was not dated when Robinson executed it. Whiting later inserted the date. The court permitted Whiting to rely on parol evidence to prove his contention that his aunt signed the deed on April 17 or 18, 1802, thus before she executed her will of March 10, 1803, in which she stated clearly her intention to free all of her slaves when she died. Robinson died on April 14, 1803. Her will was proved in the county court on July 4, 1803. The deed to Whiting was not proved in the county court until December 13, 1803.[43]

The Supreme Court of Appeals nevertheless reversed the trial court's finding that the deed was invalid, concluding that Whiting did not commit a fraud when he filled in the date on which he and his witnesses stated that his aunt signed the deed. The court also found that Robinson "had no right or power" to free her slaves in her duly executed will.[44] The court applied a "liberal" approach to a deed that defeated the slaves' claims to liberty, in contrast to the strict approach that it took when reviewing imperfectly executed manumission deeds.[45]

The Kentucky Court of Appeals also applied the strict compliance doctrine to reverse a freedom judgment in an 1810 decision that was based on the Virginia manumission law.[46] But in 1821, that court took a more liberal approach in response to an 1800 Kentucky law requiring only that a manumission be evidenced by a will or other written instrument. The court reversed a judgment for the defendant to allow the freedom claimant a new trial to present parol evidence of an alleged lost manumission deed.[47] Even in Kentucky, however, this period of liberal construction of manumission deeds was short lived. Pursuant to the 1850 constitution, the legislature again required that manumission deeds be acknowledged or proved in the county court by two subscribing witnesses.[48]

Manumission Bonding Requirements

The Southern courts were divided, however, on the issue of how to apply the statutes that required masters to post bonds for some or all of their freed slaves. As noted in chapter three, these statutes required bonds to protect the public interest. Some required security to prevent charges to the public if the slaves, who were to remain in the state after their release from bondage, could not support themselves after they were freed. Later statutes that required the removal of freed slaves from the jurisdiction used the bonding requirement as a means to fund the forced removal of the freed slaves, if they did not voluntarily leave the state as required by law.[49]

In two cases decided in 1820 and 1836, the Kentucky Court of Appeals, without extensive discussion, endorsed an interpretation of that state's 1798 manumission statute that would enforce the master's intention to free his or her slaves even if the master did not post the required bond. The courts distinguished between the relative rights of the freed slaves and their former master's heirs and successors, and the state's rights against the master's heirs and successors for the master's failure to post the bond.[50]

The Florida Supreme Court rejected this distinction and reached the contrary conclusion, however, in its 1852 decision in *Bryan v. Dennis*.[51] The suit was filed by the heirs of Jacob Bryan to recover three slaves, Dennis, Mary, and Sarah. The Chancery judge ruled in favor of Dennis and Mary, who were siblings, and against Sarah, who was their aunt. The Florida Supreme Court reversed a freedom judgment that had been entered in favor of Dennis and Mary because their master did not post the required bond in connection with their manumission.

The facts apparently were not in dispute: In January 1830, Jacob Bryan, a Georgia resident, moved to Florida, bringing with him slaves including Sarah and Susan, the mother of Dennis and Mary, both of whom later were born in Florida. On November 25, 1842, Bryan executed a manumission deed freeing slaves including Sarah, Dennis, and Mary. Nevertheless, "Bryan never gave bond, as required by law, for the transportation of these negroes beyond the limits of Florida, and ... they continued to reside here until after the death of Bryan, which took place in 1847, he dying intestate."[52]

The Court, in an opinion by Justice Albert Gallatin Semmes, held that the manumission was not valid under Florida law. The Court cited a November 1829 act, which stated that any person manumitting a slave who was brought into Florida after the act's adoption was required to pay two hundred dollars for every slave so manumitted. Before granting the manumission, the master also was required to post a bond, with two or more securities, in a sum equal to the slave's value, to be approved by the Judge of Probate. The bond was to be security for the transportation of the slave out of Florida within thirty days after the manumission. The statute also stated that any slave manumitted contrary to its provisions "shall not be deemed free," but shall be liable to be taken up, under a Circuit Court order, and sold by the sheriff at public sale, with the sale proceeds paid into the state's treasury. No proceedings were ever taken by the state under this statute against the defendants. To the contrary, the legislature, in 1850, passed a special act for the relief of Bryan's heirs, releasing to them the state's right to Bryan's slaves.[53]

Semmes first held that the statute applied to Dennis and Mary, even though they were not brought into Florida, because their mother was brought into the state before they were born. Semmes therefore read the statute against liberty. He applied the statute to slaves who were brought into the state and to their children born in Florida, even though the statute's text did not refer to children who were born in Florida.[54]

Semmes also strictly applied the letter of the law's bonding requirement. He stated that the 1829 act was in effect when Bryan executed the manumission deed. He also found that Bryan did not post the required bond. He thus concluded that: "The bond is a condition precedent to the act of manumission, and without it the deed has no legal existence, and consequently is inoperative in vesting in the contemplated beneficiaries any rights whatsoever."

The court also rejected the freedom claimants' argument "that though the State may have claimed a forfeiture of this property, yet the deed is good as against the grantor and his heirs, and that the latter are estopped, by the act of their ancestor, from asserting any property in these slaves." Semmes stated: "The law is otherwise. The deed, upon its execution, was absolutely void, for all purposes—a mere gratuity, made in contravention of law, and imposing no disabilities on the grantor over this property, further than it remained in possession, *liable* to the claim of the State."[55]

The New Jersey Approach to the Bonding and Manumission Formalities

In contrast, the New Jersey Supreme Court favored liberty when it construed the state's manumission bonding requirement, but favored slavery when it later applied the manumission formality statute. The court applied the bonding requirement in the 1775 case *King v. Esther Barber and others*.[56] That action was a habeas corpus proceeding requiring the defendants to "bring the Body of Beulah, a Negro Girl." The defendant, Esther Barber, and the residuary legatees under the will of Caleb Haines, claimed Beulah as a slave. Beulah was the daughter of David and Dinah, "a Negro Man and a Negro Woman," who "formerly belonged to Caleb Haines." Haines freed both of these slaves before his death, which occurred about the year 1756, before Beulah was born. After Haines died, David, Dinah, and their children lived as free people until the winter of 1774, when the defendants seized Beulah. The defendants claimed that Haines did not post the bond that was then required by New Jersey's 1713-1714 manumission statute. Therefore, the defendants claimed that Haines's manumission was "void."[57]

This was not a frivolous argument. The text of that act regulating slave manumissions stated that masters freeing their "Negro or Mulatto" slaves were required to give security to the king or queen of 200 pounds for each slave, with two sureties, and to pay 20 pounds yearly to each freed slave. The executors of masters freeing slaves by their wills also were required to comply with these provisions "immediately upon proving the said Will and Testament." If the masters or executors refused to comply with these requirements, "the said Manumission [was to] be void, and of none Effect."[58]

The New Jersey Supreme Court, consisting of Chief Justice Frederick Smyth and Justices David Ogden and Richard Stockton, nevertheless decided the case for Beulah. The court heard argument during its May 1775 term. Because the court found the matter to be "a case of first impression, and of considerable importance, the Judges took time to consider of it, and ordered another argument."[59]

The court heard argument again during its November 1775 term. The next day, the two judges in attendance, probably Chief Justice Smyth and Justice Stockton, ordered that Beulah "be delivered up from out of the Custody of the said Esther Barber and others, in which she hath been illegally detained." The court held that the manumission of David and Dinah "was good in law against the said Caleb Haines and those claiming under him," even though Caleb did not post the required bond. Thus, the court concluded that "Beulah is entitled to her Freedom under the said Manumission against Haines and those claiming under him."[60]

The court's opinion was not officially published, but it was reported in the press. The court found that the legislature's intent embodied in the statute "was not to prevent Negroes from being set free, but to prevent the parish from suffering by their being made so, and that the law would receive its full operation by a construction, which indemnifies the parish from the manumitted slave." The newspaper report of the judge's opinion states that they thus found that if they were

to construe the act in such a manner as to make the manumission void, as to the person manumitting, because the law directed such security to be given, or the manumission to be void and of none effect, would be, to prefer a literal construction to the clear intention of the legislature, and that nothing was more common than for Judges to construe an act according to the spirit of it, where the letter and spirit did disagree—That to prefer a literal construction of the act, so as to render the manumission void as to the master, for his neglect of entering into security required, would be, to permit him to illude [sic] the spirit, by resorting to so unjust and iniquitous a principle, as that of punishing another person for the fault he himself had committed, and would promote deceit and imposition, for, by the manumission itself, the Negroe [sic] supposes himself to be perfectly freed, the master by that act intends to make him believe the fact to be so, and to put it in the power of the master, after the Negroe [sic] had exerted his industry, and had procured something considerable for his children, begotten in this supposed state of freedom, to say that Negroe [sic] was not free, because the master, either through design or neglect, had omitted to give the security directed by law, would be a construction too absurd for a Court of Justice to make of any act of the legislature; and that it was a solid distinction, than an act may be good as to one person, and void as to another.[61]

The New Jersey Supreme Court applied this reasoning again after independence, in cases decided in 1782 and 1793.[62]

In contrast, the New Jersey Supreme Court strictly interpreted a 1798 statute that, among other things, required that masters confirm their intent to manumit slaves in a will or by a deed that was signed before two witnesses.[63] The court's 1806 decision in *State v. Emmons*,[64] by a vote of two to one, applied this statute to deny the manumission claims of two slaves, Isaac Emmons and Matthias Cramer. They based their claims on manumission deeds that were witnessed by one person rather than two. The three judges each wrote opinions.[65]

Chief Justice Andrew Kirkpatrick and Justice William S. Pennington interpreted the statute against the claimants. They rejected the claimants' argument that the court should apply the liberal approach that the New Jersey courts, as illustrated by cases including *King v. Esther Barber and others*, had applied to manumission claims asserted under the state's manumission laws. Kirkpatrick stated that the 1798 law was intended to reform evils including "the loose grounds" upon which manumission claims "were frequently made, and the expense and vexation consequent thereupon[.]" He also criticized the earlier court decisions on which the claimants relied, when he noted that applications for freedom were "sometimes but too easily listened to," and thus "they had really become a subject of public complaint, at least in one part of the State[.]"[66]

Justice Pennington agreed that the statute was so clear that he rejected the claimants' lawyer's contention that it should be construed in favor of liberty. Pennington asserted that this "humane and benign" legal principle favoring liberty "can only have operation in doubtful cases; and cannot be set up as a bar to a positive provision in an act of the Legislature." He also noted that in 1798 he was a legislator who opposed the statutory provision at issue. But as a judge, he thought he must enforce this statute, although he also stated: "If the law is a hard one, be it on those who made it[.]"[67]

Justice Rossell's dissent asserted that the court should interpret the statute "in aid of liberty and humanity, (which the law always favors)[.]" He contended that this would have been consistent with precedent in New Jersey. Thus he also stated that his interpretation would advance the "sake of uniformity in our decisions[.]"[68]

Justice Rossell's view in favor of liberty did not prevail, however, even though the legislature in 1804 had adopted New Jersey's gradual emancipation law.[69] Moreover, the New Jersey courts continued to apply the majority's approach to the state's manumission statute long after the gradual emancipation law had been adopted.[70] It was not until 1844 that New Jersey's legislature adopted an act validating manumission deeds witnessed by only one person, provided that no court ruling denying manumission had been entered.[71]

Thus, as Cobb suggested, freedom claimants were at the mercy of the ability of others, often decades before, to understand and comply with the formal legal technicalities that the legislators enacted and that the courts enforced when they considered manumission claims. Justice Rossell's rule of statutory interpretation in favor of liberty did not prevail as the majority rule in New Jersey or in the South. The courts instead applied principles of statutory and deed construction that emphasized form over substance. This approach created barriers that defeated freedom claims contrary to reliable written proof of the masters' intention.

The Slave Choice Cases

The courts decided the cases that we have discussed so far in this chapter under the relatively "liberal" statutory manumission schemes in Southern legal history. Other freedom claimants faced even higher hurdles on the road to liberty when the courts applied statutes that further restricted the masters' power to free their slaves.

In the slave choice or election cases, the slave owners' disappointed would-be heirs objected to will provisions by which the masters expressed their intention to allow their slaves to make choices or elections after the masters' death. These choices fell into two broad categories. In one, the masters expressed their intentions that their slaves remain in bondage, but, after the masters' death, the wills permitted the slaves to select "new" masters. In the other, the masters' wills permitted the slaves to decide whether to live free out of their home state, usually in Liberia, or to remain slaves at home after their masters' death.[72]

The majority of the decisions enforced both of these choice provisions without too much controversy.[73] The real issue in these cases, however, was not whether the courts would enforce the slave's right to choose; it was whether the courts would enforce the master's right to allow the slave the choice.

For example, in the 1860 pro-choice decision of *Milton (of color) v. McKarney*,[74] the Missouri courts construed the following provision in John McKarney's August 1833 will:

> As to the residue of my slaves, to-wit, Marietta and her five children, Sam, Phebe, Nance, George, and her young child, with all her increase, I will and bequeath them to my beloved wife Margaret during her natural life, with a request that she attend strictly to their morals, and instruct them all to read the English language; but I expressly prohibit the sale of them under any circumstances; and after the death of the said Margaret, all of them that are twenty-one years of age are by me set free, on condition that they will enter under the care of the Colonization Society and emigrate to the American colony in Liberia, and as fast as they or their increase arrive at the said age of twenty-one years and comply with the above condition, I hereby set free. All of them that prefer remaining with any of my children, after the death of my said wife, to complying with the foregoing condition, are permitted to do so; but I am to be distinctly understood, that they are not to be bought or sold even amongst my own children, much less to strangers.

The plaintiff, Milton, was a son of Marietta. He sued for his freedom when he was twenty-one years old. Milton alleged that Margaret McKarney had died and that he therefore was free according to John McKarney's will. "He declares his willingness to comply with the conditions of said will and prays a judgment of liberation. To this petition there was a demurrer, and it was sustained."[75]

The Missouri Supreme Court affirmed the lower court order dismissing the complaint, finding that Milton was not entitled to "a judgment of immediate liberation."[76] Nevertheless, Judge William Barclay Napton wrote that the provision in the will affording the slaves a choice was not invalid. This was so because "[i]t is the act of the master, and not of the slave, which effectuates the emancipation. If the master can emancipate upon condition at all, why may not the choice of the slave constitute that condition, as well as any other event or act with which the slave has no concern?" Napton thus held that "[t]he legal incapacity of the slave to make a choice is a theory designed to recognize and enforce the legal dominion of the master, and it is a perversion of the theory to make it have the effect of diminishing the extent of that dominion."[77]

But beginning with the 1848 Alabama Supreme Court decision in *Carroll v. Brumby, Adm'r*,[78] some courts began to hold to the contrary. The relevant clause of John F. Wallis's will stated that, as to his "kind and faithful servants, Jane Harper and her children ... it is my will that they be permitted to go to Africa, their passage paid," with support for two years. "If however, my said servants prefer to remain subject to my said daughter, as they are to me, they may be permitted to do so, but in no event shall they be sold or deprived of their privilege before or after the death of my daughter."[79]

The court's opinion by Justice Edmund S. Dargan invalidated this bequest. "It is true [that the testator] did intend to give [the slaves] the option of freedom or servitude, but they have not the legal capacity to choose—the law forbids this[.]"[80]

The courts in Virginia and Georgia later followed the Alabama court's reasoning and invalidated slave choice or election provisions. The Virginia Supreme Court of Appeals, by three to two votes, adopted the no choice rule in its 1858 decisions in *Bailey v. Poindexter Ex'r*[81] and *Williamson v. Coalter's Ex'rs*.[82] In *Bailey*, the court construed the November 1835 will of John L. Poindexter. He loaned his plantation and his slaves upon his death to his wife Jaqueline for her life. The will also stated that upon Jaqueline's death, John's slaves would "have their choice of being emancipated or sold publicly."[83] Virginia's Supreme Court reversed a judgment in favor of freedom for John's slaves and their children.[84]

Judge William Daniel, writing also for President J. J. Allen and Judge George N. Lee, held that the Virginia cases that assumed that masters could permit slaves to choose freedom or a new master did not squarely address the issue. The majority in essence distinguished or "overruled" earlier decisions in which the Virginia courts apparently assumed that masters could in their wills bestow upon their slaves the right to choose freedom or a new master.[85]

Accordingly, Daniel felt free to invalidate the will's provision by which John gave to his slaves the election to be free. He wrote:

> When we assent to the general proposition, as I think we must do, that our
> slaves have no civil or social rights; that they have no legal capacity to

make, discharge or assent to contracts; that though a master enter into the form of an agreement with his slave to manumit him, and the slave proceed fully to perform all required of him in the agreement, he is without remedy in case the master refuse to comply with his part of the agreement; and that a slave cannot take anything under a decree or will except his freedom, we are led necessarily to the conclusion that nothing short of the exhibition of a positive enactment, or of legal decisions having equal force, can demonstrate the capacity of a slave to exercise an election in respect to his manumission.[86]

Thus, he concluded: "Any testamentary effort of a master to clothe his slave with such power is an effort to accomplish a legal impossibility."

Daniel expressed a concern that the will would in effect "create a new species of property unknown to the law." He also wrote that masters could not be

allowed to introduce anomalies into the ranks under which the population of the state is ranged and classified by its constitution and laws. It is for the master to determine whether to continue to treat his slaves as property, as chattels, or, in the mode prescribed by law, to manumit them, and thus place them in that class of persons to which the freed negroes of the state are assigned. But he cannot impart to his slaves, as such, for any period, the rights of freedmen. He cannot endow, with powers of such import as are claimed for the slaves here, persons whose *status* or condition, in legal definition and intendment, exists in the denial to them of the attributes of any social or civil capacity whatever.

Judge Daniel recognized that masters could write their wills after ascertaining whether their slaves wanted to be freed upon the masters' death. In contrast, he found that John *"has endeavored to clothe his slaves with the uncontrollable and irrevocable power of determining for themselves whether they shall be manumitted. And in doing so, he has, I think, essayed the vain attempt to reconcile obvious and inherent contradictions."*[87]

Judge Richard C. L. Moncure, also writing for Judge Green B. Samuels, dissented. He stated that it was "certainly true" that "slaves have no civil rights or legal capacity," but he rejected the conclusion that slaves therefore cannot elect between slavery and freedom when they make that election after their master's death in accordance with their master's will. The slave's election thus was not an "exercise of a civil right or capacity."[88] He also stated his disagreement with the majority's reading of the precedent that Judge Daniel distinguished.[89]

In *Williamson*, the court construed the August 4, 1857 will of Hannah H. Coalter. Hannah's estate was substantial; upon her death she owned 93 slaves, and the rest of her estate was estimated to be worth between fifteen and twenty thousand dollars. She freed unconditionally her "faithful servant Charles," and directed her executors "to provide him with a fund sufficient to take him to such state or country as he may elect to live in, and pay to him an annuity of one hundred dollars during his life." Her will also directed that "the balance of my negroes ... be manumitted on the first day of January, 1858." She authorized her executors to raise a fund out of her estate sufficient to settle these slaves "in Liberia, or any other free state or country in which they may elect to live[.]" The will added, however, "that if any of my said servants shall prefer to remain in Virginia instead of accepting the foregoing provision, it is my desire that they shall be permitted, by my executors, to select among my relations their respective owners[.]"[90]

The Supreme Court reversed the lower court's pro-freedom judgment, in a majority opinion by President Allen, joined by Judges Daniel and Lee. Allen cited the court's decision in *Bailey*, and distinguished the earlier decisions that apparently supported the lower court's ruling.[91] He concluded that the will's operation as an instrument of manumission "is made to depend on the choice of the slaves," and he voided the provision affording to Hannah's slaves that choice. Judge Moncure again dissented, joined by Judge Samuels.[92]

In 1896, the Virginia Supreme Court of Appeals again addressed this issue, in a case in which Bob Jones, who was a slave of Philip H. Jones, sought payment from his former master's estate of an annuity provided for him in Philip's pro-choice will. The court in effect reversed these anti-choice decisions, stating that they were "in conflict with the prior decisions of the court, two judges dissenting in each case, and are so contrary to reason and to justice that we should hesitate long before we hold that a slave could not elect to be free when that right was given him by his owner."[93]

In contrast, the Georgia Supreme Court, without any dissenters, followed the no-choice trend in its 1860 decision in *Curry v. Curry*.[94] In that case, the heirs of Wiley Curry filed a caveat challenging the probate of two provisions of Wiley's will. One of these provisions stated:

> Item 2d. I give my servants, John, a man of yellow complexion [sic], and Betsy, a woman of yellow complexion [sic], to my executor, hereinafter named, in trust to carry said negroes, immediately after my death, to some one of the non-slaveholding States of this Union, as the said executor may select, or to whomsoever said servants may elect for a master in this State, before John T. Stephens.[95]

The Georgia Supreme Court affirmed a judgment invalidating this clause.

The court's opinion, written by newly sworn-in Justice Richard F. Lyon, held that the will's provision permitting slaves to choose a master violated the purposes of Georgia's statute prohibiting all manumissions:

> The bequest was in fact, placing a charter of the liberty of these negroes in their hands to go throughout the State and trade and traffic on it until such person should be found who would give them the largest liberty for the least consideration; one in whom they could confide, who would hold them nominally as slaves, while for all practical purpose they would be free. There is no time fixed within which they must elect. In the interim, what is their condition, slaves or free? Neither the one or the other—*quasi slave-quasi free*.

Lyon found that this state of *quasi*-freedom "is obnoxious to the provisions of the Act of 19th Dec., 1818." He relied on the legislators' intentions as expressed in the Act's preamble:

> "*And whereas*, divers persons of color, who are slaves by the Laws of this State, having never been manumitted in conformity to the same, are nevertheless in the full exercise and enjoyment of all the rights and privileges of free persons of color, without being subject to the duties and obligations incident to such persons, thereby constituting a class of people equally dangerous to the free citizens of this State, and destructive of the comfort and happiness of the slave population thereof, which it is the duty of the Legislature by all just and lawful means to suppress."

Lyons wrote that, according to Wiley's will,

> these negroes are slaves, yet they are in the full exercise and enjoyment of all the rights and privileges of free persons of color, without the burdens. They have a higher and greater right than the free negro, for the social right and legal capacity of election to be free is in their hands. I cannot imagine a condition of the negro more hurtful to a proper and necessary regulation of the slave population, or one more obnoxious to the provision of the Act.

He also warned that if the court were to permit "such a bequest ... of these slaves,"

> there would be no end to which the system would be carried. As emancipation is now prohibited by Statute, whether to take effect in or out of the State, this plan would be instantly laid hold of and followed as a happy expedient by persons, who, from improper relations with these slaves, or from other causes, desire after their death that the condition of the slaves should be altered, until a large class of this sort of population will be established throughout the State, obnoxious to the Laws, dangerous, mischievous and corrupting to the slaves. New Legislation would be required to abolish the system, not to eradicate the evil, for that would be impossible. The effect would continue, like free negrodom, a perpetual blight on the institution.

Thus he suggested: "How much better is it to strike at the evil as we do here, while it is yet in the bud, and break it up, root and branch, before it has laid a basis for its own propagation."[96]

Lyon also justified the court's holding, "should we be mistaken in this view of the question," by referring to the *Bumbry, Bailey,* and *Williamson* cases as authority for the proposition that slaves had no legal capacity to choose a master, "and the testator could not clothe them, as slaves, with any such power or capacity[.]"[97] Lyon also noted Georgia's 1859 act that by then prohibited all manumissions, and that statute may have at least in part influenced the court's thinking.[98]

Nash stated that the *Curry* decision "overruled sub silentio the earlier holding that slaves could make such an election."[99] Indeed, Lyon's opinion did not distinguish or even cite the Georgia Supreme Court's 1854 and 1855 decisions in *Cleland v. Waters*.[100] The court's majority, among other rulings, upheld a provision of George M. Waters's will that directed Waters's executors to obtain approval to free his slaves in Georgia, and if they could not obtain that approval, "to send the said slaves out of the State of Georgia, to such place as they may select[.]"[101]

Justice Lumpkin's 1855 *Cleland v. Waters* opinion cited and distinguished the *Bumbry* decision. Lumpkin noted that Waters's will allowed his slaves to select the destination where they would be freed instead of a choice of freedom or liberty. Lumpkin also cited several pro-choice decisions, including an 1830 Georgia Superior Court case, *Jordan v. Bradley*.[102] He stated that these precedents supported his conclusion "when this case was last up ... that extra-territorial emancipation was not forbidden by the Statutes of 1801 and 1818."[103]

Lumpkin nevertheless made it clear that his decision was grounded on his reading of the legislature's intention. He took the occasion to "state empathically" his personal policy opposition to "all *post mortem* manumission":

> We may not be able to prevent expatriation of the living—to restrain the master in his lifetime from removing whithersoever he pleases with his property; but when the owner has kept them as long as he can enjoy them; shall he, from an ignorance of the scriptural basis upon which the institution of slavery rests, or from a total disregard to the peace and welfare of the community which survive him, invoke the aid of the Courts of this State to carry into execution his false and fatal views of humanity? Is not every agitation of these cases in our Courts attended with mischief? Is not every exode of slaves from the interior to the seaboard, thence to be transported to a land of freedom, productive of evil? Can any doubt its tendency? Are there not now in our midst large gangs of slaves who expected emancipation by the will of their owners, and who believe they have been unjustly deprived of the boon? Are such likely to be good servants? On the contrary, are they not likely to sow the seeds of insubordination, perhaps of revolt, amongst the slaves in their neighborhood?

> Deeply impressed with these views, I have earnestly solicited the immediate attention of the present Legislature, (1855-'6) through the Chairman of the Judiciary Committee of the Senate to the subject. Still, whatever may be the strength of my convictions, I feel bound by the construction which has been put upon the law by the eminent Judges who have preceded me, until the Legislature see fit to intervene.[104]

Uncharacteristically, Lumpkin did not offer an opinion in *Curry* to explain why he came to a different conclusion when the court directly addressed the slave choice issue.[105]

The anti-slave choice decisions thus rebuked masters for giving this gratuity to those held in slavery. They are among the decisions in which the courts and legislators found it necessary to clamp down on masters who were too lenient in their relations with "negrodom."

The judges in the anti-choice cases focused on the proof of the master's intent, but they disregarded that intent to further what they perceived to be the public policies that increasingly regulated or prohibited manumission. These differing results may, to some extent, also have reflected the judges' dissimilar views about manumission, but not necessarily differences in their commitment to slavery and the master's authority over his or her slaves.

The judges who enforced the slave choice wills included North Carolina Justice Thomas Ruffin, whom Nash called "that rigorous expounder of the absolutist theory of slavery."[106] The pro-choice judges were not, as Nash implied, "'namby-pamby-on-slavery' types."[107] *They* did not vest slaves with a legal right to choose a new master or freedom; the judges instead enforced the *master's* right to give the slave that choice as a gratuity—and not by any right—just like any other gift of manumission.

The Send/Free and Free/Send Cases

The send/free and free/send issue arose in the antebellum cases interpreting wills in which masters expressed their intention in favor of the foreign manumission of their slaves. A send/free will directed the master's executor to send his or her slaves to a free state or a free country, such as Canada or Liberia, and then to free these slaves. A free/send will, on the other hand, declared that the master's slaves were to be freed upon the master's death, on a future date, or upon the happening of a contingency, and that the executor must then send the former slaves to a place where they may live as free people.

In a state that permitted manumission within the state, neither type of will would have created any controversy. But, as noted in chapter three, the Southern legislatures adopted statutes barring in-state manumissions, and some even prohibited all manumission. Accordingly, the send/free and free/send wills were controversial in states that prohibited in-state manumission or manumission by will.

The free/send wills caused the most serious concern to Southern jurists. Some courts held that a will that directed the executor to free the master's slaves and then send them to a free state or country did not interfere with their state's public policy if the law prohibited domestic manumission. These judges concluded that the testator's intention was consistent with the state's policy requiring that the freed slaves ultimately be removed from the state.[108] "The object," North Carolina Justice Richmond Pearson wrote regarding the freed slave removal laws, "was to make them go away, so as to not add to the number of free negroes, and the law imposes no restriction and continues no incapacity, except so far as is necessary to accomplish that object. With this saving, the humanity of our laws strikes off his fetters at once, and says, go 'enjoy life, liberty and the pursuit of happiness.'"[109]

The Georgia Supreme Court, however, did not share this 'live and let live as long as you leave' attitude. Instead, it invalidated what the court perceived to be a free/send will in the 1857 decision in *Drane v. Beall*.[110] The case arose when the next of kin of Thomas E. Beall filed a caveat in April 1856 challenging the probate of Beall's will of June 13, 1853. The caveat alleged that various provisions of the will were invalid.[111]

The will's alleged invalid free/send provision stated: *"Item Fifteenth:* I will that all my negroes shall receive their freedom and be emancipated from slavery, except those hereafter mentioned. And such negroes so freed and emancipated from slavery shall be sent to Liberia, California, or any free State or Territory in the United States of America, as they choose to elect." Two related clauses stated:

> *Item Sixteenth:* If those of my negroes freed and emancipated from slavery shall choose to go to Liberia, then in that case, I will to the Colonization Society the sum of fifteen hundred dollars, to be expended in transporting them there; and if they choose to go to California, or any other free State or Territory in the United States of America, then and in that case, their passage shall be paid to the place they shall elect, by my executors, hereafter named.

> *Item Seventeenth:* It is my will and desire that those negroes that I have given their freedom and emancipated, shall be kept on my plantation for the term of four years after my death, for the purpose of raising funds, and after defraying all expenses on the plantation during those four years, then the net proceeds shall be equally divided among those of my negroes freed and emancipated from slavery, share and share alike, agreeable to their situation, some being old, and some being women and children, will require more, whilst some are young, can go to work immediately and make their support; and this division is left to my executors, hereafter named, to exercise a proper and equitable division between them all. And it is my will and desire that my executors, out of the above named funds, shall furnish each of the negroes above eight years of age, two good blankets each; and the whole of the negroes freed and emancipated from slavery shall receive two good suits of clothes, a hat, a pair of shoes; and those of my negroes freed and emancipated from slavery, under eight years of age, one good blanket each.[112]

Superior Court Judge William W. Holt, on December 18, 1856, rejected the challenge to the will as a matter of law.

Judge Holt held that clause 15 was valid because "[i]t is plain" that Beall intended that "the manumission is to take effect out of the State."[113] According to Holt, Beall took "special care to direct" that the freed slaves be removed from Georgia, and he "provide[ed] for the expense of it, and for a temporary support in their new home." Holt concluded that the four-year term before the slaves were to be removed, as stated in paragraph 17, was "not an unreasonable length of time to prepare for the important change designed in their condition, the state of slavery is strictly preserved. They have neither the power over their own time, nor over the proceeds of their labor. The right of this testamentary disposition of slaves by their owners is as unquestionable as the right to remove them while the owner lives."[114]

The Georgia Supreme Court reversed these findings. Justice Lumpkin wrote the Court's opinion. He stated that the "only question" that clause 15 and the other challenged clauses raised was whether "the manumission of the slaves [was] to take effect at the death of the testator, and consequently within the State? Does the will, in other words, contemplate their removal, not to *acquire*, but to *enjoy* the freedom which it supposes to be conferred by virtue of the declared wishes of the testator? It seems to us, that there can be but one answer given to these questions." He stated that the will's words

> are too plain to admit of doubt or difficulty. That the emancipation be-
> queathed by the will, was intended to be *enjoyed* in Liberia, California, or
> some other free State or Territory, will be readily conceded: but that it was
> to take effect in Georgia, at the death of the testator, is clear, beyond cavil;
> and whether you construe the 15th item *per se*, or as explained by the
> context, the same inference is irresistible.

> It never occurred to the testator, for a moment, that it was wrong to give
> his slaves present freedom by his will, provided they were to be carried out
> of the State, within what he supposed to be a reasonable time, to enjoy it.
> He did not intend to violate the law. But the mistake he committed was in
> supposing that a gift of freedom, *in præsenti*, to his slaves, to vest at his
> death, although it be but for a moment of time, was not unlawful. In whom
> was the title of these slaves, from the death of the testator to the time con-
> templated for their removal? Not in themselves, for they were incapable of
> taking; not in the Executors, although they were clothed with a *quasi* trust
> or agency respecting them. The title vested, *eo-instanti*, at the death of
> Beall, in his personal representatives, in trust for the residuary legatees or
> distributees, and it is not in the power of the Courts to divest it. For myself,
> I entertain not a doubt but that a testator may by his will direct his Execu-
> tor to remove his negroes to some other country, where they may acquire,
> as well as enjoy their freedom, and that the performance of such trust, will
> be permitted, if not enforced against such Executor; I am equally well
> satisfied, that the bequest of freedom to slaves in this case is void, as it was
> to take effect in this State, and the slaves are made the legatees of their
> own freedom, a boon they are incapable of taking.[115]

In view of this holding invalidating clause 15, Lumpkin found that it was not "necessary to dwell at length upon the 17th item, directing the slaves, to whom the testator had given their freedom, to be kept on his plantation for four years after his death, to provide for an outfit."[116]

Nevertheless, Lumpkin expressed his concerns about that clause's legality as well:

> It is said that a reasonable time must be allowed, because some time must
> elapse, longer or shorter, according to circumstances, despite the testator,
> as in case of caveat, suit in chancery, possible insolvency of the estate, &c.,
> and this is certainly true. But the time required for the meeting and over-

coming these and other unforeseen contingencies, is one thing; and for the testator to direct by his will, that they shall be kept within the State for a specified period, four, six or ten years, to accumulate funds to defray the expenses of their transportation, and support them in their new home, is quite a different thing. This point has never been distinctly made in any previous case. By the act of 1818, already quoted, every will, deed, whether of trust or otherwise, contract, agreement or stipulation, or other instrument in writing, or by parol, made and executed for the purpose of effecting or endeavoring to effect the manumission of any slave or slaves, either directly, by conferring or attempting to confer freedom on such slave or slaves, or indirectly and virtually, by allowing or attempting to secure to them the privilege of enjoying the profits of their labor and skill, shall be utterly null and void. Cobb 991.

Suppose it be true then, that the hand of the Executor is upon these slaves, as the hand of the master, until they leave Georgia, and that they are subject to his control, still can it be denied, that during this four years, these slaves are working for themselves? That they are enjoying the profits of their own skill and labor?

Lumpkin concluded that "principle and policy, not to say positive law, are opposed to this whole scheme of emancipation."[117]

Thus, Lumpkin found the send/free and free/send distinction to be of substantive importance; this was not just a matter of imprecise drafting leading to doubts about the testator's intent. Lumpkin objected to the free/send wills because they, in effect, give the slaves a form of *quasi*-freedom effective upon the testator's death. To Lumpkin, free and send wills violated the policy behind the statute prohibiting in-state manumission because slaves were not competent to take title to themselves. Therefore, when the master died, title in the slaves vested in the executors in trust for the beneficiaries upon the testator's death. Lumpkin was concerned that this would create a kind of *quasi*-freedom in the former slaves until they were sent to a free state.

Mark Tushnet likened this close analysis of the free/send wills to legal formalism, which he stated would encourage lawyers for slave owners to practice more precise will drafting.[118] But legal formalism can have substantive purposes, and it had real world effects on people held as slaves who were denied their freedom because of this interpretation defeating their masters' intention.[119]

Most Southern courts nevertheless found the send/free bequests or deeds to be enforceable because the judges concluded that they did not defeat the state's anti-manumission policy.[120] For example, the 1858 North Carolina Supreme Court decision in *Redding v. Long*[121] rejected a challenge to a deed that created a trust. The deed, dated September 23, 1852, was executed by Anne L. Woods. She conveyed three slaves, who were not named in the report of the case other than a slave identified as Ellen, to Osmond F. Long, in trust for Woods during her life. Upon Woods's death, the deed stated that Long was to send the slaves "to Liberia or some free State, if [the slaves] make a choice to go, within one year after my death, and if Ellen should have any children, they are to go with her[.]" If the slaves decided to remain in North Carolina, "then they are all to belong to Alexander Findley, with the increase of Ellen, if any[.]" Woods died intestate in 1857, and the slaves elected to go to Liberia or to a free state. The administrator of Woods's estate, Robert Redding, filed an action seeking to void the deed. He alleged that the deed was obtained by undue influence or other unfair means, and that the deed was an illegal manumission. He sought possession of the slaves and an accounting for the profits earned after Woods died.[122]

The North Carolina Supreme Court rejected Redding's claims in an opinion by Justice Ruffin. Ruffin summarily dismissed Redding's undue influence claim. He also found that the deed creating the trust was not void, even though North Carolina law by then required a master or executor to seek superior court permission before freeing a slave.

> Neither a deed of emancipation by the owner, nor a direction in a will to that effect, constitutes a valid emancipation here, until allowed by the court, as prescribed in the statute. But when a deed is made by the owner of a slave to another person, upon a trust, to have the slave emancipated, there, the trustee becomes the owner, and he may, as such, either proceed to procure the emancipation here, under our law, or carry the slave to another country, where he may be free without observing the ceremonies which we require. It is totally immaterial to this purpose, by what kind of instrument the trust, for emancipation, may be created, whether a deed or a will. It is most commonly, indeed, a will, because most persons wish to keep the control of their property as long as they live, and, therefore, prefer a revocable, to an irrevocable instrument, on such occasions. The question, however, on each, is always the same; namely, whether the particular kind of emancipation prescribed, or contemplated, contravenes the provisions or the policy of our law. If it does not, the trust is not illegal, and will be executed; while, if it does, that trust becomes ineffectual, and will result to the donor, or go over to some other person, according to the limitations contained in the instrument.

Ruffin enforced the trust because he found that "by repeated decisions, it is the settled law of this State, that such a trust as the one before us, for carrying the negroes out of North Carolina, to live as free persons, in a free country, is not illegal, but perfectly valid."[123]

In Georgia, however, the pro-slavery ideology of the Supreme Court Justices, including Lumpkin, came to oppose even send/free freedom bequests because of the statute law and public policy that came to prohibit all attempts at manumission, both domestic and foreign. These judges perceived any manumission of slaves, even if it occurred in Liberia or Canada, as a threat to the South's slaveholding regime.

Justice Lumpkin expressed these extreme anti-manumission views in his 1858 opinion in *Sanders v. Ward*.[124] That case arose when the plaintiff, Elizabeth Sanders, filed a caveat challenging the probate of Nathaniel T. Myrick's June

21, 1856 send/free will. She objected to the following two provisions in the will:

> *Item Second:* I devise and bequeath, and require my executors hereinafter named, to remove my servants Owen, Elizabeth, Joseph, Samuel, William, Flora, George, Harriett and Leonard, to some free State, as my executors may choose and select, as they may deem proper, then and there to manumit and set them, my said named servants, free, to act for themselves, them and their heirs forever.

> *Item Third:* My executors hereinafter named shall purchase in such free State as they may select, a parcel of land sufficient for the above named servants, with a supply of provisions, household and kitchen furniture, farming utensils, horses or mules, cattle, hogs and sheep, with the money arising from the sale of my estate, as above directed, and shall pay over any surplus after paying for the removal aforesaid, land and other articles mentioned, to my servant Owen, to be manumitted aforesaid, each one to have and own an equal portion of said land and other articles to be purchased as aforesaid, and also an equal portion of the money remaining after the removal and settlement aforesaid.

After a trial, a jury found the will was valid and the plaintiff filed an appeal.[125]

Justices Lumpkin and Charles J. McDonald voted to affirm the judgment. Each wrote opinions, over the dissent of Justice Henry L. Benning. Lumpkin and McDonald chose not to overrule precedents, including an 1830 Superior Court decision in *Jordan v. Bradley*,[126] which they admitted held that a send/free will did not contravene Georgia's anti-domestic manumission policy under the 1801 and 1818 statutes.[127]

Lumpkin concluded that, although these statutes prohibited domestic manumission, they did not prohibit foreign manumission. He added that this interpretation had historically been the prevailing view:

> Had the entire State been polled in 1818, ten men would not have been found opposed to foreign manumission. Wm. H. Crawford, who decided on his circuit, and afterwards in convention of the Judges, in the *Bradley Will Case*, that emancipation in Liberia was not forbidden by the Acts of 1801 and 1818, was a practicing and prominent lawyer, and if I mistake not, a member of the Legislature in 1801. He was familiar with the condition of things and of public opinion at that period, and he and his compeers repudiated the forced construction now attempted, for the first time, to be put upon the Acts of 1801 and 1818. The North and South had not been arrayed at that period in hostile antagonism to each other, touching African slavery. If this change of circumstances demands a new policy to be introduced — and for myself I think it does — let it, as I have said and written again and again, be inaugurated by the Legislature, and not by the Courts.[128]

Lumpkin thus based his decision on deference to the legislative language and to precedent. In a remarkable passage, however, he also made known his own policy views, and called for legislative reform to close this loophole:

> During the session of the Legislature before the last, I addressed a communication to the eminent counsel who argues so earnestly against the validity of this will, and who was at that time chairman of the Senate's Judiciary Committee, calling his attention to this subject, and suggesting the propriety of passing a law forbidding all *post mortem* manumission. Were I a legislator, I should vote for such a bill. So many unforeseen obstacles arise, that it is far better that the master should, during his lifetime, consummate his scheme as to the future disposition of his slaves. From some cause or other, my friend took no action upon the matter. I have been informed by a distinguished Representative of the House, that a bill was introduced in the other branch of the General Assembly, and *voted down by an overwhelming majority of that body.* I have not consulted the journals, but take it for granted the statement is true.

Lumpkin stated that the court therefore should not "inaugurate this new policy," so that it will not "be forever importuned and harrassed [sic] with this subject, at each change of incumbents upon this Bench[.]" Lumpkin concluded that the issue was "settled, until the Legislature see fit to intervene. Let that body speak, and no one will take more pleasure than myself in obeying their behest. Sworn as I am, not to make but to administer the law, I never can torture the law, as it now stands, to a purpose for which *I know* it never was intended."[129]

Lumpkin stated that he had "no partiality for foreign any more than domestic manumission. I believe that policy, as well as humanity for the negro, forbid both." He expressed his special objection to "the colonization of our negroes upon our northwestern frontier. They facilitate the escape of our fugitive slaves. In case of civil war, they would become an element of strength to the enemy, as well as of annoyance to ourselves."[130]

Lumpkin's calls for the legislature to remedy the situation did not fall on deaf ears much longer. The legislators in 1859 responded. They adopted an act that prohibited all postmortem manumissions.[131]

The "Monstrous" Cy Pres Doctrine

Two related types of wills illustrate how judges could put into effect their pro-manumission or anti-manumission preferences. In the first, the masters' wills called for slaves to be freed in the forum slave states, and these local manumissions later came to be disallowed. In the second, the wills required that the freed slaves be removed to free states that no longer allowed free black migration.

Some courts applied the doctrine of *cy pres* in these situations in favor of liberty to effectuate the testator's overall intent to free his or her slaves, but others did not. This rule of will and trust construction generally allows a court to fashion a remedy to do "the next best thing" to enforce the testator's general intent when it is impossible or illegal to enforce the document exactly as it was written.[132] The court must determine if "it appears that the intent of the donor was sufficiently broad that he would have preferred the required modification be made rather than have the entire gift fail."[133]

Thus, in the first example cited above, the courts could permit the executor to remove a master's slaves to another state where the slaves could be freed or settle as free blacks. In the second, the court would permit the executor to in effect change the freed slaves' destination stated in the will or trust to one that allowed free black migration.[134]

The Georgia Supreme Court, in 1855, rejected the *cy pres* doctrine and invalidated the freedom bequests in the 1846 will of Robert Bledsoe.[135] In relevant part, Bledsoe's will directed that his executors buy "a sufficiency of good, arable land," either in Indiana or Illinois, for all of his slaves "to locate upon and cultivate, with a sufficiency of land for timber and firewood included[.]" And "within a reasonable time" after Bledsoe died, his executors were to remove all of these slaves "to said tract or settlement of land," which Bledsoe recommended be purchased in his executors' names "for fear that [the slaves] might be defrauded out of the land, or squander it themselves." The will also directed that after the slaves were resettled "west of the Ohio river [sic], that they be furnished an outfit of farming utensils, including the wagons and teams used in their removal as a part of said outfit," and that a year's provision be supplied for the subsistence of these slaves, after their removal.[136]

Nathan Bass qualified as executor under this will. He filed a bill for direction, stating, among other things, that Indiana, before Bledsoe's death, and Illinois, after his death, "passed laws prohibiting the introduction of negroes into either of those States; that it was impossible, therefore, to execute that portion of the will." The trial judge, Robert V. Hardeman, held that the clause freeing the slaves "was not void under the Acts of 1801 and 1818; and that it could be carried into effect by the negroes being sent to some other State or Territory, west or north-west of the Ohio river [sic]." The Georgia Supreme Court reversed this decision on appeal.[137]

All three Justices wrote opinions. They all agreed that the *cy pres* doctrine should not be applied to permit the slaves to be freed. Justice Lumpkin wrote the first opinion. He stated that: "It appears that Indiana, by her Constitution and laws, and Illinois, by Statute, have prohibited, under severe pains and penalties, the introduction of negroes into either of those States—the former *before* and the latter *subsequent* to the death of the testator." Thus, he concluded that will's freedom bequest cannot be carried out "according to the expressed wish of the testator. And that, alone, would seem to be, as it ought to be, conclusive of the case. But the Courts of Great Britain, and to some extent of this country, whether wisely or unwisely, reasonably or otherwise, have taken it upon themselves, under certain circumstances, to perform a most delicate and responsible office; that is, to make another will for the testator, where his declared intention necessarily fails." Lumpkin stated that the court would apply this *cy pres* doctrine, "[h]owever revolting this doctrine may be to common sense or repugnant to our own sense of right, we are content to administer it[.]"

Lumpkin read Bledsoe's will narrowly. He found that Bledsoe would have intended that his slaves and their progeny remain in bondage rather than be free anywhere other than Indiana or Illinois:

> Can it be collected from the will, that the paramount object of the testator was to give freedom to his negroes, and that Indiana and Illinois were selected only as the mode of carrying out that paramount purpose? We may conjecture so, especially as to substitute some other State or Territory northwest of the Ohio would be but a slight alteration of that which is directed, but which cannot be performed. But the testator has not said so, and neither this nor any other Court can undertake to determine, judicially, what would have been his will provided he had foreseen what has happened. I might be willing to have my sons educated at Princeton College; and yet, prefer that the whole of them, were they numerous as the progeny of old Priam, should grow up in ignorance of the alphabet, rather than they should be taught at Yale. Still, these institutions are within less than a day's journey of each other.[138]

Lumpkin apparently was serious with this analogy between his views of the relative merits of an education at Yale and Princeton (from which he graduated), and Bledsoe's affinity for Indiana and Illinois as the only destinations for his freed slaves:

> General Bledsoe was a large landed proprietor in Indiana and Illinois, and had often visited those States. He is known to have entertained the most inveterate hostility to the neighboring State of Ohio. The differences which existed between the two former and every other north-western State may have constituted the sole motive with the testator for making the disposition which he did of his slaves. I do not pretend to say that this was so. It is sufficient that it may have been. Speaking for the last time by his last will, and without manifesting, by a single syllable, any general intent to manumit his slaves, and without once using the words "freedom," "emancipation" or any other term indicative, that any such object was uppermost in his mind, his sole and definite proposition is to have his negroes removed to Indiana or Illinois, and located on land to be bought for them there. Liberty, of course, would be the necessary terms of this disposition; and such, unques-tionably, was contemplated by the testator. But to hold that he would have conferred the same boon, taking all the risks and disadvantages attendant on the change, anywhere else, is to assume what is incapable of proof. Upon this subject, he has not spoken and must remain silent forever; and we must be satisfied to continue ignorant of his wishes, further than he has seen fit to reveal them. All beyond is *terra ignota*, mere vague surmise, upon which we dare not act.

Lumpkin suggested that, "[h]ad the testator directed his negroes to be manumitted in some place where they could, by law, enjoy this real or *imaginary* blessing, and there stopped, his will might have been executed; certainly it could have been in England by the King as *parens patriæ*; and upon the information of the Attorney General, a scheme would have been devised for this purpose. Had he declared a general intent to free his slaves, and given specific directions for its execution, which could not be carried out, as in the present instance, still a Court of Chancery would execute the general intent as nearly as possible, in some other way." Lumpkin found, however, "that here no such general purpose is manifested; but a precise disposition made upon the testator's own plan. The Courts, in such case, cannot execute the will *Cypres* [sic]; because the testator having declared a clear and intelligible purpose, and nothing more, that purpose, and none other, *is his will*."[139]

Lumpkin also stated his own personal biases concerning manumission and the African race, which may have colored his own views about Bledsoe's intentions and what he called this "revolting" doctrine of will construction:

> I will only add that, as a man, I do not regret the failure of this bequest. Look at the stringency of the laws of Indiana and Illinois and other Northwestern States, against persons of color, and reflect upon their thriftlessness [sic] when not controlled by superior intelligence and forethought, and what friend of the African or of humanity, would desire to see these children of the sun, who luxuriate in a tropical climate and perish with cold in higher latitudes, brought in close contact and competition with the hardy and industrious population which teem in the territory northwest of the Ohio, and who loathe negroes as they would so many lepers? Courts should not be astute in so construing wills as to doom them to such a destiny. A stern and inexorable State policy equally forbids it. (*See Bryan vs. Walton*, 14 *Ga. Rep.* 185, 206.)

Lumpkin also rejected the suggestion that the slaves be transported to Liberia, stating "the wildest and most latitudinous application of the *Cypres* [sic] *doctrine*, could never, *under this will*, justify such a project as that."[140] Thus it appears that, in Lumpkin's eyes, *cy pres* was a revolting legal principle because it would lead to excessive judicial power and, at least in manumission cases, more free blacks.

Justice Starnes's concurring opinion stated his general agreement with some, but not all, of Lumpkin's beliefs:

> I, myself, doubt the policy of permitting free persons of color to be sent into the Northern and Western States of this Union, to increase the number of paupers and aid in swelling the abolition chorus by their votes and voices. Yet, several interesting and most cogent reasons can be assigned, why it would not be for the best interests of the slave holding citizens of the State to prohibit the removal of slaves from the State to any place whatever. But this is a subject which, to be properly treated, would require more to be said and shown than would become the limits of this judgment; I therefore forbear further to discuss it.[141]

Justice Benning dissented from the court's holding because he believed that the entire will was invalid under Georgia's anti-domestic manumission acts. But in a companion decision denying standing in the case to a person seeking to be appointed as guardian for the slaves and to the American Colonization Society, Benning confirmed his opposition to the application of what he called "the monstrous doctrine" of *cy pres*.[142]

The Quasi-Freedom Cases

The *quasi*-freedom cases exhibit a similar pattern. *Quasi*-freedom was said to result when a will directed an executor to hold the master's slaves in a free or *quasi*-unfree status permanently, for a fixed term, or until the slaves' labor raised sufficient money to send the slaves out of state. Again, there was disunity among the judges. Some judges were entirely hostile to wills creating *quasi*-freedom, while others found that these wills were permissible. Others made a fine distinction between the wills providing that the slaves were to be freed before the contingency occurred or after, with a similar formalism that some courts applied to the free/send wills.[143]

South Carolina Justice John B. O'Neall's decisions are interesting in this respect. For years he argued that manumission was not inherently dangerous to slavery. He thus contended that the law should permit masters to reward "good" slaves with their freedom, to further slave discipline and obedience.[144]

Unfortunately, the majority of the South Carolina legislators disagreed with O'Neall. In 1800, they adopted an act that required five freeholders to approve of the character of slaves who were to be manumitted. The act also required that masters confirm their intention to free slaves in written deeds. An 1820 statute prohibited manumission except by an act of the legislature. That act did not, however, expressly state whether the legislature intended that this provision apply to manumission by will.[145]

Justice O'Neall read this omission in favor of freedom. He thus upheld a send/free will in the 1835 case of *Fraizer v. Ex'rs of Fraizer*,[146] even though that will created a form of *quasi*-freedom until the slaves were freed. John Frazier's 1824 will directed his executors to sell his assets, except his slaves, with the proceeds to be used to support his widow for her life. "She was to have the use of one or two of the testator's slaves during [her] life to wait and attend on her 'own proper person.'" The other slaves were to be hired out during his widow's lifetime. After his widow's death, Frazier directed that the balance of the funds from the hiring of his slaves, and the rest of his estate if necessary, be used to enable his slaves to acquire a fund of $100 each to permit the slaves "with the assistance of government, to go to St. Domingo to be colonized, or to any part that they with government may choose."

Frazier died soon after executing a codicil in 1825, and his wife died in 1832. Frazier had no issue. One of his executors, Benjamin Frazier, "seized the negroes, with the view of carrying the will into effect." Frazier's next of kin then sued, seeking an accounting of the proceeds of the hiring of the slaves and declaring the will's send/free provision void.[147] Chancellor Henry De Saussure ruled in favor of the plaintiffs.[148]

The Court of Appeals reversed, in an opinion by Justice O'Neall. O'Neall first held that the 1820 act did not bar a send/free will such as Frazier's, and the executor was not required to obtain legislative approval before removing the slaves out of South Carolina. O'Neall stated that the "evil" the 1800 and 1820 acts were intended to remedy was the "increase of free negroes within the State from emancipation.... The removal of slaves belonging to citizens of this State and their emancipation in parts beyond her territorial limits, was no injury to her." He noted that the 1820 and 1823 acts also prohibited the return of freed blacks.[149]

O'Neall next concluded that the will's provision requiring the executors to hire the slaves to raise the fund necessary for their removal did not create an illegal state of *quasi*-freedom. He read the provision to direct, "in substance," that the interest on the slaves' hiring

> during the life of his wife, or on the sum of $100 each, should constitute a fund to enable them to go to St. Domingo or any other place they may choose, and to which the government may be willing that they should go, and that his executors should set them free, and pay them the sum of $100 each. In construing a will, it is an [sic] uniform rule to give it if possible, such a construction that it may have effect, and not be defeated. It is hence admissible to transpose words and sentences to subserve the intentions of the testator. In this bequest it is manifest that the testator intended that his slaves should enjoy freedom, not within the State, but in parts beyond her limits, where it might be lawful and proper that they should be free. This is not contrary to the law of this State. The direction to his executors to set them free must be taken to be part of the provision to "enable them to go to St. Domingo to be colonized, or to any part that they, with the government, may choose." To set them free within the State, is contrary to law; and this the executors cannot therefore do: but they can remove them from the State to parts where emancipation is lawful, and there set them free. This comports with the testator's intention, and is therefore admissible.

O'Neall also noted that the estate would have been liable for the removal costs, if the will had "not provided a fund in the interest on the sum of $100 each which [Frazier] had bequeathed to them. This last sum they will also be entitled to receive on being emancipated; for in the will it follows the bequest of freedom, and is intended to vest in them and be payable to them when they shall become free people." He thus concluded that this fund was not an objectionable "legacy to slaves."[150]

The legislature attempted to reverse that decision with the 1841 anti-manumission act. The statute consisted of four sections. It voided all manumissions intended to be effectuated by removal of the slave from South Carolina. Second, it voided trusts created to fund slave removal and liberation. Third, it voided attempts to create trusts to support in-state "nominal servitude." Fourth, it declared illegal all gifts to slaves through trusts to be held for the benefit of slaves.[151]

Nevertheless, in the 1842 decision *Carmille v. Adm'n of Carmille*,[152] Justice O'Neall found a way to enforce John Carmille's two 1830 deeds that conveyed his slave Henrietta and her four children while creating a trust that Carmille intended to fund a state of *quasi*-freedom for the favored slaves' benefit. Those deeds were in apparent conflict with the 1841 act that was intended to "overrule" *Fraizer* and to avoid the deeds that in 1841 were on appeal in the *Carmille* case. Justice O'Neall enforced the deeds and "rejoice[d]" to conclude that the 1841 act was prospective. "For I would have thought it a stain upon the purity of our legislation, if it had been true that the Act had been passed to defeat vested rights."

O'Neall also stated his view that if a master "dared not make provision to make more comfortable faithful slaves, hard indeed would be the condition of slavery. For then no motive could be held out for good conduct; and the good and the bad would stand alike." O'Neall added his view that this "has never been the rule applied to our slaves, and such I hope it never will be."[153]

O'Neall's worst fears soon became reality, however. Later court decisions held that the 1841 anti-manumission act prevented all in-state and out-of-state manumissions. The prevailing law in South Carolina thus came to be in harmony with Lumpkin's views.[154]

For example, in the 1854 decision in *Morton v. Thompson*,[155] the South Carolina Court of Appeals affirmed Chancellor George Washington Dargan's ruling invalidating two provisions of David Morton's will regarding four of Morton's slaves. The will left all of Morton's estate to his church and religious charities, except for these four slaves. But the will also freed two slaves, Wilson and Madison, upon the payment of their appraised cost within three years, and it stated that that Morton's "negro woman Amy" was to "be free by getting a guardian. I do this for her kindness towards me during the affliction that it has pleased God to afflict me with; and that her youngest child, David, go with her in like manner[.]"[156]

Dargan found that these manumission and the *quasi*-manumission provisions were part of "an open, barefaced infraction of the specific provisions of the Act of 1820[.]"[157] He also criticized the *Carmille* and *Frazier* decisions' interpretations of the 1820 and 1841 statutes.[158] Sounding much like Lumpkin, Dargan wrote: "A free African population is a curse to any country, slaveholding or non-slaveholding; and the evil is exactly proportionate to the number" of free blacks in the population. "This race, however conducive they may be in a state of slavery, to the advance of civilization, (by the results of their valuable labors,) in a state of freedom, and in the midst of a civilized community, are a dead weight to the progress of improvement." Dargan stated that, "[w]ith few exceptions they become drones and *lazaroni*—consumers, without being producers. Uninfluenced by the higher incentives of human action, and governed mainly by the instincts of animal nature, they make no provision for the morrow, and look only to the wants of the passing hour. As an inevitable result, they became pilferers and marauders" and they corrupt slaves.[159]

According to Peter Hoffer, "[f]ew decrees matched the chilling candor of Dargan's outburst, but in his many other decrees, and in those of his colleagues, the callousness of the racist state was imposed on the more caring consciences of dying would-be emancipators." Therefore, Hoffer concluded that the common law doctrines of equity "without the active hand of a sympathetic chancellor, could not promote systemic equality in slave cases."[160]

Consequently, the anti-manumission trend was too strong for O'Neall to defeat. In the end, the virulent racism of the pro-slavery legislators and jurists such as Lumpkin and Dargan evidenced a trend that caused Southern lawmakers to strike an atypical course in the regulation of manumission, when compared with other slave societies.

The Good Faith Rule

Nevertheless, even in Kentucky, a pro-choice state that permitted send/free wills, the Court of Appeals in 1863 held that a slave must in good faith obey his or her master's will even after the master's death, or risk re-enslavement. In *Winn v. Sam Martin (of color)*,[161] Sam sued for his freedom under the will of John Martin, who died in 1837. Martin's will permitted his slaves, when they came of age, to chose slavery in Kentucky, serving the heir who Martin designated, or transportation to and freedom in Liberia. Sam asked the defendant Winn to buy him because he preferred to remain in Kentucky as Winn's slave. After Martin's heir would not sell, Sam decided to go to Liberia, "but he refused to become a citizen of the colony, and came back to New York on the vessel that took him out." Sam wrote to Winn "expressing his desire to return to Kentucky if Winn would buy him." In 1846, Winn bought Sam, who served as Winn's slave until 1859, when Sam "sued for his freedom and the value of his services."

Sam won a freedom judgment, which the Kentucky Court of Appeals reversed. The court's opinion, written by Judge Joshua F. Bullitt, found that "Sam never intended to become a Liberia colonist[.]" Bullitt also concluded that Martin's will expressed his intention "to promote the scheme of colonization, which many then regarded as giving promise of a peaceful and happy solution of the problem of African slavery." Sam, the court found, went to Liberia "with a concealed design to return to the United States," and he thus did not comply "with Martin's will." Instead, the court found that Sam "attempted to take an unfair advantage of [Martin's] benevolent purpose, and committed a fraud upon the colonization society, instead of promoting its success according to the testator's intention."[162] Because Sam did not agree to return to Liberia, the court held that he was not entitled to relief and he thus remained Winn's slave.[163]

Conclusion

The master's power to grant or withhold manumission was thought to be consistent with slavery in most of the slavery systems in the world's history. In the United States South, however, the advocates of the pro-slavery ideology, such as Georgia Justice Joseph Lumpkin, came to view manumission as an anti-slavery act. Others, including the South Carolina jurist John Belton O'Neall, dissented from this view. But O'Neall could not stem the tide against manumission in his state. The anti-manumission forces prevailed in South Carolina in the late antebellum years, as they did in the majority of the Southern states.[164]

Even in the most pro-manumission Southern states, however, the manumission cases did not involve slave "rights" in any real sense. Nor were the Southern pro-manumission decisions libertarian or anti-slavery in their effect or purpose. To the contrary, these cases confirm that the master's right to free his or her slaves was at issue. The courts strictly applied even the most liberal manumission laws to defeat claims to freedom even when the masters' intentions were not in doubt.

These manumission cases illustrate the effect of the statutes and public policy that increasingly regulated and eventually eliminated the master's right to free his or her slaves. That right was perceived to conflict with changing perceptions of the value of slaves and the growing fears of the dangers that large numbers of free blacks posed to the orderly oppression of plantation slavery.[165]

Notes to Chapter 6

[1] *See, e.g.*, Tushnet, *Humanity, supra* at 191-228.

[2] *See* chapter 3, *supra* at notes 26-30, 74-77.

[3] *See* Cobb, *supra* at 289; *see also* MacLeod, *supra* at 125-26.

[4] 2 H. & J. 176, 1807 WL 480 (Md. 1807).

[5] *See Laws of Maryland, 1796*, ch. 67, §29; *Proceedings and Acts of the General Assembly, 1752-1754*, ch. 1.

[6] *See Negro James v. Gaither*, 1807 WL 480 at *1.

[7] The case report identified counsel for James as "*Key* and *Johnson* (Attorney General)." *Ibid.*

[8] *See Laws of Maryland, 1796*, ch. 67, §29; *Proceedings and Acts of the General Assembly, 1752-1754*, ch. 1.

[9] *See Negro James v. Gaither*, 1807 WL 480 at *1.

[10] *See Miller v. Herbert*, 46 U.S. (5 How.) 72, 12 L. Ed. 55 (1842); *Bloodgood v. Grasey*, 31 Ala. 575, 1858 WL 430 (1858); *Thrift v. Hannah*, 29 Va. (2 Leigh) 300, 1830 WL 1565 (1830); *see also Bell v. Greenfield*, 3 F. Cas. 103 (C.C.D.C. 1840) (No. 1,251) (applying Maryland law, masters did not follow the formal requirements).

[11] *Laws of Maryland, 1810*, ch. 15, §1.

[12] *Laws of Maryland, 1810*, ch. 15, §2.

[13] *See Negro Anna Maria Wright v. Rogers*, 9 G. & J. 181, 1837 WL 1204 (Md. 1837).

[14] *See, e.g., Wilson v. Negro Ann Barnett*, 9 G. & J. 158, 1837 WL 1917 (Md. 1837); Morris, *Slavery, supra* at 390-92.

[15] *See Hamilton v. Cragg*, 6 H. & J. 16, 1823 WL 1067 (Md. 1823).

[16] *See Burrough's Adm'r v. Negro Anna*, 4 H. & J. 262, 1817 WL 961 (Md. 1823) (reversing freedom judgment because Anna was older than 45 years of age when her master died).

[17] *See Negro Clara v. Meagher,* 5 H. & J. 111, 1820 WL 925 (Md. 1820).

[18] *Laws of Maryland, 1792,* ch. 41, §3; *Laws of Maryland, 1785,* ch. 72, §11.

[19] 4 H. & J. 543, 1819 WL 947 (Md. 1819).

[20] *See Wicks v. Chew,* 1819 WL 947 at *1-*2.

[21] *Id.* at *3.

[22] 6 Va. (2 Call) 319, 1800 WL 404 (1800). For discussions of this case, *see, e.g.,* Wolf, *Race, supra* at 152-53; Huebner, *Tradition, supra* at 24-25; Morris, *Slavery, supra* at 404-08; Finkelman, *Casebook* at 116-27; Cover, *Justice Accused, supra* at 69-72; Kettner, *supra.*

[23] *Pleasants v. Pleasants,* 1800 WL 404 at *1; Kettner, *supra* at 136-43.

[24] *Pleasants v. Pleasants,* 1800 WL 404 at *1-*2; *see* Kettner, *supra* at 143-47; *see also* Davis, *Revolution, supra* at 196-97; McColley, *supra* at 156-59 (discussing Robert Pleasants).

[25] *Pleasants v. Pleasants,* 1800 WL 404 at *2; Kettner, *supra* at 142-48.

[26] *Pleasants v. Pleasants,* 1800 WL 404 at *2-*8, and Kettner, *supra* at 148-52, for summaries of the arguments of counsel. On John Marshall's role, *see, e.g.,* Newmyer, *supra* at 94-96; David Scott Robarge, *A Chief Justice's Progress: John Marshall from Revolutionary Virginia to the Supreme Court* 227-28 (2000); Smith, *Definer, supra* at 251-52; Charles F. Hobson, *The Great Chief Justice: John Marshall and the Rule of Law* 165 (1996); Jean Edward Smith, "Marshall Misconstrued: Activist? Partisan? Reactionary?," 33 *John Marshall L. Rev.* 1109, 1114-15 (2000). On the rule against perpetuities, *see, e.g.,* Timothy Sandefur, "Why the Rule Against Perpetuities Mattered in Pleasants v. Pleasants," 40 *Real Prop. Pro. & Trust J.* 667 (2006).

[27] *See* Smith, *Definer, supra* at 251.

[28] *Pleasants v. Pleasants,* 1800 WL 404 at *8-*19; Kettner, *supra* at 152-54.

[29] *See* Finkelman, "Exploring," *supra* at 92.

[30] *See* Huebner, *Tradition, supra* at 24.

[31] Cover, *Justice Accused, supra* at 71.

[32] *See id.* at 72-73, citing *Charles v. Hunnicutt,* 9 Va. (5 Call) 311, 1804 WL 547 (1804).

[33] *See* Wolf, *Race, supra* at 156.

[34] *See* Huebner, *Tradition, supra* at 26.

[35] See chapter 3, *supra* at notes 40-51.

[36] 20 Va. (6 Munf.) 191, 1818 WL 1120 (1818).

[37] *Givens v. Manns,* 1818 WL 1120 at *8.

[38] *See Sawney v. Carter,* 27 Va. (6 Rand.) 173, 1828 WL 1003 at *3 (1828) (deed was not executed as required by Virginia act); *Lewis v. Fullerton,* 22 Va. (1 Rand.) 15, 1821 WL 967 at *6 (1821) (same); *but see Manns v. Givens,* 34 Va. (7 Leigh) 689, 1836 WL 1776 (1836) (eighteen years after *Givens v. Manns,* reversing judgment for defendants to permit plaintiffs to attempt to authenticate manumission deed that the master recorded in the wrong county).

[39] 27 Va. (6 Rand.) 561, 1828 WL 1025 (1828).

[40] *See Moses v. Denigree*, 1828 WL 1025 at *1-*2.

[41] *See id.* at *2; *see also Alston v. Coleman*, 7 Ala. 795, 1845 WL 154 (1845) (following *Moses v. Denigree* and distinguishing *Pleasants v. Pleasants* to deny manumission).

[42] 11 Va. (1 Hen. & M.) 390, 1807 WL 433 (1807).

[43] *See Whiting v. Daniel*, 1807 WL at *1-*8.

[44] *See id.* at *8.

[45] *But see Ben v. Peete*, 23 Va. (2 Rand.) 539, 1824 WL 539 (1824) (reversing judgment for defendants in freedom suit, proof offered to support introduction of a copy of 1774 deed allegedly transferring slaves before the master signed and filed a manumission deed in 1796 was inadequate).

[46] *Donaldson v. Jude*, 5 Ky. (2 Bibb) 57, 1810 WL 637 (1810) (reversing freedom judgment).

[47] *Winney v. Cartwright*, 10 Ky. (3 A.K. Marsh.) 493, 1821 WL 637 (1821); *see also Clarke v. Bartlett*, 7 Ky. (4 Bibb) 201, 1815 WL 722 (1815) (affirming freedom judgment under Kentucky's 1798 statute, allowing others to testify about acknowledging witnesses' signatures on a manumission deed); and chapter 3, *supra* at note 75.

[48] *See* Jones, *Fathers, supra* at 92-93; *see also Smith v. Adam (of color)*, 57 Ky. (18 B. Mon.) 685, 1857 WL 4848 (1857) (slave freed by non-conforming deed remained an asset available to the master's creditors).

[49] *See* chapter 3, *supra* at notes 63, 96, and 108.

[50] *Black v. Meaux*, 34 Ky. (4 Dana) 188, 1836 WL 2037 at *2 (1836); *Talbot v. David, a Pauper*, 9 Ky. (2 A.K. Marsh.) 603, 1820 WL 1132 at *4-*5 (1820).

[51] 4 Fla. 445, 1852 WL 1109 (1852).

[52] *See Bryan v. Dennis*, 1852 WL 1109 at *2.

[53] *See id.*

[54] *See id.* at *2-*4.

[55] *See id.* at *4.

[56] *See Cases Adjudged, supra* at 7-8. A summary of the case also was reported in *The Pennsylvania Gazette*, January 17, 1776, in *Revolutionary Document, supra* at 19-22.

[57] *See id.* at 19-20; *Cases Adjudged, supra* at 7. For the New Jersey manumission statutes, *see* chapter 3, *supra* at notes 164-75; Cooley, *supra* at 45-50; Wolinetz, *supra* at 2233-34, 2244.

[58] *An Act Regulating Slaves*, March 11, 1713-14, §14.

[59] *See King v. Barber*, in *Revolutionary Documents, supra* at 20.

[60] *See King v. Barber*, in *Cases Adjudged, supra* at 8; *see also Revolutionary Documents, supra* at 20.

[61] *Revolutionary Documents, supra* at 21.

[62] *See State v. Pitney*, 1 N.J.L. 192 (Sup. Ct. 1793), also reported in *Cases Adjudged, supra* at 31-32; *State v. McKnight*, in *Cases Adjudged, supra* at 11-12.

[63] *See* Wolinetz, *supra* at 2244-45.

64 2 N.J.L 6, 1806 WL 636 (Sup. Ct. 1806).

65 *Id.*, 2 N.J.L. at 6-7.

66 *Id.* at 9.

67 *Id.* at 15-16.

68 *Id.* at 11.

69 *See* Wolinetz, *supra* at 2246-47. Justice Rossell, who had no formal legal training, was a controversial figure. Because he was thought to lack knowledge of matters of practice and pleading, he was so unpopular with the lawyers that a statute was adopted in 1820 rotating the judges on circuit apparently "to spare the county courts more than an occasional term with Judge Rossell." Nevertheless, Rossell later served as a United States District Judge in New Jersey from 1826 to 1840; he followed Justice Pennington, who also served on that court after serving on New Jersey's Supreme Court. *See* Mark Edward Lender, *"This Honorable Court": The United States District Court for the District of New Jersey, 1789-2000* 72 (2006).

70 *See Overseers of the Poor of Perth Amboy v. Overseers of the Poor of Piscataway*, 19 N.J.L. 173, 1842 WL 2019 (Sup. Ct. 1842).

71 *See* "An act to confirm the manumission of certain slaves," February 28, 1844; Cooley, *supra* at 50, n.1.

72 *See, e.g.*, Wahl, *Burden, supra* at 163; Morris, *Slavery, supra* at 385-88; Tushnet, *Humanity, supra* at 208-16, 227-28; Cobb, *supra* at 28, 301-02; Nash, "Reason of Slavery," *supra* at 118-19, 148, n. 471, 181-84.

73 *See, e.g.*, permitting choice of freedom, *Milton (of color) v. McKarney*, 31 Mo. 175, 1860 WL 6210 (1860); *Redding v. Long,* 57 N.C. (4 Jones Eq.) 216, 1858 WL 1973 (1858); *Tongue v. Negroes Crissy, Rhody and others*, 7 Md. 453, 1855 WL 3801 (1855); *Washington v. Blunt*, 43 N.C. (8 Ired. Eq.) 253, 1852 WL 1198 (1852); *Adams v. Adams*, 49 Ky. (10 B. Mon.) 69, 1849 WL 3535 (1849); *John v. Morman*, 47 Ky. (8 B. Mon.) 100, 1847 WL 2920 (1847); *Graham's Excutor v. Sam*, 46 Ky. (7 B. Mon.) 403, 1847 WL 2843 (1847); *Wade v. American Colonization Society*, 15 Miss. (7 Smedes & M.) 663, 1846 WL 3004 (1846); *Elder v. Elder's Ex'rs*, 31 Va. (4 Leigh) 252, 1833 WL 2083 (1833); *Pleasants v. Pleasants*, 6 Va. (2 Call.) 319, 1800 WL 404 (1800); and permitting choice of a new master, *Reeves v. Long*, 58 N.C. (5 Jones Eq.) 355, 1860 WL 1973 (1860); *Harrison v. Everett*, 58 N.C. (5 Jones Eq.) 163, 1859 WL 2283 (1859); *Beaupied v. Jennings*, 28 Mo. 254, 1859 WL 6603 (1859); *Hooking v. Morgan's Ex'rs*, 33 Ky. (3 Dana) 17, 1835 WL 1806 (1835); *Blakey's Ex'rs v. Blakey*, 26 Ky. (3 J. J. Marsh) 674, 1830 WL 2221 (1830); *Jordan v. Bradley*, Dudl. Ga. 170, 1 Ga. Rep. Ann. 443 (1830).

74 31 Mo. 175, 1860 WL 6210 (1860).

75 *See Milton (of color) v. McKarney*, 1860 WL 6210 at *3.

76 *See id.* at *4. Judge Scott dissented from the holding. He would have freed Milton immediately because Milton stated that he would comply with the conditions of the will. *Id.*

77 *See id.* at *3.

78 13 Ala. 102, 1848 WL 301 (1848).

79 *Carroll v. Bumbay Adm'r*, 1848 WL 301 at *1.

[80] *Id.* at *3; *see Creswell's Ex'r v. Walker*, 37 Ala. 229, 1861 WL 362 (1861).

[81] 55 Va. (14 Gratt.) 132, 1858 WL 3940 (1858).

[82] 55 Va. (14 Gratt.) 394, 1858 WL 3953 (1858).

[83] *Bailey v. Poindexter Ex'r*, 1858 WL 3940 at *1.

[84] *See id.* at *1-*2, *36. The official case report contains the extensive and rather well-researched arguments of counsel. *See id.* at *2-*28.

[85] *See id.* at *28-*34; citing, e.g., *Osborne v. Taylor*, 53 Va. (12 Gratt.) 117, 1855 WL 3460 (1855); *Elder v. Elder's Ex'rs*, 31 Va. (4 Leigh) 252, 1833 WL 2083 (1833); *Pleasants v. Pleasants*, 6 Va. (2 Call.) 319, 1800 WL 404 (1800); *see also* Nash, "Reason of Slavery," *supra* at 183-84.

[86] *Bailey v. Poindexter Ex'r*, 1858 WL 3940 at * 34.

[87] *Id.* at *35.

[88] *Id.* at *38.

[89] *Id.* at *38-*42.

[90] *Williamson v. Coalter's Ex'rs*, 1858 WL 3953 at *1.

[91] *See id.* at *3-*8, citing, e.g., *Osborne v. Taylor's Adm'rs*.

[92] *Williamson v. Coalter's Ex'rs*, 1858 WL 3953 at *8-*14.

[93] *Jones' Adm'r v. Jones Adm'r*, 92 Va. 590, 24 S.E. 255 (1896). For another interpretation of these Virginia cases, *see* Colin (Joan) Dayan, *The Law is a White Dog: How Legal Rituals Make and Unmake Persons* 138-76 (2011).

[94] 30 Ga. 253, 1860 WL 2310 (1860).

[95] *Curry v. Curry*, 1860 WL 2310 at *1.

[96] *Id.* at *4.

[97] *Id.* at *5-*6.

[98] *See* Grindle, *supra* at 717.

[99] *See* Nash, "Reason of Slavery," *supra* at 119; *see also* 3 Catterall, *supra* at 1-4.

[100] 16 Ga. 496, 1854 WL 1651 (1854); 19 Ga. 35, 1855 WL 1788(1855).

[101] *See Cleland v. Waters*, 1854 WL 1651 at *1-*2.

[102] *See Cleland v. Waters*, 1855 WL 1788 at *3-*6, citing, e.g., *Jordan v. Bradley*, Dudl. Ga. 170, 1 Ga. Rep. Ann. 443 (1830).

[103] *Cleland v. Waters*, 1855 WL 1788 at *7.

[104] *Id.*

[105] *See* Tushnet, *Humanity, supra* at 227; Stephenson & Stephenson, *supra* at 597-608 (discussing the evolution of Lumpkin's views on manumission, but not discussing *Curry*).

[106] *See* Nash, "Reason of Slavery," *supra* at 119 [footnote omitted], citing *Redding v. Long*, 57 N.C. (4 Jones Eq.) 216, 1858 WL 1973 (1858).

[107] *See* Nash, "Reason of Slavery," *supra* at 119.

[108] *See, e.g., Leech v. Cooley*, 14 Miss. (6 S. & M.) 93, 1846 WL 2949 (1846); *Trotter v.*

Blocker, 6 Port. 269, 1838 WL 1294 (Ala. 1838), and cases cited in Nash, "Reason of Slavery," *supra* at 111-13, nn. 345-46, 200-02, nn. 670-71; and Tushnet, *Humanity, supra* at 196-202.

[109] *See Alvany, A Free Woman of Color v. Powell,* 54 N.C. (1 Jones Eq.) 35, 1853 WL 1495 at *3 (1853).

[110] 21 Ga. 21, 1857 WL 1791 (1857).

[111] *See Drane v. Beall,* 1857 WL 1791 at *1-*11.

[112] *Id.* at *6.

[113] *Id.* at *10.

[114] *Id.*

[115] *Id.* at *15.

[116] *Id.* at *16.

[117] *Id.* With this digression, Lumpkin recorded his disapproval of Judge William H. Crawford's opinion to the contrary in *Jordan v. Bradley, supra,* Dudl. Ga. at 171, 1 Ga. Rep. Ann. at 444. *See infra* note 128, and *compare* Tushnet, *Humanity, supra* at 218-19.

[118] *See* Tushnet, *Humanity, supra* at 196-98.

[119] For example, in an 1848 decision, Mississippi's High Court of Errors and Appeals refused to enforce the 1844 Virginia free/send will of a Virginia slaveholder who also had a Mississippi plantation, and who clearly expressed his intention to free his Mississippi slaves and send them to Africa. *See Mahorner v. Hooe,* 17 Miss. (9 S. & M.) 247, 1848 WL 1937 at *16-*20 (1848). As to the substantive effects of formalism generally, *see* Duncan Kennedy, "Form and Substance in Private Law Adjudication," 89 *Harv. L. Rev.* 1685 (1976).

[120] *See, e.g., Purvis v. Sherrod,* 12 Tex. 140, 1854 WL 4380 (1854); *Thompson v. Newlin,* 43 N.C. (Ired. Eq.) 32, 1851 WL 1300 (1851); *Sibley v. Maria, A Woman of Color,* 2 Fla. 553, 1849 WL 1274 (1849) (South Carolina law); *Ross v. Vertner,* 6 Miss. (5 Howard) 305, 1840 WL 2435 (1840); *Frazier v. Frazier's Ex'rs,* 11 S.C. Eq. (2 Hill Eq.) 304, 1835 WL 1399 (S.C. App. 1835); Tushnet, *Humanity, supra* at 193-95; Cobb, *supra* at 290-91, 303.

[121] 57 N.C. (4 Jones Eq.) 216, 1858 WL 1858 (1858).

[122] *Id.,* 1858 WL 1858 at *1.

[123] *Id.* at *2. Ruffin also found that the slave choice provision was not invalid. *See id.* at *3.

[124] 25 Ga. 109, 1858 WL 1914 (1858).

[125] *See Redding v. Long,* 1858 WL 1914 at *1-*2.

[126] Dudl. Ga. 170, 1 Ga. Rep. Ann. 443 (1830) (enforcing will permitting James A. Bradley's slaves to chose freedom in "the African Colony," and holding that slaves should be hired out if necessary to fund their export from Georgia).

[127] *Sanders v. Ward,* 1858 WL 1914 at *2-*10. For Benning's dissent, *see id.* at *11-*15.

[128] *See id.* at *6. Lumpkin referred to William Harris Crawford's Superior Court decision in *Jordan v. Bradley, supra.* One of Crawford's biographers stated that this decision "best shows Crawford's humanity as a judge...." *See* Chase Curran Mooney, *William H. Crawford* 334 (1974). Crawford wrote that Bradley's will did "not contemplate" that the freed

slaves would "remain in the State, to the annoyance and injury of the owners of slaves." Thus, Crawford found that the will would not create the "evil" that the statutes prohibiting in state manumission were intended to prevent. *Jordan v. Bradley, supra,* Dudl. Ga. at 171, 1 Ga. Rep. Ann. at 444. Crawford was a Georgia state court judge from 1827 until his death in 1834. Among other things, he also was a United States senator, ambassador to France, secretary of war, secretary of the treasury, and an unsuccessful presidential candidate. He served in the Georgia state legislature from 1803 to 1807. *See generally* Mooney, *supra;* Edgar J. McManus, "William Harris Crawford," in 5 *American National Biography* 711-13 (1999).

[129] *See Sanders v. Ward,* 1858 WL 1914 at *7.

[130] *See id.* at *10.

[131] *See* chapter 3, *supra* at note 133; Nash, "Reason of Slavery," *supra* at 118.

[132] *See* Morris, *Slavery, supra* at 374-80; Tushnet, *Humanity, supra* at 223; Cobb, *supra* at 302.

[133] *See* Note, "Mandatory *Cy Pres* and the Racially Restrictive Charitable Trust," 69 *Colum. L. Rev.* 1478, 1480 (1969).

[134] *See Hogg v. Capehart,* 58 N.C. (5 Jones Eq.) 71, 1857 WL 7136 (1857) (court held that executor could select place for manumission after North Carolina law barred in state manumission, citing *Revised North Carolina Code, supra* §47 at 574 stating: "Whenever it may be directed by a testator, that any of his slaves shall be emancipated and carried to any State, Territory, or country, and it may not be convenient to carry them to the place specifically appointed, the court shall designate and prescribe to what other place the slaves shall be carried after, or for emancipation.").

[135] *See Adams v. Bass,* 18 Ga. 155, 1855 WL 1641 (1855); *Hunter v. Bass,* 18 Ga. 127, 1855 WL 1639 (1855) (court would not substitute new destination when selected states prohibited free black migration).

[136] *Adams v. Bass,* 18 Ga. 155, 1855 WL 1641 at *1-*2.

[137] *See id.* at *1.

[138] *See id.* at *4.

[139] *See id.* at *5.

[140] *See id.* at *6.

[141] *See id.* at *11.

[142] *See Hunter v. Bass,* 18 Ga. 127, 1855 WL 1639 at *2.

[143] *See, e.g.,* for the anti-*quasi*-freedom approach, *Cox v. Harris,* 17 Md. 23 (1861); *Bivens v. Crawford,* 26 Ga. 225 (1858); *Knight v. Hardemann,* 17 Ga. 253 (1855); *Weathersby v. Weathersby,* 21 Miss. (13 S. & M.) 685, 1850 WL 3420 (Err. & App. 1850); *see also* Dale Edwyna Smith, *The Slaves of Liberty: Freedom in Amite County, Mississippi, 1820-1868* 21-22, 37-48, 176-78 (1999) [hereinafter Smith, *Liberty*] (discussing *Weathersby*). For the more favorable cases, *see Brown v. Brown,* 12 Md. 87, 1858 WL 4416 (1858); Tushnet, *Humanity, supra* at 203-07; *see generally* Hoffer, *supra* at 112-17.

[144] *See* Smiddy, *supra* at 598-630; Nash, "Negro Rights," *supra;* and O'Neall, *supra* at 10-12, for O'Neall's views on manumission as expressed in his judicial opinions and his

pamphlet on slave law.

[145] *See* Smiddy, *supra* at 603-04, 612-13; and chapter 3, *supra* at notes 83-85.

[146] 11 S.C. Eq. (2 Hill Eq.) 304, 1835 WL 1399 (S.C. App. 1835).

[147] *See Fraizer v. Ex'rs of Fraizer*, 1835 WL 1399 at *1-*2.

[148] *See id.* at *2-*3.

[149] *See id.* at *7.

[150] *See id.* at *8.

[151] *See* Smiddy, *supra* at 627-28; Nash, "Negro Rights," *supra* at 164; *Jolliffe v. Fanning*, 44 S.C.L. (10 Rich. L) 186, 190 (1856); *Morton v. Thompson*, 27 S.C. Eq. 146 (6 Rich. Eq.) 370, 375-376 (S.C. App. Eq 1854).

[152] 27 S.C.L. (2 McMul.) 454, 1842 WL 2408 (S.C. Err. 1842).

[153] *Carmille v. Adm'n of Carmille*, 1842 WL 2408 at *11.

[154] *See Escheator v. Dangerfield*, 29 S.C. Eq. (8 Rich. Eq.) 95 (1856); *Morton v. Thompson*, 27 S.C. Eq. (6 Rich. Eq.) 370, 1854 WL 2864 (S.C. App. Eq. 1854); *Johnson v. Clarkson*, 24 S.C. Eq. (3 Rich. Eq.) 305 (1851); *Swinton v. Egleston*, 24 S.C. Eq. (3 Rich. Eq.) 201 (1851); *Vinyard v. Passalaigue*, 33 S.C.L. (2 Strob.) 536 (1848); *Blackman v. Gordon*, 19 S.C. Eq. (2 Rich Eq.) 43 (1845); *see also Broughton v. Telfer*, 24 S.C. Eq. (3 Rich. Eq.) 431 (1851) (pre-1841 manumission upheld under *Carmille*, but ex-slave seized under 1800 act and returned to servitude).

[155] 27 S.C. Eq. (6 Rich. Eq.) 370, 1854 WL 2864 (S.C. App. Eq. 1854).

[156] *Morton v. Thompson*, 1854 WL 2864 at *1-*2.

[157] *Id.* at *5.

[158] *Id.* at *3-*5.

[159] *Id.* at *2.

[160] *See* Hoffer, *supra* at 117; *see also* Nash, "Reason of Slavery," *supra* at 101, n. 304.

[161] 61 Ky. (4 Met.) 231, 1863 WL 2544 (1863).

[162] *See Winn v. Sam Martin (of color)*, 1863 WL 2544 at *1-*2.

[163] *See id.* at *4. According to a biographer, at the start of the Civil War Judge Bullitt was pro-Union, but "his sentiments changed when the schemes of subgation [sic] and emancipation and arming negroes came to the surface as 'war measures.'" *See* John C. Dolan, "The Court of Appeals of Kentucky," 12 *The Green Bag* 408, 418 (1900).

[164] *See* Patterson, *Social Death*, *supra* at 209-39, and Nash, "Negro Rights," *supra* at 154-66, 172-77, 179-87, for O'Neall's views.

[165] Fede, "Toward a Solution," *supra* at 316.

7

The Freedom Suits and the
Presumption Disfavoring Liberty

In the freedom suits that were filed by people held as slaves in the Southern states, the courts enforced the race-based standards for enslavement and other public policies that the Southern judges and legislators established. The courts vindicated the lawmakers' and judges' rights to decide who could legally be held as slaves, often in opposition to the alleged slave owners. The judges thus controlled a safety valve with which the courts released from bondage whites and Native Americans who, because of their race, were exempted from slavery.[1] These freedom suits also discouraged acts that were perceived not to be in the public interest, such as importing slaves into a state as merchandise or disturbing the peace by kidnapping into slavery free white, Native American, African, or mixed race people. The judges and legislators perceived these acts, like slave thefts, to be threats to slavery society's orderly oppression.[2]

Some historians paint a rather benign picture of the freedom suits. Ira Berlin wrote of a 1787 decision in a successful Maryland freedom suit that was filed by some of the mixed-race descendants of a white woman known as Irish Nell. The claimants alleged that Nell had been a servant of Lord Baltimore.[3] This was Irish Nell's descendants' second suit; the first was unsuccessful.[4] According to Berlin, this victory "[a]wakened" people held as slaves "to the possibility of freedom." They

> rummaged through their family trees searching for freedom in the charter generation. Many found it in Indian ancestry and others in descent from a white woman, often an indentured servant who had taken a black man as a husband or lover. Knowledge of the charter generation which had been submerged for years came rushing to the fore as slaves searched for roots in freedom.

Berlin also asserted: "Confronted with a growing number of freedom suits, state courts responded sympathetically by liberalizing the rules of descent and expanding the range of evidence acceptable in freedom suits."[5]

Jason Gillmer and others build on Berlin's interpretation. They contrast the Revolutionary period's liberality with the later antebellum period, when, under the influence of the racist positive good theory, the courts and legislatures took a more restrictive stand on the freedom suits.[6]

This chapter will test the fairness of the law regulating the freedom suits that were based upon the local law of the forum state or other slave states. It will review the substantive grounds on which claimants could base their freedom suits, and the procedural hurdles that the courts and legislatures placed in the path of those who claimed that they were illegally held in slavery. The next chapter considers freedom suits that were based on the substantive law of free states or nations.

The Slaves' Substantive "Right" to File Freedom Suits

The first issue that lawyers and litigants might have asked when evaluating a freedom suit is on what substantive basis could people held as slaves successfully assert freedom claims without having any proof of their masters' expressed intention to free their slaves as permitted by law, either by an *inter vivos* deed of manumission or a will, or without other evidence from which a court could infer the masters' implied intention to free their slaves. The substantive law that allowed these claims vested enforceable legal rights in persons who illegally were held as slaves, but it did not interfere with the fundamentals of the master and slave relationship. "The suit for freedom is allowed only to those who are actually free, and are wrongfully detained in bondage. Hence, it does not lie to enforce an executory contract, by which freedom is promised to the slave."[7] Slaves could not enforce manumission contracts even indirectly as intended third party beneficiaries.[8]

As noted in chapters one and two, slaves in the United States South could in very limited instances be freed when their masters did not express an intention to do so. In most of the Southern freedom suits in which the claimants did not base their claim on direct or indirect expressions of the master's intention, the proofs centered on the freedom claimant's race. Race was used as a concept to identify the persons who, according to the law, could be held as slaves.[9]

Slavery law in the United States South eventually reversed the common law rule, by which the child's status followed that of his or her father. Instead, the mother's status determined her children's slave or free status, under the doctrine *partus sequitur ventrem*.[10]

A 1662 Virginia statute enacting this rule stated that "some doubts" had arisen whether the children fathered by "an Englishman upon a negro woman should be slave or ffree [sic][.]" The legislators decided that the children of these parents would be slaves. Their slave status followed from their mothers' bondage, but only if the mothers had black female ancestry.[11] In contrast, Maryland's legislators, in 1664, adopted a statute that followed the common law rule. They provided that the status of children "Born of any Negro or other slave" followed the father's status. Maryland eventually adopted the Virginia rule, however, which was followed in the statutes and case law elsewhere in the United States.[12]

This slave law principle cut a slave mother's child off from all claims of birth right, except the right of the child and his or her children to be held in bondage. It also communicated to all the social and legal debasement of people held as slaves, who, at least for these important purposes, were reduced to the property status level occupied by livestock.[13]

Furthermore, this rule limited the number of people who were born free. According to Orlando Patterson, slave societies have used five patterns for the rules of enslavement by birth for people of mixed slave and free parents. A child's slave or free status was determined:

> (1) by the mother only, regardless of the father's status; (2) by the father only, regardless of the mother's status; (3) by the mother or father, whoever had the higher status; (4) by the father or mother, whoever had the lower status; and (5) by neither, the child always being free regardless of the status of either or both parents.

Patterson called the last pattern "incipient (non-heredity) slavery," which "is not, strictly speaking, genuine slavery as we understand and use the term."[14]

The legislators and judges in the Southern colonies and states did not consider the possibility that a law favoring liberty would have followed Patterson's third pattern, presuming that a child would be free if either parent were not a slave. Moreover, Patterson, Thomas Morris, and William Nelson have read South Carolina's 1712 and 1717 slave codes as examples of Patterson's fourth pattern of enslavement by birth if either parent was a slave.[15]

Therefore, most of the people held as slaves in the United States South who sought their freedom without proof of their master's intention alleged that they had a maternal ancestor who was not black, or was a free black woman, and that the ancestor, later ancestors, or the claimant were illegally reduced to slavery.[16] Often, however, evidence of the alleged slave's family history was ambiguous at best or was just not available. This was understandable because slave families were subject to division and sale.[17] Moreover, some Southern statutes made it a crime for one to teach slaves to read or write. These laws made written slave family histories, other than a master's accounts and records, often a practical impossibility.[18]

A slave's good conduct could not lead to a right to freedom. The legislators in the seventeenth century eliminated religious conversion to Christianity as a basis for freedom.[19] Except in the early days of settlement in South Carolina and Georgia, a slave's military service also would not be a cause for state-mandated manumission in the South.[20] The good conduct of people held in slavery in the United States South was on occasion indirectly asserted in freedom suits in which the claimants sought to prove that their racial ancestry prevented them from being held in bondage. Some freedom claimants offered to prove that they had "acted white," or that they were accepted as if they were white, to defeat their alleged masters' right to hold the claimants in bondage.[21]

A Southern slave owner's misconduct also could possibly lead to freedom for his or her slaves, but only if the master illegally imported or exported the slaves into or from a state that imposed a forfeiture on illegal slave traders. Most Southern states, at one time or another, prohibited the importation of slaves into the state as merchandise and not for use by *bona fide* settlers, and they imposed fines and other penalties on those who violated these laws.[22] For example, the Kentucky statutes imposed a $600 penalty on those who illegally imported slaves into that state.[23]

Nevertheless, the laws adopted in only three Southern states—Delaware, Virginia, and Maryland—provided that owners who imported slaves into the state in violation of those states' anti-importation acts risked forfeiting those slaves.[24] The statutes in these states banning slave imports, like those adopted later in other states, "arose ... as part [of] a calculated effort to keep the state from becoming too black and to protect the value of existing slave property."[25]

Virginia's statutes prohibited the importation of slaves into Virginia, after November 1, 1778, whether by "sea or land," and no imported slaves were to be bought or sold. All slaves imported contrary to the act were to be free upon their importation. This slave forfeiture provision did not to apply, however, to a United States citizen who moved to Virginia with his or her slaves, and who, within ten days of moving, took an oath before a justice of the peace swearing that his or her removal to Virginia was not intended to evade the act preventing the further slave importation, "nor have I brought with me, or will cause to be brought, any slaves, with the intent of selling them, nor have any of the slaves now in my possession been imported from Africa, or any of the West India islands[.]" The legislators also exempted from the slave forfeiture provision "any persons claiming slaves by descent, devise, or marriage[,]" any Virginia citizens who were "the actual owners of slaves" in the United States and who removed those slaves to Virginia, and travelers "and others making a transient stay" in Virginia who brought "slaves for necessary attendance, and carrying them out again." Persons importing, selling, and buying slaves contrary to this act were to pay a fine for each illegal slave.[26]

Michael Nicholls suggested that the legislators may have viewed the forfeiture provision "as such a severe penalty that it would not have to be imposed."[27] Nicholls and Eva Sheppard Wolf have shown that, although some masters took the required oath, many did not and freedom suits soon followed. Apparently in response, the legislators several times, beginning in 1780, revised this act or enacted exemptions. These legislators lessened the statutes' effect on masters who imported slaves into Virginia without taking the required oath on a timely basis.[28] Furthermore, in 1789, the legislature extended the time within which the oath was to be taken to sixty days.[29]

The legislature in 1785 and in 1792 restricted the slaves' potential right to freedom by providing that only slaves who were brought into Virginia and were kept there "one whole year together, or so long at different times as shall amount to one year, shall be free."[30] And a 1796 statute excluded from the forfeiture and freedom provision a citizen of the United States "residing in or owning lands within this state," who removes slaves born in Virginia "into any other state, and who has not sold or hired, or shall not hereafter sell or hire out such slaves," and who later brings the slaves back to Virginia. This statute also provided, however, that if slaves who were removed from Virginia became entitled to freedom under the laws of another state to which they were removed, "such right shall remain; any thing in this act notwithstanding."[31]

Wolf stated that these amendments "indicated that the legislators had meant for the freedom provision not so much to create free blacks as to discourage illegal importation of slaves."[32] The 1806 statute by which the Virginia legislature repealed the forfeiture and freedom provision further supports Wolf's conclusion.[33] People held as slaves nevertheless continued to file freedom suits decades later, claiming that an ancestor had been illegally imported before 1806. These cases posed difficult proof issues after the passage of time.[34]

The Maryland and Delaware legislatures adopted similar anti-importation provisions beginning in 1783 and 1787 respectively. For example, the Maryland act, "An act to prohibit the bringing of slaves into this state," declared that it was illegal for any person "to import or bring into this state, by land or water, any negro, mulatto or other slave, for sale, or to reside within this state[.]" The act also stated that "any person brought into this state as a slave contrary to this act, if a slave before, shall thereupon immediately cease to be a slave, and shall be free[.]" The statute contained exceptions to this rule. The act did not prohibit any United States citizen

> coming into this state with a *bona fide* intention of settling therein, and who shall actually reside within this state for one year at least, to be computed from and next succeeding his coming into the state, to import or bring in any slave or slaves which before belonged to such person, and which slave or slaves had been an inhabitant of some one of the United States, for the space of three whole years next preceding such importation; and the residence of such slave in some one of the United States, for three years as aforesaid antecedent to his coming into this state, shall be fully proved, to the satisfaction of the naval officer, or collector of the tax, by the oath of the owner, or some one or more credible witness or witnesses.

The statute also excluded slaves who were brought into the state by a person traveling "through the state, or sojourning therein for a short time," as long as the slave was not sold and was "carried by the owner out of the state." The legislature later amended the act to exempt other slaves from liberation, including those who were inherited from out of the state. The laws of both of these states also provided, however, that freed slaves were not entitled to vote, hold public office, give evidence against white persons, or enjoy any of the other rights of free people, except the right to "hold property, and obtain redress in law or equity for any injury to his person or property."[35]

The Delaware legislators in 1787 prohibited the sale of slaves for export out of the state unless the seller received a license approved by three and later five judges.[36] Delaware later became the only Southern state that extended its involuntary slave freedom provision to people who without a license or permit either exported slaves from Delaware or sold slaves with the intention of exporting them from the state.[37] The legislature included this provision in a 1793 statute that was intended to prevent the kidnapping of Delaware's slaves.[38]

The substantive law provided a more restrictive basis for freedom suits in the United States South than in other modern slave societies. As noted in chapter two, the Spanish law *Las Siete Partidas* permitted slaves to claim their freedom if they performed good works or discovered treason, or if their masters violated standards of good conduct.[39] Brazilian law also permitted people held as slaves to assert several grounds for freedom suits. These included the enforcement of the rights of people who were the descendants of free women who could not be held as slaves because of their race, the rights of slaves who arrived in Brazil after the slave trade was outlawed, and the rights of slaves whose masters inflicted excessive violence or abuse on the slaves, including slaves whose masters held the slaves in prostitution.[40]

The narrower substantive grounds for freedom suits in the United States South limited the potentially successful freedom cases that the slaves' lawyers could file. These lawyers also faced procedural burdens that made these cases all the more challenging.

Statutes Allocating the Burdens of Production and Persuasion Based on Race

The Southern courts and legislatures created presumptions and evidence rules to resolve the issues that arose in the freedom suits that were based upon the claimants' race or on the illegal acts of others importing or exporting people held as slaves. These procedural rules often had substantive effects on a freedom claimant's chance of success.

As a general rule, the courts impose on the party advancing a claim or defense the burdens of production and persuasion as to each element of the claim or defense that party is asserting, but there are exceptions.[41] The burden of production, also called the burden of moving forward with the evidence, requires the proponent of a claim or defense to produce in court sufficient evidence supporting all of the elements of his or her claim or defense to permit the trial judge to submit the case to the trier of fact, whether a jury or a judge.[42] The burden of persuasion serves as a tie breaker instruction that the trier of fact applies if, for example under the preponderance of the evidence standard, the evidence is in equipoise. The parties on whom the courts impose this burden stand to lose their case or defense if the evidence is not so clear either way.[43]

Commentators have identified several relevant factors that the courts employ when allocating these burdens of production and persuasion. The courts may place one or both of these burdens upon the party most likely to have access to the evidence that is necessary to advance and prove the elements of the claim or defense.[44] The courts also may reallocate one or both of these burdens based upon substantive considerations, such as which class of parties the courts favor for substantive policy reasons.[45]

The courts often allocate these burdens by creating presumptions. A presumption is a procedural device that excuses the party asserting a claim or defense of one or both of these the burdens.[46] The party or class of parties favored by a presumption has a procedural and substantive advantage over the disfavored party or class of parties because the presumption, in effect, makes it easier for a litigant to get his or her case before a jury, or compels the fact finder to reach a specific conclusion in favor of the benefited party in the absence of evidence to the contrary.[47] These presumptions could come in two forms: an *irrebuttable* presumption would be conclusive, and no amount of contrary evidence could overcome it; in effect the presumption became a firm rule of law more than some evidentiary burden because legally it could not be disproved. More commonly, presumptions were *rebuttable*, allowing the presumption to be overcome or disproved with sufficient proof, but placing the burden of doing so on the party challenging it.[48]

The Southern courts and the legislatures went quite far in the alleged masters' favor when they allocated the burdens of the production of evidence and of persuasion in freedom suits. They used rebuttable presumptions and relieved masters defending an alleged black slave's trespass claim of these burdens on the affirmative defense of property ownership in the freedom claimant.

The judges and legislators accomplished this end by abrogating the common law presumption in favor of liberty when a black person sought to establish his or her right to freedom. Instead, they created a presumption of slavery for claimants who appeared to be black, on whom the courts imposed the burdens of production and persuasion to establish their freedom. If, on the other hand, a person claiming unjust enslavement appeared to be white or Native American, or in some states at least not black, the Southern courts applied the common law presumption of freedom, and required the "person claiming title [to the alleged slave] to rebut the presumption."[49]

The presumption disfavoring some people who were held in slavery first explicitly appeared in the law of Britain's North American colonies in South Carolina's 1712 slave code. That code stated that "all negroes, mulatoes [sic], mustizoes [sic] or Indians," who had previously been sold, bought, or taken as slaves, were slaves for life, along with their children. The statute excluded those who were enslaved but who had, "for some particular merit," been freed by their owners or by the governor and council of the colony pursuant to any law, "and also excepting all such negroes, mulatoes [sic], mustizoes [sic] or Indians, *as can prove* [that] they ought not to be sold for slaves."[50]

The 1740 South Carolina slave code clarified this presumption of slavery. It first stated that "all negroes and Indians, (free Indians in amity with this government, and negroes, mulattoes and mustizoes [sic] now free, excepted,) mulattoes or mustizoes [sic] who now are, or shall hereafter be, in this Province, and all their issue and offspring, born or to be born," were "hereby declared to be, and remain forever hereafter, absolute slaves," and that the free or slave status of children would follow that of their mother. The statute then stated that in freedom suits filed by a guardian for the plaintiff "the burden of the proof" was "upon the plaintiff," and that "it shall be always presumed that every negro, Indian, mulatto and mustizo [sic], is a slave, unless the contrary be made to appear, the Indians in amity with this government excepted, in which case the burthen of the proof shall be on the defendant[.]"[51] The Georgia legislators adopted an almost identical provision in that colony's 1755 slave code.[52]

The Missouri freedom statutes also included the presumption of slavery against freedom claimants. The 1807 Territory of Louisiana act, which applied in what later became Missouri, required the trial judge to instruct the jury hearing a freedom trial that "the weight of proof lies with the petitioner[.]"[53] Missouri's 1824 freedom suit law narrowed this presumption disfavoring liberty, and stated that "the petitioner, if he or she be a negro or mulatto, shall be held and required to prove his or her right to freedom[.]"[54]

According to Robert Olwell, these statutory presumptions based on race "could lead the courts to render bizarre verdicts."[55] He cited a 1767 freedom suit that "Clarinda, a black woman," filed in Charleston South Carolina. Clarinda alleged that she was a free woman who "escaped from Spanish territory." Nevertheless, "she had no evidence to support her case. A white man came forward claiming to be her master but he also could provide neither witnesses nor written proof." Therefore, the trial judge, Charles Skinner, "faced a dilemma: while Clarinda was, by law, a slave, she also had no known master. With a deft hand, the judge solved his problem by dismissing Clarinda's suit, paying the court costs himself, and claiming the woman as his own property[.]"[56]

Skinner no doubt would have ordered himself to release Clarinda if anyone was later able to produce satisfactory proof of ownership. But absent this proof, Clarinda remained a slave because she could not prove her right to liberty.

Case Law Allocating the Burdens of Production and Persuasion Based on Race

Even when no statute explicitly abrogated the common law presumption of liberty, the Southern courts, beginning with the earliest reported freedom suits, applied the presumption of slavery to some people held as slaves. That presumption imposed the burdens of production and of proof upon some or all freedom claimants, and the deciding factor most often centered on the courts' perceptions of the claimants' physical appearance. The earliest freedom suits from the Southern colonies confirm that the courts adopted this burden allocation in favor of slavery over liberty, which no doubt had substantive effects in all but the most one-sided cases.[57]

The official publication of court decisions beginning in the late eighteenth century provides evidence confirming that the courts in Maryland, North Carolina, Virginia, and Louisiana by 1810 applied this presumption of slavery for some freedom claimants. In Maryland, we have only a summary of John Babtista's freedom petition, which he filed on March 10, 1653 with the Maryland Provincial Court. The report states that Babtista "a moore [sic] of Barbary ... hath made it appeare [sic] by sufficient proofe [sic]" that Simon Overzee, who "brought him in did not sell him for his life tyme[sic][.]" Instead, Baptista established that he was to serve for seven years. It appears that all presumed that Babtista was required to prove a case for his freedom. Babtista obtained a freedom judgment, which required him to serve two more years or produce 2,000 pounds of tobacco. Overzee later died and Babtista was freed by the court after he filed a second petition in 1661 alleging that he was being "dayly [sic] troubled" by Overzee's attorneys.[58]

In 1664, Maryland's legislators adopted "An Act Concerning Negroes & other Slaves." When read literally, this act created an irrebuttable presumption that "all Negroes and other slaves" already in the colony, and those "hereafter imported," were to "serve Durante Vita," meaning for their entire lives. The statute also stated that "all children Born of any Negro or other slave shall be slaves as their ffathers [sic] were" also for their lives. These provisions were intended to distinguish slaves, whose bondage was apparently by then permanent and inheritable, from servants, whose terms of service were of a limited duration. It also confirmed the common law rule that the child's condition followed that of his or her father. Therefore, children born of slaves whose fathers were free also would be free, although Maryland law eventually was amended and interpreted to follow the Southern states' majority rule, which provided that a child's free or unfree condition followed the mother's status.[59]

It appears, however, that the 1664 act was interpreted as creating or confirming a rebuttable presumption of slavery from black skin, and that black freedom claimants had the burden to rebut the presumption. This act "evidently sanctioned what had become familiar practice. Unless a black could prove that he had contracted his labor for a matter of years, the law presumed him to be a slave."[60] For example, in 1676 Thomas Hagleton filed a freedom petition with Maryland's Provincial Court. Hagleton was born in London to free black parents, and had been an apprentice tobacco worker in Durham.[61] In his petition, Hagleton, who is described as "a negroe [sic]," claimed that he was being denied "his liberty & freedome [sic] by Major Thomas Truman," contrary to an agreement made in England by Margery Dutchesse who "consigned" Hagleton to Thomas Kemp to serve for four years. Hagleton claimed that the four-year term expired one year before he filed his petition; therefore, the agreement must have been entered into sometime in 1670 or 1671. Truman appeared on May 20, 1676 to answer the complaint "by Kenelm Cheseldyn his Procurator ...." The court heard the evidence presented, which the report of the case states included several depositions and letters, and awarded Hagleton a freedom judgment. Thus, it appears that the court assumed that the 1664 act created a presumption of slavery from Hagleton's skin color, which could be rebutted.[62]

Although the reports of the Babtista and Hagleton freedom petition proceedings do not clearly state which party had the burden of proof, the General Court of Maryland used the presumption of slavery and burden of proof to dismiss a freedom suit in its 1796 decision, *Negro Mary v. The Vestry of William and Mary's Parrish*.[63] The petitioner, Mary, claimed that she was the daughter of "Negro Mary, imported many years ago into this country from *Madagascar*; and the question was, whether she was entitled to her freedom?" The plaintiff admitted that her mother was a slave, but she alleged that her mother was imported before the adoption of the 1715 slave code.[64] The claimant's lawyer argued that this code, in relevant part, explicitly enacted the rule of *partus sequitur ventrem*, when it declared "that all negroes and other slaves already imported, or hereafter to be imported into this province and all the children now born, or hereafter to be born of such negroes and slaves, shall be slaves during their natural lives." The report of the case does not refer to or cite the 1664 act, and it does not state the facts in any further detail.[65]

Chief Justice Roger Taney, while sitting on the Maryland United States Circuit Court, wrote that he "examined the original papers" in the *Negro Mary* case. Taney found that "[i]t was proved that the mother of the petitioner was a yellow woman with straight black hair, and that she was not of the negro race[.]" He added that "the testimony shows that it was upon this fact that the petitioner chiefly relied[.]"[66] It is not clear whether the petitioner Negro Mary appeared to be black.

The Maryland General Court dismissed the petition, apparently because it found that the petitioner's mother was imported as a "negro or other slave," and because it imposed the burden of persuasion on the petitioner. The Court held: "*Madagascar* being a country where the slave trade is practised [sic], and this being a country where slavery is tolerated, it is incumbent on the petitioner to show her ancestor was free in her own country to entitle her to freedom."[67]

The 1664 statute addressed another problem as perceived by Maryland's early leaders, the marriage of free white women and slaves. According to the statute's drafters, these women were "forgetfull" [sic] of their free condition, and their "shamefull [sic] Matches" were a "disgrace to our Nation." To discourage this practice, the 1664 act stated that free women who married slaves became slaves for their husbands' lives, and all children of the marriage would be slaves for life. The children of free women and slaves who were living when the act was adopted were to serve their parents' master for thirty years. These provisions were repealed in 1681, after Lord Baltimore returned to Maryland following a visit to England. He brought to Maryland a free white domestic servant whose name was Eleanor, and who was known as Irish Nell. Nell married a black slave, and the 1664 act's provision calling for the enslavement of women such as Nell and her children was repealed.[68]

In response to these statutes many mixed race people held as slaves filed freedom suits claiming that they were decedents of white women such as Nell, or their children, who were enslaved under the repealed provision of the 1664 law. In these cases, it appears that the Maryland courts assumed that the freedom claimants had the burden of proof, even though their claim was based on their mixed racial heritage.[69]

The presumption of slavery based upon racial appearance was confirmed in North Carolina by Judge John Louis Taylor, who later served as that state's first Supreme Court Chief Justice. Taylor applied a race-based presumption of slavery in the 1802 North Carolina case of *Gobu v. Gobu*.[70] The plaintiff sued the defendant for trespass and false imprisonment. The defendant responded by alleging that the plaintiff was her slave.

The plaintiff had been abandoned in a barn when he was an eight-day-old baby. He was found by the defendant, who was a twelve-year-old girl when she made her discovery. The report does not state in whose barn the defendant found the baby. The defendant took the plaintiff home, and she "kept possession of him ever since; treating him with humanity, but claiming him as her slave." The report does not state how long this arrangement lasted. The plaintiff was described as having "an olive colour, between black and yellow, had long hair and a prominent nose."

The case was presented to a jury. Judge Taylor charged the jury that he agreed with the defendant's counsel's contention that "every black person" is presumed to be a slave. According to Judge Taylor, this presumption applies "because the negroes originally brought to this country were slaves, and their descendants must continue as slaves until manumitted by proper authority." Therefore, a black person claiming his freedom "must establish his right to it by such evidence as will destroy the force of the presumption arising from his color."

Nevertheless, Judge Taylor also instructed the jury that he was "not aware that the doctrine of presuming against liberty has been urged in relation to persons of mixed blood, or to those of any color between the two extremes of black and white[.]" Taylor said that he did not "think it reasonable that such a doctrine should receive the least countenance." He stated that persons fitting this description could be descended from "Indians" or "mulatto parents originally free." Thus, he concluded: "Considering how many probabilities there are in favor of liberty of these persons, they ought not to be deprived of it upon mere presumption, more especially as the right to hold them in slavery, if it exists, in most instances, capable of being satisfactorily proved." After hearing this charge, the jury gave a verdict for the plaintiff. He thus won his freedom apparently because of his skin color, even though he offered no proof of his maternal ancestry.[71]

Judge Taylor's charge placed the burdens of proof and persuasion on the defendant to establish her claim of ownership, if the jury found that the claimant was not black. The jury apparently found that that the defendant failed to sustain her burden because she offered no proof of the plaintiff's maternal ancestry. Thus, they found for the plaintiff because of his skin color, as neither side offered evidence of his ancestry.

This holding implies, however, that if a black plaintiff had been found by an alleged owner under the same circumstances, he or she would likely be held to be a slave for life, even if the defendant's title claim was based on merely being the finder. This rule as to black plaintiffs, thus, is analogous to the common law rule that applies to those finding personal property. According to that doctrine, the finder of abandoned property has good title against all except the rightful owner, including the owner of the real estate on which the chattel was found.[72] This also is consistent with the general rule that a person coming into possession of a stray animal may acquire ownership of the chattel.[73]

One of the earliest colonial era freedom suits for which a relatively complete record exists was pursued in Virginia in 1655 or 1656 by Elizabeth Key. She and her advisor perceived the need to prove that her father was a free Englishman, while asserting her claim that she was being held beyond her permitted term of service.[74] Elizabeth was "an Afro-Anglo woman, [who] was born around 1630 in Virginia colony."[75] In her trial before the County Court, Elizabeth relied on hearsay testimony to establish that her father was Thomas Key, a free Englishman. This case arose before the Virginia legislators adopted the rule providing that the child's status followed the maternal line.[76]

The witnesses included an eighty-year-old former servant "who testified that it was commonly known that Thomas Key had been fined by the court in Blunt Point for getting 'his Negro woman with Childe[sic],' and that child was Elizabeth."[77] Elizabeth also offered hearsay testimony of the "understanding" of "neighbors" that Elizabeth was to complete a nine-year term of service and then be sent to England.[78] Key's case was advanced by William Grinstead, a white man who was the father of her two children and whom she married after she won her case.[79] The reported cases that followed also appear to be based on the assumption that the freedom claimants had the burden of proof to rebut the presumption of slavery.[80]

The Virginia Supreme Court of Appeals applied a race-based presumption favoring slavery over liberty for blacks and some people of mixed racial heritage in *Hudgins v. Wrights*,[81] a decision that was reported in 1806. Ariela Gross called this case "probably the most influential Southern precedent in setting the presumptions of slave/free status on the basis of race[.]"[82] The greater interest in *Hudgins v. Wrights* may be because it was an appellate court decision, the author of one of the opinions was St. George Tucker, and the court resolved a constitutional issue.[83]

The plaintiffs in *Hudgins* were Jackey Wright and her children. Their lawyer, John K. Taylor, filed a writ of *ne exeat in forma pauperis* with the Virginia High Court of Chancery, to prevent the defendant, Holder Hudgins, or a slaver named Cox to whom he allegedly sold the plaintiffs, from taking them out of the state.[84] According to H. Jefferson Powell, Taylor filed this writ to prevent the plaintiffs, the property in dispute, from being removed from the state while the case was pending. He adds that, although this was an effective strategy, it created an "incongruity" because the plaintiffs' claim was based on the assertion that they were unjustly held as slaves and thus were not property.[85]

The plaintiffs traced their maternal lineage to Jackey's great-great-great-great-grandmother, a Native American woman known as Butterwood Nan. Like the maternal ancestors of the plaintiff, Gobu, evidence of Butterwood Nan's status was wanting. At the hearing before Chancellor George Wythe, no one testified whether Butterwood Nan's mother was slave or free, and her mother's race was not established. She may have lived when Indian slavery was legal in Virginia.[86] Jackey's mother, Phoebe Wilson, appeared before the court with the plaintiffs. The Chancellor found that the youngest plaintiff "was perfectly white, that there were gradual shades of difference in colour between the grand-mother, mother, and grand-daughter (all of whom were before the Court)."[87]

Chancellor Wythe upheld the plaintiffs' claims to freedom, but his opinion apparently is lost. According to the appellate report, Wythe held that the 1776 Virginia Bill of Rights established for all persons a presumption of freedom. He relied on the clause declaring that "all men are by nature equally free."[88] He thus imposed the burden of non-persuasion on the alleged owner. In essence, he found that the defendant did not prove that the plaintiffs were descended from a maternal slave ancestor.

Although the plaintiffs won below on universal principles of natural liberty, their lawyer's appellate argument began: "This is not a common case of mere blacks suing for their freedom; but of persons *perfectly* white."[89] This apparently was a wise strategy; the appellate court affirmed the judgment while disagreeing with Wythe's application of the presumptions and burdens of proof.[90]

The Court of Appeals judges published three opinions. The first, by Judge St. George Tucker, discussed the Virginia statutes determining who legally could be held as slaves, as well as his views on "the natural history of the human species," of which he did not "profess an intimate acquaintance...."[91] Tucker disagreed with Wythe's broad reading of the Virginia constitution, stating that the provision on which the Chancellor relied "was notoriously framed with a cautious eye to this subject, and was meant to embrace the cause of free citizens, or aliens only; and not by a side wind to overturn the rights of property, and give freedom to [slaves]."[92]

Tucker held that the presumption of freedom applied only to white persons and Native Americans.[93] Tucker reaffirmed the racial basis of slavery with the following example:

> Suppose three persons, a black or mulatto man or woman with a flat nose and woolly head; a copper-colored person with long jetty black, straight hair; and one with a fair complexion, brown hair, not woolly nor inclining thereto, with a prominent Roman nose, were brought together before a judge upon a writ of Habeas Corpus, on the ground of false imprisonment and detention in slavery. ... How must a judge act in such a case?

If the alleged owner did not offer evidence to the contrary, persons two and three would be freed, but person number one had the burden to prove "his descent, in the maternal line, from a free female ancestor."[94] The court imposed this burden on only the "black or mulatto" plaintiffs.

According to Tucker's reasoning, because the plaintiffs in *Hudgins* appeared to be white, or at least because they were not "black or mulatto," the defendant had to satisfy the burdens of production and persuasion, and prove that the plaintiffs were descended from a maternal slave ancestor. His failure to do so permitted the Chancellor to find for the plaintiffs, based upon the lack of conclusive proof of Butterwood Nan's mother's racial identity. Tucker thus upheld the Chancellor's judgment and his allocation of the burdens of proof in this case, while declaring a race-based rule for future cases.[95]

Judge Spencer Roane wrote an opinion agreeing with Tucker's analysis of the burdens of production and proof. Roane wrote: "In the case of a person visibly appearing to be a negro, the presumption is, in this country, that he is a slave, and it is incumbent on him to make out his right to freedom," but if the plaintiff appeared to be "a white man or Indian, the presumption is that he is free, and it is necessary for the adversary to shew [sic] that he is a slave."[96] Judges Fleming, Carrington, and Lyons, in a brief opinion by Lyons, also stated that they were "entirely disapproving" of Wythe's decision applying the presumption of freedom to "native Africans and their descendants," but they too voted to affirm the judgment.[97]

The presumptions of slavery and freedom were established in Louisiana's law consistent with *Gobu* in the 1810 decision of the Superior Court of the Territory of Orleans in *Adelle v. Beauregard*.[98] According to Jennifer Spear, who studied the original surviving documents from the proceeding, the plaintiff was

Adele Auger, a woman of color who sued the defendant, Frederick Beaurocher, who was referred to as Beauregard by the official case reporter, Judge François-Xavier Martin. Auger sued Beaurocher for her freedom and for wages earned during the time that she resided with him. She alleged that "she was a free woman of color, 'born of a free family' in Guadeloupe." According to Auger, when she was eleven years old, her mother died. Auger "and her sister were taken in by Beaurocher, their mother's brother, and sent to a boarding school in New York. A few years later, Auger moved to New Orleans at her uncle's request. Shortly after that she filed her petition asserting that her uncle was trying to sell her."[99]

Spear stated that Judge Louis Moreau-Lislet decided this case.[100] He first decided which party had the burden of proof. Beaurocher's lawyer contended that Auger, as the plaintiff, must prove "that she was born free or has been emancipated." Auger's lawyer responded that even if Beaurocher could prove that he had possession of Auger before she filed the suit, "the Spanish law [*Las Siete Partidas*] would require him to produce some written title, or at least that he acquired possession of her without fraud." Auger's lawyer relied on Part 3, Title 14, Law 5 of *Las Siete Partidas*.

Judge Moreau-Lislet did not rely on the Spanish law. He instead adopted Judge Taylor's presumption based on race, as set forth in *Gobu*, and the reported opinion cites the *Gobu* case:

> Although it is in general correct, to require the plaintiff to produce his proof before the defendant can be called upon for his, it is otherwise, when the question is slavery or freedom. The law cited by the plaintiff is certainly applicable to the present case. We do not say that it would be so, if the plaintiff were a negro, who perhaps would be required to establish his right by such evidence, as would destroy the force of the presumption arising from color; negroes brought to this country being generally slaves, their descendants may perhaps fairly be presumed to have continued so, till they show the contrary. Persons of color may have descended from Indians on both sides, from a white parent, or mulatto parents in possession of their freedom. Considering how much probability there is in favor of the liberty of those persons, they ought not to be deprived of it upon mere presumption, more especially as the right of holding them in slavery, if it exists, is in most instances capable of being satisfactorily proved. *Gobu v. Gobu*, Taylor 115.

Moreau-Lislet's *dicta* suggested that he would not impose the burden of proof on all masters asserting a claim to slave property. Nevertheless, the court applied a presumption favoring liberty to claimants like Auger, who did not appear to be black.

This presumption obviously provided Auger's lawyer with a procedural and substantive advantage. Beaurocher's lawyer was required to first offer his client's proof of ownership. He asserted that Beaurocher brought Auger from the West Indies and "placed her in a boarding school in New York[.]" A "few years" later, he "sent for her to New Orleans, where she resided a few months with him, and left his house, and in a few days after brought the present suit."[101]

These proofs apparently did not persuade Moreau-Lislet, who awarded Auger her freedom. She then withdrew her claim for wages because the judge stated that he was "inclining to view her services as the return of gratitude, for the trouble and expense attending her education[.]"[102]

Judge Moreau-Lislet was born in St. Domingue and was educated in Paris. "In the course of his career in Louisiana he held nearly every office of public trust, from parish judge to state representative, state senator, [to] attorney general," and he was one of the drafters of the state's Digest of 1808 and 1825 Civil Code.[103] The opinion was reported by Judge Martin, who like Judge Taylor, later became his state's chief justice. Judge Martin was a native of France, but he was trained in the common law in North Carolina before moving to Louisiana.[104] Martin also was one of North Carolina's "most prolific printers of legal material[.]" In 1797, he published a volume containing notes of North Carolina Superior Court decisions, which was one of the early efforts to publish state court decisions in the United States.[105]

This decision is significant because in it one of the drafters of Louisiana's Civil Code adopted the rule that Judge Taylor developed through common law reasoning. As Carl Degler noted, "the Louisiana court used some of the precise phrases of the North Carolina court, suggesting a borrowing of idea as well as language."[106] This similarity may have been the result of Martin's involvement in reporting the *Adelle* decision.

Moreover, Judge Moreau-Lislet's opinion in *Adelle* rejected the approach that the Spanish law *Las Siete Partidas* enacted in the section that Auger's lawyer cited to the court. That law imposed the burdens of production and proof on the alleged master or the alleged slave depending on the slave's status when the suit was filed. If a person "goes about as a freeman" and another person claimed him as a slave, in court the statute required the alleged master to "prove his case, and not the other who is in possession of his liberty, if the latter does not desire to do so." But if the person seeking freedom was "in the power of his master as a slave," the master had the right to produce "a document, bill of sale, or any other evidence by which it can be ascertained that he, in good faith and not through violence or fraud, obtained control of the party whom he says is his slave[.]" If the alleged master satisfied this burden of production, the statute called for a presumption of slavery to attach to the slave. In response to this evidence, the person "who asserts that he is free must prove it, and show that the other party obtained possession of him either by force or fraud." If the alleged slave could not meet this burden, "he must remain in the power of his master as a slave, since the latter has shown a lawful reason for having control of him."[107]

Therefore, the court's actual holding in *Adelle* was more beneficial to the plaintiff than the rule established in this Spanish law because her appearance, and not her free or unfree status on or about the time that she filed her suit, was the determining factor in the Court's allocation of the burdens of production and proof. This rule would obviously not benefit a black plaintiff, however, who alleged that he or she was a free person who was reduced to slavery by force or fraud.[108]

Robert J. Cottrol noted, moreover, that in Louisiana this allocation of the burdens of proof "reflected underlying social realities. According to the 1860 census in Louisiana, 77% of free Negroes were mulattoes while 74% of slaves were black: 80% of all blacks were slaves, and 70% of all mulattoes were free."[109]

Antebellum Court Decisions Applying the Racial Presumption of Slavery

Throughout the antebellum period, the Southern courts continued to apply in the freedom suits the presumption of slavery that imposed both the burdens of production and persuasion on black freedom claimants, and imposed one or both of those burdens on those claiming ownership of freedom claimants who appeared to be white.[110] Delaware is cited as the one slave state in which the nineteenth century courts rejected the slavery presumption based on skin color.[111] In a freedom suit based on Delaware's 1793 anti-exportation act, however, Justice Caleb S. Layton, in 1838, wrote that "where a negro has been claimed and held as a slave in this state, the presumption of law is that he is a slave, and the *onus probandi* rests upon him to show that he is entitled to his freedom. But this, like every other presumption may be rebutted."[112] While discussing the contrary presumption, Chief Judge Richard H. Bayard of Delaware's Court of Oyer and Terminer stated that by the 1840s the "state of things has changed" and the majority of Delaware's blacks were free, but as early as 1800, more than 50% of Delaware's blacks were free.[113]

According to Thomas Cobb's 1858 treatise, most Southern states extended the presumption of slavery "to mulattoes or persons of mixed blood," although in other states, following *Gobu*, it was "confined to the negroes."[114] In the states that had abolished slavery, the slavery presumption would not "attach, except to persons proven to be fugitives from a slaveholding State."[115] Thus, Justice Theophilus W. Smith of the Illinois Supreme Court in 1841 rejected the presumption of slavery for whites and for blacks in a damage suit filed by a person who was illegally held as a slave:

> The rule, in some or most of the slaveholding states, from considerations of public policy, is undoubtedly that the *onus probandi*, in such cases, lies with the party asserting his freedom. This rule, however, it is conceived, is founded in injustice. It is contrary to one of the fundamental principles upon which our government is founded, and is repugnant to, and subversive of, natural right; nor can there be, in my judgment, sufficient grounds of public policy, to justify a departure from the well settled rules of evidence governing all other cases, and adopting one which inverts a rule drawn from the principles of natural justice. The arbitrary character of such a rule is repugnant to moral sense, and a violation of the fundamental principles of evidence, which requires him, who asserts a right, to produce the evidence upon which he seeks to maintain his claim. If this rule is inflexibly adhered to in other cases, why should a departure be justified in

cases involving the right of personal liability? The proposition cannot be maintained, upon any rational principle; nor can considerations of public policy exist to sustain it.[116]

Nevertheless, the Southern courts continued to apply the presumption against liberty to most non-white freedom claimants.

Moreover, the Southern courts held that presumption of freedom arising from a claimant's white appearance was not conclusive in his or her favor either.[117] This followed from the rule requiring that a child's slave or free status "follows the condition of the mother," but with the added requirement that the mother's slavery was lawful. "If the mother was of the pure white race," or "was of Indian and not African blood," the child "could not be held in slavery *de jure.*"[118]

Although a "white person of unmixed blood" could not legally be held in slavery, the courts recognized that "a person apparently white may, nevertheless, have some African taint, and may, consequently, have descended from a mother who was a slave[.]" The claimants' white color and appearance therefore was only *prima facie* evidence of freedom, and defendants could offer evidence "to prove that, notwithstanding the [claimant's] visible complexion, there is African blood in the veins sufficient to doom [the claimant] to slavery."[119]

Accordingly, throughout the antebellum period, freedom claimant lawyers advanced two general strategies. These were to a great extent dictated by the race-based presumptions and burden allocations established in the *Gobu* and *Hudgins* cases. As in *Hudgins*, lawyers often offered proof that the freedom claimants could not legally be held as slaves because they had a maternal ancestor who was white, Native American, or a free black, and that that ancestor, other ancestors, or the claimant, was or were illegally denied free status or was or were kidnapped into slavery.[120]

This strategy was successfully used on behalf of a black claimant in *Fulton's Ex'ors v. Gracey,*[121] an 1859 Virginia Court of Appeals decision, which affirmed a freedom judgment. That judgment was in part based on the claimants' written proof tending to establish that their maternal mother or grandmother, known as Nan or Nancy, registered in 1817 according to statute as a free black woman.[122] The Court rejected the defendants' contention that the verdict "was contrary to the law and the evidence[,]" holding: "There is nothing in the case to show that Nan was ever a slave, except for the fact of her color and African descent; and the presumption arising from that fact, seems to be repelled by the other facts proved in the case."[123]

A lawyer had to employ other strategies in cases in which this clear evidence of the freedom claimant's race and the status of the claimant's maternal ancestry was not available, as in *Gobu*, or even if it was available, it was ambiguous, as in *Hudgins*. For example, the claimant's lawyer often offered proofs establishing the *prima facie* case of freedom based on the claimant's racial appearance alone. Lawyers apparently advanced this approach if they thought that they could convince the judge and jury that the claimant was white or a Native American, to obtain the benefits of the tie breaking jury instruction from the presumption of freedom that the courts enforced in *Gobu* and *Hudgins* when proof of the claimant's maternal ancestry was wanting.[124]

For example, in *Hook v. Pagee*,[125] the Virginia Court of Appeals in 1811 affirmed a jury verdict for the plaintiffs, Nancy Pagee and her children. Although the claimants offered no evidence of their ancestry, the court held that jury could find that Nancy and her children were white, and not slaves, based on the jury's own in court inspection of the claimants. Nancy Pagee may have been successful because she "was championed by an ex-member of the United States House of Representatives, George Hancock. Hancock appears to have been keeping her as a mistress and he opposed the claims of John Hook, a prominent Loyalist during the Revolution, to her service."[126] Hancock later sued Hook for slander regarding statements Hook made arising out of that case.[127]

Ariela Gross and others have discussed at length the 1845 Louisiana case of Sally Miller, which attracted extensive media attention as a paradigm of white slavery.[128] The Louisiana Supreme Court affirmed a judgment awarding Miller her freedom. At trial, Miller's lawyer relied in part on the testimony of white German immigrant witnesses. They identified Miller as a long-lost relative or neighbor who had been sold into slavery as a young girl after she was separated from her family off a boat that arrived from Holland.[129] Miller's lawyer's argument also emphasized her "moral behavior" and "hidden whiteness[.]"[130] This strategy was consistent with and reinforced all of the stereotypes that the judges and jury members hearing the case may have had.[131]

The outcome of a freedom claimant's case thus often centered on the judgments made by a judge and jury about the claimant's race, especially when the evidence of the claimant's maternal ancestry was ambiguous, or just was not available. This judgment included the evaluation of three components: (1) whether the claimants had a white physical appearance, (2) whether the claimants "acted white," and (3) whether others in the informal "court" of white public opinion treated the claimants as if they were white. Accordingly, a claimant's lawyer could try to win a freedom suit by offering a jury inspection of the claimant's appearance, and testimony about the claimant's behavior and how others in the community treated the claimant.[132]

Freedom suit trials in the antebellum years also often included the opinion testimony of lay witnesses and expert witnesses regarding the claimants' race. Lawyers offered expert medical opinions consistent with what in the nineteenth century was thought to be the science of detecting the "taint" of African origin, or its absence, from a person's appearance.[133]

Because the freedom presumption following from a claimant's white appearance was not conclusive, the alleged owner's lawyer often rebutted this presumption by offering evidence that the claimant's mother, or another maternal ancestor, was a slave who had some African blood. Two Arkansas cases and one each from Louisiana and Texas illustrate these strategies.

The Arkansas Supreme Court affirmed an equity court judgment holding that the defendant legally held the sixteen-year-old freedom claimant, Thomas Gary, as a slave, in the 1858 case *Gary v. Stevenson*.[134] The courts reached this conclusion even though the claimant had a white appearance—blue eyes, straight light hair, and a sandy complexion. The courts held that the alleged owner rebutted the freedom presumption that arose from Gary's physical appearance and also rejected the testimony of Gary's three scientific medical expert witnesses.[135] The defendant offered uncontested evidence of Gary's mother's servile status.[136] The Supreme Court held that "the preponderance of the testimony" supported the lower court's finding that there was some African blood in the claimant's mother's heritage, "notwithstanding the admixture of African blood [in the claimant] may be but small[.]"[137]

An alleged slave owner won a new trial in 1861 from the Louisiana Supreme Court in *Morrison v. White*.[138] The claimant Alexina Morrison's petition for freedom stated that she "was born of white parents, and that she was kidnapped and stolen from her home[.]"[139] After the jury in the first trial could not reach a verdict, the jury in a second trial decided in the claimant's favor. She relied at trial on expert testimony, which the Supreme Court derided as "speculative opinions of physicians and others, as to the indications of Caucasian extraction presented in her skin, hair, and features," and on her own physical appearance consisting of "fair complexion, blue eyes, and flaxen hair."[140] The Supreme Court held that in the second trial the judge improperly excluded the defendant's evidence of ownership, which the Court suggested might have rebutted the presumption of freedom that arose from the Morrison's white appearance.[141]

An alleged slave owner won two new trials in 1856 and in 1862 from the Texas Supreme Court, in *Gaines v. Ann*[142] and *Gaines' Adm'r v. Ann*.[143] The claimant Ann's petition for freedom stated that she "was a free white girl, without negro blood[.]"[144] After the jury in the first trial reached a verdict in Ann's favor, the Texas Supreme Court reversed in an opinion written by Justice Abner Lipscomb.

The court held that the alleged owner should have been granted a new trial because the verdict was not supported by the evidence. Justice Lipscomb reasoned:

> The question was not merely whether [Ann] was entitled to her freedom, because, if of the African race, she might still be entitled to her freedom, from having been born of a free mother, if so proven; but it was, whether she was of the pure white race, or mixed with African blood and born of a slave mother. On the question of her condition of slavery, the doctrine is too well settled to require a reference to authority, that the offspring follows the condition of the mother. If the mother was a slave, so also would be the child, with this qualification, that the mother was in lawful slavery. If the mother was of the pure white race, unmixed with African blood, her being *de facto* held in slavery would not be lawful and could not entail her own illegal slavery upon her child. So if she was of Indian and not of African blood, she could not be held in slavery *de jure*. Lawful slavery is confined to the African race.[145]

This analysis thus omits the possibility, which other courts recognized following *Hudgins*, that a claimant who had "African blood" could be freed if his or her mother, or an earlier female maternal ancestor, was white or Native American.

Accordingly, under Justice Lipscomb's more restrictive analysis, the court held that Gaines rebutted the presumption of freedom that applied based upon Ann's white appearance. Gaines offered proof that Ann's mother and grand-mother both were slaves "and of the African race; that the grandmother was a mulatto, or half-breed; that the mother of Ann was a quarteroon, and slave at the birth of Ann; that the reputed father of Ann was a white man, and she con-sequently was one-eighth of the African blood." In response, Justice Lipscomb stated that Ann's claim of being of "pure white blood" was based on the evidence

> of two medical gentlemen, who testified that they had examined her and could not detect any of the indicia of the existence of African blood in her, but that a person who was only one-eighth of the African blood might not show any signs of the existence of that blood, though in general that degree of the blood would show itself; and that the appearance of the child, in cases of mixed blood, were much more likely to be in conformity with the father than the mother. Does this evidence contradict the positive fact of the mother being a slave and of the African race? We think not. The facts sworn to by the medical gentlemen may be true, and yet not in any way contrary to the fact proven, of the status of the mother. And the evidence of the witnesses who proved the facts of the mother being of the African race and a slave, is not impeached.

The court therefore found that it was "bound to conclude that the verdict of the jury, finding Ann to be of the pure white race, is not supported by the evidence; and it is not a case of conflicting evidence, where the verdict should not be disturbed."

Justice Lipscomb also expressed "some grave reflections" about the results in the appeal:

> The girl Ann is proved to be only one-eighth of African blood, and the third generation, one of each being white, and is the last degree prohibited by law from giving evidence against a white person. Her child, if by a white man, would be a competent witness against a white person, but following the status of its mother, it would be a slave, and it would so descend, *ad infinitum*, so long as the descent from a slave mother could be traced, though the blood be of the smallest possible amount. Whether it is sound policy to permit the law to remain in its present state is a question to be answered by the wisdom of the legislature, and not by us. Believing that the verdict in this case is not supported by the evidence, the judgment is reversed and the cause remanded for a new trial.[146]

Gaines won the right to a new trial, but a jury again found in Ann's favor. The Texas Supreme Court again reversed the judgment and remanded the case for yet another trial. The Supreme Court found that the trial judge should have granted a new trial because the second verdict was contrary to the evidence, which, the Court stated, was weaker for Ann and stronger for Gaines in the second trial than in the first.[147]

In contrast, the Arkansas Supreme Court, in 1862, affirmed a jury verdict awarding freedom to Abby Guy and her four minor children,[148] This was the second jury verdict that the claimants won. The Arkansas Supreme Court reversed the first judgment because it found that the trial judge's charge to the jury was too favorable to the claimants. The trial judge based that charge on his interpretation of a statute that he thought required the jury to presume that the claimants were free if they were less than one-fourth black.[149] The defendant also obtained an order changing the venue for the second trial, but, in that second trial the claimants nevertheless again won a jury verdict awarding them their freedom.[150]

In the trials in Abby Guy's case, the claimants' lawyer had access to and introduced evidence in addition to the type of medical expert testimony that was available to Thomas Gary, Alexina Morrison, and Ann.[151] He presented undisputed evidence that Abby Guy and her children had lived for at least eight to nine years as if they were free and white, and that they were accepted by the white community.[152] The evidence confirmed, however, that Abby Guy's mother Polly was a slave, that Abby was born into slavery, and that Polly's racial heritage was ambiguous.[153] The claimants' lawyer presented the only medical and scientific evidence of the claimants' racial characteristics.[154]

The judge presiding in the second trial also allowed the claimants to exhibit to the jury their white appearance. He permitted the claimants to take off their shoes and socks and display their feet in court, over the defendant's objection.[155]

The Arkansas Supreme Court sustained the jury's verdict for the plaintiffs in the second trial, although expressing concerns about "an impression on our part that the verdict may have been contrary to the weight of the evidence."[156] The Court found that the demonstration to the jury of the claimants' personal appearance was not reversible error because "[n]o one, who is familiar with the peculiar formations of the *negro foot,* can doubt, but that an inspection of that member would ordinarily afford some indication of the race—though the evidence of race, thus afforded, would, of course, be stronger or weaker, according, to the extent of the admixture of the blood."[157] The court also rejected the defendant's claim "that there was a total want of evidence to support the verdict," although recognizing that "it is possible that the jury found against the preponderance of the evidence, through reluctance to sanction the enslaving of persons, who, to all appearance, were of the white race, and, for many years before such suit, had acted as free persons and been treated as such."[158]

Consequently, as Ariela Gross concluded, the claimants' lawyer in Abby Guy's case introduced evidence of the claimants' "physical appearance, social acceptance and reputation 'as an equal,' and exercise of the rights of free persons."[159]

> Abby Guy may have won because the jury was reluctant to remove rights to which she had a "prescriptive" claim by virtue of having exercised them for some years. She may have won because the jury believed from their own observation that she was white, regardless of her ancestry. Perhaps the jury

feared the horror of "white slavery." Or perhaps Abby Guy's medical experts and other witnesses were simply more credible than [those of the defendant].[160]

The litigation strategies and modes of trial illustrated by these cases were the result of the race-based presumptions of slavery and freedom and tie-breaking instructions that the trial judges read to the juries.

These cases also show how in *Gobu* and *Hudgins* the courts established presumptions that created a double standard favoring slavery for dark skinned plaintiffs and freedom for light skinned plaintiffs. No common law precedent or doctrine required the courts to adopt these presumptions, which were contrary to at least three basic common law principles. First, they were "[c]ontrary to the general rule" allocating the burden of proof in a tort case to the litigant asserting an affirmative defense. The defendant master, who the plaintiff alleged committed a tort, "pleads the affirmative plea, and yet need not prove it." Instead, the master asserts "in justification of his trespass, that the plaintiff is a slave, and yet on that plaintiff is devolved the *onus probandi* to show himself a freeman."[161] Second, the master was not required to prove his or her title claim to the slave, contrary to the general rule requiring a litigant asserting a claim of title to a chattel to prove his ownership rights, a rule that the courts applied, for example, to those claiming ownership of an animal, but not to those claiming ownership of a slave.[162] Third, the courts allocated the burdens of production and of proof to the alleged slave, contrary to the presumption favoring liberty.[163]

The New Jersey Courts' Approach to the Presumptions of Slavery and Freedom

This presumption of slavery and burden allocation based upon the claimants' racial appearance was not an inevitable outcome based upon common law precedent. Instead, it was a matter of choice reflecting policy preferences that the Southern legislators and judges made into law. This is further illustrated by the very different way that the New Jersey cases applied the presumption of slavery in freedom suits while New Jersey was a slave state. The New Jersey courts imposed the ultimate burden of persuasion on the owner in two freedom suits, and required the alleged owners to prove their defense of property ownership of even black claimants.

The New Jersey Supreme Court in 1789 applied this version of the presumption of slavery in *State v. Lyon*,[164] and sustained Margaret Reap's freedom claim, which was filed by a writ of *habeas corpus*. The court held that Margaret rebutted the slavery presumption because she and her parents lived as if free for many years, although Margaret appeared to be black, her mother was a slave, and she did not produce any will or deed of manumission for herself or her mother.[165]

The claimant's evidence proved that Margaret Reap's mother, Flora, was a slave who, in 1750, was given by deed to Lucy Little. Mrs. Little then lived in Massachusetts, and had a son, William Little. After her husband died, Mrs. Little married Dr. Joseph Eaton, and the family moved to New Jersey with Flora. Dr.

Eaton, in 1752, sold Flora and a child she had, who was named Rose, to John Worthley. In 1753, Worthley sold Flora to John Williams. Dr. Eaton reacquired Flora from Williams in May 1754.[166]

The claimant also presented affidavits and oral testimony of "several ancient witnesses" of Dr. Eaton's statements that he opposed slavery, and "that he never intended Flora to belong to his estate, nor should any of his children be entitled to her as their property." After Dr. Eaton died, Lucy Eaton sold a spinning wheel that Flora used, stating that she had no use for it because Flora was free. "Since that period, Flora has been considered in the neighborhood, as a free woman. No claim to hold her as a slave was heard for seventeen years." Flora worked as a free woman, and married John Reap, "a free negro, with whom she has since lived and continues to live."[167]

The Reaps had two children, one of whom was the claimant Margaret. "These children lived with their parents, and were brought up by them from the fruits of their industry, and continued with them until Margaret was seized and carried away forcibly." After Margaret was seized by Lyon, William Little signed an instrument stating that he relinquished any claim to Flora and her children, "and manumits them, so far as regards any rights belonging to him."[168]

In response to this evidence, the defendant's counsel attempted to introduce an affidavit that was taken *ex parte*. The Attorney General objected to the evidence. The court did not permit the affidavit to be used as evidence, but granted the defendant's request for an adjournment so that he could obtain and review Dr. Eaton's will.[169] The following day, both counsel reported that they reviewed Dr. Eaton's will, and neither elected to offer it as evidence.[170]

As to the burden of proof, the court stated: "It is true, as has been contended for the defendant, that negroes claiming their freedom, must prove themselves entitled to it; and this has been the invariable practice of this court. Whatever may be our opinions with regard to the propriety of the rule, we do not think ourselves entitled to change it[.]"[171]

The court found that Margaret produced "sufficient evidence to establish her freedom."[172] The record contained no evidence that Margaret had a white appearance. Nevertheless, the court found that she at least made out a *prima facie* case for freedom, "if not sufficient, independent of other testimony, to authorize discharge" of both Flora and Margaret, "sufficient to put defendant on proving a strict legal property."[173] The court found that the defendant did not establish his affirmative defense of "a strict legal property" in the claimant.[174]

The New Jersey Supreme Court further weakened the presumption of slavery on facts that essentially were similar to *Gobu* in the 1795 case of *State v. Heddon.*[175] The claimant was a young man referred to only as "negro Cork." His maternal ancestry was just as mysterious as the baby "found" in *Gobu*. A witness named Davis testified that, in 1779, Cork was with the regiment of Colonel Tarleton of the British Army, "before the surrender of New York to the American army[.]" Cork was "then about twelve or thirteen years of age," and served Colonel Tarleton training horses while Tarleton remained in this country. Davis stated that Cork "belonged to the regiment, and was considered a prisoner, and not as a slave."[176] The case report apparently refers to Colonel Banastre Tarleton, who served as a British army officer in New York and elsewhere, with some success, until he returned to England in 1781. He later was elected to serve in Parliament.[177]

When Tarleton departed for England, he left Cork with a servant woman, who was married to a man named James. James sold Cork into slavery. After a number of transactions, "[a] certain Mr. Snowden" claimed Cork as his slave. Cork ran away, was captured, and was committed to the Essex County sheriff in October 1793.[178]

The Supreme Court, in a two to one decision, ruled in Cork's favor. The majority opinion of Chief Justice James Kinsey held that Snowden failed to sustain the burden of proving his property claim.[179] "No right to the boy has been proved to exist, either in James or his wife; on the contrary, the witness says that [Cork] was in the regiment during the whole time that Tarleton stayed in America, that there was no report of his selling Cork till after his departure, and that in the regiment he was considered as not the object of sale." Kinsey thus concluded that Snowden's claim was "not proved with sufficient clearness to warrant me saying that he has any property in the boy."[180]

In his dissenting opinion, Justice John Chetwood, who voted with the majority in favor of the claimant in *Lyon*, stated that he would have denied Cork his freedom. Chetwood opined that persons held as slaves must prove their right to freedom, and that Cork failed to sustain this burden. He wrote:

> It is true that slavery is incompatible with liberty, and does not correspond with the true principles of a republican government, but it is recognized by our laws, and it exists in New Jersey. Negro slaves have always been looked upon in the same light with other personal property, and transferred in the same manner. It is a rule of law applicable to personal property, that possession constitutes a sufficient title against all persons except the rightful owner, who, whenever he appears, may claim and recover that which belongs to him. The negro, in this case, has undertaken to prove that he is free, and, failing in this, the effect of his application ceases.[181]

Chetwood thus was of the opinion that Cork should have been delivered to Snowden as his slave, based upon the presumption against liberty.[182]

Both Chief Justice Kinsey and Justice Chetwood noted that, in 1775, Lord Dunmore issued a proclamation offering freedom to slaves who joined the British Army, and that many slaves ran away to join the British forces. Both also stated that there was no evidence confirming whether Cork was a runaway slave or was a free black who was impressed into service as a prisoner or as plunder.[183] There is evidence, however, that Colonel Tarleton recruited or impressed at least one free black man, Thomas Johnson, who served Tarleton as a guide from 1780 "till the bitter end," when Johnson and his family were evacuated with the British army to Nova Scotia.[184]

These cases further illustrate the substantive effects that the procedural presumptions and burden of proof allocations had on the lives of the freedom claimants and their alleged owners. The Southern courts, following the decision in *Gobu*, would have applied the presumption of slavery if a dark skinned baby had been abandoned. This presumption probably would have applied to Cork as well if he had been abandoned in North Carolina, because he was described only as a "negro." In both the *Gobu* and *Lyon* cases, no one offered any proof of the maternal ancestry or servile status of the claimants' maternal ancestors, so the presumption and burden allocation that the courts applied was crucial to the outcome of the cases. Cork may have won his case because the New Jersey version of the slavery presumption required the defendant to prove his title, even though it appears that Cork may have been of a darker color than the claimant in *Gobu*.

Case Law Allocating the Burdens Based on Illegal Export or Import

The statutes that freed slaves who were illegally imported into Virginia, Maryland, and Delaware, and those who were illegally exported from Delaware, also created issues of proof in the freedom suits that persons held as slaves filed pursuant to those acts. The Delaware and Virginia courts applied different presumptions.

The Virginia courts adopted an approach favoring slavery over liberty when they applied the statute freeing slaves if they were imported into Virginia by an owner who did not take the required oath on a timely basis. The courts created a presumption of compliance by which a jury could conclude that the owner took the required oath within the necessary time if the circumstances suggested compliance, such as if the slave was imported twenty years before the freedom suit filing. The Virginia courts required the person held as a slave to prove that the oath was not taken.[185]

The Virginia Supreme Court of Appeals first endorsed this presumption in the 1817 decision in *Garnett v. Sam*.[186] The plaintiffs Sam and Phillis, who were husband and wife, relied on the statutes barring the importation of slaves into Virginia after 1778. They claimed that they were slaves of Mr. Peck, who, sometime between 1787 and 1790, brought them into Virginia when he moved from New Jersey. They did not file their suit until July 1811. The defendant apparently resisted the plaintiffs' claim, in part, by alleging that Peck gave the required oath when he moved into Virginia. The plaintiffs' lawyer requested that the trial court instruct the jury that if they believed that the plaintiffs were imported into Virginia after 1786, the defendant must "shew [sic] that he had taken the Oath prescribed and required" by the statutes. The court refused to give this instruction, and the jury then found for the defendant.[187]

On the plaintiffs' appeal, the Supreme Court's opinion by Judge Roane reversed the verdict, and remanded the case for further proceedings, but Roane also endorsed the presumption against liberty. The defendant's lawyer, identified as Mr. Stanard, argued that the trial court correctly rejected the plaintiffs' proposed instruction for two reasons. First, Stanard noted that the instruction was not properly worded because it required the defendant to prove that he took the required oath, rather than the person who imported the slaves. Second, he argued in favor of a presumption that the oath had been taken.

> The Jury might well presume, from the circumstances, that the Oath had been taken. No provision for perpetuating the evidence of it is made in the law, which does not even say that it shall be reduced to writing. After such a length of time, when every Magistrate, who lived in the County at the time of importation, and every person, connected with the transaction, was dead, the burthen [sic] of proof ought surely not to be imposed upon the defendant. It would be a most formidable decision, that every descendant of a slave, brought in since 1787, is entitled to freedom, unless it can *now* be proved that the Oath was taken by the importer, and within sixty days after the importation.

He concluded by noting: "Even a grant from the Commonwealth, or a Deed, will be presumed after thirty years possession."[188]

Judge Roane stated that the trial court erred in not providing the jury with the instruction that the plaintiffs' lawyer requested. But he also suggested that the defendant could prove his defense under the statute after the plaintiffs made their *prima facie* case of illegal importation "by evidence adduced to shew [sic], or by circumstances authorizing a presumption that" the requited oath "had been taken[.]" Roane stated that the instruction in question was broad enough "to include the latter description of evidence as well as the former." He added that the trial court's refusal to give the instruction "may have absolved the [defendant] from exhibiting, either such circumstances, or such evidence to the Jury, one or other of which is deemed to be indispensible [sic], the Court is of opinion, that the said refusal was erroneous, and may have injured the rights of the [plaintiffs] on the trial."[189]

The Court of Appeals applied this presumption of compliance almost one year later to affirm a judgment for the defendant slave owner in *Abraham v. Matthews*.[190] The slave claimants alleged that they were illegally imported into Virginia before 1792. The trial court instructed the jury that "the fact of the master's having taken the oath required by law withing [sic] ten days after removal, would be presumed from a lapse of *twenty years* possession so as to throw the *onus probandi* on the plaintiff suing for freedom; but this presumption might be met or avoided by circumstances." The jury then found for the defendant. The Court of Appeals affirmed this judgment on the record submitted by the plaintiffs' counsel, without augment, even though the defendant did not appear.[191]

The Virginia judges continued to apply this presumption into the 1850s.[192] With the passage of time after the alleged importation, this presumption of compliance and against liberty provided masters and their lawyers with a procedural advantage. This presumption was a judicial creation that was not even suggested by the text of the statutes.

The Delaware Errors and Appeals Court, on the other hand, in 1838, adopted a presumption favoring liberty in *Allen v. Sarah*.[193] The freedom claimants in that case relied on the 1793 statute that freed slaves if their owners failed to obtain licenses before exporting from Delaware the slaves or their ancestors. The plaintiffs claimed that they were descendants of a slave named Amelia, who Derwood Hicks illegally exported from Delaware in 1799. The suit was not filed until 1836. The defendant's lawyer argued that the court should presume that Hicks obtained the necessary license in view of the passage of time after Amelia was exported, during which no civil suit or criminal complaint was filed.[194]

The Errors and Appeals Court's opinion by Justice Caleb S. Layton rejected this contention and affirmed the freedom judgment in favor of the plaintiffs. Layton stated that, as a general rule, people held as slaves were required to satisfy the burden of proof to sustain their claims. But when plaintiffs alleged that they or their ancestors were illegally exported by someone without a license in violation of the statute and the plaintiffs prove a *prima facie* case of the illegal exportation, "the burthen [sic] of proof is then shifted upon the master, and he must satisfy the court that the negro was lawfully exported."[195]

Conclusion: Procedural Burdens, Presumptions, and Policy Aims

These rules of procedure evidenced choices among alternative rules that we may presume legislators and judges made to advance what they perceived to be important public policy aims.[196] Robert Cover noted that, on one level of analysis, the race-based presumption of slavery and the burdens of proof as allocated in *Hudgins* made sense as public policy in the antebellum Southern states such as Virginia because the majority of blacks were in fact slaves.[197] He stated that legal rules establishing presumptions and allocating the burden of proof "ordinarily conform to probabilities in some sense[.]"[198] Indeed, in affirming a decision enforcing the presumption against an unsuccessful freedom claimant, Kentucky Court of Appeals Chief Justice John Boyle noted that free blacks "constitute but a small portion of the aggregate number of the African race among us. In a great majority of instances, therefore, the characteristic marks of the African are found to be connected with slavery, and the existence of the latter may well be inferred from the proof of the former."[199]

Nevertheless, Cover also observed that some presumptions and burden allocations, including the presumption of innocence in criminal cases, are "initial allocations of the burden of uncertainty," which, in view of the consequences on the people involved in the dispute, are resolved as policy preferences without regard to the probabilities. Accordingly, although it was "more probable than not that a black person [was] a slave in the Virginia of 1806[,] ... the consequences of the characterization of 'slave' are so serious that one wishes to be more certain of such fact than is permitted by a sense of general probability based on race." According to Cover it is "impossible to conceive of a manner of allocating the risks of uncertainty without considering substantive preferences. A general rule conforming allocations solely to probabilities flies in the face of our sense that one wants to be more certain when consequences are sufficiently serious."[200]

This perceived need for certainty coincided with the probabilities when light-skinned plaintiffs claimed that they were illegally held in slavery in the South, but it did not do so in the same way when black plaintiffs sought their freedom. As Wilbert Moore noted, "persons who were visibly members of the dominant caste could legally be held as slaves. In suits for freedom, however, those persons had an advantage in the legal principle which was a corollary of the presumption of slavery arising from color: the burden of proof of slavery lay on him who held as a slave a person who by 'inspection' was visibly white."[201] The presumption of slavery and burden allocation that the Southern courts applied, as Adrienne Davis wrote, thus hindered the claims of black-looking people seeking their release from bondage while protecting the property interests of slave owners and allowing a remedy to prevent whites "from accidentally falling into the perils of slavery."[202] These rules of procedure "secure[d] rights structured to secure white economic and liberty interests," and encouraged freedom claimants "to situate themselves as people who could be removed from chattel slavery without altering its fundamental order."[203]

Accordingly, the substantive law and the trial procedures that governed freedom suits were outcome determinative in many cases. They thus had real effects on the lives of real people claiming their freedom. The New Jersey and Delaware cases show, moreover, that these presumptions were not the inevitable result of autonomous legal reasoning from common law precedent. The courts and legislators simply were not required to abrogate the presumption in favor of liberty and designate some people presumptively as slaves with the burden of proof in either the Southern states' slave codes or in the common law of slavery.

Notes to Chapter 7

[1] *See* Cheryl I. Harris, "Whiteness as Property," 106 *Harv. L. Rev.* 1707, 1720-21 (1993).

[2] *See* Fede, *People Without Rights, supra* at 83-84, 210-15 (discussing the disruption of slavery's orderly oppression by acts including slave theft); and chapter 1, *supra* at note 128.

[3] *Butler v. Craig*, 2 H. & McH. 214 (Md. Gen. Ct. 1787), *aff'd* (Md. Ct. App. 1791).

[4] *Butler v. Boarman*, 1 H. & McH. 371 (Md. Prov. Ct. 1770); *see* Berlin, *Many Thousands, supra* at 281; Martha Hodes, *White Women, Black Men: Illicit Sex in the 19th-Century South* 19-38 (1999); Whitman, *supra* 63-65; Shaw, *supra* at 48; 4 Catterall, *supra* at 3; Gillmer, "Suing for Freedom," *supra* at 577-78.

[5] Berlin, *Many Thousands, supra* at 281.

[6] Gillmer, "Suing for Freedom," *supra* at 544-45; *see also, e.g.,* Grinberg, "Freedom," *supra* at 71-73; Nicholls, "Squint of Freedom," *supra* at 55-59 (noting how legislators and judges narrowed the basis for freedom suits beginning in the 1790s). A. E. Keir Nash also wrote of the relative fairness of the decisions of some Southern judges in the manumission and freedom suits. *See* Nash, "Reason of Slavery," *supra* at 98-218. Robert Shaw summarizes the appellate decisions in the freedom suit cases. Shaw, *supra* at 47-64, 152-53. Ariela Gross and Loren Schweninger discuss lower court records and verdicts. Gross,

Blood, supra at 1-110; Schweninger, "Slave Women," *supra*; Gross, "Litigating Whiteness," *supra*. I generally agree with Jason Gillmer's comment that the evidence of trial court proceedings is best considered within the legal context created by the statutes and appellate court decisions, just as the statutes and appellate court decisions must be read in their social, political, economic, and intellectual context. Gillmer, "Suing for Freedom," *supra* at 542, n. 31; Fede, *People Without Rights, supra* at 22-25; Fede, "Toward a Solution," *supra* at 319.

[7] Cobb, *supra* at 252.

[8] *Henry v. Nunn's Heirs*, 50 Ky. (11 B. Mon.) 239, 1850 WL 3346, at *4 (1850).

[9] *See, e.g., Phillips v. Lewis*, 1 Del. Cas. 417, 1796 WL 28 (Del. Com. Pl. 1796) (Asians could not be slaves absent a statute, only "Negroes and mulattoes descended from a female Negro."); Fede, *People Without Rights, supra* at 37.

[10] *See* chapter 1, *supra* at notes 74-75.

[11] 2 Hening, *supra* at 170; *see* Morris, *Slavery, supra* at 43-44. The 1662 act further revealed the slave's dishonored condition in a provision doubling the usual penalty for fornication when a black person was involved. *See* Higginbotham, *Color, supra* at 42-43.

[12] *See* Morris, *Slavery, supra* at 45 (noting that until 1715 in Maryland the child's status followed that of the father); Patterson, *Social Death, supra* at 138; *see also* chapter 1, *supra* at notes 74-75.

[13] *See* chapter 1, *supra* at notes 74-75.

[14] *See* Patterson, *Social Death, supra* at 134, and at 132-47 (discussing how different societies used enslavement by birth patterns, which included in some societies freedom for the child if only one parent was a free person).

[15] *See* Morris, *Slavery, supra* at 46 and 457, n. 53; Patterson, *Social Death, supra* at 144; William E. Nelson, "The Height of Sophistication: Law and Professionalism in the City-State of Charleston, South Carolina, 1670-1775," 61 *S.C. L. Rev.* 1, 47 (2009).

[16] Stampp, *supra* at 94.

[17] *See* Fede, *People Without Rights, supra* at 221-40; Mark Thornton, *et al.*, "Selling Slave Families Down the River: Property Rights and the Pubic Auction," 14 *The Independent Rev.* 71 (2009); Russell, "New Image," *supra*.

[18] *See* Kolchin, *American Slavery supra* at 61, 129; Shaw, *supra* at 167; Genovese, *Roll, supra* at 41; Stroud, *supra* at 58-63. New Jersey statutes of 1788 and 1798, in contrast, *required* masters to teach slave children how to read. *See* Wolinetz, *supra* at 2227, 2241-42.

[19] *See* chapter 1, *supra* at note 76.

[20] *See* chapter 2, *supra* at notes 57-84.

[21] *See infra* at chapter 8.

[22] *See* Stampp, *supra* at 251-56; Fede, "Slave Buyers," *supra* at 350-53.

[23] *See Commonwealth v. Griffin*, 42 Ky. (3 B. Mon.) 208, 1842 WL 3310 (1842).

[24] *See* Ford, *supra* at 30-38; Shaw, *supra* at 141-47; Cobb, *supra* at 307-08.

[25] *See* Ford, *supra* at 38.

[26] *See* 9 Hening, *supra* at 471-72; *Betty v. Horton*, 32 Va. (5 Leigh) 615, 1833 WL 2132 at *2 (1833); Ford, *supra* at 38; Wolf, *Race, supra* at 25-27, 116; 2 Hurd, *supra* at 2; Nicholls, "Squint of Freedom," *supra* at 51-55, 57-59; Higginbotham & Higginbotham, *supra* at 1248-55.

[27] Nicholls, "Squint of Freedom," *supra* at 51.

[28] *See* Wolf, *Race, supra* at 26-27; Nicholls, "Squint of Freedom," *supra* at 51-52.

[29] 13 Hening, *supra* at 62; Nicholls, "Squint of Freedom," *supra* at 51.

[30] *See* 12 Hening, *supra* at 182-83; Nicholls, "Squint of Freedom," *supra* at 52-53.

[31] *See Betty v. Horton*, 32 Va. (5 Leigh) 615, 1833 WL 2132 at *2.

[32] Wolf, *Race, supra* at 26.

[33] *Id.* at 27, 116; 2 Hurd, *supra* at 7; *see McMichen v. Amos,* 25 Va. (4 Rand.) 134, 1826 WL 1001 (1826) (forfeiture provision not repealed by 1819 statute where right to freedom was vested).

[34] For the Virginia court decisions applying this statute, *see infra* at notes 185-92.

[35] For Maryland, *see Laws of Maryland, 1831*, ch. 323, §§4-5; *Id., 1823*, ch. 87; *Id., 1796*, ch. 67, §§1-11; *Id., 1792*, ch. 56; *Id., 1783*, ch. 23; *Scott v. Negro Ben,* 10 U.S. (6 Cranch.) 3, 3 L. Ed. 135, 1810 WL 1606 (1810); *Ringgold v. Barley,* 5 Md. 186, 1853 WL 3571 (1853); *Cross v. Black,* 9 G. & J. 198, 1837 WL 1922 (Md. 1837); *Bland and Woolfolk v. Dowling,* 9 G. & J. 19, 1837 WL 1911 (Md. 1837); *Baptiste v. De Volunbrun,* 5 H. & J. 86, 1820 WL 395 (Md. 1820); *Fulton v. Lewis,* 3 H. & J. 564, 1815 WL 581 (Md. 1815); *Negro Harry v. Lyles,* 4 H. & McH. 215, 1798 WL 412 (Md. Gen. Ct. 1798); *DeKerlegand v. Negro Hector,* 3 H. & McH. 185, 1794 WL 453 (Md. Gen. Ct. 1794), *aff'd* (Md. 1796); Ford, *supra* at 34; Whitman, *supra* at 10-11; Brackett, *supra* at 45-52, 64-72; Patricia A. Reid, "The Haitian Revolution, Black Petitioners and Refugee Widows in Maryland, 1796-1820," 50 *Am. J. of Legal Hist.* 431, 439-41 (2010). For Delaware, *see* 2 *Laws of Delaware, supra* at 886-87; *Newton v. Turpin,* 8 G. & J. 433, 1837 WL 1905 (Md. 1837); *Negro James v. Carr,* 2 Del. Cas. 223, 1805 WL 624 (Del. Com. Pl. 1805); *Britol v. Dickerson's Adm'rs,* 1 Del. Cas. 148, 1797 WL 676 (Del. Com. Pl. 1797); *Negro Jemima v. Ross,* 1 Del. Cas. 119, 1796 WL 726 (Del. Com. Pl. 1796); Ford, *supra* at 31; Essah, *supra* at 40-41, 50-51; 4 Catterall, *supra* at 213; 2 Hurd, *supra* at 75. For the District of Columbia, *see* Shaw, *supra* at 228-31.

[36] *See* 2 *Laws of Delaware, supra* at 885; Ford, *supra* at 31; Essah, *supra* at 40-41. Maryland's legislature considered but rejected a slave export ban. *See* Ford, *supra* at 34; Brackett, *supra* at 57-60.

[37] *See* 2 *Laws of Delaware, supra* at 1094; *Allen v. Negro Sarah,* 2 Del. (2 Harr.) 434, 1838 WL 150 (Del. Er. & App. 1838); Essah, *supra* at 41; Shaw, *supra* at 144, 148; Stampp, *supra* at 252; 4 Catterall, *supra* at 212-13.

[38] 2 *Laws of Delaware, supra* at 1093-95; *Allen v. Negro Sarah,* 1838 WL 150 at *5; Essah, *supra* at 84-86; 4 Catterall, *supra* at 212.

[39] *See* chapter 2, *supra* at notes 42-47.

[40] *See* Grinberg, "Manumission," *supra* at 221-28; and chapter 2, *supra* at note 48.

[41] Richard J. Biunno, *Current New Jersey Rules of Evidence* 24-28 (2010).

[42] *Id.* at 50-54.

[43] *Id.* at 24-27, 52.

[44] *Anderson v. Mt. Clemens Pottery Co.*, 328 U.S. 680, 686-88, 66 S. Ct. 1187, 90 L. Ed. 1515 (1946); Biunno, *supra* at 26-27, 52; 29 *Am. Jur. 2d*, "Evidence" §202 at 216 (2008 & supp. 2010).

[45] Biunno, *supra* at 26.

[46] *Id.* at 119-30; 29 *Am. Jur. 2d*, "Evidence," *supra* §202 at 216.

[47] Biunno, *supra* at 53, 119-22; 29 *Am. Jur. 2d*, "Evidence," *supra* §199 at 212-13, §215 at 230.

[48] *See, e.g.*, Biunno, *supra* at 125-30.

[49] *See* Schafer, *Supreme Court, supra* at 20; Sweet, *supra* at 161-68; Oakes, *supra* at 156-57; Tushnet, *Humanity, supra* at 143; Stampp, *supra* at 194; Cobb, *supra* at 66-67; Gillmer, "Suing for Freedom," *supra* at 604; Wiecek, "Statutes," *supra* at 263; Moore, "Slave Law," *supra* at 187-91.

[50] *See 7 Statutes at Large of South Carolina, supra* at 352 [emphasis added]. The 1712 code's provisions were for the most part continued in the 1722 and 1735 slave codes. The 1712 code authorized the "governor and council" to grant freedom claims, and the 1722 and 1735 codes authorized the courts to hear those claims. *See id.* at 371, 385; Higginbotham, *Color, supra* at 169; Davis, *Western Culture, supra* at 57; 1 Hurd, *supra* at 299, 302.

[51] *See 7 Statutes at Large of South Carolina, supra* at 397-98; chapter 4, *supra* at note 7.

[52] *See* chapter 4, *supra* at note 9.

[53] *See Laws of the Territory of Louisiana, supra* at 97, §4.

[54] *See Laws of Missouri 1824, supra* at 405, §3; *Chouteau v. Pierre of Color*, 9 Mo. 3, 1845 WL 3817 at *3 (1845); *Tramell v. Adam, a Black Man*, 2 Mo. 155, 1829 WL 1766 at *2 (1829); *Susan v. Hight*, 1 Mo. 118, 1821 WL 1446 at *1 (1821).

[55] *See* Olwell, "Becoming Free," *supra* at 2.

[56] *See id.* at 17, n. 3.

[57] Frank Sweet asserted that, until 1802, the courts in British America, followed *Las Siete Partidas* and required the alleged owner to rebut a presumption of freedom. *See* Sweet, *supra* at 161-62. In the pre-1802 cases discussed in this chapter, the claimants apparently assumed the burden of proof to establish their right to freedom by proof of a white, Native American, or other free maternal ancestor. *See also State v. Heddon*, 1 N.J.L. 377 (Sup. Ct. 1795); *State v. Lyon*, 1 N.J.L. 462 (Sup. Ct. 1789). On *Las Siete Partidas*, see *Adelle v. Beauregard*, 1 Mart. (o.s.) 183, 1810 WL 869 at *1 (La. Terr. Super. Orleans 1810); Watson, *Americas, supra* at 40-47; Davis, *Western Culture, supra* at 57.

[58] 41 *Archives of Maryland, Proceedings of the Provincial Court, 1658-1662* 499-500 (Bernard Christian Steiner, ed.) (1922); *see* 4 Catterall, *supra* at 9, 13; Alpert, *supra* at 192.

[59] 1 *Archives of Maryland, Proceedings and Acts of the General Assembly of Maryland, January 1637/8–September 1664* 533-34 (William Hand Browne, ed.) (1883); *see* 4 Catterall, *supra* at 1-2; Alpert, *supra* at 195-98.

[60] *See* Robert J. Brugger, *Maryland, A Middle Temperament: 1634-1980* 43 (1996); Brackett, *supra* at 37.

[61] *See* Lois Green Carr, Men's Career Files, Maryland State Archives, Thomas Hagleton,

MSA SC 5094-1736-1.

[62] *See* 66 *Archives of Maryland: Proceedings of the Provincial Court, 1675-1677* 291 (Elizabeth Merritt, ed.) (1954); Alpert, *supra* at 207.

[63] 3 H. & McH. 501, 1796 WL 636 (1796).

[64] *Negro Mary v. The Vestry of William and Mary's Parrish*, 1796 WL 636 at *1.

[65] *Act of Assembly of Maryland of 1715*, ch. 44, §22, quoted in Stroud, *supra* at 2; *United States v. Dow*, 25 F. Cas. 901, 903 (C.C. D. Md. 1840) (No. 14,990); *see* Morris, *Slavery*, *supra* at 45; Brackett, *supra* at 33; Wiecek, "Statutes," *supra* at 262; Alpert, *supra* at 190-95, 209.

[66] *United States v. Dow*, 25 F. Cas. at 903.

[67] *Negro Mary v. The Vestry of William and Mary's Parrish*, 3 H. & McH. 501, 1796 WL at *1; Brackett, *supra* at 36-37.

[68] *See* 4 Catterall, *supra* at 2; Alpert, *supra* at 209-10.

[69] *See, e.g., Mahoney v. Ashton*, 4 H. & Mc H. 63, 1797 WL 583 (Md. Gen. Ct. 1797), 4 H. & Mc H. 210, 1798 WL 411 (Md. Gen. Ct. 1798), 4 H. & Mc H. 295, 1799 WL 397 (Md. Gen. Ct. 1799), *rev'd* (Md. Ct. App. 1802) (freedom judgment for plaintiff reversed); *Higgins v. Allen*, 3 H. & McH. 504 (Md. Gen. Ct. 1796) (judgment for plaintiff reversed), *aff'd* (Md. Ct. App. 1798); *Queen v. Ashton*, 3 H. & McH. 439, 1796 WL 630, 1796 WL 630 (Md. Gen. Ct. 1796) (unsuccessful damage suit after freedom judgment for plaintiff); *Shorter v. Rozier*, 3 H. & McH. 238 (Md. Gen. Ct. 1794) (judgment for plaintiff); *Thomas v. Pile*, 3 H. & McH. 241 (Md. Gen. Ct. 1794) (judgment for plaintiff affirmed); *Rawlings v. Boston*, 3 H. & McH. 139, 1793 WL 394 (Md. Gen. Ct. 1793) (judgment for plaintiff affirmed); *Butler v. Craig*, 2 H. & McH. 214 (Md. Gen. Ct. 1787), *aff'd* (Md. Ct. App. 1791) (judgment for plaintiffs affirmed); *Toogood v. Scott*, 2 H. & McH. 26, 1782 WL 7 (Md. Gen. Ct. 1782) (freedom judgment for plaintiff), *aff'd* (Md. Ct. App. 1783); *Butler v. Boarman*, 1 H. & McH. 371 (Md. Prov. Ct. 1770) (judgment for defendant); 4 Catterall, *supra* at 2-3.

[70] 1 N.C. (Tay.) 100, 1802 WL 207 (1802); *see* Max R. Williams, "John Louis Taylor," in *The Yale Biographical Dictionary of American Law* 539 (Roger K. Newman, ed., 2009) [hereinafter *Yale Biographical Dictionary*].

[71] *Gobu v. Gobu*, 1802 WL 207 at *1.

[72] *See* John V. Orth, "What's Wrong with the Law of Finders and How to Fix It," 4 *Green Bag* 2d 391, 391-94 (2001); Eric W. Neilsen, "Is the Law of Acquisition of Property by Find Going to the Dogs?," 15 *T.M. Cooley L. Rev.* 479, 485-86 (1998).

[73] *See* Neilsen, 15 *T.M. Cooley L. Rev.* at 493-98.

[74] *See* Morris, *Slavery*, *supra* at 44-45; Banks, *supra* at 809-11.

[75] Banks, *supra* at 799.

[76] *Id.* at 812-20; Warren M. Billings, "The Cases of Fernando and Elizabeth Key: A Note on the Status of Blacks in Seventeenth-Century Virginia," 30 *Wm. & Mary Q.* 467, 468-69, 772-73 (1973); *see* Morris, *Slavery*, *supra* at 44-45.

[77] Banks, *supra* at 819.

[78] *Id.* at 822.

[79] *See id.* at 834-37; Billings, *supra* at 469. The record of the case is published in Warren

M. Billings, ed., *The Old Dominion in the Seventeenth Century: A Documentary History of Virginia, 1606-1689* 165-69 (1975).

[80] *See Coleman v. Dick*, 1 Va. (1 Wash.) 378 (Va. Sup. Ct. 1793) (judgment for plaintiff affirmed by divided court); *Jenkins v. Tom*, 1 Va. (1 Wash.) 90 (Va. Sup. Ct. 1792) (judgment for plaintiff affirmed); *Howell v. Netherland*, 1 Va. (Jeff.) 90 (Va. Gen. Ct. 1770) (plaintiff's claim denied at trial).

[81] 11 Va. (1 Hen. & M.) 134 (1806).

[82] *See* Gross, "Litigating Whiteness," *supra* at 129; *see also* chapter 1, *supra* at notes 81-82.

[83] Among the discussions of *Gobu v. Gobu*, *see* Randall Kennedy, *Sellout: The Politics of Racial Betrayal* 21-22 (2008); Sweet, *supra* at 163-64; Degler, *supra* at 241; Randall Kennedy, "Interracial Intimacies: Sex, Marriage, Identity, Adoption," 17 *Harv. BlackLetter L.J.* 57, 66 n. 37 (2001); Aaron Schwabach, "Jefferson and Slavery," 19 *T. Jefferson L. Rev.* 63, 73, n. 75 (1997).

[84] *Hudgins v. Wrights*, 11 Va. (1 Hen. & M.) at 134.

[85] *See* Powell, *supra* at 101. Neither Ms. Wright's first name nor the names of her children appear in the official report. Her name is spelled two ways in recently published sources. *See* Wallenstein, *supra* at 32 (Jacky); Angela Onwuachi-Willig, "Multiracialism and the Social Construction of Race: The Story of *Hudgins v. Wrights*," in Rachel F. Moran, *et al.*, eds., *Race Law Studies* 154 (2008) (Jacky); Wythe Holt, "George Wythe: Early Modern Judge," 58 *Ala. L. Rev.* 1009, 1031 (2007) (Jackey). Ms. Wright also sued with either two or three children. *See* Wallenstein, *supra* at 32 (three); Onwuachi-Willig, *supra* at 154 (two). Taylor was either Chief Justice Marshall's brother-in-law or son-in-law. *See* Powell, *supra* at 101 (brother-in-law); Wallenstein, *supra* at 32 (son-in-law).

[86] *Hudgins v. Wrights*, 11 Va. (1 Hen. & M.) at 134; Onwuachi-Willig, *supra* at 154-55.

[87] *Hudgins v. Wrights*, 11 Va. (1 Hen. & M.) at 134; *see* Holt, *supra* at 1031-34 (discussing the trial), and at 1036-38 (discussing Wythe's opinion re-created from the court files and other sources).

[88] *Id. See* Cover, *Justice Accused*, *supra* at 42-61 (discussing the constitutional provision and Wythe's life and decisions). *See also* Kermit L. Hall, *et al.*, eds., *American Legal History: Cases and Materials* 69 (2d ed. 1996); Higginbotham & Higginbotham, *supra* at 1237-42; Higginbotham & Kopytoff, *supra* at 1985-88. For a history of the Virginia "free and equal" clause, *see* Paul Finkelman, "The Centrality of the Peculiar Institution in American Legal Development," 68 *Chi-Kent L. Rev.* 1009, 1019-21 (1993). For another discussion of Wythe's career, *see* John T. Noonan, Jr., *Persons and Masks of the Law: Cardozo, Holmes, Jefferson, and Wythe as Makers of the Masks* 29-64 (1976).

[89] *Hudgins v. Wrights*, 11 Va. (1 Hen. & M.) at 135.

[90] *See* Holt, *supra* at 1036-38 (discussing the reversal of Wythe's reasoning and his mysterious death).

[91] *See Hudgins v. Wrights*, 11 Va. (1 Hen. & M.) at 136-40.

[92] *See id.* at 141.

[93] *Id.* at 139-40.

[94] *Id.* at 140.

[95] *Id.* at 141.

[96] *Id.*

[97] *Id.* at 144. These opinions do not cite the *Gobu* decision.

[98] 1 Mart. (o.s.) 183, 1810 WL 869 (La. Terr. Super. Orleans 1810). The official report of the decision is sometime referred to *Adele v. Beauregard*.

[99] *See* Spear, *supra* at 190.

[100] *Id.* at 190-91.

[101] *See Adelle v. Beauregard*, 1810 WL 869 at *1.

[102] *See id.* Judith K. Schafer notes that the plaintiff could have won her case because she attended school in New York, a free state, but "she claimed that because she was a mulatto she was legally presumed free, and won that way." *See* Schafer, *Supreme Court, supra* at 264, n. 19.

[103] *See* Vernon Valentine Palmer, "The Strange Science of Codifying Slavery—Moreau Lislet and the Louisiana Digest of 1808," 24 *Tulane Eur. & Civ. L.F.* 83, 89 (2009).

[104] *See* Schafer, *Supreme Court, supra* at 13, 20, 223.

[105] *See* Edwards, *People, supra* at 37, 304-05, n. 8, 307-08, n. 9.

[106] *See* Degler, *supra* at 241.

[107] *See Las Siete Partidas, Volume 3, supra* Part 3, Title 14, Law 5 at 655; *Hawkins v. Vanwickle*, 6 Mart. (n.s.) 418, 1828 WL 1418 at * 1 (La. 1828) (applying the rule in *Las Siete Partidas* to impose the burden of proof on the defendant when the issue was not the plaintiff's right to freedom, but was whether the plaintiff was a freed slave who could sue the defendant to recover a slave and other property from the defendant).

[108] *See Forsyth v. Nash*, 4 Mart. (o.s.) 385, 1816 WL 944 (La. 1816) (presumption of slavery in *Adelle* applied to "a negro man," but bill of sale executed in Detroit, Michigan created a presumption of freedom that the defendant master could not rebut).

[109] *See* Cottrol, "Outlawing," *supra* at 742, n. 118, citing John W. Blassingame, *Black New Orleans, 1860-1880* 21-22 (1973).

[110] *See, e.g., Heirn v. Bridault*, 37 Miss. 209, 1859 WL 3633 at *15 (1859); *Farrelly v. Maria Louisa*, 34 Ala. 284, 1859 WL 731 at *2-*4 (1859); *Daniel v. Guy*, 19 Ark. 121, 1857 WL 545 at *9 (1857); *Gaines v. Ann*, 17 Tex. 211, 1856 WL 4994 at *3 (1856); *Cross v. Black*, 9 G. & J. 198, 1837 WL 1922 at *9 (Md. 1837); *Miller v. Denman*, 16 Tenn. (8 Yer.) 233, 1835 WL 941 at *2 (1835); *Vaughn v. Phebe*, 8 Tenn. (Mart. & Yer.) 5, 1828 WL 289 at *10 (1828); *Scott v. Williams*, 12 N.C. (1 Dev.) 376, 1827 WL 613 at *1 (1827); *Davis, a man of color v. Curry*, 5 Ky. (2 Bibb) 238, 1810 WL 715 at *2 (1810); *see also Bell v. Hogan*, 3 F. Cas. 107 (C.C.D.C. 1811) (No. 1,253).

[111] *See State v. Jeans*, 4 Del. (4 Harr.) 570 (Del. O. & T. 1845); *State v. Dillahunt*, 3 Del. (3 Harr.) 551 (Del. O. & T. 1842); Essah, *supra* at 67-69; 4 Catterall, *supra* at 211; Gillmer, "Suing for Freedom," *supra* at n. 465.

[112] *See Allen v. Sarah*, 2 Del. (2 Harr.) 434, 1838 WL 150 at *3 (Err. & App.1838).

[113] *State v. Dillahunt*, 3 Del. (3 Harr.) at 552; Essah, *supra* at 69. *See State v. Kershaw*, 1 Del. Cas. 218, 1799 WL 207 (Del. Quar. Sess. 1799) (requiring defendant to post surety for peace pending slave's freedom suit, court found on the facts there was a presumption of

freedom in the slave's favor); *Phillips v. Lewis*, 1 Del. Cas. 417, 1796 WL 28 (Del. Com. Pl. 1796) (claimant demonstrated that her grandmother was imported from Asia, not Africa, so claimant could not legally be a slave); Essah, *supra* at 69 (citing Daniel Webb or Webster's successful 1851 suit in which the owner did not produce a bill of sale or other proof that the petitioner was not free).

[114] Cobb, *supra* at 67; *see, e.g., Adelle v. Beauregard*, 1 Mart. (o.s.) 183, 1810 WL 869 at *1 (La. Terr. Super. Orleans 1810); Schafer, *Supreme Court, supra* at 20; Tushnet, *Humanity, supra* at 143-44.

[115] Cobb, *supra* at 67; *see also Stoutenborough v. Haviland*, 15 N.J.L. 266 (Sup. Ct. 1836) (questioning slavery presumption after adoption of gradual emancipation law).

[116] *Kinney v. Cook*, 4 Ill. (3 Scam.) 232, 1841 WL 3305 at *2 (1841); *see Bailey v. Cromwell*, 3 Ill. (3 Scam.) 71, 1841 WL 3255 at *3 (1841) (also adopting the presumption of freedom in suit on a note, which was argued by Abraham Lincoln).

[117] *See, e.g., Morrison v. White*, 16 La. Ann. 100, 1861 WL 3671 at * 2 (1861); *Heirn v. Bridault*, 37 Miss. 209, 1859 WL 3633 at *15 (1859); *Gentry v. McMinnis*, 33 Ky. (3 Dana) 382, 1835 WL 1908 at *5 (1835).

[118] *Gaines v. Ann*, 17 Tex. 211, 1856 WL 4994 at *3 (1856).

[119] *Gentry v. McMinnis*, 33 Ky. (3 Dana) 382, 1835 WL 1908 at *5 (1835).

[120] *See, e.g., id.* (affirming judgment on jury verdict based upon proof that claimant was born in Pennsylvania after 1780, according to abolition statute she was born free and was required to serve apprenticeship until 28 years old); *Vaughn v. Phebe*, 8 Tenn. (Mart. & Yer.) 5, 1828 WL 289 (1828) (reversing judgment on jury verdict because of hearsay evidence admitted in error, verdict based upon proofs that claimant's mother was a free Native American). For excellent discussions of the trial and appellate court proceedings in the latter case, and its context, *see* Gross, *Blood, supra* at 9, 24-27; Gillmer, "Suing for Freedom," *supra* at 536-37, 565-78; Gross, "Litigating Whiteness," *supra* at 143-47.

[121] 56 Va. (15 Gratt.) 314, 1859 WL 4569 (1859).

[122] *Fulton's Ex'ors v. Gracey*, 1859 WL 4569 at *1-*9.

[123] *Id.* at *8.

[124] *See, e.g., Gaines' Adm'r v. Ann, by her Guardian ad Litem*, 26 Tex. 340, 1862 WL 2867 (1862) and *Gaines v. Ann*, 17 Tex. 211, 1856 WL 4994 (1856) (reversing two jury verdicts for claimant based in part on claimant's white appearance as being contrary to the evidence of the claimants' maternal black slave ancestry); *Morrison v. White*, 16 La. Ann. 100, 1861 WL 3671 (1861) (reversing jury verdict for claimant with "fair complexion, blue eyes, and flaxen hair" to permit alleged owner to rebut presumption of freedom with hearsay reputation evidence); *Chancellor v. Milly*, 39 Ky. (9 Dana) 23, 1839 WL 2577 (1839) (reversing jury verdict based on claimant's white skinned appearance to permit alleged owner to rebut presumption of freedom with hearsay reputation evidence).

[125] 16 Va. (2 Munf.) 379, 1811 WL 685 (1811).

[126] MacLeod, *supra* at 125.

[127] *Id.*; *Hook's Adm'rs v. Hancock*, 19 Va. (5 Munf.) 546 (1817) (judgment for Hancock reversed).

[128] *See* Shirley Elizabeth Thompson, *Exiles at Home: The Struggle to Become American in*

Creole New Orleans 82-84 (2009); Gross, *Blood, supra* at 58-63; Stephan Talty, *Mulatto America: At the Crossroads of Black and White Culture: A Social History* 13-15 (2003); Gross, "Litigating Whiteness," *supra* at 166-72, citing *Miller v. Belmonti*, 11 Rob. 339 (La. 1845) and the trial records.

For book-length treatments, *see* Carol Wilson, *The Two Lives of Sally Miller: A Case of Mistaken Racial Identity in Antebellum New Orleans* (2007); John Bailey, *The Lost German Slave Girl: The Extraordinary True Story of Sally Miller and Her Fight for Freedom in Old New Orleans* (2005).

[129] Gross, "Litigating Whiteness," *supra* at 166-72.

[130] Gross, *Blood, supra* at 60; Gross, "Litigating Whiteness," *supra* at 167-69.

[131] *See* Gross, *Blood, supra* at 60-63; Gross, "Litigating Whiteness," *supra* at 167-72, discussing the public debate over the case as evidenced in the media.

[132] Gross, *Blood, supra* at 16-72; Gillmer, "Suing for Freedom," *supra* at 608; Gross, "Litigating Whiteness," *supra* at 132-51, 156-77.

[133] *See, e.g., Morrison v. White*, 16 La. Ann. 100, 1861 WL 3671 (1861); *Gary v. Stevenson*, 19 Ark. 580, 1858 WL 613 (1858); *Daniel v. Guy*, 19 Ark. 121, 1857 WL 584 (1857); *Gaines v. Ann*, 17 Tex. 211, 1856 WL 4994 (1856); Gross, *Blood, supra* at 38-41; Sweet, *supra* at 169-77; Gillmer, "Suing for Freedom," *supra* at 607-08; Gross, "Litigating Whiteness," *supra* at 151-56 (citing cases in which expert testimony was relied upon).

[134] 19 Ark. 580, 1858 WL 613 (1858).

[135] *Gary v. Stevenson*, 1858 WL 613 at *1-*4.

[136] *Id.* at *3.

[137] *Id.* at *4. For an excellent discussion of the trial and appellate court proceedings in this case and its context, *see* Gillmer, "Suing for Freedom," *supra* at 537-38, 588-619; and *see* Tushnet, *Humanity, supra* at 143-44; Stafford, *supra* at 461-62 (stating that the claimant's lawyer may have made a "tactical error" by filing the case in the court of equity instead of as an action at law in which a jury trial would have been held).

[138] 16 La. Ann. 100, 1861 WL 3671 (1861).

[139] *Morrison v. White,* 1861 WL 3671 at *2.

[140] *Id.* at *1-*2.

[141] *Id.* at *2. For excellent discussions of the trial and appellate court proceedings in this case, and its context, *see* Thompson, *supra* at 84; Gross, *Blood, supra* at 1-3, 39-40; Wallenstein, *supra* at 52-53; Walter Johnson, "The Slave Trader, the White Slave, and the Politics of Racial Determination in the 1850s," 87 *J. of Am. Hist.* 13 (2000); Gross, "Litigating Whiteness," *supra* at 171-77. The trial after the appeal resulted in a hung jury, the defendant appealed again, but the Civil War intervened before the Louisiana Supreme Court decided the case a second time. *Id.*

[142] 17 Tex. 211, 1856 WL 4994 (1856).

[143] 26 Tex. 340, 1862 WL 2867 (1862).

[144] *Gaines v. Ann,* 1856 WL 4994 at *2.

[145] *Id.* at *3.

[146] *Id.*

147 *See Gaines' Adm'r v. Ann*, 1862 WL 2867 at *2. Nash does not discuss these cases in his article on the Texas Supreme Court's decisions between 1845 and 1860. *See* A. E. Keir Nash, "The Texas Supreme Court and Trial Rights of Blacks, 1845-1860," 58 *J. of Am. Hist.* 622 (1971).

148 *Daniel v. Guy*, 23 Ark. 50, 1861 WL 538 (1861).

149 *Daniel v. Guy*, 19 Ark. 121, 1857 WL 584 at * 5-*11 (1857).

150 *Daniel v. Guy*, 23 Ark. 50, 1861 WL 538 at *2.

151 *Id.*; *Daniel v. Guy*, 19 Ark. 121, 1857 WL 584 at *4.

152 *Daniel v. Guy*, 23 Ark. 50, 1861 WL 538 at *2; *Daniel v. Guy*, 19 Ark. 121, 1857 WL 584 at *2-*5.

153 *Daniel v. Guy*, 19 Ark. 121, 1857 WL 584 at *2-*5.

154 *Daniel v. Guy*, 19 Ark. 121, 1857 WL 584 at *4.

155 *Daniel v. Guy*, 23 Ark. 50, 1861 WL 538 at *2.

156 *Id.* at *4.

157 *Id.* at *2.

158 *Id.* at *4. For excellent discussions of the trial court and appellate court proceedings in this case, and its context, *see* Gross, *Blood*, *supra* at 9, 30-34; Teresa C. Zackodnik, *The Mulatta and the Politics of Race* 4-7 (2004); Tushnet, *Humanity*, *supra* at 146-47; Gillmer, "Suing for Freedom," *supra* at 616-19; Gross, "Litigating Whiteness," *supra* at 124-37; Stafford, *supra* at 459-61.

159 Gross, *Blood*, *supra* at 45-46.

160 *Id.* at 46.

161 *Vaughn v. Phebe*, 8 Tenn. (Mart. & Yer.) 5, 1827 WL 613 at *10 (1827).

162 *See Henderson v. Campbell*, 95 Mont. 180, 26 P.2d 351, 352 (1933); 3B *C.J.S.* "Animals," §7.

163 *See* Banks, *supra* at 809-11; William M. Wiecek, "The Origins of the Law of Slavery in the British North America," 17 *Cardozo L. Rev.* 1711, 1715-25 (1996).

164 1 N.J.L. 462 (Sup. Ct. 1789).

165 *State v. Lyon,* 1 N.J.L. at 475-76.

166 *Id.* at 466-67.

167 *Id.* at 467.

168 *Id.*

169 *Id.* at 467-72.

170 *Id.* at 472.

171 *Id.* at 475.

172 *Id.*

173 *Id.* at 475-76.

174 *Id.* at 476; *see* Graham Russell Hodges, *Slavery and Freedom in the Rural North: Afri-*

can Americans in Monmouth County, New Jersey, 1664-1865 121-22 (1997); Cases Adjudged, supra at 19-20. The court later, in a case in which a black man's testimony was admitted, held that the presumption of slavery from a person's "black color" could be rebutted if there was proof that the witness enjoyed "unquestioned and uninterrupted possession of freedom" for more than 20 years, by analogy to the law of adverse possession of real estate. The court noted, however, that the actual period of years necessary to rebut the presumption had not been settled. Fox v. Lambson, 8 N.J.L. 275 (Sup. Ct. 1826); see Potts v. Harper, 3 N.J.L. 1030 (Sup. Ct. 1813) (affirming trial court's decision to permit black witness to testify on proof that he was reputed among his neighbors to have been free from his childhood).

[175] 1 N.J.L. 377 (Sup. Ct. 1795).

[176] State v. Heddon, 1 N.J.L. at 378-79.

[177] See Anthony J. Scotti, Jr., Brutal Virtue: The Myth and Reality of Banastre Tarleton 13-29, 232 (2002).

[178] State v. Heddon, 1 N.J.L. at 378-79. The defendant in this habeas corpus proceeding was "Heddon, the gaoler of Essex County," who had possession of Cork after his capture. Id. at 378.

[179] Id. at 379-80.

[180] Id. at 380.

[181] Id. at 381 (Chetwood, J., dissenting).

[182] Id.

[183] See id at 379, and at 381 (Chetwood, J., dissenting).

[184] See Cassandra Pybus, Epic Journeys of Freedom: Runaway Slaves of the American Revolution and their Global Quest for Liberty 41, 212 (2006); Gary B. Nash, The Forgotten Fifth: African Americans in the Age of Revolution (2006); Simon Schama, Rough Crossings: Britain, the Slaves and the American Revolution (2006); Berlin, Many Thousands, supra at 257-58 (discussing runaway slaves who fought for the British forces and their fate after the war). Paul Finkelman stated that State v. Heddon demonstrates that, before 1804, "New Jersey treated blacks the way other slave states did." Paul Finkelman, "Chief Justice Horatio Hornblower of New Jersey and the Fugitive Slave Law of 1793," in Slavery and the Law, supra at 119.

[185] See, e.g., Higginbotham & Higginbotham, supra at 1248-55. For a different interpretation of the cases, see Sherry, supra at 174-76.

[186] 19 Va. (5 Munf.) 542, 1817 WL 918 (1817). In Hook v. Pagee, 16 Va. (2 Munf.) 379, 1811 WL 685 (1811), the court avoided this issue, which was raised by the parties, when it sustained the freedom judgment for the claimants on other grounds. See supra at notes 125-27.

[187] See Garnett v. Sam, 1817 WL 918 at *1-*2. The plaintiffs relied upon hearsay affidavits containing alleged admissions of Peck to prove that they were brought into the state as they alleged. The defendant objected to these affidavits, which the trial court permitted as evidence. Id.

[188] Id. at *3. It appears that the defendant's lawyer was Robert Stanard, who was a lawyer, legislator, and a Virginia Court of Appeals judge from 1839 until his death in 1846. His son,

Robert C. Stanard, also was a respected lawyer and legislator, and was a friend of Edgar Allen Poe. *See* Theodore Frelinghuysen Wolfe, *Literary Haunts and Homes of American Authors* 120 (1898); 29 *American Almanac and Repository of Useful Knowledge* 359-60 (Jared Sparks, *et al.*, eds.) (1857); Nash, "Reason of Slavery," *supra* at 129 n. 394, 154, 162-63.

[189] *Garnett v. Sam*, 1817 WL 918 at *4. Judge Roane also held that the hearsay affidavits should not be admitted regarding Peck's alleged admissions. *Id.* Suzanna Sherry does not correctly state the holding of the court, which did not free the plaintiffs. *Compare* Sherry, *supra* at 175.

[190] 20 Va. (6 Munf.) 159, 1818 WL 1109 (1818).

[191] *Id.* The trial court also refused to give an instruction requested by the plaintiff that his infancy would defeat the presumption. Instead the judge "told that Jury that infancy was a *circumstance*, the *weight* and *effect* of which should be left to them." *Id.*

[192] *See, e.g., Unis v. Charlton's Adm'r*, 53 Va. (12 Gratt.) 484, 1855 WL 3486 (1855) (presumption applied, judgment for defendant affirmed); *George v. Parker*, 25 Va. (4 Rand.) 659, 1826 WL 1065 (1826) (applying presumption, but judgment for defendant reversed, trial judge misdirected jury by stating that oath could be taken within one year of the importation); *McMichen v. Amos*, 25 Va. (4 Rand.) 134, 1826 WL 1001 (1826) (presumption did not apply because the time after the importation was short of twenty years and it was alleged that the wife of the owner took the oath); *see also* Higginbotham & Higginbotham, *supra* at 1248-55; Sherry, *supra* at 174-76 (discussing these and other cases decided under these statutes).

[193] 2 Del. (2 Harr.) 434, 1838 WL 150 (Del. Er. & App. 1838).

[194] *See Allen v. Sarah*, 1838 WL 150 at *1-*2; Essah, *supra* at 67-68.

[195] *Allen v. Sarah*, 1838 WL 150 at *3. For other cases decided under the Delaware act, *see, e.g., State v. Turner*, 5 Del. (5 Harr.) 501, 1854 WL 860 (Del. Gen. Sess. 1854); *Sarah Thoroughgood, Negro v. Anderson*, 5 Del. (5 Harr.) 97, 1848 WL 818 (Del. Super. 1848) (and the decisions reported in the notes thereto); *Shockley v. Travers*, 2 Del. 673, 1821 WL 1530 (Err. & App. 1821).

[196] Cover, "Reflections," *supra* at 732-40; *see* Martinez, *supra* at 1077-92.

[197] Cover, "Reflections," *supra* at 729-30.

[198] *Id.* at 730. Cover stated that "virtually all presumptions include *both* some policy preference *and* assessments of probability." *Id.*, citing Charles McCormick, *Evidence* §§343-46, at 806-33 (2d ed. 1972), a leading treatise on evidence law.

[199] *Davis, a man of color v. Curry*, 5 Ky. (2 Bibb) 238, 1810 WL 715 at *2 (1810). The claimant in that case based his claim to freedom on the fact that he was removed from Delaware to Kentucky, and Delaware was the only slave state to eventually reject the presumption of slavery based on appearance.

[200] *See* Cover, "Reflections," *supra* at 730.

[201] Moore, "Slave Law," *supra* at 190.

[202] Davis, "Identity Notes," *supra* at 707.

[203] *Id.* at 708.

8

Freedom Suits Based on the Movement of Slaves

Some freedom claimants based their cases on their time spent in free states, territories, or nations, either with their masters or with their masters' consent. These freedom claimants can be placed into in three categories. First are the claimants who, while on free soil, either sued for their freedom or resisted their masters' attempts to retain them in slavery and return them to a slave jurisdiction. These claimants relied on the local laws of the forum free jurisdiction. Second are those who were brought to (or sent to) free soil by their masters, and who later sued for their freedom after they left free soil and returned to a slave state. These claimants asserted rights in the forum slave states based upon the substantive law of the free states, territories, or nations. Third are the claimants who were former slaves residing in free states. They sued in the slave state courts to recover property that their former masters devised or gave to them. They also asserted rights under the free states' substantive law.[1]

This chapter primarily will review the issues raised in the cases in categories two and three. Excluded from this analysis are cases involving slaves who ran away to free jurisdictions; they were subject to capture and return as fugitive slaves.[2]

This chapter also will exclude, with two exceptions, cases in which the freedom claimants based their claims on the substantive laws of the forum slave states or the laws of slave states other than the forum slave states in which they filed their action. We will consider an 1855 decision in which the Georgia Supreme Court held that slaves forfeited their "right" to freedom granted to them in their deceased master's will, if they were moved from a slave state that permitted manumission to another that did not.

The scholars who have evaluated the freedom cases discussed in this chapter have noted that many plaintiffs asked the forum slave state courts, or the federal courts, to decide their cases based upon the laws of a free nation, territory, or state. The courts in the antebellum years generally either explicitly or implicitly evaluated these requests under choice of law principles, including the doctrine of comity.[3] Comity in this sense means the voluntary decision by the forum state courts to decide a suit with another jurisdiction's laws.[4]

Scholars have evaluated these cases in their legal context by referring to the works of nineteenth century American legal treatise writers, including James Kent and Joseph Story, who discussed choice of law principles.[5] The forum state courts that decided whether or not to extend comity to foreign law made choices between alternative results in a case or class of cases. These choices could reflect both the public policy views of the forum state's lawmakers as well as the individual judges' views. For example, Story's treatise stated that "the laws of every people in force within its own limits, ought to have the same force every where, so far as they do not prejudice the power or rights of other governments, or of their citizens."[6]

According to Paul Finkelman and others, the courts in the North and the South found that this comity principle became more difficult to apply in freedom suits in the latter antebellum years.[7] By then, the northern states adopted laws abolishing slavery, and the pro-slavery doctrine gained force in the southern states:

> The critical question was how to determine these limits [on the application of foreign law], especially for the separate jurisdictions that made up the United States in the antebellum period. What were the elements of a law or judicial opinion that made it "prejudice" another jurisdiction? There was no set answer for this question. How a court responded to such an argument depended on the philosophical foundations of the political entity, as well as the ideological assumptions of the judges. Not surprisingly, in the antebellum era, attitudes towards race and slavery could put the jurisprudence or laws of one state beyond the pale of acceptability in another. The most crucial tests of these theories involved slavery and race.[8]

Therefore, Finkelman concluded that, in the later antebellum years, the Northern and the Southern courts were less willing to honor the principles of comity and apply foreign law when they decided whether to enforce freedom claims. Foreign law included the law of another nation or another state or territory in the United States. This trend extended in the South to freed slaves who asserted rights to property that was left to them by their former masters.

I suggest that, in addition to considering different approaches to comity, we can analyze these suits as examples of the different views that the Southern courts entertained about the masters' implied intentions when they traveled to or relocated to free soil with their slaves, and the perceived public policy implications of the courts' continued enforcement of both the masters' implied and expressed intentions to free their slaves in these and other circumstances. I will not in this chapter analyze this legal change to the extent that Finkelman did in his book-length treatment of the subject. I will instead highlight statutes and case law decisions that show how the legislators' and judges' attitudes toward these suits paralleled the legal trend that was increasing the limits on manumission, as discussed in the earlier chapters.

As Thomas Cobb suggested in his treatise, some Southern judges inferred from the masters' acts, including permanent or indeterminate relocations to free states or territories, that the masters intended to free the slaves that the masters took with them to live on free soil. But the courts found that other travels by masters and slaves to free lands were not evidence of implied manumissions because the masters made only visits of limited duration. The courts held that the masters did not clearly intend to change their residence and free their slaves merely by setting foot on free soil.[9]

The Southern courts initially distinguished relatively permanent changes in the masters' or slaves' domicile or residence and more temporary visits. Paul

Finkelman listed four categories—"transient, visitor, sojourner, or resident"—to analyze the treatment of masters who entered free territory.

> A transient was someone traveling from one state to another (usually from a slave state to a slave state), passing through a free state. Being "in transit" implied continuous movement. A visitor was someone entering a free state with a definite intention to return to his or her home state at some time in the near future. A sojourner intended to leave a free state at some unspecified time in the future. A resident, of course, planned to remain in the free state.[10]

Thus, when the courts made distinctions among these categories, the master's intention was a relevant factor.[11] Moreover, it also was held, as a general rule, that "[t]he itinerant and unsettled condition of the master will give character to the condition of his slaves. They are to be considered as attached to his person; dependent on his movements; and their will is merged in his."[12]

In my view, Southern judges based their decisions among these categories upon their own notions of what they thought that the masters intended, and not out of comity to foreign law, unless that law explicitly recognized the masters' rights to the courts' satisfaction. When the Southern opinion leaders embraced the pro-slavery ideology and became more hostile toward manumission, the legislators and judges increasingly began to refuse to enforce the masters' intentions to free or otherwise benefit their slaves or freed slaves, even when the masters' intentions were apparent. Consequently, the cases in this chapter are consistent with the antebellum trend that we have seen elsewhere in the Southern manumission and freedom suits limiting liberty and favoring bondage.

Somerset v. Stewart and The Slave Grace

Two influential British cases set the legal context for the study of these American freedom suits—*Somerset v. Stewart*[13] and *The Slave Grace*.[14] In *Somerset*, Chief Justice Lord Mansfield declared the legal theory that underlies the freedom claims that were based on the laws of a free state or nation. That 1772 decision, as noted in chapter four, influenced the development of the procedural remedy of *habeas corpus* in the United States, both in slavery cases and in general. It also highlighted substantive issues that exposed slavery's legal status in the English common law of the seventeenth, eighteenth, and nineteenth centuries.

James Somerset sought his freedom in that case. He was a slave of Charles Steuart. Steuart's name was spelled in the reports of the case as Stewart, and Somerset's name has been spelled in various ways. Steuart was a Scottish merchant and slave trader who moved to Virginia in 1741. In 1749, he bought Somerset, who then may have been between eight years old and his early teens. After 1765, Steuart served as the surveyor general of customs and was responsible for a territory from Quebec to Virginia. In 1767, Steuart was promoted to the office of receiver general of customs and he moved to Boston. Steuart then won a transfer to England. In the fall of 1769, he left Boston and arrived in London with

Somerset.

Steuart held Somerset as a slave in London until October 1, 1771, when Somerset escaped. Steuart hired slave catchers who captured Somerset on November 26, 1771, and placed him on a ship that was bound for Jamaica.

Two days later and while the ship still was docked in the River Thames, three Londoners who were Somerset's godparents obtained a writ of *habeas corpus* from Chief Justice Mansfield. The writ was served on the ship's captain, John Knowles. In effect, the writ forced Steuart, through Knowles, to assert the basis for his case in favor of slavery before Mansfield and two other judges of the Court of King's Bench.[15]

The lawyers argued the case before the court in February and May 1772. The initial arguments were made on February 7, 1772. Knowles had filed a return or response to the writ asserting first that slavery was practiced in Africa, and that Jamaican and Virginian laws authorized the purchase of African slaves who were held as personal property. Knowles alleged that Somerset was an African slave who Steuart bought in Jamaica, and that Somerset remained Steuart's slave until Somerset ran away on October 1, 1771. Knowles thus claimed that Steuart had the right to capture Somerset by force, hold him against his will on Knowles's ship, and then send him off to Jamaica for sale. This return was deceptive, according to Steven Wise, because it did not mention that Steuart and Somerset lived in Massachusetts before they sailed to England. Thus, it was assumed that Virginia was their last colony of residence, and that Virginia law might apply to determine Somerset's status.[16]

The matter was argued further beginning on May 9, 1772. At the end of the argument, Mansfield declared that the court would not immediately provide its decision.[17] He stated his concern for the "effects" of a decision "setting loose" 14,000 to 15,000 slaves who were then living in England. Mansfield signaled strongly his leanings when he suggested that the "merchants," not the abolitionists, might seek legislation to settle "the point for the future," and that Steuart should "end the question, by discharging or giving freedom to the negro."[18] Mansfield nevertheless advised the lawyers that if they could not resolve the dispute, the court would decide it; "*fiat justitia, ruat coelum*' he told the lawyers for both sides—let justice be done, though the heavens may fall!"[19]

The parties could not settle the dispute. Both the abolitionists, including Granville Sharp, and those supporting the British slave trading and slave holding interests apparently agreed that this was "a climacteric test case."[20] This clash of the interests forced Mansfield to decide the case, which he did when he read the court's oral opinion on June 22, 1772.[21]

The court's task was not an easy one. No statute prohibited or authorized and defined the master and slave relationship on British soil, and the available case law and other authorities discussing slavery were ambiguous.[22] Moreover, Mansfield had recently avoided deciding the issue of slavery's legality, much to the chagrin of abolitionists such as Sharp.[23]

The published accounts of Mansfield's oral opinion vary to some degree.[24] It is clear, however, that Mansfield thought that he found a way to free Somerset without directly ruling on the legality of the status of all of the other people held as slaves in England. Mansfield began by reviewing Steuart's return on the writ, and the case law and other authorities addressing slavery in England. He held that this return was insufficient under the common law of England.[25]

Mansfield explained that "on a return to *habeas corpus*; the only question before us is, whether the case on the return is sufficient? If it is, the negro must be remanded; if not he must be discharged." Mansfield then summarized the return, stating "that the slave departed and refused to serve; whereupon he was kept to be sold abroad." Mansfield's response to this return was:

> So high an act of dominion must be recognized by the law of the country where it is used. The power of the master over his slave has been extremely different, in different countries. The state of slavery is of such a nature, that it is incapable of being introduced on any reasons, moral or political; but only positive law, which preserves its force long after the reason, occasion, and time itself from whence it was created, is erased from memory: It's so odious, that nothing can be suffered to support it, but positive law. Whatever inconveniences, therefore may follow from a decision, I cannot say this case is allowed or approved by the law of England[.]

Accordingly, he concluded that "the black must be discharged."[26]

Scholars including David Brion Davis and William Wiecek concluded that Mansfield ordered Somerset's release in response to the narrow grounds raised by Steuart's return to the writ. Davis asserted that when Mansfield referred to "so high an act of dominion" he did not mean to include "slavery in general," but he referred only "to the specific cause in the return."[27] According to Wiecek, this decision "illustrates the ambiguities of slave case law," and that it has often been "misunderstood[.]" He asserted that the decision "settled only two narrow points of English law: a master could not seize a slave and remove him from the realm against the slave's will, and a slave could secure a writ of habeas corpus to prevent that removal."[28]

But Wiecek also noted, "Despite the restricted scope of the holding, and the later efforts of Mansfield and others to clarify the case and foreclose more liberating possibilities, *Somerset* burst the confines of Mansfield's judgment."[29] This was so because the return on the writ in essence asked the court to legitimize as a matter of common law the master's unique power to breach the peace and force his or her slave to comply with the master's command to do anything the master wished. To release Somerset, Mansfield had to reject this essential substance of the right claimed in Knowles's return, which sought a decision legitimizing, through the common law, the master's powers, including the right to buy and retain a slave as personal property and to forcibly recapture, restrain, and sell a runaway slave. Mansfield's decision was supported by the notion that, by the end of the eighteenth century, and probably long before, the unique power relationship between the master and the slave was erased from the common law. The master's extreme and immediate physical power over a slave, unlike contracts and other commercial transactions based on slave trade, was not enforceable in

English law without a statute legitimizing this relationship.[30]

Because no statute legitimized slavery in England, Mansfield held that the common law alone could not support it. This reasoning did not preclude decisions enforcing slavery in the British colonies in which statutes eventually explicitly legalized slavery. Nor did it stop Parliament from passing a law legitimizing slavery in Britain, either permanently or—like the law in Holland and France—only for transients, visitors, or sojourners who wished to bring their slaves to free European soil.[31]

Mansfield's reasoning thus is consistent with the cases and statutes that authorized freedom and manumission claimants to file suits alleging assault and battery or false imprisonment as the basis for their freedom even in the slave states. As noted in chapter four, because the common law did not explicitly recognize the master's powers that were slavery's essence, masters routinely committed actions that otherwise would be common law torts, such as false imprisonment, assault, or battery, unless the positive slave code legalized these practices.[32]

Somerset was indeed lucky in two respects. First, he had white friends who were willing and able to expend their own time, money, and effort in filing on his behalf and then continuing to pursue to the end an emergent application for a writ of *habeas corpus*. Second, the writ was served on Knowles before he set sail for Jamaica. This issue of timing became a crucial factor after the British High Court of Admiralty's 1827 decision in the case that is known as *The Slave Grace*.[33]

That case was among those that had "caused great excitement" in 1826 among the slaveholders in the British colony of Antigua. The British government's officials in Antigua, in twenty-seven cases, began enforcing the nineteenth century British laws abolishing the slave trade. "The object of the proceedings was to secure the freedom of certain slaves who, having been absent for a time from the colony, had afterwards returned to it, and it was contended by the Government that that circumstance alone was sufficient to entitle them to their freedom."[34]

The Slave Grace was one of these cases. Sometime in 1822, the wife of Antiguan slave owner John Allan went to England with her female attendant Grace Jones, who John Allan owned and held as a slave on Antigua. In 1823, Mrs. Allan returned to Antigua with Grace. On August 8, 1825, Antiguan customs officials seized Grace as a slave who had been forfeited to the king. In June 1826, George Wyke, the Collector of Customs, filed an information alleging that, in 1823, Grace had been illegally imported into Antigua. John Allan responded with a claim against the king. The Vice-Admiralty Court of Antigua, on August 5, 1826, found in favor of Allan, returned Grace to him, and awarded him costs and the damages caused by Grace's detention. Antigua's Attorney General then filed an appeal to the High Court of Admiralty.[35]

Lord Stowell wrote a decision dated November 6, 1827 affirming the judgment. His wordy forty page opinion was much longer than Mansfield's oral opinion in *Somerset*. Stowell endorsed what has been called the reattachment principle as an exception to the *Somerset* rule. According to this rule, Grace's slavery status was only suspended while she was in Britain. Because she was not there manumitted, her freedom "totally expired when that residence ceased and she was imported into Antigua[.]"[36]

The *Somerset* and *Slave Grace* decisions soon influenced the substantive law in the United States, both in the Northern and Southern courts. Most of the Northern states eventually followed the *Somerset* reasoning, and the reattachment principle would be irrelevant as long as the slave remained on free soil.[37] But the Southern courts' acceptance of the *Somerset* doctrine was not clear at all, and Lord Stowell's reattachment doctrine gained support.

Somerset v. Stewart and Freedom Suits on Free Soil

The issue of freedom by a master and slave's transit to free soil did not arise in America, of course, until there was free soil. The courts' need to confront the issue was further delayed because the free states explicitly established "safe harbor" periods, such as six months in Pennsylvania and nine months in New York, during which slave masters who were just visiting could hold their slaves on free soil. The courts in other free states, such as Ohio and Illinois, initially recognized these rights even without statutory authority.[38]

Things later began to change in the antebellum years, however, as evidenced by Massachusetts Chief Justice Lemuel Shaw's 1836 opinion in *Commonwealth v. Aves*,[39] which applied a broad reading of the *Somerset* doctrine. "Like Somerset, this was a case brought by opponents of slavery—this time the Boston Female Anti-Slavery Society—to secure the freedom of a slave visiting in a free jurisdiction."[40]

The case arose when Mary Slater, who was then a New Orleans, Louisiana resident, traveled to Boston in May 1836 to visit her father, Thomas Aves. Mrs. Slater brought with her Med, a six-year-old slave girl. In August 1836, Levin H. Harris filed a petition seeking a writ of *habeas corpus* claiming that Thomas Aves was unlawfully retaining Med and depriving her of her liberty. A judge issued the writ, and Aves was served with the writ while Mrs. Slater and Med were in Massachusetts. Aves's return alleged that Samuel Slater, Mrs. Slater's husband, purchased Med in 1833. Aves claimed that Mrs. Slater intended to return to Louisiana with Med, and that, as Mr. Slater's "agent and legally authorized representative," he was entitled to custody of Med.[41]

Massachusetts did not have a sojourner or transit safe harbor statute. Applying Mansfield's common law analysis, Shaw therefore held that "slavery was illegal in Massachusetts, and no one could be held a slave in that state, except a fugitive who escaped into Massachusetts and whose slave status was preserved by the U.S. Constitution."[42] Med was not a fugitive slave because Mrs. Slater brought her from New Orleans. Consequently, Shaw found that the comity principles did not require him to recognize Med's slave status under Louisiana law.[43] According to Finkelman:

> Med was free, not because the law of Massachusetts made her free, but

because the law of Louisiana ceased to have any force over her once her master voluntarily removed her from that state. The status of slave could only be maintained under positive law, and no such law was available to Med's owner in Massachusetts. As in *Somerset*, this was a decision in which local human rights law trumped international law principles that denied the liberty to slaves and generally allowed people to move their property (including slaves) from one jurisdiction to another.[44]

Shaw also quoted the 1824 Louisiana Supreme Court decision in *Lunsford v. Coquillon*[45] and the 1820 Kentucky Court of Appeals decision in *Rankin v. Lydia, a pauper*[46] in support of his application of the *Somerset* principles.[47]

Shaw suggested that a different result might follow if a slave owner was traveling through Massachusetts with his or her slaves on a journey from one slave state to another.[48] He asserted that he did not have to predict how he would resolve a transit case such as this, and that "our geographical position exempts us from the probable necessity of considering such a case[.]"[49]

The New York courts did have to confront this issue after 1841, however, when the legislature repealed the nine-month safe harbor statute for slave masters visiting or traveling through the state. In the antebellum years, New York's geographic position was on a convenient route from the eastern slave states, such as Virginia, to the western slave states, such as Texas. Accordingly, in 1852, Jonathan Lemmon, his wife, and eight of their slaves stopped for just three days in New York on a journey from their native Virginia to Texas. The New York courts applied the *Somerset/Aves* doctrine to this transit situation that Shaw avoided in *Aves*. The trial level court released the slaves on a writ of *habeas corpus*. The litigation ended eight years later, when the New York Court of Appeals affirmed this decision in *Lemmon v. The People*.[50]

Somerset, The Slave Grace, and the Master's Intent in the Southern States

According to Paul Finkelman: "Initially most southern states accepted the concept articulated by *Somerset v. Stewart* that a slave voluntarily brought to a free jurisdiction became free[,]" and he stated that this right was enforced even in freedom suits that the claimants filed in the slave state courts.[51] Nevertheless, an alternative reading of the cases is possible, beginning with *Mahoney v. Ashton*.[52] This was the first reported Southern case discussing the *Somerset* doctrine. The Maryland Court of Appeals rejected a broad reading of *Somerset* and fore-shadowed the reattachment doctrine that Lord Stowell advanced in *The Slave Grace*.[53]

Mahoney was a freedom suit that Charles Mahoney filed in 1791 against the Reverend John Ashton, a Catholic priest who claimed Mahoney as his slave. Mahoney's first lawyer was Gabriel Duvall, who later became a Maryland state court judge and a United States Supreme Court justice. Duvall apparently devised a plan to bottom the case on a broad reading of *Somerset*.[54]

He began a four and one-half year search for evidence to prove that Mahoney was a great-great grandson of Ann Joice, who had been freed by the laws of England because in the 1670s she was brought from Barbados to England and then to Maryland by Lord Baltimore. A jury in the first trial found in a special verdict that "Joice came into this country with Charles Lord Baltimore, son of Cecilius Lord Baltimore, from England, between the year 1676, and the 15th of February 1679." General Court Chief Justice Jeremiah Townley Chase and Justice Charles Goldsborough then adjourned the case for a year.[55]

The General Court reconvened in October 1798. It heard argument and ordered a new trial because the Court believed that it was not clear whether the jury found that Joice had in fact ever been in England.

A second trial was held before the General Court in May 1799. Mahoney's lawyers relied on the general verdict and "a register of servants brought to Maryland by Lord Baltimore in 1688. Although Ann Joice's name was not listed, a 'Mary Joice' did appear, lending further credence to the belief that Joice's family had at one time resided in England."[56] Mahoney's lawyers also relied on the English cases including *Somerset*.[57] They thus asked the court to instruct the jury: "That if, from the evidence, the jury are of opinion that the woman *Joice,* from whom the petitioner is descended, was in England, and came from thence, they must find a verdict for the petitioner." Chief Justice Chase read this instruction to the jury.

Chase also refused to give the instruction requested by Ashton's counsel, which foreshadowed the reattachment rule. That instruction would have advised the jury that if they believed that Joice "was a negro woman carried with her owner, claiming her as a slave, from the island of Barbadoes [sic] to England, and afterwards brought into this country by Lord *Baltimore,* claiming her as a slave, between the years 1678 and 1681, and that she, during her life was held, used and treated, as a slave, and that her issue have been held as slaves ever since, that then they must find a verdict for the defendant." The jury returned a verdict for Mahoney.[58]

"Mahoney's victory did not last long."[59] Ashton appealed the Maryland Court of Appeals. That court reversed the judgment after hearing oral argument in 1802.[60]

The Court of Appeals held that the trial court should have read the charge requested by Ashton's lawyers. The court recognized that much was at stake in this dispute: "Great industry hath been used, and great ability displayed by the counsel, in the argument of this cause. The decision, involving on the one hand the question of freedom or slavery to the plaintiff below, and on the other great pecuniary interests to persons claiming negroes under similar circumstances, demanded it."[61]

The court's opinion first discussed the ambiguity of British law on the fundamental issue of slavery's status under the common law.[62] The court then concluded that British law, including the *Somerset* doctrine, would not govern the dispute. Instead, the court held that Maryland's positive law legitimized slavery, and that this positive law applied to Joice when she arrived there:

In this collision of individual opinions, and opposing decisions, in the

British books, this court will not say what would have been the decision of a British tribunal on the question stated in the exception; and acting as a court of an independent country, unfettered by any political stipulations on subjects of this nature, and bound to decide according to the laws of this state, they do not consider themselves at liberty to adopt an opinion that might possibly prevail in a foreign tribunal.

By a positive law of this state in 1715, then the province of Maryland, the relation of master and slave is recognized as then existing, and all negro and other slaves, then imported, or thereafter to be imported into this province, and all children then born, or thereafter to be born, of such negroes or slaves, are declared to be slaves during their natural lives.

The court held that the case "must be governed by the law of this state[,]" thus rejecting the notion that, under comity principles, British law applied. "[H]owever the laws of Great Britain in such instances operating upon such persons there, might interpose so as to prevent the exercise of certain acts by the master, not permitted, as in the case of *Somerset*; yet upon the bringing *Ann Joice* into this state, then the Province of Maryland, the relation of master and slave continued in its extent as authorised [sic] by the laws of this state[.]"[63]

Robert Shaw critiqued this case, stating that it was "based on [Ann Joice's] brief sojourn … in England, over a century earlier[.]" Shaw called future Maryland judge and Supreme Court Justice Duvall's theory of the case "certainly far fetched in the light of prevailing attitudes and it is remarkable that it ever reached the courts at all."[64] But Duvall's theory had a sound basis when we recall that Stowell had not yet announced the reattachment theory. A broad reading of Mansfield's *Somerset* decision in favor of liberty was certainly a plausible one to a court that was true to the principle of once free always free.[65]

At the very least, it appears that Ann Joice, like James Somerset, was held as a slave on a ship that was docked in British waters. The captain could have been served with a writ of *habeas corpus*, and a court, anticipating Mansfield's reasoning, could have granted the writ. But the court in *Mahoney* and some later Southern decisions did not adopt a broad reading of *Somerset*. They required freedom claimants to prove that the master, like Charles Steuart, expressed in his or her actions an intention to reside on free soil, or have the slave reside on free soil, thus excluding masters who were merely visitors on or in transit over free territory or waters. The courts also applied the reattachment rule to slaves whose masters merely were sojourners or travelers on free soil or waters.

The Maryland appellate court's decision rejecting comity, foreshadowing *Slave Grace*, and adopting a narrow reading of *Somerset* contrasts with the 1818 Mississippi Supreme Court decision in *Harry v. Decker & Hopkins*.[66] *Harry* is the first officially reported Southern decision applying the *Somerset* doctrine to free claimants who previously had been on free soil, although the court's opinion does not cite the *Somerset* case.

The plaintiffs won a freedom judgment, which the Mississippi Supreme Court affirmed. The claimants were "three negroes" who were slaves in Virginia.

In 1784, John Decker took them "to the neighbourhood of Vincennes," in the southwest portion of what later became the State of Indiana, where they remained until July 1816, when Decker moved these slaves to Mississippi.[67] Finkelman suggested that the defendant probably made this move because the Indiana constitution prohibiting slavery was ratified on June 29, 1816, with an effective date of July of that year.[68]

The plaintiffs sued for freedom after being brought to Mississippi, claiming that they were freed by operation of the law that was in effect in Indiana. They apparently relied on the slavery prohibitions in the Northwest Ordinance of 1787 and on the Indiana constitution's anti-slavery provision.

The relevant Northwest Ordinance provision stated:

> There shall be neither slavery nor involuntary servitude in the said territory, other than in punishment of crimes, whereof the party shall have been duly convicted. Provided always, that any person escaping into the same, from whom labor or service is lawfully claimed in any one of the original states, such fugitive may be reclaimed and conveyed to the person claiming his or her labor as aforesaid.[69]

The Indiana constitution of 1816 also barred slavery in the state. The first article, section 1, declared: "That all men are born equally free and independent, and have certain natural, inherent and unalienable rights, among which, are the enjoying and defending of life and liberty, and of acquiring, possessing and protecting property, and pursuing and obtaining happiness and safety." Section 24 of that article stated that these rights shall forever remain inviolable. Article 11, section 7, prohibited slavery stating: "There shall be neither slavery nor involuntary servitude in this State, otherwise than for the punishment of crimes, whereof the party shall have been duly convicted."[70]

The defendants opposed the plaintiffs' first contention by arguing that the Northwest Ordinance's slavery prohibition applied only to slaves imported into the territory after 1787, a position that the Illinois Supreme Court had adopted until 1845.[71] The defendants responded to the plaintiffs' second argument by asserting that the Indiana constitution could not bar slavery without violating the treaty of cession between Virginia and the United States, an argument that the Indiana Supreme Court later rejected in 1820.[72]

The Mississippi Supreme Court found for the plaintiffs. The Court's unsigned opinion, echoing *Somerset*, stated: "Slavery is condemned by reason and the laws of all nature. It exists and can only exist, through municipal regulations, and in matters of doubt, is it not an unquestionable rule, that courts must lean 'in favorem vitae et libertatis[?]'" The opinion recognized that at least the plaintiffs' constitutional argument was not without some doubt, but the court nevertheless declared that, when weighing property rights and rights to freedom, the court "would be in favour of liberty."[73]

Finkelman noted that the court's *Harry* opinion "was extraordinary for its explicit condemnation of slavery and its interpretation of the Northwest Ordinance." He added: "Unfortunately for Mississippi's slaves," this "was the first and the last case of this type to free slaves" in Mississippi based upon the laws of a free state or nation.[74]

Judge Michael Mills suggested that this opinion "could only have been penned by Justice [Joshua G.] Clarke."[75] I agree with this assessment, which provides the key to an understanding of this opinion's language favoring liberty. Clarke was a Pennsylvania native who served on the Mississippi Supreme Court between 1818 and 1821, when he resigned to become the state's first chancellor. Clarke's only signed Mississippi Supreme Court opinion was *State v. Jones*.[76] That criminal law decision also is singular in its reference to slave rights, and, in my view, it has caused confusion when it is read out of the context of the later Mississippi decisions.[77]

Similarly here, it appears that Clarke may have been sincere in his own preference for liberty over slavery and for the broad reading of *Somerset*. But Clarke's approach is misleading because it was atypical; ultimately, this preference for liberty when the master's intentions were in doubt did not prevail in Mississippi or in the United States South.

According to Finkelman, the courts in Missouri, Virginia, Kentucky, and Louisiana also initially applied *Somerset* and this comity doctrine to free slaves who based their freedom suits on the law of free states or territories. He also stated that the courts in Missouri and Mississippi, and the legislature in Louisiana, changed the law to eliminate comity as a doctrine that would lead to freedom judgments in cases such as *Harry*.[78]

Finkelman contrasts this legal change with Kentucky law, which he stated, "[t]hroughout the antebellum period ... remained, with respect to comity, one of the most consistent and fair-minded of any of the slave-state courts."[79] Others have argued, however, that Kentucky law, like that of the other southern states, "took a sudden turn toward forum law in its 'in transit' cases."[80] And A. E. Keir Nash advanced yet another view, stating that the courts in Texas, Tennessee, North Carolina, Florida, Arkansas, Maryland, Kentucky, and Delaware did not reject comity.[81]

In my view, the Kentucky courts, like those in Virginia and Missouri, never really applied the comity doctrine. They thus did not take a sudden turn away from comity. Finkelman points to the 1820 Kentucky Court of Appeals decision in *Rankin v. Lydia*[82] as evidence of the Kentucky courts' application of comity principles to free slaves. Even this case can be read as having rejected comity toward the law of free states or nations in favor of decisions based on local law and on the court's view of a fair reading the master's intentions.

Lydia filed an action of trespass, assault, battery, and false imprisonment, claiming that she was free. Lydia was born a slave in Kentucky, in 1805. She belonged to John Warrick, a Kentuckian who, in 1807, moved to the Territory of Indiana, where he settled, shortly after September 17, 1807, with Lydia and her mother Flora.[83]

After moving to Indiana, in accordance with a statute adopted on September 17, 1807, Warrick went before the clerk of the county where he resided. He made an agreement with Flora that she would serve him for twenty years. This agreement was recorded in November 1807. Warwick also registered Lydia as a slave under fifteen years of age, again according to the 1807 act.[84] Warrick sold his rights to Lydia on December 6, 1814 to Thomas Miller, an Indiana resident, who then sold Lydia to Robert Todd of Kentucky. Todd brought Lydia to Kentucky, and then sold her to Rankin, "who still holds and claims her as a slave for life[.]"[85]

The Court of Appeals, in an opinion by Judge Benjamin Mills, affirmed a freedom judgment for Lydia, which included an award of one cent in damages, as agreed by the parties, and costs.[86] The decision apparently was based on two acts of the legislature of Indiana Territory, a September 17, 1807 act titled "An act concerning the introduction of negroes and mulattoes into this territory" and a December 14, 1810 act repealing the 1807 act, and on the anti-slavery provisions of the 1787 Northwest Ordinance and the Indiana 1816 constitution. As noted above, the Northwest Ordinance provision on which Lydia's lawyer primarily relied and the 1816 constitution barred slavery and involuntary servitude in the territory or state, other than in punishment of crimes, and saving the rights of masters to recover fugitive slaves. These provisions did not explicitly recognize the rights of masters to visit with their slaves or travel through the state with their slaves.[87]

The 1807 act required slave owners bringing slaves into Indiana to register the slaves as servants, as Warrick did. Slaves under the age of fifteen were to serve until they were thirty-two years old if they were females and until they were thirty-five years old if they were males. The 1810 act repealed this 1807 statute, and stated that "negroes and mulattoes" could not be removed from Indiana without their consent.[88]

Judge Mills stated that his decision was not based on any presumption in favor of liberty; to the contrary, he declared that "we disclaim the influence of the general principles of liberty, which we all admire," and that "we conceive [that the case] ought to be decided by the law as it is, and not as it ought to be." He added, moreover:

> Slavery is sanctioned by the laws of this state, and the right to hold them under our municipal regulations is unquestionable. But we view this as a right existing by positive law of a municipal character, without foundation in the law of nature, or the unwritten and common law. If, by their positive provisions in our code, we can and must hold our slaves in the one case, and statutory provisions equally positive decide against that right in the other, and liberate the slave, he must, by an authority equally imperious, be declared free. Every argument which supports the right of the master on one side, based upon the force of written law, must be equally conclusive in favor of the slaves when he can point out in the statute the clause which secures his freedom.[89]

Judge Mills thus suggested that the court's decision was based on its application of Indiana's constitution and laws, which prohibited slavery.[90]

He also stated, however, that Warrick's own conduct was relevant. When

Warrick registered his slaves under Indiana law, he agreed to accept the slaves' temporary servitude as an admission of their freedom; and he and his vendee were estopped to deny it.[91]

If the opinion stopped at this point, it could be read to be an unambiguous application of foreign law under comity principles, similar to the opinion in the *Harry* case—not because of the operation of Indiana law alone, but because of Warrick's stated intention to relocate to Indiana. Judge Mills nevertheless continued to address, *in dictum*, an argument that Rankin's lawyer raised about the inconvenience that this holding would pose to traveling slave owners:

> The argument which has been relied on as most formidable is that arising *ab inconvenienti*. It is contended that there is no difference between a transient passing or sojourning in Indiana, under the ordinance in question, and a residence there. That the slave which would be there an hour would be as much under the influence of the ordinance as the one who resided ten years; that if the ordinance could give freedom at all it could and would do it in a moment when the slave touched the enchanted shore, and that the consequence would be that the slave of the traveler who attended his master—the slave of the officer who marched in the late armies of the United States—those sent of errands to the opposite shores— or attending their masters while removing beyond the Mississippi through the territory, would all have an equal right to freedom with Lydia; and that by a decision in her favor the right of such property would be much jeopardized.

Mills rejected this argument by concluding that the ordinance applied to the slaves of residents, but not to those of sojourners, visitors, or transients.[92]

Judge Mills did not cite any provision of Indiana law that expressly enacted this exception for the slaves of visitors or travelers passing through the state or territory. Instead, he concluded that Indiana's slavery prohibition, "like most other municipal regulations,"

> was designed to operate on the inhabitants and settlers of the territory, and on them exclusively; and when the ordinance declares that slavery shall not exist there it evidently means among the inhabitants and settlers, and not among the travelers and sojourners there. Their case is not affected by the provisions of the ordinance; against them no provision exists.[93]

On the notion of comity, Mills explained:

> If the comity between this and the state of Indiana is to have any bearing on this subject it will be most promoted by this construction. It appears in the record that the territory adopted laws prohibiting the removal of their domiciled negroes. If, then, such are removed, and it is once known that their vested rights are denied by the functionaries of this government, it is calculated to produce retaliatory measures, and to cause them to detain and refuse our transient slaves, who are not and never were subject to their

municipal regulations with regard to their resident blacks and resident claimants. In any view of the case, which this court has been able to take, we consider Lydia as free. Not because she acquired that freedom by the laws of Kentucky, but during her absence from the state, by the voluntary and unequivocal acts of her master, and that when it is thus acquired it ought to be held equally sacred here, whether she is brought against her will, as it would be, had it been her birthright. It is enough if it exists now— it is equally as precious, valuable and sacred as if it commenced with her existence.[94]

Thus, Mills's gesture of comity was tied to Warrick's own "voluntary and unequivocal acts" moving to Indiana and accepting the benefits of Indiana's laws as well as its burdens, including the effects of the laws freeing his slaves. The free state's law alone did not free Lydia; Mills's view of the evidence of the master's intention was of crucial importance. If the master's actions indicated to the court an intention to return to a slave state, then under Mills's *dicta*, which he wrote before *The Slave Grace* decision, the court would apply the reattachment doctrine in favor of slavery.

As Finkelman noted, the Indiana Supreme Court, in an 1829 decision, endorsed the traveler and sojourner exception in *dictum*, and in 1831 the legislature adopted a statute making it the law of Indiana. Mills accurately predicted how Indiana law would later evolve, but in 1820 this Indiana authority did not exist.[95]

Therefore, Mills endorsed a limit on Indiana law that was based upon Kentucky law and public policy. His decision did, however, free a slave, and it contained language endorsing *Somerset*. This may have been one of the reasons why Mills lost his seat on the court in 1828, when the state senate failed to confirm his nomination for another term.[96]

The Kentucky Court of Appeals later applied the Mills *dictum* granting safe harbor protection to travelers and sojourners and adopting the reattachment principle.[97] For example, in its 1851 decision in *Maria v. Kirby*,[98] the court denied Maria's freedom claim that she asserted in Kentucky under Pennsylvania law after a visit to Pennsylvania, even though that state's laws no longer contained the six-month safe harbor provision protecting the property rights of slaveholders who were temporary visitors in or travelers passing through Pennsylvania. The court went so far as to ignore a Pennsylvania court order that had granted a writ of *habeas corpus* in favor of Maria. This decision did not, in my view, constitute a sharp break with the past. Instead, we can reconcile the *Maria* and *Rankin* decisions based upon the court's overriding concern about the master's property rights, including his or her intentions to free or retain his or her slaves.

The Virginia cases followed a similar pattern rejecting comity when the master's intention to free his or her slave was not established to the court's satisfaction. In 1820, the Supreme Court of Appeals affirmed a freedom judgment without an opinion, in *Griffith v. Fanny*.[99] Fanny claimed that, in August 1816, she was sold by her owner, Kincheleo, to Skinner, who lived in Ohio. Because Ohio law prohibited slavery, the bill of sale was made out to the defendant Griffith. In October 1818, Fanny was returned to Virginia, and she sued for her freedom, based upon the Ohio constitution's provision prohibiting slavery. Although the court did not explain its reasoning, it appears that the court found that Fanny's two-year residence in Ohio was conclusive evidence of her owner's intention to reside in Ohio.

The 1821 Virginia Supreme Court of Appeals decision in *Lewis v. Fullerton*,[100] which is discussed in chapter two, did not apply the *Somerset* rule when it did not appear to the court's satisfaction that the master intended to move to Ohio. Lewis, who was a child, sought his freedom in a suit that his mother Milly filed on his behalf. The defendants were William Fullerton and Jane Rodgers. A jury trial ended in a verdict for the defendants. Lewis then filed an appeal with the Supreme Court of Appeals of Virginia, which affirmed the judgment, in an opinion by Judge Spencer Roane.

Some time during or before March 1808, John Rodgers brought Milly and her husband Naise to Ohio, apparently from John's home in Virginia. Milly and Naise then obtained a writ of *habeas corpus*, seeking an order releasing them from John's custody, who claimed them as his slaves. A Gallia County Ohio judge held "a hearing of the parties and witnesses at a subsequent day[.]" The judge rendered a judgment that Milly and Naise "go hence, be discharged, and set at liberty."

The next day, John went to Edward Tupper and asked "him to prevail on Milly to live with him as an indentured servant for two years[.]" John also promised that if Milly agreed to do this "he would execute to her a complete deed of manumission, which should put the question of her liberty at rest[.]" John also promised not to file an appeal from the Ohio court's order. Milly and Naise agreed to these terms, provided that John would sign a manumission deed.

John signed the promised manumission deed on April 2, 1808, and this execution was attested to by two witnesses. John also acknowledged the deed's execution before an associate judge in Gallia County, and this was certified by the county recorder, the county clerk, and the President of the Court of Common Pleas.[101]

Milly and Naise returned to Virginia with John, and Lewis later was born in Virginia. Milly apparently performed her end of the bargain, but John or his successors in interest later reneged on his promise and would not free Lewis. It also appears from the case report that Milly was not freed, nor is it clear who the defendants were, other than John's successors in interest to Lewis.

Lewis's lawyer asserted three claims to Milly's freedom, which the defendants conceded, if meritorious, would also free Lewis "as a necessary consequence."[102] The arguments relevant to this chapter are the assertions that Milly was freed by "having sojourned" in Ohio, where slavery was prohibited and where at least for one day she worked for her master, and that the Ohio court entered a judgment that freed Milly. The claim based on John's own manumission deed and the exchange of promises is discussed in chapter two.[103]

Judge Roane's opinion rejected the contention and Milly's residence on Ohio soil freed her, stating that

we must throw entirely out of view the *subsequent* residence of the mother within the state of Ohio, with the alleged consent of Rodgers her former master. Whatever may be the effect of a residence therein, for a great length of time, and with the assent aforesaid; whatever may be the effect of this circumstance in relation to a person who may thereby have become one of the permanent members of that state, the residence now in question is of a far different character.[104]

He also rejected the notion that Milly was freed because she "was once seen, on a Sunday, working at a sugar camp" in Ohio "in the absence of her master, and without any evidence that it was with his permission." He added:

Such an occupation for a short time, and even for the benefit of the master, and probably in his presence, could never operate an emancipation of his slave. It could not so operate, when the *animus revertendi* strongly existed in him, both in relation to himself, and to his slave. There is indeed but a shade of difference between such a residence as this, (if indeed it can be called a residence,) and the mere right of passage through the state: and such a construction, as that now contended for, would whittle down to nothing the right of the citizens of each state, within every other state guaranteed to them by the constitution.

Roane concluded that Milly's work cannot "carry with it evidence of the assent of the master, that she should cease to remain his property, and become a member of the state of Ohio, without which the regulations of that state on the subject of emancipation cannot attach."

Roane also rejected Lewis's reliance on the Ohio court's habeas corpus judgment.

[T]hat judgment has not *affirmed* the mother's right to freedom. Even if it had, and this mode of proceeding was legalized by the laws of that state, (as it *seems* not to be by the laws of this,) in favour of a slave against his master, those laws are not found in the case before us: and even if they were, it might well be questioned whether the judgment aforesaid could have concluded the right of the master in the present instance. The right of our citizens under the constitution to reclaim their fugitive slaves from other states, would be nearly a nullity, if that claim was permitted to be intercepted by a proceeding like the one in question; a proceeding of so extremely summary a character, that it affords no fair opportunity to a master deliberately to support his right of property in his slave.

He thus held that "[s]uch a proceeding ought not, therefore, to be conclusive on the subject."[105]

The seemingly inconsistent results in these cases can be reconciled by reference to the courts' perception of the paramount importance of the masters' intentions. This is further illustrated by the 1853 decision in *Foster's Adm'r v. Fosters*.[106] William Foster, Martha Ann Johnson, Ellen Johnson, Richard Johnson, Betsey Johnson, Thomas Johnson, Eliza Johnson, and Francis Johnson sued *in forma pauperis* to recover their freedom. The defendant was Richard

Adams, Francis Foster's administrator, who claimed the plaintiffs as slaves belonging to Foster's estate. A jury found for the plaintiffs after a trial. The Virginia Supreme Court of Appeals affirmed the judgment, in an opinion by Judge Green B. Samuels.

On and before November 3, 1831, Foster was the owner of a number of slaves, including William Foster, Betsey Johnson, Francis Johnson, and Thomas Johnson. Martha Ann Johnson, Ellen Johnson, Eliza Johnson, and William Johnson, the other plaintiffs, were Betsey Johnson's children, who were born after 1831. Foster acknowledged that he was the father of William and Betsey, as well as others of his slaves who were not parties to the suit. On or about November 3, 1831, Foster, "having previously determined to emancipate his natural children, their mother also his slave, and the issue of his children, took with him to the city of New York these objects of his favor, including William, Betsey, Francis and Thomas, the only parties to this suit then in existence."

While he was in New York, on November 3, 1831, Foster executed a manumission deed, "which was attested by one witness and acknowledged before the mayor of the city, and ordered to be recorded." In this deed, Foster stated his intention to free "amongst others, William Foster, Betsey Johnson, Francis Johnson and Thomas Johnson."

Foster's New York "sojourn" lasted "for a few days only." He "spoke of the trip ... as intended for the sole purpose of giving freedom to the objects of his favor." Foster took his slaves to New York to free them there, rather than in Virginia, because he believed that the Virginia law requiring that freed slaves "leave the state in twelve months would not extend to the case which he had devised."

After returning from New York, Foster and the freed slaves "lived together as a family upon terms of equality, and not as a master with his slaves." Foster's July 27, 1835 will was admitted to probate on May 9, 1836. "By this will he emancipated by name, in express terms, his slaves other than his own children, their mother, and their descendants: To some of these last mentioned he bequeathed a portion of his personal property." Although Foster did not register the plaintiffs as free negroes, "they had always after the death of Foster up to the year 1850, acted as free people, and were not included in the inventory or appraisement of Foster's estate[.]" Nevertheless, "in July 1850 they were taken into custody by the defendant below, claiming to hold them as slaves."[107]

Judge Samuels found that Foster's conduct freeing his slaves in New York and then returning to Virginia with them as free people was not necessarily contrary to Virginia law. Virginia's statutes did not prohibit manumission, although freed slaves were required to leave the state.[108] Nevertheless, Samuels stated:

> There was nothing in the law to prevent Foster from taking his slaves whithersoever he chose for any reason that to him seemed good: To hold otherwise would be an unjust interference with his rights of property. If then the law allowed emancipation within the state, and moreover allowed Foster to carry the slaves out of the state, it is impossible to perceive a

reason why an emancipation without the state, according to the law of the place where made, should not be fully recognized here.[109]

Thus, Samuels combined fidelity to comity principles with fidelity to the master's intent.

Samuels also rejected the notion that the plaintiffs should be denied their freedom because Foster's manumission plan was a fraud. Instead, he reviewed the "general principles" that he derived from the cases in which freedom claimants were successful and unsuccessful.[110] Samuels concluded that the master's intention was the governing factor in these cases:

> A safe, plain and practicable test of these questions will be found by ascertaining whether the owner intended to surrender his right of property under the operation of the laws of a nonslaveholding state; if he so intended, no wrong is done by giving effect to his intention. If he did not so intend, his right of property should be held unimpaired, whatever may have been done to divest him thereof under color of law in any nonslaveholding state.[111]

Samuels based this "safe, plain and practicable test" primarily on the court's perceptions of evidence of the owner's intention "to surrender" his property rights on free soil. This test also helps us to reconcile these freedom cases in the majority of the Southern states.

The Missouri cases decided before 1852 followed a similar pattern rejecting comity when the master's intention to free his or her slave was not established to the court's satisfaction. The Missouri Supreme Court's 1824 decision in *Winny v. Whitesides*[112] was the first leading case. This was an assault and battery and false imprisonment action filed on behalf of Winny in 1818. She obtained a freedom judgment after a trial in the Circuit Court of St. Louis County at the April term in 1821.[113] The defendant, Phoebe Whitesides, filed an appeal, and the Missouri Supreme Court affirmed the judgment.

"[A]bout twenty-five years before," Phoebe and her husband, John Whitesides, moved from North Carolina to Illinois, which was then part of what was known as the Indiana Territory. The Whitesides brought Winny with them. They all resided in Illinois for "about three or four years[.]" The Whitesides retained Winny in slavery while they resided in Illinois. "From Illinois, the defendant and her then husband removed to Missouri, bringing with them the plaintiff in this action, and still holding her as a slave."[114]

The defendant's counsel asked the trial judge to instruct the jury that this Illinois residence did not free Winny under the Northwest Ordinance, and "that the law did not give the plaintiff more than nominal damages in this action." The trial judge did not give these instructions. Instead, he "charged the jury, that if they believed the defendant and her then husband, resided in Illinois, with an intention to make that place the home of themselves and of the said Winny, they should find the issue for the plaintiff, and assess damages to her in this form of action, on the same principles as any other plaintiff might recover in an action of false imprisonment."[115]

The Missouri Supreme Court's opinion by Justice George Tompkins affirming the judgment cited the Northwest Ordinance's anti-slavery provision as one basis for his ruling, but his interpretation of the owners' intentions also was a salient concern:

> The sovereign power of the United States has declared that "neither slavery nor involuntary servitude["] shall exist there; and this court thinks that the person who takes his slave into said territory, and by the length of his residence there indicates an intention of making that place his residence and that of his slave, and thereby induces a jury to believe that fact, does, by such residence, declare his slave to have become a free man. But it has been urged that by such a construction of the ordnance every person traveling through the territory, and taking along with him his slave, might thereby lose his property in his slave. We do not think the instructions of the Circuit Court can be, by any fair construction, strained so far; nor do we believe that any advocate for this portion of the species ever seriously calculated on the possibility of such a decision.[116]

Therefore, like Mills and Roane, Tompkins based his opinion on the court's reading of the owners' intentions.

In *dictum*, Tompkins also endorsed the notion that the law should permit safe transit and visits on free soil for slave owners with their slaves. The Missouri courts followed this approach until the 1852 decision *Scott v. Emerson*,[117] which will be discussed below.[118]

The Louisiana Supreme Court's Liberal Approach and the Legislature's Response

In contrast, the Louisiana Supreme Court again provides an exception among the Southern states. This indicates that another interpretation that was more in favor of liberty was possible. In its 1824 decision in *Lunsford v. Coquillon*,[119] the court applied the comity principle without the reattachment rule if the free state's or nation's law did not explicitly contain a transient or sojourner exception. This more liberal approach prevailed even after *The Slave Grace* decision, until the legislature abolished this route to freedom in 1846. Indeed, Louisiana's about face initiated the trend restricting the path to freedom based on the master's implied, and often even expressed, intentions to free slaves as evidenced in these travel cases.[120]

The plaintiff in *Lunsford* filed a freedom suit alleging "that some years ago, her then owner removed from Kentucky into Ohio, with the intention of residing there, taking her thither as a part of his family." She contended that Ohio's constitution provided that "there shall be neither slavery nor involuntary servitude, in the state[.]" She also alleged "that she resided for several years in this man's family, in Ohio, continuing to serve him as before-that, having made an attempt to assert her freedom, he defeated it by her forcible removal into Kentucky, from whence she was brought back into Ohio, and afterwards into Louisiana."[121]

Writing for the Louisiana Supreme Court, Justice François-Xavier Martin affirmed a freedom judgment for the plaintiff. Although he did not cite Mansfield's opinion in *Somerset*, he included its essential holding in his opinion:

> The relation of owner and slave is, in the states of this union, in which it has a legal existence, a creature of the municipal law. Although, perhaps, in none of them a statute introducing it as to the blacks can be produced, it is believed that, in all: statutes were passed for regulating and dissolving it. The issue of a female slave is held to be born in the condition of the mother, the maxim of the Roman law, *partus sequitur ventrem*, being universally recognized. Indians taken captives in war, have been declared slaves, and the absolute property of the captor; and a kind of temporary slavery has been made the doom of persons of color guilty of certain breaches of the law. 2 *Martin's revisal of N. C. Laws.* 2 *Martin's digest of the laws of Louisiana*, 102. In most of the states recognizing slavery, laws have been passed to authorise [sic], regulate, or check the emancipation of slaves. In some, as in Pennsylvania, laws have been made to abolish or modify slavery.[122]

Martin recognized that Ohio also had the right to prohibit slavery.[123]

According to Martin, Ohio's constitution "emancipates, *ipso facto*, such slaves whose owners remove them into that state, with the intention of residing there[.]" Therefore, the constitution's "*ipso facto*" effect was, in Martin's analysis, combined with the following evidence of the master's intentions:

> [T]hat the plaintiff having been voluntarily removed into that state, by her then owner, the latter submitted himself, with every member of his family, white and black, and every part of the property brought with him, to the operations of the constitution and laws of the state; and that, as according to them slavery could not exist in his house—slavery did not exist there[.]

Martin thus held that "the plaintiff was accordingly as effectually emancipated, by the operation of the constitution, as if by the act and deed of her former owner—that she could not be free in one state, and a slave in another[.]"

Martin also rejected what would become *The Slave Grace* reattachment doctrine. He reasoned further that the plaintiff's freedom "was not impaired" by her alleged owner's actions "forcibly removing her into Kentucky to defeat her attempt to assert her freedom, nor by her subsequent removal, voluntary or forced, into this state."

Martin declined the invitation to opine, as did Mills, Roane, and Tompkins, on what might happen if the plaintiff's master claimed that he was only a visitor or was in transit through Ohio with his or her slaves:

> The plaintiff's counsel has laid great stress on the former owner of the plaintiff removing into Ohio, with the intention of settling, and it is this circumstance which governs the case. In the decision of the court of appeals of Kentucky, it is expressly said that slaves attending their masters sojourning in, or travelling [sic] to Ohio, are not thereby emancipated—as this point has no bearing on the present case, it is useless to consider it.[124]

Moreover, as Catterall, Finkelman, Schafer, and others have noted, the Louisiana Supreme Court continued to afford comity to the law of free states and nations, including France, even for slaves in transit.[125]

The Louisiana legislators responded with two statutes that changed this approach. An 1842 act, among other things, stated that masters could not remove slaves from Louisiana to free states or nations and then return to Louisiana.[126] The legislators in 1846 went a step further; they adopted an act stating that "no slave shall be entitled to his or her freedom under the pretence that he or she has been, with or without the consent of his or her owner, in a country where slavery does not exist, or in any of the States where slavery is prohibited."[127]

According to Finkelman, "[t]he state policy, as determined by the legislature, was to cease enforcing the freedom created by foreign and out-of-state laws. It was a rejection of precedent and comity."[128] After 1850, judges in other Southern states began expressly to deny any pretense of comity to free state law in suits filed in the South. These judges, under the influence of the pro-slavery doctrine, came to believe that manumission was not compatible with slavery or with their state's public policy.

The Southern Courts' Balance of Public Policy and the Master's Intent

In Missouri and Mississippi, the high court justices took it upon themselves to adopt the public policy that the Louisiana legislature enacted in 1846. These judges did not wait for legislative action; they repudiated precedent and blocked the route to freedom based on a slave's residence on free soil.

The Missouri Supreme Court, in its 1852 decision *Scott v. Emerson*,[129] overruled the line of cases that awarded people held as slaves their freedom, following the Court's 1824 decision in *Winny v. Whitesides*.[130] The United States Supreme Court's 1857 decision certainly is more significant in the nation's legal history.[131] Nevertheless, the Missouri Supreme Court's about face also is an important indicator of the type of legal reform that was gaining force in the Southern law regarding manumission, freedom, and slavery. Dennis Boman has argued, moreover, that the Court's decision overruling precedent had been foreshadowed in the 1840s as the dominant perceptions of public policy in Missouri came to oppose freedom suits.[132]

The extensive research of historians including Don E. Fehrenbacher, Walter Ehrlich, and Lea VanderVelde permits a better understanding of the facts and context of the case than we can derive from the factual summaries in the reported appellate court decisions. Accordingly, I will refer to those facts to supplement the officially reported facts.[133]

The slave known as Dred Scott was one of the slaves owned by Peter Blow, who died on June 23, 1832 as a resident of St. Louis, Missouri.[134] Dred's connection to the Blow family would later be a crucial benefit to him and to his family. Peter Blow's children and their friends later helped support the Scotts' litigation efforts. For example, Taylor Blow, one of Peter's sons, posted a bond for costs in the Scotts' federal court suit, effectuated the manumission of Dred and his family after both the Missouri Supreme Court and the United States Supreme Court denied the Scotts' claims to freedom, and posted a bond so that Dred and his wife could remain in Missouri after he freed them. He even saw to Dred's re-internment after the cemetery in which he initially was buried was abandoned.[135]

Dred apparently was sold by Peter Blow, or by the Blow estate, to Dr. John Emerson, who also was a St. Louis resident.[136] In December 1833, Dr. Emerson obtained a commission to serve as an Army surgeon. He reported with Scott to Fort Armstrong in Rock Island, Illinois, which by then was a free state. One of the privileges of Dr. Emerson's rank was the right to have an enlisted man assigned to him or to receive a monthly stipend to help pay for a slave or hired man.[137]

Dr. Emerson, in 1836, was transferred to Fort Snelling, in what later became the site of St. Paul, Minnesota. This Fort also was on free soil. It was a part of the territory that was acquired in the 1803 Louisiana Purchase from France. Slavery had been abolished in that territory by the 1820 Missouri Compromise.

Dred Scott married Harriet Robinson while they lived at Fort Snelling. Major Lawrence Taliaferro had brought Harriet to Fort Snelling in 1835 when she was fourteen years old. Taliaferro was a United States Indian Agent. His service in the area ended after a treaty was signed with the local Native American tribes. Taliaferro was in the process of breaking up his frontier household, which still included Harriet, when he apparently gave Harriet to Dred so that he could marry her. Taliaferro performed the marriage for the Scotts, as he had done for others while he served as an Indian Agent on the frontier.[138]

It was by then a settled rule in the United States South that slaves could not be legally married. VanderVelde and Subramanian suggested, however, that one can presume that Taliaferro's own actions marrying Harriet on free territory and then relinquishing control over her provided strong evidence of his intention to free her, at least under the laws of a free state or territory.[139] Nevertheless, there is no evidence that Taliaferro signed a manumission deed in favor of Harriet. Nor is there any evidence that Taliaferro signed a deed transferring ownership of Harriet to Dr. Emerson or anyone else. Taliaferro may have believed that he could not legally sell Harriet on free soil. The marriage to Dred may have been perceived as a way for Taliaferro to "transfer" possession of Harriet to Dred's owner.[140]

It nevertheless appears that Dr. Emerson gained possession of Harriet after the wedding. She and Dred served Dr. Emerson while he was stationed on free soil at Fort Snelling. After just one winter at Fort Snelling, however, Dr Emerson sought a transfer to St. Louis. In 1837, Dr. Emerson won his transfer, but the Army sent him to Fort Jesup in Louisiana instead. Dr. Emerson left his property and slaves behind, including the Scotts, and in 1838 he married Eliza Irene Sanford, who was known as Irene. Also in that year, Dr. Emerson had the Scotts sent to him in Louisiana.

Dr. Emerson eventually obtained a transfer back to the free soil of Fort Snelling. On the journey there, Harriet gave birth to the Scotts' first child, Eliza, apparently while she was on a boat on the Mississippi River, between the free territory that became Iowa and the free state of Illinois. The Scotts continued to reside with Emerson on free soil until the spring of 1840, when Dr. Emerson was transferred to Florida to serve in the Second Seminole War. Irene and the Scotts did not go to Florida with Dr. Emerson; instead, they moved to Missouri, where Irene held the Scotts as slaves.

Dr. Emerson was discharged from the Army in 1842. He was attempting to restart his civilian life when he died on December 29, 1843, at the age of 40. Dr. Emerson died while he was in Davenport, Iowa, where he owned land and was building a house. Emerson left a life estate in his entire estate to Irene. His estate inventory in Missouri did not mention his slaves and his Iowa estate inventory was lost.[141]

Nevertheless, Irene apparently continued to claim ownership of Dred, Harriet, and their children, although her claim to Harriet and the children was tenuous at best. She even refused Dred's 1846 offer to buy his family, which eventually consisted of Harriet and their two children, Eliza and Lizzie, who was born after the Scotts returned to Missouri.[142]

On April 6, 1846, Francis Murdoch, the first attorney for Dred and Harriet Scott, filed petitions seeking permission to file freedom suits on their behalf in the Missouri Circuit Court in St. Louis. On that date, Judge John Krum granted the Scotts permission to sue. Irene Emerson was the defendant in both cases.[143]

The Missouri statute regulating freedom suits required slaves suing for their freedom to obtain a judge's order permitting the suit to proceed. The legislature amended the statutes in 1845 to, among other things, also require that slaves post a bond to cover the costs of the suit if they lost the case, and it provided that the plaintiffs could not recover damages against their alleged owner. This statute may have discouraged some slaves or lawyers who intended to file and pursue freedom suits.[144] Murdoch initially posted bonds for the Scotts, and Joseph Charless, Jr., the husband of Charlotte Blow Charless and Taylor Blow's partner, posted a bond in 1847.[145]

Several lawyers handled the Scotts' cases during these suits' long tenure in the courts.[146] At the start, Murdoch probably thought that the cases would quickly be decided in his clients' favor. The Missouri Supreme Court had resolved the legal issues that could be raised in the Scotts' cases in its 1836 decision in *Rachel v. Walker*.[147] The court reversed a judgment denying the freedom claim of Rachel. She contended that, between 1830 and 1834, she was held as a slave by J.B.W. Stockton, a United States Army officer, on free soil at Fort Snelling and at Prairie du Chien, on the Wisconsin side of the Mississippi River. The court rejected the notion that it should create a military officer exception to the general rule that applied to masters taking up residence on free soil, because Stockton decided, "as his voluntary act," to take his slave with him to live on free soil where the Army stationed him.[148] But Kenneth Kaufman has argued that by 1846 the "dominant slavery attitudes" in St. Louis had changed, and that "the legal signposts were pointing in the opposite direction and had been for some time."[149]

The trial in the Scotts' first suit was not held until June 1847. It resulted in a judgment for Irene Emerson, however, because the Scotts' lawyers did not prove, through competent and admissible evidence, that Mrs. Emerson was their owner.

The Scotts' lawyers faced procedural hurdles that freedom claimants' lawyers faced in even the most "liberal" Southern states—their clients were presumed to be slaves, they had the burden of proof, and the freedom claimants could not testify in court in support of their own cases. Instead, all of the evidence supporting the freedom claimants' cases had to be derived from admissible documents or the testimony of white witnesses. In the Scotts' trial, these procedures "produced the absurd effect of allowing Mrs. Emerson to keep her slaves simply because no one had proved that they *were* her slaves."[150]

The trial judge Alexander Hamilton later granted the Scotts' motion for a new trial. The Missouri Supreme Court in 1848 affirmed this ruling.[151]

The Scotts' second trial ended in freedom judgments, but not until January 12, 1850, almost four years after the suits began.[152] Irene Emerson then filed an appeal with the Missouri Supreme Court. The attorneys for all parties signed a stipulation that the court's decision in Dred's case would also apply to Harriet's case, on the faulty premise that the facts in these cases were "identical."[153]

Don Fehrenbacher and Lea VanderVelde have demonstrated that the facts that underlie the Scotts' cases were not identical. For Harriet and her children, this stipulation, which "submerged Harriet's case for the sake of expediency," may now be viewed as a tactical error. "[I]t was not at all clear that anyone owned Harriet, yet a freedom case needed a defendant."[154]

The stipulation may have been seen as a way to limit the cost of the proceedings and move the appeal to a decision more quickly. As it turned out, more expediency would not have worked to the Scotts' advantage. The Missouri Supreme Court heard oral argument in October 1850. It was poised to rule against the Scotts when the court's make-up changed after the voters approved a constitutional amendment in 1849 providing for the election of the Missouri Supreme Court's justices. Two of the members of the new court, William Scott and John Ryland, also were ready to advance a new judicial philosophy in the freedom suits. The Scotts' case provided the new court with the opportunity to change the law.[155]

On March 22, 1852, the court reversed the judgment in favor of the Scotts, in a two to one decision. Justice Scott's majority opinion overruled the court's precedents favoring comity toward the enforcement of a free jurisdiction's law and the enforcement of the masters' apparent intentions to free their slaves as evidenced by relatively permanent moves to free soil. Justice Scott tied these notions together in his analysis of the precedents that he had to confront:

> Cases of this kind are not strangers in our courts. Persons have been frequently here adjudged to be entitled to their freedom on the ground that their masters held them in slavery in territories or States in which the institutution [sic] was prohibited. From the first case decided in our courts, it might be inferred that this result was brought about by a presumed assent of the master, from the fact of having voluntarily taken his slave to a place where the relation of master and slave did not exist. But subsequent cases base the right "to exact the forfeiture of emancipation," as they term it, on the ground it would seem, that it is the duty of the courts of this State to

carry into effect the Constitution and laws of other States and territories, regardless of the rights, the policy or the institutions of the people of this State.[156]

Justice Scott did not state which decisions he believed strayed from the master's intention test to comity. He overruled a line of cases without discussing or even mentioning these cases.[157]

Justice Scott held that changing times required new legal rules and results. He stated that the facts did not indicate sufficient proof that Emerson intended to free his slaves. He suggested that the case could have been decided by a narrow decision overruling the 1836 decision in *Rachel v. Walker* and creating a military officer exception to *Winny v. Whitesides*, because Emerson "was ordered by superior authority to posts where his slave was detained in servitude[.]"[158] But Justice Scott did not so limit his reasoning and holding, nor did he advance an incremental change in the law. Instead, his opinion is an example of what today would be labeled judicial activism when he overruled precedent and cited with approval and applied the reattachment doctrine.[159]

Justice Scott declared that comity to foreign law was a matter of discretion under Missouri law:

> If it is a matter of discretion, that discretion must be controlled by circumstances. Times are not now as they were when the former decisions on this subject were made. Since then not only individuals but States have been possessed with a dark and fell spirit in relation to slavery, whose gratification is sought in the pursuit of measures, whose inevitable consequences must be the overthrow and destruction of our government. Under such circumstances it does not behoove the State of Missouri to show the least countenance to any measure which might gratify this spirit. She is willing to assume her full responsibility for the existence of slavery within her limits, nor does she seek to share or divide it with others. Although we may, for our own sakes, regret that the avarice and hard-heartedness of the progenitors of those who are now so sensitive on the subject, ever introduced the institution among us, yet we will not go to them to learn law, morality or religion on the subject.

He also wrote in favor of the pro-slavery doctrine, which justified the court's decision to read narrowly the evidence of Dr. Emerson's intention to free his slaves simply by living with them on free soil:

> As to the consequences of slavery, they are much more hurtful to the master than the slave. There is no comparison between the slave in the United States and the cruel, uncivilized negro in Africa. When the condition of our slaves is contrasted with the state of their miserable race in Africa; when their civilization, intelligence and instruction in religious truths are considered, and the means now employed to restore them to the country from which they have been torn, bearing with them the blessings of civilized life, we are almost persuaded, that the introduction of slavery amongst us was,

in the providence of God, who makes the evil passions of men subservient to His own glory, a means of placing that unhappy race within the pale of civilized nations.[160]

When Justice Scott phrased the issue as the master's will versus God's will, it is clear which was secondary in his pro-slavery world view.[161]

Justice Hamilton R. Gamble's dissenting opinion began by noting that in other slave societies the law recognized the master's right to free his or her slaves.[162] He found that laws in the United States regulated manumission, but that when a master freed a slave according to the legal requirements of one state, it was effective in the other states.[163]

Gamble then stated: "In this State, it has been recognized, from the beginning of the government, as a correct position in law, that a master who takes his slave to reside in a State or territory where slavery is prohibited, thereby emancipates his slave[.]"[164] He cited a list of decisions supporting his conclusion, and stated that "[t]hese decisions, which come down to the year 1837 seem to have so fully settled the question, that since that time there has been no case bringing it before the court for any reconsideration until the present."[165] Gamble also discussed similar cases from other states. He stated that the courts decided all of these precedents "when the public mind was tranquil, and when the tribunals maintained in their decisions the principles which had always received the approbation of an enlightened public opinion. Times may have changed, public feeling may have changed, but principles have not and do not change; and, in my judgment, there can be no safe basis for judicial decisions, but in those principles, which are immutable."[166]

Gamble derived from these authorities the "principle" that "is either expressly declared or tacitly admitted in all these cases, that where a right to freedom has been acquired, under the law of another State or community, it may be enforced by action, in the courts of a slaveholding State[.]" He also asserted that a freedom judgment from a free state's courts was not a prerequisite "for, in every one of these cases, the party claiming freedom had not procured any adjudication upon his right in the country where it accrued."[167]

Gamble thus found from his "very brief examination of the questions involved in this case" that it was his "duty to declare, that the voluntary removal of a slave, by his master, to a State, territory or country in which slavery is prohibited, with a view to a residence there, entitles the slave to his freedom, and that that right may be asserted by action in our courts under our laws." Gamble also rejected the potential military officer exception to this rule, stating that in *Rachel v. Walker*, a case that he unsuccessfully argued on behalf of the military officer slave owner, the court held that military "officers were not authorized, any more than private individuals, to hold slaves, either in the Northwest territory or in the territory west of the Mississippi and north of thirty-six degrees thirty minutes, north latitude." He added that "the Missouri Compromise, was, in that case, held as operative as the Ordinance of 1787."[168]

The Missouri Supreme Court's *Dred Scott* decision "did not close all doors to freedom in Missouri," but especially for people held as slaves in Missouri, which on three sides was bordered by free soil, "it did close a major one."[169] Judge Duane Benton critiqued Justice Scott's opinion from a twenty-first century judge's perspective. He disapproved of Justice Scott's failure to adhere to or even cite precedent and his failure to defer to the legislature's policy judgments providing statutes authorizing freedom suits.[170] Nevertheless, as noted above, the legislature had, in 1845, modified the freedom suit statutes to add more hurdles in the way of freedom claimants. The legislature never adopted a statute to overrule Justice Scott's judicial activism that created yet another roadblock for freedom claimants.

The Missouri Supreme Court's treatment of precedent is consistent with that of the Mississippi High Court of Errors and Appeals in its 1838 decision in *Hinds v. Brazealle*[171] and the 1859 decision in *Mitchell v. Wells*.[172] The former "became an infamous case among abolitionists (and even the subject of a subplot in Harriet Beecher Stowe's *Dred: A Tale of the Great Dismal Swamp*)."[173] The latter is one of the clearest expressions of the racist pro-slavery ideology's influence on Southern judges and case law, and of the emerging Southern judicial hostility toward manumission.

The *Hinds* opinion by Chief Justice William L. Sharkey "severely limited *Decker*...."[174] In *Hinds* "as in all other Mississippi cases, *Harry v. Decker* and its pro-freedom rhetoric were conveniently ignored."[175]

The case centered on the undisputed acts of Elisha Brazealle, a Mississippi slave owner who, in 1826, traveled to Ohio with "a 'negro' woman and her son, John Munroe Brazealle, with the intention of [freeing] them and bringing them back to [Mississippi]." Elisha signed a manumission deed while he and these slaves were in Ohio. He then returned with them to Mississippi, where he lived until his death.

Elisha's will confirmed that he signed the manumission deed, and that he devised all of his property to John, whom he acknowledged was his son. Elisha's disgruntled would-be heirs filed a bill in chancery. They challenged the will, claiming that John still was a slave and that he could not inherit any property under the will. The chancery judge overruled the defendants' demurrer to this bill, and the Mississippi high court affirmed this decision.[176]

Chief Justice Sharkey stated that "[u]pon principles of national comity, contracts are to be construed according to the laws of the country or state where they are made," and the parties' rights are to be "defined and enforced" by that law. Elisha confirmed in the manumission deed and in his will that he intended to free John under Ohio law. As Judge Mills noted, "*Decker* would appear to have been controlling. However, Sharkey found slavery to be such an ingrained part of the law of Mississippi that questions of freedom versus bondage must be settled in favor of bondage, foreign laws and *Decker* notwithstanding." Indeed, Sharkey did not attempt to distinguish Clarke's decision in *Decker*, or even cite that precedent.[177]

Instead, Sharkey based his decision on his view of Mississippi's public policy. He found that this policy

is indicated by the general course of legislation on a given subject, and we find that free negroes are deemed offensive, because they are not permitted to emigrate to, or remain in the state. They are allowed few privileges, and subject to heavy penalties for offences [sic]. They are required to leave the state within thirty days after notice, and in the meantime give security for good behavior, and those of them who can lawfully remain, must register and carry with them their certificates, or they may be committed to jail. It would also violate a positive law, passed by the legislature, expressly to maintain this settled policy, and to prevent emancipation. No owner can emancipate his slave, but by a deed or will properly attested, or acknowledged in court, and proof to the legislature, that such slave has performed some meritorious act for the benefit of the master, or some distinguished service for the state; and the deed or will can have no validity until ratified by special act of the legislature. It is believed that this law and policy are too essentially important to the interests of our citizens, to permit them to be evaded.

Sharkey also found that the manumission deed "had its origin in an offence [sic] against morality, pernicious and detestable as an example."

But even worse, Sharkey found that Elisha intended "to evade the rigor of the laws of this state." He added that the state's laws "cannot be thus defrauded of their operation by one of our own citizens." Thus, the court held that "the consequence is, that the negroes John Munroe and his mother, are still slaves, and a part of the estate of Elisha Brazealle."[178]

Judge Mills concluded that: "Sharkey's holding, while inconsistent with *Decker*, was not out of step with Mississippi law in the late 1830s." He explained:

Paranoia about free blacks in the state was growing in the 1830s as the slave population increased. Both the 1817 Constitution and the 1832 Constitution prohibited the Legislature from passing laws for the emancipation of slaves, absent consent of the owners. State law prohibited emancipation of slaves by last will and testament or manumission, absent legislative approval. The 1832 Constitution prohibited the importation of slaves into the state as merchandise for sale after May 1, 1833, but allowed actual settlers to bring slaves into the state until 1845. The Legislature passed an act on May 13, 1837, prohibiting the importation of slaves into the state for sale. Sharkey's opinion not only represented political fears of the state leadership in 1838, it also reflected judicial deference to state statutory law over Clarke's appeal to "natural rights."[179]

Sharkey's opinion thus was consistent with Mississippi's 'no in state' manumission policy.

Indeed, Mississippi's high court continued to permit masters to free their slaves by will as long as the free slaves ultimately were not going to reside in Mississippi and increase that state's free black population. The court even decided that freed slaves living on free soil could inherit and recover property in Mississippi and sue in the Mississippi courts to enforce their legal rights.[180]

According to Judge Mills, "[t]his high-minded judicial independence in matters of manumission would continue until the dawn of the war."[181] This change came with the court's 1859 decision in *Wells*. The court held that even a master's out-of-state manumission of a Mississippi slave violated the state's anti-manumission policy. Justice William L. Harris wrote the court's majority opinion, which held that Nancy Wells, a freed former slave, could not claim her inheritance under the will of Edward Wells, who was a Mississippi resident. Edward was Nancy's father, and he owned her when she was a slave. In 1846, Wells brought Nancy to Ohio and he freed her under that state's laws. Edward died in 1848. In 1857, Nancy, now as an Ohio citizen and resident, sued Edward's former executor to claim her legacy under Edward's will, consisting of a watch, a bed, and three thousand dollars.[182]

As in *Scott v. Emerson*, Nancy's lawyers must have gained comfort with their case when Mississippi's Errors and Appeals Court in 1858 decided *Shaw v. Brown*,[183] which was a similar case in which the court found in favor of the claimant. But the court's membership also changed in 1858 when Justice Harris, "a staunch secessionist," joined the court.[184]

The Mississippi Errors and Appeals Court reversed a lower court judgment in Nancy's favor and "overruled *Shaw* and its precedents[.]"[185] Justice Harris's opinion "struck down and overruled all prior cases granting certain rights to free persons of color, including *Shaw*."[186] The court held "both upon principle and the weight of authority, that a slave, once domiciled as such, in this State, can acquire no right, civil or political, within her limits, by manumission elsewhere. That manumission and citizenship, *elsewhere conferred*, cannot even upon principles of comity, under our laws and policy, vest any right *here*."[187]

Harris expressed the following pro-slavery and overtly racist sentiments to explain why the Mississippi courts did not need to afford comity to Ohio's laws:

> The State of Ohio, forgetful of her constitutional obligations to the whole race, and afflicted with a *negro-mania*, which inclines her to descend, rather than elevate herself to the scale of humanity, chooses to take to her embrace, as citizens, the neglected race, who by common consent of the States united, were regarded, at the formation of our government, as an inferior caste, incapable of the blessings of free government, and occupying, in the order of nature, an intermediate state between the irrational animal and the white man.[188]

Harris made no pretense about any relevance of even a freed slave's "rights" to freedom or property, even though those rights were derived from the slave's owner's exercise of his or her property rights and powers.

But Harris's opinion did not stop there. He explained further that some, "[i]n violation of good faith, as well as of the guarantees of the Constitution," were seeking "to destroy the rights of property in this race, which, at the time of the adoption of that instrument, was in servitude, in all or nearly all the States originally parties to the compact of Union." He added the following thoughts, which must be considered at length:

> Mississippi and other States, under the firm conviction, that the relation of

master and slave, which has existed within her limits, from the organization of the State government to this day, is mutually productive of the happiness and best interests of both, continues the institution, and desires to perpetuate it. She is unwilling to extend to the slave race freedom and equality of rights, or to elevate them into political association with the family of States.

Ohio persists; and not only so introduces slaves into her own political organization, but her citizens extend encouragement and inducement to the removal of slaves from Mississippi into the limits of Ohio; and then, in violation of the laws and policy of Mississippi, and in violation of the laws of the United States in relation to the rendition of fugitive slaves, introduces them into her limits as citizens.

Looking at the transaction in the light of comity, courtesy, founded on mutual respect and mutual good-will, regarding it as a question of neighborly politeness and good breeding, or in the more intimate relation of constitutional brotherhood, in which the advocates of this doctrine of comity choose to place it, and it seems to me that comity is terminated by Ohio, in the very act of degrading herself and her sister States, by the offensive association, and that the rights of Mississippi are outraged, when Ohio ministers to emancipation and the abolition of our institution of slavery, by such unkind, disrespectful, lawless interference with our local rights.

But when I am told that Ohio has not only the right thus to degrade and disgrace herself, and wrong us, but also, that she has the right to force her new associates into the Mississippi branch of the American family, to claim and exercise rights *here*, which our laws have always denied to this inferior race, and that Mississippi is bound to yield obedience to such demand, I am at a loss to understand upon what *principle* of law or reason, of courtesy or justice, such a claim can be founded.

Suppose that Ohio, still further afflicted with her peculiar philanthropy, should determine to descend another grade in the scale of *her peculiar* humanity, and claim to confer citizenship on the chimpanzee or the ourang-outang (the most respectable of the monkey tribe), are we to be told that "comity" will require of the States not thus demented, to forget their own policy and self-respect, and lower their own citizens and institutions in the scale of being, to meet the necessities of the mongrel race thus attempted to be introduced into the family of sisters in this confederacy?

The doctrine of comity is not thus unreasonable. Like the benign principles of moral duty, which regulate the miniature government of family in social life, it commands no duty, the observance of which will tend to degrade a sister in the family of nations.

If the sister, in violation of morality, and respect for herself, as well as her associates of the old household, will insist on the meretricious embrace, we are neither bound to sanction nor respect it, much less to receive her new associate into our immediate circle.

The duty to respect the rights of its constituent members, is no less obligatory upon states than families. The same immutable laws of natural reason and justice, which regulate the one, should govern and control the other. They are what the law denominates, imperfect obligations as sanctioned by reason and the common good, but, from their very nature, incapable of strict enforcement by penal sanctions. The obligations of comity being mutual and reciprocal, as well as voluntary, no State in this confederacy may violate that comity towards others, and thereby impose obligations on such others not previously existing.

Thus, he concluded that Ohio, by allowing manumission "in her jurisdiction, and conferring rights of citizenship *there,* contrary to the known policy of Mississippi, can neither confer freedom on a Mississippi slave, nor the right to acquire, hold, sue for, nor enjoy property in Mississippi."[189]

Justice Alexander Handy's dissenting opinion also expressed his strong personal opposition to any manumission. Nevertheless, Handy asserted that the courts should retain the comity principle to maintain the Union as he understood it.[190] Finkelman showed that Handy was no moderate. Rather than violate the "spirit and principles" of the Union, Handy suggested that it might be better for the South to dissolve "the compact[.]"[191] Justice Handy's support for comity in the travel cases therefore was in his mind consistent with slavery and even with secession.

The opinions in *Mitchell v. Wells* show how even when the slave master testator's intent to free his slave was clear, the antebellum judges increasingly believed that an order enforcing that intent violated good public policy principles. Handy's position was consistent with the notion that slaves had no legal rights unless their masters elected to free them as then authorized by the laws of the place in which the slaves were freed. But Harris's approach reflected the pro-slavery ideology's influence. He disallowed the master's intentions because, in his world view, any black freedom was an anathema.

Chief Justice O'Neall Resisting the Anti-Manumission Trend

This pro-slavery anti-manumission view had not persuaded all Southern judges when the Civil War intervened. John B. O'Neall was a leading example. In his 1860 opinion in *Willis v. Jolliffe,*[192] O'Neall—then Chief Justice—and Justice Job Johnstone enforced the master's intent in a case that was similar to *Mitchell v. Wells*, over Justice Francis H. Wardlaw's dissent.[193]

The master in the *Willis* case, Elijah Willis, was a South Carolina native who "accumulated considerable property, consisting chiefly of lands and slaves." Willis never married. On August 18, 1846, he executed a South Carolina will leaving his estate to his siblings and their children. After he executed that will, Willis "began to live in concubinage with one of his slaves, named Amy, who bore, during their intercourse, several children." On February 23, 1854, Willis executed a will in Ohio that expressed his intention to free Amy and her children and to leave his estate to them. The will was prepared by James M. Gitchell of the Cincinnati firm of Jolliffe and Gitchell. John Jolliffe, a lawyer who opposed slavery, was one of the executors. The will directed the executors to sell Willis's property and to use the sale proceeds to bring Amy and her children to Ohio to be freed, and to purchase land for them on which they could reside in Ohio.[194]

In May 1855, Willis left his home in South Carolina for Cincinnati, "taking with him Amy and her mother, and Amy's children, the eldest three having been begotten by a man of color." Willis "arrived with them at a wharf in Cincinnati, in the steamboat Strader, and, having disembarked, he died betwixt the landing and a hack, in which he was about to proceed with said negroes to lodgings."[195]

After Willis died, Jolliffe qualified as the estate's sole executor and he probated the Ohio will in Ohio. Willis's heirs under the earlier will also probated that will in South Carolina. Jolliffe then sought to admit the Ohio will to probate in South Carolina. Willis's next of kin filed a bill in equity seeking an order invalidating the will. After a trial, a jury found the will was invalid. Joliffe filed an appeal to the South Carolina Court of Appeals of Law, which reversed the judgment and ordered a new trial in the 1856 decision *Jolliffe v. Fanning*.[196]

Another trial was held during the February 1858 term in the equity court before Chancellor Wardlaw. He wrote an extensive opinion finding for the plaintiffs, to which were attached extracts from the testimony presented at the hearing.[197] Jolliffe then filed an appeal with the South Carolina Court of Appeals of Equity, which reversed Wardlaw's decision and judgment.

Jolliffe argued "that Amy and her children were in the condition of free persons" when Willis died, "and were consequently capable of taking by devise or bequest." Jolliffe apparently conceded that if Amy and her children continued to live in South Carolina until Willis's death his send/free will would have been unenforceable under the state's 1841 act. Accordingly, as slaves, Amy and her children would have no right to their inheritance. He argued, instead, that Wills "himself took them to Ohio, after having declared his purpose to manumit them, and settle them in some free State[.]" Therefore, "this exercise by the owner of the *jus disponendi* escapes all the provisions of the Act, and that the intended beneficiaries became free and competent the moment they touched the soil of Ohio." Willis's relatives argued that Amy and her children were Willis's slaves when he died and that his will was void under the "Act of 1841, to prevent the emancipation of slaves, and for other purposes[.]"[198]

Chief Justice O'Neall's majority opinion allowed Amy and her children to receive property that Willis devised to them. In so ruling, O'Neall upheld Willis's intent to free his slaves. O'Neall stated that the anti-slavery provisions of the Northwest Ordinance and the Ohio constitution did not "reach cases of persons passing through Ohio with slaves, or where a slave accompanies his master or mistress on a temporary sojourn for business or pleasure." These acts of the master would not free the slaves because, according to O'Neall, "the master, and the slave, as his property, are entitled by the comity of States, and also by the Constitution of the United States, to be protected."[199]

O'Neall decided nevertheless to enforce what he believed was the master's intent in cases such as *Willis*, "when the master puts his slaves on the soil of Ohio with the purpose of making them free. It is then true, that they become free by [the master's] own act." O'Neall noted that Thomas Cobb, "[t]he eloquent counsel for the defendant, in his own work on negro slavery, ... states the principle which applies to and governs such a case 'where there is a change of domicil [sic] from a slave holding to a non-slave holding nation, the *animus remanendi* works of itself and instanter [sic],'" to cause the slave's manumission.[200]

O'Neall applied this principle to the *Willis* case, in which the master apparently did not intend to change his domicile, but he changed his slaves' domicile, with the intention of manumitting them on free soil:

> It is true Mr. Willis did not change his own domicil [sic], although his last act was reaching the soil of Ohio. He intended to return [to South Caro-lina], and therefore his domicil [sic] was not changed, but his act and in-tention both concurred in placing his slaves, who before were mere chattels personal, in a country where they assumed the character of free persons. This was making Ohio their domicil [sic], *and they are now in the full enjoyment of freedom which cannot be disturbed....* [T]hey . . . were free from the moment when, by the consent of their master, they were placed upon the soil of Ohio to be free. I have no idea that the soil of Ohio *per se* confers freedom. It is the act of the master which has that effect.[201]

Chief Justice O'Neall thus expressed his strong preference to enforce the master's intention in the *Willis* case.[202]

As one would predict, Wardlaw voted to affirm his own decision. Wardlaw's dissent expressed his disagreement with O'Neall's conclusion, and he accused O'Neall with adopting Lord Mansfield's *Somerset* doctrine.[203] In a remarkable passage, in light of O'Neall's Irish heritage, Wardlaw stated:

> My brethren seem more inclined to adopt the extravagance of the Irish orator, which revolts most men of sober mind and correct taste, and to declare as the law of South Carolina: "The first moment a slave touches the sacred soil of Britain (or Ohio) the altar and the god sink together in the dust; his soul walks abroad in her own majesty; his body swells beyond the measure of his chains that burst from around him; and he stands re-deemed, regenerated, and disenthralled by the irresistible genius of uni-versal emancipation."[204]

Wardlaw overstated O'Neall's views. O'Neall did not call for the courts to apply *Somerset* broadly to free slaves who traveled on free soil if it was not clear to the court that the master intended to free his slaves.

To the contrary, O'Neall's fidelity to the master's intent was the basis for the *Willis* decision. This is confirmed by his opinion in *Guillemette v. Harper*,[205] a case to which O'Neall referred after the passage quoted above from the *Willis* case. The master in *Guillemette* brought his slaves to Ireland and executed a will and codicil indicating his intent to free his slaves. O'Neall questioned the status of Patrick, one of these slaves, under these facts:

> According to *Somerset* vs. *Stewart*, ... he became thereby free. That *that* case carries the law further than I should willingly acknowledge, it is true. But if the master carries a slave to Great Britain to set him free, or while there assents in any way to his freedom, there can be no objection to the validity of the freedom acquired. For if the law of the place does not prohibit emancipation, no one can object to the dissolution of the tie of slavery. It is true, if a master carried his slave to Great Britain, or elsewhere, where slavery does not exist, and against his will, his slave is allowed to go as free, I have no doubt he may reclaim him—or if the slave returns to a country where slavery is recognized, he *ipso facto* is remitted to his original condition.[206]

Therefore, even one of the most "liberal" of Southern judges rejected a broad reading of *Somerset* and adopted *The Slave Grace* reattachment doctrine. He based his defense of comity upon his respect for the master's intent, when the master's wishes did not pose a threat to the interests of slave society as O'Neall perceived those interests.[207]

Georgia's Chief Justice Joseph Lumpkin, in his 1855 opinion in *Cleland v. Waters*,[208] advocated a view toward these cases that was similar to O'Neall's. Lumpkin also agreed that a master could remove his or her slaves from Georgia to a free state and if he or she intended that the slaves live on free soil they were free. But, like O'Neall, he rejected the broad reading of *Somerset*. He called on the courts to focus on the evidence of the master's intention, not the liberating effects of free soil:

> For myself, I utterly repudiate the whole current of decisions, English and *Northern*, from Somerset's case down to the present time, which hold that the bare removal of a slave to a free country, either by way of transit in travelling [sic], or the convenience of temporary sojourn, will give freedom to the slave. *African* slavery may, in the rhapsodical language of British Jurists, be inconsistent with the genius of their Constitution—*if so, it is the only species of slavery that is.* But this is certainly not true, under the Constitution of the United States. Upon the principle of international law, properly expounded and applied, to promote the free and unembarassed [sic] intercourse between the citizens and subjects of foreign States, we maintain, that the judgment in Somerset's case was wrong. Much more so are the decisions in this country, to the same effect, under a compact formed to abolish *alienage*, and to establish a more perfect union between the States constituting our confederacy, recognizing slavery as it does, in the broadest terms, and guaranteeing its enjoyment. The *status* of the slave under our system, united as we are under the same federal authority, and governed by the same laws, should never have been held to be affected by

the temporary residence of the owner in a free State. It was not necessary to the maintenance of any local policy, that the Northern States, in the exercise of their undoubted right to abolish slavery, should have held that citizens of the slave States were thereby prevented from coming among them or passing through with their families and servants. Prior to 1836, the Courts even in Massachusetts had made no such decision. This fungus has been engrafted upon their Codes by the foul and fell spirit of modern fanaticism. Indeed, the Legislatures of many of the free States passed laws securing to citizens of the slave States, who came within their territories, upon business or pleasure, and brought slaves with them, means and facilities to take those slaves back to their domicil [sic].[209]

Lumpkin thus concluded "that whenever slaves are removed to a free country, with a view to change their former domicil [sic] and to remain there permanently, they cease to be slaves, naturally and necessarily." This he stated will follow "*a fortiori*" when a master "carried" his or her slaves "to a free state, for the express purpose of being liberated." According to Lumpkin, the master's exercise of his or her "right of removal" of the slaves "to a free State, was all that was needed to bestow freedom upon these slaves. No express power to emancipate was required."[210]

As I previously noted, Lumpkin's approach to manumission evolved over the years. He came to be against all manumissions anywhere. Indeed, O'Neall's views favoring the master's intentions were on the wane in the South during the late antebellum years.[211] According to Robert Shaw, Harris's opinion in *Mitchell v. Wells* "was certainly more representative of southern legal dicta than O'Neall's ruling in the *Willis* case."[212] Lumpkin's and Harris's views represented the emerging legal reform trend to the contrary.

Lumpkin Extends the Anti-Manumission Trend to Another Slave State's Law

Chief Justice Lumpkin's 1855 opinion in *Knight v. Hardeman*[213] further advanced the anti-comity and anti-manumission trend to include the negation of slave "rights" to freedom upon their movement from one slave state to another. In that case, the court effectively denied the claimants their freedom, even though they based their case on a clear showing of the master's intention to free his slaves in accordance with the laws of another slave state, and not the laws of a free state.

On June 5, 1822, Henry Duvall of Maryland executed a will apparently in accordance with Maryland law stating: "It is my will that my black woman Rebecca shall be free on the 1st day of January, 1828; and all her issue to be free as they arrive at the age of 30 years; and all or any of my young blacks that are not manumitted, shall be free as they arrive at the age of thirty years." Duvall died a Maryland resident. His date of death is not stated in the official case report.

The freedom claimants were Margaret Phillips and her children. Margaret was Rebecca's daughter. She arrived at the age of thirty in 1835, but she was held in slavery contrary to Duvall's will and was sent to Georgia. Margaret was sold more than once as a slave. In 1840, she was sold to Michael J. Healey, who died in 1850. Healey named Judge Robert V. Hardeman and others as the executors of his will.

Healey's executors were about to sell Margaret and her children when the plaintiff, John Knight, filed a bill in chancery as the claimants' next friend. Knight sought an order from Hardeman, who was the Judge of the Circuit where Margaret was domiciled, appointing Knight to serve as the claimants' guardian. Hardeman denied Knight's request. Knight then appealed to the Georgia Supreme Court, which affirmed Hardeman's decision.

Knight sought relief in equity. He alleged "that a suit at Law would not protect [the claimants]—1st. Because all the witnesses are resident in Maryland, and their testimony could not be procured before the sale. 2d. Because they would be sold and removed from the State before a hearing could be had. The prayer [for relief] was for an injunction and a decree, declaring complainants free."[214]

Lumpkin wrote the court's opinion rejecting both of these grounds. He noted executor-judge Hardeman's obvious conflict of interest, but blamed Knight for not trying to file his bill with another judge. In sum, Lumpkin found that the claimants had an adequate remedy at law under Georgia's freedom suit statutes.[215]

But Lumpkin's opinion went further, however; and he raised and addressed an argument that the lawyers in the cases apparently did not advance:

> I must be pardoned for suggesting, that to my mind, there lies, at the foundation of this case, a much stronger objection to this whole proceeding, than any which have been discussed by the learned Counsel. And that is, the want of equity in the bill, not because the complainants have ample redress *at Law*, if any where; but because neither Courts of Law nor of Equity have any right to grant the relief which they seek.
>
> We have, in this State, the most stringent Statutes which the ingenuity of our wisest statesmen could devise, to prevent domestic manumission. For fifty years, the policy of our legislation has manifested no variableness nor shadow of turning in this respect. Can the laws of a sister State, then, allowing the freedom of these slaves, be executed by the Courts of Georgia? Dare we say, in the face of the Acts of 1801 and 1818, that these foreign laws are not prejudicial to our own rights and interests? Are we not under paramount obligation to enforce our own policy?
>
> To my mind, this is a plain case.
>
> No one pretends that negroes can be carried to New York or any other free State, and held there in perpetual bondage by their owner, in defiance of the laws and policy of that State. With what more propriety can slaves be brought here and emancipated? Such a doctrine is wholly inadmissible. It

might be used to subvert the domestic institutions of every slave State in the Union. Our Courts of Justice are powerless to exercise an authority so repugnant to the declared will of their own Government.

After raising and discussing this point, Lumpkin added: "But I forbear to discuss this point, inasmuch as the decision below may be sustained upon the other ground."[216]

Accordingly, Lumpkin would deny comity to another slave state's laws, such as Maryland's, which still permitted manumission by will, thus defeating that state's policy and the intent of a master who resided only in that state, and whose freed slaves were illegally taken to Georgia and sold into lifetime slavery. Lumpkin extended Lord Stowell's reattachment rule when slaves were taken from one slave state to another.

Lumpkin's holding was contrary to an 1849 Mississippi High Court of Errors and Appeals decision in *Sam, a Man of Color v. Fore*.[217] In a short opinion by Justice Alexander M. Clayton, the High Court reversed the lower court's order dismissing Sam's suit on the defendant's demurrer. Sam based his manumission claim on the May 7, 1821 will of his then owner, Mary Kennedy, a Kentucky resident. That will stated that Sam was to be freed when he reached the age of 31. Sam claimed that he was sold and was brought to Mississippi, where he was illegally held in slavery by the defendant Wright Fore because, under Kennedy's will, Sam was entitled to freedom on December 7, 1844. In remanding the case for a trial, Justice Clayton wrote that "it will be necessary for the petitioner to produce the law of Kentucky, which establishes his right to freedom, in a shape which will entitle it to be considered by the court."[218] Justice Clayton did not question Sam's right to rely on Kennedy's Kentucky will and Kentucky law, despite the 1842 Mississippi law that barred all manumissions by will.[219]

As A. E. Keir Nash noted, Lumpkin's opinion in *Knight v. Hardeman* denied the claimants relief "when no good reason existed why [the claimants] could not be returned to Maryland to receive [their] liberty."[220] Moreover, according to John Phillip Reid, "Lumpkin did precisely what he had criticized Northern judges for doing. He refused to grant interstate comity for reasons of a public policy[.]"[221] That public policy was manifested in the anti-manumission rule that, in turn, was based on the pro-slavery ideology that Lumpkin and other judges increasingly advanced thorough their judicial decisions.

Conclusion

According to Paul Finkelman, in the early antebellum years the Southern courts allowed slaves whose masters removed them to a free state, territory, or country and who thus were freed pursuant to the free state's laws to enforce their rights to liberty and to inherit property, out of respect or comity toward the free state's laws. During the later antebellum years, however, Finkelman cited cases confirming that the Southern courts became more reluctant to grant rights to former slaves who claimed that they who were freed in this way. Finkelman argued that, although this process was not complete by the beginning of the Civil

War, it was a clear trend.[222] He concluded that, by the 1850s, most of the Southern courts and legislatures had, to one degree or another, decided that interstate comity could not extend to cases involving slaves who claimed to be free.[223]

In my view, that trend also was consistent with the increasing hostility to manumission exhibited in the antebellum Southern statute and case law. The decline of implied manumission and the prohibition of in-state and even out-of-state manumission shows how the nineteenth century slave law reform trend in the South increasingly confined the masters' freedom to manumit their slaves. The Southern decisions that refused to apply the doctrine of comity to uphold freed slaves' claims to property or freedom, when those claims were based upon a free state's laws, also illustrate the effects of the pro-slavery ideology and this anti-manumission trend in the law and in society.

It is not surprising, then, that Kentucky's courts continued to recognize claims that freed slaves asserted under free state or territory laws, consistent with the court's view of the evidence of the master's intentions. Kentucky's legislators did not adopt statutes prohibiting all manumissions, although the legislature in 1851 prohibited in-state manumission. Therefore, the courts in Kentucky were not confronted with legislative edicts stating or strongly suggesting that the manumission of any Kentucky or former Kentucky slaves anywhere offended the state's public policy. This same logic would appear to apply to other states like Virginia, Tennessee, and Missouri, which also did not prohibit manumission. But the Missouri Supreme Court's majority itself advanced this pro-slavery and anti-slavery view, and the legislature did not dissent.[224]

In contrast, the legislators in other Southern states, including Mississippi, adopted laws that attempted to ban all manumissions. These anti-comity/anti-implied manumission statutes, and the cases enforcing them, are in harmony with the pro-slavery ideology that Lumpkin and Harris so clearly expressed in their opinions. These opinions demonstrate the racist pro-slavery ideology's influence on case law, as well as the emerging legislative and judicial hostility toward manumission.

Notes to Chapter 8

[1] *See, e.g.*, Shaw, *supra* at 111-39.

[2] *See, e.g.*, Finkelman, *Imperfect Union*, *supra* at 6, 132-34; Paul Finkelman, "When International Law was a Domestic Problem," 44 *Val. U. L. Rev.* 779, 791-97 (2010) [hereinafter Finkelman, "International Law"].

[3] In addition to Finkelman's writings, *see* Weinberg, *supra* at 1331-32; Note, "American Slavery and Conflict of Laws," 71 *Colum. L. Rev.* 74, 85-98 (1971) [hereinafter "Conflict of Laws"]; Harold W. Horrowitz, "Choice-of Law Decisions Involving Slavery: 'Interest Analysis' in the Early Nineteenth Century," 17 *U.C.L.A. L. Rev.* 587 (1970).

[4] *See* Finkelman, *Imperfect Union*, *supra* at 13-16.

[5] *See id.*; Cover, *Justice Accused, supra* at 83-86; Mark W. Janis, "Dred Scott and International Law," 43 *Colum. J. Transnat'l L.* 763, 764-79 (2005); Wiecek, *"Somerset," supra* at 128-41; *see also* Bush, "First Slave," *supra* at 620-69.

[6] *See* Finkelman, "International Law," *supra* at 789, quoting Joseph Story, *Commentaries on the Conflicts of Laws* 29 (1834).

[7] *See* Weinberg, *supra* at 1332-45, 1332, n. 73.

[8] *See* Finkelman, "International Law," *supra* at 789.

[9] *See* Cobb, *supra* at 134-37, 199-200.

[10] Finkelman, *Imperfect Union, supra* at 9.

[11] *See, e.g., Ringgold v. Barley*, 5 Md. 186, 1853 WL 3571 at *5-*6 (1853); *Baptiste v. De Volunbrun*, 5 H. & J. 86, 1820 WL 395 at *4 (Md. 1820).

[12] *See, e.g., Cross v. Black*, 9 G. & J. 1298, 1837 WL 1922 at *11 (Md. 1837).

[13] Lofft 1, 98 Eng. Rep. 499, 20 How. St. T. 1 (K.B. 1772); *see* chapter 4, *supra* at notes 111-16.

[14] 2 Hagg. Adm. 94 (1827). For a summary of the British slavery cases, *see* 1 Catterall, *supra* at 1-52.

[15] *See Somerset v. Stewart*, Lofft at 1, 18; Wise, *Heavens, supra* at 1-11, 114-25; Mark S. Weiner, *Black Trials: Citizenship from the Beginnings of Slavery to the End of Caste* 70-83(2004) [hereinafter Weiner, *Black Trials*]; Davis, *Revolution, supra* at 480-81; Finkelman, "International Law," *supra* at 797; Mark S. Weiner, "New Biographical Evidence on *Somerset's Case*," 23 *Slavery & Abolition* 121, 122, 126-31 (2002).

[16] *Somerset v. Stewart*, Lofft at 1, 18; Wise, *Heavens, supra* at 127-44; Weiner, *Black Trials, supra* at 81-83; *see also* Kristen Sword, "Remembering Dinah Nevil: Strategic Deceptions in Eighteenth-Century Antislavery," 97 *J. of Am. Hist.* 315, 321 (2010) (discussing James Somerset's time in Philadelphia in 1766 and 1767).

[17] *See Somerset v. Stewart*, Lofft at 1-17; Wise, *Heavens, supra* at 145-71; Weiner, *Black Trials, supra* at 83-84.

[18] *Somerset v. Stewart*, Lofft at 18; Wise, *Heavens, supra* at 174.

[19] *See* Finkelman, "International Law," *supra* at 797, quoting *Somerset v. Stewart*, 98 Eng. Rep. at 509.

[20] *See* Wiecek, *"Somerset," supra* at 103; *see also* Drescher, *supra* at 99; Wise, *Heavens, supra* at 174-77; Higginbotham, *Color, supra* at 316-20, 351-53.

[21] *See Somerset v. Stewart*, Lofft at 18-19; Wise, *Heavens, supra* at 171-77.

[22] *See Somerset v. Stewart*, Lofft at 18-19; Wise, *Heavens, supra* at 13-30; Oldham, *Common Law, supra* at 309-10; Higginbotham, *Color, supra* at 320-29; Wiecek, *"Somerset," supra* at 88-95.

[23] *See* Wise, *Heavens, supra* at 31-114; Oldham, *Common Law, supra* at 310-13; Higginbotham, *Color, supra* at 329-32; Wiecek, *"Somerset," supra* at 95-101.

[24] *See* James Oldham, "New Light on Mansfield and Slavery," 27 *J. of British Studies* 45, 54-60 (1988); Wiecek, *"Somerset," supra* at 141-46.

[25] *See Somerset v. Stewart*, Lofft at 18-19; Wise, *Heavens, supra* at 181-82.

[26] *See Somerset v. Stewart*, Lofft at 19; Wise, *Heavens*, *supra* at 182.

[27] *See* Davis, *Revolution*, *supra* at 498, n. 52.

[28] *See* Wiecek, "*Somerset*," *supra* at 87.

[29] *See id.* at 108; *see also* Wong, *supra* at 24-36; Drescher, *supra* at 102-14; Brown, *Moral Capital*, *supra* at 96-104; Weiner, *Black Trials*, *supra* at 85-90; 1 Catterall, *supra* at 1-5; Charles R. Foy, "'Unkle Sommerset's Freedom: Liberty in England for Black Sailors," 13 *J. of Maritime Research* 21 (2011). According to Mark Weiner, Mansfield's decision was consistent with the notion that "[j]udges generally are appropriately cautious, loath to make sweeping pronouncements where a case may be decided on narrow grounds." Weiner, *Black Trials*, *supra* at 85. Nevertheless, "the most carefully delimited judicial pronouncements have a way of assuming lives beyond the intent of their authors: just as it is for judges to be judicious, so, too, is it natural for the people to infer what larger principles they will from their opinions. This is the nature of legal conversation, a push-and-pull between the law and moral aspiration." *Id.* at 86.

[30] *See, e.g.*, Drescher, *supra* at 101; Higginbotham, *Color*, *supra* at 353-60; J. R. Pole, "Review, Slavery and Revolution: The Conscience of the Rich," 20 *Historical J.* 503, 504-05 (1977); *see also* Diane J. Klein, "Paying Eliza: Comity, Contracts, and Critical Race Theory—19th Century Choice of Law Doctrine and the Validation of Antebellum Contracts for the Purchase and Sale of Human Beings," 20 *Nat'l Black L.J.* 1 (2006-2007) (cases enforcing slave sale contracts after emancipation). On the British abolition of slave trade and slavery, *see* Davis, *Inhuman Bondage*, *supra* at 231-49; Drescher, *supra* at 205-66; Davis, *Progress*, *supra* at 168-226; Higginbotham, *Color*, *supra* at 363-68; Elkins, *supra* at 140-222, 252-66.

[31] *See* Drescher, *supra* at 93-100; Peabody, *supra* at 15-136.

[32] *See* Fede, *People Without Rights*, *supra* at 29-30.

[33] 2 Hagg. Adm. 94 (1827). The case also is designated as *The King, and His Majesty's Procurator-General, and George Wyke v. John Allan, Esq. Claimant*, in *Haggard's Admiralty Reports*.

[34] *See* H.C. Rothery, "The Antigua Slave Cases," in 14 *Reports from Commissioners, Inspectors and Others: Elections (Boston) and Fugitive Slaves* 229 (1876).

[35] *The Slave Grace*, 2 Hagg. Adm. at 94-95. The November 1827 *Anti-Slavery Monthly Reporter*, which was published in England by the Anti-Slavery Society, asserted that Grace "was induced to return to Antigua, on an understanding which is asserted by Grace, but has not been proved, that she should henceforward enjoy, in Antigua, the liberty of which she was put into possession by her arrival in England." *See* "The Slave Grace," in 30 *Anti-Slavery Monthly Reporter* 143, 143 (November 1827); *see also* Wong, *supra* at 42.

[36] *See The Slave Grace*, 2 Hagg. Adm. at 101; Wong, *supra* at 36-47; Finkelman, *Imperfect Union*, *supra* at 16-17, 185-87; Higginbotham, *Color*, *supra* at 360-63; Davis, *Revolution*, *supra* at 499-500; 1 Catterall, *supra* at 5-8. The Antiguan Vice-Admiralty Court also entered judgments in 1826 favor of the alleged owners of James and Robert, and, in 1827, in favor of the alleged owners of Jack Martin and Rachel and John Smith. *See* Rothery, *supra* at 229-30. Jack Martin's case and others were appealed to the High Court of Admiralty, and Lord Stowell affirmed the lower court rulings, based upon his *Slave Grace* decision. *See* Wong, *supra* at 46-47; Parks, *supra* at 127-29. Martin's case "was remitted, together with that of the slave Grace, and other cases, to the Vice-Admiralty Court of Antigua in

order that the respective claimants might obtain the costs and damages which had been awarded to them." Rothery, *supra* at 230; *see also* Henry J. Bourguignon, *Sir William Scott, Lord Stowell: Judge of the High Court of Admiralty, 1798-1828* xi (2004) (author notes that he omits Lord Stowell's slavery cases).

[37] *See* Wong, supra at 47-48; Wise, *Heavens, supra* at 185-204; Finkelman, *Imperfect Union, supra* at 101-80; Higginbotham, *Color, supra* at 353-68; Finkelman, "International Law," *supra* at 800.

[38] *See, e.g., Foster's Adm'r v. Fosters*, 51 Va. (10 Gratt.) 485, 1853 WL 3241 at *2 (1853) (discussing New York law); *Butler v. Hopper*, 4 F. Cas. 904 (C.C.D. Pa. 1806) (No. 2,241) (discussing Pennsylvania law); Finkelman, *Imperfect Union, supra* at 41-100; Fernbacher, *supra* at 54.

[39] 35 Mass. (18 Pick.) 193, 1836 WL 2441 (1836).

[40] Finkelman, "International Law," *supra* at 798-99.

[41] *See Commonwealth v. Aves*, 35 Mass. at 193-95.

[42] Finkelman, "International Law," *supra* at 799.

[43] *See Commonwealth v. Aves*, 35 Mass. at 217-19.

[44] Finkelman, "International Law," *supra* at 800.

[45] 2 Mart. (n.s.) 401, 1824 WL 1642 (La.1824).

[46] 9 Ky. (2 A.K. Marsh.) 467, 1820 WL 1098 (1820).

[47] *See Commonwealth v. Aves*, 35 Mass. at 217; Finkelman, "International Law," *supra* at 812.

[48] *See Commonwealth v. Aves*, 35 Mass. at 218.

[49] *See id.* at 225.

[50] 20 N.Y. (6 E.P. Smith) 562, 1860 WL 7815 (1860); *see* Finkelman, *Imperfect Union, supra* at 296-310; William H. Manz, "'A just cause for war': New York's Dred Scott Decision," 79 *N.Y. St. B.J.* 10 (Nov./Dec. 2007).

[51] *See* Finkelman, "International Law," *supra* at 812.

[52] *Mahoney v. Ashton*, 4 H. & Mc H. 295, 1799 WL 397 (Md. Gen. Ct. 1799), *rev'd* (Md. Ct. App. 1802), 4 H. & Mc H. 210, 1798 WL 411 (Md. Gen. Ct. 1798), 4 H. & Mc H. 63, 1797 WL 583 (Md. Gen. Ct. 1797).

[53] *See* Shaw, *supra* at 115-16.

[54] *See* Papenfuse, *supra* at 38-39.

[55] *See id.* at 39-41.

[56] *See Mahoney v. Ashton*, 1799 WL 397 at *2; Papenfuse, *supra* at 41.

[57] *See id.* at 41-45.

[58] *See Mahoney v. Ashton*, 1799 WL 397 at *2-*7; Papenfuse, *supra* at 45.

[59] Papenfuse, *supra* at 45.

[60] *See Mahoney v. Ashton*, 1799 WL 397 at *7-*18; Papenfuse, *supra* at 45-46.

[61] *See Mahoney v. Ashton*, 1799 WL 397 at *17.

[62] *See id.*, where the court wrote:

> If this case was before a British court, it would seem, that the question should be decided according to the British law, as it stood between the years 1678 and 1681, and not by the law as it may have been modified or altered subsequent to that period. No adjudged case in the British books hath been cited, nor have the court been able to find one coming up to the case in the exception. Opposing cases as well as opinions of particular judges and law writers, have been cited as applicable to the case. About the period of *Ann Joice's* being in England, a diversity of opinions prevailed on that subject. At one period it was held by a judge, that a slave, by being brought to England thereby became free. Sometimes it hath been held that trover would lie, at other times that it would not; that the sale of a negro was a sufficient consideration to support assumpsit to pay the price; that a master, deprived of his slave, might support an action *per quod servitium amisit.* By British charters, and British acts of parliament, the slave trade hath been authorised [sic] and encouraged, and slaves have been considered there as merchandise, as chattels, as property, and have, by a British statute operating in this state, been subjected to be sold and disposed of as other property for the payment of debts. Lord Chief Justice *Talbot,* and Sir *Philip Yorke,* in 1729, expressly declare, that a slave coming from the West-Indies, with or without his master, to Great-Britain or Ireland, doth not become free, and that his master's property or right in him is not thereby determined or varied, &c. And that his master may legally compel him to return. This opinion is recognized by *Hardwicke,* acting as chancellor, in 1749, and that trover would lie for a negro. Judge *Blackstone* in his Commentaries, in 1765, (11 *edition, vol.* 1, *page* 127,) says, that a slave or negro the moment he lands in England falls under the protection of the laws, and so far becomes a freeman; though the master's right to his service may probably still continue. And in *page* 424, repeats the same, and adds, that the law will protect him in the enjoyment of his person and property; but yet with regard to any right which the master may have lawfully acquired to the perpetual service of John or Thomas, this will remain exactly in the same state as before; for this is no more than the same subjection for life, which every apprentice submits to for the space of seven years or more, &c.
>
> In the British books slaves are sometimes called slaves or servants; and it is said by Lord *Mansfield* in *Somerset's* case, that there may be a villein in gross by confession. In the case of *Somerset* in 1772, Lord *Mansfield* mentioned the opinions of Sir *Philip Yorke,* and Lord Chief Justice *Talbot,* in 1729, and recognized by Lord *Hardwicke* in 1749, and calls them two of the greatest men of their own or any times, and says he pays all due attention to their opinions. Lord *Mansfield* puts several questions as to the law with respect to their settlements, their wages, actions for any slight

coercion by their masters. In *Somerset's* case the court declined deciding the question, whether by being carried to England he thereby became free; but say, that they would judge upon the return of the *habeas corpus*, and according to their own laws, which did not admit of so high an act of dominion as in that case had been exercised by the master over his slave, and therefore that *Somerset* must be discharged. Lord *Mansfield,* in *Somerset's* case, says, that the state of slavery is so odious that nothing can be suffered to support it but positive law.

[63] *Mahoney v. Ashton,* 1799 WL 397 at *17-*18; Cover, *Justice Accused, supra* at 88-89; Papenfuse, *supra* at 45-46.

[64] *See* Shaw, *supra* at 116.

[65] *See* 1 Catterall, *supra* at 7; *see also Negro David v. Porter,* 4 H. & McH. 418, 1799 WL 418 (Md. Gen. Ct. 1799) (awarding freedom judgment under Pennsylvania law to claimant who was taken to that state and hired out in 1788 before being returned to Maryland).

[66] 1 Miss. (Walker) 36, 1818 WL 1235 (1818).

[67] *See Harry v. Decker & Hopkins,* 1818 WL 1235 at *1.

[68] *See* Finkelman, *Imperfect Union, supra* at 228.

[69] *See* Finkelman, *Slavery and the Founders, supra* at 32-80; Finkelman, *Imperfect Union, supra* at 83-84; Schwemm, *supra* at 356-57, discussing *Northwest Ordinance,* art. IV.

[70] *See State v. Lasselle,* 1 Blackf. 60, 1820 WL 828 at *1 (Ill. 1820); Finkelman, *Imperfect Union, supra* at 93; 2 Hurd, *supra* at 127.

[71] *See* Finkelman, *Imperfect Union, supra* at 150-51 (citing *Jarrot v. Jarrot,* 2 Gil. 1 (Ill. 1845)), and *id.* at 228.

[72] *See id.* at 93 (citing *State v. Lasselle,* 1820 WL 828 at *1-*2), and *id.* at 228; *see also* Sandra Boyd Williams, "The Indiana Supreme Court and the Struggle Against Slavery," 30 *Ind. L. Rev.* 305, 305-07 (1997).

[73] *Harry v. Decker & Hopkins,* 1818 WL 1235 at *1.

[74] *See* Finkelman, *Imperfect Union, supra* at 229. Further, Meredith Lang stated that *Harry* "could have no sequel. The moral philosophy expressed in the opinion on the institution of slavery was only a romantic historical error of 1818," which was "antagonistic to the forces at work in the state" that eventually would "venerate slavery as one of the noblest inventions of man and consign *Harry* to oblivion." Lang, *supra* at 78.

[75] *See* Mills, *supra* at 178.

[76] 1 Miss. (Walker) 83, 1820 WL 1413 (1821).

[77] *See* Mills, *supra* at 176-79; *see also* Fede, *People Without Rights, supra* at 3, 73-75 (discussing *State v. Jones*). Carl Degler, for example, gave primary emphasis to opinions such as *Jones* and *Harry* as typical exemplars of judicial attitudes and decisions in the United States South, to demonstrate what he stated were the essential similarities between Brazilian and North American slavery conditions and law. *See* Degler, *supra* at 27-29.

[78] *See* Finkelman, *Imperfect Union, supra* at 190-228.

79 *See id.* at 205.

80 *See* Weinberg, *supra* at 1343; "Conflict of Laws," *supra* at 97.

81 *See* Nash, "Radical Interpretations," *supra* at 299-09.

82 9 Ky. (2 A.K. Marsh.) 467, 1820 WL 1098 (1820); Finkelman, *Imperfect Union, supra* at 192-95; Schwemm, *supra* at 364-66.

83 *Rankin v. Lydia,* 1820 WL 1098 at *1.

84 *Id.* at *3.

85 *Id.* at *1. Robert Todd was Abraham Lincoln's father-in-law. *See* Schwemm, *supra* at 365, n. 77.

86 *Rankin v. Lydia,* 1820 WL 1098 at *3.

87 *Id.*

88 *Id.* at *1-*3; *see* 2 Hurd, *supra* at 124-27.

89 *Rankin v. Lydia,* 1820 WL 1098 at *3.

90 *See id.* at *3-*5.

91 *Id.* at *5.

92 *Id.* at *6.

93 *Id.*

94 *Id.* at *7.

95 *See* Finkelman, *Imperfect Union, supra* at 94-95 (citing *Sewell's Slaves,* 3 Am. Jur. 404 (1830)).

96 *See* chapter 3, *supra* at note 188.

97 *See, e.g., Norris (of color) v. Patton's Adm'r,* 54 Ky. (15 B. Mon.) 575 (1855) (denying freedom claim); *Ben Mercer (of color) v. Gilman,* 50 Ky. (11 B. Mon.) 210 (1850) (granting freedom claim); *Collins v. America, a woman of color,* 48 Ky. (9 B. Mon.) 565 (1849) (denying freedom claim); Finkelman, *Imperfect Union, supra* at 195-205 (citing cases).

98 51 Ky. (12 B. Mon.) 542, 1851 WL 2366 (1851).

99 21 Va. (Gilmer) 143, 1820 WL 809 (1820).

100 22 Va. (1 Rand.) 15, 1821 WL 967 (1821).

101 *Lewis v. Fullerton,* 1821 WL 967 at *1.

102 *See id.* at *4.

103 *See id.* at *3-*4.

104 *See id.* at *4.

105 *See id.* at *5.

106 51 Va. (10 Gratt.) 485, 1853 WL 3241 (1853).

107 *Foster's Adm'r v. Fosters,* 1853 WL 3241 at *1.

108 *See id.* at *1-*3.

109 *See id.* at *3.

[110] *See id.* at *4, stating:

> No case can be found like this in its circumstances; yet general principles applicable thereto may be deduced from some of the cases. In *Griffith v. Fanny*, Gilm. 143, the owner having permitted his slave to reside in the state of Ohio, a nonslaveholding state, for no merely temporary purpose, it was held that the constitution of Ohio conferred the right of freedom. In *Ben Mercer v. Gilman*, 11 B. Monr. R. 210, the master having permitted his slave to go at large in the state of Illinois, (a nonslaveholding state,) and act as a free man, and having recognized his right to freedom, was held to have lost his title to his slave, and the slave to have become free. Where the master allowed his slave to reside in Maryland under circumstances to give the slave his freedom according to the law there, the master was held to have lost his right. *Hunter v. Fulcher*, 1 Leigh 172.

> On the other hand, cases are found in which the owner is held not to have lost title to the slave; as where the slave absconds from the master to a nonslaveholding state; the title in such case being protected by the federal constitution; or where the owner for a temporary purpose takes or sends his slave into a nonslaveholding state; or where under forms of law the courts of nonslaveholding states have adjudged *in invitum* that the master's right was lost: In all such cases the owner's right has been preserved. *See Lewis v. Fullerton*, 1 Rand. 15; *Maria v. Kirby*, 12 B. Monr. R. 542.

[111] *See Foster's Adm'r v. Fosters*, 1853 WL 3241 at *4.

[112] 1 Mo. 472, 1824 WL 1839 (1824). *See* Finkelman, *Imperfect Union, supra* at 217-18; Konig, "Dred Scott," *supra* at 71-73.

[113] Konig, "Dred Scott," *supra* at 71-72. The official report of the Missouri Supreme Court decision states that judgment was entered for Winny during the trial court's February 1822 term. *Winny v. Whitesides*, 1824 WL 1839 at *1.

[114] *See v. Whitesides*, 1824 WL 1839 at *1; Konig, "Dred Scott," *supra* at 72.

[115] *Winny v. Whitesides*, 1824 WL 1839 at *1.

[116] *Id.* at *3.

[117] 15 Mo. 576, 1852 WL 4171 (1852).

[118] *See, e.g., Wilson v. Melvin*, 4 Mo. 592 (1837); *Rachael v. Walker*, 4 Mo. 350 (1836); *Nat. v. Ruddle*, 3 Mo. 400 (1834); *Julia v. McKinney*, 3 Mo. 270 (1833); *Ralph v. Duncan*, 3 Mo. 194 (1833); *Tramell v. Adam, a Black Man*, 2 Mo. 155 (1829);*Milly v. Smith*, 2 Mo. 36 (1828); *LaGrange v. Chouteau*, 2 Mo. 116 (1829); *LaGrange v. Chouteau*, 2 Mo. 20 (1828); *see also* Finkelman, *Imperfect Union, supra* at 218-22; 5 Catterall, *supra* at 105-17; Konig, "Dred Scott," *supra* at 73-79; Boman, "Dred Scott," *supra* at 414-15 (discussing the post-*Winny* decisions).

[119] 2 Mart. (n.s.) 401, 1824 WL 1642 (La. 1824).

[120] Finkelman, *Imperfect Union, supra* at 206-16.

[121] *Lunsford v. Coquillon,* 1824 WL 1642 at *1.

[122] *Id.*

[123] *Id.* at *1-*2.

[124] *Id.* at *3; *see* Finkelman, *Imperfect Union, supra* at 208-09.

[125] *See* Schafer, *Supreme Court, supra* at 263-75; Shaw, *supra* at 124-25; Finkelman, *Imperfect Union, supra* at 209-16; 3 Catterall, *supra* at 389-96.

[126] *See* Finkelman, *Imperfect Union, supra* at 211.

[127] *See* Schafer, *Supreme Court, supra* at 275-88; Finkelman, *Imperfect Union, supra* at 212.

[128] *See* Finkelman, *Imperfect Union, supra* at 212.

[129] 15 Mo. 576, 1852 WL 4171 (1852).

[130] *See supra* at notes 112-16.

[131] *See Dred Scott v. Sandford,* 60 U.S. (19 How.) 393, 15 L. Ed. 691 (1857); *see also* sources cited in chapter 1, *supra* at note 1, and the articles in *Dred Scott Perspectives, supra*; Lea VanderVelde & Sandhya Subramanian, "Mrs. Dred Scott," 106 *Yale L.J.* 1033 (1997).

[132] *See* Boman, "Dred Scott," *supra* at 405-20; *see also* Benton, *supra* in *Dred Scott Perspectives, supra* at 199-200.

[133] *See, e.g.,* Paul Finkelman, "The Strange Career of *Dred Scott*: From Fort Armstrong to Guantanamo Bay," in *Dred Scott Perspectives, supra* at 231-35 [hereinafter Finkelman, "Strange Career"], for a recent summary of the facts.

[134] *See* Ehrlich, *supra* at 9-11; Fehrenbacher, *supra* at 239-40.

[135] *See* VanderVelde, *Mrs. Dred Scott, supra* at 248-49; *See* Kaufman, *supra at* 138; 156-58; Ehrlich, *supra* at 183-84; Fehrenbacher, *supra* at 240-41, 276, 421, 568-69, 653, nn. 4 and 6; Michael A. Wolff, "Missouri Law, Politics, and the *Dred Scott* Case," in *Dred Scott Perspectives* at 222, 226, n. 112.

[136] *See* Ehrlich, *supra* at 11-15; Fehrenbacher, *supra* at 239-40, 652, n. 2, noting that the historical record is not clear. VanderVelde suggested that Henry Blow may have sold Dred to Dr. Emerson "earlier than customarily believed." VanderVelde, *Mrs. Dred Scott, supra* at 408, n. 49.

[137] *See Scott v. Emerson,* 1852 WL 4171 at *5; Ehrlich, *supra* at 16-19; Fehrenbacher, *supra* at 239-44; *see also* VanderVelde, *Mrs. Dred Scott, supra* at 74-75. In fact, for a time, three other officers also claimed Dred Scott as their slave at Fort Armstrong, and all four received the same monthly stipend. Thus, as Lea VanderVelde noted, "[t]he U.S. Army actually subsidized slave ownership on the frontier." *Id.* at 75.

[138] *See Scott v. Emerson,* 1852 WL 4171 at *5; VanderVelde, *Mrs. Dred Scott, supra* at 9-57, 115, 355 nn. 2-4; Ehrlich, *supra* at 19-21; Fehrenbacher, *supra* at 244.

[139] VanderVelde & Subramanian, *supra* at 1100-17.

[140] *See* VanderVelde, *Mrs. Dred Scott, supra* at 115-18; Ehrlich, *supra* at 21; Finkelman, "Strange Career," *supra* at 232-33; *see also* chapter 2, *supra* at note 117 on slave marriage.

[141] *Scott v. Emerson,* 1852 WL 4171 at *5; VanderVelde, *Mrs. Dred Scott, supra* at 200-11;

Ehrlich, *supra* at 21-28; Fehrenbacher, *supra* at 244-49.

[142] *See* VanderVelde, *Mrs. Dred Scott, supra* at 212-32; Kaufman, *supra* at 117-20; Fehrenbacher, *supra* at 249-50.

[143] *See* VanderVelde, *Mrs. Dred Scott, supra* at 233-37; Kaufman, *supra* at 135-43; Fehrenbacher, *supra* at 250-51. Murdoch had represented freedom claimants in 16 suits. *See* VanderVelde, *Mrs. Dred Scott, supra* at 400, n. 1; Kaufman, *supra* at 136-37.

[144] *See* Ehrlich, *supra* at 34; chapter 4, *supra* at notes 48-52.

[145] *See* VanderVelde, *Mrs. Dred Scott, supra* at 248-49, 407, n. 44; Kaufman, *supra* at 143-44. Charless had in the past practiced law, and, in the 1820s, he represented "at least seven slaves in freedom suits." VanderVelde, *Mrs. Dred Scott, supra* at 407, n. 43.

[146] *See* Kaufman, *supra* at 135-48; 155-61, 180-228.

[147] 4 Mo. 350, 1836 WL 2300 (1836).

[148] *Rachel v. Walker,* 1836 WL 2300 at *3; *see* VanderVelde, *Mrs. Dred Scott, supra* at 237-41; Ehrlich, *supra* at 41-44; Fehrenbacher, *supra* at 252-53.

[149] *See* Kaufman, *supra* at 147.

[150] Fehrenbacher, *supra* at 254, *see also* VanderVelde, *Mrs. Dred Scott, supra* at 252-54; Kaufman, *supra* at 155-59; Ehrlich, *supra* at 44-46; Fehrenbacher, *supra* at 253-54.

[151] *Emmerson v. Harriet (of color),* 11 Mo. 413, 1848 WL 3953 (1848); *Emmerson v. Dred Scott,* 11 Mo. 413, 1848 WL 3954 (1848); VanderVelde, *Mrs. Dred Scott, supra* at 253-54; Kaufman, *supra* at 159-60; Ehrlich, *supra* at 47-50; Fehrenbacher, *supra* at 254-55.

[152] *See* VanderVelde, *Mrs. Dred Scott, supra* at 273-75; Kaufman, *supra* at 160-61; Ehrlich, *supra* at 51-54; Fehrenbacher, *supra* at 255-57.

[153] *See* VanderVelde, *Mrs. Dred Scott, supra* at 277; Ehrlich, *supra* at 55-56; Fehrenbacher, *supra* at 257.

[154] *See* VanderVelde, *Mrs. Dred Scott, supra* at 277.

[155] *See* VanderVelde, *Mrs. Dred Scott, supra* at 276-87; Kaufman, *supra* at 162-76; Ehrlich, *supra* at 56-64; Fehrenbacher, *supra* at 257-64; Wolff, *supra* at 212-26; Boman, "Dred Scott," *supra* at 417-24.

[156] *Scott v. Emerson,* 1852 WL 4171 at *5.

[157] *Id.* at *5-*8; *see* Kaufman, *supra* at 177; Benton, *supra* at 198-200.

[158] *Scott v. Emerson,* 1852 WL 4171 at *7.

[159] *Id.*

[160] *Id.* at *8.

[161] Scott was removed from the Missouri Supreme Court in 1862 after he refused to swear an oath of allegiance to the Union. *See* Wolff, *supra* at 221.

[162] *Scott v. Emerson,* 1852 WL 4171 at *8. Gamble was the brother-in-law of Edward Bates, Abraham Lincoln's attorney general. Gamble left the Court in 1855 and later was Missouri's Civil War provisional governor. *See* Dennis K. Boman, *Lincoln's Resolute Unionist: Hamilton Gamble: Dred Scott Dissenter and Missouri's Civil War Governor* 93-238 (2006) [hereinafter Boman, *Gamble*]; Louis Gerteis, "The Legacy of the Dred Scott Case: The Uncertain Course of Emancipation in Missouri," in *Dred Scott Perspectives,*

supra at 69; Wolff, *supra* at 221-22.

[163] *Scott v. Emerson*, 1852 WL 4171 at *9.

[164] *Id.* at *10, citing *Wilson v. Melvin*, 4 Mo. 592 (1837); *Rachael v. Walker*, 4 Mo. 350 (1836); *Nat v. Ruddle*, 3 Mo. 400 (1834); *Julia v. McKinney*, 3 Mo. 270 (1833); *Ralph v. Duncan*, 3 Mo. 194 (1833); *Milly v. Smith*, 2 Mo. 36 (1828); *LaGrange v. Chouteau*, 2 Mo. 20 (1828); *Winny v. Whitesides*, 1 Mo. 472 (1824).

[165] *Scott v. Emerson*, 1852 WL 4171 at *10.

[166] *Id.* at *11.

[167] *Id.*

[168] *Id.* at *12; *see* Boman, *Gamble, supra* at 73-75. For the other cases in which Gamble represented both freedom claimants and slave owners, *see id.* at 70-73.

[169] *See* Finkelman, *Imperfect Union, supra* at 227; Benton, *supra* at 202.

[170] *See* Benton, *supra* at 197-204.

[171] 3 Miss. (2 Howard) 837, 1838 WL 1199 (1838).

[172] 37 Miss. (8 George) 235, 1859 WL 3634 (1859).

[173] Alfred L. Brophy, "What Should Inheritance Law Be? Reparations and Intergenerational Wealth Transfers," 20 *Law & Literature* 197, 204 (2008).

[174] *See* Mills, *supra* at 180; *see also, e.g.*, Shaw, *supra* at 132; Finkelman, *Imperfect Union, supra* at 229-31 (discussing *Hinds*).

[175] *Id.* at 230.

[176] *Hinds v. Brazaelle*, 1838 WL 1199 at *1.

[177] *Id.* at *3.

[178] *Id.* at *4.

[179] Mills, *supra* at 181-82; *see* Finkelman, *Imperfect Union, supra* at 229.

[180] *See id.* at 231-34; Mills, *supra* at 182-88, citing *Shaw v. Brown,* 35 Miss. (6 George) 246, 1858 WL 3074 (1858); *Leiper v. Hoffman,* 26 Miss. (4 Cushm.) 615, 1853 WL 3718 (1853); *Wade v. American Colonization Society*, 15 Miss. (7 S. & M.) 663, 1846 WL 3004 (1846); *Ross v. Vertner*, 6 Miss. (5 Howard) 305, 1840 WL 2435 (1840); *see also* Alan Huffman, *Mississippi in Africa: The Saga of the Slaves of Prospect Hill Plantation and their Legacy in Liberia Today* 4-6, 53-70 (2004) (discussing the *Ross* and *Wade* cases); Smith, *Liberty, supra* at 15-25 (discussing the *Ross, Brown,* and *Wade* cases); Lang, *supra* at 78-88 (same).

[181] *See* Mills, *supra* at 189; *see also* Lang, *supra* at 78-93.

[182] *Mitchell v. Wells*, 1859 WL 3634 at *1-*2.

[183] 35 Miss. (6 George) 246, 1858 WL 3074 (1858). *See* Smith, *Liberty, supra* at 22-25; Lang, *supra* at 87-88.

[184] *See* Mills, *supra* at 223.

[185] *See id.* at 223-229; *see also* Jones, *Fathers, supra* at 98-125; Shaw, *supra* at 88, 132-33; Finkelman, *Imperfect Union, supra* at 287-95.

186 Mills, *supra* at 225; *see* Lang, *supra* at 89-93.

187 *Mitchell v. Wells,* 1859 WL 3634 at *2.

188 *Id.* at *19.

189 *Id.* at *20-*21.

190 *Id.* at *21-*37 (Handy, J., dissenting).

191 *Id.* at *35; *see also Heirn v. Bridault,* 37 Miss. (8 George) 209 (1859) (opinion by Harris holding that free blacks cannot inherit property, also with Handy dissenting). For post emancipation decisions not following *Mitchell* and *Heirn, see Cowan v. Stamps,* 46 Miss. 435, 1872 WL 6140 at * 7 (1872); *Berry v. Alsop,* 45 Miss. 1, 1871 WL 5874 at *6 (1871).

192 32 S.C. Eq. (11 Rich. Eq.) 447, 1860 WL 3897 (S.C.1860).

193 *See Willis v. Jolliffe,* 1860 WL 3897 at *35-*39 for Wardlaw's dissent. Johnstone concurred in the result. *Id.* at *35; *see also* Jones, *Fathers, supra* at 125-50; Shaw, *supra* at 87-88; Nash, "Negro Rights," *supra* at 175-76.

194 *See Willis v. Jolliffe,* 1860 WL 3897 at *1-*2; Jones, *Fathers, supra* at 129. On Jolliffe's law practice, *see* Jones, "Southern Free Women," *supra* at 788-94.

195 *See Willis v. Jolliffe,* 1860 WL 3897 at *2; Jones, *Fathers, supra* at 129-34.

196 44 S.C.L. (10 Rich.) 186, 1856 WL 3237 (S.C. App. 1856); Jones, *Fathers, supra* at 41-42, 129.

197 *See Willis v. Jolliffe,* 1860 WL 3897 at *1-*31.

198 *See id.* at *31-*32.

199 *See id.* at *33 (citing Cobb, *supra* at 134-36).

200 *See id.* (citing Cobb, *supra* at 136-37).

201 *See Willis v. Jolliffe,* 1860 WL 3897 at *33.

202 *See id.* at *34-*35.

203 *See id.* at *35-*39.

204 *See id.* at *39.

205 38 S.C.L. (4 Rich.) 186, 1850 WL 2766 (1850).

206 *Guillemette v. Harper,* 1850 WL 2766 at *3.

207 *See Willis v. Jolliffe,* 1860 WL 3897 at *33.

208 19 Ga. 35, 1855 WL 1788 (1855).

209 *Cleland v. Waters,* 1855 WL 1788 at *6, citing 1 *Rev. Laws of New York,* 657; *Laws of Rhode Island,* 607; *Purdon's Dig. of Laws of Pennsylvania,* 650; *Laws of New Jersey,* 679.

210 *Cleland v. Waters,* 1855 WL 1788 at *6.

211 See chapter 3, *supra* at notes 195-213, and chapter 6, *supra* at notes 102-05, 110-31.

212 *See* Shaw, *supra* at 88.

213 17 Ga. 253, 1855 WL 1818 (1855).

214 *See Knight v. Hardeman*, 1855 WL 1818 at *1-*3.

215 *See id.* at *4-*8. Judge Hardeman ruled in favor of the freedom claimants in *Adams v. Bass*, 18 Ga. 155, 1855 WL 1641 (1855), and the Supreme Court reversed his decision. *See* chapter 6, *supra* at notes 135-42.

216 *See Knight v. Hardeman*, 1855 WL 1818 at *8.

217 20 Miss. (12 Smedes & M.) 413, 1849 WL 2261 (Err. & App. 1849).

218 *Sam, a Man of Color v. Fore*, 1849 WL 2261 at *2.

219 *See* chapter 3, *supra* at note 137. *But see Mahorner v. Hooe*, 17 Miss. (9 S. & M.) 247, 1848 WL 1937 at *16-*20 (1848) (refusing to enforce Virginia will declaring Virginia slave owner's intent to free his Mississippi slaves and send them to Africa).

220 *See* Nash, "Reason of Slavery," *supra* at 117. Under the Maryland law then in effect, freed slaves were required to be sent to Liberia, unless they obtained a license to remain, conditioned on their continued good behavior. *See* chapter 3, *supra* at note 115.

221 *See* John Phillip Reid, "Lessons of Lumpkin: A Review of Recent Literature on Law, Comity, and the Impending Crisis," 23 *Wm. & Mary L. Rev.* 571, 581 (1982); *see also* Shaw, *supra* at 135.

222 *See* Finkelman, *Imperfect Union*, *supra* at 2-6, 181-235, 285-98. *See also, e.g.,* the works cited in chapter 1, *supra* at note 21.

223 Finkelman, *Imperfect Union*, *supra* at 189-90.

224 *See Laura Jane v. Hagen*, 29 Tenn. (10 Hum.) 332, 1849 WL 2188 (1849) (affirming claim to annuity by freed slave who moved to Ohio).

9

Rules of Evidence and Damages Recoverable in the Freedom and Manumission Suits

The rules of law establishing the evidence that is admissible in a civil case and the amount of damages that a plaintiff may potentially recover have obvious practical effects when a lawyer and client decide whether to file a civil suit. This chapter will survey two important issues in the manumission and freedom suits: What evidence was admissible and what damages could the plaintiffs recover if they proved their claims of wrongful slavery?

The Slave Testimony Bar

The Southern legislators and judges adopted evidence rules that created substantive hurdles for freedom and manumission claimants. Evidence rules, like other procedural rules, can make it harder or easier for one class of parties to prove their claims or defenses. "The power to exclude crucial evidence is the power to defeat a claim."[1]

The most obviously disadvantageous evidence rule that plaintiffs seeking their freedom faced was the general rule prohibiting slave testimony in the Southern courts except for testimony against other slaves.[2] The Southern states also extended this bar to free black testimony against whites.[3] For example, Maryland's statutes barred the testimony of a "negro or mulatto slave, free negro or mulatto, born of a white woman during his time of servitude," which referred to the term of mandatory service that Maryland's laws required of white women and their children with "a negro or other slave or free negro...."[4] The legislators originally prohibited this testimony against "any white Christian person," but, in 1846-47, they extended it to include all whites.[5] A 1787 Delaware statute barred the testimony of slaves who were freed under Delaware law, and that of their issue, against any white person, except in order "to obtain redress in law and equity for any injury to his person or property."[6]

This exclusionary rule limited the proofs that persons held as slaves could present to support their claims. Therefore, unless the claimant in a freedom or manumission suit was willing to rely on his or her appearance alone, in most cases a claimant would need to enlist at least one white person to testify against the alleged owner or his or her heirs.[7]

Thomas Cobb recognized that this exclusionary rule "may, in many supposable cases, operate harshly and to defeat justice"; nevertheless, he thought that it was necessary because "the indiscriminate admission and giving credit to negro testimony would not only in many cases, defeat justice, but would be productive of innumerable evils in the relation of master and slave."[8] According to Cobb, this rule was consistent with the "general rule" that blacks were "mendacious," a fact that he found was "too well established to require the production of proof, either from history, travels, or craniology." Cobb suggested, however, that slaves be permitted "to testify as to the cruel treatment of himself or his fellows, by persons other than his master, when no competent white witness is present to testify as to the transaction." He expressed confidence in the jurors' ability to evaluate this testimony if it were to be "specially submitted to the jury[.]"[9]

Hearsay Evidence in Freedom and Manumission Suits

When a freedom claimant or a defendant raised the issue of the identity, race, or status of someone in the chain of the claimant's maternal ancestry, the courts also were required to grapple with the hearsay rule. Hearsay is defined, under modern terminology, as "a statement, other than one made by the declarant while testifying at the trial or hearing, offered in evidence to prove the truth of the matter asserted." A "statement" could be an oral or written assertion, or nonverbal conduct that the actor intended as an assertion.[10]

Hearsay evidence of the claimant's maternal racial ancestry often was the only proof available to the parties on both sides of a freedom suit. This type of evidence also could be relevant in a suit alleging that a slave's maternal ancestor was a free black person. The courts did not establish a novel and more liberal hearsay rule exception for the benefit of the alleged slaves. Instead, they applied a recognized common law exception, which permitted hearsay evidence of family history, reputation, or pedigree. This is "[o]ne of the oldest exceptions to the hearsay rule," and it "encompasses statements concerning family history, such as the date and place of birth and death of members of the family and facts about marriage, descent, and relationship."[11]

The Southern courts generally permitted the parties in freedom suits to advance hearsay pedigree evidence in support of their claims or defenses, but the cases reveal two approaches to the rule. This hearsay exception involved two key issues: Who could testify and what could they say?

The most liberal decisions answered the first question by holding that this hearsay evidence of family history could be offered by anyone who knew the family and the reputation of its members. The second key issue is on what matters would the courts permit the witnesses to testify? The courts in the earliest freedom suits of which we have records applied an expansive version of this hearsay exception. This exception included hearsay evidence of the identity of the claimant's family members as well as evidence of the reputation or general understanding in the relevant community of their race and servile or free status. These latter attributes of a claimant's maternal ancestors were obviously uniquely relevant in freedom suits.

In one of the earliest successful freedom suits of which there is a record, which was pursued in 1655 or 1656 in Virginia, Elizabeth Key relied on hearsay testimony to establish that her father was Thomas Key, a free Englishman. Elizabeth was "an Afro-Anglo woman, [who] was born around 1630 in Virginia colony."[12] This case arose before the Virginia legislators adopted the rule providing that the child's status followed the maternal line.[13]

The witnesses at her trial before the County Court included an eighty-year-old former servant "who testified that it was commonly known that Thomas Key had been fined by the court in Blunt Point for getting 'his Negro woman with Childe[sic],' and that child was Elizabeth."[14] Elizabeth also offered hearsay testimony of the "understanding" of "neighbors" that Elizabeth was to complete a nine-year term of service and then be sent to England.[15]

As in Elizabeth Key's case, the Virginia and Maryland courts permitted this type of pedigree and reputation hearsay evidence, as confirmed by several reported decisions from the 1780s and into the early 1800s. Among the Virginia cases is the 1792 Virginia Supreme Court of Appeals decision in *Jenkins v. Tom*,[16] which permitted hearsay pedigree and reputation evidence of the claimants' alleged Native American ancestors. At the trial, the plaintiffs produced "sundry depositions of ancient people to prove, that certain women named *Mary* and *Bess,* when they came first into this country, were called *Indians*; and had a tawny complexion, with long straight black hair[.]" The plaintiffs also "produced a witness to prove, that he heard a certain other person now dead, say in the year 1701, that when he was a lad about 12 years old, these women were brought to this colony in a ship, and were called *Indians*; that they had the appearance of *Indians,* and that the former of them was called the grandmother of the latter." The trial judge admitted the evidence over the defendant's objection.[17]

The appellate court affirmed a judgment for claimants, but the court's opinion was not reported because the reporter was not in court when the opinion was delivered.[18] Nevertheless, this decision was followed in later Virginia cases.[19]

The Maryland cases include *Mahoney v. Ashton*.[20] This was a freedom suit filed by Charles Mahoney in 1791. The Maryland General Court issued decisions in 1797, 1798, and 1799, and the Court of Appeals issued an 1802 decision in this case that was tried three times before a jury. The courts permitted litigants on both sides to introduce hearsay reputation evidence from non-family members relating to Mahoney's claim that his great-great grandmother, Ann Joice, who came to Maryland from England as a cook for the third Lord Baltimore, was or should have been free.[21]

In the first trial that was held in October 1797, Mahoney's lawyers offered to read to the jury the deposition of Henry Davis. The defense counsel objected to the part of the deposition in which Davis said that he "has heard his uncle *David Davis* (who is deceased) say, that it was the report of the neighbourhood [sic] that if she (meaning *Joice*) had justice done her, she ought to have been free; and this he heard sundry times from his uncle when talking the matter over[.]" Judge Jeremiah Townley Chase overruled the objection and permitted the jury to hear the deposition. Judge Chase agreed with the defense, however, when Mahoney's counsel offered the deposition of John Wheat. That deposition "contained the opinions of persons uncoupled with the facts from whence their conclusions were drawn or opinions formed." The court found that "opinions were not evidence; but that the facts upon which they were formed were evidence."[22]

In his argument on the appeal that followed the second trial and a freedom judgment for Mahoney, Attorney General Luther Martin, on behalf of the defendant, objected to the "evidence of opinions as to a right, and not of facts whereon such opinions were grounded. General reputation may be given in evidence of facts in certain cases, but not the legal inference deducible from facts." He added:

> A witness has no right to give an opinion to the jury of a right; he must relate facts, and the jury are to form their opinion from those facts. Whether a person exercises the right of freedom is a fact; but his right to freedom is not a fact. Persons are frequently declaring that all negroes are entitled to freedom—Forty years hence this will be reputation, and be brought forward to prove they are entitled to freedom. Our courts have determined that general reputation, that such persons are descended from white women, or that they have exercised the right of freedom, is evidence to the jury. It is giving the power to ignorant persons to judge of rights. In the case of the *Butler's,* reputation was given in evidence that they were descended from a white woman; so also in the case of the *Toogood's.* In the case of the *Queen's,* that they were descended from a native Indian of South America. In all these, and in many other similar cases, hundreds of negroes have been let loose upon community by the hearsay testimony of an obscure illiterate individual.[23]

Martin was referring to several of the successful freedom suits in Maryland, in which the claimants relied in part upon pedigree evidence.[24]

The Court of Appeals did not address this argument in its 1802 opinion reversing the freedom judgment and remanding the case for a third trial. But, as will be noted below, Ashton's counsel decided to use this expansive version of the hearsay rule to their client's advantage by offering their own pedigree evidence in the third trial.[25]

The General Court also approved of the use of hearsay pedigree evidence in *Shorter v. Rozier,*[26] a freedom suit filed by Basil Shorter against Henry Rozier. Shorter claimed that he was descended from a free white woman named Elizabeth Shorter, who, in 1681, allegedly married "a Negro man" known as "Little Robin."

At the trial, Shorter's lawyer submitted evidence that Shorter "was the son of a mulatto woman named *Linda,* who was the daughter of a mulatto woman named *Moll,* or *Mary.*" Shorter also proved that Rozier "holds and claims him," under Edward Neale, Rozier's father-in-law; that Edward's father was Anthony Neale, of Saint Mary's County; "and that *Moll* was held and claimed by *Anthony Neale,* for many years in his lifetime." Shorter also offered evidence to prove that Moll had two sisters, Jenny and Patt, who were held and claimed by Anthony, "and who, with their issue, have been since held and claimed by his descendants and others under him; and that the said *Anthony Neale* departed this life in or about the year 1723." Shorter "also offered evidence to prove the existence of such a free white woman as *Elizabeth Shorter,* in the family of the *Neales,* and in the lifetime of the said *Anthony Neale.*"[27]

This evidence apparently went to the jury without any objection from Rozier's lawyer. Rozier's lawyer did object, however, when Shorter's attorney offered a copy of a document that apparently was recorded in 1703. It consisted of two affidavits from June 1702. In the first, Nicholas Geulick stated that, in 1681, he was a priest in Saint Mary's County who married Elizabeth Shorter, "a white woman," and Little Robin, "a negro man." The other affidavit was given by Emma Roswell. She stated that she was a witness to this marriage by Father Geulick. She also asserted that when Elizabeth married Robin, they both were servants of her late husband, William Rosewell, who gave them to Anthony Neale when Anthony married Rosewell's daughter Elizabeth. In addition, Rosewell stated that Elizabeth Shorter and Robin "have remained in the said *Neale's* service ever since;" and that after this marriage Elizabeth Shorter "had three mulatto girl children, named *Mary, Jane and Martha,* who are now living to the best of this deponent's knowledge."[28] The General Court Judges Chief Judge Samuel Chase and Judge Jeremiah Townley Chase allowed the evidence to be read to the jury, which found for Shorter.[29]

It therefore may have come as a surprise when, in *Shorter v. Boswell,*[30] a freedom suit filed by a female Shorter family member whose first name is not mentioned in the reported case, the county court excluded the Geulick and Rosewell affidavits and the other hearsay pedigree evidence offered by the claimant. The claimant in that case proffered the written deposition of Mary Lancaster, who was deceased, and the testimony of her son, Thomas Lancaster, to prove that the claimant was Elizabeth Shorter's great-great-great granddaughter.[31]

The Maryland Court of Appeals in 1808 reversed the judgment for the defendant, Boswell, and remanded the case for a new trial. The appellate court disagreed with the trial judge's decision rejecting all of this hearsay evidence. There is no officially published opinion of the court; it is reported only that the appeals court "dissented from the opinions expressed by the court below, in all of the *bills of exceptions.*"[32]

Some courts later limited the scope of this pedigree reputation evidence in freedom suits, however. The United States Supreme Court advanced the more restrictive version of this hearsay rule exception in two opinions authored by Chief Justice John Marshall. In *Mima Queen v. Hepburn,*[33] which the Supreme Court decided in 1813, the plaintiffs offered at trial hearsay evidence to prove that their ancestor, Mary Queen, was a free woman who was sold for a term of seven years of service. The trial court excluded the hearsay evidence. After a jury verdict for the defendant, the plaintiffs filed an appeal to the Supreme Court.[34]

Chief Justice Marshall affirmed the trial court's decision. He started his analysis by asserting the "general principle" that "hearsay evidence is incompetent to establish any specific fact, which ... is in its nature susceptible of being proved by witnesses who speak from their own knowledge." He stated that the same evidence rules of general application applied to freedom suits and to suits in which only rights to non-human property were at stake:

> However the feelings of the individual may be interested on the part of a
> person claiming freedom, the court cannot perceive any legal distinction

between the assertion of this and of any other right, which will justify the application of a rule of evidence to cases of this description which would be inapplicable to general cases in which the right to property may be established.

He then quoted a "great judge" who stressed how the "rules of evidence are of vast importance to all orders and degrees of men: our lives, our liberty, and our property are all concerned in support of these rules," which reflect the "wisdom of the ages[.]"[35]

Chief Justice Marshall acknowledged that the hearsay rule exceptions "are said to be as old as the rule itself. There are cases of pedigree, of prescription, of custom, and in some cases of boundary." He also referred to "matters of general and public history which may be received without that full proof which is necessary for the establishment of a private fact."[36]

The Chief Justice found that these exceptions did not apply to the hearsay evidence of Mary Queen's reputed free status as the plaintiffs' ancestor.[37] He expressed concerns about the reliability of hearsay evidence, stated that the evidence at issue did not fall within the common law hearsay exceptions he cited, and observed that the court "was not inclined to extend the exceptions further than they have already been carried."[38]

Justice Gabriel Duvall responded with the only dissenting opinion he authored in his almost twenty-three years on the court.[39] Duvall had been a Maryland lawyer and state court judge, among other governmental positions, before he was appointed to the United States Supreme Court in 1811. He brought a unique perspective to the case. He represented Charles Mahoney in one of the Maryland freedom suits in which the courts admitted hearsay reputation evidence.[40]

Duvall asserted that under Maryland law, it was

for many years settled that on a petition for freedom where the petitioner claims from an ancestor who has been dead for a great length of time, the issue may be proved by hearsay evidence, if the fact is of such antiquity that living testimony cannot be procured. Such was the opinion of the judges of the general Court of Maryland, and their decision was affirmed by the unanimous opinion of the judges of the High Court of Appeals in the last resort, after full argument by the ablest counsel at the bar. I think the decision was correct. Hearsay evidence was admitted upon the same principle, upon which it is admitted to prove a custom, pedigree and the boundaries of land;—because from the antiquity of the transactions to which these subjects may have reference, it is impossible to produce living testimony. To exclude hearsay in such cases, would leave the party interested without remedy. It was decided also that the issue could not be prejudiced by the neglect or omission of the ancestor. If the ancestor neglected to claim her right, the issue could not be bound by length of time, it being a natural inherent right. It appears to me that the reason for admitting hearsay evidence upon a question of freedom is much stronger than in cases of pedigree or in controversies relative to the boundaries of land. It will be universally admitted that the right to freedom is more important than the right of property.[41]

Justice Duvall also noted that "people of color from their helpless condition under the uncontrolled authority of a master, are entitled to all reasonable protection." He predicted that the majority's decision "cuts up by the root all claims of this kind, and puts a final end to them, unless the claim should arise from a fact of recent date, and such a case will seldom, perhaps never, occur."[42]

Chief Justice Marshall, in his very brief 1816 opinion in *Davis v. Wood*,[43] reaffirmed the majority's *Mima Queen* decision. Marshall affirmed the dismissal of a freedom suit, again endorsing the more restrictive hearsay rule pedigree exception.

Scholars have debated how best to understand Chief Justice Marshall's *Mima Queen* and *Davis* opinions. Was Marshall "imposing the slaveholder's values on the hearsay rule," or was he "simply applying the technical rules of evidence in accordance with the English precedents he cites[?]"[44] The answer is not clear. It is clear, however, that Marshall's decisions placed yet another potential procedural hurdle in the way of freedom claimants. These decisions had a potential substantive effect directly in the federal courts, and indirectly in the state courts if they adopted this version of the rule in their state.

The Southern courts offered mixed responses to Marshall's *Mima Queen* and *Davis* decisions. Two Maryland Court of Appeals decisions from 1817 and 1820 were consistent with *Mima Queen*.[45] These decisions rejected evidence of the claimants' maternal ancestors' general reputation. The court nevertheless approved of evidence "identifying an ancestor from whom the pedigree is attempted to be traced[.]"[46] Thus, a 1932 Maryland Court of Appeals decision discussing the hearsay rule in Maryland stated: "in the old special proceeding in Maryland on petitions for freedom of slaves, which was one of the most familiar of our civil proceedings prior to 1863, hearsay covering an extraordinary range of facts was commonly received out of necessity and custom, but the courts stopped at receiving such hearsay as neighborhood reputation on the ultimate question in controversy, whether the petitioner was a slave or free."[47]

Other Southern courts did not follow the United States Supreme Court's restrictive reading of the hearsay rule pedigree exception. For example, the Tennessee Supreme Court of Errors and Appeals applied the broader hearsay exception in the 1827 decision in *Vaughan v. Phebe*.[48] The appellate court reversed a freedom judgment in the plaintiff's favor, in essence because the court found that the trial judge improperly admitted hearsay evidence.[49]

Nevertheless, Justice Henry Crabb's opinion for the court stated that Chief Justice Marshall's decisions in *Mima Queen* and *Davis* do not have "the approbation of our judgments, and we must dissent from them."[50] The court noted that "[s]lavery, in our sense of the word, is not known in England."[51] Therefore, the court held that it would apply the hearsay rule and exceptions in view of the realities of slavery in America.[52]

The claimant in *Phebe* offered hearsay evidence, which included the assertion that Phebe was born in Virginia, the daughter of Beck, "who was always called an Indian by descent[.]" Phebe's great grandmother was Murene, who, it was said, "was always reputed an Indian, and was free," and "was a copper color[.]" Phebe also presented evidence that other members of Phebe's family won their freedom, including her maternal aunt, Tab, who won a judgment for freedom in the Superior Court of Prince George County Virginia, in the case *Tab et al. v. Littlebury Tucker*, on the proof that Tab was a descendant of Murene.[53]

Crabb stated that the trial judge did not err in permitting hearsay evidence referring to the "pedigree or common reputation as to freedom" of Phebe and her maternal ancestors, but the court held that the trial judge should not have permitted "evidence of several family members having recovered their freedom by due course of law." This evidence, according to Crabb, should have been proven by the court records of these cases themselves, such as was presented for Tab's case.[54]

The Tennessee Supreme Court followed *Vaughan v. Phebe* eight years later in a related context in *Miller v. Denman*.[55] The plaintiff, Denman, sued Miller for damages. Denman claimed that Miller enticed out of Denman's possession a slave named Harriet, knowing that Harriet was Denman's slave. The jury returned a verdict for Denman, which the Supreme Court reversed, in an opinion by Justice Nathan Green. The court held that the trial judge erred in excluding hearsay evidence that the defendant offered to prove that Harriet was not a slave. Justice Green stated that the rule established in *Vaughn* applied in this suit as well.[56] Justice Green also noted, however, that this decision may have, at least in part, been based upon respect for precedent. He expressed his view that the court in *Vaughn* "extends the right to introduce hearsay evidence to the utmost limit and further than other courts of high authority have gone, yet, as that case was fully argued and maturely considered, and has been acquiesced in ever since that decision was made, we will not now disturb it."[57]

The Southern judges' diverse views on this hearsay rule exception are well illustrated by the 1831 decisions in the Virginia case of *Gregory v. Baugh*.[58] The Virginia Supreme Court of Appeals reversed a jury verdict in favor of the freedom claimant, whose proofs included hearsay evidence establishing that he was the descendant of free female Native Americans. The members of the court agreed to reverse the judgment based on the trial judge's error in mischaracterizing some of the evidence, and not on the hearsay issue. The appellate court judges were equally divided on the scope of the pedigree hearsay exception, with Judges Francis T. Brooke and Dabney Carr endorsing Chief Justice Marshall's view, and Judges John W. Green and William H. Cabell favoring the broader version of this hearsay rule exception.[59] The Virginia appellate court never decided to overrule or affirm the earlier decisions that permitted the use at trial of hearsay evidence of pedigree and reputation.

As late as in the 1859 case of *Farrelly v. Maria Louisa (Woman of Color)*,[60] the Alabama Supreme Court endorsed the broader hearsay pedigree exception. The court reversed a freedom judgment in favor of the claimant, but not because the trial judge permitted her to introduce hearsay testimony. To the contrary, the court stated that the claimant could rely on hearsay evidence to establish that her mother, who it was said "was a woman of yellow complexion" or "seemed to be of an Indian or Mexican descent," "was generally considered and called a free person[.]"[61]

Writing for the court, Justice George W. Stone explained that because the plaintiff's status was at issue, hearsay evidence was "clearly competent ... to prove that the mother of the petitioner, before and about the time she gave birth to Louisa, went at large, uncontrolled in her movements, and that she was dealt with and treated as a free person; and that generally, her deportment was that of a person having control of her own movements." This evidence was "permissible to show, either that she was, or was not, under the direction and control of another." The court concluded that the jury would decide if this evidence or the defendant's evidence of ownership was of greater weight. The opinion does not cite the *Mima Queen* decision.[62]

Even the broader version of this hearsay rule pedigree exception was a mixed blessing for freedom and manumission suit claimants. The slave owner defendants also could rely on this rule to offer hearsay evidence to prove the plaintiffs' maternal ancestors' slave status.

Charles Mahoney's eleven-year unsuccessful freedom suit illustrates this point. Mahoney filed his suit on October 18, 1791. The case was tried three times before juries, and it produced three published General Court decisions and one Court of Appeals decision. The jury in the second trial found for Mahoney, apparently based upon the pedigree and reputation evidence testimony that Mahoney's lawyers presented regarding the status of Mahoney's great-great-grandmother, Ann Joice. This verdict was reversed, however, and in October 1802, the jury in the third trial found for the defendant, the Reverend John Ashton.

That jury apparently was convinced by the pedigree and reputation evidence that Ashton's lawyers presented at that trial, including that of Samuel Douglass and Thomas Lane, to rebut the evidence that Mahoney's lawyers produced at the first two trials. These witnesses testified in support of Ashton's lawyers' claim "that Joice was actually a 'Guinea negro' whom Lord Baltimore had purchased on his way to Maryland. Wanting to 'conform the manners and customs of the place', he stopped a ship 'from the Coast of Guinea loaded with negroes' and purchased three slaves, one of whom was named Ann." Ann "obtained the surname 'Joice' on account of her intimacy with Daniel Joice, a sailor on board Lord Baltimore's ship who 'took a great liking' to her. At no time had she ever set foot on English soil."

Douglass claimed that he heard the story "from an old woman who used to live in the area." Lane testified that his father knew a tailor, John Stephens, who was a steward on Lord Baltimore's ship. Stephens kept a journal of what occurred on the journey, which he gave to Lane's father for safe keeping. "These papers survived in the Lane family for many years, and Thomas often 'amused himself' by reading it. Unfortunately, however, the journal could not be entered as evidence because 'the rats got at it ... and [it] is not now in existence.'"[63]

Mahoney's case continued to have effects even after its long duration. The Circuit Court of the District of Columbia, in the 1808 case of *Joice v. Alexander*,[64] permitted Francis Scott Key to use at trial the deposition of Lane, who by then was deceased. Key offered this deposition on behalf of his slave owner client, Robert Alexander, to defeat the freedom claim of Clem Joice, who also was a descendant of Ann Joice. The court also sustained Key's objection to a question by Joice's lawyer concerning the "general reputation of the neighbourhood" about Ann Joice, and "whether she was a free white woman." The court ruled "that evidence of general reputation of a fact, can only be given when the reputation was among free white persons who are dead, or presumed from the length of time to be dead."[65] The jury found for Alexander in that case, apparently because Lane's testimony again was persuasive.[66]

The Kentucky Court of Appeals also approved the alleged owner's use of hearsay pedigree evidence in its 1839 decision in the case *Chancellor v. Milly*.[67] The plaintiff was "apparently a white woman, about forty years old[.]" She had been treated as a slave from her birth. Nevertheless, she filed a freedom suit, relying on her white color as her only evidence in support of her claim. The trial judge held that the defendant could not rebut the presumption of freedom that arose from Milly's white color with hearsay evidence offered "to prove that, in the family in which she was born and reared from infancy, [the plaintiff] had ever been called and reputed the child of a woman of color, who was a slave and the property of the family."[68]

The Kentucky Court of Appeals opinion by Chief Justice George Robertson reversed a judgment for the plaintiff. He held that the trial judge should have allowed the jury to hear the reputation evidence. "After the lapse of forty years, such a fact would scarcely ever be susceptible of any other proof than that of reputation." The Chief Justice could "perceive no reason" to exclude the evidence "in a suit for freedom, as well as in all other suits in which proof of pedigree becomes material." He also observed that evidence of reputation would have been admissible in the plaintiff's favor "if her reputed mother had been free; and that which she might have proved to create a presumption in her favor, her adversary should be permitted to show against her."[69]

Jason Gillmer has argued that after the *Mima Queen* decision "the courts had effectively put an end to freedom suits brought by people claiming their liberty based on descent."[70] He cites as evidence the "lack of appellate cases" after that decision, although he acknowledges that this "does not mean that no slave attempted to prove descent through hearsay at the trial level. However, given the degree to which this question was litigated at the appellate level in the first quarter of the nineteenth century, its lack of attention in later years strongly suggests the suits were not successful."[71]

Nevertheless, as Gillmer also notes, even after the *Mima Queen* decision, some Southern courts continued to apply the broader version of this hearsay rule exception, thus making it possible for plaintiffs in freedom suits to introduce evidence about their free maternal ancestors that otherwise would not have been admissible.[72] But the alleged owners also used this hearsay evidence to fight freedom suits. This may explain why the Southern courts were not so willing to explicitly embrace the *Mima Queen* court's version of the hearsay rule.

Moreover, Duncan MacLeod suggested that the slave law pedigree decisions had an effect on the development of the rules of evidence in the United States. He cited Zephaniah Swift's 1810 evidence treatise, which stated: "In respect to pedigrees, it is very evident that direct testimony, founded on personal knowledge, cannot be obtained, to trace families to any remote period: this must be done by common reputation, and hearsay evidence, or such facts cannot be proved."[73] According to MacLeod, "Swift's knowledge of Southern court procedures may well have derived from his interest in the Negro. He was a member of, and publicist for, the Connecticut Abolition Society[.]"[74] Swift did not cite any of the slavery cases, however, in support of his assertions.[75]

Theron Metcalf's 1826 American version of Thomas Starkie's evidence treatise also advocated the broader pedigree hearsay exception, to include testimony of general reputation by non-family members. That treatise suggested that without this evidence "it is impossible to prove the relationships of past generations," and that the courts are required to resort to hearsay evidence from those, including non-family members, who were likely to know the truth, "or to evidence of *general reputation*."[76] Concerns about the reliability of this evidence were addressed as follows: "[I]n the absence of any motive for committing a fraud upon society, it is in the highest degree improbable that the parties should have been guilty of practicing a continued system of imposition upon the rest of the world, involving a conspiracy in its very nature difficult to be executed."[77] The treatise writers do not, however, rely on the slavery cases in their discussion of this rule.[78]

MacLeod concluded that evidence law treatise writers, such as Swift, "apparently assumed that the contemporary practice of the Southern courts constituted a precedent of general applicability to American law."[79] Nevertheless, the majority of the courts in the United States adopted the more restrictive rule regarding both the scope of pedigree evidence and the identity of those who could testify. The more restrictive decisions limited this pedigree testimony to that of family members, and this became the majority rule in the United States for some time. A minority of the jurisdictions in the United States, however, continued to follow the broader rule, including some Southern states, long after slavery ended, and some evidence law commentators criticized the more restrictive majority rule.[80]

The majority rule limiting the pedigree testimony to that of family members would, of course, create unique burdens for slaves seeking their release from bondage. Their own black family members most likely could not testify in support of freedom claimants. Moreover, if the claimants were of mixed racial heritage, their white family members were likely to be their opponents in the litigation, who were seeking to preserve their rights in the slaves as family property assets.

The minority rule eventually gained support in the United States, and it was adopted in the current Federal Rules of Evidence.[81] Therefore, a recent treatise on evidence states: "Matters of family history traditionally have also been provable by reputation in the family and sometimes in the community." The exception applies to evidence of reputation, "and not simply assertions of individuals."[82]

Although it is not clear what direct influence the freedom and manumission cases had on the development of this rule of evidence, the more liberal version of the pedigree hearsay rule exception now is the prevailing exception to the hearsay rule in the United States courts.[83]

Damages for Wrongful Detention in Slavery

Because the Southern courts and legislatures classified the freedom and manumission suits as intentional tort actions, it should have followed without much debate that the successful claimant would be entitled to some monetary compensation for the damages he or she suffered as a result of the defendant's wrongful acts. The torts of assault, battery, and false imprisonment were derived from the trespass action, and a plaintiff establishing a claim under any of these causes of action would at least be entitled to "nominal damages."[84] The plaintiff also would be entitled to compensatory damages, and potentially punitive damages if there was proof that the defendant acted with "bad intent or wanton misconduct." If the defendant acted by mistake, then punitive damages would be denied.[85]

These basic legal principles were not so clear to the Southern judges and legislators. The statutes and court decisions, at different times and in different places, established an assortment of rules of law establishing what damages, if any, that persons who proved that they were wrongfully held in slavery could recover with their freedom.

The courts in Louisiana, Virginia, and Maryland denied successful freedom claimants the right to damage judgments in connection with a finding of wrongful enslavement.[86] The Virginia rule can be traced to Judge Spencer Roane's opinion in the leading case of *Pleasants v. Pleasants*.[87] The Virginia Supreme Court of Appeals in 1799 affirmed in part Chancellor Wythe's decision freeing the slaves of a father and son, John and Jonathan Pleasants. The decision was based on the Pleasants' wills of 1771 and 1776, which called for the manumission of their slaves if and when Virginia adopted a statute permitting manumission by will, and on the 1782 Virginia statute that permitted manumission by will.[88]

The appellate court reversed the Chancellor's order that the liberated slaves be paid some compensation for the time that they toiled as slaves of the Pleasants' heirs after 1782, when the courts held that they were entitled to their freedom. Judge Roane rejected this claim for compensation because he stated there were "no precedents, either of the courts of England or this country, to guide us." He stated that there were no English cases "because slavery is not there tolerated;" and that "in this country, I believe no instance can be produced of profits being adjudged to a person held in slavery, on recovering his liberty. Among a thousand cases of palpable violations of freedom, no jury has been found to award, and no Court has yet sanctioned a recovery of profits of labour, during the time of detention."[89]

He qualified this holding in dictum, however, noting that "this [case] is not a palpable violation of freedom." He asked: "[O]ught the Court, in such a doubtful case, to award that, which the whole equity to the country, flowing through a thousand channels, has not yet awarded a single instance? It seems to be a solecism, to award ordinary profits to recompense the privation of liberty; which, if it is to be recompenced, the power of money cannot accomplish."[90]

The "decisive" point to Judge Roane was the fact that children of the claimants who were born after 1782 were reared at the expense of the heirs of the Pleasants. He stated that this "will form perhaps not an unreasonable set-off against profits of those who were capable of gaining a profit by their labor."[91]

There is evidence that Roane may have overstated the total lack of precedent for the idea that a jury could award a successful freedom claimant damages. The 1808 report of the Virginia Supreme Court of Appeals decision in *Pegram v. Isabell*[92] refers to the testimony of George Keith Taylor. Taylor was the lawyer for the claimant's mother Nanny, who won her freedom in the District Court in 1799. The defendant defaulted in that case. According to Judge Roane's opinion in *Pegram*, Taylor's testimony referred to the evidence that he presented in court on a proof hearing to fix Nanny's damages. The jury found that the claimant sustained damages of "one penny."[93]

Andrew Kull noted that, in his *Pleasants* opinion, "Roane touched on a theme that would become a standard justification. The judicial method was to cast the issue of restitution in terms of the potential hardship to the slaveholding defendant."[94] Indeed, the Virginia Supreme Court of Appeals reaffirmed this rule in two cases decided in 1833 and 1848. In these cases, Judges Briscoe Baldwin, Dabney Carr, William Cabell, and Henry St. George Tucker all wrote opinions supporting this rule, both as a matter of precedent and as a salutary public policy.[95]

These Virginia judges had to confront the anomaly caused by the form action that Virginia law permitted for the assertion of a freedom suit, which was an action in trespass. Why would the successful claimant not be entitled to recover all of the reasonably foreseeable damages that flowed from the defendant's tort, including, at the very least, the net profit after deducting the claimant's living expenses, which the defendant derived from the claimant's labor?

The judges evaded this hurdle by labeling the form of action a "legal fiction."[96] This no damages rule gave a dual benefit to the slaveholder defendants; they did not need to pay damages in tort, as if the form of action were a writ of *habeas corpus*, and they did not have to comply with the pretrial procedures in a *habeas corpus* proceeding, as if the action really were a tort action in trespass.

On the issue of precedent, these judges did not read the dictum in Judge Roane's decision to limit the logic of the no damages rule to the considerations evidenced by the unique and complicated facts of the *Pleasants* case. Instead, they read Roane's opinion to establish a strict rule prohibiting damage awards in all freedom suits. For example, Judge Baldwin wrote that these damage claims were "expressly repudiated" by the "uniform course of our Courts, in denying them under all circumstances, and however gross and palpable the violation of the right to freedom."[97]

On the public policy issue, the Virginia judges opined that the no damage rule was necessary to prevent injustice to the slave owner defendants, who would have paid for the cost of wrongfully maintaining the successful claimants in slavery. As Judge Baldwin stated:

> In point of abstract justice, it may seem reasonable enough that slaves re-covering their freedom should be entitled to an account of *mense* profits: but a slight examination will serve to shew [sic] that the question is anom-alous in its character, and arises out of a peculiar organization of society, affecting the condition and rights of persons in a way unknown to the principles of the common law. Slavery is with us an institution founded upon a distinction of races, one of which is subject to the control and domi-nation of the other. The servile race, from colour, and other physical traits, carry with them indefinitely the marks of inferiority and degradation; and even when relieved from bondage can never aspire to association and citizenship with the white population. Freedom to them is a benefit rather in name than in fact; and in truth, upon the whole, their condition is not thereby improved in respectability, comfort, or happiness. While they re-main in what is here their original *status*, provided for as they are in in-fancy, old age and infirmity, they are exempt from the cares and anxieties of a precarious subsistence, and the wretchedness of actual want; and those most familiar with the usually mild despotism to which they are sub-ject, can best appreciate their sources of enjoyment from the commonly humane indulgence, and kind regards of their former masters.

Judge Baldwin thus stated that, as free people, former slaves will not suffer any "practical injustice" if the courts strike "an even balance of profit and loss between them and their former masters." He also noted that if the former slaves were to receive, in addition to their freedom, "a pecuniary recovery for past servile labors," this "would not promote those habits of industry, temperance and humility, without which their recently acquired liberty must prove a curse in-stead of a blessing."[98]

Judge Baldwin recognized, however, that "judicious and well guarded" legis-lation might be considered to prevent cases "of peculiar hardship and oppres-sion[.]"[99] In 1849, the Virginia legislature followed through on this suggestion and adopted a statute, which, after fifty years, ameliorated in part the no dam-ages rule that the courts derived from Judge Roane's opinion in *Pleasants*.

This act provided a remedy to slaves who, like the slaves in *Pleasants*, were manumitted by will and who were hired out as slaves before being awarded their freedom by a court. It permitted the slaves to recover "the nett [sic] proceeds of the aggregate of their hires and profits, with which the personal representative of the testator is chargeable," unless this payment was "inconsistent with the mani-fest intention of the testator," and excluding funds that were required to pay the estate's debts. These net proceeds were to be apportioned among the slaves who were freed "as a court of equity having cognizance of the case may deem just."[100]

In an 1855 decision in *Osborne v. Taylor's Adm'rs*,[101] the Virginia Supreme Court of Appeals affirmed a lower court ruling that allowed the former slaves of Thomas O. Taylor to receive the net proceeds of their hiring for the years 1851 and 1852. This was part of the period after their right to freedom accrued under Taylor's will. Even though their rights accrued in 1849 before the above cited statute was adopted, the majority opinion of Judge Green B. Samuels, which was joined in by Judges J.J. Allen and Richard Moncure, advanced a narrow interpretation of Judge Roane's opinion in *Pleasants*. Samuels attempted to distinguish the *Osborne* case from *Pleasants* because Taylor's former slaves were compensated for the time that they were hired out under the court's supervision, and because the Virginia statutes then permitted manumission.[102] Judges William Daniel and George N. Lee authored short opinions dissenting only from the court's holding compensating the slaves. They found that the 1849 act did not apply, and apparently they did not endorse Judge Samuels's narrow reading of Judge Roane's *Pleasants* opinion.[103]

According to Andrew Kull, the "Maryland judges displayed an exceptional willingness to dismiss out of hand the notion that former slaves might have enforceable rights to their own labor during a period of wrongful detention."[104] Nevertheless, there is evidence that this rule was not always the law in Maryland.

Two cases in which the Reverend John Ashton was the defendant illustrate this ambiguity. In *Queen v. Ashton*,[105] Edward Queen filed an action seeking damages for assault and battery and unjust imprisonment. Queen filed this suit after he won a freedom judgment in an earlier suit that he filed against Ashton. Queen claimed damages from October 15, 1791 to May 16, 1794, the time during which Queen alleged that Ashton illegally detained him in slavery. Ashton defended by pleading not guilty, and by alleging that the suit was filed after the time permitted by the statute of limitations. The county court refused to give the instructions requested by Queen, that he could recover damages for this assault and imprisonment. The court also refused Ashton's requested charge that Queen could not recover damages. In April 1796, the jury found for the defendant. Queen then appealed to the General Court, which affirmed the judgment. While the case was pending on appeal before the Court of Appeals, Queen died and the further appeal was not decided.[106]

In June 1799, the jury in Charles Mahoney's second trial, also against Ashton, "declared Mahoney 'a free man' and awarded him $159 and 8,929 pounds of tobacco as compensation for his wrongful enslavement."[107] This was a short lived victory, however, because the judgment was reversed on appeal on other grounds. Mahoney lost his case in the third trial.[108]

The Maryland Court of Appeals removed all ambiguity, however, with its decision 1849 in *Negro Andrew Franklin v. Freeborn G. Waters*.[109] The Court affirmed a judgment dismissing the damage claim of Andrew Franklin, a term slave whose master held him in slavery beyond the promised manumission date. Franklin was a slave of Charles Waters, who signed a deed on June 9, 1812 stating that he "manumitted and set free my negro boy, *Andrew*, from and after the 1st day of January, 1840[.]" Franklin then "offered evidence, by competent witnesses, tending to prove that he was the same person named in said deed of manumission, the value of his services," and that Waters detained Franklin in slavery until May 12, 1846, when Waters died. Franklin also alleged that he "was kept in ignorance of said deed of manumission, and of his right to freedom, until he was discharged by the defendant," Water's executor, on September 2, 1846.[110]

The jury found for the defendant, and Franklin appealed.[111] The Court of Appeals affirmed the judgment, in an opinion by Judge Ezekiel F. Chambers. Chambers explained and approved of the General Court's decision in *Queen v. Ashton* as follows:

> That case was argued by distinguished counsel in the late general court, where the most intelligent members of the bar from all the counties were assembled, and the principles on which it was argued and adjudged, were, in all probability, well known at that time in every part of the State. How else is it to be accounted for, that such actions have been unknown from that period, although it is scarcely possible to doubt that occasions for it have frequently occurred?
>
> We have inspected the record in that case, because there is some obscurity in the report of it, and we have no doubt the general court decided that the action would not lie. The claimant had been turned out of court by the judgment below, from which he appealed. That judgment was the result of a refusal to declare the law as he claimed it. If the general court supposed the law of the case was with the plaintiff, it was an obvious duty to send the case back on a *procedendo,* with directions to the court below to instruct the jury accordingly, which instruction, according to the facts of the case, must have entitled the plaintiff to a verdict and judgment; but, on the contrary, they affirmed the judgment, thereby deciding that the plaintiff was not entitled to the verdict and judgment, and was properly turned out of court. The obscurity of the case arises from the expression of the reporters, "affirmed on both exceptions," an error into which they appear to have been led by looking to the docket, an entry on which seems to have been made erroneously at first, then altered, but not correctly altered at last.[112]

Chambers then explained that the rule denying damages was consistent with Maryland's statutory procedure for trying freedom claims.[113]

Chambers also rejected Franklin's lawyer's argument that damages should be allowed in cases such as this, in which there was no doubt about the defendant's wrongful conduct:

> Who is to judge whether the case be clear or one of doubt? When is it to be ascertained, and how? Is the form of action only to be ascertained by the result of the trial? The parties will certainly differ. It is of frequent occurrence that juries are unable to agree upon questions of fact, and judges are not always unanimous in regard to questions of law. The only persons at all likely to be held and claimed as slaves in this State, are such as have been

manumitted by last will and testament, or a deed recorded, and whose freedom is to commence at some date subsequent to the execution of the will or deed.

But as all such instruments are exposed on the public records, to which all persons have ready access, and of which any one is able to procure copies, there is very small probability in this age of benevolence and charity, that there will be wanting persons to remind them of their rights, should they be otherwise uninformed. Experience has fully demonstrated, that they have never failed in the recovery of their legal rights, for the want of generous professional aid. We do not therefore admit the necessity, if, on other accounts, we could perceive the propriety or claim the authority of changing the recognised [sic] principles of common law applicable to this question, especially as our statute law enforces the necessity of adhering to it.[114]

This result is especially puzzling because Maryland's statutes provided a means by which masters owning term slaves could apply to the courts to extend a slave's term of bondage on a showing of good cause. Therefore, Chambers ignored the fact that the master's conduct in *Franklin* violated this statute—as well as the conditions of his own manumission deed, which was duly prepared and recorded according to Maryland law.[115]

The court nevertheless reaffirmed and extended this rule in an 1853 decision, *State v. Van Lear*.[116] The plaintiff, Alex Clements, was a former slave who won a decision in the trial court directing his former master's executor, John Van Lear, Jr., to sign a deed of manumission. Van Lear appealed that judgment and posted a bond pending the appeal. The bond provided that if the judgment were to be affirmed, the obligor would pay to Clements "the damage or full value of the freedom and liberty" he lost "for the time [his] freedom shall be suspended by the said appeal, and also all costs[.]"[117] After Clements won on the appeal, Van Lear paid the costs but not the damages. The State sued on behalf of Clements pursuant to the bond to recover damages for the value of his services rendered while the appeal was pending. The Court of Appeals, in an opinion by Judge William H. Tuck, held that, under the logic of the court's decision in *Franklin*, Clements could not recover damages for the time he was held in slavery after he won his case, but while the appeal was pending.[118]

Tuck admitted that under this rule, "[c]ases of hardship may occur and injustice be the consequence." But, citing *Franklin*, he held that "such a result in the present case is not more oppressive than withholding compensation for the time, perhaps a number of years, that a petitioner may be held in bondage, before his right to freedom finally attached."[119]

In 1855, the Court of Appeals, in *Negro Louisa Jason v. Henderson*,[120] extended the no damages rule to a free person of color's claim that she was enjoying her freedom when she was wrongfully seized and enslaved. Judge John Thomas Mason, writing for the court, rejected Jason's lawyer's attempt to distinguish the holdings in *Franklin* and *Van Lear*. Although Mason conceded that Jason "was in actual enjoyment of her freedom" when the defendant seized her, he found it relevant that the defendant did not act "wantonly, and without color of title[.]" Judge Mason nevertheless suggested that damages might be recovered if "a negro, avowedly free," was "forcibly and wantonly captured, without color of title, and reduced to slavery[.]"[121]

The Louisiana Supreme Court also adopted a rule that generally denied damages to people who were wrongfully held in slavery, but in some cases freedom claimants did recover damages.[122] In the Court's 1856 decision in *Maranthe v. Hunter*,[123] Justice James Lea's opinion suggested that the rule providing that freedom claimants could not recover damages followed from Article 177 of the Code, which permitted persons held as slaves to sue for their freedom only and for no other relief. Lea stated until freedom claimants "are recognized as free, or until they are emancipated, they cannot maintain a suit for wages." He suggested, however, that: "It would be otherwise in the case of a free person who had been illegally reduced to a condition of slavery."[124]

The courts and legislatures in the other Southern states, as a general rule, permitted persons winning freedom suits to also recover some measure of damages from the person who a judge or jury found had wrongfully detained the plaintiff in slavery.[125] But in Kentucky, first the courts and then the legislature adopted a bad faith rule that limited the damages that non-white enslaved freedom claimants could recover.

The Kentucky Court of Appeals declared this damage limitation in the 1809 decision in *Thompson v. Wilmont*.[126] The court stated such a limit while in the process of affirming a judgment of $691.25 in favor of a slave named Will, whom the court found was wrongfully detained in slavery by the defendant Thompson. Chief Justice George M. Bibb's opinion suggested, in *dicta*, that the court based its holding on Thompson's bad faith breach of his agreement to free Will after seven years:

> If the claim to emancipation had depended upon general municipal regulations, upon the construction of statutes, or was of obscure or occult derivation, so that the holder might reasonably have believed that he had a property in the negro Will, we should have declared without hesitation that only nominal damages should have been allowed for the detention in slavery. But the present case is devoid of all such excuses. The claim to freedom originated in the agreement of [Thompson], the very letters offered by him in his defense, were an admonition to him to perform his agreement; he was reminded of it from time to time, it had been asserted in the name of the negro in a Court of Justice, but was defeated by the very breach of faith of which [Thompson] had been guilty, and from the expiration of the term in the contract mentioned, to the time of rendering the decree in the Court below, we can see no color of claim on which his conscience could have reposed.

Bibb also noted that Thompson did not ask the trial court to set aside the damage award, "and *here* the error assigned goes only to the principle upon which the damages were decreed, not to the *quantum* assessed according to that principle."[127]

The Kentucky Court of Appeals later applied this bad faith rule to limit or reverse the damages that successful freedom claimants could recover.[128] The court endorsed this bad faith rule in two 1836 opinions by Chief Justice George Robertson. In *Aleck v. Tevis*,[129] Aleck, "a boy of color," filed a bill in chancery in 1832 against Samuel Tevis. Aleck claimed that he was freed by the will of Cloe Pen, who Aleck alleged was his former owner. Aleck enjoyed his freedom from 1813, when Pen died, until September 1818, when Tevis reduced him again to slavery. "[T]he Circuit Court dismissed the bill without prejudice, to a suit at law."[130]

The Court of Appeals reversed this judgment and found that Tevis acted in bad faith when he enslaved Aleck.[131] Robertson also noted that the bad faith rule generally applied in Kentucky freedom suits as announced by Bibb's *dictum*.[132] Nevertheless, Robertson also stated that Tevis was not entitled to the benefit of the good faith exemption.

> [N]ot only was Aleck in the enjoyment of freedom when [Tevis] took possession of him as a slave, but there is no proof that he had any authority to claim his services, or to control him. He is therefore liable for the value of his services, as long as he has enjoyed the benefit of them—counting from the time of the decree back, not longer than five years prior to the institution of this suit. A Court of Equity will give no more than the profits; and if Aleck desire more, or be, in fact, entitled to damages for personal wrong, he ought, in our opinion, to have sued at law, and appealed to a jury. By profits, we of course mean the actual value which, all things being considered, Tevis derived from the services of Aleck. And, as this has not been ascertained, it will be proper, on the return of the cause to the Circuit Court, to ascertain it by agreement, or by inquiry through the instrumentality of a commissioner. The value of the hire, which has been agreed, is not necessarily the true test; for it is obvious, that the actual profits may have been more or less, but most probably less, than that sum.[133]

The court in Robertson's opinion in *Hudgens v. Spencer*[134] also held that when an enslaved person sued in the chancery court his or her recovery should be limited to the master's actual profits instead of the damages for a "personal wrong" that a slave suing at law could recover.[135]

The Kentucky Court of Appeals applied this bad faith rule in *Hundley v. Perry*[136] to reverse a chancery judge's damage award in favor of a successful freedom claimant, Perry. The chancery court judge awarded Perry $300 in damages for the three years that he was wrongfully enslaved by the defendant, Hundley. Perry based his claim, in part, on a manumission deed that Perry's prior master, Hammond, executed and recorded in Maryland, before he transferred possession of Perry and his mother and a sibling to Dorsey. Dorsey later sold these slaves to Hammond.[137]

Judge Alexander K. Marshall's decision for the Court of Appeals affirmed the chancellor's freedom judgment but reversed Perry's damage award. Marshall wrote that

> it does not appear that, when Hundley took possession of Perry, or while he held him in servitude, prior to the commencement of this suit, he knew or believed that Perry was entitled to be free, or had knowledge of the particular facts on which his right is now made manifest, or had good reason to suppose that he was holding a free man in servitude[.]

Thus, the court concluded "this case is not one which, according to the principles heretofore applied to the subject, entitles Perry to damages, from Hundley, for the value of his services."[138] Therefore, a defendant could avoid a money damages judgment if the black plaintiff could not prove that the defendant acted with the requisite knowledge or intent.[139]

Kentucky's legislature adopted this damage limitation in an 1840 statute that provided the "master" with a good faith defense to a damage claim asserted by a "free person of color." The statute stated that the defendant in a freedom or manumission suit who wrongfully retained the plaintiff in slavery "with a knowledge of the [plaintiff's] right to freedom, shall be liable to the [plaintiff for the] value of the services of such free person of color, whilst retained in slavery, by way of damages."[140]

Georgia and South Carolina statutes, and as noted above to a limited extent Virginia's 1849 statute, permitted wrongfully enslaved persons to recover damages.[141] Missouri's 1824 freedom statute also allowed successful freedom petitioners to win damage awards caused by their wrongful detention in slavery "as in other cases." But the legislature eliminated this damages provision in the 1835 and 1845 freedom suit acts.[142]

The South Carolina and Georgia freedom suit statutes required the plaintiff's next friend to seek damages in the freedom suit, thus setting up a potential trap for litigants who did not seek damages in the freedom suit. The Arkansas Supreme Court applied this rule in a trover suit that Abby Guy, by then known as Abby Roper, filed against William Daniel after she won her freedom suit against Daniel.[143] The Court affirmed the dismissal of Roper's equity bill, which sought to bar the statute of limitations defense that Daniel asserted in response to Roper's claim that Daniel took a colt, yoke of oxen, and a cart, which were Roper's property when Daniel asserted his claim to Roper and her children. The Supreme Court suggested that Roper "could have sued Daniel for her property when she and her children sued for themselves."[144] Mark Tushnet stated that this decision "is slightly less silly than it seems; the effect of the rule would have been to induce claimants to freedom to join their damage action in the same proceeding."[145] It also created another procedural trap for the unwary.

The Tennessee courts, on the other hand, permitted serial litigation in which the plaintiff, after first winning a freedom suit, could file another suit to recover his or her damages.[146] This doctrine made sense. As Abby Roper's lawyer argued, it was consistent with the notion that slaves could sue only for their freedom, and that the "owner," who was by then found to be a wrongdoer, should not be permitted to benefit from the statute of limitations defense because of his own actions subjecting the claimant to slavery, and taking the claimant's labor and property without justification.[147] After being awarded their freedom, the claimants' right to sue for other relief, along with other legal rights, sprang into existence.[148]

The courts also adopted different rules establishing the measure of damages that the wrongfully enslaved person could recover. The Missouri Supreme Court held that damages cannot be awarded from the date the suit is filed until the trial.[149] Some decisions allowed the plaintiff to recover a damage judgment for the whole time during which the plaintiff was unlawfully held as a slave, others allowed damages beginning only on the date the suit was filed, and in others "the question of damages is made to depend upon the *bona fides* of the defendant's claim."[150]

In his slave law treatise, Cobb declared his apparent approval of the Virginia decisions denying freed "slaves" the right to recover any damages for the period of their wrongful detention in slavery. He cited "the peculiar condition of the slave, and the relation that he bears to the white race, the difficulties surrounding the master, and the interest of the freedman himself[.]"[151]

Nevertheless, the majority of cases and statutes permitted successful freedom claimants to recover some damages caused by their wrongful detention in slavery. This law was consistent with the notion that people legally held as slaves were people without rights, and that slavery for all others was associated with tortious conduct by the "master."

If the rule were otherwise, white people, along with non-white people illegally confined to slavery, would not be able to recover the damages proximately caused by the wrongdoers capturing or kidnapping them into slavery.[152] It follows that most judges and legislators would not be hostile to all of these damage claims.

Conclusion

The cases and statutes determining the legal rules of evidence and of the damages that applied in the manumission and freedom suits imposed additional practical hurdles for people held as slaves to surmount on the road to freedom. The rules limiting the evidence on which claimants could rely could backfire on masters seeking to establish their property claims in "their people." Therefore, the courts were divided on how strictly to apply the hearsay rule.

Similarly in damage suits, the rule prohibiting all damages for all of those illegally held in slavery did not earn universal support among the Southern judges and legislators. This rule also would deny relief to people found to be illegally held in slavery even if they were white.

Nevertheless, only former slaves who were illegally held in slavery or who were improperly denied the benefits of freedom and property devised to them under their master's wills could obtain monetary relief in the courts. The Georgia Supreme Court emphasized this distinction in an 1869 decision in *Green v. Anderson*.[153] The court affirmed an order that permitted a freed slave to sue to enforce a trust created for his benefit in his former master's pre-Civil War will. The court nevertheless felt compelled to add:

> [W]e hold that a freedman has no right of action in our Courts, to recover damages for injuries done to his person while he was a slave, or for wages on account of labor done by him as a slave. As the law then stood, his labor belonged to his owner, and the owner alone had a right of action to recover damages for injuries to his person. By his transition from slavery to freedom, no such right of the owner has been transferred to him.

The court also noted that "under our last statute of limitations, all such actions for personal injuries, not already commenced, are forever barred and foreclosed."[154]

Notes to Chapter 9

[1] *See* 30 Wright, *supra* at §6321, quoting Roger Park, "A Subject Matter Approach to Hearsay Reform," 86 *Mich. L. Rev.* 51, 112 (1987); Cover, "Reflections," *supra* at 730-32.

[2] *See* Morris, *Slavery, supra* at 227-39; Fede, *People Without Rights, supra* at 194-95; Cobb, *supra* at 226-33; Wheeler, *supra* at 193-99; Finkelman, "Crime of Color," *supra* at 2089-91, 2094; Wiecek, "Statutes," *supra* at 269.

[3] *See* Berlin, *Slaves Without Masters, supra* at 96.

[4] *Laws of Maryland*, 1796, ch. 67, §5; *Id.*, 1728, ch. 4, §2-3; *Id.*, 1717, ch. 13, §2-3; *Id.* 1715, ch. 44, §25-27; *see* 1 Hurd, *supra* at 252-53; Snethen, *supra* at 11.

[5] *Laws of Maryland*, 1846-1847, ch. 27, §1 (1847); *see* 2 Hurd, *supra* at 23.

[6] *See* Zechariah Chaffee, Jr., "Delaware Cases, 1792-1830," 57 *Harv. L. Rev.* 399, 406 (1944) (book review), quoting 2 *Laws of Delaware, supra*, at 887, §8, and citing cases interpreting the statute, *Collins v. Hall*, 1 Del. Cas. 326 (Sup. Ct. 1793) (applying testimonial bar to person freed in Maryland); *State v. Bender*, 1 Del. Cas. 16 (Quar. Sess.1793) (free black could testify against whites in criminal case for assault because no other white witnesses were available). The statute also stated that freed slaves could not vote, hold an elected or appointed office of "trust or profit," or "enjoy any other rights of a freeman, other than to hold property[.]" 2 *Laws of Delaware, supra*, at 887.

[7] *See Thomas v. Pile*, 3 H. & McH. 241, 1794 WL 260 (Md. Gen. Ct. 1774) (freedom judgment for petitioner who offered testimony of a white witness, and the court rejected the defendant's attempt to impeach the witness "who, by general reputation of the neighbourhood, associated and kept company with negroes."); *Laws of Maryland*, 1796, ch. 67, §5 (slaves manumitted under Maryland law were not permitted "to give evidence against any white person," or "be received as competent evidence to manumit any slave petitioning for his freedom."); Snethen, *supra* at 11; Finkelman, "Crime of Color," *supra* at 2094; *but see Sprigg v. Negro Mary*, 3 H. & J. 491, 1814 WL 681 (Md. Ct. App. 1814) (agreeing with trial judge's decision permitting member of Shorter family who had been freed as a descendent of a white woman who was required to serve a term of servitude to testify in freedom suit,

but reversing freedom judgment for petitioner on other grounds), and Papenfuse, *supra* at 61, n. 69 (noting that in Charles Mahoney's freedom case, a freed slave mixed race relative of Mahoney's, Peter Harbard, gave a deposition, which would not have been admissible under the 1796 law), *See also* Jason A. Gillmer, "Base Wretches and Black Wenches: A Story of Sex and Race, Violence and Compassion, During Slavery Times," 59 *Ala. L. Rev.* 1501 (2008) (analyzing a post-Civil War case in Texas, in which non-whites testified and served on the jury).

[8] Cobb, *supra* at 232-33.

[9] *Id.* at 233.

[10] 2 McCormick on Evidence §246 (Kenneth S. Broun, ed., 6th ed. 2006), quoting *Federal Rule of Evidence* 801.

[11] *Id.* at §322.

[12] Banks, *supra* at 799.

[13] *Id.* at 812-20; Billings, *supra* at 468-69, 772-73.

[14] Banks, *supra* at 819.

[15] *Id.* at 822. Key's case was advanced by William Grinstead, a white man who was the father of her two children and whom she married after she won her case. *See id.* at 834-37; Billings, *supra* at 469; and chapter 7, *supra* at notes 74-79.

[16] 1 Va. (1 Wash.) 123, 1792 WL 327 (1792).

[17] *Jenkins v. Tom*, 1792 WL 327 at *1.

[18] *See id.* at *2.

[19] *See, e.g., Pegram v. Isabell*, 11 Va. (1 Hen. & M.) 387, 1807 WL 432 (1807), 12 Va. (2 Hen. & M.) 193, 1808 WL 578 (1808); *Hudgins v. Wrights*, 11 Va. (1 Hen. & M.) 134, 1806 WL 562 (1806); *Nanny v. Mayes* (1799), cited in 1 Catterall, *supra* at 107; MacLeod, *supra* at 112-16; Nicholls, "Squint of Freedom," *supra* at 47-51; Nicholls, "Passing Through," *supra* at 50, 56-60.

[20] 4 H. & Mc H. 295, 1799 WL 397 (Md. Gen. Ct. 1799), *rev'd* (Md. Ct. App. 1802), 4 H. & Mc H. 210, 1798 WL 411 (Md. Gen. Ct. 1798), 4 H. & Mc H. 63, 1797 WL 583 (Md. Gen. Ct. 1797).

[21] *See id.*; 4 Catterall, *supra* at 5; Papenfuse, *supra* at 39-42, 54.

[22] *Mahoney v. Ashton*, 1797 WL 583 at *1.

[23] *Id.* at *12.

[24] *See Butler v. Craig*, 2 H. & McH. 214 (Md. Gen. Ct. 1787), *aff'd* (Md. Ct. App. 1791); *Queen v. Ashton*, 3 H. & McH. 439, 1796 WL 630, 1796 WL 630 (Md. Gen. Ct. 1796); *Toogood v. Scott*, 2 H. & McH. 26, 1782 WL 7 (Md. Gen. Ct. 1782), *aff'd* (Md. Ct. App. 1783).

[25] *Mahoney v. Ashton*, 1799 WL 397 at *16-*18.

[26] 3 H. & McH. 238, 1794 WL 463 (Md. Gen. Ct. 1794).

[27] *Shorter v. Rozier*, 1794 WL 463 at *1.

[28] *Id.* at *1-*2.

29 *Id.* at *2.

30 2 H. & J. 359, 1808 WL 669 (Md. 1808).

31 *Shorter v. Boswell,* 1808 WL 669 at *1-*2.

32 *Id.* at *4; *see* 4 Catterall, *supra* at 2-5; Gillmer, "Suing for Freedom," *supra* at 579-80; *see also* MacLeod, *supra* at 117.

33 11 U.S. (7 Cranch) 290 (1813).

34 *Id.* at 290-93.

35 *Id.* at 295.

36 *Id.* at 296.

37 *See id.* at 296-98.

38 *See id.* at 296-97.

39 *Id.* at 298-99 (Duvall, J., dissenting).

40 Duvall was appointed to serve as a Maryland General Court judge in 1796. Before that appointment, he was counsel for the freedom claimant in *Mahoney v. Ashton.* He did not sit when the General Court heard the case. *See Mahoney v. Ashton, supra;* Papenfuse, *supra* at 39, 55, n. 6.

41 *Mima Queen v. Hepburn,* 11 U.S. (7 Cranch) at 298-99.

42 *Id.* at 299.

43 14 U.S. (1 Wheat.) 6 (1816).

44 *See* Wright, *supra* at §6321 at nn. 83-84 (citing Leonard Baker, *John Marshall: A Life in Law* 726-27 (1974)); Irving Younger, *Hearsay* 4-5 (1988); *see also, e.g.,* Newmyer, *supra* at 426-31; MacLeod, *supra* at 117-18; Leslie Freidman Goldstein, "Slavery and the Marshall Court: Preventing 'Oppressions of the Minor Party'?," 67 *Md. L. Rev.* 166, 177 (2007); Cover, "Reflections," *supra* at 725-26, 730-32; Kent Newmyer, "On Assessing the Court in History: Some Comments in the Roper and Burke Articles," 21 *Stan. L. Rev.* 540, 542-43 (1969); Donald M. Roper, "In Quest of Objectivity: The Marshall Court and the Legitimation of Slavery," 21 *Stan. L. Rev.* 532, 533, 537 (1969).

45 *Walkup v. Pratt,* 5 H. & J. 51, 1820 WL 912 (Md. 1820); *Walls v. Hemsley,* 4 H. & J. 343, 1817 WL 959 (Md. 1817).

46 *Walkup v. Pratt,* 1820 WL 912, at *5; *see also Glover v. Millings,* 2 Stew. & P. 28, 1832 WL 551 at *6-*7 (Ala. 1832) (citing *Mima Queen* with approval).

47 *Waddell George's Creek Coal Co., Inc. v. Chisholm,* 163 Md. 49, 161 A. 276, 278 (1932).

48 8 Tenn. (Mart. & Yer.) 5, 1827 WL 613 (1827).

49 *Vaughan v. Phebe,* 1827 WL 613 at *13-*14.

50 *Id.* at *12.

51 *Id.* at *11.

52 *Id.* at *12.

53 *Id.* at *1-*2, citing the testimony of Seth R. Pool, Martha Jones, and Phebe Tucker.

54 *Id.* at *13.

55 16 Tenn. (8 Yer.) 233, 1835 WL 941 (1835).

56 *See Miller v. Denman,* 1835 WL 941 at *1-*2.

57 *Id.* at *2.

58 29 Va. (2 Leigh) 665, 1831 WL 1924 (1831).

59 *See id.*; Nash, "Reason of Slavery," *supra* at 137-38.

60 34 Ala. 284, 1859 WL 731 (1859).

61 *Farrelly v. Maria Louisa (Woman of Color),* 1859 WL 731 at *1.

62 *Id.* at *2.

63 *See* Papenfuse, *supra* at 39-42, 54; *see id.* at 52, discussing the Maryland General Court's 1796 judgment in *Queen v. Ashton* against Ashton and in favor of the freedom claimant Edward Queen and at least nine of his family members. *See also Queen v. Ashton,* 3 H. & McH. 439, 1796 WL 630, 1796 WL 630 (Md. Gen. Ct. 1796) (Queen's unsuccessful damage suit after freedom judgment). On Ashton's alleged "illicit dealings" with his slaves, *see* Papenfuse, *supra* at 52-54.

64 13 F. Cas. 907 (C.C.D.C. 1808) (7,435).

65 *Id.* at 907.

66 *See id.* at 908; Papenfuse, *supra* at 62, n. 95.

67 39 Ky. (9 Dana) 23, 1839 WL 2577 (1839).

68 *Chancellor v. Milly,* 1839 WL 2577 at *1.

69 *Id.* Bernie D. Jones does not include this opinion in her listing and analysis of the Kentucky Court of Appeals decisions issued during Chief Justice Robertson's tenure. She concluded that the decisions she reviewed exhibited a "trend of supporting flexible manumission policies, ruling on the side of freedom and humanity." *See* Jones, *Fathers, supra* at 86; *see generally id.* at 68-97, 159.

70 *See* Gillmer, "Suing for Freedom," *supra* at 587.

71 *Id.*; MacLeod, *supra* at 117-24.

72 Gillmer, "Suing for Freedom," *supra* at 587 and n. 338.

73 *See* MacLeod, *supra* at 113, quoting Zephaniah Swift, *Digest of the Law of Evidence in Civil and Criminal Cases and a Treatise on Bills of Exchange, and Promissory Notes* 122 (1810).

74 *See* MacLeod, *supra* at 215, n. 10.

75 *See* Swift, *supra* at 122.

76 *See* 3 Thomas Starkie, *A Practical Treatise of the Law of Evidence and Digest of Proofs in Civil and Criminal Proceedings* 1099 (Theron Metcalf, ed.) (1826).

77 *See id.* at 1101.

78 *See id.* at 1102-03; *but see id.* at 1116, citing the *Pegram* and *Mima Queen* decisions.

79 *See* MacLeod, *supra* at 113.

80 *See* W. R. Habeeb, "Admissibility of Declarations of Persons Other Than Members of Family as to Pedigree," 15 *A.L.R.* 2d 1412 (1951 & supp. 2009) (listing and discussing

majority rule and minority rule decisions). For Southern cases adopting the minority rule in cases other than manumission and freedom suits, *see, e.g., Saunders v. Fuller*, 23 Tenn. (4 Hum.) 516, 1844 WL 1853 (1844); *Kaywood v. Barnett's Adm'r*, 20 N.C. (3 & 4 Dev. & Bat.) 88, 1838 WL 494 (1838); *Horry v. Glover*, 11 S.C. Eq. (2 Hill Eq.) 515, 1837 WL 1538 (1837); and for cases citing slavery hearsay cases, *see, e.g., Waddell George's Creek Coal Co., Inc. v. Chisholm*, 163 Md. 49, 161 A. 276 (1932); *Stewart v. Profit*, 146 S.W. 563 (Tex. Ct. Civ. App. 1912); *Cole v. District Bd. of School dist. No. 29, McIntosh County*, 32 Okla. 692, 123 P. 426 (1912); *see also* MacLeod, *supra* at 112-26.

81 *See, e.g.,* Glen Weissenberger, "Federal Rules of Evidence 804: Admissible Hearsay from an Unavailable Declarant," 55 *U. Cin. L. Rev.* 1079, 1129-1134 (1987).

82 2 *McCormick on Evidence, supra* at §246.

83 *See, e.g.,* Biunno, *supra* at 824-25, discussing *Federal Rule of Evidence* 803(c)(19) and *New Jersey Rule of Evidence* 803(c)(19). The latter rule permits the introduction of: "Evidence of a person's reputation, among members of the person's family by blood, adoption, or marriage, or among that person's associates, or in the community, concerning a person's birth, adoption, marriage, divorce, death, legitimacy, ancestry, relationship by blood, adoption, or marriage, or other similar fact of the person's personal or family history."

84 *See* Prosser, *supra* at 48.

85 *See id.* at 48-49; Kull, *supra* at 1281-82, citing *Hickam v. Hickam*, 40 Mo. App. 496 (Ct. App. 1891), for the proposition that a person wrongfully held in slavery should ordinarily be entitled to restitution for the value of his or her services provided for the defendant's benefit for the entire period of illegal confinement.

86 *See* Schafer, *Supreme Court, supra* at 245; Kull, *supra* at 1282-86.

87 6 Va. (2 Call) 319, 1800 WL 404 (1800).

88 *Pleasants v. Pleasants,* 1800 WL 404 at *1-*13.

89 *Id.* at *13.

90 *Id.*

91 *Id.* at *14. *See* Huebner, *Tradition, supra* at 24-25 (discussing other portions of Roane's opinion and his decisions in other cases).

92 12 Va. (2 Hen. & M.) 193, 1808 WL 578 (1808).

93 *Id.,* 1808 WL at *9. The report also contains opinions of Judges St. George Tucker and Fleming.

94 Kull, *supra* at 1284-85.

95 *Peter v. Hargrave,* 46 Va. (5 Gratt.) 12, 1848 WL 2754 (1848); *Paup's Adm'rs v. Mingo,* 31 Va. (4 Leigh) 163, 1833 WL 2076 (1833).

96 *Peter v. Hargrave,* 46 Va. (5 Gratt.) 12, 14, 1848 WL 2754 at *1-*2; *Paup's Adm'rs v. Mingo,* 31 Va. (4 Leigh) 163, 1833 WL 2076 at *12.

97 *Peter v. Hargrave,* 46 Va. (5 Gratt.) 12, 1848 WL 2754 at *7.

98 *Id.* at *6.

99 *See id.* at *7.

[100] 1 *Virginia Code 1849, supra*, title 30, ch. 106, §8, at 465; *see Osborne v. Taylor's Admr's*, 53 Va. (12 Gratt.) 117, 1855 WL 3460 at *1, n. 1, and at *8 (1855) (quoting and discussing this act).

[101] 53 Va. (12 Gratt.) 117, 1855 WL 3460 (1855).

[102] *See Osborne v. Taylor's Adm'rs*, 1855 WL 3460 at *1-*9.

[103] *See id.* at *9.

[104] Kull, *supra* at 1282-83, n. 21.

[105] 3 H. & McH 439, 1796 WL 630 (Md. Gen. Ct. 1796).

[106] *Id.*; *see* Papenfuse, *supra* at 52 (discussing Ashton's involvement with the Queen family and asserting that Ashton may have been the father of Charles and Elizabeth Queen because, when he died in 1815, Ashton left them bequests in his will).

[107] *See* Papenfuse, *supra* at 45.

[108] *See id.* at 45-54.

[109] 8 Gill 322, 1849 WL 3212 (Md. 1849).

[110] *Negro Andrew Franklin v. Freeborn G. Waters*, 1849 WL 3212 at *2.

[111] *Id.* at *3.

[112] *Id.* at *4.

[113] *Id.* at *4-*6.

[114] *Id.* at *7.

[115] *See* chapter 2, *supra* at note 201.

[116] 5 Md. 91, 1853 WL 3563 (1853).

[117] *State v. Van Lear*, 1853 WL 3563 at * 1.

[118] *Id.* at * 2-*3.

[119] *Id.* at *3.

[120] 7 Md. 430, 1855 WL 3800 (1855).

[121] *Negro Louisa Jason v. Henderson*, 1855 WL 3800 at *7.

[122] *See Bateman v. Frisby*, 15 La. Ann. 58, 1860 WL 5498 at *2 (La. 1860) (affirming award of $300 damages to claimant who was held in slavery after he should have been freed according to his master's Arkansas will); *Arsene v. Pigneguy*, 2 La. Ann. 620, 1847 WL 427 at *1 (La. 1847) (affirming award of $8.00 damages per month from the date of the "judicial demand" to claimant who was brought to France and then returned to slavery in Louisiana); *Phillis v. Gentin*, 9 La. 208, 1836 WL 775 at *2 (1836) (suggesting that *statu libera* who was sold into slavery after she should have been freed could obtain "vindictive damages" against the vendor who first sold her into slavery).

[123] 11 La. Ann. 734, 1856 WL 4829 (La. 1856).

[124] *See Maranthe v. Hunter*, 1856 WL 4829 at *1, Schafer, *Supreme Court*, *supra* at 245.

[125] *See Matilda v. Crenshaw*, 12 Tenn. (4 Yer.) 299, 1833 WL 1102 at *3 (1833) (plaintiffs can recover damages for wrongful slavery from the time of the demand or when the suit is filed, without a showing of bad faith by the defendant); *Scott v. Williams*, 12 N.C. (1 Dev.)

376, 1827 WL 613 at *1 (1827) (affirming jury's freedom verdict with "substantial damages"); Kull, *supra* at 1278-90; Higginbotham & Higginbotham, *supra* at 1247-49; Nash, "Reason of Slavery," *supra* at 102-04.

126 4 Ky. (1 Bibb.) 422, 1809 WL 759 (1809).

127 *Thompson v. Wilmont*, 1809 WL 759 at *3. In 1820, the Court affirmed a freedom judgment that awarded only "one cent damages, agreed by the parties, and costs[.]" *Rankin v. Lydia*, 9 Ky. (2 A.K. Marsh.) 467, 1820 WL 1098 (1820); Schwemm, *supra* at 365.

128 *See* McDougle, *supra* at 279.

129 34 Ky. (4 Dana) 242, 1836 WL 2053 (1836).

130 *Aleck v. Tevis*, 1836 WL 2053 at *1.

131 *Id.* at *2-*5.

132 *Id.* at *5-*6.

133 *Id.* at *7. For discussions of this decision, *see* Jones, *Fathers, supra* at 82; Kull, *supra* at 1286-90. Jones does not note the damages portion of the decision.

134 34 Ky. (4 Dana) 589, 1836 WL 2119 (1836).

135 *Hudgens v. Spencer*, 1836 WL 2119 at *5 (citing bad faith rule, but allowing the successful freedom claimant who was hired out by the court while the suit was pending to recover the net value of his services).

136 37 Ky. (7 Dana) 359, 1838 WL 2321 (1838).

137 *Hundley v. Perry*, 1838 WL 2321 at *1-*3.

138 *Id.* at *6.

139 *See Warfield v. Davis*, 53 Ky. (14 B. Mon.) 40 (1853); *Dowrey v. Logan*, 51 Ky. (12 B. Mon.) 236 (1851); *see also Moore's Adm'r v. Minerva*, 17 Tex. 20, 1856 WL 4959 at *4-*5 (1856) (plaintiffs can recover damages for wrongful slavery from the time of the demand or when the suit is filed, without a showing of bad faith by the defendant, but the court noted that the defendant's bad faith may be required for the recovery of damages beginning at an earlier date). *But see* Nash, "Trial Rights," *supra* at 637-38.

140 *See* Kull, *supra* at 1282, n. 20, quoting a Kentucky act of Feb. 12, 1840; *see also* Schwemm, *supra* at 365, n. 76 (noting the statute but not the good faith exception).

141 For South Carolina, *see* 7 *Statutes at Large of South Carolina, supra* at 398; *see also Pepoon v. Clarke*, 8 S.C.L. (1 Mill.) 137 (1837); Stroud, *supra* at 52. For Georgia, *see* Prince, *supra* at 777; *Knight v. Hardeman*, 17 Ga. 253, 1855 WL 1818 at *4 (1855). *See also* Cobb, *supra* at 255-56; Stroud, *supra* at 53; Kull, *supra* at 1282, n. 20; Higginbotham & Higginbotham, *supra* at 1247-48.

142 *See Statutes of Missouri 1845, supra*, "Freedom," §14 at 284; *Statutes of Missouri, 1835, supra*, "Freedom," §14 at 286; 1 *Laws of Missouri 1825, supra*, "Freedom," §3 at 405; Fehrenbacher, *supra* at 251, 657, n. 5; Konig, "Dred Scott," *supra* at 68.

143 *Daniel v. Roper*, 24 Ark. 131, 1863 WL 440 (1863).

144 *Daniel v. Roper*, 1863 WL 440 at *4.

145 Tushnet, *Humanity, supra* at 147, n. 89.

146 *See Woodfolk v. Sweeper*, 21 Tenn. (2 Hum.) 88 (1840); *Matilda v. Crenshaw*, 12 Tenn. (4 Yerg.) 249 (1833).

147 *See Daniel v. Roper*, 24 Ark. 131, 1863 WL 440 at *2.

148 *See* Fede, *People Without Rights, supra* at 142; Finley, *supra* at 97.

149 *Tramell v. Adam, a Black Man*, 2 Mo. 155, 1829 WL 1766 at *3 (1829); *but see Gordon v. Duncan*, 3 Mo. 385, 1834 WL 2549 (1834) (claimant who was hired out under a court order while his freedom suit was pending could recover wages earned during the hiring).

150 *See Reuben v. Parrish*, 25 Tenn. (6 Hum.) 122, 1845 WL 1873 (1845) (defendant liable for all funds received for labor during claimants' wrongful detention in slavery); Cobb, *supra* at 255-56; *see* Kull, *supra* at 1282-83.

151 Cobb, *supra* at 256; *see* Kull, *supra* at 1282, n. 19.

152 *See Aleck v. Tevis*, 34 Ky. (4 Dana) 242, 1836 WL 2053 at *6.

153 35 Ga. 655, 1869 WL 1611 (1869).

154 *See Green v. Anderson*, 1869 WL 1611 at *6.

10

Conclusion

Many people who were held as slaves in the United States filed suits in search of their liberation before slavery was abolished in their state or in the nation. Some were successful and some were not. But they all had to confront the legal roadblocks that the legislators and judges placed along the path to freedom.

The nature of these roadblocks varied over time in each of the Southern colonies and states. Indeed, as explained in chapter three, the lawmakers exhibited considerable creativity as they struggled to find the right regulatory regime. At times they required masters to post bonds before freeing their slaves; they limited the age and condition of slaves who could be freed; they prohibited manumission by will; they required that manumission deeds be signed, witnessed, and recorded; they required that judges or even the state legislators approve all manumissions; and they prohibited in state manumission and required freed slaves to leave the state or colony.

Moreover, in the years before the Civil War the lawmakers in a number of the Southern states ultimately voted to prohibit all manumissions. They also enacted a simple path to bondage for free blacks, who could "voluntarily" elect to relinquish what Frederick Douglass called "the heaven of comparative freedom" for "the dark and pestiferous tomb of slavery," which the Southern lawmakers and opinion leaders came to believe was the only suitable legal status for all blacks.[1]

This pattern of legal change, by the start of the Civil War, in effect created a barrier to manumission suits as a route to freedom in most of the Southern states. But the Southern lawmakers and judges did not bar all freedom suits. If they had done so, they would have closed off a necessary outlet to liberty for people who the law defined as white but who were illegally caught in the "tomb of slavery."

This law's unique pattern of development prompted David Brion Davis to conclude that "the slave system in the United States became distinctive by virtually closing off the possibility of manumission, which in many societies had been at least a theoretical check on dehumanization, since it showed that a slave *was* capable of being a free person." Although Davis acknowledged that "various kinds of highly privileged slaves were freed," he asserted that slavery in the United States South became the "ultimate form of inhuman bondage."[2]

According to Davis, these legal developments occurred "after about 1815," but he also cited Virginia's 1691 statute essentially requiring that slaves leave the colony after they were freed.[3] We can illustrate this unique trend against liberty in the South that began with this 1691 act by considering the lives and work of three Southern judges, St. George Tucker, John Belton O'Neall, and Joseph Henry Lumpkin, including the freedom and manumission suits that they decided and their efforts to reform slavery law.

Tucker was a slave owner who was one of Virginia's most prominent early lawyers, judges, law professors, and legal scholars.[4] He wrote an American version of *Blackstone's Commentaries*, which contained one of the first widely-published scholarly summaries of slavery law in the United States.[5]

Tucker also was a critic of the slave system of social organization and its law who tried to persuade his own state of Virginia to reform itself. In 1796, he published a monograph candidly discussing slavery's essential nature, summarizing Virginia's slave law, and urging that his state's legislature adopt a gradual emancipation statute.[6] According to Tucker, a republic recently founded upon the ideals of rights to life, liberty, and the pursuit of happiness could not tolerate slavery, which denied those rights to people who were slaves, "unless we first degrade them below the rank of human beings, not only politically, but also physically and morally."[7]

"Tucker's condemnation of slavery was powerful," but "[w]hen he turned to freeing slaves, Tucker made many concessions to racial prejudice, and admitted that he was somewhat infected by it."[8] Tucker cited Thomas Jefferson's *Notes on the State of Virginia* as authority on the alleged inferiority of blacks.[9] In his unpublished papers, Tucker wrote that freed blacks "[are] not remarkable for their industry.... They appear to have no ambition for civil rights."[10]

Tucker's plan called for very gradual reform indeed. No slave who was alive upon its adoption would have been freed. "The first generation of male slaves born after the adoption of the plan would remain enslaved for life."[11] All female children born of female slaves after the plan's effective date would be born free, and they would "transmit freedom to all of [their] descendants, both male and female[.]" These free mothers and children would, however, be required to serve their owners until they reached the age of 28, when they would receive freedom dues of twenty dollars, "two suits of clothes, suited for the season, a hat, a pair of shoes, and two blankets."[12] During this 28-year term of service, these people were to be on the same "footing as white servants and apprentices" regarding "food, raiment, correction, and the assignment of their service from one another."[13]

According to Gary B. Nash, the plan would have granted "liberty to female slaves born after a certain date only after they had reached 28 years of age, thus allowing masters to recapture their investment, and requiring even the male and female children of these black women born free to serve 28 years." This plan thus "would be cost-free to the present generation of slaveholders and required not a penny of Northerners in taxes or appropriations from the government's general fund."[14] Tucker estimated that his plan would have perpetuated slavery for at least 105 years, but, according to Paul Finkelman, slavery would have lasted "120 years or more."[15]

Unlike the earlier published emancipation proposals of Tucker's fellow Virginians Thomas Jefferson and Ferdinando (or Fernando) Fairfax, Tucker did not call for the forced removal of the freed slaves from Virginia.[16] Nevertheless, Edmund S. Morgan concluded that Tucker's plan would have transformed slavery "into a kind of serfdom."[17]

Tucker also proposed that the law deny freed slaves equal legal rights. His plan would have denied them the right to hold public office; to own an interest in real estate, other than a lease not to exceed twenty-one years; to keep or bear arms, unless authorized by special legislation lasting no more than three years; to enter into marriage contracts other than with "a Negroe [sic] or mulattoe [sic];" to be an attorney, juror, or a witness in court except in an action between "Negroes and mulattoes"; to make a will; or to be an executor, administrator, or trustee.[18] He hoped that laws imposing these legal disabilities on free blacks would "render it their inclination and their interest to seek those privileges in some other climate."[19]

Tucker's emancipation proposal, with all of its limitations, had little support in Virginia.[20] While he was a legislator, George K. Taylor, a lawyer who also represented slaves in freedom and manumission suits, tried to convince Virginia's legislature to consider and adopt this proposal. "His failure had caused him considerable chagrin."[21] Even Judge Spencer Roane, "who often saw eye to eye with his colleague St. George Tucker" on manumission cases, did not endorse Tucker's emancipation plan.[22]

In contrast, Tucker's cousin, George Tucker, advocated a plan in 1801 that explicitly called for the removal of Virginia's blacks to western lands. This idea "found a more receptive audience than his cousin's had five years earlier."[23]

According to David Brion Davis, "[m]uch has been made of the plans of men like Thomas Jefferson and St. George Tucker for the gradual emancipation and colonization of Negroes[,]" but Tucker's plan is most relevant as one example of the South's failure to reform its law in favor of freedom.[24] Indeed, Tucker did not free his slaves and he participated in the "derailment" of a stepson's plan to free Tucker's wife's slaves while the South's post-revolution leaders continued to legitimize slavery, unlike those in Northern states, who, in the decades after the signing of the Declaration of Independence, advanced laws providing for slavery's immediate or gradual abolition.[25]

Tucker's notion that the law should confine freed slaves to second class citizenship, however, was the one portion of his gradual emancipation plan that became law, in the form of the pre-Civil War statutes limiting the rights of free blacks and the South's post-emancipation black codes and Jim Crow laws.[26] By the 1880s, the term Jim Crow was "synonymous with a complex system of racial laws and customs in the South that ensured white social, legal, and political domination of blacks. Blacks were segregated, deprived of their right to vote, subjected to verbal abuse, discrimination, and violence without redress in the courts or support by the white community."[27] These pre- and post-emancipation laws denying free blacks equal legal rights echoed Tucker's proposal for the second class citizenship of freed slaves. And as Tucker suggested, these laws may have been one of the factors that motivated many Southern blacks to seek their legal rights elsewhere in the pre- and post-Civil War migrations to the Northern states, while others sought to secure their rights at home in the South in the civil rights movement.[28]

In the 1806 case of *Hudgins v. Wrights*,[29] moreover, Tucker and Roane, who, according to a biographer, expressed a "preference for liberty," wrote the leading opinions enforcing a presumption of slavery based on racial appearance in the freedom suits.[30] Judge John Louis Taylor's 1802 jury charge in *Gobu v. Gobu*[31] foreshadowed this race-based presumption. According to one biographer, Taylor's "compassionate views toward Africans and his decisions sometimes stretched the bounds of social acceptance."[32]

These venerated Southern judges created one of the principal rules that hampered the claims of non-white freedom claimants while maintaining a route to freedom for whites who somehow came to be held as slaves. Slavery in the United States South continued to be tied to racism, in part because of the race-based slavery presumption that Tucker, Roane, and Taylor advanced in the freedom suits.

South Carolina Chief Justice John B. O'Neall advocated slave law reforms—not emancipation—to address what he perceived to be slavery's harshest aspects in order to protect and defend slavery as a legal and social institution. O'Neall was from an Irish-American Quaker family.[33] He was a legislator, long-time judge, legal reformer, and temperance advocate who often declared his own policy views in his judicial opinions. For example, in an 1842 opinion Justice O'Neall explained why he thought slave law should permit masters to reward some or all of their slaves with freedom. O'Neall believed that "[k]indness to slaves" was "the true policy of slave owners," and "its spirit should go (as it generally has) into the making of the law, and ought to be a ruling principle of its construction. *Nothing will more assuredly defeat our institution of slavery, than harsh legislation rigorously enforced.* On the other hand, as it hitherto has been, with all the protections of law and money around it, it has nothing to fear from *fanaticism abroad or examination at home.*"[34]

O'Neall explained further his benign vision of slave law in an 1848 monograph that he prepared as authorized by his state's Agricultural Society.[35] O'Neall called for reforms to South Carolina's slavery laws, including revisions that would better protect slave families and enforce the master's right to free his or her slaves. He stated that his "experience as a man, and a Judge, leads me to condemn the Acts of 1820 and 1841[,]" which restricted manumission. He called on the legislature to repeal these acts and restore the 1800 act's milder provisions.[36]

According to O'Neall, public policy should favor manumission as a way to preserve slavery:

> The State has nothing to fear from emancipation, regulated as the law directs it to be. Many a master knows that he has a slave or slaves, for whom he feels it to be his duty to provide. As the law now stands, that cannot be done. In a slave country, the good should be especially rewarded. Who are to judge this, but the master? Give him the power of emancipation, under well regulated guards, and he can dispose the only reward, which either he, or his slave appreciates. In the present state of the world, it is especially our duty, and that of slave owners, to be just and merciful, and in all things to be *exceptione majori*. With well regulated and mercifully applied slave laws, we have nothing to fear for negro slavery. Fanatics

of our own, or foreign countries, will be in the condition of the viper biting the fire. They, not us, will be the sufferers. Let me, however, assure my countrymen, and fellow-slave-holders, that unjust laws, or unmerciful management of slaves, fall upon us, and our institutions, with more withering effect than anything else. I would see South Carolina the kind mother, and mistress of all her people, free and slave. To all, extending justice and mercy. Against our enemies, I would say to her, *be just and fear not.* Her sons faltered not on a foreign shore; at home, they will die in the last trench, rather than her rights should be invaded or despoiled.[37]

When O'Neall referred to "emancipation" in this paragraph he of course meant "manumission," as I have used those terms. He did not advocate the end of slavery; to the contrary, he called for an approach to slave treatment and the law that he believed would better perpetuate slavery by combating its enemies from without or from within.

A South Carolina Senate Judiciary Committee report, signed by Senator Wilmot G. DeSaussure, criticized O'Neall's proposed reforms, but not his slave law summary. O'Neall's publication prompted a public debate on the merits of his suggested reforms, but, in the end, South Carolina's legislature did not enact O'Neall's slave law reform proposals.[38]

Like Tucker's very gradual emancipation plan, O'Neall's law reform proposals—including his "liberal" manumission views—did not prevail in the public policy debates of the late antebellum years. "Celebrated as an educator, a judge, and as a temperance advocate, his ideas on slavery did not appear to be the focus of discussion during his lifetime or upon his death."[39] Thus, in a profile of O'Neall that was published twenty years after O'Neall's death, former Governor Benjamin Franklin Perry referred to O'Neall's authorship of "two works of great interest to the people of South Carolina," but he did not include the slavery law monograph.[40]

The South Carolina legislators joined with the other Southern state legislators and judges who advanced what O'Neall found to be a harsh version of legal reform, which called for laws barring manumission and encouraging voluntary slavery for free blacks. This legal change illustrates O'Neall's generation's failure to ameliorate slavery's characteristics in law, after Tucker's generation failed to abolish it peacefully in the South, or at least set in motion a means to end it 100 years in the future.

Georgia Chief Justice Joseph Henry Lumpkin, on the other hand, was a more successful reformer. A legislator, lawyer, legal educator, and a long-time judge, he, like O'Neall, was a temperance advocate who called for reforms in law and in society in general. Early in life, he even publicly criticized slavery.[41]

But Lumpkin later was converted to the notions that slavery was a positive good that was mandated by the bible, and that servitude was God's gift to the inherently inferior blacks. Thus, he successfully advocated slavery law reforms that closed what he perceived to be unwarranted loopholes in Georgia's manumission laws.[42] In an 1855 opinion, Lumpkin "emphatically" stated:

> [W]hatever opinions I may have expressed heretofore upon this subject, that I am fully persuaded that the best interests of the slave, as well as a stern public policy, resulting from the whole frame-work of our social system, imperatively demand that all *post mortem* manumission of slaves should be absolutely and entirely prohibited. Slavery is a cherished institution in Georgia—founded in the Constitution and laws of the United States; in her own Constitution and laws, and guarded, protected and defended by the whole spirit of her legislation; approved by her people; intimately interwoven with her present and permanent prosperity. Her interests, her feelings, her judgment and her conscience—not to say her very existence, alike conspire to sustain and perpetuate it.[43]

Lumpkin came to believe that these practical concerns and slavery's "divine origins" excluded manumission as "an acceptable option."[44]

Lumpkin also argued, however, that masters should treat their slaves "with paternalistic kindness to provide moral uplift."[45] But, in part because of Lumpkin's efforts, the law in Georgia and in the majority of the Southern states eventually provided that slaves could not be uplifted out of bondage, even if their masters thought that this was the right thing to do, or if their masters believed that manumission was an acceptable means to encourage good behavior by slaves and deter slave rebellion. Lumpkin, like O'Neall, did not perceive the judiciary as "a neutral forum on questions involving slavery. Rather, his court was a court of policy aiding the other agencies of government to protect and defend a system implanted with the seeds of its own destruction."[46]

O'Neall was no less dedicated to protecting and defending slavery than Lumpkin; in my view both were sincerely dedicated to slavery. O'Neall in 1846, using words that are strikingly similar to Lumpkin's, stated that slavery "is here so interwoven with every part of society, and so essential to life itself, that its destruction would be ours."[47] These reformers simply had different policy beliefs on how best to support slavery through the law. Lumpkin's was the majority view in the South in general, and among the legislators and judges as well, in the years leading up to the Civil War.

The debate between O'Neall and Lumpkin about slavery law reform and the manumission and freedom suits also occurred against the background of the contrasting views of the nineteenth century pro-slavery and anti-slavery writers who considered the relative merits of slavery and its law.[48] Pro-slavery writers praised the freedom and manumission suits as evidence of the superiority of Southern slave society and law, which provided a legal means to release from bondage people who were illegally held as slaves, while protecting the property interests of rightful slave owners and providing a paternalistic and honorable slave system to protect and advance the allegedly inferior black race.[49] In contrast, anti-slavery writers, such as George Stroud, condemned the "harsh and unreasonable" procedures that he said hampered plaintiffs asserting claims to freedom.[50] The abolitionists also wrote of these suits to motivate others to oppose slavery because these cases demonstrated how even people appearing to be white could be wrongfully captured and held as slaves in the United States.[51]

Stroud, in my view, had the better argument. The Southern courts and legislatures adopted and applied law in the freedom suits that was fundamentally unfair to freedom claimants who were not perceived to exhibit a white appearance. In the freedom suits, the courts enforced the race-based standards that determined who legally could be a slave. The law regulated the individual master's right to decide whom to enslave, just as it regulated his or her right to treat his or her lawfully held slaves as indulgently or as poorly as he or she wished. These legal standards were analogous to laws that regulated the rights of other property owners in the public interest.

The Southern courts and legislatures adopted and enforced substantive and procedural principles that narrowed the types of freedom suits that lawyers could successfully file. This law hindered the chances of those seeking their release from slavery when it is measured, not against today's norms, but against those of the past. This was especially so for the claimants who appeared to be black. The law in the freedom suits created a double standard based upon the claimants' perceived racial appearance.

The Southern law thus restricted the potential freedom claims that did not rely on direct proof of the masters' intentions to free their slaves. Children of *statu liberi* were in most states and at most times slaves for life even after their mothers were freed. Except in Louisiana, and to a limited extent in Delaware and Maryland, the law did not enforce slave self-purchase rights or manumission contracts over the owner's objection.

The cases and statutes also put procedural hurdles in the way of freedom claimants. They did so in a way that favored claimants who appeared to be white, when they imposed the burden of proof based on the claimants' racial appearance. They also often required plaintiffs to sue by next friends, or required lawyers and sometimes even judges to pre-screen freedom suits before the alleged owner even was required to respond. They even suspended the writ of *habeas corpus*, as a general rule, for all freedom claimants who appeared to be black, and prohibited or limited the monetary damages that successful freedom claimants could recover after proving that they were wrongfully detained in slavery. Although some courts applied the common law hearsay rule fairly to freedom suits, hearsay evidence about a claimant's family history could be admitted for or against the freedom claimant.

In the manumission suits, the courts enforced the master's intention to free his or her slaves, to the extent permitted by law. The law regulated and even at times prohibited this right, however, to prevent what the lawmakers perceived to be undue harm to the public interest. These regulations varied over time, but the trend of legal change in the nineteenth century Southern courts and legislatures further limited and eventually prohibited some or all manumissions by slave owners, even if the evidence of the master's intentions was clear.

The various issues raised in the Southern manumission cases have received very thorough discussions in the works of authors including A. E. K. Nash, Arthur Howington, Mark Tushnet, and, more recently, Bernie Jones.[52] Nash found that some judges and courts, in Georgia for one example, were anti-manumission and pro-slavery, while others in states such as Tennessee were pro-manumission and even "libertarian." Howington, studying Tennessee, wrote that Nash went too far in calling even that state's decisions libertarian. But he concluded that the courts addressed a concern, at least in part, for slave's "rights" in the Tennessee manumission cases, and that this "was completely compatible with and supportive of the peculiar institution." Tushnet cited the manumission cases to make further arguments, but he agreed that these cases reveal the judge's pro-slavery or anti-slavery biases.[53] Nash and Tushnet argued the law in Georgia was less "liberal" than that of Tennessee.[54]

Jones compared the Kentucky cases and statutes regulating manumission with the other slave states. She stated the Kentucky law was less restrictive of the master's manumission rights, and that the Kentucky judges "used their consciences, their senses of right and wrong, to blunt the edges of legislation and counteract the will of proslavery southerners who opposed manumission in the Commonwealth of Kentucky. They did this on a case-by-case basis."[55]

One key point must be kept in mind, however, so that our enthusiasm for the Tennessee and Kentucky court decisions is not overemphasized. The slave claiming his or her freedom because of an alleged manumission was a surrogate for the deceased master's intention and interest in the enforcement of his or her own will. When the courts gave the slave a "fair" hearing in a manumission case, they were primarily reviewing evidence of the deceased master's intent. It is thus unremarkable, then, that the courts fairly aired the issues in manumission cases while closing their doors to slaves in other civil cases in which the master and slave did not have an identical interest.

Southern lawmakers and judges disagreed, however, when they decided how far the law should restrict the masters' intentions to manumit their slaves. The Georgia decisions tended to be more restrictive than those of the Tennessee or Kentucky courts. The issue in these cases, however, was not the legislators' and judges' concern for slave freedom. Instead, the issue was whether the courts would effectuate the masters' plainly expressed intentions to free their slaves, weighed against what the judges perceived to be the salient social and political interests and the claims and interests of the masters' heirs, executors, or interested third parties including the masters' creditors. Some judges may have talked about "slave rights" and the dictates of "humanity" while allowing manumission, but these judges enforced the masters' power to do what they wished with their slaves—even after the masters' death. As the prevailing perceptions of the relevant interests changed, the legislatures and courts more often tended to further regulate the masters' will when they thought that public policy so required.[56]

The antebellum Southern courts and legislatures increasingly limited the masters' right to manumit their slaves by will if the slaves were to stay in the forum state, and in some states, even if the masters intended that their slaves leave their home state after the slaves were freed. This legal trend occurred without any concern for the slaves' "right" to be free. In fact and in law, only people who were illegally held as slaves had a right to be set free. Those who legally were held in slavery could be freed only if their masters chose to bestow liberty upon them, and if the state did not veto the masters' benevolence. Accordingly, this law is another example of how slave law can best be understood as a compact between the slaves' rulers. The lawmakers balanced the competing property interests of the masters and others, which were embodied in the slave, with the perceived public policy concerns that were raised by some or all manumissions. With the limited exceptions noted in this book, Southern slaves had no independent legal right to freedom.

The antebellum Southern lawmakers who increasingly circumscribed the master's right to free his or her slaves also expanded the scope of the master's liability for slave abuse and provided more comprehensive procedural safeguards in slave criminal trials. These two currents of legal change were consistent. Both limited the individual owner's right to use his or her property and the state's right to take that property, in an effort to further what the lawmakers perceived to be salient social ends, including the perpetuation of slavery and the protection of slave property. The law seems contradictory only if the irrelevant concept of "slave rights" is considered.

As St. George Tucker accurately predicted, a society based upon the inalienable rights of all men could not accommodate slavery into its law and culture "unless we first degrade [those held as slaves] below the rank of human beings, not only politically, but also physically and morally."[57] This racism reached its apex with the nineteenth century "positive good" doctrine. This theory's underpinning was the alleged racial inferiority of blacks, who, it was argued, could not achieve social and legal equality with whites.[58]

This theory was manifested in law by the statutes banning all manumissions and the laws adopted in nine Southern states permitting free blacks to seek in court or by special legislation approval for their "voluntary" enslavement.[59] "These acts represented a culmination of the 'positive good' theory of slavery— that people of African descent lived happily as slaves and found freedom inconvenient or miserable."[60]

The statutes permitting these enslavement petitions show how far the notions of slave law reform had strayed from Tucker's and even O'Neall's proposals to Lumpkin's reforms. These petitions were the antithesis of the freedom suits, but slavery's racial basis was a constant. This probably explains why the South Carolina legislature rejected three enslavement petitions that Lucy Adams, a free person of color, filed between 1858 and 1863. She could not be a "voluntary" slave because her mother was white.[61]

By the end of the antebellum years, the South's intellectual, religious, and political leaders no longer condemned or even criticized slavery; instead, they praised it. They cited the freedom suits as examples of the beneficence of their law, which they reformed to bar all manumissions and to ease the voluntary enslavement of blacks.

The South that would not condemn itself could not reform itself in favor of freedom and equal rights for all. To the contrary, according to the majority of the Southern legislators and judges, the necessary legal reforms included measures that would perpetuate slavery and facilitate its expansion by blocking the road to freedom and creating an easy route to "voluntary" enslavement for all blacks. The effects of this tragic failure lasted longer than the 105 years that slavery would have survived under St. George Tucker's very gradual emancipation plan.[62]

Notes to Chapter 10

[1] *See* Frederick Douglass, *The Life and Times of Frederick Douglass Written by Himself: His Early Life as a Slave, his Escape from Bondage, and his Complete History* 97 (reprint ed. 2003) (1892).

[2] *See* Davis, *Inhuman Bondage, supra* at 3.

[3] *See id.* at 3, 132. It appears that Davis's views on the manumission and freedom suits in the American South evolved over the years. *See* Davis, *Western Culture, supra* at 262-88.

[4] Cover, *Justice Accused, supra* at 37-41; Paul Finkelman, "St. George Tucker," in *Encyclopedia of Antislavery and Abolition* 684-86 (Peter P. Hinks, *et al.*, eds. 2007); Charles F. Hobson, "St. George Tucker's Legal Papers," 47 *Wm. & Mary L. Rev.* 1245, 1245-47 (2006); Finkelman, "Tucker," *supra* at 1218-20; Curtis, *supra* at 1158; Davidson M. Douglas, "Foreword: The Legacy of St. George Tucker," 47 *Wm. & Mary L. Rev.* 1111, 1111-16 (2006); Doyle, *supra* at 422-42; *see also* Melvin Patrick Ely, "Richard and Judith Randolph, St. George Tucker, George Wythe, Syphax Brown, and Hercules White: Racial Equality and the Snares of Prejudice," in *Revolutionary Founders: Rebels, Radicals, and Reformers in the Making of the Nation* (Alfred F. Young, Ray Raphael, and Gary Nash, eds.) 323-36 (2011).

[5] St. George Tucker, *Blackstone's Commentaries: With Notes of Reference, to the Constitution and Laws, of the Federal Government of the United States; and of the Commonwealth of Virginia* (1803). The slave law summary is at 3 *Id.* at Note E, 73-97.

[6] Tucker, *Dissertation, supra; see* Wedgwood, *supra* at 1391-92; Nash, "Reason of Slavery," *supra* at 127; *see also*, discussing Tucker's plan and its context, George William Van Cleve, *A Slaveholders' Union: Slavery, Politics, and the Constitution in the Early American Republic* 206-11, 269 (2010); Egerton, *supra* at 141-43; Wolf, *Race, supra* at 101, 104-07; Phillip Hamilton, *The Making and Unmaking of a Revolutionary Family: The Tuckers of Virginia 1752-1830* 81-83 (2003) [hereinafter Hamilton, *Revolutionary Family*]; Nash, *Race and Revolution, supra* at 43-46, 151-65; Jordan, *White Over Black, supra* at 555-61.

[7] Tucker, *Dissertation, supra* at 50-51; Curtis, *supra* at 1160.

[8] Curtis, *supra* at 1164.

[9] Tucker, *Dissertation, supra* at 86-88, n. a, and 89. For Jefferson's views on race, slavery, and the law, *see, e.g.*, Finkelman, *Founders, supra* at 129-96; Kolchin, *American Slavery, supra* at 88-89; Aaron Schwabach, "Jefferson and Slavery," 19 *T. Jefferson L. Rev.* 63, 76-90 (1997).

[10] Mark Douglas McGarvie, "Transforming Society Through Law: St. George Tucker, Women's Property Rights, and an Active Republican Judiciary," 47 *Wm. & Mary L. Rev.* 1393, 1394, n. 10 (2006), quoting 1 St. George Tucker, *Notes on the State of Slavery in Virginia*,

nbk. 7, at 10, unpublished Tucker-Coleman papers, located at the Earl Gregg Swem Library at The College of William and Mary.

[11] Wolf, *Race, supra* at 105.

[12] Tucker, *Dissertation, supra* at 91.

[13] *Id.* at 92.

[14] Nash, *Race and Revolution, supra* at 46.

[15] Tucker, *Dissertation, supra* at 99-104; Finkelman, "Tucker," *supra* at 1235-36; Nash, "Reason of Slavery," *supra* at 127, n. 391.

[16] Thomas Jefferson proposed a failed anti-slavery provision for the 1784 Territorial Governance Act. *See* Finkelman, *Founders, supra* at 148-09; William G. Merkel, "Jefferson's Failed Anti-Slavery Proviso and the Nascence of Free Soil Constitutionalism," 38 *Seton Hall L. Rev.* 555, 602 (2008); Annette Gordon-Reed, "Logic and Experience: Thomas Jefferson's Life in the Law," in *Slavery, South, supra* at 13-14.

As a Virginia legislator, Jefferson co-authored a proposal to abolish slavery in Virginia and transport the freed slaves out of the state. He did not advance the proposal, although he published it in his *Notes on the State of Virginia* and he included a version in his 1783 draft of a constitution for Virginia. *See* Wolf, *Race, supra* at 102; Finkelman, *Founders, supra* at 145; Nash, *Race and Revolution, supra* at 11-12; Noonan, *supra* at 52-54; Jordan, *White Over Black, supra* at 546-47; Jefferson, *supra* at 148-55. Tucker's plan's publication also followed Fairfax's publication in 1790 of a gradual voluntary emancipation and colonization plan. *See* Egerton, *supra* at 141; Joseph J. Ellis, *Founding Brothers: The Revolutionary Generation* 104-08 (2000); Wolf, *Race, supra* at 107-09; Nash, *Race and Revolution, supra* at 42-43, 146-50; Jordan, *White Over Black, supra* at 554-55.

[17] Morgan, *American Slavery, supra* at 385.

[18] Tucker, *Dissertation, supra* at 93-94; Berlin, *Slaves Without Masters, supra* at 105; Katz, *supra* at 928.

[19] Tucker, *Dissertation, supra* at 94; Berlin, *Slaves Without Masters, supra* at 104; Curtis, *supra* at 1168. On May 30, 1797, Robert Pleasants wrote a letter to Tucker criticizing Tucker's emancipation plan for being too gradual and for denying civil rights to freed slaves. Tucker's letter in response blamed the latter provisions on his perceived need to obtain support for the plan, but he also admitted his own prejudice against "inter-marriages." *See* Curtis, *supra* at 1170-71.

[20] Hamilton, *supra* at 82-83; Jordan, *White Over Black, supra* at 346, n.11; Curtis, *supra* at 1169, 1188-93. The Virginia legislature also did not adopt Tucker's proposal that free blacks be denied the right to own real estate. *See* Katz, *supra* at 928. Tucker reprinted his plan as Note H of his 1803 version of *Blackstone's Commentaries*. Between 1819 and 1821, he wrote a "supplement" to this plan, which he never published. *See* Phillip Hamilton, "Revolutionary Principles and Family Loyalties: Slavery's Transformation in the St. George Tucker Household of Early National Virginia," 55 *Wm. & Mary Q. 3d Ser.* 531, 555 (1998).

[21] *See* MacLeod, *supra* at 219, n. 49.

[22] Huebner, *Tradition, supra* at 26.

[23] Jordan, *White Over Black, supra* at 562; *see* Wolf, *Race, supra* at 107; Berlin, *Slaves Without Masters, supra* at 106.

[24] *See* Davis, *Revolution, supra* at 87; *see also* Gordon-Reed, "Logic and Experience: Thomas Jefferson's Life in the Law," in *Slavery, South, supra* at 14; Malick W. Ghachem, "The Slave's Two Bodies: The Life of an American Legal Fiction," 60 *Wm. & Mary Q.* 809, 839 (2003).

[25] *See* Hamilton, *Revolutionary Family, supra* at 155, *see also, e.g.,* Gordon S. Wood, *Empire of Liberty: A History of the Early American Republic, 1789-1815* 508-542 (2009); Drescher, *supra* at 124-45; Davis, *Inhuman Bondage, supra* at 141-56; Davis, *Revolution, supra* at 255-342.

[26] *See,* on the black codes, Berlin, *Slaves Without Masters, supra;* and on the Jim Crow laws, *id.* at 381-83; C. Vann Woodward, *The Strange Career of Jim Crow* (3d. ed. 1974).

[27] Richard Wormser, *The Rise and Fall of Jim Crow* xi (2004).

[28] *See, e.g., id.;* Michael J. Klarman, *From Jim Crow to Civil Rights: The Supreme Court and the Struggle for Racial Equality* 10-15 (2004); Curtis, *supra* at 1200-02, 1204-05. Some confronted and confounded these racial categories by passing as white or black. *See, e.g.,* Elizabeth M. Smith-Pryor, *Property Rites: The Rhinelander Trial, Passing, and the Protection of Whiteness* (2009); Martha A. Sandweiss, *Passing Strange: A Gilded Age Tale of Love and Deception Across the Color Line* (2009); Baz Dreisinger, *Near Black: White-to-Black Passing in American Culture* (2008); Berlin, *Generations, supra* at 66-67.

[29] 11 Va. (1 Hen. & M.) 134 (1806).

[30] *See* Huebner, *Tradition, supra* at 24-25 (discussing some of Roane's slavery opinions).

[31] 1 N.C. (Tay.) 100, 1802 WL 207 (1802).

[32] *See* Williams, "Taylor," *supra* at 539 (discussing Taylor's life and opinions, but not his *Gobu* opinion); Wiethoff, *supra* at 3, 11, 83-84, 131, 133; (same); Nash, "Equitable Past?", *supra* at 206-11 (same).

[33] *See generally* Jones, *Fathers, supra* at 140-46; Benjamin F. Perry, *Reminiscences of Public Men* 202-07 (1883); Alexander M. Sanders, Jr., "John Belton O'Neall," in *Yale Biographical Dictionary, supra* at 410-11; *see also* Edwards, *People, supra* at 34-35 (discussing O'Neall's role within the broader context of the lawyers and judges who advocated antebellum legal reforms).

[34] *Carmille v. Carmille's Adm'r*, 27 S.C.L. (2 McMul.) 454, 1842 WL 3402 at *11 (S.C. Err. 1842).

[35] O'Neall, *supra* at 1-56.

[36] *Id.* at 12.

[37] *Id.*

[38] *See Statutes on Slavery, supra* at 173-76, for the report, and Nash, "Negro Rights," *supra* at 177-87, for an analysis of the report and the public debate it caused.

[39] Jones, *Fathers, supra* at 146.

[40] *See* Perry, *supra* at 206.

[41] *See* William E. Wiethoff, *The Insolent Slave* 149-59 (2002); Huebner, *Tradition, supra* at 70-86; *see also* Reid, *supra* at 590-91 (discussing Lumpkin's law reform proposal of 1850); *see generally* Paul DeForest Hicks, *Joseph Henry Lumpkin: Georgia's First Chief Justice* (2002).

[42] *See* Huebner, *Tradition, supra* at 86-95; Stephenson & Stephenson, *supra* at 582-86.

[43] *Cleland v. Waters*, 19 Ga. 35, 1855 WL 1788 at *7 (1855).

[44] *See* Huebner, *Tradition, supra* at 95; Hicks, *supra* at 45-56, 134-35, 151-52; Reid, *supra* at 591-602.

[45] *See* Huebner, *Tradition, supra* at 95.

[46] *See* Stephenson & Stephenson, *supra* at 608, quoting, in a footnote, Edmund Burke, *Reflections on the Revolution in France* 19-20 (1935) ("A state without the means of some change is without the means of its conservation.").

[47] See Elizabeth Fox-Genovese and Eugene D. Genovese, *The Mind of the Masterclass: History and Faith in the Southern Slaveholders' Worldview* 111 (2005), quoting J. B. O'Neall, "Address," in *Proceedings of the Agricultural Society of South Carolina* 219 (1846).

[48] The leading slave law treatise writers in the nineteenth-century United States also discussed the freedom suits. *See* Cobb, *supra* at 247-59; Stroud, *supra* at 52-57; Goodell, *supra* at 295-99; Wheeler, *supra* at 11-22.

[49] Gross, *Blood, supra* at 35-36; Gillmer, "Suing for Freedom," *supra* at 600.

[50] Stroud, *supra* at 53.

[51] Gross, *Blood, supra* at 35-36; Gillmer, "Suing for Freedom," *supra* at 603.

[52] *See* Morris, *Slavery, supra* at 371-423; Fede, *People Without Rights, supra* at 131, 138-58; Shaw, *supra* at 76-109; Stampp, *supra* at 94-96.

[53] For Nash, *see* "Reason of Slavery," *supra* at 93-184; "Trial Rights," *supra* at 629-37; "Negro Rights," *supra* at 154-66, 172-77; *see also* "Radical Interpretations," *supra* at 296-314. *See generally* Tushnet, *Humanity, supra* at 188-228; Howington, *What Sayeth, supra* at 26-27; Smiddy, *supra*; Grindle, *supra*.

[54] *See* "Reason of Slavery," *supra* at 98-184; Tushnet, *Humanity, supra* at 188-228.

[55] *See* Jones, *Fathers, supra* at 96.

[56] *Id.* at 96-97.

[57] Tucker, *Dissertation, supra* at 50-51; Curtis, *supra* at 1160.

[58] *See* chapter 3, *supra* at notes 196-213.

[59] *See* chapter 3, *supra* at notes 214-45.

[60] Schafer, *Becoming Free, supra* at 150.

[61] *Petitions to Legislatures, supra* at 233-34; Morris, *Slavery, supra* at 35.

[62] On the failure of reform in the South, *see* Morris, *Slavery, supra* at 434-39; Fede, *People Without Rights, supra* at 235-45; Kolchin, *American Slavery, supra* at 129. *Compare* Russell Smandych, "'To Soften the Extreme Rigor of their Bondage': James Stephen's Attempt to Reform the Criminal Slave Laws of the West Indies, 1813-1833," 23 *Law & Hist. Rev.* 537 (2005) (discussing Stephen's work as legal advisor to the British Colonial Office).

TABLE OF CASES

Case names and page citations for all cases which are discussed in the body of the text.

INDEX

Topics, concepts and persons, and their relevant page numbers, found in the body of text. Case names are indexed separately in the preceding Table of Cases.

About the Author

ANDREW T. FEDE is the author of *People Without Rights: An Interpretation of the Fundamentals of the Law of Slavery in the U.S. South* (1992), which was republished by Routledge in 2011. His writings on legal history include "Slave Codes," in *Macmillan Encyclopedia of World Slavery* (1998); articles and book reviews published in the *American Journal of Legal History*, the *Law and History Review*, and *Cardozo Law Review*; and biographies of New Jersey lawyers and judges in *American National Biography* (1999) and *The Yale Biographical Dictionary of American Law* (2009).

A New Jersey lawyer since 1982, Andrew Fede now practices in the Hackensack, N.J. office of Archer & Greiner, P.C. Since 1986, he has been an adjunct professor at Montclair State University, Upper Montclair, N.J., where he now teaches classes in the Department of Political Science and Law. He lives in northern New Jersey with his wife Daniele.

Visit us at *www.quidprobooks.com.*

CPSIA information can be obtained at www.ICGtesting.com
Printed in the USA
LVOW100956200613

339469LV00005B/161/P